When should I travel to get the best airfare?
Where do I go for answers to my travel questions?
What's the best and easiest way to plan and book my trip?

frommers.travelocity.com

Frommer's, the travel guide leader, has teamed up with **Travelocity.com**, the leader in online travel, to bring you an in-depth, easy-to-use resource designed to help you plan and book your trip online.

At **frommers.travelocity.com**, you'll find free online updates about your destination from the experts at Frommer's plus the outstanding travel planning and purchasing features of Travelocity.com. Travelocity.com provides reservations capabilities for 95 percent of all airline seats sold, more than 47,000 hotels, and over 50 car rental companies. In addition, Travelocity.com offers more than 2,000 exciting vacation and cruise packages. Travelocity.com puts you in complete control of your travel planning with these and other great features:

Expert travel guidance from Frommer's - over 150 writers reporting from around the world!

Best Fare Finder - an interactive calendar tells you when to travel to get the best airfare

Fare Watcher - we'll track airfare changes to your favorite destinations

Dream Maps - a mapping feature that suggests travel opportunities based on your budget

Shop Safe Guarantee - 24 hours a day / 7 days a week live customer service, and more!

Whether traveling on a tight budget, looking for a quick weekend getaway, or planning the trip of a lifetime ~~Frommer's guides and Travelocity.com~~ will make your travel dreams a ~~reality. Visit us today and now book~~ the trip!

Travelocity.co~~m~~
A Sabre Compa~~ny~~

D1445865

~~Frommer~~'s®

Cape Cod, Nantucket & Martha's Vineyard

2001

by Laura M. Reckford

HUNGRY MINDS, INC.

New York, NY • Cleveland, OH • Indianapolis, IN
Chicago, IL • Foster City, CA • San Francisco, CA

ABOUT THE AUTHOR

Laura M. Reckford is a writer and editor who lives on Cape Cod. Formerly the managing editor of *Cape Cod Life Magazine*, she has also been on the editorial staffs of *Good Housekeeping* magazine and *Entertainment Weekly*.

Published by:

HUNGRY MINDS, INC.

909 Third Ave.
New York, NY 10022
www.frommers.com

ISBN 0-7645-6288-6
ISSN 1091-5907

Editor: Amy Lyons
Production Editor: Todd A. Siesky
Photo Editor: Richard Fox
Design by Michele Laseau
Cartographer: John Decamillis
Production by Hungry Minds Indianapolis Production Department

SPECIAL SALES

For general information on Hungry Minds' products and services please contact our Consumer Care department; within the U.S. at 800-762-2974, outside the U.S. at 317-572-3993 or fax 317-572-4002. For sales inquiries and reseller information, including discounts, bulk sales, customized editions, and premium sales, please contact our Customer Care department at 800-434-3422.

Manufactured in the United States of America

5   4   3   2   1

Contents

Appendix A: Cape Cod in Depth   291

Appendix B: Planning Your Trip—An Online Directory   296

Index   309

List of Maps

The author would like to thank J. Robert Ostergaard for his assistance.

AN INVITATION TO THE READER

In researching this book, we discovered many wonderful places—hotels, restaurants, shops, and more. We're sure you'll find others. Please tell us about them, so we can share the information with your fellow travelers in upcoming editions. If you were disappointed with a recommendation, we'd love to know that, too. Please write to:

Frommer's Cape Cod, Nantucket & Martha's Vineyard 2001
Hungry Minds, Inc.
909 Third Ave.
New York, NY 10022

AN ADDITIONAL NOTE

Please be advised that travel information is subject to change at any time—and this is especially true of prices. We therefore suggest that you write or call ahead for confirmation when making your travel plans. The authors, editors, and publisher cannot be held responsible for the experiences of readers while traveling. Your safety is important to us, however, so we encourage you to stay alert and be aware of your surroundings. Keep a close eye on cameras, purses, and wallets, all favorite targets of thieves and pickpockets.

WHAT THE SYMBOLS MEAN

✪ Frommer's Favorites

Our favorite places and experiences—outstanding for quality, value, or both.

The following abbreviations are used for credit cards:

AE	American Express	EC	Eurocard
CB	Carte Blanche	JCB	Japan Credit Bank
DC	Diners Club	MC	MasterCard
DISC	Discover	V	Visa
ER	EnRoute		

FIND FROMMER'S ONLINE

www.frommers.com offers up-to-the-minute listings on almost 200 cities around the globe—including the latest bargains and candid, personal articles updated daily by Arthur Frommer himself. No other Web site offers such comprehensive and timely coverage of the world of travel.

The Best of Cape Cod, Nantucket & Martha's Vineyard

Only 70 miles long, Cape Cod is a curling peninsula that encompasses hundreds of miles of beaches and more freshwater ponds than there are days in the year. The ocean's many moods rule this thin spit of land, and in summer, it has a very sunny disposition indeed. And little wonder. The "arm" of the Cape has beckoned wayfarers since precolonial days. More than 17 million visitors flock from around the world to enjoy nature's non-stop carnival, a combination of torrid sun and cool, salty air.

On the Cape, days have a way of unfurling aimlessly but pleasantly, with a round of inviolable rituals. First and foremost is a long, restful stint at the beach (you can opt for either the warmer, gently lapping waters of the bayside or the pounding Atlantic surf). The beach is generally followed by a stroll through the shops of the nearest town and an obligatory ice-cream stop. After a desalinating shower and perhaps a nap (the pristine air has a way of inspiring impromptu snoozes), it's time for a fabulous dinner. There are few experiences quite so blissful as sitting at a picnic table overlooking a bustling harbor and feasting on a just-caught, butter-dripping, boiled lobster.

Be forewarned, however, that the Cape can be a bit too popular at full swing. Although it's hard to fathom why the settlers waited nearly 3 centuries to go splashing in the surf, ever since the Victorians donned their bathing costumes, there's been no stopping the waves of sun-, sand-, and sea-worshippers who religiously pour onto this peninsula and the islands beyond every summer.

Experienced travelers are beginning to discover the subtler appeal of the off-season, when the population—and prices—plummet. For some, the prospect of sunbathing with the midsummer crowds on sizzling sand can't hold a candle to the chance to take long, solitary strolls on a windswept beach, with only the gulls as company. Come Labor Day (or Columbus Day, for stragglers) the crowds clear out, and the whole place hibernates until Memorial Day weekend, the official start of "the season." It's in this downtime that you're most likely to experience the "real" Cape. For some, it may take a little resourcefulness to see the beauty in the wintry, shuttered landscape (even the Pilgrims, who forsook this spot for Plymouth, didn't have quite the necessary mettle), but the people who do stick around are an interesting, independent-minded lot worth getting to know.

As alluring as it is on the surface, the region becomes all the more so the more you learn about it. One visit is likely to prompt a

Cape Cod

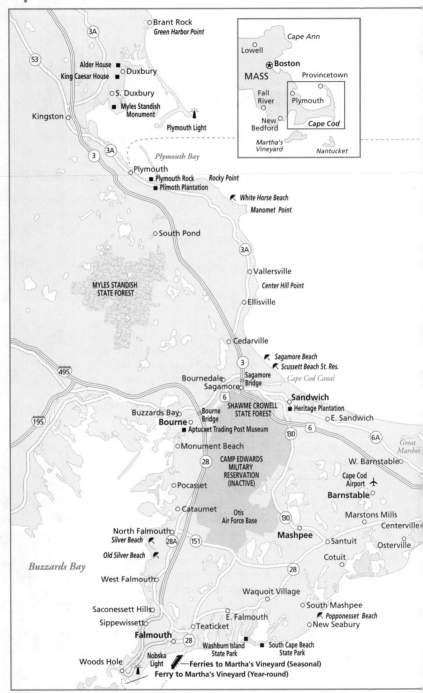

Brant Rock
Green Harbor Point

3A

Cape Ann

Lowell

Boston

MASS

Provincetown

Alder House
King Caesar House
Duxbury
S. Duxbury
Myles Standish Monument

Kingston

53

Fall River

Plymouth

New Bedford

Martha's Vineyard

Cape Cod

Nantucket

Plymouth Light

3 3A

Plymouth Bay

Plymouth
Plymouth Rock
Plimoth Plantation

Rocky Point

White Horse Beach

Manomet Point

South Pond

MYLES STANDISH STATE FOREST

Vallersville

Center Hill Point

Ellisville

Cedarville

495

3

Sagamore Beach
Scussett Beach St. Res.

Cape Cod Canal

Bournedale
Sagamore

Sagamore Bridge

6

SHAWME CROWELL STATE FOREST

Sandwich

Heritage Plantation

Buzzards Bay

195

Bourne
Bourne Bridge

Aptucxet Trading Post Museum

E. Sandwich

130

6

6A

Great Marshes

Monument Beach

28

CAMP EDWARDS MILITARY RESERVATION (INACTIVE)

Cape Cod Airport ✈

W. Barnstable

Pocasset

Barnstable

Cataumet

Otis Air Force Base

130

Marstons Mills

Centerville

North Falmouth
Silver Beach

28A 151

Mashpee

Santuit

Osterville

Old Silver Beach

Cotuit

Buzzards Bay

West Falmouth

28

Waquoit Village

Saconessett Hills

Sippewissett

E. Falmouth

South Mashpee

Popponesset Beach
New Seabury

Falmouth

28

Teaticket

Washburn Island State Park

South Cape Beach State Park

Woods Hole

Nobska Light

Ferries to Martha's Vineyard (Seasonal)
Ferry to Martha's Vineyard (Year-round)

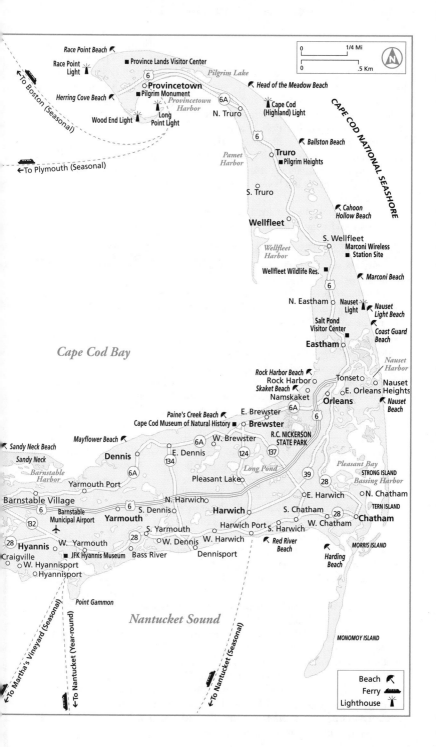

Race Point Beach 🏖
Race Point Light 🗼
■ Province Lands Visitor Center
Pilgrim Lake
6
Head of the Meadow Beach 🏖
Provincetown
■ Pilgrim Monument
Herring Cove Beach 🏖
6A
Cape Cod (Highland) Light 🗼
Provincetown Harbor
N. Truro
Wood End Light 🗼
Long Point Light 🗼
To Boston (Seasonal) →

Ballston Beach 🏖
6
Pamet Harbor
Truro
■ Pilgrim Heights
←To Plymouth (Seasonal)

S. Truro

CAPE COD NATIONAL SEASHORE

Cahoon Hollow Beach 🏖
Wellfleet

Wellfleet Harbor
S. Wellfleet
Marconi Wireless ■ Station Site
Wellfleet Wildlife Res. ■
Marconi Beach 🏖
6

N. Eastham
Nauset Light 🗼
Nauset Light Beach 🏖
Salt Pond Visitor Center
Coast Guard Beach

Cape Cod Bay

Eastham

Nauset Harbor

Rock Harbor Beach 🏖
Rock Harbor
Skaket Beach 🏖
Namskaket
6A
Tonset
Nauset Heights
E. Orleans
Nauset Beach
Paine's Creek Beach 🏖
E. Brewster
Orleans
Cape Cod Museum of Natural History ■
Brewster
6
Mayflower Beach 🏖
6A
W. Brewster
R.C. NICKERSON STATE PARK
Pleasant Bay
Dennis
E. Dennis
124
137
STRONG ISLAND
Bassing Harbor
Sandy Neck Beach 🏖
134
Long Pond
39
28
Sandy Neck
6A
Pleasant Lake
Barnstable Harbor
Yarmouth Port
N. Harwich
E. Harwich
N. Chatham
Barnstable Village
6
S. Dennis
Harwich
S. Chatham
28
TERN ISLAND
B2
Barnstable Municipal Airport
Yarmouth
Harwich Port
S. Harwich
W. Chatham
28
Chatham
28
Hyannis
W. Yarmouth
28
S. Yarmouth
W. Dennis
W. Harwich
Red River Beach 🏖
MORRIS ISLAND
Craigville
■ JFK Hyannis Museum
Bass River
Dennisport
Harding Beach
W. Hyannisport
Hyannisport

Point Gammon

Nantucket Sound

MONOMOY ISLAND

←To Martha's Vineyard (Seasonal)
←To Nantucket (Year-round)
←To Nantucket (Seasonal)

Beach 🏖
Ferry ⛴
Lighthouse 🗼

follow-up. Although you can see all of the Cape, and the Islands as well, in a matter of days, you could spend a lifetime exploring its many facets and still just begin to take it all in. Early Pilgrims saw in this isolated spot the opportunity for religious freedom, whaling merchants the watery road to riches, and artists the path to capturing the brilliance of nature's palette. Whatever the incursions of commercialism and overdevelopment, the land is suffused with spirit, and it attracts seekers still.

Narrowing down possible "bests" is a tough call, even for a native of the region. The selections in this chapter are intended merely as an introduction to some of the highlights. They're listed from closest to farthest along the Cape, followed by the Islands. A great many other outstanding resorts, hotels, inns, attractions, and destinations are described in the pages of this book. Once you start wandering, you're sure to discover bests of your own.

Basic contact information is given for the enterprises listed below. You'll find more information by referring to the appropriate chapters of the book.

1 The Best Beaches

It is difficult to identify the best beaches without specifying for whom: fearless surfers or timid toddlers, party types or incurable recluses? The bayside and sound beaches, for instance, tend to be much more placid than those on the ocean, and thus preferable for little ones who only plan to splash and muck about.

- **Sandy Neck:** This relatively unpopulated, 6-mile barrier beach, extending from the eastern edge of Sandwich to shelter Barnstable Harbor, features pretty little dunes seldom seen on the bayside. Hike in far enough (but avoid the nests of piping plovers), and you're sure to find a secluded spot. Adventurous types can even camp overnight with permission (☎ **508/362-8300**). See chapter 4.
- **Falmouth Heights:** On a clear day, you can see Martha's Vineyard from this hip beach in Falmouth's most picturesque neighborhood. Grand turn-of-the-century homes compete for the view with newer motels, and the beach fills up with families throughout the day. Off-season, this beach is virtually deserted, perfect for romantic arm-in-arm strolling. See chapter 4.
- **Nauset:** Located along the outer "elbow" of the Cape, this barrier beach descends all the way from East Orleans to a point parallel to Chatham—about 9 miles in all, each mile increasingly deserted. The entry point, however, is a body squeeze: It's here that the young crowd convenes to strut their stuff. Administered by the town of Orleans, but still considered part of the Cape Cod National Seashore, Nauset Beach has paid parking, rest rooms, and a snack bar. See chapter 6.
- **Cahoon Hollow:** Spectacular Cahoon Hollow Beach on the rough, frigid Atlantic Ocean is a winding trek down a 75-feet dune. This is a Wellfleet favorite, which boasts a most unusual music club housed in an 1897 lifesaving station called the **Beachcomber**—referred to fondly as the 'Comber, or better yet, 'Coma (☎ **508/349-6055**). Twenty-somethings are the primary patrons, but lingering families also enjoy the reggae and rock that starts to leak out late in the afternoon on summer weekends. See chapter 7.
- **Race Point:** Free of the sexual politics that predominate the beaches closer to Provincetown (certain sections of Herring Cove Beach are tacitly reserved for gays of each sex), Race Point—another Cape Cod National Seashore (CCNS) beach-cum-visitor-center (☎ **508/487-1256**) at the northernmost tip of the Cape—is strictly non-denominational. Even whales are welcome—they can often be spotted with the bare eye, surging toward Stellwagen Bank. See chapter 7.

- **Jetties Beach** (Nantucket)**:** Nantucket's beaches as a rule have the best amenities of any beaches in the region; most have rest rooms, showers, lifeguards, and food concessions. For families and active types, Jetties Beach (just half a mile from the center of town) can't be beat. There are boat and windsurfing rentals, tennis courts, volleyball nets, a playground, and great fishing (off the eponymous jetties). It's also scenic (those jetties again) with calm, warm water. See chapter 8.
- **Gay Head/Aquinnah Beach** (Martha's Vineyard): These landmark bluffs on the western extremity of Martha's Vineyard (call the **Chamber of Commerce** at ☎ **508/693-0085** for directions) are threatened with erosion, so it's no longer politically correct to engage in multicolored mud baths, as hippies once did. Still, it's an incredibly scenic place to swim—come early to beat the crowds. See chapter 9.

2 The Best Bike Routes

Blessed with gently rolling hills (on most), the Cape and Islands are custom-made for a bike trek—whether as a way to get to the beach or as an outing unto itself.

- **Cape Cod Canal:** On this 14-mile loop maintained by the **U.S. Army Corps of Engineers** (☎ **508/759-5991**), you can race alongside the varied craft taking a shortcut through the world's widest sea-level canal. See chapter 4.
- **Shining Sea Bicycle Path** (☎ **508/548-8500**): Connecting Falmouth to Woods Hole by way of the shore and the picturesque Nobska Lighthouse, this 3.6-mile path lets you dash to the ferry or dally at the beach of your choice. See chapter 4.
- **Cape Cod Rail Trail** (☎ **508/896-3491**): Reclaimed by the Rails-to-Trails Conservancy, this paved railroad bed currently stretches some 25 miles from South Dennis all the way to Wellfleet, with innumerable detours that beckon en route. See chapters 5 through 7.
- **Province Lands Trail** (☎ **508/487-1256**): Offering by far the most rigorous workout, this 7-mile network swoops among the parabolic dunes and stunted forests at the very tip of the Cape. Take your time enjoying this somewhat spooky moonscape, and be sure to stop off at Race Point Beach for a bracing dip, and at the **Province Lands Visitor Center** (☎ **508/487-1256**). See chapter 7.
- **Nantucket Town to Madaket** (☎ **508/228-1700**): Only 3 miles wide and 14 miles long, Nantucket is a snap to cover by bike. The 6-mile Madaket path crosses undulating moors to reach a beach with boisterous surf. See chapter 8.
- **Nantucket Town to Surfside** (☎ **508/228-1700**): An easy, flat few miles from town, Surfside Beach is a perfect mini-excursion for the whole family. There are even benches along the route if you'd like to stop and admire the scrub pine and beach plums. When you return to town pause at Brant Point to watch the yachts maneuver in and out of Nantucket Harbor. See chapter 8.
- **Oak Bluffs to Edgartown** (Martha's Vineyard; ☎ **508/693-0085**): All of Martha's Vineyard is easily accessible for two-wheel recreationalists. This 6-mile path hugs the water almost all the way, so you're never far from a refreshing dip. See chapter 9.
- **Chilmark to Gay Head** (Martha's Vineyard; ☎ **508/693-0085**): The Vineyard's awe-inspiring vistas of ponds, inlets, and ocean greet you at every turn as you bike along State Road and then turn onto the Moshup Trail, a road that takes you along the coast up to Gay Head. It's a strenuous ride with perhaps the best scenic views in the region. On the way back, treat yourself to a bike-ferry ride to the fishing village of Menemsha. See chapter 9.

3 The Best Small Towns & Villages

The prettier towns of the Cape and Islands combine the austere traditionalism of New England—well-tended historic houses punctuated by modest white steeples—with a whiff of their own salty history.

- **Sandwich:** For a "gateway" town, Sandwich is remarkably composed and peaceful. Not-too-fussy preservation efforts have ensured the survival of many of this first settlement's attractions, such as the pond that feeds the 17th-century **Dexter Grist Mill** (☎ **508/888-1173**). Generous endowments fund an assortment of fascinating museums, including the multifaceted **Heritage Plantation** (☎ **508/888-3300**), which, with its splendid rhododendrons, doubles as a botanical garden. See chapter 4.

- **Yarmouth Port:** It may look somewhat staid on the surface (Hallet's, the local soda fountain, hasn't changed much since 1889, except to start renting videos), but a trio of unabashedly "grumpy old men"—author/illustrator Edward Gorey, restaurateur Jack Braginton-Smith (of the ultra-casual Jack's Place), and vintage bookseller Ben Muse (of the gloriously jumbled Parnassus Books)—keep things interesting. Stop in at Inaho, all but hidden within an ordinary frame house, for the Cape's best sushi. See chapter 5.

- **Chatham:** Only Provincetown offers better strolling-and-shopping options, and Chatham's versions are G-rated. In summer, Friday-night band concerts draw multigenerational crowds by the thousands. For a glimpse of nature's awesome forces at work (it's busy rearranging the shoreline, with little eye to local real-estate values), take an aerial tour with the **Cape Cod Flying Circus** (☎ **508/945-9000**)—loop-de-loops are optional. Look for the hordes of seals on uninhabited Monomoy Island. See chapter 6.

- **Wellfleet:** A magnet for creative artists (literary as well as visual), this otherwise classic New England town is a haven of good taste—from its dozens of shops and galleries to its premier restaurant, Aesop's Tables. All is not prissy, however: certainly not the iconoclastic offerings at the **Wellfleet Harbor Actors' Theatre** (☎ **508/349-6835**) or the goings-on at the 'Comber (see "The Best Beaches," above). See chapter 7.

- **Provincetown:** At the far tip of the Cape's curl, in intensely beautiful surroundings, is Provincetown. Provincetown's history goes back nearly 400 years, and in the last century, it's been a veritable headquarters of bohemia—more writers and artists have holed up here than you could shake a stick at. It's also, of course, among the world's great gay and lesbian resort areas—people come here for the pleasure of being "out" together in great numbers. If you're discomfited by same-sex public displays of affection, do everyone a favor and stay home. Straights who are more open-minded will have a great time—Provincetown has savory food, fun shopping, terrific company, and fascinating people watching. See chapter 7.

- **Nantucket Town:** It looks as though the whalers just left, leaving behind their grand houses, cobbled streets, and a gamut of enticing shops offering luxury goods from around the world. Tourism may be rampant, but not its tackier side effects, thanks to stringent preservation measures. Time has not so much stood still here as vanished. So relax and shift into island time, dictated purely by your desires. See chapter 8.

- **Oak Bluffs,** Martha's Vineyard: This harbor town on Martha's Vineyard evolved from a Methodist campground that sprang up in the mid–19th century. Pleased with the scenic and refreshing oceanside setting (and who wouldn't be?), the faithful started replacing their canvas tents with hundreds of tiny, elaborately decorated and gaudily painted "gingerbread" cottages. Still operated primarily as a religious community, the revivalist village is flanked by a commercial zone known for its rocking nightlife. See chapter 9.

- **Edgartown,** Martha's Vineyard: For many visitors, Edgartown *is* Martha's Vineyard, its regal captain's houses and manicured lawns a symbol of a more refined way of life. Roses climb white picket fences, and the tolling of the Whaling Church bell signals dinnertime. By July, gleaming pleasure boats fill the harbor passing Edgartown Lighthouse, and shops overflow with luxury goods and fine art. Edgartown's old-fashioned 4th of July parade harkens back to small-town America, as hundreds line Main Street cheering the loudest for the floats with the most heart. It's a picture-perfect little town, a slice of homemade apple pie to go with nearby Oak Bluff's hot-fudge sundae. See chapter 9.

4 The Best Luxury Hotels & Inns

- **Chatham Bars Inn** (Chatham; ☎ **800/527-4884** or 508/945-0096): The last of the grand old oceanfront hotels, this is hands-down the most elegant place to stay on Cape Cod. A 5-year multimillion-dollar renovation has only added to the splendor of this resort. You can stay in one of the luxury suites for $1,500 a night or off-season in a regular room for under $100. Lunch at the Beach House Grill with sand underfoot is a delight, and by all means, have an evening cocktail on the majestic porch overlooking the Atlantic Ocean. The service throughout the hotel is impeccable, and the best part is that this is a family-friendly place—bring the kids and treat yourself. You only live once. See chapter 6.

- **Wequassett Inn Resort and Golf Club** (Chatham; ☎ **800/225-7125** or 508/432-5400): This Chatham institution occupies its own little peninsula on Pleasant Bay and offers excellent sailing and tennis clinics. You'll be tempted just to goof off, though—especially if you score one of the clapboard cottages, done up in an upscale country mode, right on the water. The restaurant, housed in the 18th-century Eben Ryder House, holds its own with the top Cape contenders. See chapter 6.

- **Captain's House Inn** (Chatham; ☎ **800/315-0728** or 508/945-0127): An elegant country inn that positively drips with good taste, this is among the best small inns in the region. Most rooms have fireplaces, elegant paneling, and antiques throughout; they're sumptuous yet cozy. This may be the ultimate spot to enjoy Chatham's Christmas Stroll festivities, but you may need to book your room a couple of years in advance. See chapter 6.

- **Brass Key Guesthouse** (Provincetown; ☎ **800/842-9858** or 508/487-9005): What do you get when you take a charming inn and add a couple million dollars plus a lot of good taste? The Brass Key Guesthouse, now a compound consisting of five historic buildings, has been transformed into *the* place to stay in Provincetown. With Ritz-Carlton–style amenities in mind, Michael MacIntyre and Bob Anderson have created a paean to luxury. These are the kind of innkeepers who think of everything: Pillows are goose down, showers have wall jets, and gratis iced tea is delivered poolside. See chapter 7.

- **The Wauwinet** (Nantucket; ☎ **800/426-8718** or 508/228-0145): Far from the bustle of Nantucket Town, and nestled between a bay beach and an ocean beach, this opulently restored landmark proffers the ultimate retreat. Everything a summering sybarite could want is close at hand, including tennis courts, a launch to drop you off on your own secluded beach (part of a 1,100-acre wildlife refuge), and an outstanding New American restaurant, Topper's. See chapter 8.

- **Charlotte Inn** (Edgartown, Martha's Vineyard; ☎ **508/627-4751**): Edgartown tends to be the most formal enclave on Martha's Vineyard, and this Anglicized compound of exquisite buildings is by far the fanciest address in town. The rooms are distinctively decorated: One boasts a baby grand piano, another its own thematic dressing room. The conservatory restaurant, **L'étoile** (☎ **508/627-5187**), is among the finest you'll find on this side of the Atlantic. See chapter 9.

5 The Best Hotel Deals

- **Simmons Homestead Inn** (Hyannisport; ☎ **800/637-1649** or 508/778-4999): Bill Putman may be the most personable and hospitable innkeeper on Cape Cod. He is determined that his guests have an excellent vacation, a factor that may make the Simmons Homestead Inn one of the best deals around. A former race-car driver/ad exec, Putman, who has filled his inn with a merry mishmash of animals (stuffed, sculpted, or painted), has thoughtfully written up all his choices for the best things to see and do on Cape Cod. After you've toured around on his recommendations, join him for cocktails and tell him about your day. He'd love to hear about it. *Note:* This is one of the few local inns that allow smoking. See chapter 5.
- **Lamb and Lion Inn** (Barnstable; ☎ **800/909-6923** or 508/362-6823): Part B&B, part motel, this historic Cape cottage has been turned into a comfortable lodging with a pool. Hallways are muralled, and rooms are creatively decorated. You'll be charmed by innkeeper Alice Pitcher and her three tiny Yorkies. See chapter 5.
- **Isaiah Hall B&B Inn** (Dennis; ☎ **800/736-0160** or 508/385-9928): Fancy enough for the Broadway luminaries who star in summer stock at the nearby Cape Cod Playhouse, this former farmhouse in Dennis is the antithesis of glitz. The great room doubles as a green room—an actors' hangout—and breakfast is celebrated communally in the country kitchen. The more-plain rooms will set you back less than a pair of orchestra tix. See chapter 5.
- **The Orleans Inn** (Orleans; ☎ **508/255-2222**): You can't miss this mansard-roofed beauty, perched right on the edge of Town Cove. Absolutely, get one of the rooms facing the water. Built in 1875, the inn was recently restored to its former grandeur. The water view and great location make this a terrific value. See chapter 6.
- **White Horse Inn** (Provincetown; ☎ **508/487-1790**): Look for the blue-shuttered sea captain's house with the bright-yellow door with the intriguing oval window. The very embodiment of Provincetown funkiness, this inn has hosted such celebrities as cult filmmaker John Waters and poet laureate Robert Pinsky. Rooms are short on amenities (no cable TV here) but long on artiness. Innkeeper Frank Schaefer has been in Provincetown for 35 years and can give you a quick history of art by pointing out the original works that grace the walls of the inn. See chapter 7.
- **Cliff Lodge** (Nantucket; ☎ **508/228-9480**): A freshened up 1771 captain's house about a block from the center of town, this cheerful inn has knowledgeable, friendly innkeepers. Rooms range in size, but all are spotless with colorful quilts and splatter-painted floors. This is a well-run establishment with reasonable prices, a rarity on Nantucket. See chapter 8.
- **Edgartown Inn** (Martha's Vineyard; ☎ **508/627-4794**) This is a quirky old-fashioned inn, centrally located in the heart of Edgartown. Smells of fresh baked goodies swirl around, and the staff is friendly and helpful. Most important, prices have stayed reasonable, a rarity on the Vineyard. See chapter 9.

6 The Best Restaurants

It wasn't long ago that "fancy" food in these parts began and ended with classic French. Several spots still uphold the old standards, but the New American revolution has sparked ever-more inventive ways to highlight local delicacies. The best luxury hotels (see above) all maintain superlative restaurants, and soaring on par with them are the following choices, some chef-owned and all truly memorable.

- **Regatta of Falmouth-by-the-Sea** (Falmouth; ☎ **508/548-5400**): Perched over Falmouth Harbor, this dining room features exquisite nouvelle and fusion cuisine and atmosphere that's more relaxed than reverential. Signature dishes include a memorable crab-and-corn chowder, plus succulent lamb *en chemise*. See chapter 4.

- **The Regatta of Cotuit at the Crocker House** (Cotuit; ☎ **508/428-5715**): What most distinguishes the two Regattas from their competition is the sensational service, far exceeding most local establishments. In addition, the Regatta of Cotuit has a quintessential old Cape Cod setting; the building was once a stagecoach inn and the decor is formal Federal style. Food here is consistently excellent, with fresh ingredients, generous portions, and creative preparations. See chapter 5.

- **Roadhouse Cafe** (Hyannis; ☎ **508/775-2386**): This is the most dependable choice in Hyannis' crowded restaurant scene. The food is always tasty with good portions. Prices are reasonable, and service is excellent. The clubby atmosphere can't be beat, especially on Monday nights when a jazz quartet plays. See chapter 5.

- **abbicci** (Yarmouth Port; ☎ **508/362-3501**): It's a bit of a shock to find this sophisticated northern Italian restaurant tucked into an antique cape on the Old King's Highway. Those in-the-know have discovered abbicci, though, and it can be tough to get a reservation here on a summer weekend. Instead, go during the week when the skilled staff is a little more relaxed, and you can linger over this delicate cuisine and the fine wine that should accompany it. See chapter 5.

- **The Bramble Inn Restaurant** (Brewster; ☎ **508/896-7644**): An elegantly established entry in the Lower Cape dining scene, this is a favorite for those who don't mind a rather steeply priced, four-course fixed-price dinner. The five intimate dining rooms are decorated with antique china and fresh flowers. Chef Ruth Manchester is a local favorite for her extraordinary evolving cuisine. See chapter 6.

- **The Mews** (Provincetown; ☎ **508/487-1500**): Its romantic downstairs dining room is set on the beach with views to the harbor. Waiters are pros here, a rarity on Cape Cod. And the food by Chef Laurence is consistently excellent, with a creative continental flair. There's also a hopping bar scene upstairs with entertainment and a lighter-fare menu. See chapter 7.

- **Òran Mór** (Nantucket; ☎ **508/228-3919**): Chef/owner Peter Wallace has worked his magic on this humble space, transforming it into an elegant and very romantic setting for his unusual and creative cuisine. His eclectic style ranges from very spicy, hot fusion to simple international dishes, with many grilled items on the menu. An excellent sommelier is on hand to assist wine lovers. See chapter 8.

- **L'étoile** (Edgartown, Martha's Vineyard; ☎ **508/627-5187**): This exquisite conservatory at the elegant Charlotte Inn has long been the best restaurant on the Vineyard, if not the entire region. The fixed-price dinner, a triumph of French cuisine, may be a tad extravagant; for a special occasion, you can't do any better than this. See chapter 9.

7 The Best Clam Shacks

- **The Clam Shack** (Falmouth Harbor; ☎ **508/540-7758**): The ultimate clam shack sits on the edge of the harbor and serves up reasonably priced fried seafood with all the fixings. Order the fried clams (with bellies, please!), and squeeze into the picnic tables beside the counter to await your feast. See chapter 4.
- **Mill Way** (Barnstable Harbor; ☎ **508/362-2760**): Sort of a gourmet clam shack, Mill Way offers succulent specialties beyond the usual picnic-table fare. This is a seasonal joint (open May to mid-October), and when it's open, it's packed, so go early and hungry. See chapter 5.
- **Cap't Cass Rock Harbor Seafood** (Orleans; no phone): Take a photo of the family in front of this shack covered with colorful buoys, then go inside and chow down. Fresh fish, simply prepared, and hearty portions keep them coming back year after year. See chapter 6.
- **Moby Dick's Restaurant** (Wellfleet; ☎ **508/349-9795**): Unfortunately, word has spread about this terrific restaurant, and it can get pretty mobbed here around suppertime. Still, it's a terrific place to bring the family, screaming kids and all. The clambake special is a 1¼-pound lobster, native Monomoy steamed clams, and corn on the cob. Perfect. See chapter 7.
- **Sayle's Seafood** (Nantucket; ☎ **508/228-4599**): Take a 10-minute walk from town on Washington Street Extension, and you'll arrive at this fish-store-cum-clam-shack. Charlie Sayles is a local fisherman, and everything here is deliciously fresh. Get your fried clams to go, and eat them picnic-style at the beach. See chapter 8.
- **The Bite** (Menemsha, Martha's Vineyard; ☎ **508/645-9239**): A travel writer once called it the best restaurant on Martha's Vineyard, perhaps in retaliation for a high-priced meal in Edgartown. Nevertheless, this is a top-shelf clam shack, tucked away in a picturesque fishing village. Order your meal to go and stroll over to the beach, which has the best sunset views on the island. The fried clams are delicious; some say the secret is the batter. Of course, the fish, unloaded just steps away, couldn't be fresher. What more could you want? See chapter 9.

8 The Best Shopping

No matter how spectacular the scenery or splendid the weather, certain towns have so many intriguing shops that you'll be lured away from the beach, at least temporarily. The inventory is so carefully culled or created that just browsing can be sufficient entertainment, but slip a credit card into your cutoffs just in case.

- **Chatham:** Old-fashioned, tree-shaded Main Street is packed with inviting store-fronts, including **The Spyglass** (☎ **508/945-9686**) for nautical antiques, and gourmet treats-to-go at **Chatham Cookware** (☎ **508/945-1550**). See chapter 6.
- **Wellfleet:** The commercial district is 2 blocks long; the art zone is twice that. Pick up a walking map to locate the galleries in town: **Cherrystone Gallery** (☎ **508/349-3026**) tops the don't-miss list. Seekers of low-key chic will want to check out two designers, **Hannah** (☎ **508/349-9884**) and **Karol Richardson** (☎ **508/349-6378**). For designer produce and impeccable seafood, peruse the array at the homey **Hatch's Fish & Produce Market** (☎ **508/349-2810**) behind Town Hall. See chapter 7.
- **Provincetown:** Overlooking the import junk that floods the center of town, the 3-mile gamut of Commercial Street is a shopoholic's dream. It's all here, seemingly direct from SoHo: sensual, cutting-edge clothing (for every sex and permutation

thereof), art, jewelry, antiques, antique jewelry, and more. And whatever you really need but didn't know you needed can be found at **Marine Specialties** (☎ **508/487-1730**), a warehouse packed with surplus essentials. See chapter 7.

- **Nantucket:** Imagine Martha Stewart cloned a hundredfold, and you'll have some idea of the tenor of shops in this well-preserved 19th-century town. Centre Street—known as "Petticoat Row" in whaling days—still caters to feminine tastes, and the town's many esteemed antiques stores would never deign to present anything less than the genuine article. See chapter 8.

- **Vineyard Haven:** Though it's the dowdiest of Martha's Vineyard's towns, this ferry port boasts the best shops, from **Bramhall & Dunn** for housewares (☎ **508/693-6437**) to **The Great Put On** for designer and contemporary women's wear (☎ **508/627-5495**); and, of course, Carly Simon's **Midnight Farm** (☎ **508/693-1997**) for country home and personal furnishings. You might want to save some cash, though, for the multi-ethnic boutiques of Oak Bluffs or the pricey preppy redoubts of Edgartown. See chapter 9.

9 The Best Bars & Clubs

- **Roadhouse Cafe** (Hyannis; ☎ **508/775-2386**): Most consider this the best bar in town, and, even better, it's for grown-ups. There is live music nightly in the new "Back Door Bistro" and a sizzling Monday-night Jazz Series popular with locals and those in the know. See chapter 5.

- **The Beachcomber** (Wellfleet; ☎ **508/349-6055**): Perched atop the towering dunes of Cahoon Hollow Beach, this bar and dance club is one of the most scenic watering holes on Cape Cod. Although the crowd tends to be on the young and rowdy side, the young at heart are also welcome. You *will* end up on the dance floor, so wear comfortable shoes. See chapter 7.

- **Antro** (Provincetown; ☎ **508/487-8800**): Currently, this is the hottest nightclub in town, featuring Big Boned Barbies and Kandi Kane. Drag Comedy happens nightly in season, and all are welcome. See chapter 7.

- **The Chicken Box** (Nantucket; ☎ **508/228-9717**): The Box is the rocking spot for the 20-something crowd, but depending on the band or theme (reggae, disco, and so on), sometimes it seems like the whole island is shoving their way in here. Jimmy Buffett has been known to make an appearance late at night at least once every summer to jam with the band. See chapter 8.

- **Hot Tin Roof** (Martha's Vineyard; ☎ **508/693-1137**): Carly Simon's nightclub at the airport is the hottest after-dark scene on the Vineyard. It's a great space, particularly the outside area with its own funky bar. Be aware that cover prices can skyrocket depending on the act; also, some nights are reserved for comedy. See chapter 9.

2 Planning a Trip to Cape Cod & the Islands

Once you've made it over one of the bridges guarding the Cape Cod Canal, getting around is relatively easy—and you can bypass the bridges, of course, by flying or boating in. The Cape is really many capes: tacky in spots, ordinary in others; sometimes it's a nature lover's dream, sometimes a living historical treasure, or a hotbed of creativity. This chapter will introduce you to the Cape's top spots and should steer you there smoothly; the town-by-town chapters should help you to zone in on the area that will suit you best.

1 The Lay of the Land

Newcomers—known locally as "wash-ashores"—invariably struggle with the terms "Upper" and "Lower," used to describe, respectively, the westernmost and easternmost sections of the Cape. The distinction is thought to allude to the longitude, which decreases as you head east. Many find it helpful to use the analogy of the "arm" of Cape Cod, with the Upper Cape towns of Sandwich, Falmouth, Bourne, and Mashpee forming the upper arm, Chatham the elbow of the lower arm, and Provincetown the "fist." In Martha's Vineyard, similar confusion reigns over what's meant by "up-island" and "down-island." Down-island consists of the touristy port towns of Vineyard Haven, Oak Bluffs, and Edgartown. In the summer months, locals try to stay up-island, avoiding down-island at all costs.

Even the term "land" may be a bit misleading; the Cape and Islands are actually just heaps of sand, sans bedrock. Described geologically as "terminal moraine," they're what remains of the grit heaved and dumped by the motion of massive glaciers that finally receded some 12,000 years ago, leaving a legacy of "kettle ponds"—steep-sided freshwater pools formed when sharp fragments of the glacier were left to melt in place. Under the relentless onslaught of storms and tides, the landmass's outlines are still subject to constant change and eventual erasure.

The modern landscape is vastly different than what was visible a century ago. Virtually all the trees represent new growth. The settlers, in their rush to build both houses and ships, and to fuel both hearths and factories, plundered all the lumber. Were it not for the recession during the late 19th century, you'd be looking at turnip fields and "poverty grass"—so called because it will grow anywhere, needing next to nothing to survive. Instead, the Lower Cape and Mid Cape are now lushly forested, and if the tree cover gets spindly along the Outer

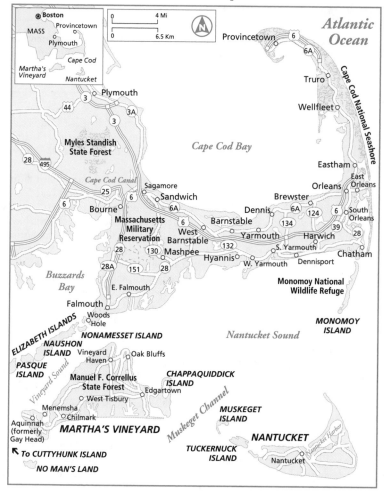

Cape, it's the result of battery by salt winds rather than human depredation. The Islands also show the effects of the ocean winds—predominantly those out of the southwest. Harbor towns and down-island areas enjoy a canopy of trees, while the more exposed portions consist primarily of grassy sand plains and moors.

Each of the 15 towns on Cape Cod really represents many different capes, with often quite distinct personalities to match the varied landscape. Few similarities exist, for instance, among rural Truro, rowdy Hyannis, and historic Sandwich Village. Most frequent vacationers to Cape Cod return to the same village every year, rarely venturing beyond town lines. But the resourceful visitor who explores the region, perhaps driving the Old King's Highway (Route 6A), shopping in Chatham, beaching it at the National Seashore, and checking out an island or two, will have a good idea of the area's diversity.

Visitors may be confused by the similarity of place names on the Cape, particularly in the Mid Cape area. When you are booking a room, it may be helpful to understand these distinctions. Barnstable County consists of the 15 towns on Cape Cod, all of

Here Today, Gone Tomorrow

The shoreline has eroded about a full mile since colonial times, and current scientific predictions give the Cape and Islands a projected life span of as much as 5,000 more years—or as little as 500. Not to make light of the situation, but this is all the more reason to enjoy them while you can!

which are made up of individual villages. The largest town on Cape Cod is called Barnstable, and it is made up of the following eight villages: Cotuit, Osterville, Marstons Mills, Centerville, Hyannis, Hyannisport, West Barnstable, and (is there an echo in here?) Barnstable Village.

Despite the similar names, towns, and even villages on the Cape retain their distinct characters. For instance, charming and historic Barnstable Village along Route 6A (the historic Old King's Hwy.) couldn't be more different from Hyannis (off Rte. 28; transportation hub and home of the mall). Both are villages in the town of Barnstable. In the same vein, the village of West Barnstable (off Rte. 6A; sleepy, rural, and historic) doesn't have much in common with Osterville (off Rte. 28 on the coast; wealthy and preppy). Other notable villages in Barnstable include Cotuit (off Rte. 28; historic and charming), Marstons Mills (off Rte. 28 but inland; mainly residential), Centerville (off Rte. 28; beachy, yet with some commercial sprawl), and Hyannisport (off Rte. 28 on the coast; a residential neighborhood made famous by the Kennedys).

A number of other villages and towns are notable for their unique characteristics. Woods Hole—where bohemians and scientists coexist in a bustling ferry port—is a village in the town of Falmouth, a historic but not musty town with a pleasant Main Street and picturesque town green. Chatham and Osterville both have main streets that are destinations for shoppers seeking expensive, quality wares. Gay-friendly Provincetown has a colorful main street with great people-watching opportunities. Sandwich may well be the quaintest town; Wellfleet, the most artsy. West Barnstable, Barnstable, Yarmouth Port, Dennis, and Brewster are all prototypical New England villages along the historic Old King's Highway. Of these, Dennis Village has the most going on—with museum, cinema, and playhouse all in one historic complex. The Outer Cape towns (Eastham, Wellfleet, Truro, and Provincetown) have the National Seashore beaches, but many families prefer the accessibility of villages like West Dennis and Harwich Port on Nantucket Sound, which offer pretty beaches with calm surf and warmer waters.

On the Islands, location is also an important factor. Most visitors to Nantucket will want to choose lodging in town, where everything is within walking distance. On Martha's Vineyard, down-island towns (Vineyard Haven, Oak Bluffs, and Edgartown) host the majority of the action—shops, restaurants, and fellow tourists. If a serene escape from the grind is what you seek, you may want to be up-island (West Tisbury; Chilmark, including the village of Menemsha; or Gay Head), but you'll need a car— or a passion for biking—to enjoy these locations.

Socially, a parallel could be drawn between the slightly more conservative types that populate the older, more protected communities and the renegades who gravitate to the wilder extremes. Towns like Sandwich, Falmouth, and Edgartown will suit conventional visitors, while 20-somethings and adventurous types of all ages will probably feel more at home in an open-minded, forward-thinking setting such as Wellfleet or Provincetown. Families are sure to have a fabulous time at whatever spot they choose because to keep most kids happily absorbed all it takes is some splashing surf and an expanse of sand.

Route 28 east of Hyannis, an eyesore of tacky strip-mall development, represents a warning of what the future holds unless residents continue to clamp down on zoning. Though the pressures of development are unrelenting, Cape lovers have done a pretty good job, so far, of fending off more egregious offenders. The Cape Cod National Seashore—though hotly protested when it was instituted in 1961—serves as a living reminder of the beauty that otherwise would have almost inevitably been lost or reserved solely for the enjoyment of the ultra-rich.

Today, it is the unspoiled natural beauty and historical charm of the area that attracts visitors. Cape Cod's yearly haul of 17 million visitors infuses the region with more than $700 million in revenues. Tourism has been the leading business sector since the late 19th century and is likely to remain so for centuries to come.

2 Visitor Information

For the free *Getaway Guide,* which covers the whole state, contact the **Massachusetts Office of Travel and Tourism,** 100 Cambridge St., 13th Floor, Boston, MA 02202 (☎ 800/447-MASS ext. 454 or 617/727-3201; www.massvacation.com).

The **Cape Cod Chamber of Commerce,** Routes 6 and 132, Hyannis, MA 02601 (☎ 888/332-2732 or 508/862-0700; fax 508/362-2156; www.capecodchamber.org; e-mail: info@capecodchamber.org); **Martha's Vineyard Chamber of Commerce,** Beach Road, Vineyard Haven, MA 02568 (☎ 508/693-0085; fax 508/693-7589; www.mvy.com); and **Nantucket Island Chamber of Commerce,** 48 Main St., Nantucket, MA 02554 (☎ 508/228-1700; fax 508/325-4925; www.nantucketchamber. org), can provide location-specific information and answer any questions that may arise. In addition, most towns on the Cape have their own chambers of commerce, which are listed in the relevant chapters that follow. Also check out "Cape Cod Life Magazine" at www.capecodlife.com.

If you're a member of the **American Automobile Association (AAA)** (☎ 800/222-8252), they'll provide a complimentary map and guide covering the area.

HOSTEL INFORMATION Hostelling International/American Youth Hostels (☎ 202/783-6161) offers low-cost dorm accommodations in five sites on the Cape and Islands. Rates are $15 per person per night for non-members; members (membership $25 a year for adults, $15 for adults over 54, $10 for children under 18) pay somewhat less. Note that there's a "lockout" period (typically 10am to 5pm daily), and, likely, a limit on the length of stay. HI/AYH properties are located on the outskirts of Hyannis; in Eastham, just off the bike trail; in a former Coast Guard station overlooking Ballston Beach in Truro; adjoining 4,000-acre Manuel F. Correllus State Forest in West Tisbury on Martha's Vineyard; and in an 1874 lifesaving station on Surfside Beach on Nantucket. For details, see "Where to Stay" in the relevant chapters.

SPORTS INFORMATION Cape Cod Chamber of Commerce (☎ 508/862-0700; fax 508/362-2156; www.capecodchamber.org) offers a *Sportsman's Guide* outlining fishing and hunting options. Those interested in outdoor activities will find reams of info through the **World Wide Web's Great Outdoor Recreation Pages** (www.gorp.com). Birders should call the **Cape Cod Museum of Natural History** (☎ 508/896-3867) for info about the Cape Cod Bird Club or call the **Birdwatchers General Store** in Orleans (☎ 508/255-6974) for top spots and the latest sightings. Many of the Cape's **golf clubs** are open to the public; for an annotated listing and advice, call ☎ 800/TEE-BALL, "the chamber of golf."

3 Money

Though the Cape and Islands—especially the Islands—might seem pricey compared to non-tourist areas, visitors used to city prices will find costs quite reasonable. Basically, you can get by on very little if your comfort needs are minimal (rooms in older motels go for as little as $50 a night). Then again, you could spend $1,000 or more on a room—per night. Most of the nicer rooms fall between $150 and $250 a night.

Restaurant prices offer as wide a range. You could dine on clam rolls, for instance, at less than $10 a head, or blow that much or more on a mere appetizer. With such a great variety of dining styles available everywhere, the choice is yours.

TRAVELER'S CHECKS   Traveler's checks are accepted at hotels, motels, restaurants, and most stores, as are credit cards. They are something of an anachronism these days, but since many banks now impose a fee every time you use your card to withdraw money from an ATM in a different city or bank, you may be better off with traveler's checks. You can get traveler's checks at almost any bank; American Express cardholders can charge them over the phone and avoid the 1% fee by calling ☎ **800/ 221-7282.** If you opt to carry traveler's checks, make sure to record their serial numbers and keep them separate from the checks themselves.

ATMs   ATMs are available throughout the area, at banks and supermarkets, so you can get cash as you travel. Call one of the major networks, such as **Cirrus** (☎ **800/ 424-7787;** www.mastercard.com/atm/) or **PLUS** (☎ **800/843-7587;** www.visa.com/ atms), to find the nearest location. Be sure to check your bank's daily withdrawal limit before you leave. Foreign travelers should check with their banks beforehand to make sure their PINs will work abroad.

Should you require personal service, the banks with the greatest number of branches include **Fleet** (☎ **800/841-4000;** www.fleet.com) and the 25-odd branches of **Cape Cod Bank & Trust Company** (☎ **800/458-5100;** www.ccbt.com). Both banks will exchange all foreign currencies, although you might want to stop off at the exchange booth at Logan Airport in Boston.

CREDIT CARDS   Credit cards are invaluable when traveling. They are a safe way to carry money and provide a convenient record of all your expenses. You can also withdraw cash advances from your credit cards at any bank (though you'll start paying hefty interest on the advance the moment you receive the cash, and you won't receive frequent-flyer miles on an airline credit card). At most banks, you don't even need to go to a teller; you can get a cash advance at the ATM if you know your PIN number. If you've forgotten your PIN number or didn't even know you had one, call the phone number on the back of your credit card and ask the bank to send it to you. It usually takes 5 to 7 business days, though some banks will provide the number over the phone if you pass some security clearance such as telling them your mother's maiden name.

THEFT   Almost every credit-card company has an emergency 800-number that you can call if your wallet or purse is stolen. They may be able to wire you a cash advance off your credit card immediately, and in many places, they can deliver an emergency credit card in a day or two. The issuing bank's 800-number is usually on the back of the credit card—though, of course, that won't help you very much if the card has been stolen. The toll-free information directory will provide the number if you dial ☎ **800/555-1212.** Citicorp Visa's U.S. emergency number is ☎ **800/336-8472.** American Express cardholders and traveler's check holders should call ☎ **800/ 221-7282** for all money emergencies. MasterCard holders should call ☎ **800/ 307-7309.**

Odds are that if your wallet is gone, it won't be recovered. However, after you realize that it's gone and you cancel your credit cards, it is still worth informing the police. Your credit-card company or insurer may require a police report number.

4 When to Go: Climate & Events

Once strictly a seasonal destination, opening with a splash on Memorial Day weekend and shuttering up come Labor Day, the Cape and Islands now welcome more and more tourists to witness the tender blossoms of spring and the fiery foliage of autumn. During these "shoulder seasons," lodging tends to cost less, and a fair number of restaurants and attractions remain open. Most important, traffic is manageable. In addition, the natives tend to be far more accommodating in the off-season, and shopping bargains abound.

August is by far the most popular month, followed by July (especially the July 4th weekend). You are virtually guaranteed good beach weather in July and August. September and October, though, are splendid, too: The ocean retains enough heat to make for bearable swimming during the sunny days of Indian summer, and the subtly varied hues of the trees and moors are always changing, always lovely. The Atlantic will be bone-chillingly cold, but May and June are also enticing as gardening goes way beyond hobby in this gentle climate, and blooms are profuse from May right through the summer. Unless your idea of the perfect vacation requires a swim in the ocean, you'll be better off (for example, fewer people and better deals) if you visit the Cape slightly off-season: May, June, September, or October.

OFF-SEASON   In the last few years, a number of entertaining town festivals and events have attracted crowds in the spring and fall. Provincetown has the **Arts Festival** in late September and **Women's Week** in October. Truro's town festival, **Truro Treasures,** is also held in September. Of course, the **cranberry festivals** all take place in the fall. Harwich has the largest event, usually spanning 2 weekends in September. Nantucket's Cranberry Weekend in October is also popular. Some say the most crowded time on Nantucket is during the **Christmas Stroll** in early December; the entire month before Christmas is known as **Nantucket Noel,** with lots of holiday events. Martha's Vineyard also rolls out the red carpet in December with events in Edgartown and Vineyard Haven, including Santa arriving on the ferry. Many towns on the Cape, including Sandwich, Osterville, Falmouth, and Chatham, also have big holiday festivals. Spring brings **daffodil festivals** in Brewster, Osterville, and on Nantucket (book your ferry reservations way in advance for this one).

Some establishments persist straight through the truly quiet season—January through March—and it's a rare treat to enjoy these historic towns and pristine landscapes with almost no one but natives stirring about. To avoid disappointment in the off-season, however, always be sure to call ahead to check schedules.

WILDLIFE   The wetlands of the Cape and Islands are part of one of the country's greatest annual wildlife spectacles: the passage of thousands of migratory sea-, shore-, and songbirds in spring and fall. Warblers, herons, terns and oystercatchers, shorebirds like avocets and the endangered piping plover, dozens of species of ducks, huge flocks of snow geese, owls, and hawks—these are just a few of the birds that take a rest stop on the Cape as they pass along the Atlantic Flyway, which for some birds extends from winter homes in South America to breeding grounds in the vast, marshy tundra within the Arctic Circle. March, April, October, and November are all good months to see migrating waterfowl. August is the month to observe migrating shorebirds, with thousands stopping to feed at places like Monomoy Island, Nauset Marsh, and Sandwich's Great Marsh. Fewer shorebirds stop on the Cape in spring, but those that do

---

Shopping Bargains _____

Insider's tip: Provincetown's October sales are to die for.

Discounts often range from 50% to 70% off as merchants clear the shelves before closing for the winter. And remember, Provincetown is not just tacky T-shirt stores. There are excellent men's and women's clothing stores, as well as a surfeit of fancy home-accessories stores that have opened up in the past few years. See "Shopping" in the Provincetown section in chapter 7 for more information.

---

will be decked out in the bird equivalent of a tux—their breeding plumage. Songbirds pass through in May, in their brightest plumage and in full-throated song (both color and voice are muted in the fall migration). If you're birding on the Cape during the height of the summer season, you'll find plenty of herons, egrets, terns, and osprey wherever you find sand and wetlands.

The other great wildlife-watching opportunity this region is known for is **whale watching.** The humpbacks, huge finbacks, and small minkes all cluster to feed around the Stellwagen Bank north of Provincetown from April all the way through November.

Monomoy Island is worth a special trip in late winter, when thousands of **harbor seals** take their version of a holiday in the sun, retreating to Monomoy from Maine and points north. At that time of year, they share the island with many thousands of wintering sea ducks. For info on a tour, call the **Cape Cod Museum of Natural History** (☎ **508/896-3867**).

CLIMATE

The Gulf Stream renders the Cape and Islands generally about 10° warmer in winter than the mainland, and offshore winds keep them about 10° cooler in summer (you'll probably need a sweater most evenings). The only downside of being surrounded by water is the tendency for fog; typically, it's sunny about 2 days out of 3—not bad odds. And the foggy days can be rather romantic. Pack some good books for when it pours.

THE SEASONS

SUMMER   The official beginning of summer on Cape Cod is heralded by the **Figawi sailboat race** from Hyannis to Nantucket on Memorial Day weekend. Traffic all over the Cape is horrendous, and ferries are booked solid. It's a rowdy party weekend, but then, strangely, things slow down for a few weeks until late June. The first few weeks of June can be a perfect time to visit the region, but be forewarned: You may need to request a room with a fireplace. Weather this time of year, particularly in the Outer Cape, can be unpredictable at best. At worst, it's cold and rainy. Don't count on swimming in the ocean unless you're a member of the Polar Bear Club. Late June weather is usually lovely. July 4th is another major mob scene weekend to be avoided. July and August can be perfect—sunny and breezy—or damp, foggy, and humid. Usually it's a combination of the two. Heavily trafficked Labor Day is another weekend you'll probably want to avoid.

AUTUMN   It usually starts feeling like fall around mid-September on Cape Cod. Leaves start to change color, roads start to unclog, and everyone seems happier. Day temperatures are perfect for long hikes along the seashore. By October, you'll need a sweater during the day, and evenings can be downright chilly. But this is a lovely time of year on the Cape and Islands.

WINTER   It's not supposed to snow on Cape Cod, but it does. A few years ago, some towns got close to 100 inches. During another recent winter, the Cape received virtually no snow until a surprise blizzard on April 1. The holidays are quite popular for family gatherings on the Cape and Islands. January through March are on the bleak side. This is when a lot of locals head south to sunnier climes.

SPRING   April is a cheerful time on the Cape and Islands. Daffodil festivals abound. Folks are gearing up for the summer season. It's a time for last-minute fix-up jobs: painting and repairing. In May and June, the entire Cape blossoms, but the weather can be quite rainy this time of year.

Hyannis's Average Monthly Temperatures

	Jan	Feb	Mar	Apr	May	June	July	Aug	Sept	Oct	Nov	Dec
High Temps. (°F)	40	41	42	53	62	71	78	76	70	59	49	40
Low Temps. (°F)	25	26	28	40	48	56	63	61	56	47	37	26

Cape Cod & the Islands Calendar of Events

April

- **Brewster in Bloom,** Brewster. Open houses, a crafts fair and flea market, a parade, and hot air balloons. The Old King's Highway (Rte. 6A) is lined with thousands of daffodils. Call ☎ **508/896-3500.** Late April.
- ✪ **Daffodil Festival,** Nantucket. Spring's arrival is heralded with masses of yellow blooms adorning everything in sight, including a cavalcade of antique cars. Call ☎ **508/228-1700.** Late April.

May

- **Herb Festival,** Sandwich. Exhibits, talks, and garden walks at the Green Briar Nature Center. Call ☎ **508/888-6870.** Mid-May.
- ✪ **Cape Maritime Week,** Cape-wide. A multitude of cultural organizations mount special events—such as lighthouse tours—highlighting the region's nautical history. Activities include Coast Guard open houses, lectures, walking tours, and more. Sponsored by the Cape Cod Commission. Call ☎ **508/362-3828.** Mid-May.
- **Spring Fling,** Chatham. A family-oriented festival featuring clowns, pets, and a crazy hat parade. Call ☎ **508/945-5199.** Mid-May.
- **Nantucket Wine Festival,** Nantucket. Vintners from all over converge on Nantucket for wine tastings and cuisine provided by some of the island's top chefs. The Grand Cru is the main event. Call ☎ **508/228-1128.** Late May.
- **Figawi Sailboat Race,** Hyannis to Nantucket. The largest—and wildest—race on the East Coast. Intense partying in Hyannis and on Nantucket surrounds this popular event. Call ☎ **508/771-3333.** Late May.
- **Dexter Rhododendron Festival,** Sandwich. **Heritage Plantation**—at the peak of bloom—sells offshoots of its incomparable botanical collection. Call ☎ **508/888-3300.** Late May.

June

- **Brewster Historical Society Antiques Fair,** Brewster. An outdoor extravaganza featuring 80 top dealers. Call ☎ **508/896-3500.** Early June.
- **Hyannis Harbor Festival,** Hyannis. A boat parade and sailboat races, live music, crafts, and maritime exhibits. Call ☎ **800/449-6647** or 508/362-5230. Early June.
- **Heritage Week,** Cape-wide. Ten days of special tours and events hosted by historic sites and museums. Additional events, called Heritage Cape Cod, are spread throughout the year. Call ☎ **508/375-0010.** Mid-June.

- **A Taste of the Vineyard,** Martha's Vineyard. Island restaurateurs offer samplings of their specialties at Edgartown's Whaling Church to benefit the Martha's Vineyard Preservation Trust. Call ☎ **508/627-8017.** Mid-June.

✪ **Harborfest Celebration,** Nantucket. A chance to sample competing chowders and board tall ships. Call ☎ **508/228-1700.** Mid-June.

- **Provincetown Film Festival**, Provincetown. Focusing on alternative film, this fête has brought out celebrities like John Waters and Lilly Tomlin. Call ☎ **508/487-FILM.** Mid-June.

- **Nantucket Film Festival,** Nantucket. Annual event focuses on storytelling through film and includes showings of short- and feature-length films, documentaries, staged readings, panel discussions, and screenplay competition. Sponsors include *Vanity Fair* magazine, so you may see a celebrity or two. Call ☎ **508/228-1700.** Late June.

- **Strawberry Festival,** Bourne. **The Aptucxet Trading Post Museum,** a replica of the country's first store, hosts crafts demonstrations, accompanied by fresh strawberry shortcake. Call ☎ **508/759-9487.** Late June.

- **Provincetown Portuguese Festival,** Provincetown. This new cultural event celebrates Provincetown's Portuguese heritage with music, dancing, exhibits, food, a parade, fireworks, and the traditional Blessing of the Fleet. Call ☎ **508/487-3424.** Late June.

- **Rock & Roll Ramble,** Sandwich. Vintage cars from the '50s and '60s converge on Heritage Plantation for a concert and mutual admiration. Call ☎ **508/888-3300.** Late June.

July

- **Edgartown Regatta,** Martha's Vineyard. A highly social sailing event. Call ☎ **508/627-4364.** Early July.

- **Wampanoag Pow Wow,** Mashpee. Native American tribes from around the country converge to enjoy traditional dances and games. Call ☎ **508/477-0208.** July 4th weekend.

- **Independence Day,** Falmouth. Festivities include a Blessing of the Fleet and fireworks at Falmouth Heights Beach. Your best bet is to park in town earlier in the evening and walk over to the Heights. Call ☎ **508/548-8500.** July 4th weekend.

- **Independence Day,** Provincetown. Festivities include a spirited parade, entertainment, and fireworks over the harbor. Call ☎ **508/487-3424.** July 4th weekend.

- **Independence Day,** Barnstable. A spectacular fireworks display over either Barnstable Harbor or Hyannis Harbor (depending on the nesting of the piping plovers). Call ☎ **800/4-HYNNIS.** July 4th weekend.

✪ **Barnstable County Fair,** East Falmouth. An old-fashioned 6-day agricultural extravaganza, complete with prize produce and livestock. Call ☎ **508/563-3200.** Mid-July.

August

- **Beach Plum Music Festival,** Provincetown. Town Hall hosts some top jazz and folk acts. Call ☎ **508/487-3424.** Early August.

- **Jazz by the Sea and Pops by the Sea,** Hyannis. Celebrity "conductors"—such as Julia Child wielding a wooden spoon—enliven these two outdoor concerts. Call ☎ **800/4-HYNNIS.** Early August.

- **Possible Dreams Auction,** Martha's Vineyard. Resident celebrities give—and bid—their all to support the endeavors of Martha's Vineyard Community Services. Call ☎ **508/693-7900.** Early August.

- **In the Spirit Arts Festival,** Martha's Vineyard. Oak Bluffs celebrates its cultural diversity with food, music, and children's fun. Call ☎ **508/693-0085.** Early August.

- **Falmouth Road Race,** Falmouth. Joggers and world-class runners turn out in droves—9,000 strong—for this annual 7.1-mile sprint. Entry registration is by lottery and ends in May. No unregistered runners are allowed to participate. Call ☎ **508/540-7000.** Mid-August.

- **Carnival Week,** Provincetown. The gay community's annual blowout, featuring performers, parties, and an outrageous costume parade. Call ☎ **508/487-2313.** Mid-August.

- ✪ **Agricultural Society Livestock Show and Fair,** Martha's Vineyard. In West Tisbury, a classic country carnival, and a great leveler. Call ☎ **508/693-9549.** Mid-August.

- **Sandcastle and Sculpture Day,** Nantucket. A fairly serious contest, but fun; categorization by age group ups the odds of winning. Call ☎ **508/228-1700.** Mid-August.

- **Festival Days,** Dennis. Fun-for-the-family activities, including a kite-flying contest, canoe race, crafts fair, and more. Call ☎ **800/243-9920** or 508/398-3568. Late August.

- **Illumination Night,** Martha's Vineyard. The Oak Bluffs campground is lit with hundreds of Japanese lanterns. Campground officials keep this event a secret until the last minute, so it's hard to plan ahead. Call ☎ **508/693-0085.** Late August.

- **New England Jazz Festival,** Mashpee. Sponsored by the Boch Center for the Performing Arts. A weekend of big-name performers. Call ☎ **508/477-2580.** Late August.

- **Oak Bluffs Fireworks and Band Concert,** Martha's Vineyard. The summer's last blast. Call ☎ **508/693-5380.** Late August.

September

- **Bourne Scallop Festival,** Bourne. This annual weekend event features food, crafts, rides, musical entertainment, and more. Call ☎ **508/759-6000.** Early September.

- **Provincetown Arts Festival,** Provincetown. Building up to the **Provincetown Art Association and Museum Annual Consignment Auction** (☎ **508/ 487-1750**), this festival is an extraordinary opportunity to collect works spanning the past century. Local artists hold open studios, actors stage readings of Eugene O'Neill, and stalwart swimmers participate in the **Harbor Swim for Life** (☎ **508/487-3684**) to raise money for local AIDS organizations. The race is followed by a festive Mermaid Brunch and a sunset "Festival of Happiness" on Herring Cove Beach. This is a relatively new festival for Provincetown, but it looks to be a keeper. Early September.

- **Windmill Weekend,** Eastham. This jolly community festival includes a sand-art competition, road races, band concerts, an arts-and-crafts show, a tricycle race, and professional entertainment. The highlight of this weekend is the square dance held under the historic windmill. Call ☎ **508/255-6133.** Early September.

- **Cranberry Festival,** Harwich. A chance to observe and celebrate the colorful harvest, with 9 days of events ranging from pancake breakfasts to fireworks. Call ☎ **800/441-3199** or 508/430-2811. Mid-September.

- **Sandwich Boardwalk Celebration,** Sandwich. This community did some serious bonding 7 years ago when their boardwalk was damaged by a storm, and everyone pitched in to build a new one. This festival, with professional kite flying and entertainment for families, has become an annual tradition. Call ☎ **508/888-1233.** Late September.

October

- **Trash Fish Banquet,** Provincetown. Unsung, or perhaps undersung, species are creatively cooked to benefit the Center for Coastal Studies. Call ☎ **508/487-3622.** Mid-October.
- **Women's Week,** Provincetown. A gathering of artists, entertainers, and educators, as well as women who just want to have fun. Call ☎ **800/933-1963** or 508/487-2313. Mid-October.
- **Walking Weekend,** Cape-wide. Over 45 guided walks (averaging 2 hours in length) sponsored by the Cape Cod Commission to foster appreciation for the Cape's unique ecology and cultural accomplishments. Call ☎ **508/362-3828.** Mid-October.
- **Nantucket Harvest Festival,** Nantucket. Features inn tours, and a big chowder contest, just when the foliage is at its burnished prime. Call ☎ **508/228-1700.** Mid-October.
- **Nantucket Arts Festival,** Nantucket. This weeklong event includes a wet-paint sale, mini-film-festival, writers and their works, gallery exhibitions, artist demonstrations, theater, concerts, photography, and more. Call ☎ **508/228-1700.** Mid-October.
- **Yarmouth Seaside Festival,** Yarmouth. Parade, fireworks, arts and crafts, contests, and sporting events. Call ☎ **508/778-1008.** Mid-October.
- **Happy Haunting Weekend,** Martha's Vineyard. Edgartown hosts Halloween festivities, including a pumpkin-carving contest and trick or treating. Call ☎ **508/627-4711.** Late October.

November

- **Chatham's Christmas by the Sea,** Chatham. Ten days of townwide events include historic-inn tours, carolers, hayrides, open houses, a dinner dance, and Santa. Call ☎ **508/945-5199.** Late November.
- **Lighting of the Pilgrim Monument,** Provincetown. The Italianate tower turns into a monumental holiday ornament, as carolers convene below. Call ☎ **508/ 487-1310.** Thanksgiving Eve (late November).
- **Harbor Lighting,** Hyannis. The boats parade by, a-twinkle with lights, and Santa arrives via lobster boat. Call ☎ **508/362-5230.** Late November.
- **Fall Festival,** Edgartown. Family activities at the Felix Neck Wildlife Sanctuary, including a treasure hunt, wildlife walks, and wreath making. Call ☎ **508/ 627-4850.** Late November.

December

- **Christmas Stroll,** Nantucket. The island briefly stirs from its winter slumber for one last shopping/feasting spree, attended by costumed carolers, Santa in a horse-drawn carriage, and a "talking" Christmas tree. This event is the pinnacle of ✪ **Nantucket Noel,** a month of festivities starting in late November. Ferries and lodging establishments book up months before this event, so you'll need to plan ahead. Call ☎ **508/228-1700.** Early December.
- **Falmouth Christmas by the Sea,** Falmouth. A weekend of caroling, tree lighting, Santa, entertainment, and a parade that centers on the historic and lavishly decorated Falmouth Village Green. Call ☎ **508/548-8500.** Early December.
- **Christmas in Sandwich,** Sandwich. Seasonal open houses, exhibits, community caroling, and merchant promotions take place throughout the town. Call ☎ **508/ 759-6000.** Early December.

- **Holly Folly,** Provincetown. The 2nd Annual Gay and Lesbian Holiday Festival has events open to all, including guest house tours, holiday parties, the Reindeer Run, concerts, and more. Call ☎ **800/933-1963.** Early December.
- **Yarmouth Port Christmas Stroll,** Yarmouth Port. Stroll along the Old King's Highway for open houses, visits with Santa, and caroling. Call ☎ **508/778-1008.** Early December.
- **Christmas Weekend in the Harwiches,** Harwich. This townwide celebration features entertainment, merchant promotions, hayrides, visits with Santa, and more. Call ☎ **508/432-1600.** Mid-December.
- **First Night,** Chatham. Following Boston's lead, Chatham puts on a festive evening featuring local performers. Call ☎ **508/945-5199.** New Year's Eve.
- **First Night,** Vineyard Haven and Edgartown. The two island towns mount their own Boston-inspired jamborees featuring local artists and performers. Call ☎ **508/693-0085.** New Year's Eve.

5   Health & Insurance

STAYING HEALTHY

Even in this northerly clime, sunburn is a real hazard—as is, increasingly, **sun expo-sure,** whatever the latitude. For most skin types, it's safest to start with a lotion with a high SPF and work your way down. Be sure to reapply often, according to the directions; and no matter how thoroughly you slather up, try to stay in the shade during prime frying time—11am to 2pm. Kids should always wear sunscreen with a high SPF number, or a cover-up such as a T-shirt, if they're going to be playing outside for long periods of time (and just try to stop them!). Sunglasses with UVP (Ultra Violet Protection) lenses will help shield your eyes.

The sea breezes keep most **mosquitoes** on the move, but not always (said Thoreau: "I have never been so much troubled by mosquitoes as in such localities."), so pack some bug spray. The most dangerous insect you're likely to encounter may not be so easily dissuaded. Unfortunately, pinhead-size **deer ticks,** which transmit Lyme disease (named for the Connecticut community where the malady was diagnosed), are quite widespread along the Massachusetts coast, and they're especially active just when you're apt to be there: April through October. Nantucket has the dubious distinction of having the highest concentration of Lyme disease in the country. A vaccine tested there is now on the market. Ask your doctor if you should consider the vaccine. If caught in its early stages—symptoms include a ring-shaped rash and flu-like achiness—the disease is easily countered with antibiotics; if it's left untreated, however, the effects could eventually prove fatal.

The best protection, so far, is prevention. Avoid walking in brush or high grass—it's bad for the dunes, anyway. If you insist on bushwhacking, cover up in light-colored clothing (the better to spot any clinging ticks), consisting of a long-sleeved shirt and long pants tucked into high white socks. Camping stores such as EMS sell bush pants that are perfect for this purpose—they're actually comfortable in warm weather. For double protection, spray your clothes and hands (but not face) with a DEET-based insect repellent. Check your clothes before removing them, and then check your body; it helps to use a mirror, or call upon a significant other. Showering after such an outing is a good safeguard. If, despite your best precautions, you find you've brought home a parasite, remove it with tweezers by pulling directly outward, if you can manage to do so without squeezing the body (that would only serve to inject more bacteria into your bloodstream). Dab the bite with alcohol to help disinfect it, and save the tick in a closed jar. If you're within a few minutes of a medical facility, have a doctor deal with the extraction; if you do it yourself, go for testing and treatment as soon as you can and take the tick with you.

The **Lyme Disease Foundation** (☎ 860/525-2000) distributes brochures to tourist areas and is also able to field questions. Other good sources of information are the **Centers for Disease Control** (☎ 888/232-3228 or 404/332-4555) and the **Massachusetts Department of Public Health** (☎ 508/947-1231).

There's one other very good reason not to go in for splendor in the grass: **poison ivy.** The shiny, purplish, three-leafed clusters are ubiquitous and potent; if you so much as brush past a frond, the plant's oil is likely to raise an itchy welt. Clothing that has been in contact with the plant can spread the harmless but irritating toxin to your skin; it's even transmitted by smoke. If you think you've been exposed, your best bet is to wash with soap immediately (otherwise the oil may spread elsewhere on your body). Calamine lotion—available without prescription at all drugstores—should help soothe the itching. You won't spread the rash by scratching, since it's the oil that does the spreading, but scratches could get infected, so resist the temptation.

There's one key health precaution you can take if you're planning to do any bicycling while on the Cape and Islands: a **helmet.** In Massachusetts, children 12 and under are required to wear one. All the good bike shops rent out helmets as well, and those few extra bucks could save your life.

Pack an adequate supply of any **prescription drugs** you'll need in your carry-on luggage, and also bring copies of your prescriptions. If you wear contact lenses, pack an extra pair in case you lose one. If you have a serious medical condition or allergy, wear a **Medic Alert Identification Tag** (☎ 800/825-3785; www.medicalert.org), which will immediately alert doctors to your condition and give them access to your records through Medic Alert's 24-hour hot line. Membership is $35, plus a $15 annual fee. If you have dental problems, a nationwide referral service known as **1-800-DENTIST** (☎ 800/336-8478) will provide the name of a nearby dentist or clinic.

INSURANCE

There are three kinds of travel insurance: trip cancellation, medical, and lost luggage coverage. **Trip cancellation insurance** is a good idea if you have paid a large portion of your vacation expenses up front. The other two types of insurance, however, don't make sense for most travelers. Rule number one: Check your existing policies before you buy any additional coverage.

Your existing health insurance should cover you if you get sick while on vacation (though if you belong to an HMO, you should check to see whether you are fully covered when away from home). For independent travel health-insurance providers, see below. Your homeowner's insurance should cover stolen luggage. The airlines are responsible for $1,250 on domestic flights if they lose your luggage; if you plan to carry anything more valuable than that, keep it in your carry-on bag.

The differences between travel assistance and insurance are often blurred, but in general, the former offers on-the-spot assistance and 24-hour hot lines (mostly oriented toward medical problems), while the latter reimburses you for travel problems (medical, travel, or otherwise) after you have filed the paperwork. The coverage you should consider will depend on how much protection is already contained in your existing health insurance or other policies. Some credit- and charge-card companies may insure you against travel accidents if you buy plane, train, or bus tickets with their cards. Before purchasing additional insurance, read your policies and agreements over carefully. Call your insurers or credit-/charge-card companies if you have any questions.

If you do require additional insurance, try one of the companies listed below. But don't pay for more than you need. For example, if you need only trip-cancellation insurance, don't purchase coverage for lost or stolen property. Trip-cancellation insurance costs approximately 6% to 8% of the total value of your vacation.

Among the reputable issuers of travel insurance are:

Access America, 6600 W. Broad St., Richmond, VA 23230 (☎ **800/284-8300**).

Travel Guard International, 1145 Clark St., Stevens Point, WI 54481 (☎ **800/826-1300**).

Travel Insured International, Inc., P.O. Box 280568, East Hartford, CT 06128 (☎ **800/243-3174**).

Travelex Insurance Services, P.O. Box 9408, Garden City, NY 11530-9408 (☎ **800/228-9792**).

6 Tips for Travelers with Special Needs

FOR TRAVELERS WITH DISABILITIES

A disability shouldn't stop anyone from traveling. The free *Getaway Guide* offered by the **Massachusetts Office of Travel and Tourism** (☎ **800/447-MASS** or 617/727-3201) is keyed for handicapped accessibility. Though the larger, more popular establishments, as well as newer (1990s) construction, are generally up to code, a great many of the Cape's older, historic buildings are difficult to retrofit, and the task is prohibitively expensive for many small-business owners, much as they might like to upgrade. Your best bet is to check accessibility when calling ahead to confirm hours or make reservations. You'll find most places eager to do whatever they can to ease the way; but if you run into problems, you might want to contact the **Cape Organization for Rights of the Disabled** (☎ **800/541-0282** or 508/775-8300). For information on services available in the state, call the **Massachusetts Network of Information Providers** (☎ **800/642-0249** or 800/764-0200) during business hours.

A World of Options, a 658-page book of resources for disabled travelers, costs $35 ($30 for members) and is available from **Mobility International USA,** P.O. Box 10767, Eugene, OR 97440 (☎ **541/343-1284,** voice and TDD; www.miusa.org). Annual membership for Mobility International is $35, which includes their quarterly newsletter, *Over the Rainbow.* In addition, **Twin Peaks Press,** P.O. Box 129, Vancouver, WA 98666 (☎ **360/694-2462**), publishes travel-related books for people with disabilities.

You can join **The Society for the Advancement of Travel for the Handicapped** (SATH), 347 Fifth Ave., Suite 610, New York, NY 10016 (☎ **212/447-7284;** fax 212/725-8253; www.sath.org) for $45 annually, $30 for seniors and students, to gain access to their vast network of connections in the travel industry. They provide information sheets on travel destinations and referrals to tour operators that specialize in traveling with disabilities. Their quarterly magazine, *Open World for Disability and Mature Travel,* is full of good information and resources. A year's subscription is $13 ($21 outside the U.S.).

The **Moss Rehab Hospital** (☎ **215/456-9600**) has been providing friendly and helpful phone advice and referrals to disabled travelers for years through its **Travel Information Service** (☎ **215/456-9603;** www.mossresourcenet.org).

Travelers with disabilities may also want to consider joining a tour that caters specifically to them. One of the best operators is **Flying Wheels Travel,** 143 W. Bridge (P.O. Box 382), Owatonna, MN 55060 (☎ **800/535-6790**). They offer various escorted tours and cruises, with an emphasis on sports, as well as private tours in minivans with lifts. Other reputable specialized tour operators include **Access Adventures** (☎ **716/889-9096**), which offers sports-related vacations; **Accessible Journeys** (☎ **800/TINGLES** or 610/521-0339), for slow walkers and wheelchair travelers; **The**

Guided Tour, Inc. (☎ 215/782-1370); **Wilderness Inquiry** (☎ 800/728-0719 or 612/379-3858); and **Directions Unlimited** (☎ 800/533-5343).

Hertz and **Avis** both provide hand-controlled cars with up to 3 days of advance notice (see "Getting Around," below), and both **Amtrak** (☎ 800/USA-RAIL) and **Greyhound** (☎ 800/752-4841), which serves Boston, offer special fares and services for travelers with disabilities; call at least a week in advance for details.

You can obtain a copy of Air Transportation of Handicapped Persons by writing to Free Advisory Circular No. AC12032, Distribution Unit, U.S. Department of Transportation, Publications Division, M-4332, Washington, D.C. 20590.

The National Park Service issues free "Golden Access Passports," which entitle disabled people and a guest of their choice to free admission into national parks, forests, and wildlife refuges. (You will have to provide proof of disability.) The passport can be obtained at park entrances.

Vision-impaired travelers should contact the **American Foundation for the Blind,** 11 Penn Plaza, Suite 300, New York, NY 10001 (☎ 800/232-5463), for information on traveling with Seeing Eye dogs.

FOR SENIORS

With relatively mild winters and splendid summers, Cape Cod and the Islands are popular retirement spots. In fact, as of the 1990 U.S. Census, a third of the population was 55 or older. Businesses from museums to B&Bs cater to this clientele with attractive discounts, and many restaurants offer early-bird specials (smaller portions at lower prices, offered before the ordinary dinner hour). Mention that you're a senior when you first call to make your travel reservations, and be sure to carry some form of identification that establishes your birth date, such as a driver's license or passport.

Both **Amtrak** (☎ 800/USA-RAIL) and **Greyhound** (☎ 800/752-4841), which serves Boston, offer discounted fares to persons over 62.

You should also inquire about the resources of **Elder Services of Cape Cod and the Islands** (☎ 800/244-4630 or 508/394-4630).

Members of the **American Association of Retired Persons (AARP),** 601 E St. NW, Washington, D.C. 20049 (☎ 800/424-3410 or 202/434-2277), get discounts not only on hotels but on airfares and car rentals, too. AARP offers members a wide range of special benefits, including *Modern Maturity* magazine and a monthly newsletter.

The National Council of Senior Citizens, 8403 Colesville Rd., Suite 1200, Silver Spring, MD 20910 (☎ 301/578-8800), a non-profit organization, offers a newsletter six times a year (partly devoted to travel tips) and discounts on hotel and auto rentals; annual dues are $13 per person or couple.

Golden Companions, P.O. Box 5249, Reno, NV 89513 (☎ 702/324-2227), helps travelers 45 plus find compatible companions through a personal voice-mail service. Contact them for more information.

"The Mature Traveler," a monthly 12-page newsletter on senior citizen travel is a valuable resource. It is available by subscription ($30 a year) from GEM Publishing Group, Box 50400, Reno, NV 89513-0400. GEM also publishes "The Book of Deals," a collection of more than 1,000 senior discounts on airlines, lodging, tours, and attractions around the country; it's available for $9.95 by calling ☎ 800/460-6676. Another helpful publication is "101 Tips for the Mature Traveler," available from Grand Circle Travel, 347 Congress St., Suite 3A, Boston, MA 02210 (☎ 800/221-2610 or 617/350-7500; fax 617/346-6700).

Elderhostel is a national organization that offers affordably priced educational programs for people over 55. Programs generally last a week, and prices average about $350 per person, including classes, room, and board. For information on programs held on the Cape and Islands, contact the main office at 75 Federal St., Boston, MA 02110-1941 (☎ **617/426-7788;** www.elderhostel.org) and request a free catalog.

FOR GAY & LESBIAN TRAVELERS

Gay and lesbian travelers, singly or in pairs, will feel right at home in Provincetown, a world-renowned gay vacation capital. They should also feel comfortable wandering farther afield. This is a sophisticated, semi-urban population, and you'll rarely encounter an overtly bigoted innkeeper, shopkeeper, or restaurateur—if you do, report them to the **Massachusetts Commission Against Discrimination,** 1 Ashburton Place, Room 601, Boston, MA 02108 (☎ **617/727-3990**). To avoid unpleasant sit-uations, read between the lines of promotional literature ("fun for the whole family" may mean rampant bedlam and not much fun for you), or be blunt in stating your expectations (for example, "It will be for myself and my partner [name goes here], and we'd like a queen bed, if possible"). The descriptions of each establishment listed in this book should give some idea of their suitability and compatibility. For a detailed insider's look at Provincetown beyond the scope of this book, consult *Gay USA* by George Hobica, published by First Books, P.O. Box 578147, Chicago, IL 60657 (☎ **773/276-5911**).

The **International Gay & Lesbian Travel Association (IGLTA)** (☎ **800/448-8550** or 954/776-2626; fax 954/776-3303; www.iglta.org) links travelers up with the appro-priate gay-friendly service organization or tour specialist. With around 1,200 members, it offers quarterly newsletters, marketing mailings, and a membership directory that's updated quarterly. Membership often includes gay or lesbian businesses but is open to individuals for $150 yearly, plus a $100 administration fee for new members. Members are kept informed of gay and gay-friendly hoteliers, tour operators, and airline and cruise-line representatives. Contact the IGLTA for a list of its member agencies, who will be tied into IGLTA's information resources.

General gay and lesbian travel agencies include **Family Abroad** (☎ **212/459-1800** or 800/999-5500; gay and lesbian), **Above and Beyond Tours** (☎ **800/397-2681;** mainly gay men), and **Yellowbrick Road** (☎ **800/642-2488;** gay and lesbian).

There are also two good, biannual English-language gay guidebooks, both focused on gay men but including information for lesbians as well. You can get the *Spartacus International Gay Guide* or *Odysseus* from most gay and lesbian bookstores, or order them from Giovanni's Room (☎ **215/923-2960**), or A Different Light Bookstore (☎ **800/343-4002** or 212/989-4850). Both lesbians and gays might want to pick up a copy of *Gay Travel A to Z* ($16). The *Ferrari Guides* (www.q-net.com) is yet another very good series of gay and lesbian guidebooks.

Out and About, 8 W. 19th St. #401, New York, NY 10011 (☎ **800/929-2268** or 212/645-6922), offers guidebooks and a monthly newsletter packed with good information on the global gay and lesbian scene. A year's subscription to the newslet-ter costs $49. Our World, 1104 N. Nova Rd., Suite 251, Daytona Beach, FL 32117 (☎ **904/441-5367**), is a slicker monthly magazine promoting and highlighting travel bargains and opportunities. Annual subscription rates are $35 in the U.S., $45 out-side the U.S.

FOR FAMILIES

Basically a giant sandbox with a fringe of waves, the Cape and Islands are ideal family vacation spots. A number of the larger hotels and motels offer deals whereby kids can share their parents' room for free. But beware of the fancier B&Bs: Although it's quite illegal for them to do so, some actively discriminate against children (see "Tips on Accommodations," below). The kind that do are apt to be the kind that children dislike, so it's no great loss. For the most part, the local tourism industry is big on serving family needs, so there's not much you'll need to do by way of advance preparation. For establishments that are extra-welcoming, as well as especially appealing, see the "Family-Friendly Hotels & Restaurants" (chapters 4 through 7) features.

Family Travel Times is published six times a year by TWYCH (Travel with Your Children; ☎ 888/822-4388; 212/477-5524) and includes a weekly call-in service for subscribers. Subscriptions are $40 a year for quarterly editions. A free publication list and a sample issue are available by calling or sending a request to the above address.

Families Welcome!, 92 N. Main, Ashland, OR 97520 (☎ 800/326-0724 or 541/482-6121), is a travel company specializing in worry-free vacations for families.

FOR SINGLE TRAVELERS

Many people prefer traveling alone—save for the relatively steep cost of booking a single room, which usually costs well over half the price of a double. **Travel Companion** (☎ 631/454-0880) is one of the nation's oldest roommate finders for single travelers. Register with them and find a trustworthy travel mate who will split the cost of the room with you and be around as little, or as often, as you like during the day.

Several tour organizers cater to solo travelers as well. **Experience Plus** (☎ 800/685-4565; fax 907/484-8489) offers an interesting selection of singles-only trips. **Travel Buddies** (☎ 800/998-9099 or 604/533-2483) runs single-friendly tours with no singles supplement. **The Single Gourmet Club,** 133 E. 58th St., New York, NY 10022 (☎ 212/980-8788; fax 212/980-3138), is an international social, dining, and travel club for singles, with offices in 21 cities in the USA and Canada, and one in London.

You may also want to research the Outdoor Singles Network (P.O. Box 781, Haines, AK 99827). An established quarterly newsletter (since 1989) for outdoor-loving singles ages 19 to 90, the network will help you find a travel companion, pen pal, or soulmate within its pages. A 1-year subscription costs $45, and your own personal ad is printed free in the next issue. Current issues are $15. Write for free information or check out the group's Web site at **www.kcd.com/bearstar/osn.html**.

7 Getting There

BY CAR

Visitors from the west (New York, for example) will approach the Cape Cod Canal via Route 25 and the Bourne Bridge; those coming from Boston can either come that way (reaching Rte. 25 via I-95 or I-93 South, then Rte. 24 and I-495) or head directly south from Boston on I-93 and Route 3, leading to the Sagamore Bridge. The bridges are only 3 miles apart, with connecting roads on both sides of the canal, so either will do. The one you choose will most likely depend on whether you're planning to head farther south on the Cape to Falmouth along Route 28 or its more rural parallel, Route 28A (in that case, take the Bourne Bridge), or farther east of the Sagamore along Route 6 and its scenic sidekick, Route 6A, which merges with Route 28 in Orleans. From Orleans, the main road is Route 6 all the way to Provincetown.

The big challenge, actually, is getting over either bridge, especially on summer weekends, when upwards of 100,000 cars are all trying to cross at once. Savvy residents avoid at all costs driving onto the Cape on Friday afternoon or joining the mass exodus on Sunday (or Monday, in the case of a holiday weekend), and you'd be wise to follow suit. Call **SmarTraveler** (☎ 617/374-1234 or cellular *1) for up-to-the-minute news on congestion and alternate routes, as well as parking availability in the pay-per-night parking lots that serve the island ferries.

Traffic can throw a major monkey wrench into these projections, but on average, driving time to Hyannis is about 7 hours from New York and 2 hours from Boston. It'll take about 1 to 1½ hours more to drive all the way to Provincetown.

Traffic can truly be a nightmare on peak weekends. Cars are enough of a bother on the Cape itself: If you're not planning to cover much ground, forego the "convenience" and rent a bike instead (some B&Bs even offer "loaners"). On the Islands, cars are truly superfluous. Quite expensive to ferry back and forth ($158 one-way to Nantucket in season, and that's *if* you manage to make a reservation months, even a year, in advance or are willing to sit in "stand-by" for many hours), a car will only prove a nuisance in the crowded port towns, where urban-style gridlock is not uncommon. Should you change your mind and want to go motoring once you arrive, you can always rent a car on the island (see "Getting Around," below), usually for *less than the cost of bringing your own vehicle over.*

If you do come by car, have a mechanic check it out beforehand. If you're a member of the **American Automobile Association (AAA)** (☎ **800/222-4357**) or another national auto club, call beforehand to ask about travel insurance, towing services, free trip planning, and other services that may be available.

BY BOAT

Arriving by water gives you a chance to decompress from city worries, while taking in glorious views both coming and going. All the ferries are equipped to carry bikes, for

A Word About Traffic

Cape Cod traffic is nothing if not predictable. You do not want to be driving over the Bourne or Sagamore bridges to come onto the Cape on a summer Friday between 4 and 8pm. Saturday between 10am and 3pm is also not a good time to arrive. Most of all, you do not want to trying to get off the Cape on a Sunday or holiday Monday between 2 and 8pm. If you find yourself in one of the infamous Cape Cod traffic jams (on Memorial Day in 2000, traffic was backed up 18 miles east from the Sagamore Bridge), there are options. Here are my personal traffic-beating tips. Don't tell anyone.

1. Always take the Bourne Bridge. It is almost always a less crowded route.

2. When heading off the Cape on Route 6, turn off at exit 5. Take Route 149 south to Route 28. At the Mashpee Rotary, take Route 151 to Route 28 in North Falmouth. Take Route 28 to the Bourne Bridge.

3. To get on the Cape to points east of Yarmouth, follow the above in reverse.

4. If you are travelling to Nantucket and plan to park your car in Hyannis, watch the signs on Route 6 to see if the parking lot at Cape Cod Community College is open. If it is, take exit 6 and make a right turn onto Route 132. Cape Cod Community College is about a ½ mile on the right. A free shuttle will take you to the ferry.

5. If you are heading to Martha's Vineyard, consider taking a passenger ferry from New London or New Bedford (see chapter 9). Otherwise, be alert to the signs on Route 28 about parking lots. These signs are accurate. If it says the lot is full in Woods Hole, that means they will not let you park there, so don't bother driving down to check it out. Follow the signs to the open parking lots, and a free shuttle bus will take you to the ferry.

about one-third the cost of a ticket. **Bay State Cruises** (☎ 617/748-1428 or 508/ 487-9284 (seasonal); www.baystatecruisecompany.com) runs a fast ferry to Province-town from Boston, in addition to a daily round-trip passenger ferry (Commonwealth Pier at the World Trade Center) late June through Labor Day, and on weekends late May to late September. The voyage ($18 one-way or $30 round-trip for adults; $14 one-way, $21 round-trip for children 3 to 12; $15 one-way, $23 round-trip for seniors) takes about 3 hours each way, and there's a 3-hour lunchtime layover. The fast ferry makes the trip in under 2 hours and costs $39 one-way, $75 round-trip. You can also ferry directly to Provincetown from Plymouth, in season, with **Captain John Boats** (☎ 508/747-2400); it takes 1½ hours and costs $15 one-way (for any age); $26 round-trip for adults; seniors, $21; children 12 and under, $16. Bikes cost an extra $3. In July and August, only round-trip tickets are sold.

For detailed information on ferries to the islands, see the "Getting There" sections in chapters 8 and 9. The three "down-island" ports of Martha's Vineyard are hooked up to the Cape and mainland in various ways. Oak Bluffs has the busiest harbor in season. It's served by the **Hy-Line** from Hyannis or Nantucket (☎ 508/778-2600), the *Island Queen* from Falmouth Harbor (☎ 508/548-4800), and the state-run **Steamship Authority** car ferry from Woods Hole (☎ 508/477-8600). Edgartown is serviced by the Falmouth Ferry Service, a passengers-only ferry called the *Pied Piper* (☎ 508/548-9400), which leaves from the Falmouth Heights side of Falmouth Harbor and makes a 1-hour crossing (six crossings a day in season). Vineyard Haven welcomes Steamship Authority car and passenger ferries from Woods Hole year-round (over 30 crossings a day on weekends in season). If you want to bring your car, you'll need a reservation (☎ 508/477-8600), although there's limited stand-by space available for those willing to wait around, except during certain peak-demand stretches in summer. Passengers not planning to bring a car do not need a reservation. The **Cape Island Express** (☎ 508/997-1688) runs a passenger ferry, called *Schamonchi,* from New Bedford daily in summer. There are four trips a day on weekends in season. The Cape Island Express takes about 1½ hours but spares travelers coming from New York the long drive onto the Cape. The *Island Queen* makes the quickest crossing, at about 35 minutes. Round-trip fares on all ferry choices range from about $10 to $23, depending on the distance, and the round-trip rate for cars in season is $104. Parking averages $10 per day. Including all of the ferry services, there are dozens of crossings a day in summer.

Nantucket is linked in season to Harwich Port by the **Freedom Cruise Line** (☎ 508/432-8999), which makes three trips a day in season, one trip a day in the spring and the fall. Nantucket is also linked to Hyannis and Oak Bluffs by **Hy-Line** (☎ 508/778-2600). When taking the Hy-Line ferry, you'll need to reserve a parking spot in advance. The Steamship Authority passenger/car ferry from Hyannis operates year-round, making six crossings each day in season.

There are now competing high-speed ferries to Nantucket. Ordinarily, the ferries to Nantucket take over 2 hours, but the passengers-only MV Grey Lady II (☎ 800/ 492-8082), Hy-Line's high-speed catamaran, cuts the time in half, for more than twice the slow-boat price ($55 round-trip, versus $25). It's a smooth, comfortable trip, which will probably come down in price with the new competition. The Steamship Authority now runs its own high-speed catamaran, the Fast Ferry, which also makes the trip in 1 hour. Fares are $42 round-trip for adults and $31.50 round-trip for children.

The best deal may be Hy-Line's passenger ferry, the MV Great Point, which makes the trip in under 2 hours and offers a first-class lounge for $10 extra. Incidentally, transporting a car costs an astronomical $316 round-trip in season—pretty silly when you consider that the island is only 3 miles wide and 15 miles end to end. A bike ($10 round-trip) will more than suffice.

A certain frenzy usually accompanies the ferry departures, but if you arrive about an hour ahead of time, you should have plenty of time to drop off your luggage at the pier beforehand, so you won't have to lug it around. This may not always work in Woods Hole, which is a cul-de-sac: Call SmarTraveler (see "By Car," above) or listen to the radio station 1610 AM to find out what's up and whether traffic is clogged. The Steamship Authority boats offer a luggage trolley, which often fills to capacity half an hour or more before departure, so it pays to get there early. The Hy-Line staff cheerfully attends to all the loading of luggage and bikes. It's a lot less hassle.

Note: See the note on bus-ferry connections under "By Bus," below. The same holds true for return journeys: Ferry arrival times tend to be more reliable, but give yourself plenty of time, and don't take a chance on the last bus of the day.

BY PLANE

Most major carriers offer service to **Boston's Logan Airport,** and from there, it's a quick (½ hour) commuter flight to Hyannis (about $100 round-trip), Provincetown (about $160 round-trip), or the Islands (to the Vineyard, about $100 round-trip; to Nantucket, about $125 round-trip). It's also easy to shuttle in from New York (from La Guardia to Hyannis, about $160 round-trip; from La Guardia to Martha's Vineyard, about $210 round-trip; from La Guardia to Nantucket, about $315 round-trip). Non-stop flights from either La Guardia or Newark to Hyannis, Martha's Vineyard, or Nantucket take about 1 hour and 15 minutes. Connections are also available between these airports and to New Bedford, and private charters are easy to arrange. Comparison shopping by phone (or computer) can pay off, since preliminary research will help you find the best deal. For example, Continental offers service to Hyannis from La Guardia Airport and a seasonal service from Newark Airport to Martha's Vineyard and Nantucket. US Airways services Hyannis from Logan, La Guardia, and Newark; they also service Martha's Vineyard and Nantucket from both Logan and La Guardia. Cape Air is the only airline currently offering service from Logan Airport to Provincetown.

Among the larger airlines serving Logan Airport are **American** (☎ 800/433-7300; www.aa.com), **Continental** (☎ 800/525-0280; www.continental.com), **Delta** (☎ 800/221-1212; www.delta.com), **Northwest** (☎ 800/225-2525; www.nwa.com), **TWA** (☎ 800/221-2000; www.twa.com), **United** (☎ 800/241-6522; www.ual.com), and **US Airways** (☎ 800/428-4322; www.usairways.com).

Carriers to the Cape and Islands include all of the above except TWA, plus **Cape Air** (☎ 800/352-0714 or 508/771-6944; www.flycapeair.com), **Colgan Air** (☎ 800/272-5488 or 508/775-7077; www.colganair.com/), **Island Airlines** (☎ 800/248-7779 or 508/775-6606; www.nantucket.net/trans/islandair/), and **Nantucket Airlines** (☎ 800/635-8787 or 508/790-0300; www.nantucketairlines.com). Flying over to Nantucket from Hyannis takes only 12 minutes, costs about $65 round-trip, and is a great way to avoid the hectic ferry scene. Island Air and Cape Air make the most frequent trips from Hyannis to Nantucket, and between these two air carriers alone, there are over 30 flights per day. Charter flights are offered by Island Air and Nantucket Airlines (see above), as well as by **Air New England** (☎ 508/693-8899) and **Westchester Air** (☎ 800/759-2929). The commuter flights have their own little fare wars, so it's worth calling around. And though flights may lessen in frequency during the off-season, fares descend as well.

Flying for Less: Tips for Getting the Best Airfares

Passengers who can book their ticket long in advance, who don't mind staying over Saturday night, or who are willing to travel on a Tuesday, Wednesday, or Thursday after 7pm, will pay a fraction of the full fare. On most flights, even the shortest hops, the full fare is close to $1,000 or more, but a 7-day or 14-day advance-purchase ticket is closer to $200 to $300. Here are a few other easy ways to save.

1. Periodically, airlines lower prices on their most popular routes. Check your newspaper for advertised discounts or call the airlines directly and ask if any **promotional rates** or special fares are available. You'll almost never see a sale during the peak Cape Cod summer vacation months of July and August; but if your schedule is flexible, ask if you can secure a cheaper fare by staying an extra day or by flying midweek.

   Note: The lowest-priced fares are often non-refundable, require advance purchase of 1 to 3 weeks and a certain length of stay, and carry penalties for changing dates of travel.

2. **Consolidators,** also known as bucket shops, are a good place to find low fares. Consolidators buy seats in bulk from the airlines and then sell them back to the public at prices below even the airlines' discounted rates. Their small boxed ads usually run in the Sunday travel section at the bottom of the page. Before you pay, however, ask for a confirmation number from the consolidator, and then call the airline itself to confirm your seat. Be prepared to book your ticket with a different consolidator—there are many to choose from—if the airline can't confirm your reservation. Also be aware that bucket shop tickets are usually non-refundable or rigged with stiff cancellation penalties, often as high as 50 to 75 percent of the ticket price.

   Council Travel (☎ **800/226-8624;** www.counciltravel.com) and **STA Travel** (☎ **800/781-4040;** www.sta.travel.com) cater especially to young travelers, but their bargain-basement prices are available to people of all ages. **Travel Bargains** (☎ **800/AIR-FARE;** www.1800airfare.com) was formerly owned by TWA, but now offers the deepest discounts on many other airlines, with a 4-day advance purchase. Other reliable consolidators include **1-800-FLY-CHEAP** (www.1800flycheap.com); **TFI Tours International** (☎ **800/745-8000** or 212/736-1140), which serves as a clearinghouse for unused seats; or "rebators" such as **Travel Avenue** (☎ **800/333-3335** or 312/876-1116) and the **Smart Traveller** (☎ **800/448-3338** in the U.S. or 305/448-3338), which rebate part of their commissions to you.

3. Search the Internet for cheap fares—though it's still best to compare your findings with the research of a dedicated travel agent, if you're lucky enough to have one, especially when you're booking more than just a flight. A few of the better-respected virtual travel agents are Travelocity (www.travelocity.com) and Microsoft Expedia (www.expedia.com). For more information on surfing for cyberbargains, see the online directory in the back of this book.

From Logan Airport in Boston, the Cape is about a 1½- to 2½-hour drive, depending on how far along it you intend to go. Hyannis, the Cape's transportation hub, is about a 2-hour drive, or 2½ hours via the **Plymouth & Brockton bus line** (☎ **508/771-6191**); from there, you can take a 2-hour ferry ride to either island.

BY BUS

Greyhound (☎ 800/231-2222) connects Boston with the rest of the country, and **Bonanza Bus Lines** (☎ 800/556-3815 or 508/548-7588) covers a good portion of southern New England. Logan Airport to Falmouth costs about $17 each way. Bonanza links Boston's Logan Airport and South Station with Bourne, Falmouth, and Woods Hole; its buses from New York reach the same destinations, plus Hyannis. From New York to Hyannis or Woods Hole, the 6-hour ride costs about $45 each way. **Plymouth & Brockton** (☎ 508/771-6191) offers service from Logan and South Station to Hyannis by way of Sagamore and Barnstable, and offers connections from there to the towns of Yarmouth, Dennis, Brewster, Orleans, Eastham, Wellfleet, Truro, and Provincetown.

Note: If you're planning to catch a ferry, don't count on the bus arriving on time (there's no telling what the traffic may do). Plan to take the second-to-last ferry of the day, so you have a backup; and even so, schedule your arrival with an hour to spare.

8 Getting Around

BY CAR

Traveling by car does offer the greatest degree of flexibility, although you'll probably wish no one else knew that. While traffic can often be frustrating, parking is another problem. In densely packed towns like Provincetown, finding a free, legal space is like winning the lottery. Parking is also problematic at many beaches. Some are closed to all but residents, and visitors will almost always have to pay a day rate of about $5 to $10. Renters staying a week or longer can arrange for a discounted weeklong or monthlong sticker through the local town hall (you'll probably need to show your lease, as well as your car registration). You can usually squeeze into the Cape Cod National Seashore lots if you show up early (by 9am); here the fee is only $7 a day, or $20 per season.

Further complicating the heavy car traffic on the Cape is the seemingly disproportionate number of bad drivers. A few key traffic rules: A right turn is allowed at a red light after stopping, unless otherwise posted. In a rotary (think traffic circle with Boston drivers), cars within the circle have the right of way until they manage to get out. Four-way stops call for extreme caution or extreme courtesy, and sometimes both.

Rental cars are available at the Hyannis Airport and at branch offices of major chains in several towns. The usual maze of rental offers prevails. Almost every rental firm tries to pad its profits by selling Loss-Damage Waiver (LDW) insurance at a cost of $8 to $15 extra per day. Before succumbing to the hard sell, check with your insurance carrier and/or credit-card companies; chances are, you're already covered. If not, the LDW may prove a wise investment. Exorbitant charges for gasoline are another ploy to look out for; be sure to top off the tank just before bringing the car in.

Certain car-rental agencies have also set maximum ages or may refuse to rent to those with bad driving records. If such restrictions might affect you, ask about requirements when you book to avoid problems later.

It's worth calling around to the various rental companies to compare prices and to inquire about any discounts available (members of AAA or AARP, for instance, may be eligible for reduced rates). The national companies represented on the Cape and Islands include **Avis** (☎ 800/331-1212), **Budget** (☎ 800/527-0700), **Hertz** (☎ 800/654-3131), **National** (☎ 800/227-7368), and **Thrifty** (☎ 800/367-2277).

Internet resources can make comparison-shopping easier. **Travelocity** (www.travelocity.com) and **Microsoft Expedia** (www.expedia.com) help you compare prices and locate car-rental bargains from various companies nationwide. They will even make your reservation for you once you've found the best deal.

BY BOAT

For ferries linking the Cape and Islands, see "Getting There," above. Other local water-taxi services and cruise opportunities are listed by town in the appropriate chapters.

BY BIKE

The perfect conveyance for the Cape and Islands, for distances great and small. The Cape has some extremely scenic bike paths, including the glorious Cape Cod Rail Trail, which meanders through seven towns for over 25 miles. Two wheels are the best way to explore Nantucket's flat terrain, and there are scenic bike routes through all six towns on Martha's Vineyard. You'll find a rental shop in just about every town (see the listings under "Bicycling" in subsequent chapters), or better yet, bring your own.

BY MOPED

They're legal on the Islands and can be rented at many bicycle-rental shops, but locals loathe them: They're noisy, polluting, traffic-clogging, and a menace both to their riders and to innocent bystanders. In other words, *caveat renter,* and expect some dirty looks.

BY TAXI

You'll find taxi stands at most airports and ferry terminals. The Islands also offer jitney services with set rates, such as **Adam Cab** on Martha's Vineyard (☎ **800/ 281-4462** or 508/693-3332) and **Aardvark Cab** on Nantucket (☎ **508/728-9999**). Several, like Aardvark, offer bike racks or can arrange for bike transportation with advance notice—call around until you find what you need. Some companies offer sightseeing tours. Among the larger taxi fleets on the Cape are **Falmouth Taxi** (☎ **800/618-8294** or 508/548-4100), **Hyannis Taxi Service** (☎ **800/773-0600** or 508/775-0400), and Provincetown's **Mercedes Cab** (☎ **508/487-3333**), which delivers elegance at no extra charge. Other cab companies are listed in the Yellow Pages, as are limousine liveries.

BY BUS

To discourage congestion and provide a pleasant experience, a growing number of towns offer free or low-cost in-town shuttles in season. You'll find such services in Falmouth, Woods Hole, Mashpee, Hyannis, Dennis, Yarmouth, Harwich, Martha's Vineyard, and Nantucket. Each town's chamber of commerce can fill you in, or call the **Cape Cod Regional Transit Authority** (☎ **800/352-7155** or 508/385-8326). For commercial bus service between towns, see "Getting There," above.

TRAVEL TIMES   Please note that traffic is very heavy driving over the bridges onto the Cape on Friday afternoons and going over the bridges off the Cape on Sunday afternoons. Saturdays can also have heavy traffic because it is the start and end of most rental units. The Bourne Bridge is usually less crowded than the Sagamore Bridge, but unless you are going to Falmouth, you'll have to merge with the Sagamore Bridge traffic on Route 6 anyway. If you are trying to catch a ferry, particularly in Hyannis, always leave plenty of extra time.

9 Tips on Accommodations

The listings in this book feature a range of summer rates for a double room. Keep in mind that this figure does not take into account the sales tax, which can go as high as 9.7%, depending on the town. Prices off-season are typically discounted by about 20% to 30%, sometimes more.

Travel Times to Cape Cod & the Islands

New York to Hyannis	5 to 7 hours, depending on traffic
Boston to Hyannis	1½ hours with no traffic
Sagamore Bridge to Orleans	1 hour; with high-season traffic, 2 to 3 hours
Sagamore Bridge to Provincetown	1½ hours with little traffic
Hyannis to the Sagamore Bridge	½ hour; on Sunday afternoons in season, 3 hours
Bourne Bridge to Woods Hole	45 minutes; Friday afternoons in season, 1¾ hours
Hyannis to Nantucket by plane	12 minutes
Hyannis to Nantucket by Steamship Authority ferries	2¼ hours
Hyannis to Nantucket by Hy-Line ferries	1¾ hours
Hyannis to Nantucket by Steamship Authority or Hy-Line high-speed catamaran	1 hour
Woods Hole to Martha's Vineyard aboard the Steamship Authority ferries	45 minutes
Falmouth to Edgartown, Martha's Vineyard, aboard the *Pied Piper*	1 hour
Falmouth to Oak Bluffs, Martha's Vineyard, aboard the *Island Queen*	35 minutes

Virtually every town on the Cape has lodgings to suit every taste and budget. The essential trick is to secure reservations months—possibly as much as a year—in advance for the peak season of July through August (June and September are beginning to get crowded, too). You can't count on luck; in fact, unless you're just planning a day trip, you probably shouldn't even visit at the height of summer unless you've prearranged a place to stay.

Accommodations range from sprawling, full-facility resorts to cozy little B&Bs with room for only a handful of guests. The price differential, surprisingly enough, may not be that great. A room at a particularly exquisite inn might run more than a modern hotel room with every imaginable amenity.

Because there are hundreds of lodging establishments of every stripe throughout the Cape and Islands, I've focused only on those with special qualities: superb facilities, for example, or especially friendly and helpful hosts. I've personally visited every place listed in this guide, but worthy new inns—as well as resurrected old ones—are constantly popping up.

RESERVATIONS SERVICES   Several reservations services cover the region, but the only one I can personally vouch for—their standards being as exacting as mine—is **Destinnations** (☎ **800/333-4667** or 508/790-0566). Representing hundreds of top inns throughout New England, Destinnations can also design custom tours that cater to special interests, such as golf or antiquing.

Otherwise, it's buyer beware when it comes to such promotional terms as "water view" or "beachfront" (Provincetown's in-town beach, for instance, is quite scenic for strolls, but a bit too close to an active harbor to make for pleasant swimming). To spare yourself disappointment, always call ahead to request a brochure, if you have time. Some inns and hotels offer special packages, which they may or may not list, so always inquire. Most require a 2-night minimum on weekends, 3 if it's a holiday weekend. All provide free parking, although in a congested area such as Provincetown, you may have to play musical spaces.

FAMILY-FRIENDLY   Although all lodgings in the state are prohibited by law from discriminating on the basis of age, a lot of the fancier, fussier B&Bs will be none too happy if you show up with a young child or infant in tow. You might not be too happy either, spending your entire vacation attending to damage control. It can't hurt to inquire—perhaps anonymously, before calling to book—about an establishment's attitude toward children and its suitability for their needs. If you get the impression that your child won't be welcome, there's no point in pushing it: The child, sensing correctly that he/she is not wanted, is likely to exceed your worst expectations. If, on the other hand, you know your child to be a reliable model of "company behavior," you might want to risk an unannounced arrival.

It's probably easier from the outset, though, to seek out places that like having kids around. Motels are always a safe bet (it's what they're designed for), and the descriptions provided here should give some indication of other likely spots. For a sure thing, see the list of "Family-Friendly Hotels & Restaurants" that accompanies each chapter.

A popular family option—but again, you must make plans as much as a year in advance—is to **rent a cottage or house** by the week, or even month (see below).

RENTING A COTTAGE OR HOUSE   Families planning a Cape Cod vacation, especially families with young children, should consider renting a cottage or house rather than choosing an inn or hotel. The trick to finding a great rental can be summed up in two words: Book Early. Start calling Realtors in January and February (if not sooner—some vacationers who return every summer book a year in advance). If you can visit earlier in the year to check out a few places, that helps, but if not, you may be able to view choices on a Realtor's Web site or see photos that the Realtor can mail to you.

Believe it or not, there are parts of Cape Cod that are not close to a beach. When talking to a Realtor, ask specifically for rentals on the water, with views of the water, or within a ½ mile from a beach. You'll have a better Cape Cod vacation if you are within walking distance of a beach.

Prices on rentals vary, but they are always much lower off-season. Depending on the rental, off-season could mean late June or even late August, so ask what the cut-off dates are for high-season prices. Location is the single biggest factor in determining price: A two-bedroom cottage could cost $800 a week in Dennis or $8,000 a week on Nantucket. Tell your Realtor your price range and what you are looking for, and they will select appropriate listings for you to choose from.

Each town's chamber of commerce can put you in touch with local Realtors. You can also call the **Cape Cod and the Islands Board of Realtors,** 450 Station Ave.,

---

Hit the Pavement

Sometimes the best way to find a good rental is to drive around the area you want to rent in and look for handwritten signs advertising rentals by owner. These rentals tend to be cheaper (no Realtor commission), and you'll know just what you are getting into before you sign on the dotted line.

South Yarmouth, MA 02664 (☎ **508/394-2277;** www.ccibor.com) for a complete list of Realtors in the area.

Here is a list of good Realtors with rentals in different regions of the Cape and on the Islands: Real Estate Associates in North Falmouth (☎ 508/563-7173), Norton Realtors in Sandwich (☎ 508/888-1555), Bay Village Realty in Brewster (☎ 800/833-4958), Duarte/Downey Real Estate in Truro (☎ 508/349-7588), Linda R. Bassett Vacation Rentals on Martha's Vineyard (☎ 800/338-9201); and Nantucket Real Estate Co. on Nantucket (☎ 508/228-3131).

CAMPING INFORMATION   A number of state parks and recreation areas maintain campgrounds; for a full listing for the state, contact the **Department of Environmental Affairs,** Division of Forests and Parks (☎ **617/727-3180**).

The largest such area on the Cape is the 2,000-acre **Nickerson State Park** (☎ **508/896-3491**), offering over 400 campsites. The Massachusetts Audubon Society offers limited tenting at its 1,000-acre **Wellfleet Bay Wildlife Sanctuary** (☎ **508/349-2615**).

Note: Camping is expressly forbidden within the Cape Cod National Seashore (with the exception of a few "grandfathered" commercial campgrounds) and on Nantucket. Seashore camping is not allowed on Martha's Vineyard either. The Vineyard has one campground, called Martha's Vineyard Family Campground on Vineyard Haven-Edgartown Road (☎ **508/693-3772**), which is in the middle of the island and not near a beach.

A partial list of private campgrounds that belong to the **Massachusetts Association of Campground Owners** appears in the Massachusetts Office of Travel and Tourism's free "Getaway Guide" (☎ **800/447-6277**).

Fast Facts: The Cape & Islands

American Express   The **American Express Travel Service** office is at 1600 Falmouth Rd. in Centerville (☎ **800/937-1255** or 508/778-2310) and is open Monday to Wednesday and Friday from 9am to 5:30pm, Thursday from 9am to 8pm, and Saturday from 9am to 5pm. Closed Thursday and Saturday in July and August.

Area Code   The telephone area code for the Cape and Islands is **508.** You must always dial 1 and this area code first unless you are making a call within the same town.

Business Hours   Business hours in public and private offices are usually Monday to Friday from 8 or 9am to 5pm. Most stores are open Monday to Saturday from 9:30 or 10am to 5:30 or 6pm; many are also open on Sunday from noon to 5pm—or earlier, now that Massachusetts's "blue laws" (intended to curb the sale of alcohol) have been relaxed. Virtually every town has some kind of convenience store carrying food, beverages, newspapers, and some household basics; and the larger communities have supermarkets, which generally stay open as late as 10 or 11pm.

Currency Exchange   See chapter 3.

Dentists   Dentists are listed in the Yellow Pages; among those serving emergencies is **Dr. William J. Scheier** of Orleans (☎ **508/255-2511**). Most hospitals will gladly provide referrals, or call ☎ **800/DENTIST.**

Doctors   For a referral, contact **Cape Medsource** at the Falmouth Hospital (☎ **800/243-7963** or 508/457-7963), **Ask-a-Nurse** at Cape Cod Hospital

(☎ 800/544-2424), or the **Physician Referral Service** at Massachusetts General Hospital in Boston (☎ 617/726-5800). Physicians and surgeons are also listed by specialty in the Yellow Pages.

Drugstores   All the larger towns have pharmacies that are open daily. The ones with the longest hours are likely to be located within a supermarket. A 24-hour **CVS** drugstore is located at 182 North St. in Hyannis (☎ 508/775-8346 pharmacy; 508/775-8977 store phone).

Emergencies   Phone ☎ 911 for fire, police, emergency, or ambulance; be prepared to give your number, address, name, and a quick report. If you get into desperate straits—if, for example, your money is stolen and you need assistance arranging to get home—contact the **Travelers Aid** office in Boston (☎ 617/542-7286).

Fishing Licenses   Contact the local town hall of the area in which you want to fish (see individual chapters under "Fishing" for addresses). Massachusetts residents pay $13.50 for a 3-day pass or $28.50 for a season pass; non-residents pay $24.50 for a 3-day pass or $38.50 for a season pass.

Hospitals   The **Cape Cod Hospital** at 27 Park St., Hyannis (☎ 508/771-1800, ext. 5235), offers 24-hour emergency medical service and consultation, as does the **Falmouth Hospital** at 100 Ter Heun Dr. (☎ 508/457-3524). On the Islands, contact the **Martha's Vineyard Hospital** on Linton Lane in Oak Bluffs (☎ 508/693-0410) or **Nantucket Cottage Hospital** on South Prospect Street (☎ 508/228-1200).

Hot Lines   The **Poison Hot Line** is ☎ 800/682-9211; the **Samaritans Suicide Prevention line,** ☎ 508/548-8900. For a range of other hot lines related to social and health problems, see the front section of the local phone book.

Information   See "Visitor Information," earlier in this chapter, and specific chapters for local information offices.

Liquor Laws   The legal drinking age in Massachusetts is 21. Bars are allowed to stay open until 1am every day, with "last call" at 12:30. Beer and wine are sold at grocery as well as package stores; hard liquor, at package stores only. No liquor can be sold on Sunday, though bars can serve drinks. A few towns on Martha's Vineyard are "dry" by choice or tradition (no alcohol can be sold or served), but at most establishments lacking a liquor license, you're welcome to bring your own wine or beer; if in doubt, call ahead.

Maps   Maps of the Cape and Islands are available from the **Cape Cod Chamber of Commerce,** Routes 6 and 132, Hyannis, MA 02601 (☎ 888/332-2732 or 508/362-3225); the **Martha's Vineyard Chamber of Commerce,** P.O. Box 1698, Beach Rd., Vineyard Haven, MA 02568 (☎ 508/693-0085; fax 508/696-0433; www.mvy.com); and the **Nantucket Island Chamber of Commerce,** 48 Main St., Nantucket, MA 02554 (☎ 508/228-1700). For maps of Massachusetts, contact the **Massachusetts Office of Travel and Tourism,** 100 Cambridge St., 13th Floor, Boston, MA 02202 (☎ 617/727-3201; fax 617/727-6525).

Newspapers/Magazines   The *Cape Cod Times* is published daily and runs regular supplements on arts and antiques, events and entertainment, and restaurants. Provincetown, Martha's Vineyard, and Nantucket each put out two weekly papers; all six offer insight into regional issues. *Cape Cod Life* is a glossy bimonthly that provides a sophisticated take on the area's cultural and scenic offerings. Each island has its own glossy as well, but they're not quite up to *CCL's* standards. *Provincetown Arts,* published yearly, is a must for those interested in local arts and letters. In addition, a great many summer-guide magazines are available (don't expect much novel information), and free booklets with discount coupons are ubiquitous; the nicest of these, with a friendly tone and a lot of useful information, is the *Cape Cod Guide.*

Overnight Delivery   For the location of the nearest **Federal Express** drop-off box, or to arrange a pickup, call ☎ **800/238-5355.**

Police   For police emergencies, call ☎ **911.**

Radio   Out of about a score of local AM and FM radio stations, two can be counted on for local color (in the "alternative album" mode): WOMR (91.9 FM) out of Provincetown and WMVY (92.7 FM) from Martha's Vineyard. The classical choice is WFCC (107.5 FM), which also features twice-daily birding reports. All three stations come in clearly on the Cape and Islands.

Safety   A great many people on the Cape and Islands still don't even lock their houses, let alone their cars. However, the idyll may not last long: Real crime, from petty theft to rape, has made inroads everywhere, even on isolated Nantucket. So, all your city smarts should apply. Do lock up, keep a close hold on purses and cameras (especially in restaurants: don't just sling them over a chair), and don't frequent deserted areas alone, even in broad daylight. For the most part, the natives' good faith is warranted.

Smoking   In the past 2 years, 10 out of 15 Cape Cod towns have gone "smoke-free" to some extent. The towns of Falmouth, Barnstable, Yarmouth, Dennis, Brewster, Chatham, Orleans, Eastham, Wellfleet, and Truro have all passed some variation on laws forbidding smoking in public places as a way to protect non-smokers from secondhand smoke. This means that in the majority of restaurants and even bars in these towns, you cannot light up. A few bars have installed a ventilation system and/or a separate area where smoking is allowed, but these are few and far between. While some large hotels have some rooms set aside for smokers, the vast majority of lodging establishments on Cape Cod are non-smoking. There is one establishment in Barnstable where smoking is currently allowed. At **Puff the Magic,** 649 Main St., Hyannis (☎ **508/771-9090**), a cigar bar where no food is served, you can puff to your heart's discontent.

On Martha's Vineyard, all restaurants are smoke-free except those in Oak Bluffs and Edgartown that have separately enclosed and ventilated bar areas. Since the other four towns on the Vineyard are "dry," meaning no alcohol can be sold, there are no bar areas in those towns and therefore no smoking at all in restaurants. There is also no smoking allowed in the commons areas of inns on the Vineyard. There may be some inns where certain rooms are designated for smokers, and visitors wishing to smoke should inquire when they book their rooms.

Despite the attempts by the Nantucket Board of Health, the island of Nantucket has no official smoking ban. But many inns on the island do not allow smoking, and visitors should inquire when they book. Restaurants often have smoking and non-smoking sections as designated by management.

Taxes   In Massachusetts, the state sales tax is 5%. This tax applies to restaurant meals (but not food bought in stores) and all goods, with the exception of clothing items priced lower than $175. The hotel tax varies from town to town; the maximum, including state tax, is 9.7%.

Taxis   See "Getting Around," earlier in this chapter.

Telephone   Local pay-phone calls cost 25¢, and "local" typically means a small radius; a call to the next town over could cost a dollar or more. Beware of "slamming" (the usurpation of phone services by a small, overpriced carrier): Whatever the label on the phone, use the 800 number on your calling card. Smaller inns and B&Bs may not have phones in the rooms, but they generally provide a communal courtesy phone on which you can make local calls and charge long-distance calls. If you do have an in-room phone, check whether there's a per-call surcharge—they can quickly add up.

Tides   If you have any question about the effect of the tides on beaches you plan to hike (they differ dramatically from town to town and could leave you stranded), check the tide chart in a local newspaper before heading out.

Transit Information   An ever-growing number of towns are providing free or low-cost shuttle services to reduce congestion. To find out if there's one that serves the place where you're planning to stay, contact the **Cape Cod Regional Transit Authority** (☎ **800/352-7155**). On the Islands, the phone number for **Martha's Vineyard Transit Authority** is ☎ **508/627-7448,** and for **Nantucket Regional Transit Authority,** it's ☎ **508/228-7025.** The respective **chambers of commerce**—for Martha's Vineyard (☎ **508/693-0085**) and Nantucket (☎ **508/228-1700**)—can also provide maps and schedules for public transportation.

Weather   For the latest reports and forecasts, call the WQRC (99.9FM) **Forecast Phone** (☎ **508/771-5522**), available around the clock.

For Foreign Visitors   3

The pervasiveness of American culture around the world may make you feel that you know the USA pretty well, but leaving your own country requires an additional degree of planning. This chapter will help prepare you for the more common problems that visitors may encounter and illuminate some of the more puzzling aspects of daily life.

1 Preparing for Your Trip

ENTRY REQUIREMENTS

Immigration laws are a hot political issue in the United States these days, and the following requirements may have changed somewhat by the time you plan your trip. Check at any U.S. embassy or consulate for current information and requirements. You can also plug into the **U.S. State Department's** Web site at www.state.gov.

VISAS The U.S. State Department has a **Visa Waiver Pilot Program** allowing citizens of certain countries to enter the United States without a visa for stays of up to 90 days. At press time these included Andorra, Argentina, Australia, Austria, Belgium, Brunei, Denmark, Finland, France, Germany, Iceland, Ireland, Italy, Japan, Liechtenstein, Luxembourg, Monaco, the Netherlands, New Zealand, Norway, San Marino, Slovenia, Spain, Sweden, Switzerland, and the United Kingdom. Citizens of these countries need only a valid passport and a round-trip air or cruise ticket in their possession upon arrival. If they first enter the United States, they may also visit Mexico, Canada, Bermuda, and/or the Caribbean islands and return to the United States without a visa. Further information is available from any U.S. embassy or consulate. Canadian citizens may enter the United States without visas; they need only proof of residence.

Citizens of all other countries must have (1) a valid passport that expires at least 6 months later than the scheduled end of their visit to the United States, and (2) a tourist visa, which may be obtained without charge from any U.S. consulate.

OBTAINING A VISA To obtain a visa, the traveler must submit a completed application form (either in person or by mail) with a 1½-inch-square photo, and must demonstrate binding ties to a residence abroad. Usually you can obtain a visa at once or within 24 hours, but it may take longer during the summer rush from June through August. If you cannot go in person, contact the nearest U.S. embassy or consulate for directions on applying by mail. Your travel agent or airline office may also be able to provide you with visa applications and instructions. The U.S. consulate or embassy that issues your visa will determine whether you will be issued a multiple- or single-entry visa and any restrictions regarding the length of your stay.

British subjects can obtain up-to-date passport and visa information by calling the **U.S. Embassy Visa Information Line** (☎ **0891/200-290**) or the **London Passport Office** (☎ **0990/210-410** for recorded information).

IMMIGRATION QUESTIONS   Telephone operators will answer your inquiries regarding U.S. immigration policies or laws at the **Immigration and Naturalization Service's Customer Information Center** (☎ **800/375-5283**). Representatives are available from 9am to 3pm, Monday through Friday. The INS also runs a 24-hour automated information service, for commonly asked questions, at ☎ **800/755-0777.**

MEDICAL REQUIREMENTS   Unless you're arriving from an area known to be suffering from an epidemic (particularly cholera or yellow fever), inoculations or vaccinations are not required for entry into the United States. If you have a disease that requires treatment with narcotics or syringe-administered medications, carry a valid, signed prescription from your physician to allay any suspicions that you may be smuggling narcotics (a serious offense that carries severe penalties in the U.S.).

For HIV-positive visitors, requirements for entering the United States are somewhat vague and change frequently. According to the latest publication of *HIV and Immigrants: A Manual for AIDS Service Providers,* although INS doesn't require a medical exam for everyone trying to come into the United States, INS officials may keep out people whom they suspect are HIV positive. INS may stop people because they look sick or because they are carrying AIDS/HIV medicine.

If an HIV-positive non-citizen applying for a non-immigrant visa knows that HIV is a communicable disease of public health significance but checks "no" on the question about communicable diseases, INS may deny the visa because it thinks the applicant committed fraud. If a non-immigrant visa applicant checks "yes," or if INS suspects the person is HIV positive, it will deny the visa unless the applicant asks for a special waiver for visitors. This waiver is for people visiting the United States for a short time, for instance, to attend a conference, to visit close relatives, or to receive medical treatment. It can be a confusing situation, so for up-to-the-minute information concerning HIV-positive travelers, contact the Centers for Disease Control's **National Center for HIV** (☎ **404/332-4559;** www.hivatis.org) or the **Gay Men's Health Crisis** (☎ **212/367-1000;** www.gmhc.org).

DRIVER'S LICENSES   Foreign driver's licenses are mostly recognized in the U.S., although you may want to get an international driver's license if your home license is not written in English.

PASSPORT INFORMATION

Safeguard your passport in an inconspicuous, inaccessible place like a money belt. If you lose it, visit the nearest consulate of your native country as soon as possible for a replacement. Passport applications are downloadable from the Internet sites listed below.

FOR RESIDENTS OF CANADA

You can pick up a passport application at one of 28 regional passport offices or most travel agencies. The passport is valid for 5 years and costs $60. Children under 16 may be included on a parent's passport but need their own to travel unaccompanied by the parent. Applications, which must be accompanied by two identical passport-size photographs and proof of Canadian citizenship, are available at travel agencies throughout Canada or from the central **Passport Office, Department of Foreign Affairs and International Trade,** Ottawa, ON K1A 0G3 (☎ **800/567-6868;** www. dfait-maeci.gc.ca/passport). Processing takes 5 to 10 days if you apply in person, or about 3 weeks by mail.

FOR RESIDENTS OF THE UNITED KINGDOM

If you already possess a passport, it's always useful to carry it. To pick up an application for a regular 10-year passport (the Visitor's Passport has been abolished), visit your nearest passport office, major post office, or travel agency. You can also contact the London Passport Office at ☎ **0171/271-3000** or search its Web site at www.open.gov.uk/ ukpass/ukpass.htm. Passports are £21 for adults and £11 for children under 16.

FOR RESIDENTS OF IRELAND

You can apply for a 10-year passport, costing IR£45, at the Passport Office, Setanta Centre, Molesworth Street, Dublin 2 (☎ **01/671-1633;** www.irlgov.ie/iveagh/ foreignaffairs/services). Those under age 18 and over 65 must apply for a IR£10 3-year passport. You can also apply at 1A South Mall, Cork (☎ **021/272-525**), or over the counter at most main post offices.

FOR RESIDENTS OF AUSTRALIA

Apply at your local post office or passport office or search the government Web site at www.dfat.gov.au/passports/. Passports for adults are A$126, and A$63 for those under 18.

FOR RESIDENTS OF NEW ZEALAND

You can pick up a passport application at any travel agency or Link Centre. For more info, contact the Passport Office, P.O. Box 805, Wellington (☎ **0800/225-050**). Passports for adults are NZ$80, and NZ$40 for those under 16.

CUSTOMS
WHAT YOU CAN BRING IN

Every visitor over 21 years of age may bring in, free of duty, the following: (1) 1 liter of wine or hard liquor; (2) 200 cigarettes, 100 cigars (but not from Cuba), or 3 pounds of smoking tobacco; and (3) $100 worth of gifts. These exemptions are offered to travelers who spend at least 72 hours in the United States and who have not claimed them within the preceding 6 months. It is altogether forbidden to bring into the country foodstuffs (particularly fruit, cooked meats, and canned goods) and plants (vegetables, seeds, tropical plants, and the like). Foreign tourists may bring in or take out up to $10,000 in U.S. or foreign currency with no formalities; larger sums must be declared to U.S. Customs on entering or leaving, which includes filing form CM 4790. For more specific information regarding U.S. Customs, call your nearest U.S. embassy or consulate, or the **U.S. Customs** office at ☎ **202/927-1770** or www.customs.ustreas.gov.

WHAT YOU CAN BRING HOME

U.K. citizens returning from a non-EC country have a customs allowance of: 200 cigarettes; 50 cigars; 250 grams of smoking tobacco; 2 liters of still table wine; 1 liter of spirits or strong liqueurs (over 22 percent volume); 2 liters of fortified wine, sparkling wine, or other liqueurs; 60cc (ml) perfume; 250cc (ml) of toilet water; and £145 worth of all other goods, including gifts and souvenirs. People under 17 cannot have the tobacco or alcohol allowance. For more information, contact HM Customs & Excise, Passenger Enquiry Point, 2nd Floor Wayfarer House, Great South West Road, Feltham, Middlesex, TW14 8NP (☎ **0181/910-3744;** 44/181-910-3744 from outside the U.K.), or consult their Web site at **www.open.gov.uk**.

For a clear summary of **Canadian** rules, write for the booklet *I Declare,* issued by **Revenue Canada,** 2265 St. Laurent Blvd., Ottawa, ON K1G 4KE (☎ **613/ 993-0534**). Canada allows its citizens a $500 exemption, and you're allowed to bring back duty-free 200 cigarettes, 2.2 pounds of tobacco, 40 imperial ounces of liquor, and 50 cigars. In addition, you're allowed to mail gifts to Canada from abroad at the rate of Can$60 a day, provided they're unsolicited and don't contain alcohol or tobacco (write on the package "Unsolicited gift, under $60 value"). All valuables should be declared on the Y-38 form before departure from Canada, including serial numbers of valuables you already own, such as expensive foreign cameras. *Note:* The $500 exemption can be used only once a year, and only after an absence of 7 days.

The duty-free allowance in **Australia** is A$400 or, for those under 18, A$200. Personal property mailed back from the United States should be marked "Australian goods returned" to avoid payment of duty. Upon returning to Australia, citizens can bring in 250 cigarettes or 250 grams of loose tobacco, and 1,125ml of alcohol. If you're returning with valuable goods you already own, such as foreign-made cameras, you should file form B263. A helpful brochure, available from Australian consulates or Customs offices, is *Know Before You Go.* For more information, contact **Australian Customs Services,** GPO Box 8, Sydney, NSW 2001 (☎ **02/9213-2000**).

The duty-free allowance for **New Zealand** is NZ$700. Citizens over 17 can bring in 200 cigarettes, or 50 cigars, or 250 grams of tobacco (or a mixture of all three if their combined weight doesn't exceed 250 grams); plus 4.5 liters of wine and beer, or 1.125 liters of liquor. New Zealand currency does not carry import or export restrictions. Fill out a certificate of export, listing the valuables you are taking out of the country; that way, you can bring them back without paying duty. Most questions are answered in a free pamphlet available at New Zealand consulates and Customs offices: *New Zealand Customs Guide for Travellers, Notice no. 4.* For more information, contact New Zealand Customs, 50 Anzac Ave., P.O. Box 29, Auckland (☎ **09/359-6655**).

INSURANCE

Although it's not required of travelers, health insurance is highly recommended. Unlike many European countries, the United States does not usually offer free or low-cost medical care to its citizens or visitors. Doctors and hospitals are expensive, and in most cases will require advance payment or proof of coverage before they render their services. Policies can cover everything from the loss or theft of your baggage and trip cancellation to the guarantee of bail in case you're arrested. Good policies will also cover the costs of an accident, repatriation, or death. See "Health & Insurance" in chapter 2 for more information. Packages such as **Europ Assistance** in Europe are sold by automobile clubs and travel agencies at attractive rates. **Worldwide Assistance Services, Inc.** (☎ **800/821-2828**), is the agent for Europ Assistance in the United States.

Though lack of health insurance may prevent you from being admitted to a hospital in non-emergencies, don't worry about being left on a street corner to die: The American way is to fix you now and bill the living daylights out of you later.

INSURANCE FOR BRITISH TRAVELERS　Most big travel agents offer their own insurance and will probably try to sell you their package when you book a holiday. Think before you sign. **Britain's Consumers' Association** recommends that you insist on seeing the policy and reading the fine print before buying travel insurance. **The Association of British Insurers** (☎ **0171/600-3333**) gives advice by phone and publishes the free *Holiday Insurance,* a guide to policy provisions and prices. You might also shop around for better deals: Try **Columbus Travel Insurance Ltd.** (☎ **0171/ 375-0011**) or, for students, **Campus Travel** (☎ **0171/730-2101**).

INSURANCE FOR CANADIAN TRAVELERS   Canadians should check with their provincial health plan offices or call **HealthCanada** (☎ **613/957-2991**) to find out the extent of their coverage and what documentation and receipts they must take home in case they are treated in the United States.

MONEY

CURRENCY   The U.S. monetary system is painfully simple: The most common bills (all ugly, all green) are the $1 (colloquially, a "buck"), $5, $10, and $20 denominations. There are also $2 bills (seldom encountered), $50 bills, and $100 bills (the last two are usually not welcome as payment for small purchases). Note that a newly redesigned $100 and $50 bill were introduced in 1996, and a redesigned $20 bill in 1998. Redesigned $10 and $5 notes were introduced in 2000. Despite rumors to the contrary, the old-style bills are still legal tender.

There are six denominations of coins: 1¢ (1 cent, or a penny); 5¢ (5 cents, or a nickel); 10¢ (10 cents, or a dime); 25¢ (25 cents, or a quarter); 50¢ (50 cents, or a half dollar); and, prized by collectors, the rare $1 piece (the older, large silver dollar and the newer, small Susan B. Anthony coin). A new gold $1 piece was introduced in 2000.

Note: The "foreign-exchange bureaus" so common in Europe are rare even at airports in the United States, and non-existent outside major cities. It's best not to change foreign money (or traveler's checks denominated in a currency other than U.S. dollars) at a small-town bank, or even a branch in a big city; in fact, leave any currency other than U.S. dollars at home—it may prove a greater nuisance to you than it's worth.

TRAVELER'S CHECKS   Though traveler's checks are widely accepted, make sure that they're denominated in U.S. dollars, as foreign-currency checks are often difficult to exchange. The three traveler's checks that are most widely recognized—and least likely to be denied—are **Visa, American Express,** and **Thomas Cook.** Be sure to record the numbers of the checks, and keep that information separately in case they get lost or stolen. Most businesses are pretty good about taking traveler's checks, but you're better off cashing them in at a bank (in small amounts, of course) and paying in cash. Remember: You'll need identification, such as a driver's license or passport, to change a traveler's check.

CREDIT CARDS & ATMs   Credit cards are the most widely used form of payment in the United States: **Visa** (BarclayCard in Britain), **MasterCard** (EuroCard in Europe, Access in Britain, Chargex in Canada), **American Express, Diners Club, Discover,** and **Carte Blanche.** You must have a credit or charge card to rent a car. There are, however, a handful of stores and restaurants that do not take credit cards, so be sure to ask in advance. Most businesses display a sticker near their entrance to let you know which cards they accept. (*Note:* Often businesses require a minimum purchase price, usually around $10, to use a credit card.)

It is strongly recommended that you bring at least one major credit card. Hotels, car-rental companies, and airlines usually require a credit-card imprint as a deposit against expenses, and in an emergency, a credit card can be priceless.

You'll find automated teller machines (ATMs) on just about every block—at least in almost every town—across the country. Some ATMs will allow you to draw U.S. currency against your bank and credit cards. Check with your bank before leaving home, and remember that you will need your personal identification number (PIN) to do so. Most accept Visa, MasterCard, and American Express, as well as ATM cards from other U.S. banks. Expect to be charged up to $3 per transaction, however, if you're not using your own bank's ATM.

Travel Tip

Be sure to keep a copy of all your travel papers separate from your wallet or purse, and leave a copy with someone at home should you need it faxed in an emergency.

One way around these fees is to ask for cash back at grocery stores that accept ATM cards and don't charge usage fees. Of course, you'll have to purchase something first.

SAFETY

GENERAL   Tourist areas in the United States are generally safe, and the Cape and Islands are safer than most. Although a number of towns, particularly the larger ones, suffer their share of crime (much of it drug- and alcohol-related), there's no such thing as a "bad neighborhood" here, per se. However, with crime on the increase everywhere, you need to stay alert and take the usual precautions. Avoid carrying valuables with you on the street or at the beach, and be discreet with expensive cameras and electronic equipment. When milling in crowds (in Hyannis or Provincetown, for example), place your billfold in an inside pocket, and hang onto your purse; anything kept in a backpack should be buried beyond reach. In closely packed places, such as restaurants, theaters, and ferries, keep your possessions in sight, and never sling a bag over the back of your chair: It's too easy a target. Alas, anything left visible in a car, locked or unlocked, is an open invitation, even in secluded Nantucket.

It would be rare in this region to find security staff screening all those who enter a hotel, especially if there's a restaurant on the premises, so don't relax your guard until your door is securely locked. Many areas are still so countrified that homeowners don't even lock their doors, and you'll find that most B&Bs are fairly laissez-faire; a few lack bedroom door locks altogether. If you're traveling light, it shouldn't matter, but if you're the cautious type, inquire about security measures before setting out.

Women, unfortunately, are no more safe here than anywhere else, so avoid visiting deserted areas alone, even during the day. Despite its reputation for tolerance, Provincetown has experienced sporadic incidents of **gay-bashing;** safety in numbers is probably the watchword here. Hyannis can get a bit rowdy when its dance clubs are in full swing, and even more so when they let out. For the most part, though, this is a peaceful place, more like the 1950s than the 1990s, and as long as you keep your wits about you, you should be able to relax, relatively speaking.

DRIVING SAFETY   Though Massachusetts is quite strict, drunk driving is a definite hazard: The police logs are full of offenses, from foolish to fatal. The best tactic is to avoid the offenders as much as possible, primarily by staying off the roads late at night. It's probably not a good idea to cover long distances at night, in any case, since there are no 24-hour gas stations to help out in case of emergency. In the event of a breakdown, drivers are usually advised to stay in the car with the doors locked until the police arrive. This is a small and friendly enough place, though, that it would probably be all right to take a chance on the kindness of strangers. Use your judgment, and err, if at all, on the side of caution.

Carjacking has yet to make an appearance on the Cape, but car theft runs high in Massachusetts as a whole, so lock your doors even if the natives never bother.

2 Getting to the Cape & Islands

The idea of traveling abroad on a budget is something of an oxymoron, but travelers can reduce the price of a plane ticket by several hundred dollars if they take the time to shop around. Overseas visitors can take advantage of the **APEX** (advance-purchase excursion) fares offered by all the major U.S. and European carriers. Aside from these, attractive values are offered by Virgin Atlantic from London to Boston and New York. For the best rates, compare fares and be flexible with the dates and times of travel.

A number of U.S. airlines offer service from Europe to the United States. If they do not have direct flights from Europe to Boston's Logan Airport (the closest international airport to the Cape and Islands), they can book you straight through on a connecting flight. You can make reservations by calling one of the following numbers in London: **American Airlines** (☎ 0181/572-5555), **Continental** (☎ 4412/9377-6464), **Delta** (☎ 0800/414-767), or **United** (☎ 0181/990-9900).

Logan Airport is served by more than 40 carriers, including **British Airways** (☎ 081/897-4000 in the U.K.) and **Air Canada** (☎ 800/776-3000). Any airline not served by this airport—the 15th busiest in the world—is likely to fly into New York, only a 30-minute commuter flight away.

IMMIGRATION & CUSTOMS

The visitor arriving by air, no matter what the port of entry, should cultivate patience and resignation before setting foot on U.S. soil. Getting through **immigration control** may take as long as 2 hours on some days, especially summer weekends, so have this guidebook or something else to read handy. Add the time it takes to clear Customs, and you will see that you should make a very generous allowance for delay in planning connections between international and domestic flights—figure on 2 to 3 hours at least.

In contrast, for the traveler arriving by car or by rail from Canada, the border-crossing formalities have been streamlined to the vanishing point. And for the traveler by air from Canada, Bermuda, and some places in the Caribbean, you can sometimes go through Customs and Immigration at the point of departure, which is much quicker.

3 Getting Around the United States

BY PLANE   On transatlantic or transpacific flights, some large U.S. airlines (for example, Northwest and Delta) offer **special discount tickets** for any of their U.S. destinations under the name **Visit USA.** The tickets or coupons are not on sale in the United States and must be purchased before you leave your point of departure. This system is the best, easiest, and fastest way to see the United States at low cost. You should obtain information well in advance from your travel agent or the office of the airline concerned, since the conditions attached to these discount tickets can be changed without advance notice.

BY TRAIN   International visitors can also buy a **USA Railpass,** good for 15 or 30 days of unlimited travel on Amtrak (☎ 800/USA-RAIL; www. amtrak.com). The pass is available through many foreign travel agents. Prices in 2000 for a 15-day pass were $295 off-peak (mid-October to late May), and $440 during peak travel periods; for a 30-day pass, $375 off-peak and $550 peak. With a foreign passport, you can also buy passes at some Amtrak offices in the United States, including locations in San Francisco, Los Angeles, Chicago, New York, Miami, Boston, and Washington, D.C. Reservations are generally required and should be made for each part of your trip as early as possible. Amtrak also offers an **Air/Rail Travel Plan** that allows you to travel by both train and plane; for information call ☎ 800/440-8202.

BY BUS   Although bus travel is often the most economical form of public transit for short hops between U.S. cities, it can also be slow and uncomfortable—certainly not for everyone (particularly when Amtrak, which is far more luxurious, offers similar rates). **Greyhound/Trailways** (☎ **800/231-2222;** www.greyhound.com), the sole nationwide bus line, offers an **Ameripass** for unlimited travel for 7 days at $209, 10 days at $259, 15 days at $319, 30 days at $429, 45 days at $469, and 60 days at $599. Special rates are available for senior citizens, children, and students. Passes can be purchased at a Greyhound terminal or on the Greyhound Web site. (If you plan to purchase your ticket on the Web site, please do so well in advance.)

See the "Getting There" and "Getting Around" sections in chapter 2 for more information on getting from Logan Airport to the Cape and Islands and other transportation questions.

Fast Facts: For the Foreign Traveler

Automobile Organizations   Auto clubs will supply maps, suggested routes, guidebooks, accident and bail-bond insurance, and emergency road service. The major auto club in the United States, with roughly 1,000 offices nationwide, is the **American Automobile Association (AAA).** Members of some foreign auto clubs have reciprocal arrangements with the AAA and enjoy its services at no charge. If you belong to an auto club in your home country, inquire about AAA reciprocity before you leave. You may be able to join the AAA even if you're not a member of a reciprocal club; to inquire, call the AAA (☎ **800/222-8252**).

In addition, some automobile-rental agencies now provide many of these same services. Inquire about their availability when you rent your car.

Automobile Rentals   To rent a car, you need a major credit card and a valid driver's license. Sometimes a passport or an international driver's license is also required if your driver's license is in a language other than English. You usually need to be at least 25 years of age, although some companies do rent to younger people (they may add a daily surcharge). Most of the major car-rental companies are represented on the Cape and Islands (see "Getting Around" in chapter 2).

Business Hours   Banks are typically open weekdays from 9am to 3 or 4pm, and there's 24-hour access to the automated teller machines (ATMs) at most banks and other outlets. Generally, offices are open weekdays from 9am to 5pm. Most stores are open 7 days a week and late into the evening in season. See "Business Hours" in "Fast Facts: The Cape & Islands," in chapter 2.

Climate   See "When to Go: Climate & Events," in chapter 2.

Currency Exchange   With many extensive banking chains, such as **Fleet** (☎ **800/841-4000;** www.fleet.com) and **Cape Cod Bank & Trust** (☎ **800/ 458-5100;** www.ccbt.com), now offering exchange services for virtually all foreign currencies, you can wander without fear of running out of cash. To get started, you might want to get some pocket money at the currency-exchange booths at Logan Airport.

Drinking Laws   See "Liquor Laws" in "Fast Facts: The Cape & Islands," in chapter 2.

Electricity   The United States uses 110 to 120 volts AC, 60 cycles, compared to 220 to 240 volts AC, 50 cycles, as in most of Europe. In addition to a 100-volt transformer, small appliances of non-American manufacture, such as hair dryers and shavers, will require a plug adapter, with two flat parallel pins.

Embassies and Consulates   All embassies are located in Washington, D.C.; some consulates are located in major U.S. cities, and most nations have a mission to the United Nations in New York City. There are no consulates on the Cape or Islands; however, Boston boasts three dozen. There is no consular representation in Massachusetts for **New Zealand,** but there are **British** and **Canadian** consulates in Boston (see below).

The **embassy of Australia** is at 1601 Massachusetts Ave. NW, Washington, D.C. 20036 (☎ **202/797-3000**). There is a consulate at 20 Beacon St., Boston, MA 02108 (☎ **617/248-8655**).

The **embassy of Canada** is at 501 Pennsylvania Ave. NW, Washington, D.C. 20001 (☎ **202/682-1740**). There's a consulate at Copley Place, Boston, MA 02116 (☎ **617/262-3760**).

The **embassy of Great Britain** is at 3100 Massachusetts Ave. NW, Washington, D.C. 20008 (☎ **202/462-1340**). There's a consulate at 600 Atlantic Ave., Boston, MA 02110 (☎ **617/248-9555**).

The **embassy of Ireland** is at 2234 Massachusetts Ave. NW, Washington, D.C. 20008 (☎ **202/462-3939**). There's a consulate at 535 Boylston St., Boston, MA 02116 (☎ **617/267-9330**).

The **embassy of New Zealand** is at 37 Observatory Circle NW, Washington, D.C. 20008 (☎ **202/328-4800**).

For information on other consulates, call **information** (☎ **411** within Boston, or 617/555-1212 outside of Boston), or consult the "Blue Pages" of the Boston phone book.

Emergencies   Call ☎ **911** to report a fire, contact the police, or get an ambulance. This is a toll-free call (no coins are required at a public telephone).

If you encounter serious problems while traveling, call the **Travelers Aid Society of Boston** (☎ **617/542-7286**), part of a nationwide, non-profit, social-service organization dedicated to helping travelers in difficult straits. Services might include reuniting families inadvertently separated while traveling; providing food and/or shelter to people temporarily stranded without cash; and even emotional counseling. The society maintains offices at terminals A and E at Logan Airport and an information booth at South Station. Though there are no offices on the Cape, give them a call if you need help.

Gasoline (Petrol)   One U.S. gallon equals 3.8 liters or 0.85 Imperial gallons. There are usually several grades (and price levels) of gasoline available at most gas stations, and the names change from company to company. The unleaded ones with the highest octane rating are among the most expensive and probably unnecessary (most rental cars take the least expensive "regular" unleaded gas).

Holidays   On the following legal national holidays, banks, government offices, and post offices are closed (stores, restaurants, and museums may be as well): January 1 (New Year's Day), the third Monday in January (Martin Luther King, Jr. Day), the third Monday in February (Presidents' Day), the last Monday in May (Memorial Day), July 4 (Independence Day), the first Monday in September (Labor Day), the second Monday in October (Columbus Day), November 11 (Veterans Day), the fourth Thursday in November (Thanksgiving), and December 25 (Christmas). Massachusetts institutions also observe Patriots' Day on the third Monday in April, and Boston's municipal offices may be closed for Evacuation Day (March 17) and Bunker Hill Day (June 17). Also, in presidential election years (1996, 2000, and so on), the Tuesday following the first Monday in November is Election Day, a national legal holiday.

Legal Aid   The foreign tourist will probably never become involved with the American legal system. If you are "pulled over" for a minor infraction (such as driving over the speed limit), never attempt to pay the fine directly to the police officer; this could be construed as attempted bribery, a much more serious crime. Pay fines by mail or directly to the local clerk of the court. If accused of a more serious offense, say and do nothing before consulting a lawyer. Here the burden is on the state to prove a person's guilt beyond reasonable doubt, and everyone has the right to remain silent, whether he or she is suspected of a crime or actually arrested. Once arrested, a person can make telephone call to a party of his or her choice: Call your consulate or embassy.

In less urgent situations, you may wish to consult the **Legal Aid hot line** (☎ **800/742-4107**).

Mail   If you'd like your mail to follow you on your vacation but aren't sure what your address will be, arrange to have it sent in your name c/o General Delivery at the post office of a town you expect to stay in or pass through (call ☎ **800/ 275-8777** for information on the nearest post office); be sure to include the five-digit ZIP (postal) code after the state abbreviation (MA). You'll have to pick up your mail in person and provide an ID, preferably with a photo (a driver's license or passport, for example). There is no charge for this service.

Mailboxes are not as ubiquitous on the Cape and Islands as they are in the city, so you may have to go to the post office in any case to send your own mail—or give it to your innkeeper for inclusion with theirs. The domestic postage rates are currently 20¢ for a postcard and 33¢ for a letter; again, be sure to include the ZIP code to speed delivery. Overseas rates vary, so ask your innkeeper or inquire at the post office.

The post office offers express mail, or you might use a commercial service such as **Federal Express** (call ☎ **800/238-5355** to arrange for a pickup, at a slight surcharge, or to find out the location of the nearest drop-off box). Credit cards can be used as payment. To be delivered to you, FedEx packages must be labeled with your full address, including ZIP code and telephone number.

Newspapers and Magazines   Distributed throughout New England, the *Boston Globe* (owned by the *New York Times*) does an excellent job of reporting international as well as domestic news. For local periodicals offering events listings and coverage of regional issues, see "Newspapers/Magazines" in "Fast Facts: The Cape & Islands," in chapter 2.

Measurements   The United States, with rare exception, does not operate on the metric system. For a detailed chart explaining U.S. measurements, see the inside front cover.

Radio and Television   Audiovisual media, with four coast-to-coast networks (ABC, CBS, NBC, and Fox), joined by the Public Broadcasting System (PBS) and local channels on UHF, offer a choice of about a dozen channels, and cable ups the choice to dozens more. Because broadcast reception tends to be poor on the Cape and non-existent on the Islands, most establishments subscribe to cable, including, quite often, "premium channels" such as HBO. Only the more luxurious smaller inns provide TVs in the rooms; most have a set in the sitting room. Many hotels and motels provide in-room cable, both basic and premium, as well as the option of pay-per-view movies. Most lodgings come with a clock radio. You'll find a wide choice of national and local radio stations offering various kinds of talk shows and music, from classical and "country" to jazz and rock. News and weather updates are usually broadcast on the hour, and all but certain educational stations are punctuated by frequent commercials. For local favorites, see "Radio" in "Fast Facts: The Cape & Islands," in chapter 2.

Safety   See "Safety" under "Preparing for Your Trip," above.

Taxes   In the United States there is no VAT (value-added tax) or other indirect tax at a national level. Every state, and each city in it, has the right to levy its own local tax on all purchases, and none of it is refundable to foreign visitors. In Massachusetts, the statewide sales tax, with certain exceptions, is 5%. For further details, see "Taxes" in "Fast Facts: The Cape & Islands," in chapter 2.

Telephone, Telegraph, Telex, Fax & E-Mail   On Cape Cod, you have to dial the area code **508** before every phone number, unless you are calling a number within the same town where you are making the call.

The telephone system in the United States is run by private corporations, so rates, especially for long-distance service and operator-assisted calls, can vary widely—even on calls made from public telephones. Local calls in Massachusetts usually cost 25¢. Pay phones do not accept pennies, and few will take anything larger than a quarter.

Hotel surcharges on long-distance and even local calls can be steep (often $1 per call); they should be posted on the phone, and if not, ask the hotel operator before calling around. You're usually better off using a public pay telephone: There should be one in your hotel's lobby, and you'll find them in most restaurants and gas stations as well. Outdoor pay phones usually are found in a glass booth or a waist-level console.

Most long-distance and **international calls** can be dialed directly from any phone. For calls to Canada and other parts of the United States, dial 1 followed by the area code and the seven-digit number. For international calls, dial 011 followed by the country code, city code, and the telephone number.

Note that all calls to area codes **800, 788,** or **888** are **toll-free.** However, calls to numbers with the area codes **700** and **900**—commercial lines that reverse the charges—can be very expensive (several dollars or more per minute), and they may exact a minimum charge of $15 or more.

For **reversed-charge or collect calls,** and for **person-to-person** calls, dial ☎ **0** (zero, not the letter *O*) followed by the area code and number; an operator will come on the line to assist you, and you should specify the particular type(s) of service you want. To make an international call, ask for an overseas operator.

For **local directory assistance** ("Information"), dial ☎ **411;** for long-distance information, dial 1, then the appropriate area code and ☎ **555-1212.**

Like the telephone system, **telegraph and telex services** are provided primarily by **Western Union.** You can dictate your message over the phone (☎ **800/325-6000**) or inquire about local offices where you can both send and receive messages as well as money (note, however, that the service charges for wiring money may run as high as 15% to 20% of the total). There are 15 Western Union offices on the Cape and two on each of the Islands.

Most of the larger hotels offer **fax service,** but the fee is usually quite high. Copy shops often offer fax service, as do packing services such as Mail Boxes Etc., which has four offices on the Cape. (Look in the Yellow Pages under "Packing Services.")

Of course, if you have a laptop with a modem and phone jack, you can send and receive your own, or access the Internet to send e-mail. The largest online service in the U.S. is **America Online** (☎ **800/827-3338**), which now also owns **CompuServe** (☎ **800/848-8990**).

Telephone directories for the Cape and Islands combine several types of listings. Usually, emergency numbers are listed inside the front cover, followed by community service listings, dialing instructions, and information on rates. The **White Pages,** which list subscribers in alphabetical order, are in some cases divided between private and business users (the latter appear grouped at the end, with a dark border). At the back of the book, the **Yellow Pages** list businesses by categories, such as automobile repairs, drugstores (pharmacies), restaurants, bookstores, and places of worship. In addition, the telephone directories that cover this region also include a supplement offering useful tourist information and discount coupons.

Time   The United States (with the exception of Alaska and Hawaii) falls into **four time zones:** eastern standard time (EST), central standard time (CST), mountain standard time (MST), and Pacific standard time (PST). All of Massachusetts (like New England as a whole) observes eastern standard time, which runs, for example, 5 hours behind London time, or 3 hours ahead of Los Angeles. Daylight saving time, when clocks are set forward an hour, remains in effect from the first Sunday in April to the last Sunday in October.

Tipping   Except in cases of exceptionally neglectful or downright rude service, tipping restaurant servers is not so much an option as an expectation (some would say, obligation). The wait staff, as a rule, receives less than the minimum hourly wage, with the assumption that tips will make up the difference. In a seasonal economy such as that prevailing on the Cape and Islands, workers may need to make enough in 3 or 4 months to get through the winter, when the job market all but disappears. Only a handful of restaurants and hotels applies an across-the-board gratuity of 15%. That amount is standard, however, for adequate service, and if you have substantial complaints, it would be far better to take it up with the management than take it out on the servers. For especially friendly or helpful service, go to 20% or more of the pre-tax total, including beverages. A bartender should be tipped at the same rate. As a rule, maitre d's and sommeliers do not expect a separate tip; they'll usually get a share of the total. A tip of $1 per vehicle for valet parking, or $1 per garment for coat-checking (a rarity here), is appreciated. No tipping is expected in self-service or fast-food restaurants, though college-bound employees may leave a cup beside the cash register to collect contributions.

In hotels, tip the bellhops $1 per piece (the same goes for skycaps at airports and railroad stations) and leave the housekeeping staff $1 to $2 per night. Cab drivers typically receive 15% of the fare; hairdressers and barbers, 15% to 20% of the bill. Tipping movie and theater ushers or gas-station attendants is not expected.

Toilets   You won't find public toilets or "rest rooms" on the streets in most U.S. cities, but they can be found in hotel lobbies, bars, restaurants, museums, department stores, railway and bus stations, or service stations. Note, however, that restaurants and bars in resorts or heavily visited areas may reserve their rest rooms for the use of their patrons. Some establishments display a notice that toilets are for the use of patrons only. You can ignore this sign or, better yet, avoid arguments by paying for a cup of coffee or a soft drink, which will qualify you as a patron. Large hotels and fast-food restaurants are probably the best bet for good, clean facilities. If possible, avoid the toilets at parks and beaches, which tend to be dirty.

The Upper Cape: Sandwich, Bourne, Falmouth & Mashpee

4

Just over an hour from Boston by car, the Upper Cape towns have become bedroom as well as summer communities. They may not have the let-the-good-times-roll feel of towns farther east, but then again they're spared the transient qualities that come with seasonal flows. Shops and restaurants—many catering to an older, affluent crowd—tend to stay open year-round.

The four Upper Cape towns are all quite different. Bourne straddles the canal; a couple of its villages (Bournedale and Buzzards Bay) are on the mainland side, and the others (Cataumet, Pocasset, Monument Beach, and Sagamore) are on the Cape side. The Canal provides this area with most of its recreational opportunities: biking, fishing, canal cruises, and the herring run. Cataumet is perhaps the prettiest village in Bourne, while many of Bourne's businesses, including popular factory outlets, are located on the mainland side of the bridge in Buzzards Bay.

Sandwich, the oldest town on the Cape, has a lovely historic village, with lots of unique shops and charming inns, at its core. Still, the town is primarily a pastoral place, with several working farms; in East Sandwich, miles of conservation land lead out to Sandy Neck, a barrier beach extending into Barnstable. The Old King's Highway (Route 6A) winds its way through Sandwich past a number of fine gift shops, galleries, and specialty stores.

Falmouth, the site of Cape Cod's first summer colony, is one of the larger towns on the Cape; it has a sizable year-round population of 30,000. Main Street—with a number of high-end boutiques and galleries, in addition to the usual touristy T-shirt shops—offers prime strolling and shopping. Falmouth's village green is quintessential New England, with two imposing historic churches: St. Barnabas, a sturdy reddish stone, and the First Congregational, a white-clapboard, steepled church boasting a Paul Revere bell. Just north of Falmouth center, along Route 28A, lies West Falmouth, perhaps the most attractive of Falmouth's eight villages; it has several good antiques stores, a fine general store, and a picture-perfect little harbor.

The most scenic drive in Falmouth leads to the beach at Falmouth Heights, a bluff covered with grand, shingled Victorians built during the first wave of tourist fever in the late 1800s. Falmouth's southern-most village is Woods Hole, which is the main ferry port for Martha's Vineyard. Home at any given time to several thousand research scientists, it has a certain neo-bohemian panache, lively bars, and an air of vigorous intellectual inquiry. It's also a working fishing village and one of the most picturesque spots on the Cape.

Mashpee is the ancestral home of the Cape's Native American tribe, the Wampanoags. Much of the town's coastline is occupied by a huge resort called New Seabury, while inland, the Mashpee National Wildlife Refuge sponsors frequent walking tours through its thousands of woodland acres.

1 Sandwich

3 miles (5km) E of Sagamore; 16 miles (26km) NW of Hyannis

Sandwich is both the oldest town on the Cape and, arguably, the most quaint. Towering oak trees and historic houses line its winding Main Street. Two early–19th-century churches and the columned Greek Revival Town Hall, in service since 1834, surround the town square. A 1640 gristmill still grinds corn beside bucolic Shawme Pond, which is frequented by swans, geese, ducks, and canoeists. To the north, villagers have built a boardwalk over the extensive salt marsh, and further east Sandy Neck, one of the Cape's most beautiful beaches, reaches out into the Cape Cod Bay.

Sandwich was founded in 1637 by a contingent of Puritans looking for a quiet place to worship. There is still an element of peacefulness in this little town located just a few miles from the Sagamore Bridge.

Sandwich's claim to fame is its prominence as the home to the nation's first glass factories in the early– to mid–19th centuries. The famous Boston and Sandwich Glass Company and others employed over 500 craftsmen in town. In fact, the town still supports a number of highly skilled glassmakers. Sandwich is fortunate to have two very well-endowed museums—the ✪ **Heritage Plantation** and the **Sandwich Glass Museum**—as well as several quirkier sites, like the **Green Briar Nature Center** and **Jam Kitchen.**

Many historic homesteads have been converted into charming bed-and-breakfasts that welcome guests year-round. There are also many excellent antique shops in the area. The town is also a convenient base for exploring other parts of the Cape that may offer more lively activities, like the nightlife of Hyannis or the ocean beaches of Wellfleet.

ESSENTIALS

GETTING THERE   If you're driving, turn east on Route 6A toward Sandwich after crossing either the Bourne or Sagamore bridge. You can also fly into Hyannis (see "Getting There" in chapter 2).

VISITOR INFORMATION   Contact the **Cape Cod Chamber of Commerce,** Routes 6 and 132, Hyannis, MA 02601 (☎ **888/332-2732** or 508/862-0700; fax 508/362-2156; www.capecodchamber.org; e-mail: info@capecodchamber.org), open year-round, mid-April to mid-November daily 9am to 5pm; mid-November to mid-April Monday to Saturday 10am to 4pm. Stop in at the **Route 25 Visitor's Center** (☎ **508/759-3814;** fax 508/759-2146), open daily, year-round 8am to 6pm. The **Cape Cod Canal Region Chamber of Commerce,** 70 Main St., Buzzards Bay (☎ **508/759-6000;** fax 508/759-6965; www.capecodcanalchamber.org; e-mail: canalreg@ capecod.net) open year-round, daily 10am to 5pm, can provide literature on both Sandwich and Bourne. A consortium of Sandwich businesses has put together an excellent walking guide (with map) available at most inns in town.

A GET-ACQUAINTED STROLL

This walk starts at the Sandwich Glass Museum, ends at the Dunbar Tea Shop, and takes 2 to 4 hours, depending on the number of stops you make; you'll cover about 1¼ miles. Your best bet is to explore the village on any midsummer day between 10am and 4pm, except Sunday, when some spots are closed.

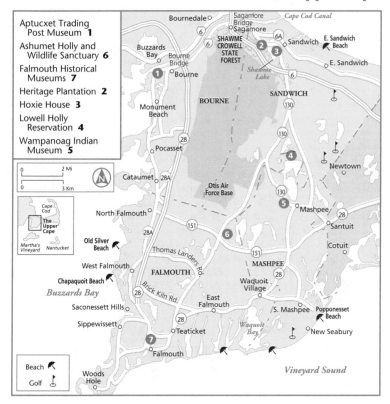

Aptucxet Trading Post Museum **1**

Ashumet Holly and Wildlife Sanctuary **6**

Falmouth Historical Museums **7**

Heritage Plantation **2**

Hoxie House **3**

Lowell Holly Reservation **4**

Wampanoag Indian Museum **5**

You may park (free with admission) at the **Sandwich Glass Museum,** 129 Main St. (☎ **508/888-0251**), a well-curated collection tracing the town's history with an emphasis on glass made in Sandwich from 1825 to 1888.

Farther down Grove Street is **Old Cemetery Point,** overlooking peaceful Shawme Pond, about one-third of a mile down the road. Read the historic headstones and keep an eye out for box turtles. Head back through the center of town and observe the exterior of **Old Town Hall,** on Main Street—a magnificent Greek Revival edifice, complete with Doric columns. It still houses some town offices. Continue down Main Street, past the **First Church of Christ,** which is topped by an impressive spire. Built by a colleague of renowned Boston architect Charles Bulfinch in 1847, it was reportedly modeled on Sir Christopher Wren's St. Mary-le-Bow, in London. The next church you'll pass, to your left, is an 1833 meetinghouse, which has been converted into the **Yesteryears Doll Museum** (☎ **508/888-1711;** closed November to mid-May), one of New England's largest collections of antique dolls, dollhouses, miniatures, and toys. The display cases of dolls dating back to the 17th century are propped on church pews in this charming small town museum.

Further down Main Street, across the street from the popular Dan'l Webster Inn, you'll find **The Weather Store** at 146 Main Street (☎ **508/888-1200**), a unique shop that stocks weathervanes, globes, sundials, and more and is devoted to the observation and understanding of New England's famously quirky weather.

Continue down Main Street, take a left on Jarves Street to admire the **Belfry Inn and Bistro** (☎ **800/844-4542** or 508/888-8550), a church and rectory converted into a very smart inn and restaurant. The restaurant, with its soaring ceilings and stained glass, is surely the prettiest and most unique dining space on Cape Cod.

Retracing your steps along Jarves Street, make a left-right zigzag along Main and School streets to reach Water Street, which skirts the eastern edge of Shawme Pond. Directly opposite, on the shore side of Water Street, you'll spot the **Hoxie House** at 18 Water Street (☎ **508/888-1173**), one of the oldest houses on the Cape. The interior is spare—not out of any aesthetic ideal, but because resources were so hard to come by in colonial New England. The settlers didn't even have closets because they were taxed as an additional room, windows were tiny to avoid the tax on glass, and pockets were considered a waste of good material. Entertaining docents explain all the details in frequent tours.

After the Hoxie House tour, head northward along Water Street, passing (on the same side) the **Thornton W. Burgess Museum,** 4 Water St. (☎ **508/888-4668**), celebrating the life and work of native son Burgess (1874–1965), a highly successful author of children's books and creator of such still-beloved characters as Jimmy Skunk and Grandfather Frog. Just past the Burgess Museum is the **Dexter Grist Mill** (☎ **508/888-1173**), a lovingly restored water mill (ca. 1640). The millstones still grind corn; buy a bag of meal to go, but only if you'll have a chance to whip up something later in the day (it doesn't keep well). Now that you're back at the center of town, this is a good time to pause for a spot of tea. The **Dunbar Tea Shop,** 1 Water St. (☎ **508/833-2485**), serves hearty lunches, teas, and breakfast. The attached shop features British imports and antiques, including vintage books. It's a wonderful place to while away a good portion of the afternoon.

BEACHES & RECREATIONAL PURSUITS

BEACHES   For the Sandwich beaches listed below, non-resident parking stickers—$20 for the length of your stay—are available at **Sandwich Town Hall Annex,** 145 Main St. (☎ **508/833-8012**). Note that there's no swimming allowed within the Cape Cod Canal as the currents are much too swift and dangerous.

✪ **Sandy Neck Beach,** off Sandy Neck Road in East Sandwich: This 6-mile stretch of silken barrier beach with low, rounded dunes is popular with endangered piping plovers—and, unfortunately, their nemesis, off-road vehicles (ORV). ORV permits ($80 per season for non-residents) can be purchased at the gatehouse (☎ **508/362-8300**) as long as it's not nesting season. ORV drivers must be equipped with supplies like a spare tire, jack, shovel, and tire-pressure gauge. Parking costs $10 per day in season, and up to 3 days of camping in self-contained vehicles is permitted at $10 per night.

- **Town Neck Beach,** off Town Neck Road in Sandwich: A bit rocky but ruggedly pretty, this narrow beach offers a busy view of passing ships, plus rest rooms and a snack bar. Parking costs $4 per day, or you could hike from town (about 1½ miles) via the community-built boardwalk spanning the salt marsh.
- **Wakeby Pond,** Ryder Conservation Area, John Ewer Road (off South Sandwich Rd. on the Mashpee border): The beach, on the Cape's largest freshwater pond, has lifeguards, rest rooms, and parking ($4 per day).

BICYCLING   The **U.S. Army Corps of Engineers** (☎ **508/759-5991**) maintains a flat, 14-mile loop along the ✪ **Cape Cod Canal,** equally suited to bicyclists, skaters, runners, and strollers. The most convenient place to park (free) is at the Bourne Recreation Area, north of the Bourne Bridge, on the Cape side. You can also park at the Sandcatcher Recreation Area at the end of Freezer Road in Sandwich. The closest bike rentals can be found at Cape Cod Bike Rental (☎ **508/833-2453**) at 40 Route 6A in Sandwich, which rents mountain bikes for around $22 per day.

BOATING **Paddle Cape Cod** (☎ 888/226-6593 or 508/564-4051; www.
paddlecapecod.com; e-mail: cccanoe@capecod.net) runs naturalist-guided trips
throughout the Cape. Trips (3 to 3½ hours)—daily, weather permitting, April
through October—cost $30 for a solo kayak or $50 for a tandem kayak or canoe.
Sunset trips are particularly popular. All equipment is supplied, and trips include juice
and snacks. Call for a schedule.

If you want to explore on your own by canoe, you can rent one in Falmouth and
paddle around Old Sandwich Harbor, Sandy Neck, or the salt-marsh maze of Scorton
Creek, which leads out to Talbot Point, a wooded spit of conservation land.

FISHING Sandwich has eight fishable ponds; for details and a license, inquire at
Town Hall in the center of town (☎ 508/888-0340). Permits cost non-residents
$38.50 for the season, $24.50 for a 3-day pass. Children, seniors and Massachusetts
residents receive discounts. No permit is required for fishing from the banks of the
Cape Cod Canal. Here your catch might include striped bass, bluefish, cod, pollock,
flounder, or fluke. Call the **Army Corps of Engineers** (☎ 508/759-5991) for canal
tide and fishing information. Local deep-water charters include the *Tigger Two,*
docked in the Sandwich Marina (☎ 508/888-8372).

FITNESS The local fitness center is the **Sportsite Health Club** at 315 Cotuit Rd.
in Sandwich (☎ 508/888-7900). It offers 15,000 square feet of Nautilus and other
fitness equipment, along with steam baths, saunas, classes, and free child care.

GOLF The **Sandwich Hollows Golf Club,** on Service Road in East Sandwich
(☎ 508/888-3384), is a 6,200-yard, par-71 town-owned course. In season, a round
costs $40 to $47. The 18-hole, par-3 **Holly Ridge Golf Course,** on Country Club
Road in South Sandwich (☎ 508/428-5577), is, at 2,900 yards, shorter and easier.
A round costs $27 in season.

NATURE & WILDLIFE AREAS The **Shawme-Crowell State Forest,** off Route
130 in Sandwich (☎ 508/888-0351), offers 285 campsites and 742 acres to roam.
Entrance is free; parking costs $2. The **Sandwich Boardwalk,** which the community
rebuilt in 1991 after Hurricane Bob blew away the 1874 original, links the town and
Town Neck Beach by way of salt marshes that attract a great many birds, including
great blue herons. The 76-acre grounds of the **Heritage Museum of Sandwich**
(☎ 508/888-3300; seasonal, admission charged) afford a pleasant stroll, especially
when the rhododendrons burst forth in multicolored bloom in May and June. To
obtain a map of other conservation areas in Sandwich (some 16 sites encompassing
nearly 1,300 acres), stop by the **Sandwich Conservation Commission** at 16 Jan
Sebastian Dr. (off Rte. 130; ☎ 508/888-4200).

As if to signify how oddly enchanted this little corner of the world is, there's a sweet
little (57-acre) nature center here—and within it is an even sweeter kitchen, where
local ladies have been cooking up jams and jellies since 1903. The **Green Briar Nature
Center & Jam Kitchen** is at 6 Discovery Hill (off Rte. 6A, about 1½ miles east of
town center; ☎ 508/888-6870); once you've caught a whiff of the jam, you'll want
to take some home. (Try the local delicacy, beach-plum jelly.) Children will be
intrigued by the expansive kitchen, as well as some old-fashioned nature exhibits on
such animals as rabbits, turtles, iguanas, and snakes. The center is open mid-April to
December, Monday to Saturday 10am–4pm, Sunday 1–4pm; January to mid-April
Tuesday to Saturday 10am–4pm. Admission by donation. Summer storytimes at
10:30am on Mondays, Wednesdays, and Saturdays cost $1 per person.

TENNIS Sandwich has public courts at the Wing School, Oak Ridge School,
Forestdale School, and Sandwich High School; call the **Sandwich Recreation
Department** (☎ 508/888-4361) for details.

SANDWICH HISTORICAL SIGHTS

✪ **Dexter Grist Mill.** Water St. (on Shawme Pond, near Main St.). ☎ **508/888-1173.** Admission $1.50 adults, 75¢ children 6–12; combination ticket ($2.50 adults, $1 children) available from the Hoxie House (see below). Mid-June to mid-Sept Mon–Sat 10am–4:45pm. Closed mid-Sept to mid-June.

This charmingly weathered building has survived some 3½ centuries and at least as many lives. At present, it's serving its original purpose, grinding corn with turbine power; you can watch the wooden gears in action and buy a bag to take home and cook up into colonial "jonnycakes" (short for "cakes for the journey") or trendy polenta. During the glassmaking boom of the 1800s, this venerable mill was but one of many pressed into service to keep the factory workers well fed. When the laborers dispersed, the mill sat useless, until a local entrepreneur thought to convert it into a tearoom to serve the new tide of tourists arriving by motorcar. The mill was fully restored in 1961 and will probably be good for a few more centuries of stalwart service.

✪ **Heritage Plantation of Sandwich.** Grove and Pine sts. (about ½ mile SW of the town center). ☎ **508/888-3300.** Admission $9 adults, $8 senior citizens, $4.50 children 6–18. Mid-May to mid-Oct daily 10am–5pm; no tickets sold after 4:15pm. Closed late Oct to mid-May.

This is one of those rare museums that appeals equally to adults and the children they drag along: The latter will leave clamoring for another visit. All ages have the run of 76 beautifully landscaped acres, crisscrossed with walking paths and riotous with color in late spring, when the towering rhododendrons burst forth in blooms that range from soft pink to gaudy orange. Scattered buildings house a wide variety of collections, from Native American artifacts to Early American weapons. The art holdings, especially the primitive portraits, are outstanding. The high point for most children will be a ride on the 1912 carousel (safely preserved indoors). Also sure to dazzle is the replica Shaker round barn packed with gleaming antique automobiles, including some once owned by celebrities (don't miss Gary Cooper's Duesenberg). Next door is the Carousel Cafe, good for a restorative snack, including soups, sandwiches, and salads; the gift shop at the gatehouse is also worth checking out. Call ahead for a schedule of the outdoor summer concerts usually held Sundays around 2pm, free with admission.

Hoxie House. 18 Water St. (on Shawme Pond, about ¼ mile S of the town center). ☎ **508/888-1173.** Admission $1.50 adults, 75¢ children 12–16, free for children under 12. Combination ticket ($2.50 adults, $1 children) available here for Dexter Grist Mill (see above), too. Mid-June to Sept Mon–Sat 10am–4:30pm; Sun 1–4:30pm. Closed mid-Oct to mid-June.

A lapsed contender for the title of the Cape's oldest house (a couple of privately owned Provincetown houses appear to have a stronger claim), this saltbox (ca. 1680) is nonetheless a noteworthy beauty, with its diamond-pane windows and broad interior planking—made of "king's wood," so called because England's king had, under pain of severe penalty, reserved the larger trees for his warships. The house was occupied, pretty much as is, with neither electricity nor plumbing, into the 1950s, which explains how it remained so remarkably intact. Even so, it had to be taken apart and reassembled to serve as the model colonial home you see today. Fortunately, restorers opted not for the cluttered "colonial revival" look, but a stark austerity that's much more historically accurate and shows off to advantage a handful of antiques on semi-permanent loan from Boston's Museum of Fine Arts.

✪ **Sandwich Glass Museum.** 129 Main St. (in the center of town). ☎ **508/888-0251.** Admission $3.50 adults, $1 children 6–16, children under 6 free. Apr–Dec daily 9:30am–5pm; Feb–Mar Wed–Sun 9:30am–4pm. Closed Jan, Thanksgiving, and Christmas.

Even if you don't consider yourself a glass fan, make an exception for this fascinating museum, which captures the history of the town above and beyond its legendary industry. A brief video introduces Deming Jarves's brilliant endeavor, which flourished from 1828 to 1888, bringing glassware—a hitherto rare commodity available only to the rich—within reach of the middle classes. Jarves picked the perfect spot, surrounded by old-growth forest, to fuel the furnaces (the greenery has only recently recovered), with a harbor handy for shipping in fine sand from farther up the coast and salt-marsh hay with which to pack outgoing orders. Demand was such that Jarves imported hordes of immigrant workers, housing them in the rather shameful shanties of "Jarvestown." All went well (for him) until Midwestern factories started using coal; unable to keep up with their level of mass production, he switched back to hand-blown techniques just as his workforce was ready to revolt.

None of this turmoil is evident in the dainty artifacts displayed in a series of sunny rooms; and of course, the fact that the factory's output was finite makes surviving examples all the more valuable. Since the museum is run by the Sandwich Historical Society, one room is given over to changing exhibits highlighting other eras in the town's history, such as its stellar seafaring days. An excellent little gift shop stocks Sandwich-glass replicas, as well as original glassworks by area artisans. During the summer season, volunteers demonstrate glassmaking techniques, including glass bead-making and "lamp work," which refers to the making of finely detailed miniature glass flowers and animals.

Thornton W. Burgess Museum. 4 Water St. (on Shawme Pond, near the center of town). ☎ **508/888-4668.** Suggested donation $2 adults, $1 children. Mid-Apr to Oct Mon–Sat 10am–4pm; Sun 1–4pm. Closed Nov to mid-Apr.

Prominent in the early half of the 20th century, this prolific and locally bred children's book author racked up 170 tomes to his credit, as well as 15,000 stories. His somewhat simple texts, featuring anthropomorphic animals prone to preaching, may seem a bit dated, but they still go over big with little listeners, especially at the summer-afternoon story hours (call for details). The gift shop carries reissues of his work, should they desire a memento. It's also worth a peek inside to see Harrison Cady's spirited illustrations and exhibits attesting to Burgess's other life work, conservation. He may have inherited this interest from his aunt (the original inhabitant of this 1756 cottage), who gained a certain notoriety for claiming that she could communicate directly with the animal and plant worlds.

Yesteryears Doll Museum. Main and River sts. (in the center of town). ☎ **508/888-1711.** Admission $3 adults, $2 senior citizens and children 12–17, $1 children under 12. June to mid-Sept Tues–Sat 10am–4pm (last tour 3:30pm). Closed mid-Sept to May.

Barely funded by a "doll hospital" and appraisal service, this musty museum is nonetheless a gem. The holdings are extraordinary, from a 17th-century Queen Anne doll to several "Nuremberg kitchens," complete with tiny crockery, and right on up to the recent past—embodied in a passel of Barbies. The collection is housed in a recently restored Gothic Revival meetinghouse; glass cases are set athwart wooden church benches, and there's a certain mazelike quality that could send shivers down the spines of the easily spooked. Those of a certain age may suffer frisson after frisson of recognition and loss; those accompanying them may wonder at the fuss, but eventually get caught up in the scaled-down drama of it all.

KID STUFF

The venerable 18-hole **Sandwich Minigolf** (☎ **508/833-1905**), at the corner of Main Street and Route 6A, is a grassy 1950s classic that encapsulates Cape Cod history. Built on a former cranberry bog, it boasts an unusual floating green. Admission is $5 for adults, $4 for children.

SHOPPING

Small as it is, Sandwich has a handful of appealing shops, all individually stocked—some with items you're unlikely to find anywhere else. Most of the shops are concentrated in the center of town. Several of the museums listed above (see "Sandwich Historical Sights," above) also have worthwhile gift shops.

ANTIQUES & COLLECTIBLES   H. Richard Strand Antiques, 2 Grove St., at Main Street, in the center of town (☎ **508/888-3230**), is a treasure-packed federal manse—it's so museumlike, you may be moved to whisper. The prices may stun you into silence, but so will the quality.

The **Sandwich Antiques Center,** 131 Rte. 6A, at Jarves Street (☎ **508/833-3600**), showcases wares from over 100 dealers in 6,000 square feet of rooms; it's headed by a congenial auctioneer and offers virtual one-stop shopping for the likes of Sandwich glass, primitives, country furnishings—you name it. The center is open daily year-round.

ARTS & CRAFTS   The Giving Tree Gallery, 550 Rte. 6A, East Sandwich, about 4 miles east of the town center (☎ **508/888-5446**), is an art and fine-craft gallery with something extra: a nature walk through the woods. Intriguing sculptures are placed strategically around the property. The path through a bamboo forest is for those who appreciate a Far Eastern aesthetic. In fact, there's something very Zen about the whole Giving Tree experience. Closed January to March.

For the finest in art glass and the perfect souvenir of your Sandwich vacation, visit **The Glass Studio,** 470 Rte. 6A, East Sandwich (☎ **508/888-6681**), where master glassblower Michael Magyar crafts one-of-a-kind pieces like his "sea bubbles" series and his Venetian-style goblets.

BOOKS   Titcomb's Book Shop, 432 Rte. 6A, East Sandwich, about 4 miles east of the town center (☎ **508/888-2331**), has a terrific selection of books (both new and used) relating to Cape Cod and much more. Look for the life-size statue of Ben Franklin out front.

FOOD & WINE   Crow Farm, 192 Rte. 6A, a quarter mile east of the town center (☎ **508/888-0690**), is a picture-perfect farm stand harboring superb local produce like sweet corn, tomatoes, peaches, and apples, as well as flowers. It's closed Sunday in summer but open daily in spring and fall. Closed late December through April.

GIFTS/HOME DECOR   The Weather Store, 146 Main St. (☎ **508/888-1200**), has a fascinating collection of meteorological paraphernalia, old and new, ranging from antique instruments to coffee-table books. It's open year-round, but from January through April, it's open by chance or appointment.

SEAFOOD   Joe's Lobster & Fish Market, off Coast Guard Road, near Sandwich Marina (☎ **800/491-2971** or 508/888-2971), is where to go for the freshest fish and shellfish to prepare at your cottage rental.

WHERE TO STAY

Sandwich has a number of motels along Route 6A, but the one with the best location is **Sandy Neck Motel** at 669 Route 6A, East Sandwich (☎ **800/564-3992** or 508/362-3992; www.sandyneck.com; e-mail: snmotel@capecod.net), which sits at the entrance to the road leading to Sandy Neck, the best beach in these parts. Rates are $89–$99 double and $125–$214 for one- and two-room efficiencies. Closed November through March.

EXPENSIVE

✪ **Bay Beach.** 1–3 Bay Beach Lane (on Town Beach), Sandwich, MA 02563. ☎ **800/475-6398** or 508/888-8813. Fax 508/888-5416. www.baybeach.com. E-mail:

info@baybeach.com. 7 units. A/C TV TEL. Summer $175–$345 double. Rates include full breakfast. MC, V. Closed Nov–Apr. No children under 16.

These two homes, overlooking Town Neck Beach with a view of the Sagamore Bridge and the boat traffic along the canal, are filled with amenities, from minifridges and hair dryers to CD players. As Sandwich's only on-beach lodging option, Bay Beach offers immaculate, modern rooms perfect for romantic interludes. Some have fireplaces and double Jacuzzis. For the fitness-minded, there's an exercise room on the premises.

The Dan'l Webster Inn. 149 Main St. (in the center of town), Sandwich, MA 02563. ☎ **800/444-3566** or 508/888-3622. Fax 508/888-5156. www.danlwebsterinn.com. E-mail: dwi@capecod.net. 54 units. A/C TV TEL. Summer $149–$189 double; $219–$349 suite. AE, CB, DC, DISC, MC, V.

This large and popular lodging and dining spot in the center of Sandwich village is a dependable bet for a comfortable stay or a hearty meal. The inn encompasses a modern main building, designed to look historic, as well as several historic homes nearby that have been outfitted with modern amenities. The main building sits on the site of a colonial tavern favored by Daniel Webster, the famous orator and prominent Boston lawyer, who enjoyed fishing on the Cape. The inn is operated by the Catania family (owners of the Hearth'N Kettle restaurants dotted about the Cape), with professionalism and style. All the rooms are ample and nicely furnished with reproductions. The suites located in nearby historic houses are especially appealing; they feature fireplaces and canopy beds. There are also eight deluxe one-room suites in the main building with amenities like balconies, gas fireplaces, oversize whirlpool baths, and heated tile floors in the bathrooms. All inn rooms have hair dryers, and there is daily room service available from 8am to 9pm.

A small heated pool suffices for a quick dip, and those seeking a real workout can repair to a local health club, where admission is gratis for guests. The inn's common spaces are convivial, if bustling; sometimes tour buses stop here. The restaurant, which turns out surprisingly sophisticated fare, is quite good, especially considering the high volume (see "Where to Dine," below).

MODERATE

✪ **The Belfry Inne.** 8 Jarves St. (in the center of town), Sandwich, MA 02563. ☎ **800/844-4542** or 508/888-8550. Fax 508/888-3922. www.belfryinn.com. E-mail: info@belfryinn.com. 14 units. Summer $95–$165 double. Rates include full breakfast. AE, MC, V.

You can't miss it: It's the gaudiest "painted lady" in town, restored to its original flamboyant glory after skulking for decades under three layers of siding. This turreted 1879 rectory has turned its fancy to romance, with queen-size retrofitted antique beds, a claw–foot tub (or Jacuzzi) for every room, and a scattering of fireplaces and private balconies. The third floor, with its single attic rooms and its delightful Alice in Wonderland mural leading up to the belfry, is perfect for families with children. Next door is the Abbey, a former church, that owner Chris Wilson has converted into six fun and deluxe guest rooms, and a very fine restaurant (see below). The Abbey rooms are painted vivid colors and tucked cleverly into sections of this old church. One room features a stained-glass window; another has angel windows. All of the Abbey rooms have Jacuzzis.

Isaiah Jones Homestead. 165 Main St. (in the center of town), Sandwich, MA 02563. ☎ **800/526-1625** or 508/888-9115. Fax 508/888-9648. www.isaiahjones.com. E-mail: info@isaiahjones.com. 7 units. Summer $99–$170 double. Rates include full breakfast. AE, DISC, MC, V. Children under 12 cannot be accommodated.

Of the many B&Bs in Sandwich Center, this one is a particularly good value, though the fancier rooms tend to be more expensive (and more elegant) than those at other small B&Bs in town. Innkeepers Jan and Doug Klapper have carefully appointed this courtly 1849 Victorian with fine antiques and reproductions. Some rooms have romantic touches like fireplaces and whirlpool baths; all have hair dryers. Two mini-suites in the Carriage Barn have sitting alcoves. The room named for industrial magnate Deming Jarves boasts an inviting floral-curtained half-canopy bed and an oversize whirlpool tub. The gentility that prevails at the candlelight breakfast, served with fine china and crystal, completes the picture.

Wingscorton Farm Inn. 11 Wing Blvd. (off Rte. 6A, about 5 miles E of the town center), East Sandwich, MA 02537. ☎ **508/888-0534.** Fax 508/888-0545. 2 units, 1 carriage house, 1 cottage. Summer $135 suite; $175 carriage house; $1000 weekly cottage. Rates for suite and carriage house include full breakfast. AE, MC, V. Pets welcome.

This 7-acre farmhouse inn will delight youngsters and animal lovers of all ages. It's been a working farm since 1758 and still houses a cheerful brood of sheep, goats, dogs, cats, chickens, a pet turkey, and a potbellied pig on its tree-shaded grounds. The main house is a classic colonial with a "keeping room" boasting a 9-foot-long hearth. Upstairs are two paneled bedrooms with canopy beds, working fireplaces, braided rugs, and antiques. Modernists might prefer the carriage house, with its skylight-suffused loft bedroom, kitchen (with woodstove), and private deck and patio; it doesn't cost appreciably more. There is also a cottage on the grounds. Guests staying in the main inn and carriage house can enjoy a hearty multicourse breakfast at the long farmhouse table in the kitchen. A private bay beach is a short walk down a country lane.

INEXPENSIVE

Captain Ezra Nye House. 152 Main St. (in the center of town), Sandwich, MA 02563. ☎ **800/388-2278** or 508/888-6142. Fax 508/833-2897. www.captainezranyehouse.com. E-mail: captnye@aol.com. 6 units. A/C. Summer $110–$125 double. Rates include full breakfast. AE, DISC, JCB, MC, V. Children under 10 cannot be accommodated.

This handsome 1829 federal manse with its fanlight and twin chimneys is set in the center of the village, within walking distance of many historic sites. Innkeepers Elaine and Harry Dickson are most gracious and set high standards in hospitality. Rooms, if not ultra-luxurious, are nicely appointed with eclectic antiques. Rates are a bargain, and breakfast tends to be quite substantial, along the lines of goat cheese soufflé or upside-down apple-French toast.

The Inn at Sandwich Center. 118 Tupper Rd. (in the center of town), Sandwich, MA 02563. ☎ **800/249-6949** or 508/888-6958. Fax 508/888-2746. www.innatsandwich.com. E-mail: info@innatsandwich.com. 5 units. A/C. Summer $100–$135 double. Rates include full breakfast. AE, MC, V. Children under 12 cannot be accommodated.

This historic B&B started out as a plain 1750s saltbox and got a fancy Federal makeover a century later. Happily, the interior decor has been similarly updated. Some rooms have four-poster beds. Rooms are spacious and tastefully decorated with antiques and reproductions. Amenities include turndown service, handmade chocolates, robes, and hair dryers. A full breakfast, featuring homemade specialties like pecan maple French toast, is served in the keeping room, with its original fireplace and beehive oven. New owners Joe and Louise Trapp are particularly proud of their gardens, featuring a rose garden with arbor and 32 different hybrids of roses, hundreds of tulips, and thousands of daffodils. The Sandwich Glass Museum is directly across the street.

ⓘ Family-Friendly Hotels & Restaurants

Betsy's Diner in Falmouth *(see p. 85)*   This classic 1950s diner offers all the old faves, plus home–baked pastries.

The Clam Shack in Falmouth *(see p. 86)*   Children will love the size of this place (it's Lilliputian), the plain fare, and all the activity on the harbor.

The Silver Lounge in North Falmouth *(see p. 85)*   This is the favorite restaurant for generations of kids because of the little red caboose attached to the side. There are just nine booths in the caboose, so you'll need to get there early if you want to snag one.

Spring Garden Inn in East Sandwich *(see below)*   With its spacious tree-shaded backyard and pool, this well-maintained motel is understandably popular with families.

Wingscorton Farm Inn in East Sandwich *(see p. 62)*   What could beat a working farm—with a beach within walking distance—for both education and fun?

Seth Pope House. 110 Tupper Rd. (in the center of town), Sandwich, MA 02563. ☎ **888/ 996-7384** or 508/888-5916. www.Sethpope.com. E-mail: info@sethpope.com. 3 units. A/C. Summer $85–$95 double. Rates include full breakfast. MC, V. Closed Nov–Apr.

Perhaps not everyone would be comfortable sleeping in a 300-year-old home, but traditionalists will be delighted with these gracious accommodations provided by innkeepers John and Beverly Dobel. Each room in this lovingly maintained 1699 saltbox has a distinctive decor. The Colonial Room features exposed beams, a pencil-post bed, and a cherry bonnet chest. The Victorian is pink-accented with plenty of marble. Also pleasant is the "Pineapple Room," with twin pineapple-post beds and a salt-marsh view. Breakfast in the old keeping room features a couple of courses: a parfait of fruit, granola, and yogurt; and then a baked omelet or stuffed French toast.

Spring Garden Inn. 578 Rte. 6A (P.O. Box 867; about 5 miles E of the town center), East Sandwich, MA 02537. ☎ **800/303-1751** or 508/888-0710. Fax 508/833-2849. www.springgarden.com. E-mail: springg@capecod.net. 11 units. A/C TV TEL. Summer $104 double; $124 efficiency. Rates include continental breakfast. DISC, MC, V. Closed Dec–Mar.

This well-maintained, beautifully landscaped motel overlooks acres of conservation land known as the Great Sandwich Salt Marsh. Every room comes with a southern-oriented patio or porch that takes in the lush view. All units have coffeemakers and minifridges, and outside, barbeque grills and picnic tables are available. With its spacious, tree-shaded backyard and pool, the motel with its reasonable rates is understandably popular with families. Guests will also appreciate the complimentary homemade continental breakfasts.

Spring Hill Motor Lodge. 351 Rte. 6A (about 2½ miles E of the town center), East Sandwich, MA 02537. ☎ **800/647-2514** or 508/888-1456. Fax 508/833-1556. www.sunsol.com/ springhill/. E-mail: raldhurs@capecod.net. 24 units, 4 cottages. A/C TV TEL. Summer $95–$125 double; $160 efficiency; $1100/weekly for 1-bedroom cottage; $1,400/weekly for 2-bedroom cottage. AE, CB, DC, DISC, MC, V.

This motel boasts all sorts of amenities and the owners keep it in top condition. Most impressive are the oversize, night-lit tennis court, with plenty of room for spectators, and a large, elegantly landscaped heated pool surrounded by comfortable lounge chairs. All rooms have minifridges and coffeemakers. The interiors are cheerfully contemporary, the grounds verdant. In addition to the motel rooms, there are four cottages with full kitchens that are light, airy, and comfortable.

✪ **The Village Inn at Sandwich.** 4 Jarves St. (in the center of town), Sandwich, MA 02563. ☎ **800/922-9989** or 508/833-0363. Fax 508/833-2063. www.capecodinn.com. E-mail: capecodinn@aol.com. 8 units, 2 with shared bathroom. Summer $85–$105 double. Rates include full breakfast. AE, DISC, MC, V.

Why envy the guests relaxing in rockers on the wraparound porch of this gracious 1837 Federal house when you could be among them? Better yet, you'll have recourse to surprisingly light and airy sleeping quarters, with gleaming bleached floors, California-ish splashes of colorful fabric, and enveloping duvets. From the French country-style dining room to the cozy dormer attic, the mood is one of carefree comfort. Innkeeper Susan Fehlinger, an artist, runs a program called Sandwich Artworks with workshops by well-known Cape Cod artists like Karen North Wells, Joyce Zavorskas, and Rosalie Nadeau. Workshops and B&B packages are available.

WHERE TO DINE
MODERATE

Aquagrille. 14 Gallo Rd. (next to Sandwich Marina). ☎ **508/888-8889.** Reservations recommended. Main courses $7–$20. AE, MC, V. May–Oct Mon–Fri noon–2:30pm and 5–9pm; Sat–Sun noon–9pm; call for off-season hours. SEAFOOD.

Overlooking Sandwich's picturesque marina and not-so-picturesque power plant, this dining spot, owned by the respected Zartarian family of The Paddock Restaurant in Hyannis, is trying hard to be the premier place for fish in Sandwich. All the elements are in place: a spacious, attractive dining room decorated in pleasing aqua shades with a glass-enclosed harbor-view deck; a long, curving bar; and an attentive wait staff. The food is delicious and plentiful, with fish (grilled or fried) the obvious choice, plus lots of pasta dishes. The towering lobster salad with haricot vert, tomato, avocado, chives, and crème fraîche is the perfect antidote to a steamy summer night. Those with larger appetites may want to choose their grilled fish (tuna, salmon, swordfish, or scrod) and then choose their sauce (Cajun rémoulade, chipotle aioli, béarnaise, dill mayonnaise, roasted red bell pepper, or tomato-and-basil stew). Try to get a table that doesn't face the power plant.

✪ **The Belfry Bistro.** 8 Jarves St. (in the center of town). ☎ **508/888-8550.** Reservations recommended. Main courses $14–$25. AE, MC, V. Apr to mid-Oct Tues–Sat 5–10pm; Sun 11am–2pm; call for off-season hours. NEW AMERICAN.

Sandwich's most romantic dining option is located in a renovated Abbey, formerly a Catholic Church. The gothic space is quite spectacular with flying buttresses supporting the ceiling's high arches. Once seated, guests can concentrate on the snowy, dense linens, intimate lighting, and pleasing menu. Portions are generous and elegantly presented. Chef Michael Arbarchuk's menu changes seasonally, but among the appetizers you might find a lobster, scallop, and leek strudel wrapped in phyllo dough, baked golden brown, and served on a bed of sautéed leeks and scallions with a chardonnay cream sauce. The entrees run the gamut from the delicate shrimp scampi with artichoke hearts; to the hearty grilled filet mignon served with garlic and leek mashed potatoes on a white bean ragout. You might be tempted by the Seafood Champagne (salmon, tilapia, and scallops), but it is perhaps an overindulgent choice. Desserts here are clearly a specialty; especially good is the old-fashioned Victorian gingerbread with fresh berries.

The Dan'l Webster Inn. 149 Main St. (in the center of town). ☎ **508/888-3623.** Reservations recommended. Main courses $18–$27. AE, CB, DC, DISC, MC, V. Daily 8am–9pm; call for off-season hours. INTERNATIONAL.

You have a choice of four main dining rooms—from a casual, colonial-motif tavern to a skylight-topped conservatory fronting a splendid garden. The atmospheric Tavern at the Inn, with its own pub-style menu, is fast becoming the most popular. All of the dining rooms are served by the same kitchen, under the masterful hand of chef/co-owner Robert Catania. A restaurant on this scale could probably get away with ho-hum, middle-of-the-road food, but his output is on a par with that of the Cape's best boutique restaurants. Try a classic dish like the *fruits de mer* (seafood) in white wine, or try a seasonal highlight (the specials menu changes monthly). The desserts are as superb, as is all that precedes them.

INEXPENSIVE

The Bee-Hive Tavern. 406 Rte. 6A (about ½ mile E of the town center), East Sandwich. ☎ **508/833-1184.** Main courses $7–$16. MC, V. Mon–Fri 11:30am–9pm; Sat–Sun 8am–9pm. INTERNATIONAL.

A cut above the rather characterless restaurants clustered along this stretch of road, this modern-day tavern employs some atmospheric old-time touches without going overboard. Green-shaded banker's lamps, for example, illuminate the dark wooden booths, and vintage prints and paintings convey a clubby feel. The food is good if not spectacular, and well priced for what it is. The menu features straightforward steaks, chops, and fresh-caught fish among the pricier choices, while burgers, sandwiches, and salads cater to lighter appetites (and wallets). This is a great option for lunch, when you should try one of the Cape's best lobster rolls.

The Dunbar Tea Shop. 1 Water St. (in the center of town). ☎ **508/833-2485.** Main courses under $10. DISC, MC, V. June–Oct daily 10am–6pm; call for off-season hours. BRITISH.

Whether you choose the cozy confines of the Tea Room on a crisp autumn day or the shady outside grove in summer, you'll enjoy the hearty English classics served here. Mornings in season, a traditional English breakfast is served. Lunch features homemade soups, salads, and sandwiches like the Farmer's Lunch (crusty warm bread, roast beef, horseradish sauce, and English mustard). The Tea Room also serves tea, of course, with all the traditional fixings and accompaniments you'd expect. A tea-themed gift shop is attached.

Marshland Restaurant. 109 Rte. 6A. ☎ **508/888-9824.** Most items under $10. No credit cards. Tues–Sat 6am–9pm; Sun 7am–1pm; Mon 6am–2pm. Open year-round. DINER.

Locals have been digging this diner for 2 decades. This is home-cooked grub, slung fast and cheap. You'll gobble up the hearty breakfast and be back in time for dinner.

SWEETS

Sweet tooth acting up? Stop by Sandwich's appropriately named **Ice Cream Sandwich** at 66 Rte. 6A, across from the Stop & Shop (☎ **508/888-7237**), for a couple of scoops of the best local ice cream. Try the Cape Cod chocolate chunk. Closed November through March.

SANDWICH AFTER DARK

Horizons on Cape Cod Bay. 98 Town Neck Rd. ☎ **508/888-6166.** No cover. Closed Nov–Mar.

On summer weekends, a light bar menu is served until midnight at this beachside party spot with decks overlooking the town beach. The lower level sometimes has live music, like acoustic guitar, on summer weekends. Upstairs is a large bar area, pool table, and large-screen TV.

Sandwich Auction House. 15 Tupper Rd. (at Rte. 6A). ☎ **508/888-1926.** Fax 508/888-0716. E-mail: sandauct@capecod.net. Free admission. MC, V. June–Aug Wed at 6pm; Sept–May Sat at 6pm; previews start at 2pm the same day.

Do you have the guts—not to mention the funds—to be a player? You'll find out soon enough as the bidding grows heated over an ever-changing parade of antique goods, from chests to portraits to spinning wheels. Antique-rug auctions take place once a month. The record set here so far was for an antique toy pedal car that fetched $77,000. Sit on your hands if you must.

2 Bourne

4 miles (7km) W of Sagamore; 16 miles (26km) NW of Hyannis

Bourne, a primarily residential community with seven villages, hugs Buzzards Bay on both sides of the Cape Cod Canal. But for the maddening traffic and sundry other evidence of encroaching modernization, this bucolic community is probably not all that different from what President Grover Cleveland encountered when, evidently attracted by the trout, he decided to set up his summer White House at Monument Beach in the 1890s. That house is long gone, but one vestige—his personal train station, a great way to maintain crowd control—is on view at the Aptucxet Trading Post Museum, a reconstructed version of this country's first place of commerce, where Pilgrims traded with Native Americans and the Dutch. Also visible from here—and from the Cape Cod Canal bike path, which runs right past the post—is the intriguing Vertical Lift Railroad Bridge (built in 1935), whose whole track moves up or down to permit the passage, respectively, of ships or trains. Cataumet with its winding roads is the most upscale village in Bourne. Though a tad run-down, Buzzards Bay with its Main Street paralleling the Canal has most of the shops. Developer's recently unveiled plans to build a 1-million-square-foot mall next to the Bourne Bridge rotary—a controversial topic, to say the least, in this unassuming town.

Somewhat introverted and intent on its own old-fashioned pleasures, Bourne is best savored by those seeking the very, very quiet life.

ESSENTIALS

GETTING THERE   After crossing either the Bourne or Sagamore bridge, turn west on Route 6A toward Bourne. You can also fly into Hyannis (see "Getting There" in chapter 2).

VISITOR INFORMATION   Contact the **Cape Cod Chamber of Commerce** (see "Visitor Information" in the "Sandwich" section, above) or stop in at the **Route 25 Visitor's Center.** The **Cape Cod Canal Region Chamber of Commerce,** 70 Main St., Buzzards Bay (☎ **508/759-6000**), can provide literature on both Sandwich and Bourne.

BEACHES & RECREATIONAL PURSUITS

BEACHES   Bourne has only one public beach: Monument Beach, off Shore Road. Half the parking lot is free (this fills up fast), and the other half requires a sticker from **Bourne Town Hall** at 24 Perry Ave. in Buzzards Bay (☎ **508/759-0623**).

Though it's a small, pebbly beach, it's picturesque. Full public-beach facilities accompany the relatively warm waters of Buzzards Bay.

BICYCLING   See "Bicycling" under "Sandwich," above. The **Cape Cod Canal Bike Path,** 14 miles on both sides of the canal, is one of the best on the Cape. On the mainland side of the canal, on Main Street in Buzzards Bay, access is at the far end of

Buzzards Bay Park. The closest bike-rental shop is **P&M Cycles** at 29 Main St. in Buzzards Bay (☎ 508/759-2830), opposite the railroad station. The shop also offers free parking. On the Cape side of the canal, access is at the Bourne Recreation Area, just north of the Bourne Bridge, along Canal Road.

BOATING   Paddle Cape Cod (☎ 888/226-6393 or 508/564-4051; www. paddlecapecod.com; e-mail: cccanoe@capecod.net) runs naturalist-guided trips throughout the Cape. Call for the schedule and more information or see "Beaches & Recreational Pursuits" in the "Sandwich" section, above.

If you have your own canoe or kayak, or want to rent one in Falmouth, you'll enjoy exploring Back River and Phinney's Harbor at Monument Beach.

FISHING   So plentiful are the herring making their spring migration up the **Bournedale Herring Run,** Rte. 6 in Bournedale, about 1 mile southwest of the Sagamore Bridge rotary (☎ 508/759-5991), that you can net them once they've reached their destination, Great Herring Pond. You can obtain a shellfish permit from **Bourne Town Hall** at 24 Perry Ave., Buzzards Bay (☎ 508/759-0613). Also plentiful here are pickerel, white perch, walleye, and bass. For freshwater fishing at Flax Pond and Red Brook Pond in Pocasset, you'll also need a license from the **Bourne Town Hall** (see above). You can also obtain a license at **Red Top Sporting Goods** at 265 Main St. in Buzzards Bay (☎ 508/759-3371). Surf-casting along the Cape Cod Canal requires no permit.

ICE-SKATING   The **John Gallo Ice Arena,** 231 Sandwich Rd. in Bourne (☎ 508/ 759-8904), is open to the public daily from September through March; call for hours.

NATURE & WILDLIFE AREAS   The Bourne Conservation Trust has managed to get hold of a handful of small plots; for information, contact the town **Conservation Commission** (☎ 508/759-0625). The largest tract is the **Four Ponds Conservation Area/Town Forest,** which consists of 280 acres off Barlows Landing Road in Pocasset. The 40-acre **Nivling-Alexander Reserve** (off Shore Rd. at Thaxter Rd.) has three walking trails and flanks Red Brook Pond, where fishing is permitted (see above); it offers a ½-mile wooded walk passing several cranberry bogs. The **Army Corps of Engineers** (☎ 508/759-5991), which is in charge of the **Cape Cod Canal,** gives free naturalist-guided nature walks and slide shows about the canal.

TENNIS   In the Bourne area, public courts are located near the old schoolhouse on County Road in Cataumet, and in Chester Park, opposite the railroad station in Monument Beach. For information, call the **Bourne Memorial Community Center** on Main Street in Buzzards Bay (☎ 508/759-0650), which also has courts.

WATER SPORTS   The **Aquarius Dive Center** at 3239 Cranberry Hwy., Buzzards Bay (☎ 508/759-3483), a PADI five-star facility, offers rentals, instruction, and charters to Sandwich Town Beach, the Plymouth coast, and a wreck site off Provincetown.

VISIT A MUSEUM

Aptucxet Trading Post Museum. 24 Aptucxet Rd., off Perry Ave. (about ½ mile W of the town center), Bourne Village. ☎ **508/759-9487.** Admission $2.50 adults, $2 seniors and AAA members, $1 children 6–18. July–Aug Mon–Sat 10am–5pm; Sun 2–5pm; call for off-season hours. Closed mid-Oct to Apr.

Long before the canal was a twinkle in Myles Standish's (and later, George Washington's and Augustus Belmont's) eye, Native Americans had been portaging goods between two rivers, the Manomet and Scusset, that once almost met at this site; its name in Algonquian means "little trap in the river." The Pilgrims were quick to notice that Aptucxet made an ideal trading spot, especially since, as Governor William

Ocean Quest

No visit to the Cape would be complete without some type of seafaring excursion on the Atlantic. If you're not a sailor or if you just don't have the time or budget for an all-day boat trip, consider a unique, hands-on cruise with ✪ **Ocean Quest,** Water Street (in the center of town), Woods Hole (☎ **800/376-2326** or 508/457-0508; www.capecod.net/oceanquest). Departing from Woods Hole, these 1½-hour harbor cruises are perfect for families, as real marine research is conducted with passengers serving as bona fide data collectors.

Here's how it works. Participants are split into two teams. Up in the bow, company founder Kathy Mullin, or a scientist borrowed from one of the revered local institutes, trains the new crew in the niceties of reading water temperature, assessing turbidity, and taking other key measurements; in the stern, passengers get to examine the specimens hauled up by the dredger. Midway into the trip, the teams switch stations, so that everyone gets to contemplate topics such as the sex life of a spider crab or why the water looks a particular shade of blue or green. Kids get a real kick out of being addressed as "Doctor," and even adults who think they know it all will probably come away much better informed.

The 90-minute cruise cost $19 for adults and $14 for children 3 to 12; boats shove off four times a day Monday through Friday from mid-June to early September; call for schedule.

Bradford pointed out, it would allow them to trade with the Dutch to the south without "the compassing of Cape-Codd and those dangerous shoulds [shoals]." In 1627, as soon as the Pilgrims had essentially declared their independence by assuming the debts of the Merchant Adventurers, they built an **outpost** here, hoping to cash in as conduits for native-caught pelts. The present building is a replica, built after a pair of local archaeologists, using ancient maps, uncovered the original foundation in 1926. The other detritus they dug up (arrowheads, pottery shards, and so on) is displayed in a roomful of rather dim, crowded display cases. Also be sure to have a look at the **Bournedale Stone,** which was discovered serving as a threshold for a Native American church built in the late–17th century. Overturned, it revealed strange, runelike inscriptions—fueling the legend (unsubstantiated as yet) that Vikings roamed the Cape around A.D. 1000.

Even though the building is not authentic, the curator does a very good job of conjuring up the hard, lonely life led by the pair of sentinels assigned here. Several other odd artifacts are scattered about the grounds, such as **President Grover Cleveland's personal train station** from his estate at Gray Gables, and a **windmill** used as an art studio by his good friend and fishing companion, the hugely successful actor Joseph Jefferson. Redlined out of Sandwich for his scandalous profession (he was a Democrat to boot!), Jefferson was avenged when he was buried there with a tart epitaph: "We are but tenants; let us assure ourselves of this, and then it will not be so hard to make room for the new administration, for shortly the Great Landlord will give us notice that our lease has expired."

The **Cape Cod Canal path** runs right behind the museum. This is a good spot from which to observe the **Vertical Lift Railroad Bridge,** which represented state-of-the-art technology for its time (1935, when it cost $1.5 million) but is now obsolescent, so scanty is the train traffic. Rush hour, between 5 and 6pm, is your best chance to catch the bridge lowering its trestle (for the garbage cars headed off-Cape); in the off-season, you might get a colorful sunset thrown in for good measure.

TAKE A CRUISE

Cape Cod Canal Cruises. Onset Bay Town Pier (on the northern side of the canal, about 2 miles W of the Bourne Bridge), Onset. ☎ **508/295-3883.** www.hy-linecruises.com. Tickets $10–$13 adults, free–$7 children 5–12. Mid-June to Sept departures daily 10am and 1:30pm; Mon–Sat 4pm, Tues–Thurs 7pm; Fri–Sat 8pm; call for off-season schedule. Closed mid-Oct to Apr.

Get an underbelly view of the Cape's two swooping car bridges and its unusual railroad bridge as you wend your way among a wide array of interesting craft, and a narrator fills you in on the canal's history. Basically, it was the brainchild of New York financial wizard Augustus Perry Belmont, who completed it in 1914 at a cost of $16 million and never saw a penny of profit. Found to be too narrow and perilous (the current reverses with the tides, roughly every 6 hours), the over ambitious waterway was handed over to the U.S. Army Corps of Engineers for expansion in 1928, at the discount price of $11.5 million. It continues to serve as a vital shortcut, sparing some 30,000 boats yearly the long, dangerous circuit of the Outer Cape.

The 4pm **family cruise,** offered Monday to Saturday, is a real bargain, at $10 per adult and free for children 12 and under. The Sunday afternoon trip is accompanied by New Orlean-style jazz, and the sunset "Moonlight'n Music" cruise on Saturday (adults only) features live bands.

TAKE YOURSELF OUT TO A BALL GAME

Sports fans of all ages will enjoy taking in nine innings of the Grand Old Game. Part of the elite-amateur **Cape Cod Baseball League** (☎ 508/432-6909; **www. capecodbaseball.org**), the Braves play at Coady School Field, in Buzzards Bay, in July and August. Call the **Cape Cod Canal Region Chamber of Commerce** (☎ **508/ 759-6000**) to check the schedule.

KID STUFF

Stuck with a gray day? Pack the family off to **Adventure Isle** on Route 28, about 2 miles south of the Bourne Bridge (☎ **800/535-2787** or 508/759-2636). Older kids can tackle the laser–tag arena, go-carts, bumper boats, bumper cars, minibikes, batting cages, and video games, among other juvenile delights. Little kids have their own little amusement park, complete with mini-ferris wheel, giant slides, minigolf, and a train with clanging bell. Prices are reasonable ($1.75 to $3.75 per ride), but they're sure to add up quickly. Buy an unlimited-rides pass for $9.95 to $11.95 to save money. The **Thunder Mine Adventure Miniature Golf** course, at the intersection of County Road and Route 28A in Cataumet (☎ **508/563-7450**), offers 18 holes of Astroturf with a gold-rush theme. This is cheap fun: $5 adults, $4 children gets you two rounds if it's not too crowded. *Be forewarned:* There's an ✪ **Emack & Bolio's** (a branch of the primo Boston ice-cream parlor) next door, and you can't expect to escape without a lick. On the mainland side of the bridge, visit the **National Marine Life Center Visitor Center** at 120 Main St. in Buzzards Bay (☎ **508/743-9888** or 508/759-8722) for an outing both fun and educational. Hours are late May to mid-September Monday to Saturday 10am to 6pm and Sunday noon to 6pm. Children will enjoy exhibits about whales, dolphins, seals, and sea turtles; they include things to touch (skeletons, baleen, whales' teeth, turtle shells, and so on) and to watch (videos of whales and dolphins in the wild). This is the future home of a rehabilitation hospital for stranded marine animals in need of TLC. Admission is free.

SHOPPING

Instead of the usual cutesy Cape Cod shops, Bourne is known for its factory outlets. **Tanger Outlet Center,** located at the Bourne rotary on the mainland side of the Bourne Bridge (☎ **800/482-6437**), has the following outlets: Liz Claiborne, Coach, Nine West, and Izod. **Cape Cod Factory Outlet Mall,** just off Route 6, exit 1, Sagamore (☎ **508/888-8417**), has Van Heusen, L'Eggs/Hanes/Playtex/Bali, Osh Kosh B'Gosh, Bass Shoe, and Samsonite. Here are a few other notable stops:

GIFTS You can observe artisans continuing the tradition of the Boston & Sandwich Glass Company at **Pairpoint Glass Works,** 851 Sandwich Rd. (Route 6A, at the foot of the Sagamore Bridge), Sagamore (☎ **800/899-0953** or 508/888-2344). Thomas J. Pairpoint was a leading designer in the 1880s. The output is on the conservative side and includes skillful replicas. Bargain-lovers flock to the **Christmas Tree Shops** at the Sagamore Bridge, Sagamore (☎ **508/888-7010**). The stock here is not just holiday-related. Housed in an oversize thatch-roofed Tudor cottage, complete with spinning windmill (you can't miss it), the array is Woolworthian in scope, but of much higher quality. There are six more outlets elsewhere on the Cape.

SEAFOOD You couldn't hope for a fresher catch than what you'll find at **Cataumet Fish,** 1360 Route 28A, Cataumet (☎ **508/564-5956**). Buy a whole fish and fib a little (they'll even gut it), or cart home a couple of lobsters—who's going to care?

WHERE TO STAY

The Beachmore. 11 Buttermilk Way, Buzzards Bay, MA 02532. ☎ **508/759-7522.** 6 units. Summer $85 double; $125 suite. Rates include continental breakfast. AE, DISC, MC, V.

New owners have awakened this sleepy property located right at the mouth of the Cape Cod Canal next to the Massachusetts Military Academy. Views (particularly sunsets) from one of the bedrooms, the commons room, and from the superb casual restaurant on the first floor (see "Where to Dine," below) are memorable. Rooms are decorated individually and with flair, and there's a loving attention to detail throughout. For instance, iron bedsteads are romantically draped with gauzy fabric, and curtains are handmade with lacy netting. Out front is a private beach perfect for sunning.

WHERE TO DINE

The Beachmore. 11 Buttermilk Way, Buzzards Bay. ☎ **508/759-7522.** Reservations recommended. Main courses $15–$26. AE, MC, V. Apr–Sept Tues–Fri and Sun 11:30am–10pm; Sat 5pm–10pm; call for off-season hours. Closed Jan–Mar. NEW AMERICAN.

If you happen to be anywhere near the Bourne Bridge and in need of sustenance (lunch or dinner), you'll want to head over to the Beachmore in Buzzards Bay. They're serving up terrific food along with a wonderful view of the Cape Cod Canal. Chef Keith Pacheco's specialties at dinner include Beachmore Stew (shrimp, clams, scallops, lobster, and fish in a saffron broth) and the daily trilogy, which might include poached salmon with béarnaise sauce, grilled swordfish with basil butter, and broiled scallops in lemon butter. Save room for dessert, and if baked pear is on the menu, don't hesitate. It's a heavenly concoction with crisp-on-the-outside, doughy-on-the-inside squares surrounding the delicate baked pears, served with vanilla ice cream and raspberry sauce. There's evening entertainment here on Fridays (Nick Lombardo sing-along) and Saturdays (Al "Fingers" Russo at the piano bar).

The Chart Room. 1 Shipyard Lane (in the Cataumet Marina, off Shore Rd.), Cataumet. ☎ **508/563-5350.** Main courses $10–$20. AE, MC, V. Mid-June to mid-Sept daily 11:30am–10pm; mid-May to mid-June and mid-Sept to mid-Oct Thurs–Sun 11:30am–10pm. Closed mid-Oct to mid-May. SEAFOOD.

An Insider's Guide to the Cape Cod Baseball League

Many consider the Cape Cod Baseball League the premier NCAA summer base-ball league in the country. For those of us enjoying the sun and surf on Cape Cod from mid-June through mid-August every year, the baseball games are just another diversion, something different to do on a Saturday night. But once you start attending the games, it can be hard to break away. Of the 10 hometown teams in the league, one of them is bound to capture your fancy. The diehard fans plan vacations around league playoff games (early to mid-August) and an all-star game (late July). The teams attract top college talent and serious professional prospects; coaches start scouting colleges from Labor Day to October 15.

Every team has its own hometown field, and several of the diamonds are definitely a cut above. Aesthetes may prefer **Veterans Field** in Chatham, charming and quintessentially Cape-y like the town itself, with the bleachers tucked neatly into a hillside. Orleans's **Eldredge Park Field** is the most impressive: It has terraced seating along the first-base line.

The league has been going for over a century, and longtime fans and rivalries can be intense. Some say the loudest, most enthusiastic fans are for the Cotuit Kettleers, but that could be a result of the tightly packed seats in those stands. Rivalries bring out the crowds, particularly when the **Wareham Gatemen** come to town; the last few years, they've won it all. Other intense rivalries include the **Harwich Mariners** vs. the **Chatham Athletics;** the **Orleans Cardinals** vs. the **Brewster White Caps;** and the **Cotuit Kettleers** vs. the **Falmouth Commodores.**

Crowd size varies over the course of the season, from early games, when a couple hundred locals turn out, to playoff games, when attendance might hit 4,500 to 5,000 at a large venue like Orleans's Eldredge Field. Saturday night games usually play to a full house.

Each team plays 44 games (22 at home). Game times are usually evenings around 7pm or afternoons starting around 5pm. All games are free; when they pass the hat, throw in a few bucks to help defer costs for equipment and uniforms. Concession stands sell steamed hot dogs, popcorn, cookies, candy, and soda pop at reasonable prices. For schedule information, call the league at ☎ **508/432-6909,** or check out their Web site at www.capecodbaseball.org.

Great sunset views over Red Brook Harbor and fresh fish are reason enough to visit this dockside restaurant, housed in a former railroad barge in a busy marina. A piano bar lends a bit of elegance, as does the well-heeled clientele.

The Parrot Bar and Grill. 1356 Rte. 28A, Cataumet. ☎ **508/563-6464.** Reservations not accepted. Main courses $10–$15. AE, DISC, MC, V. Tues–Sun 11:30am–10pm; Mon 4:30–10pm. NEW AMERICAN.

For years the Blue Parrot, a gritty bar with a sour reputation, occupied this crossroads in Cataumet. New owner Eddie Hannon has cleaned the place up and resuscitated it as an upbeat Caribbean-themed restaurant specializing in seafood and pasta. Try the lobster pie or the blackened swordfish with Southwestern salsa. Thursday to Saturday, live local bands entertain.

BOURNE AFTER DARK

On weekends, local bands draw young adults to the intimate **Courtyard Restaurant and Bar,** Cataumet Square, Cataumet (☎ **508/563-1818**). There's no cover charge. From here you can barhop next door to **The Parrot Bar and Grill,** 1356 Rte. 28A (see "Where to Dine," above), which has live music Thursday to Saturday in season. No cover.

3 Falmouth

18 miles (30km) S of Sagamore; 20 miles (33km) SW of Hyannis

Falmouth is a classic New England town, complete with church steeples encircling the town green and a walkable and bustling Main Street. Founded in 1660 by Quaker sympathizers from Sandwich (where Congregationalists considered theirs the one true path), Falmouth proved remarkably arable territory: By the 19th century, it reigned as the strawberry capital of the world. Today, with over 20,000 year-round residents, it's the second largest town on the Cape, after Barnstable.

After more than a century of catering to summertime guests (it was the first "fashionable" Cape resort, served by trains from Boston starting in the 1870s), Falmouth residents have hospitality down to an art—a business, too, but people are so genuinely welcoming, you'll tend to forget that. The area around the historic Village Green (given over to military exercises in the pre-Revolutionary days) is a veritable hotbed of B&Bs, with each vying to provide the most elaborate breakfasts and solicitous advice. Put yourself in the hands of your hosts, and you'll soon feel like a native.

Officially a village within Falmouth (one of nine), tiny Woods Hole has been a world-renowned oceanic research center since 1871, when the U.S. Commission of Fish and Fisheries set up a primitive seasonal collection station. Today the various scientific institutes crowded around the harbor—principally, the National Marine Fisheries Service, the Marine Biological Laboratory (founded in 1888), and the Woods Hole Oceanographic Institute (a newcomer as of 1930)—have research budgets in the tens of millions of dollars and employ thousands of scientists. Woods Hole's scientific institutions offer a unique opportunity to get in-depth—and often hands-on—exposure to marine biology.

Belying stereotype, the community is far from uptight and nerdy; in fact, it's one of the hipper communities on the Cape. In the past few decades, a number of agreeable restaurants and shops have cropped up, making the small, crowded gauntlet of Water Street (don't even think of parking here in summer) a very pleasant place to stroll.

West Falmouth (which is really more north of town, stretched alongside Buzzards Bay) has held on to its bucolic character and makes a lovely drive, with perhaps an occasional stop for the more alluring antiques stores. Falmouth Heights, a cluster of shingled Victorian summerhouses on a bluff east of Falmouth's harbor, is as popular as it is picturesque; its narrow ribbon of beach is a magnet for all, especially the younger crowd. The Waquoit Bay area, a few miles east of town, has thus far eluded the over-commercialization that blights most of Route 28, and with luck and foresight will continue to do so. Several thousand acres of this vital estuarine ecosystem are now under federal custody.

ESSENTIALS

GETTING THERE   After crossing either the Bourne or Sagamore bridge, take Route 28 or 28A south. Or fly into Hyannis (see "Getting There" in chapter 2).

To get around Falmouth and Woods Hole (where parking in summer is a mathematical impossibility due to ferry traffic to Martha's Vineyard), use the **Whoosh**

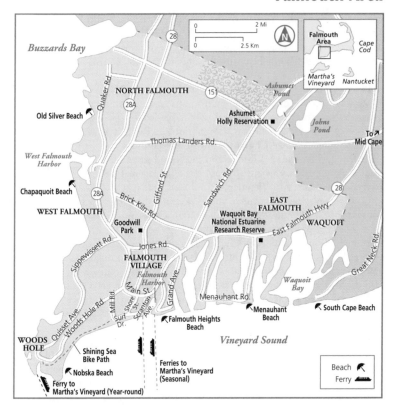

Trolley, which makes an hourly circuit from 9:30am to 6:30pm daily from late May to late September. You can pick up the trolley at the Falmouth Mall on Route 28, where there is plenty of parking. The fare is only $1 for adults, or 50¢ for seniors; children under 5 ride free. The **Sea Line Shuttle** (☎ 800/352-7155) connects Woods Hole, Falmouth, and Mashpee with Hyannis year-round (except Sunday and holidays); the fare ranges from $1 to $3.50, depending on distance; children under 5 ride free.

VISITOR INFORMATION   Contact the **Falmouth Chamber of Commerce,** Academy Lane, Falmouth, MA 02541 (☎ 800/526-8532 or 508/548-8500; fax 508/ 548-8521; www.falmouth-capecod.com; falmouth@capecod.net), or the **Cape Cod Chamber of Commerce** (see "Visitor Information" in the "Sandwich" section, above).

A STROLL AROUND FALMOUTH

You can start this walk at the Chamber of Commerce, and it'll take you 1 to 3 hours to do the circuit; a museum tour or long walk in the woods will add to your time. The distance is about 1 mile; more if you decide to take a hike. The Falmouth Historical Society Museums are only open Wednesday to Sunday from 2 to 5pm from mid-June to mid-September, if you want to fit them in. Otherwise, any time of day (or year) is fine.

From Main Street in the center of town, head to the **Chamber of Commerce** on Academy Lane (☎ 508/548-8500), a columned Greek Revival building that was once a temple of learning (it was built to house a boys' academy). You can school yourself in Falmouth's sights with the help of the chamber staff, having first taken advantage of the free parking out back (the spaces on Main Street tend to fill up fast), as well as the phones and rest rooms. Firm up your plans while enjoying a park-bench view of Shiverick Pond, then with brochures in hand, go back to Main St. and turn right.

In an ⅛ mile, you'll near the triangular point of the **Village Green,** laid out in 1749, where the all-volunteer Falmouth Militia readied itself for the War of Independence. So well-trained were they that they succeeded in repelling a British would-be invasion in 1779. Seventeen years later, patriot hero Paul Revere cast the bell that tops the First Congregational Church on the green's northern side. Its inscription reads: "The living to the church I call, and to the grave I summon all." The green is encircled by a catalog of architectural styles, including colonial, Federal, Georgian, Greek Revival, and Italian Villa Victorian; several houses are now B&Bs.

Continuing beyond the church, you'll encounter the **Falmouth Historical Society Museums** (☎ 508/548-4857), two buildings' and a barn's worth of fascinating artifacts. The Julia Wood House is the yellow Georgian style house with the widow's walk. Built in 1790 by a local doctor, the building now houses exhibits encompassing 300 years of Falmouth's history. Docents will gladly relate many intriguing stories. Rest and smell the roses at the historically accurate colonial garden. Continue up North Main to visit the little shops in the Queens Buyway, including several good antique shops.

Turn left onto Palmer Avenue, then cross over to Depot Avenue. Keep walking about an ⅛ mile west, bearing right on Depot Avenue Extension, where you'll spot **Highfield Hall,** one of a pair of twin mansions (the other was razed) built by two summering brothers in the 1870s. Locals are mobilizing to restore this old gem. Farther to the right, in the mansion's former stable, is the **Highfield Theatre** (☎ 508/548-0668), where the College Light Opera Company mounts musicals throughout the summer. It's often sold out, but see if there's a ticket to spare.

If you still have energy to spare, wander **Beebe Woods,** a 650-acre preserve bought for the town by local philanthropist Josiah K. Lilly. Or go back to Palmer Avenue (Rte. 28), zigzag briefly right, then left on West Main Street, and you'll be headed back toward the Village Green. On your left, look for plaques commemorating the Falmouth-raised luminary **Katharine Lee Bates,** author of the poem-turned-anthem "America the Beautiful"; she spent her formative years (1859–71) in this modest house. (A statue of Bates stands in front of the library in Falmouth center.) Across the street is **Mostly Hall,** a grand Southern-style mansion built by a New England captain in 1849 to please his New Orleans–born wife. It's now a superb B&B (see the review under "Where to Stay," below), and the owners are more than happy to greet curiosity-seekers, most of whom will want to come back someday and spend the night.

☕ **WINDING DOWN** For a well-earned pick-me-up, take a biscotti break at **The Coffee Obsession** (☎ 508/540-2233), a hip yet friendly coffee bar back in the Queens Buyway at the corner of North Main and Palmer Avenue.

BEACHES & RECREATIONAL PURSUITS

BEACHES While Old Silver Beach, Surf Drive Beach, and Menauhaut Beach will sell a 1-day pass for $10, most other Falmouth public beaches require a parking sticker. Renters can obtain temporary beach parking stickers, for $50 per week or $75 per month, at **Falmouth Town Hall,** 59 Town Hall Sq. (☎ 508/548-7611), or at the **Surf Drive Beach Bathhouse** in season (☎ 508/548-8623). The town beaches for which a parking fee is charged all have rest rooms and concession stands. Here is a list of some of Falmouth's public shores:

- **Old Silver Beach,** off Route 28A in North Falmouth: Western-facing (great for sunsets) and relatively calm, this warm Buzzards Bay beach is a popular, often crowded, choice. This is the chosen spot for the college crowd and other rowdy young folk. Mothers and their charges cluster on the opposite side of the street where a shallow pool formed by a sandbar is perfect for toddlers. A 1-day pass costs $10.
- **Surf Drive Beach,** off Shore Street in Falmouth: About a mile from downtown, and appealing to families, this is an easy-to-get-to choice with limited parking. A 1-day pass costs $10.
- ✪ **Falmouth Heights Beach,** off Grand Avenue in Falmouth Heights: Once a rowdy spot, this is primarily a family beach these days. Parking is sticker-only. This neighborhood supported the Cape's first summer colony; the grand Victorian mansions still overlook the beach, though now they are joined by a bevy of motels.
- **Menauhant Beach,** off Central Avenue in East Falmouth: A bit off the beaten track, Menauhant is a little less mobbed than Surf Drive Beach and better protected from the winds. A 1-day pass costs $10.

BICYCLING   The ✪ **Shining Sea Bicycle Path** (☎ 508/548-8500) is a 3.3-mile beauty skirting the sound from Falmouth to Woods Hole; it also connects with a 23-mile scenic-road loop through pretty Sippewissett. You can park at the trailhead on Locust Street in Falmouth or any spot in town (parking in Woods Hole is scarce). The closest bike shop—convenient to the main cluster of B&Bs, some of which offer "loaners"—is **Corner Cycle** at Palmer Avenue and North Main Street (☎ **508/540-4195**). For a broad selection of vehicles—from six-speed cruisers to six-passenger "surreys"—and good advice on routes, visit **Holiday Cycles** at 465 Grand Ave. in Falmouth Heights (☎ **508/540-3549**).

The Falmouth Chamber of Commerce offers a map and brochure about the Shining Sea Bike Path, which is the only bikeway on Cape Cod that runs along the seashore. Along the way, following prehistoric Wampanoag Indian trails, it passes 21 acres of woodlands, marsh, swamp, salt ponds and seascape.

The path's name is a nod to Falmouth's own Katharine Lee Bates, who wrote the lyrics to America the Beautiful with its verse, "And crown thy good with brotherhood, from sea to shining sea!"

BIRD WATCHING   The **Shining Sea Bike Path** (see above) is a great spot to bird watch. Keep an eye out for yellow-breasted chats, orange-crowned warblers, as well as waterfowl like mallards and buffleheads. You may also see majestic herons, egrets, and osprey.

Massachusetts Audubon (☎ **508/362-1426**) offers day-long trips to Cuttyhunk out of Falmouth Harbor most Sundays from mid-July to mid-October. The 50-foot boat can take 45 people and has an enclosed cabin. The trips feature naturalist-led guided walks, and participants have a choice of taking a short, medium or long walks on the island. Boats leave Falmouth Harbor at 9am and return at 5pm. The cost is $45 for adults. There are discounts for seniors, children, and Audubon members.

BOATING   **Patriot Party Boats,** 227 Clinton Ave. (at Scranton Ave. on the harbor), Falmouth (☎ **800/734-0088** or 508/548-2626), offers one-stop shopping for would-be boaters. The Patriot fleet includes a poky fishing/sightseeing vessel, the *Patriot Too* and a sleek replica 1750s Pinky schooner, the *Liberte* (2-hour sails; $20 adults, $14 children 12 and under). While wending among the Elizabeth Islands, some privately owned by the Forbes family, owner Jim Tieje can give you the scoop on local gossip and lore. Even if the scenery wasn't so lovely, his stories would make the time fly. Two-hour sunset cruises on the Patriot II, which are BYOB, take place in July and August and cost $15 for adults, $10 for kids 12 and under. The boat, which can take 49 people, departs at 6pm. Trips to Cuttyhunk Island (5 hours) for hiking, birding, and/or beaching are offered weekdays in July and August. The boat leaves at noon and returns at 5pm. Trips cost $35 for adults and $20 for kids. For info on fishing trips, see below.

Paddle Cape Cod (☎ **888/226-6393** or 508/564-4051; www.paddlecapecod.com; e-mail: cccanoe@capecod.net) runs naturalist-guided trips throughout the Cape. Call for a schedule and more information, or see "Beaches & Recreational Pursuits" in the "Sandwich" section, above.

Cape Cod Kayak (☎ **508/540-9377;** www.capecodkayak.com) rents kayaks (free delivery) by the day or week, and offers lessons and eco-tours on local waterways. Canoe and kayak rentals are $25–$35 for a half day, $35–$45 for a full day. Lessons are $30 per hour. Four-hour trips are $50. They also rent small sailboats and fishing rods.

If you want to explore on your own, **Edward's Boat Yard,** 1209 E. Falmouth Hwy, East Falmouth (☎ **508/548-2216**), rents out canoes ($30 half day, $40 full day, and $175 week) and kayaks ($25 half day, $35 full day, and $150 week) for exploring Waquoit Bay (see "Nature & Wildlife Areas," below). Washburn Island, a protected reserve just offshore, is about a ½-hour paddle via canoe.

FISHING   Falmouth has six fishable ponds. A complimentary fishing map and guide are available from the Falmouth Chamber of Commerce. Freshwater fishing and shellfishing licenses can be obtained at **Falmouth Town Hall,** 59 Town Hall Sq. (☎ **508/548-7611,** ext. 219). Freshwater fishing licenses can also be obtained at Eastman's Sport & Tackle, 150 Main St. (☎ **508/548-6900**).

Surf Drive Beach is a great spot for surf casting, once the crowds have dispersed. Other good locations are Nobska Point in Woods Hole and Bristol Beach on Menauhant Road in East Falmouth.

To go after bigger prey, head out with a group on one of the **Patriot Party Boats** based in Falmouth's Inner Harbor (☎ **800/734-0088** or 508/548-2626). Boats leave twice daily in season. The clunky *Patriot Too,* with an enclosed deck, is ideal for family-style "bottom fishing," (4-hour sails $25 adults, $15 children under 12; equipment provided).

For sport fishing, call Captain Bob MacGregor of the Hop-Tuit (☎ **508/540-7642**), who trolls for striped bass, bluefish, bonito, and school tuna on half-day, full-day, and night trips. Captain Dan Junker of Cool Running Charters (☎ **508/457-9445**) takes his boat "Relentless" out of Falmouth Harbor and around Nantucket Sound, Vineyard Sound, and the Elizabeth Islands for bass, blues, tuna, and shark.

FITNESS   If you're jonesing for some time in the gym, the **Falmouth Sports Club** at 33 Highfield Dr. (☎ **508/548-7433**) offers weight-training facilities for $7 per day. Racquet sports cost an extra $6 per person.

GOLF   Falmouth abounds in golf courses—six public ones at last count. Among the more notable is the challenging 18-hole championship course at **Ballymeade Country Club,** 125 Falmouth Woods Rd. (☎ **508/540-4005**). Greens fees are $75 (weekdays) and $110 (weekends) and include carts.

ICE-SKATING   Public skating ($3 per person) is offered October to mid-March at the **Falmouth Ice Arena,** 9 Skating Lane off Palmer Avenue (☎ **508/548-9083**), the home rink of Coleen Coyne, who was part of the gold medal 1998 Olympic hockey team; call for information.

NATURE & WILDLIFE AREAS   ✪ **Ashumet Holly and Wildlife Sanctuary,** operated by the Massachusetts Audubon Society at 186 Ashumet Rd., off Route 151 (☎ **508/362-1426**), is an intriguing 49-acre collection of more than 1,000 holly trees spanning 65 species and culled worldwide. Preserved by the state's first commissioner of agriculture, who was concerned that commercial harvesting might wipe out native species, they're flourishing here, along with over 130 species of birds and a carpet of Oriental lotus blossoms, which covers a kettle pond come summer. The trail fee is $3 for adults and $2 for seniors and children under 16.

Right in the town of Falmouth (just follow Depot Road to the end) is the 650-acre **Beebe Woods,** a treasure for hikers and dog walkers. From here, you can wind your way to the **Peterson Farm,** (entrance off Woods Hole Road; take a right at the Quisset farmstand) purchased by the town of Falmouth in 1997. The 90-acre farm has paths through woods and fields, as well as a flock of sheep grazing in a meadow near historic farm buildings. Bluebird boxes line the path on the way to a quiet pond.

Quite tiny but dazzling, the privately owned **Spohr Garden** on Fells Road, off Oyster Pond Road in Woods Hole, invites visitors to explore 6 magical acres beside Oyster Pond. In the spring, thousands of daffodils bloom, followed by rhododendrons and daylilies. Paths wind past a collection of nautical treasures, like huge anchors, and mill stones. Remarkably, this private garden is free and open to the public. Donations for the maintenance of the gardens are accepted.

Named for its round shape that sticks out into the harbor, **The Knob,** 13 acres of trails at Quissett Harbor at the end of Quissett Road, provides a perfect short walk and lovely views of Buzzards Bay. There's very limited parking at this small, secluded harbor, so try it early or late in the day. The Knob is owned by the non-profit group, Salt Pond Areas Bird Sanctuaries.

The 2,250-acre **Waquoit Bay National Estuarine Research Reserve (WBNERR),** at 149 Waquoit Hwy. in East Falmouth (☎ **508/457-0495;** www.capecod.net/ waquoit), maintains a 1-mile, self-guided nature trail. Also inquire about WBNERR's cruise over to Washburn Island on Saturdays in season by reservation. The 12-passenger motorboat leaves at 9am and returns by 12:30pm. After the 20-minute boat trip to the island, naturalist-led guided walks are offered. The reserve also manages 11 primitive campsites on Washburn Island. Permits cost a mere $6 a night. Reservations are required 3 or 6 months in advance (depending on the campsite) and can be made by calling ☎ **877/422-6762.** The reserve also offers a number of walks and interpretive programs, including the popular "Evenings on the Bluff," geared toward families.

TENNIS   Among the courts open to the public are those at the **Falmouth High School,** 874 Gifford Rd., Falmouth Recreation Dept.; and the Lawrence School on Lakeview Avenue, a few blocks from the center of town. Call Falmouth Chamber of Commerce (☎ **508/548-8500**) for information. Both are first-come, first-served. Among the commercial enterprises offering outdoor courts—clay, Har-Tru, and hard—are the **Falmouth Tennis Club,** Dillingham Avenue Extension (☎ **508/ 548-4370**) and the **Ballymeade Country Club** (see "Golf," above). The **Falmouth Sports Club** (see "Fitness," above) has six indoor courts in addition to three outside. Rates are $20 an hour per person for singles' play.

WATER SPORTS   Falmouth is something of a sailboarding mecca, prized for its unflagging southwesterly winds. While Old Silver Beach in North Falmouth is the most popular spot for windsurfing, it is allowed there only prior to 9am and after 5pm. The Trunk River area on the west end of Falmouth's Surf Drive Beach is the only public beach where Windsurfers are allowed during the day.

SEA SCIENCE IN WOODS HOLE

Marine Biological Laboratory. 100 Water St. (at MBL St., in the center of town), Woods Hole. ☎ **508/289-7623.** Free admission. Visitor center hours July–Aug Mon–Sat 10am–4pm; Sun 11am–3pm; call for off-season hours. Closed Jan. Tours by reservation (no children under 10) mid-June to Aug Mon–Fri at 1, 2, and 3pm.

The Robert W. Pierce Visitors Center and Gift Shop offers visitors short on time a chance to gain some insight into the goings-on at this preeminent scientific facility, part of which is housed in an 1836 candle factory. Visitors can observe marine organisms and learn how they help scientists to understand nature. The *Into The Lab* exhibit allows visitors to peer into a microscope, like the scientists on staff here. A guided tour requires a little more forethought—the MBL prefers that reservations be made a week in advance—but will definitely reward the curious. After a slide presentation, a retired scientist leads visitors through the holding tanks, and then to the lab to observe actual research in progress. The MBL's area of inquiry is not limited to the aquatic, but encompasses the "biological process common to all life forms"; some of what you see may have an immediate bearing on your own life, or those of your descendants.

✪ **National Marine Fisheries Service Aquarium.** Albatross St. (off the western end of Water St.), Woods Hole. ☎ **508/495-2001.** Free admission. Mid-June to early Sept daily 10am–4pm; mid-Sept to mid-June Mon–Fri 10am–4pm.

A little beat up after 1¼ centuries of service and endless streams of eager schoolchildren, this aquarium—the first such institution in the country—may not be state of the art, but it's a treasure nonetheless. The displays, focusing on local waters, might make you think twice before taking a dip. Children show no hesitation, though, in getting up to their elbows in the "touch tanks"; adults are also welcome to dabble. A key exhibit that everyone should see concerns the effect of plastic trash on the marine environment. You might time your visit to coincide with the feeding of two seals, Coco and Sandy, who live here. The fish fly at 11am and 4pm.

Woods Hole Oceanographic Institution Exhibit Center and Gift Shop. 15 School St. (off Water St.), Woods Hole. ☎ **508/289-2663.** $2 donation requested. Late May–early Sept Mon–Sat 10am–4:30pm; Sun noon–4:30pm; call for off-season hours. Closed Jan–Mar.

This world-class research organization—locally referred to by its acronym, WHOI (pronounced "Hooey")—is dedicated to the study of marine science. And with some $80 million in annual funding at stake, there's some serious science going on here. This is a small but interactive exhibit center. Kids might enjoy looking through microscopes at organisms or listening to sounds of marine animals on a computer. Titanic fans will enjoy the brief video, displays, and a life-size model of the submersible that discovered the wreck. You can climb into the model and flick switches, if you like. One-hour walking tours of WHOI are offered twice a day on weekdays in July and August, reservations required; call ☎ **508/289-2252.**

FALMOUTH HISTORICAL SIGHTS

The Falmouth Historical Society runs air-conditioned 1½-hour trolley tours of Falmouth's historic sites on select dates in summer and fall. The trolley runs every other Saturday from late June to mid-December and tickets are $10 for adults and $8 for children. Stop by the Historical Society, 55–65 Palmer Ave., or the Chamber of Commerce, Academy Lane, for this year's schedule.

Falmouth Historical Society Museums. 55–65 Palmer Ave. (at the Village Green). ☎ **508/548-4857.** Admission $3 adults, 50¢ children under 12. Mid-June to mid-Sept Mon–Thurs 10am–4pm; Sun 1–4pm. Open mid-Sept to mid-June by appointment.

Knowledgeable volunteers will lead you through three buildings that contain fascinating vestiges of Falmouth's colorful history. Tours begin at the 1790 Julia Woods House, built by Revolutionary physician Dr. Francis Wicks; a simulacrum of his office, complete with terrifying tools, is not for the faint of heart. Next door, past an authentic colonial garden, is the mid–18th-century Conant House, which evolved from a half-Cape built to accommodate the town's minister; it now houses nautical collections, including intricate "sailor's valentines" made of shells, and whaling exhibits. There's also a china hutch in the dining room with a display of romantic Staffordshire china. One room is dedicated to native daughter Katharine Lee Bates, who in 1893 wrote the poem that would become the popular anthem "America the Beautiful." Also on the grounds is the Dudley Hallett Barn, which contains vintage farm tools and the sleigh that Dr. Wicks used for house calls.

Woods Hole Historical and Maritime Museum. 573 Woods Hole Rd. (on the eastern edge of town), Woods Hole. ☎ **508/548-7270.** Donation $1. Mid-June to mid-Sept Tues–Sat 10am–4pm; off-season by appointment.

Exhibits change and can be just a touch amateur—this is, after all, a local labor of love. However, the permanent 1895 diorama of the town should give you the former flavor of this combination seaport/scientific community and tourist destination. The neighboring barn shelters a Small Boat Museum including an Old Town canoe, a Cape Cod "knockabout," a Herreshoff 12½, and a fine example of a "spritsail" boat. There's also the reconstructed 1893 hobby workshop of a local doctor. To delve into town lore in more detail, reserve a place on one of the free walking tours offered Tuesdays at 4pm in July and August.

BASEBALL
Part of the elite-amateur **Cape Cod Baseball League** (☎ **508/432-6909;** www.capecodbaseball.org), the Commodores play at Fuller Field, off Main Street, in July and August. Call the **Falmouth Chamber of Commerce** (☎ **508/548-8500**) to check the schedule, or pick one up at the **Falmouth Recreation Center,** 790 E. Main St. (☎ **508/457-2567**).

SHOPPING
Falmouth's spiffy Main Street has a number of good clothing, home goods and gift stores. There are several good art and craft galleries in West Falmouth and Woods Hole.

ANTIQUES/COLLECTIBLES   On her way to the Martha's Vineyard ferry in Woods Hole, Jackie O. often stopped into the **Antiquarium,** at 204 Palmer Ave., located next to the Steamship Parking lots (☎ **508/548-1755**), the exquisite red-clapboard Greek Revival house with the red fence. This is a quirky place, open only when the flag is out, but inside are treasures. Mr. O. D. Garland carries a general mixture of American and European antiques, as well as decorative arts. **Chrisalis Country Home,** 550 Rte. 28A, West Falmouth (☎ **508/540-5884**), a pleasantly packed shop, is owned by Dorothy Donlan. She operates an interior-design business from these digs—it ought to be booming, judging from her astute antiques selection and inspired pairings of old and new.

Village Barn Antiques, 606 Rte. 28A, West Falmouth (☎ **508/540-3215**), housed in a beautiful old barn, has a large selection of odds and ends.

ARTS & CRAFTS   The **Woods Hole Gallery,** 14 School St. (north of Water Street), Woods Hole (☎ **508/548-7594**), is far enough off the beaten path so you won't stumble onto it by accident, but collectors will want to call on Edith Bruce, an art restorer who operates a distinguished gallery out of her home. Landscapes—dunescapes, specifically—are a specialty; closed mid-September to late June.

BOOKS   Eight Cousins Children's Books, 189 Main Street, Falmouth (☎ **508/548-5548**), not only has a wide range of children's books, videos, and audio tapes, but also stocks best-sellers and local lore for adults. There are story hours and activities year-round. Call for a schedule. **Booksmith** located at Falmouth Plaza, 33 Davis

Straits (Rte. 28), Falmouth (☎ **508/540-6064**) has the largest selection of new books and magazines in town.

FASHION   Don't be intimidated to browse in **Maxwell & Co.,** 200 Main St. (in the center of town), Falmouth (☎ **508/540-8752**), which may be the highest-end clothier on the Cape. Comfortable Italian fashions are displayed here in an elegant setting. Their end-of-summer sale in mid-August offers up to 70% off these exquisite goods.

The clothing at **Caline for Kids,** 149 Main St. (in the center of town), Falmouth (☎ **508/548-2533**), ranges from practical to elegant, and sometimes manages to be both. Sizes from newborn to 14 are available.

Europa Imports Outlet, 628 Rte. 28A, West Falmouth (☎ **508/540-7814**), features imports from all over the world—including straw bags from Africa and handmade fashions from Central America. It adds up to a sophisticated look, liberated from cookie-cutter predictability. There's also a small but adorable selection of clothes for very young children.

FOOD & WINE   People drive from all over the region for the wine selection (and prices) at **Kappy's,** 21 Spring Bars Rd., off Route 28 (☎ **508/548-2600**), the Cape's largest liquor, beer, and wine store. "Pick your own" is the password at the long-established **Tony Andrews Farm and Produce Stand,** 398 Old Meeting House Rd. (about 1½ miles north of Rte. 28), East Falmouth (☎ **508/548-5257**), where it's strawberries early in the summer, tomatoes, sweet corn, and more as the season progresses. Of course, you could just buy them here, too, though the Puritans wouldn't have approved.

GIFTS   Bojangles, 239 Main St. (☎ **508/548-9888**), a high-end gift shop/women's clothing boutique, is a significant addition to Falmouth's Main Street shopping. Stop here for funky gifts and fine crafts, including exceptional hand-painted glassware.

WHERE TO STAY

For a basic motel with a great location, try the Tides Motel (☎ **508/548-3126**) at the west end of Grand Avenue in Falmouth Heights. The 1950s-style motel sits on the beach at the head of Falmouth Harbor facing out toward Vineyard Sound. Rates are in season are $131 to $186.

EXPENSIVE

Coonamessett Inn. Jones Rd. and Gifford St. (about ½ mile N of Main St.), Falmouth, MA 02540. ☎ **508/548-2300.** Fax 508/540-9831. www.capecodrestaurants.org. E-mail: cmicathi@aol.com. 27 units, 1 cottage. A/C TV TEL. Summer $180–$260 double. Rates include continental breakfast. AE, MC, V.

A gracious inn built around the core of a 1796 homestead, the Coonamessett Inn is Falmouth's most traditional lodging choice. The original inn was a few miles away and flanked the namesake river. Its future was in question until the late Josiah K. Lilly, a local resident, funded it with a trust designed to keep its body and soul intact. Set on 7 lushly landscaped acres overlooking a pond, it has the feel of a country club where all comers are welcome. Some of the rooms, decorated in reproduction antiques, can be a bit somber, so try to get one with good light. Most have a separate sitting room attached, and all have hair dryers and coffeemakers.

Dining/Diversions: The Coonamessett Inn Dining Room is unabashedly formal and fairly good, though the quality of the food can be inconsistent. Entrees are $17 to $30. A better choice is the adjoining Eli's, a clubbily decorated tavern, where a mellow jazz combo holds forth on weekends. Entrees are $7 to $15.

⚪ **Inn at West Falmouth.** 66 Frazar Rd. (off Rte. 28A), West Falmouth, MA 02574. ☎ **800/397-7696** or 508/540-7696. www.innatwestfalmouth.com. 8 units. TEL. Summer $175–$300 double. Rates include continental breakfast. AE, MC, V.

One of the loveliest small inns on the Cape, this turn-of-the-century shingle-style house is set high on a wooded hill with distant views to Buzzards Bay. Though it suffered some hard knocks in its day, serving at one point as a children's camp, stylish innkeeper Stephen Calvacca has purged it of the last trace of institutionalism. Throughout the house you'll find spacious rooms lavished with custom linens and accented by a few judicious, unusual antiques, and the large living room, set about with fresh flowers, has heaps of best-sellers begging to be borrowed. After a leisurely continental breakfast highlighted by fresh-baked pastries, you might carry off a tome to the small, sparkling heated pool set in the deck or wander the beautiful landscaped grounds. There's a clay tennis court, and Chappaquoit Beach is about a 10-minute walk down a country lane. You are also walking distance from the antiques shops and galleries of West Falmouth village. On blustery days, you can sink into one of the voluminous couches by the fireplace or retreat to your own private marble whirlpool bath.

MODERATE

⚪ **Grafton Inn.** 261 Grand Ave. S., Falmouth Heights, MA 02540. ☎ **800/642-4069** or 508/540-8688. Fax 508/540-1861. www.graftoninn.com. E-mail: ALAMKID@aol.com. 10 units. A/C TV. Summer $164–$210 double. Rates include full breakfast. AE, MC, V. Closed mid-Nov to mid-Feb. No children under 16.

Reminiscent of a more leisurely age, this turreted Victorian grande dame has a front-row seat on Falmouth Heights' lively beach. View seekers will be delighted with the vista beyond: Martha's Vineyard, glimmering across the sound. All rooms have extra touches like hair dryers, extra pillows, homemade chocolates, and fresh flowers—as well as coveted ocean views. Breakfast is served at individual tables on the screened porch overlooking the beach. The alternating elaborate breakfast menu might include Sonoma eggs (with sun-dried tomato, basil, chives, and salsa), Belgian waffles, or Hawaiian toast. In the afternoon, wine and cheese is served. The ferry to Martha's Vineyard, leaving from Falmouth Harbor, is only a short walk away.

⚪ **Inn on the Sound.** 313 Grand Ave., Falmouth Heights, MA 02540. ☎ **800/564-9668** or 508/457-9666. Fax 508/457-9631. www.innonthesound.com. E-mail: innontheso@aol.com. 10 units. TV. Summer $95–$195 double. Rates include full breakfast. AE, DISC, MC, V. No children under 16.

The ambience here is as breezy as the setting, high on a bluff beside Falmouth's premier sunning beach, with a sweeping view of Nantucket Sound from the large front deck. Innkeeper Renee Ross is an interior decorator, and it shows: There's none of the usual frilly/cutesy stuff in these well-appointed guest rooms, most of which have ocean views, several with their own private decks. Many of the bathrooms have been renovated with large, luxurious tiled showers. The focal point of the living room is a handsome boulder hearth (nice for those nippy nights). The breakfasts served, especially the surprise French toast (baked and stuffed with cream cheese and berries) and the crab-and-cream-cheese soufflé, offer incentive to dawdle, but the outdoors exerts an even stronger pull.

La Maison Cappellari at Mostly Hall. 27 W. Main St. (W of the Village Green), Falmouth, MA 02540. ☎ **800/682-0565** or 508/548-3786. Fax 508/548-5778. www.mostlyhall.com. E-mail: mostlyhall@aol.com. 6 units. A/C. Summer $185–$225 double. Rates include full breakfast. AE, DISC, MC, V. Closed mid-Dec to mid-Mar. No children under 16.

New innkeepers Christina and Bogdan Simcic have turned this traditional inn on the Village Green into a truly continental experience. The plantation-style house itself is unusual. It was built by a sea captain to please his New Orleans–born bride. Taking inspiration from the Greek Revival architecture, the Simcics have muraled the rooms and added hand-painted furniture. For breakfast, there may be unusual offerings like caviar, octopus salad, and black olive spreads. Loaner bikes are provided for exploring the nearby Shining Sea Bikeway to Woods Hole. The six stately, high-ceilinged, corner bedrooms each boast a canopied four-poster bed. The mature gardens are particularly lovely in spring when the dogwoods, azaleas, and cherry trees are in bloom. The garden gazebo makes a pleasant retreat.

Nautilus Motor Inn. 539 Woods Hole Rd., Woods Hole, MA 02543. ☎ **800/654-2333** or 508/548-1525. Fax 508/457-9674. www.nautilusinn.com. E-mail: JPNautilus@aol.com. 54 units. A/C TV TEL. Summer $100–$160 double. AE, DC, DISC, MC, V. Closed mid-Oct to mid-Apr.

The Nautilus is a crescent-shaped motel poised above Woods Hole's picturesque Little Harbor. The two tiers of rooms are standard motelish, but each comes with a private balcony for taking in the view and/or sunning, and a very spacious wooden deck flanks the fair-size pool. There are also two private tennis courts. A rather curious restaurant, The Dome, is right on the premises. An architectural landmark, this very sturdy geodesic dome was R. Buckminster Fuller's first and must have seemed grandly futuristic in 1953. The Martha's Vineyard ferry is a very short stroll away. Not so much a destination in and of itself, the Nautilus makes an ideal launching pad for day trips.

Sands of Time Motor Inn & Harbor House. 549 Woods Hole Rd., Woods Hole, MA 02543. ☎ **800/841-0114** or 508/548-6300. Fax 508/457-0160. www.sandsoftime.com. E-mail: reservations@sandsoftime.com. 36 units (2 with shared bathroom). A/C TV TEL. Summer $120–$170 double. Rates include continental breakfast. AE, CB, DC, DISC, MC, V. Closed Nov–Mar.

This property, which is across the street from the Woods Hole ferry terminal, consists of two buildings, a 2-story motel in front of a shingled 1879 Victorian mansion. The motel rooms feature crisp, above-average decor, plus private porches overlooking the harbor. The rooms in the Harbor House are more lavish and romantic—some with four-posters, working fireplaces, wicker furnishings, and harbor views. There is a small heated pool on the grounds, and guests can also use the tennis court at the motel property next door. All rooms are equipped with computer jacks.

Village Green Inn. 40 Main St. (at the Village Green), Falmouth, MA 02540. ☎ **800/237-1119** or 508/548-5621. Fax 508/457-5051. www.villagegreeninn.com. E-mail: VGI40@aol.com. 5 units. A/C TV TEL. Summer $150–$160 double; $195–$225 suite. Rates include full breakfast. AE, MC, V. Closed Jan–Feb. No children under 12.

An 1804 Federal house decked out with Victorian trim, this B&B proudly presides over the historic Village Green. The ambience is comfy rather than stuffy. For room to really stretch out, opt for the sunny suite. It comes complete with desk and daybed for (respectively) tackling the homework you imprudently lugged along or, alternately, ditching it in favor of a novel and bonbons—provided you're still peckish after a breakfast of, say, caramelized French toast, plus a sweet afternoon snack on the geranium-bedecked porch. Two rooms have working fireplaces. The suite also has a minifridge. All rooms have hair dryers. Loaner bikes are provided to explore the nearby Shining Sea Bikeway.

Wildflower Inn. 167 Palmer Ave. (2 blocks N of Main St.), Falmouth, MA 02540. ☎ **800/294-5459** or 508/548-9524. Fax 508/548-9524. www.wildflower-inn.com. E-mail: WLDFLR167@aol.com. 5 units, 1 cottage. A/C. Summer $140–$195 double; cottage $225. Rates include full breakfast. AE, MC, V.

Though located on a busy stretch of road, this B&B is immaculately appointed inside, and its exterior with colorful gardens consistently wins beautification awards from the town. The inn is full of welcoming touches like the row of red wooden rocking chairs lining the front porch. The rooms are creatively and individually decorated with summery items like wicker furnishings and country quilts. There's even a safari-style room with an iron canopy bed draped with decorative mosquito netting and accents of burlap, bamboo, and rattan. Two dormer rooms on the top floor come with whirlpool baths, and the attached apartment features a loft bedroom served by a spiral staircase. The five-course breakfast, served on the wraparound porch in summer, starts with a fruit compote and might include such treats as apple-pie French toast garnished with edible flowers. All rooms have hair dryers and robes. Loaner bikes are available, and the inn is across the street from the satellite parking lot for the Martha's Vineyard ferries, so you can easily hop a bus down to the terminal in Woods Hole.

Woods Hole Passage. 186 Woods Hole Rd. (about 2 miles N of Woods Hole center), Woods Hole, MA 02540. ☎ **800/790-8976** or 508/548-9575. Fax 508/540-4771. www. woodsholepassage.com. E-mail: inn@woodsholepassage.com. 5 units. A/C. Summer $125–$145 double. Rates include full breakfast. AE, DC, DISC, MC, V.

Innkeeper Deb Pruitt has put her stamp on this quaint B&B. The walls of the individual rooms and the great room remain boldly painted from the former owner, but the furniture reflects the new innkeeper's more down-to-earth persona. In season, you can dine outside on the slate porch overlooking the grounds, which include a croquet course, bocci, horseshoes, and a hammock for lazing. The two cathedral-ceiling loft rooms in the adjoining 18th-century barn are definitely the most comfortable and seem custom-made for honeymooning (or otherwise cocooning) couples. All rooms have hair dryers. There are loaner bikes and an outdoor shower. A 15-minute walk brings you to Vineyard Sound.

INEXPENSIVE

Inn at One Main. 1 Main St. (1 block NW of the Village Green), Falmouth, MA 02540. ☎ **888/281-6246** or 508/540-7469. Fax 603/462-5680. www.bbonline.com/ma/onemain. E-mail: innat1main@aol.com. 6 units. A/C. Summer $110–$150 double. Rates include full breakfast. AE, DISC, MC, V.

Though a centenarian (built in 1892), this shingled house with Queen Anne flourishes has a crisp, youthful air. The bedrooms embody barefoot romance, rather than the Victorian brand. Lace, chintz, and wicker have been laid on lightly, leaving plenty of room to kick about. All rooms have hair dryers. The Turret Room, with its big brass bed, is perhaps the most irresistible. Breakfasts would instantly convert a "just coffee, please" morning grouch. Gingerbread pancakes, orange-pecan French toast, homemade scones—it's a good thing the Shining Sea Bikeway is right at hand.

WHERE TO DINE
VERY EXPENSIVE

✪ **Regatta of Falmouth-by-the-Sea.** 217 Clinton Ave. (end of Scranton Ave. on Falmouth Harbor, about 1 mile S of Main St.). ☎ **508/548-5400.** Reservations recommended. Dress: "Attractively formal or informal." Main courses $20–$30. AE, MC, V. Late May to mid-Sept daily 4:30–10pm; call for off-season hours. Closed mid-Oct to Apr. INTERNATIONAL.

A dazzler since its debut in 1970, this exemplary restaurant has it all: views (it's right on the harbor), polished yet innovative cuisine, and superb service. Some guests arrive by boat and tie up at their 90-foot dock. You're likely to find owner Brantz Bryan affably making the rounds: He's the one who seems to have wandered in off a golf course, vigorous and "attractively informal" in tastefully lurid preppy attire. His wife and partner, Wendy Bryan, designed the decor, from the rose-petal pale walls to the custom Limoges china on which two roses entwine. The excellence and innovation continues in the kitchen. Favorites include the Menemsha Bay scallop bisque with fresh chervil; and for a main course, grilled 1¾ pound lobster basted with lime buerre blanc sauce and served with hand-cut tarragon fettuccini, baby eggplant, and asparagus. For dessert, nothing beats the carmelized banana puff pastry tart filled with chocolate ganache and covered with rum sauce.

For those who would dine here every summer night but for the prices, note that there is a three-course "early dinner" from 4:30 to 5:30pm—an elegant meal deal priced at $22 to $26.

MODERATE

Chapaquoit Grill. 410 Rte. 28A, West Falmouth. ☎ **508/540-7794.** Reservations not accepted. Main courses $8–$16. MC, V. Daily 5–10pm. NEW AMERICAN.

One of the few worthwhile dining spots in this sleepy neck of the woods, this little roadside bistro has Californian aspirations, wood-grilled slabs of fish accompanied by trendy salsas, and crispy personal pizzas delivered straight from the brick oven. People drive from miles around for this flavorful food; a no-reservations policy means long waits nightly in season and weekends year-round.

✪ **Fishmonger's Cafe.** 56 Water St. (at the Eel Pond drawbridge), Woods Hole. ☎ **508/540-5376.** Main courses $10–$19. AE, MC, V. Mid-June to Oct Mon–Fri 7–11am, 11:30am–4pm, and 5–10pm; Sat–Sun 7–11:30am, noon–4:30pm, and 5:30–10:30pm; call for off-season hours. Closed mid-Dec to mid-Feb. NATURAL.

A cherished carryover from the early 1970s, this sunny, casual cafe attracts local young people and scientists, as well as Bermuda-shorted tourists, with an ever-changing array of imaginatively prepared dishes. Chefs Anne Hunt and Harold Broadstock change the eclectic dinner menu every few days and have added some Thai entrees. Regulars sit at the counter to enjoy a bowl of the Fisherman's Stew, while schmoozing with staff bustling about the open kitchen. Newcomers usually go for the tables by the window, where you can watch boats come and go from Eel Pond. The menu ranges widely (lunch could be a tempeh burger, made with fermented soybeans, or ordinary beef), and longtime customers look to the blackboard for the latest innovations, which invariably include delectable desserts like pumpkin-pecan pie.

The Flying Bridge. 220 Scranton Ave. (about ½ mile S of Main St.). ☎ **508/548-2700.** Main courses $8–$20. AE, MC, V. Apr–Dec daily 11:30am–10pm; call for off-season hours. AMERICAN/CONTINENTAL.

Seafood, appropriately enough, predominates at this shipshape harborside megarestaurant (capacity: nearly 600). With three bars tossed into the mix and live music upstairs on weekends, things can get a bit crazy; you'll find comparative peace and quiet—as well as tip-top nautical views—out on the deck. In addition to basic bar food (Buffalo chicken wings and the like), you'll find hefty hunks of protein and fish in many guises, from fish-and-chips—with optional malt vinegar—to appealing blackboard specials. This is a great place to bring the kids, because they'll enjoy wandering onto the attached dock to watch the ducks in the harbor.

Landfall. Luscombe Ave. (½ block S of Water St.), Woods Hole. ☎ **508/548-1758.** Reservations recommended. Main courses $10–$24. AE, MC, V. Mid-May to Sept daily 11am–10pm; call for off-season hours. Closed Nov to mid-Apr. AMERICAN.

A terrific setting overshadows the middling cuisine and ho-hum entertainment. Besides the usual fish and pasta dishes, there's "lite fare" like burgers and fish-and-chips for under $15. This is a great place to bring the kids; there's a children's menu that comes with games and crayons. Or come for a drink at the half-dory bar to enjoy this massive wooden building constructed of salvage, both marine and terrestrial. The "ship's knees" on the ceiling are the ribs of an old schooner which broke up on the shores of Cuttyhunk Island; the big stained-glass window came from a mansion on nearby Penzance Point. A large bank of windows looks out onto the harbor, and the Martha's Vineyard ferry, when docking, appears to be making a beeline straight for your table.

The Nimrod. 100 Dillingham Ave. (off Gifford St., 1 mile N of Falmouth center). ☎ **508/540-4132.** Reservations recommended. Main courses $13–$22. AE, DISC, MC, V. June–Aug Sun–Wed 5–9pm, Thurs–Sat 5–10pm; Sept–May Sun–Wed noon–9pm, Thurs–Sat noon–10pm. NEW AMERICAN.

Slightly off the beaten track, this traditional restaurant, set in a charming 18th-century home, has a pleasing combination of Ye Olde atmosphere, attentive service, and innovative cuisine. Seafood fans have a nice selection here, highlighted by grilled shrimp Nimrod (in a ginger-citrus vinaigrette), or grilled native swordfish limone (with lemon-shallot butter). Steak lovers will be happy with the 12-oz. New York sirloin. Tavern fans will want to sit in the bar area where there is live jazz 6 nights a week in season and sometimes a 16-piece big band. The several other dining rooms are more sedate choices. In the winter, diners like to sit near one of seven working fireplaces; in the summer, they prefer the screened-in deck.

The Silver Lounge Restaurant. 412 Rte. 28A, North Falmouth. ☎ **508/563-2410.** No reservations. Main courses $8–$18. AE, DISC, MC, V. Daily 11:30am–1am. REGIONAL.

In the middle of winter when many Cape restaurants are struggling to survive, this place has an hour's wait and a line out the door. It's long been a favorite with locals, and visitors often "discover" it while driving scenic Route 28A. Although it's a publike place with a large stone hearth, families come in droves because kids love to sit in the railroad caboose where there are just nine booths (come early if you want one). This is a meat-and-potatoes crowd, and the most popular menu item is the Black Diamond steak. This is the only place in the area that serves a full menu until 1am. There is also an extensive sandwich menu (most under $6) served all day. Weekends in summer, you might find the talented kids from the College Light Opera Company at the piano, entertaining the late-night dinner crowd with show tunes.

Trabica. 327 Gifford St. (5 blocks N of town) ☎ **508/548-9861.** Main courses $9–$18. AE, MC, V. Daily 5–9pm. ITALIAN/AMERICAN.

The unfortunate name of this establishment is supposed to be a cute way of saying "We're a trattoria, a bistro, and a cafe!" What this actually is a decent Italian restaurant serving hearty food with an emphasis on garlic. In addition to pasta dishes, the small menu features such traditional dishes as rosemary roasted chicken and eclectic dishes like grilled pork loin chop with pineapple-vanilla salsa. The restaurant is located in an old house that has been divided into several small and romantic candlelit rooms and a tiny bar area.

INEXPENSIVE

Betsy's Diner. 457 Main St. (in the center of town). ☎ **508/540-0060.** Main courses $4–$10. AE, MC, V. Daily 6am–8pm. AMERICAN.

I once had the best baked piece of scrod ever at this vintage 1950s diner. It was breaded with corn flakes. This is hearty food like your mother used to make, if your mother was a variation of June Cleaver. The menu features turkey dinner, breakfast all day, and homemade soups. Many people come here for the large selection of scrumptious homemade pies, which are the best on Cape Cod. Each red vinyl booth is equipped with its own juke box with retro hits.

The British Beer Company. 263 Grand Ave. (across from the beach), Falmouth Heights. ☎ **508/540-9600.** All items under $15. AE, MC, V. Daily 11:30am–10pm. PUB FARE/PIZZA.

The view is great at this faux British pub across the street from Falmouth Heights beach. The food quality, though, is inconsistent. Stick with the fish and chips, and you'll be fine. Of course, there is also beer, over 18 drafts available, like Guinness and John Courage, as well as bottled selections.

✪ **Cap'n Kidd.** 77 Water St. (W of the Eel Pond drawbridge), Woods Hole. ☎ **508/548-9206.** Main courses $8–$15. AE, MC, V. Daily 11:30am–3pm and 5–9pm. SEAFOOD.

The semiofficial heart of Woods Hole, this well-worn bistro really comes into its own once the tourist hordes subside. It's then that the year-round scientists and fishing crews can huddle around the woodstove, or congregate in the glassed-porch overlooking Eel Pond and order up reasonably priced seafood, or belly up to the hand-carved mahogany bar (thought to date from the early 1800s) and drink to their heart's content—mostly the latter, judging from the degree of general bonhomie. The notorious 17th-century pirate, who is rumored to have debarked in Woods Hole on his way back to England to be hanged, would probably get a warm reception were he to wander in today. In season, you'll want to sit in the glassed-porch in back that overlooks Eel Pond. Although the Kidd shares a kitchen with a fancier restaurant called The Waterfront, the fare here is pub grub and some seafood, with individual pizzas, burgers, and sandwiches the mainstays. Homemade clam chowder is thick as paste, with large chunks of potato and clam; stuffed quahogs are piled high, and french fries are the real deal, thickly sliced.

✪ **The Clam Shack.** 227 Clinton Ave. (off Scranton Ave., about 1 mile S of Main St.). ☎ **508/540-7758.** Main courses $5–$15. No credit cards. Daily 11:30am–7:45pm. Closed mid-Sept to late May. SEAFOOD.

This classic clam shack sits at the head of Falmouth harbor and offers steaming plates of fried seafood that you carry to a picnic table inside, outside, or up on the roof deck. The food is basic clam-shack fare, but the fish is fresh and you can't beat the view.

McMenamy's Seafood Restaurant. 70 Davis Straits (Rte. 28; 1 mile E of the town center). ☎ **508/540-2115.** Main courses $8–$16. AE, DISC, MC, V. May–Oct 11:30am–10pm; Oct–May 11:30am–9pm. SEAFOOD.

The McMenamy family has been serving up heaping plates of fried, broiled, and baked seafood at this location for 25 years. Deliveries of fresh fish are brought in daily and make their way onto the specials board. The lobster roll is superb here, as is the fish sandwich. The chowders, both fish and quahog, are made from scratch by head chef Patrick McMenamy. Fish sandwiches here are the best in town. Onion rings are made fresh on-site. On a clear night, you may want to sit out on the screened porch. There is acoustic entertainment on weekends in season.

Peking Palace. 452 Main St. (in the center of town). ☎ **508/540-8204.** Main courses $5–$15. AE, MC, V. June–Aug daily 11:30am–2am; Sept–May Sun–Thurs 11:30am–midnight, Fri–Sat 11:30am–1:30am. CHINESE.

Incontrovertibly the best Chinese restaurant on the Cape, this smallish restaurant has been infused with TLC at every turn. From the fringes of bamboo gracing the parking lot to the gleaming rosewood tables, no detail has been overlooked to create a cosseting, exotic environment. It's a wonder the staff finds the time, what with 300-plus items on the menu, spanning three regional Chinese cuisines (Cantonese, Mandarin, and Szechuan), as well as Polynesian. Sip a fanciful drink to give yourself time to take in the menu, and be sure to solicit your server's opinion: That's how I encountered some heavenly spicy chilled squid.

TAKE-OUT & PICNIC FARE

Cape Cod Bagel Co., 419 Palmer Ave. (☎ **508/548-8485**), carries the usual bagel sandwiches, soups, coffee, and other beverages, but the bagels here, made on the premises, are definitely the best in town. **Box Lunch,** 781 Main St. (☎ **508/457-7657**), is one of a number of franchises on the Cape that carry the pita "rollwiches." These are excellent sandwiches (over 50 selections) made fast, and they're perfect for picnics. In season, Thursday and Saturday from 8am to 2pm, there's a **Farmers Market** on Main Street in Peg Noonan Park with salad greens, homemade jams, breads, plants, and more.

A COFFEEHOUSE

Laureen's, at 170 Main St. in the center of town (☎ **508/540-9104**), is a sophisticated coffee bar/deli, ideal for a quick bite or sip. It specializes in vegetarian and Middle Eastern fare. Try one of the feta pizzas. You can also take some of this good stuff home. Kitchen gear and gifts, including some great stuff for kids, round out the stock.

SWEETS

Locals know to get to **Pie in the Sky Dessert Café and Bake Shop,** 10 Water St., Woods Hole (☎ **508/540-5475**) by 9am for sticky buns, the best anywhere. Those bound for Martha's Vineyard know to stop at this small cafe for treats before hopping on the ferry.

Falmouth residents are the beneficiaries of a struggle for ice-cream bragging rights: **Ben & Bill's Chocolate Emporium,** at 209 Main St., in the center of town (☎ **508/548-7878**), draws crowds even in winter, late into the evening. They come for the homemade ice cream, not to mention the hand-dipped candies showcased in a wraparound display—a chocoholic's nightmare or dream come true, depending. Those who can trust themselves not to go hog-wild might enjoy watching the confections being made. **Dutchland Farms Ice Cream,** at 809 E. Main St., about 1 mile east of the town center (☎ **508/548-9032**), a seemingly undistinguished shop, is the descendant of a Brockton concern established in 1897 and has flavors that give those two guys in Vermont a run for their money. Honolulu Crunch, for instance, comes fortified with crushed macadamias, coconut, and chocolate chips; the "zundap" consists of coffee ice cream laced with fudge and studded with cookies.

There's also **Smitty's Homemade Ice Cream,** at 326 E. Falmouth Hwy. (☎ **508/457-1060**) and 402 N. Falmouth Hwy. (☎ **508/564-7661**) whose proprietor, the cheerful Smitty, is an ice-cream man from central casting.

FALMOUTH AFTER DARK

DRINKS   Grab a stool at **The British Beer Company,** 263 Grand Ave., Falmouth Heights (☎ **508/540-9600**), and choose from a revolving selection of over 18 drafts from the British Isles, as you ponder views of the beach across the street.

God knows whom you'll meet in the rough-and-tumble old **Cap'n Kidd,** 77 Water St., in Woods Hole (☎ **508/548-9206**): maybe a lobsterwoman, maybe a Nobel Prize winner. Good grub, too—see "Where to Dine," above.

Everyone heads to **Liam McGuire's Irish Pub,** on 273 Main St. in Falmouth (☎ **508/548-0285**) for a taste of the Emerald Isle. Liam's the jolly backslapper with a touch of the blarney.

Grumpy's, at 29 Locust St. (☎ **508/540-3930**), is a good old bar/shack with live music (rock, blues, and jazz) Thursday to Sunday nights. Cover is $2 to $10.

FILM   The Cape's only year-round art-house cinema is **Nickelodeon Cinemas,** 742 Rte. 151, East Falmouth (☎ **508/563-6510**). With six small screens, this is a great alternative to the usual mall movies.

PERFORMANCE   The Woods Hole Folk Music Society (☎ 508/540-0320) mounts biweekly concerts October through May (the first and third Sunday of each month), attracting a real grassroots crowd to Community Hall on Water Street, by the Eel Pond drawbridge. General admission is $8; discounts for members, seniors, and children.

The **Cape Cod Theatre Project** (☎ 508/457-4242) is a relatively new playwrights' workshop open to the public. These staged play readings are performed for just a few weeks in July, usually at the Woods Hole Community Hall. In 1998, they premiered a Lanford Wilson play. The rest of the year the talent behind these productions is most likely strutting the boards in New York City. Call for schedule. Suggested donation $10.

Starting at about 7:30pm on Thursday evenings in July and August, the spirited volunteers of the **Falmouth Town Band** swing through big-band numbers as small fries (and some oldsters) dance about. Concerts are held at the Harbor Band Shell, on Scranton Avenue at the harbor in Falmouth, and are free.

The top talent from college drama departments across the country form the **College Light Opera Company** (☎ 508/548-0668), which puts on a fast-paced summer repertory—a classic musical a week, from late June through August. So winning is the work of these 32 young actors and 17 musicians (many of them ultimately Broadway-bound) that the house is usually booked solid, so call well ahead or keep your fingers crossed for a scattering of singles. Its venue, the Highfield Theatre, on the Depot Avenue Extension off North Main Street in Falmouth, is a former horse barn, and for the past half century has been a terrific straw-hat theater. Performances are held Tuesday to Saturday at 8:30pm; there's also a Thursday matinee at 2:30pm. Tickets are $22.

4 Mashpee

11 miles (18km) SE of Sagamore; 12 miles (20km) W of Hyannis

Mashpee is a study in contrasts and awash in controversy. A sizable chunk of it is occupied by the Otis Air Force Base (a source, it turns out, of troublesome groundwater pollution), and the major portion of its shoreline has been claimed by the New Seabury Resort development. Further housing developments are rapidly carving up the inland woods, leaving less and less room for the region's original residents, the Mashpee Wampanoags, whose nomadic ancestors began convening in summer camps by these shores millennia ago. In 1660, concerned by the natives' rapid disenfranchisement and heartened by their willingness to convert, missionary Richard Bourne got the Plymouth General Court to grant his "praying Indians" a 10,500-acre "plantation" in perpetuity. The provision proved far from perpetual, as settlers—and much later, developers—began chipping away at their holdings.

After lengthy litigation in the 1970s and early 1980s, the Mashpee Wampanoags—whose tribal roster now numbers about 1,000—were denied tribal status (unlike the Gay Head Wampanoags of Martha's Vineyard) and were stymied in their efforts to preserve the land. It was only in 1995, with the backing of senators Edward Kennedy and John Kerry (both of whom summer on the Cape), that the sizable—5,871 acres—Mashpee National Wildlife Refuge was carved out of the disputed territory. Influential supporter Gerry Studds hailed the move as "a harbinger of things to come. . . . Creation of this refuge ranks in significance with the Cape Cod National Seashore."

ESSENTIALS
GETTING THERE   After crossing the Sagamore bridge, take Route 6 to exit 2, and Route 130 south. Or fly into Hyannis (see "Getting There," in chapter 2).

VISITOR INFORMATION   Contact the **Mashpee Chamber of Commerce** at the Cape Cod Five Cent Savings Bank, Mashpee Commons, P.O. Box 1245, Mashpee, MA 02649 (☎ **800/423-6274** or 508/477-0792; fax 508/477-5541; www.mashpeechamber.com; e-mail: info@mashpeechamber.com), or the **Cape Cod Chamber of Commerce** (see "Visitor Information" in the "Sandwich" section, above).

BEACHES & RECREATIONAL PURSUITS

BEACHES   The small part of the shoreline not reserved for the New Seabury Resort is an undersung sleeper—and a bargain, too: ○ **South Cape Beach,** off Great Oak Road (5 miles south of the Mashpee rotary). Mashpee is set amid the 450-acre South Cape Beach State Park (☎ **508/457-0495,** ext. 4). This lengthy stretch of beach has miles of hiking trails. Parking costs $2 per day.

BOATING   Paddle Cape Cod (☎ **888/226-6393** or 508/564-4051; www.paddlecapecod.com; e-mail: cccanoe@capecod.net) runs naturalist-guided trips throughout the Cape. Call for a schedule and more information, or see "Beaches & Recreational Pursuits" in the "Sandwich" section, above. **Cape Cod Kayak** (☎ **508/540-9377;** www.capecodkayak.com) rents kayaks (free delivery) by the day or week, and offers lessons and eco-tours on local waterways. Call for a schedule and more information, or see "Beaches & Recreational Pursuits" in the "Falmouth" section, above.

If you'd rather explore on your own, you can rent a canoe in Falmouth (see the "Falmouth" section, above) and paddle around the Mashpee River, Popponesset Bay, and Mashpee/Wakeby Pond.

FISHING   Mashpee/Wakeby Pond (boat landing off Rte. 130, Fisherman's Dr.) is considered one of the top-10 bass-fishing lakes in the country. Saltwater fishing licenses can be obtained at Sandwich, Falmouth, or Barnstable town halls. South Cape Beach in Mashpee (see "Beaches," above) is a primo spot for surf casting.

GOLF   Though one has to question the wisdom of its placement amid delicate wetlands, the **New Seabury Resort** at 155 Rock Landing Rd. (☎ **508/477-9110**) is, from all reports, tops. In fact, the championship-level Blue Course has consistently ranked among the top-100 courses in the country. Relative slackers have recourse to the Green Course, a regulation par-70 course. Greens fees go up to $150 at the Blue Course and $90 at the Green Course in season.

NATURE TRAILS   The **Mashpee Conservation Commission** (☎ **508/539-1414,** ext. 540) sponsors free naturalist-guided nature tours throughout Mashpee from May through December. Call for a schedule. A shady peninsula jutting into the Cape's largest body of freshwater (the adjoining Wakeby/Mashpee Pond), the 135-acre **Lowell Holly Reservation** off South Sandwich Road in the northern corner of the township harbors some 500 holly trees and a number of magnificent centennial beeches. The stewards of this enchanted place, the **Trustees of the Reservation** (☎ **978/921-1944**), charge $6 per day for the 2-mile trail loop on summer weekends; weekday admission is free. **South Cape Beach State Park** (see "Beaches," above) also offers a network of sandy trails.

WATER SPORTS   The town of Mashpee offers swimming lessons at **Attaquin Park** at Mashpee/Wakeby Pond off Route 130, and also at South Cape Beach; call the **town leisure services department** (☎ **508/539-1400,** ext. 519) for details.

MUSEUMS

Wampanoag Indian Museum. Rte. 130 (opposite The Flume, on Lake Ave.). ☎ **508/477-1536.** Donation requested. Mon–Fri 10am–2pm or Sat by appointment.

Centuries of heartbreaking history are encapsulated in this unprepossessing museum, housed in a 1793 half-Cape built by a great-grandson of pioneer missionary Richard Bourne. Though the native population embraced the colonists' religion wholeheartedly, they never fully grasped the ethos of private property; thus over the years the land vouchsafed to them by the Plymouth court in 1660 was steadily whittled away—most egregiously, starting in the 1960s, when the ratio of undeveloped to developed land in Mashpee was roughly 80 to 20. The percentages have since been reversed, despite a long legal wrangle.

The museum sells copies of Russell M. Peters's tribal history, *The Wampanoags of Mashpee*—must-reading for anyone who hopes to understand the divided nature of this semirural/semisuburban region, much less the role that indigenous peoples played in ensuring the colonists' foothold in the wilderness. The story is far from over, and tourists who take the time to look beneath the surface will gain a deeper appreciation of an area still in flux.

FOR KIDS   The Cape Cod Children's Museum, 577 Great Neck Rd. S. (☎ 508/ 539-8788; www.capecodchildrensmuseum.pair.com) has a toddler castle and a 30-foot pirate ship, among other kid pleasers. It also sponsors many special events. The museum is open Monday through Saturday 10am to 5pm and Sunday noon to 5pm. Admission is $3 for those over 4; $2 for kids under 4.

SHOPPING

Shopping in Mashpee is pretty much limited to the **Mashpee Commons,** at the Mashpee rotary, Routes 151 and 28 (☎ 508/477-5400). Designed to resemble an ideal New England village (right down to the sidewalk measurements, modeled on Woodstock, Vermont), Mashpee Commons is a gussied-up shopping complex with a facadelike feel: The been-here-forever look to which it aspires has never quite materialized, despite massive influxes of capital. This is where you'll find chains like **Gap, Talbots, Banana Republic,** and **Starbucks Coffee.** There's also **M. Brann** for retro accessories and the **Signature Gallery** for superb American crafts.

WHERE TO STAY

New Seabury Resort. Great Neck S. Rd. (about 4 miles S of the Mashpee rotary), New Seabury, MA 02649. ☎ **800/999-9033** or 508/477-9111. Fax 508/477-9790. www. newseabury.com. About 160 units (depending on rental pool). TV TEL. Summer $255–$275 1-bedroom villa; $330–$405 2-bedroom villa. AE, DC, MC, V.

One of the few full-bore "destination resorts" on the Cape, this 2,300-acre complex, packing some 1,600 condos, occupies more than half the town's shoreline—land formally granted to the Mashpee Wampanoags in 1660. Being the beneficiary of such a troubled legacy might make some uncomfortable, and one would also have to question the wisdom of positioning and maintaining golf courses in the midst of fragile wetlands. Still, the damage is mostly done, and vacationers not saddled with such concerns are sure to enjoy themselves here. The tastefully decorated condos are clustered into "villages" of varying personalities: Maushop, for instance, with its crushed-shell walkways and clambering roses, is meant to mimic Nantucket. Relatively speaking, the rates are a real "steal"—provided you don't factor in the long-term impact of such intensive development on the environment.

Dining/Diversions: Five restaurants can be found within the development, the most notable of which is the Popponesset Inn, the upscale venue of choice in this region for a good half century. The Popponesset Marketplace harbors several casual eateries, such as the congenial Raw Bar, and mounts concerts and other family-fun events.

Amenities: In addition to its two 18-hole golf courses, the complex encompasses 16 all-weather tennis courts, a health club, two outdoor pools, a 3½-mile stretch of private beach, bike trails (with rentals), scheduled children's activities, plus a minimal offering of miniature golf.

WHERE TO DINE

✪ **Contrast.** Market St. Mashpee Commons (at the intersection of Rtes. 151 and 28). ☎ **508/477-1299.** Main courses $7–$22. AE, MC, V. Daily 11:30am–10pm. ECLECTIC.

Besides sporting the funkiest interior (all bright splashes of color), the dining spot also has the area's most creative and sophisticated menu, with Mexican and Asian influences. Bistro fare such as cod cakes with citrus roumalade and chicken pot pie, shares the menu with soy-marinated salmon with stir-fried spinach. There are also specialty pizzas like grilled shrimp with pine nuts and aioli. "Deconstructed sushi" usually appears as an appetizer, and there's always a different preparation of Black Angus club steak. The bar here is top-notch, especially the comfortable niche in the corner with a couch and armchairs.

The Flume. Lake Ave. (off Rte. 130, about 2½ miles N of the Mashpee rotary). ☎ **508/477-1456.** Main courses $9–$26. MC, V. Apr–Nov Tues–Sat 5–9pm; Sun 5–8pm. Closed Dec–Mar. REGIONAL.

At this small, friendly restaurant set above a herring run, chef Earl Mills, who is also Chief Flying Eagle of the Wampanoag tribe, dishes up solid Yankee fare, from a classic clam chowder to fried smelts, pot roast, lobster Newburg, and a colonial-era Indian pudding spiced with molasses and ginger. Seasonal specialties include, in the spring, herring roe plucked right from the flume (a stream that fish climb to spawn), which runs right beside its namesake.

Gone Tomatoes. Mashpee Commons. (at the intersection of Rtes. 151 and 28). ☎ **508/477-8100.** Main courses $8–$15. MC, V. Mon–Thurs 11:45am–10:30pm; Fri–Sat 11:45am–11pm; Sun 11am–10:30pm. ITALIAN.

A shopping mall is about the last place I'd go hunting for a good Italian restaurant, but at this very stylish cafe, both the Sicilian and Tuscan repertoires are expertly rendered, in preparations such as wild-mushroom scampi served atop an angel-hair pasta pancake or a piquant veal picatta. It's not exactly the Old Country, but the food itself travels well.

5

The Mid Cape:
Barnstable, Hyannis,
Yarmouth & Dennis

If the Cape had a capital, Hyannis would be it. It's a sprawling concrete jungle where the Kennedy mystique of the 1960s led to heedless development that has nearly doubled the Cape's year-round population to over 200,000 and climbing. The summer population is about three times that, and you'd swear every single person had daily errands to run in Hyannis. That said, this overrun town still has plenty of pockets of charm. The waterfront area in particular, where the Island ferries dock, has benefited greatly from an influx of civic pride and attention, and Main Street in Hyannis, long eclipsed by the megastores along Route 132, is once again a pleasant place to stroll.

The town of Barnstable, the seat of Cape Cod's Barnstable County government, is made up of eight villages: Hyannis, Hyannisport, Barnstable Village, West Barnstable, Osterville, Centerville, Cotuit, and Marstons Mills. Along the north side of the Cape on Route 6A (the Old King's Hwy.) are Barnstable Village, with a compact Main Street anchored by an imposing granite county courthouse, and West Barnstable, containing a handful of delightful specialty stores and views of acres of salt marsh leading out to Cape Cod Bay. Along the south coast (off Route 28) are Cotuit, Marstons Mills, Osterville, and Centerville, all with gracious residential sections. Osterville has the best strolling Main Street in these parts, and Centerville has the hippest public beach, at Craigville.

While Barnstable is an ideal location for exploring the rest of the Cape and the Islands, there's also fun to be had nearby. If you are staying in the vicinity of Hyannis, you'll certainly want to head over to the north side of the Cape for a drive along the Old King's Highway, but you'll also want to stroll around Hyannis Harbor, stopping for lunch at Tugboat's or Baxter's, where seagulls will compete for a bite of your lobster roll. Main Street Hyannis has had its good and bad years; currently, things are looking good, so you'll find a number of interesting shops and galleries (see "Shopping," below), as well as cafes and bars (see "Hyannis & Environs After Dark," below).

Some of the finest seaside mansions on the Cape are in the old-money villages of Cotuit, Osterville, Centerville, and Hyannisport. To explore this "Gold Coast" by car, take some detours off Route 28, driving south toward Nantucket Sound. These winding country roads are also good for biking (see "Bicycling," below).

The towns of Yarmouth and Dennis straddle the Cape from north to south, with the northside villages along the historic Old King's

The Mid Cape

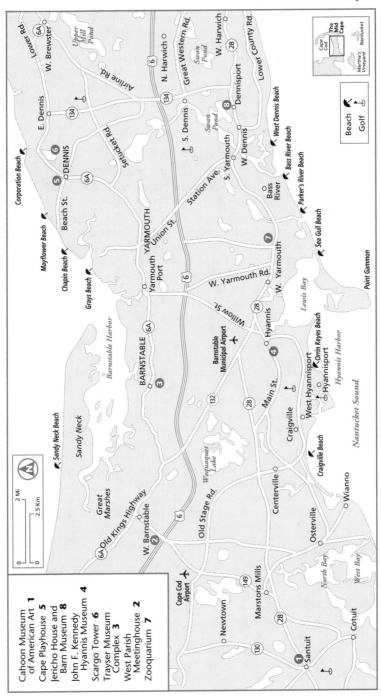

Cahoon Museum of American Art **1**
Cape Playhouse **5**
Jericho House and Barn Museum **8**
John F. Kennedy Hyannis Museum **4**
Scargo Tower **6**
Trayser Museum Complex **3**
West Parish Meetinghouse **2**
Zooquarium **7**

Beach
Golf

Highway and the southside villages along commercialized and overdeveloped Route 28. That's not to say there aren't some very nice enclaves along the south shore. Some of the beaches along this stretch of Nantucket Sound (West Dennis Beach and Parker's River Beach in South Yarmouth) are quite popular with families, but the villages themselves (Dennisport and South and West Yarmouth) have definitely seen better days. Developers in the last 30 years have gotten carried away. In stark contrast, Yarmouth Port and Dennis Village on the north side are perfect little time capsules, loaded with old-fashioned New England charm, an encyclopedic array of historic homes, and terrific small businesses.

1 Barnstable, Hyannis, Neighboring Villages & Environs

15 miles (25km) E of Sagamore; 44 miles (71km) S of Provincetown

As the commercial center and transportation hub of the Cape, hyperdeveloped Hyannis—a mere "village"—grossly overshadows the actual seat of government in the bucolic village of Barnstable. The two locales couldn't be more dissimilar. As peaceful as Hyannis is hectic, the bay area along historic Route 6A unfolds in a blur of greenery and well-kept colonial houses. It's no wonder many visitors experience "post-Camelot letdown" the first time they venture southward to Hyannis. The downtown area, sapped by the strip development that proliferated at the edges of town after the Cape Cod Mall was built in 1970, is making a valiant comeback, with attractive banners and a pretty public park flanking the wharf where frequent ferries depart for the Islands. If you were to confine your visit to this one town, however, you'd get a warped view of the Cape. Along Routes 132 and 28, you could be visiting Anywhere, USA: They're lined by the standard chain stores, restaurants, and hotels, and mired with maddening traffic.

Hyannis has more beds and better "rack rates" (in the travel–industry jargon) than anywhere else on the Cape, but there's little rationale for staying right in town or along the highways—unless you happen to have missed the last ferry out. Even full resort facilities can't begin to compensate for the lack of local color, and propinquity means little when the scenery is so dispiriting as to deter the most determined of walkers.

The best strategy is to stay somewhere peaceful near the edge of town, in one of the moneyed villages—Hyannisport, Osterville, Marstons Mills, and Cotuit—to the west, or in the bayside villages of Barnstable and West Barnstable due north, and just go into the "city" to sample the restaurants and nightlife. Hyannis and environs can offer plenty of both, to suit every palate and personality.

ESSENTIALS

GETTING THERE   After crossing either the Bourne or Sagamore bridge, head east on Route 6 or 6A. The latter passes through Barnstable; Route 132 south of Route 6A leads to Hyannis.

You can fly into Hyannis, and there is good bus service from Boston and New York (see "Getting There" in chapter 2 for more information).

The **Sea Line** (☎ 800/352-7155) makes a circuit of Barnstable, Mashpee, and Falmouth, Monday thru Saturday, and the fare is a reasonable $1 to $4 (depending on the distance); children under 6 ride free. The **Hyannis Area Trolley** (☎ 800/352-7155 or 508/385-8326) covers two loops—the Route 132 malls and the Main Street/waterfront area—every half hour from 10am to 9pm from late June to early September. Rates are 50¢ for adults, 25¢ for senior citizens, and gratis for children under 6.

VISITOR INFORMATION   For information, contact the **Hyannis Area Chamber of Commerce,** 1481 Rte. 132, Hyannis, MA 02601 (☎ **800/449-6647,** 877/492-6647, or 508/362-5230; fax 508/362-9499; www.hyannis.com; e-mail: chamber@hyannis.com); or the **Cape Cod Chamber of Commerce,** Rtes. 6 and 132, Hyannis, MA 02601 (☎ **888/332-2732** or 508/862-0700; fax 508/362-2156; www.capecodchamber.org; e-mail: info@capecodchamber.org), open year-round, mid-April to mid-November daily 9am to 5pm; mid-November to mid-April Monday to Saturday 10am to 4pm.

BEACHES & RECREATIONAL PURSUITS

BEACHES   Barnstable's primary Bay beach is **Sandy Neck Beach,** accessed through East Sandwich (see "Beaches & Recreational Pursuits" under "Sandwich" in chapter 4). Most of the Nantucket Sound beaches are fairly protected and thus not big in terms of surf. Beach parking costs $10 a day, usually payable at the lot; for a weeklong parking sticker ($40), visit the **Recreation Department** at 141 Basset Lane, at the Kennedy Memorial Skating Rink (☎ **508/790-6345**).

- **Craigville Beach,** off Craigville Beach Road in Centerville: Once a magnet for Methodist "camp" meetings (conference centers still line the shore), this broad expanse of sand boasts lifeguards and rest rooms. A destination for the bronzed and buffed, it's known as "Muscle Beach."
- **Orrin Keyes Beach** (a.k.a. Sea Beach), at the end of Sea Street in Hyannis: This little beach at the end of a residential road is popular with families.
- **Kalmus Beach,** off Gosnold Street in Hyannisport: This 800-foot spit of sand stretching toward the mouth of the harbor makes an ideal launching site for Windsurfing enthusiasts, who sometimes seem to play chicken with the steady parade of ferries. The surf is tame, the slope shallow, and the conditions are ideal for little kids. There are lifeguards, a snack bar, and rest rooms to facilitate family outings.
- **Veterans Beach,** off Ocean Street in Hyannis: A small stretch of harborside sand adjoining the John F. Kennedy Memorial (a moving tribute from the town), this spot is not tops for swimming, unless you're very young and easily wowed. Parking is usually easy, though, and it's walkable from town. The snack bar, rest rooms, and playground will see to a family's needs.

BICYCLING   While there are no paved bike paths in Barnstable (the Rail Trail in Dennis is the closest), the winding roads in Marstons Mills and Osterville make for a pleasant scenic ride. There's free public parking at the Marstons Mills millpond at the intersection of Routes 28 and 149 or behind the stores in Osterville Center. From the intersection of Routes 28 and 149, bear right on Route 149 where it turns into Main Street. Main Street soon intersects with Route 28; cross Route 28 (carefully), and then cruise down South County Road into Osterville. There are several roads here that afford wonderful bay views, not to mention views of some of the finest homes on Cape Cod. For the best views, bike to the end of Bay Street, West Bay Road, and Eel River Road to Sea View Avenue. You can rent bikes at **One World Bike Rental** at the corner of Main and Sea streets, in Hyannis (☎ **508/771-4242**). They charge $12 for 3 hours, $20 for 24 hours, and only $5 per day after the first 24 hours. They also provide a map and directions for a lovely 3-hour ride (about 8½ miles) through Craigville and Hyannisport, with lots of ocean views. A leisurely bike ride through this area is perhaps the best way to see some of the most impressive seaside mansions on the Cape.

BOATING   Paddle Cape Cod (☎ **888/226-6393** or 508/564-4051; www.paddlecapecod.com; e-mail: cccanoe@capecod.net) runs naturalist-guided trips throughout the Cape. Trips (3 to 3½ hours)—daily, weather permitting, April through October—$30 for a solo kayak or $50 for a tandem kayak or canoe. All equipment is supplied, and trips include juice and snacks. Sunset trips are particularly popular. Call for a schedule.

If you want to explore on your own, you can rent a kayak from Eastern Mountain Sports (see "Water Sports," below) for $35 to $45 a day and paddle around Scorton Creek, Sandy Neck, and Barnstable Harbor on the north side of the Cape. On the south side of the Cape, paddlers enjoy the waters around Great Island in Osterville. In Centerville, you can navigate the Centerville River. For experienced paddlers, Barnstable's Great Marsh—one of the largest in New England—offers beautiful waterways out to Sandy Neck.

FISHING   The township of Barnstable has 11 ponds for freshwater fishing; for information and permits, visit **Town Hall** at 367 Main St., Hyannis (☎ 508/790-6240), or **Sports Port,** 149 W. Main St., Hyannis (☎ 508/775-3096). Shellfishing permits are available from the **Department of Natural Resources** at 1189 Phinneys Lane, Centerville (☎ 508/790-6272). Surf casting, sans license, is permitted on Sandy Neck (see "Beaches & Recreational Pursuits" under "Sandwich" in chapter 4).

Among the charter boats berthed in Barnstable Harbor is the *Drifter* (☎ 508/398-2061), a 36-foot boat offering half- and full-day trips. The **Tightlines Sport Fishing Service,** 65 Camp St., Hyannis (☎ 508/790-8600), conducts saltwater fly-fishing expeditions. **Hy-Line Cruises** offers seasonal sonar-aided "bottom" or blues fishing from its Ocean Street dock in Hyannis (☎ 508/790-0696). The cost for a ½-day trip is $22 to $26 for adults, $14 to $16 for children 12 and under. **Helen H Deep-Sea Fishing** at 137 Pleasant St., Hyannis (☎ 508/790-0660), offers year-round expeditions aboard a 100-foot boat with a heated cabin and full galley. For a smaller, more personalized expedition, get in touch with Capt. Ron Murphy of **Stray Cat Sportfishing Charters** (☎ 508/428-8628).

FITNESS   The Cape at its most urban incarnation, Hyannis abounds in health clubs, including the **Galaxy Fitness Center** at 45 Plant Rd., off Airport Road (☎ 508/778-8100); a state-of-the-art **Gold's Gym** at the Radisson Inn, 287 Iyannough Rd./Rte. 28 (☎ 508/790-4477), which offers access to an indoor pool; and the single-sex **Woman's Body Shop** at 155 Attucks Lane, off Route 132 (☎ 508/771-1600). Non-member rates are $10 to $12 per day.

GOLF   Open year-round, the **Hyannis Golf Club,** Route 132 (☎ 508/362-2606), offers a 46-station driving range, as well as an 18-hole championship course. High-season greens fees are $65 to $75. Smaller, but scenic, is the 9-hole **Cotuit High Ground Country Club,** 31 Crockers Neck Rd., Cotuit (☎ 508/428-9863). An 18-hole round costs $15.

HARBOR CRUISES   For a fun and informative introduction to the harbor and its residents, take a leisurely, 1- to 2-hour, narrated tour aboard one of **Hy-Line Cruises'** 1911 steamer replicas *Patience* or *Prudence*. There are five family trips a day in season, but for a real treat take the Sunday 3:30pm "Ice Cream Float," which includes a design-your-own Ben & Jerry's Ice Cream Sundae, or the Thursday 9pm "Jazz Boat," accompanied by a Dixieland band. The latest offering is a lobster luncheon cruise, which leaves at 12:15pm on Monday and Wednesday. Hy-Line Cruises depart from the Ocean Street Dock (☎ 508/790-0696; www.hy-linecruises.com), and you should call for a reservation and schedule. Tickets range from $10 to $16 for adults and free to $8 for children 12 and under; departures daily from late June to September; closed November to mid-April.

NATURE & WILDLIFE AREAS   Sandy Neck, accessed through East Sandwich (see "Beaches & Recreational Pursuits" under "Sandwich" in chapter 4), is great for hiking; take care to avoid the endangered piping plovers.

TENNIS   Seven local schools open their courts to the public; all are first-come, first-served. For information, call the **Barnstable Recreation Department** (☎ **508/790-6345**). In addition, **King's Grant Racquet Club** on Main Street in Cotuit (☎ **508/428-5744**) has seven courts (three hard, four clay).

WATER SPORTS   Eastern Mountain Sports, 1513 Iyannough Rd./Rte. 132 (☎ **508/362-8690**), offers rental kayaks—tents and sleeping bags, too—and sponsors free clinics and walks, like a full moon hike.

WHALE WATCHING   Although Provincetown is about an hour closer to the whales' preferred feeding grounds, it would take you at least an hour (possibly hours on a summer weekend) to drive all the way down-Cape. If your time and itinerary are limited, hop aboard at **Hyannis Whale-Watch Cruises,** Barnstable Harbor (about a ½ mile north of Rte. 6A on Mill Way), Barnstable (☎ **888/942-5392** or 508/362-6088; fax 508/362-9739), for a 3½- to 4-hour voyage on a 100-foot high-speed cruiser. Naturalists provide the narration, and should you fail to spot a whale, your next trek is free. Tickets cost $26 for adults, $21 for seniors (62 and older), and $16 for children 4 to 12 from May through October; call for schedule and off-season rates. Closed November through April.

MUSEUMS & HISTORIC BUILDINGS

Barnstable Superior Courthouse. 3195 Rte. 6A (in the center of town), Barnstable. ☎ **508/362-2511.** Free admission. Open during business hours.

This grand public edifice, built between 1831 and 1832, still serves its original purpose vis-à-vis Barnstable County, which is to say the entire Cape. Attributed to Alexander Parris, this Greek Revival temple of justice indeed resembles his previous granite masterpieces, Boston's Quincy Market and Plymouth's Pilgrim Hall Museum, down to the grand Doric colonnade. Anyone is free to listen in on the arguments and deliberations. It's an educational pastime of which the Puritans would no doubt have approved.

Cahoon Museum of American Art. 4676 Falmouth Rd. (Rte. 28, near Rte. 130), Cotuit. ☎ **508/428-7581.** Free admission. Tues–Sat 10am–4pm.

For some 4 decades, post–World War II, this 1775 Georgian colonial house served as an atelier for two popular primitivists, Ralph and Martha Calhoun. Their playful, decorative works, featuring such Cape staples as cavorting mermaids and swaggering tars, are on permanent display, along with other American works spanning early portraiture to impressionism. Local contemporary artists are often shown as well. The interior itself is worth a look: It still boasts its 1810 stenciling, and the upstairs "ballroom"—a makeshift affair typical of Early American taverns—remains intact. Occasional gallery talks are free and open to the public.

Centerville Historical Society Museum. 513 Main St. (about ⅓ mile S of Rte. 28), Centerville. ☎ **508/775-0331.** Admission $3 adults, $2 seniors and students, free children under 12. June–Oct Wed–Sat 12:30–4:30pm (last admission at 4pm). By appointment only Nov–May.

Downright palatial compared to its peers, this local-history museum boasts 14 rooms filled with varied collections spanning 2 centuries or more, including maritime and military collections, perfume bottles, quilts, early currency (including lottery tickets used to finance the Revolution), ball gowns, 18th- and 19th-century costumes, and

Camelot on Cape Cod: The Kennedys in Hyannisport

It's been almost 40 years since those days of Camelot, when JFK was in the White House and America seemed rejuvenated by the Kennedy style, but the Kennedy sites on Cape Cod still attract record numbers of visitors every summer. In July 1999, when John Jr.'s plane crashed into Vineyard Sound, thousands visited the Kennedy Hyannis Museum to mourn the loss by viewing classic photos of the family in Hyannisport. Museum staff have compiled a special exhibit of photos of John Jr., which will be displayed through 2001.

Images of Jack Kennedy sailing his jaunty *Wianno Senior* on Nantucket Sound off Hyannisport form part of this nation's collective memory. The vacationing JFK was all tousled hair, toothy grin, earthy charisma, and attractive *joie de vivre*. Remember Jackie sitting beside him, wearing a patterned silk scarf around her head and looking like she'd rather be in Newport, where no one had ever heard of touch football?

The Kennedys always knew how to have fun, and they had it in Hyannisport. And ever since Hyannisport became the summer White House, Cape Cod has been inextricably linked to the Kennedy clan. While the Kennedys spend time elsewhere—working in Washington or wintering in Palm Beach—when they go home, they go to Cape Cod. Generations of Kennedys have sailed these waters, sunned on these beaches, patronized local businesses, and generally had a high old time.

Meanwhile, much has changed since the early 1960s on Cape Cod, especially in the Mid Cape area. In those 30-plus years, the mall was built in Hyannis, and urban sprawl infested Routes 132 and 28. Yet much, thankfully, remains the same. The Kennedy compound, with its large, gabled Dutch Colonial houses, still commands the end of Scudder Avenue in Hyannisport. Nearby is the private **Hyannisport Golf Club,** where Rose loved to play a short round on the foggy oceanfront course. The beaches here are still pristine.

---

bird carvings. The toy collection is especially strong, and among the eerier tableaux is a complete colonial revival kitchen as envisioned by clutter-inclined Victorians; it's chockablock with handsome antiques and intriguing artifacts.

Osterville Historical Society Museum. 155 W. Bay Rd. (at Parker Rd., about ⅛ mile S of the town center), Osterville. ☎ **508/428-5861.** Admission $3. Members and children free. Mid-June to mid-Oct Thurs–Sun 1:30–4:30pm. Closed mid-Oct to mid-June.

This 1824 house displays the Osterville Historical Society's cache of China Trade treasures, as well as other valuable antiques of local interest; don't miss the toys and dolls on the second floor. The rustic 1790 Cammett House, next door, is a one-room "narrow house," notable mainly for its clear exposition of the colonists' building techniques. Also on the grounds (beautifully and historically landscaped by the Osterville Garden Club) is the original Herbert F. Crosby Boat Shop, progenitor of such worthy craft as the trusty *Catboat* and the *Wianno Senior,* President Kennedy's preferred pleasure boat. Tours of the entire complex are given on the hour. The museum's annual antiques show (call for details) is held yearly on the fourth Thursday in August.

Sturgis Library. 3090 Rte. 6A (about ½ mile W of Hyannis Rd.), Barnstable. ☎ **508/362-6636.** Free admission. Mon and Thurs 10am–2pm; Tues 1–9pm; Wed, Fri, and Sun 1–5pm; Sat 10am–4pm.

To bask in the Kennedys' Cape Cod experience, visit the **John F. Kennedy Hyannis Museum,** 397 Main St., Hyannis (☎ 508/790-3077). Admission is $3 (children under 17 free), and hours are from April to October Monday to Saturday 10am to 4pm and Sundays and holidays from 1 to 4pm. Last admission is at 3:30pm. Call for off-season hours. The museum shows a documentary on Kennedy narrated by Walter Cronkite and contains several rooms' worth of photos of the Kennedys on Cape Cod. The candid shots included in this permanent display capture some of the quieter moments, as well as JFK's legendary charm. Most of us have seen some of these photos before, but here they are all blown up, mounted, and neatly labeled; if you get confused about lineage, consult the family tree on the wall at the end of the exhibit. The last 3 years of JFK's life were a bit chaotic (some 25,000 well-wishers thronged the roads when the senator and president-to-be returned from the 1960 Democratic Convention), but he continued to treasure the Cape as "the one place I can think and be alone."

Busloads of tourists visit the **Kennedy Memorial** just above Veterans Beach on Ocean Avenue; it's a moving tribute, beautifully maintained by the town, but crowds in season can be distracting. Finally, you may want to drive by the simple white clapboard church, **St. Francis Xavier,** on South Street; Rose attended mass daily, and Caroline Kennedy and several other cousins got married here.

Spend your day in the Mid Cape recreating like a privileged Kennedy scion. Rent a Windsurfer at Kalmus Beach. Play a round of golf at the **Hyannis Golf Club,** a public course on Route 132. ✪ **Four Seas Ice Cream,** at 360 S. Main St. in Centerville, apparently a favorite of secret-service agents, is a must. For lodging right in Hyannisport, stay at ✪ **Simmons Homestead Inn,** 288 Scudder Ave., Hyannisport (☎ **800/637-1649** or 508/778-4999).

Rose Kennedy once told a reporter, "Our family would rather be in Hyannisport in the summer than anyplace else in the world." And yours?

In 1863, William Sturgis, a cabin boy turned megamerchant who was an eighth-generation descendent of the town founder, willed Congregational minister John Lothrop's 1646 "half-house" to the town as the nucleus of a public library. Surrounded by subsequent additions containing extraordinary genealogical and maritime collections, the one-room home still holds the rarest book of all, Lothrop's 1609 Bible, charred by tallow drippings during the tumultuous ocean journey, then diligently patched and restored from memory.

Trayser Museum Complex. 3353 Rte. 6A (at Hyannis Rd.), Barnstable. ☎ **508/362-2092.** Donations requested. Mid-June to mid-Oct Tues–Sun 1:30–4:30pm. Closed mid-Oct to mid-June.

Named for local historian Donald G. Trayser, this former customhouse, built in 1856, showcases the collections of the Barnstable Historical Commission. The painted–brick Italian Renaissance building is quite a beauty itself, both outside and in; the interior's grandly scaled rooms, elaborate balustrades, and massive pillars attest to the harbor's prosperous past. Artifacts have been gathered to illustrate every era, from Native American tools sculpted from stone to nautical art (paintings, models) and the spoils of the China Trade. A Children's Corner filled with dolls and toys is intriguing—though not intended for touching. Behind the museum proper is a carriage house containing a horse-drawn hearse, a couple of early prototype bicycles, and antique fishing gear. Adjoining it is a wooden "gaol" built in the last decade of the 17th century, the oldest surviving structure of its sort on the continent. Perhaps it lasted so long because, as Henry David Thoreau noted during his 1850s peregrinations, "Sometimes, when the court comes together at Barnstable, they have not a single criminal to try, and the jail is shut up."

West Parish Meetinghouse. 2049 Meetinghouse Way (at Rte. 149), West Barnstable. ☎ **508/362-4445.** Free admission. Late May to mid-Oct 9am–5pm.

Up until the mid-1800s in most New England towns, there was literally no separation between church and state: Typically, the Congregational church, supported by local taxes, doubled as town hall. Such was the case with this meetinghouse, built between 1717 and 1723. Once it had lost its civic function, it was subjected to disastrous neoclassical, then Victorian, renovations, both of which were finally reversed in the 1950s, unveiling the building's original glorious oak and pine woodwork. The ½-ton Paul Revere bell, forged in 1806, still summons parishioners to worship, and visitors are welcome to enter at will to admire the handsome, honey-toned interior of the oldest public building on the Cape.

BASEBALL

The two locally based Cape Cod Baseball League elite amateur teams are the Hyannis Mets (who play at McKeon Field on Old Colony Blvd.) and the Cotuit Kettleers (Lowell Park). For a schedule, contact the **Hyannis Area Chamber of Commerce** (☎ **800/449-6647** or 508/362-5230) or the **Barnstable Recreation Department** (☎ **508/790-6345**).

KID STUFF

The **Cape Cod Storyland minigolf course,** in the middle of town at 70 Center St. (☎ **508/778-4339**), actually provides a bit of a local-history lesson, with traps that replicate notable sites on the Cape and Islands; adjoining the course is a little lagoon set up for refreshing bumper-boat rides. About a mile north, off Route 132, the **Cape Cod Potato Chips factory** on Breed's Hill Road at Independence Drive (☎ **508/775-7253**) offers free quickie tours that end with a tasting. Tours are held in July and August, Monday to Friday from 9am to 5pm and Saturday from 10am to 4pm. Call for off-season hours. On Wednesday mornings in summer, the **Cape Cod Melody Tent** at the West End rotary (☎ **508/775-9100**) offers children's theater productions.

SHOPPING

Although Hyannis is undoubtedly the commercial center of the Cape, the stores you'll find there are fairly standard for the most part; you could probably find their ilk anywhere else in the country. It's in the wealthy enclaves west of Hyannis, and along the antiquated Old King's Highway (Rte. 6A) to the north, that you're likely to find the real gems.

ANTIQUES/COLLECTIBLES   The Farmhouse, 1340 Main St. (about 1 mile south of Rte. 28), Osterville (☎ **508/420-2400**), Carolyn and Barry Crawford's 1742 farmhouse, is set up like an adult-scale dollhouse, and the "life-like" settings should lend decorative inspiration. Self-confident sorts will go wild in the barn; it's packed with intriguing architectural salvage.

Of the hundreds of antiques shops scattered through the region, perhaps a dozen qualify as destinations for well-schooled collectors. ✪ **Harden Studios,** 3264 Rte. 6A (in the center of town), Barnstable Village (☎ **508/362-7711**), is one. Owner Charles M. Harden, ASID, used to supply to-the-trade-only dealers in the Boston Design Center. An architect by training, he renovated this antique house, built around

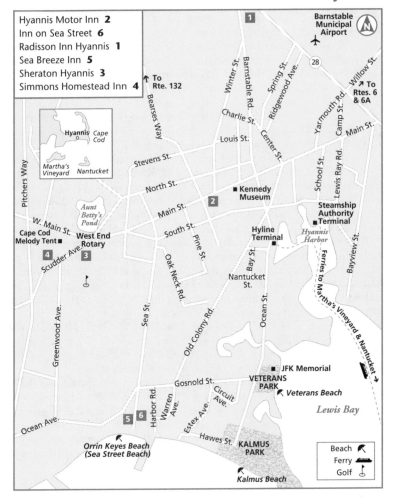

Hyannis Motor Inn	**2**
Inn on Sea Street	**6**
Radisson Inn Hyannis	**1**
Sea Breeze Inn	**5**
Sheraton Hyannis	**3**
Simmons Homestead Inn	**4**

1720, to display his finds. Some items, such as primitive portraits and mourning embroidery, are all but extinct outside of museums. Other sturdy, serviceable pieces, such as colonial corner cabinets and slant-top desks, are competitively priced, as are the antique Oriental carpets underfoot. An adjoining barn gallery features nature-centered works by area artists, including Harden's son, an accomplished etcher.

Prince Jenkins Antiques, 975 Rte. 6A (at the intersection of Rte. 149), West Barnstable (no phone), is one spooky shop, the piled-high kind that captivates scavengers. Wend your way (carefully) around the narrow path still discernible amid the heaped-up inventory, and you'll come across case upon case of vintage jewelry and watches, paintings, tapestries, urns and jade carvings, musty 18th-century garb, a Pilgrim chair or two, and all sorts of oddments. The aged proprietor, Dr. Alfred King, DFA, claims that the admittedly ancient-looking house next door belonged to Governor William Bradford in 1626—a dubious boast, given that the town wasn't settled until 1639, and Bradford was awfully busy in Plymouth. But what would you expect from a man whose card reads "In Business Since 1773"? Closed mid-November to March.

ARTS & CRAFTS   The intricate, infinitely variable patterns of Jacquard weaving not only prompted the Industrial Revolution, but prefigured the computer chip. Today there's only one weaver in the United States creating Jacquard designs by hand, and that's Bob Black, who began his trade at age 14 and refined it at the Rhode Island School of Design. He works out of **The Blacks' Handweaving Shop,** 597 Rte. 6A (about ⁷/₁₀ of a mile west of Rte. 149), West Barnstable (☎ **508/362-3955**), and specializes in custom coverlets on commission; the double-sided designs can be used as blankets, throws, even tapestries. Customers often ask for special motifs to be worked in, with the ultimate goal a one-of-a-kind, commemorative artifact. Bob's wife, Gabrielle, contributes colorful fashion accessories—hats, scarves, shawls, and even ties.

The caliber of the shows at the **Cape Cod Art Association,** 3480 Rte. 6A (about ⅓ of a mile west of Hyannis Rd.), Barnstable (☎ **508/362-2909**), may vary—this is, after all, a non-profit community venture—but it's worth visiting just to see the skylit studios, designed by CCAA member Richard Sears Gallagher in 1972. Everyone raves about "Cape light," and here you'll see it used to optimal advantage. If the setting fires up artistic yearnings, inquire about classes and workshops, which are held year-round.

Ex-Nantucketer Bob Marks fashions the only authentic Nantucket lightship baskets, crafted off-island; and as aficionados know, they don't come cheap (a mere handbag typically runs in the thousands). The other handmade furnishings found at **Oak and Ivory,** 1112 Main St. (about 1 mile south of Rte. 28), Osterville (☎ **508/428-9425**), from woven throw rugs to pared-down neo-Shaker furniture, fit the country-chic mode at more approachable prices.

At 374 Main St. in Hyannis, **Red Fish, Blue Fish** (☎ **508/775-8700**) wins the funky-gallery award, hands down. Owner Jane Walsh makes jewelry in the front window, but inside every inch of this closetlike space is covered with something unusual and handmade. There is usually a teenager or two hanging out here.

Fine-crafts shops are a dime a dozen on the Cape, but stop at the **Stone Gallery,** 1611 Main St./Rte. 6A, West Barnstable (☎ **508/375-0038**) and browse among some truly unique items and beautiful displays. Specialties here include glass, ceramics, and contemporary jewelry—some of the crafts are locally made. You can't miss the building. It's the intriguing facade made of fieldstone, built as a garage around 1920, that still has a vestige of its former life: The 1960 MG convertible parked just inside the front door is left over from the previous business.

Tao Water Art Gallery, 1989 Route 6A, West Barnstable (☎ **508/375-0428**) is a former garage that has been converted into a very Zenlike space. It features paintings by Chinese artists as well as museum reproductions of Chinese antiques and jade.

Richard Kiusalas and Steven Whittlesey salvage antique lumber and turn it into cupboards, tables, and chairs, among other things; old windows are retrofitted as mirrors. Most of the stock at **West Barnstable Tables,** 2454 Meetinghouse Way (off Rte. 149 near the intersection of Rte. 6A), West Barnstable (☎ **508/362-2676**), looks freshly made, albeit with wood of unusually high quality. Pieces are priced accordingly: A dining room set—pine trestle table with six bow-back chairs—would run over $4,000. When the wood still bears interesting traces of its former life, it's turned into folk-art furniture. A cupboard made out of old painted red boards, secured with Model-T Ford hinges, for example, might fetch $3,600.

BOOKS & EPHEMERA   Named for the revolutionary printer who helped foment the War of Independence, ✪ **Isaiah Thomas Books & Prints,** 4632 Falmouth Rd. (Rte. 28, near Rte. 130), Cotuit (☎ **508/428-2752**), has a 60,000-volume collection, housed in an 1850 home. The shop is full of treasures, clustered by topic. Owner/expert James S. Visbeck is happy to show off his first editions, rare miniatures, and maps; you get the sense that sales are secondary to sheer bibliophilic pleasure. You can buy a 200-year-old map of your favorite Cape Cod village at **Maps of Antiquity,** 1022 Rte. 6A, West Barnstable (☎ **508/362-7169**). Chains are also represented: You'll find **Barnes & Noble Booksellers,** 768 Iyannough Rd., Rte. 132 (☎ **508/ 771-1400**), and **Borders Books, Music & Café,** 990 Iyannough Rd., Rte. 132 (☎ **508/862-6363**). Borders is a huge store with lots of scheduled events, including children's storytimes, book signings, readings, and live performances in the Café.

FASHION   Europa, 37 Barnstable Rd. (at North St., in the center of town), Hyannis (☎ **508/790-0877**), is a boutique where women can bone up on that world-traveler look, even if they've never been abroad. **Mark, Fore & Strike,** 21 Wianno Ave. (at Main St., in the center of town), Osterville (☎ **508/428-2270**), stocks preppie classics for both genders.

FOOD   Cape Cod Potato Chips, Breed's Hill Rd. (at Independence Way, off Rte. 132), Hyannis (☎ **508/775-7253**), really are the world's best. Long a local favorite—they're chunkier than the norm—these snacks actually do originate here. Free factory tours are offered Monday to Friday from 9am to 5pm and Saturday from 10am to 4pm in July and August. Call for off-season hours.

HOME DECOR   As a Nantucket innkeeper whiling away the winter, Claire Murray took up hooking rugs and turned her knack into an international business. At **Claire Murray,** 867 Main St. (in the center of town), Osterville (☎ **508/420-3562**), and her new store at 770 Route 6A in West Barnstable (☎ **508/375-0331**), hobbyists can find all the fixings for various needle-crafts here including kits, and advice as needed. Those of us with little time-on our hands can just buy the finished goods, from sweaters and quilts to the signature folk-motif rugs.

Flowery pastels are the hallmark of **Joan Peters,** 885 Main St. (in the center of town), Osterville (☎ **508/428-3418**), favored by the *Town & Country* set. She designs a wide array of compatible fabrics and ceramics—right down to the bathroom sink, if need be—so that it's easy to achieve a pervasive, light-splashed look that doesn't look too overtly matched and mixed.

On Main Street in Hyannis, you'll find a world of wonderful kitchen products at **Nantucket Trading Company,** 354 Main St. (☎ **508/790-3933**).

MALLS/SHOPPING CENTERS   With nearly 100 shops and two cineplexes, the **Cape Cod Mall,** Rte. 132 (about 1 mile northwest of the airport), Hyannis (☎ **508/ 771-0200**), is the mother mall of all, the largest shopping center on the whole Cape.

SEAFOOD   Besides Mill Way at Barnstable Harbor (see "Take-Out & Take-Home Food," below), the best place to buy fresh seafood in the vicinity of Hyannis is **Cape Fish & Lobster** at 406 W. Main St. in Centerville (☎ **508/771-1122**). This is where the top restaurateurs in Hyannis get their seafood. The prices are reasonable, and the catch is the freshest in town.

WHERE TO STAY
IN HYANNIS, HYANNISPORT & CRAIGVILLE

There are a variety of large, generic, but convenient hotels and motels in Hyannis.

Right smack on Main Street within strolling distance of restaurants, shopping, and the ferries is the **Hyannis Inn Motel,** 473 Main St., Hyannis (☎ **800/922-8993** or 508/775-0255; www.hyannisinnmotel.com). Summer rates are $88 to $135 double. During the Kennedy administration, this motel served as the press headquarters. It has an indoor pool, a breakfast restaurant (not included with room rates), and a cocktail lounge.

If you prefer more amenities, there's the **Sheraton Hyannis Resort** at the West End Circle just off Main Street (☎ **800/598-4559** or 508/775-7775; www.sheraton.com). Summer rates are $189 to $209 double. Out the back door is an 18-hole, par-3 executive golf course. There are also four tennis courts, an indoor and an outdoor pool, four restaurants, and a fitness center.

Another upscale alternative is the **Radisson Inn Hyannis,** 287 Iyannough Rd. (Rte. 28), Hyannis, just east of the airport rotary (☎ **800/333-3333** or 508/771-1700; www.radisson.com/capecod), which features a full health club (a branch of Gold's Gym) and a bistro/pizzeria. Summer rates are $145 to $185 double, $185 to $205 suite. You'll have to overlook the uninspiring location in strip-mall hell, but it's within spitting distance of the airport. Rooms are clean and comfortable, with attractive blonde-wood furniture and plush carpeting.

Expensive

✪ **Simmons Homestead Inn.** 288 Scudder Ave. (about ¼ mile W of the West End rotary), Hyannisport, MA 02647. ☎ **800/637-1649** or 508/778-4999. Fax 508/790-1342. www.capecodtravel.com/simmonsinn. E-mail: simmonsinn@aol.com. 14 units. Summer $180–$220 double; $325 2-bedroom suite. Rates include full breakfast. AE, DISC, MC, V. Dogs welcome.

A former ad exec and race-car driver, innkeeper Bill Putman has a silly side and isn't afraid to show it. He started collecting animal artifacts—stuffed toys, sculptures, even needlepoint and wallpaper—to differentiate the rather traditional rooms in this rambling 1820s captain's manse, and kind of got carried away. Outside, his classic car collection is housed in two large garages. This is an inn where you'll find everyone mulling around the hearth sipping complementary wine (served at "6-ish") while they compare notes and nail down dinner plans. To help his guests plan their days and evenings, Putman has typed up extensive notes on day trips (including the Islands), bike routes (he supplies the bikes), and his own personal, quirky restaurant reviews. Guests who prefer privacy may book the spiffily updated "servants' quarters," a spacious, airy wing with its own private deck. Rooms vary in size, but all have extras like irons and hair dryers. There's a regulation billiards parlor (one foot on the floor and no spitting), and an outdoor six-person hot tub. In accordance with the permissive (fun) atmosphere here, dogs are allowed, and so is smoking in the common room.

Moderate

Inn on Sea Street. 358–363 Sea St., Hyannis, MA 02601. ☎ **508/775-8030.** Fax 508/771-0878. www.capecod.net/innonsea. E-mail: innonsea@capecod.net. 9 units, 2 with shared bathroom; 1 cottage. Summer $85–$135 double; $130 cottage. Rates include full breakfast. AE, DISC, MC, V.

Just a short walk from Sea Street beach, this establishment comprises two well-maintained historic houses across the street from each other, with a tiny cottage nestled behind one. The main house, more formally decorated in a Victorian style with interesting antiques, has high ceilings throughout. Some of the rooms have four-poster or canopy beds and claw-foot tubs. The house across the street, mansard-roofed with a wraparound porch, has larger rooms decorated with English country antiques. All rooms in this house have TVs and air-conditioning. The cute little cottage in back, with kitchen and sitting room, is a white-on-white delight. The elaborate breakfast might feature such treats as rhubarb coffee cake and breakfast quiche with cheese and bacon.

Sea Breeze Inn. 270 Ocean Ave. (about 1 mile S of the West End rotary), Hyannis, MA 02601. ☎ **508/771-7213.** Fax 508/862-0663. www.seabreezeinn.com. E-mail: seabreeze@capecod.net. 14 units, 4 cottages. A/C TV TEL. Summer $80–$140 double; cottages $1,200–$2,500 weekly. Rates include continental breakfast (except in large cottages). AE, DISC, MC, V.

Within whistling distance of the beach, this classic shingled beach house has been decked out with the totems of small-town America: a picket fence, exuberant plantings, and even a wooden rocker built for two couples—or better yet, one. All this attention to the exterior is mirrored in the neat and cheerful interior. The coast used to be lined with superior guest houses of this sort, and to find one still in its prime is a real treat. Also on the intensively gardened grounds are four cottages (a five-bedroom, a three-bedroom, and two one-bedrooms) that rent by the week, including one with a "honeymooners" double Jacuzzi.

Tradewinds Inn. 780 Craigville Beach Rd. (across the street from Craigville Beach), Centerville, MA 02632. ☎ **877/444-7966** or 508/775-0365. www.twicapecod.com. 46 units. A/C TV TEL. Summer $119–$189 double; $199–$235 suite. Rates include continental breakfast in season. AE, MC, V. Closed Oct–Apr.

Many rooms in this attractive motel have wonderful views of Craigville Beach, one of the Cape's most popular strips of sand. However, since it's hard to see the sand once the summer crowds hit, this property also has its own immaculate 500-foot private stretch of beach. Beach chairs and beach towels are provided. On cloudy days, guests may enjoy strolling up to the Craigville Campground next door, a compound of 19th-century gingerbread-style cottages that still serves as a Methodist meeting camp preserve. The motel also abuts tiny Lake Elizabeth where young Jack and Ted Kennedy learned to sail.

IN BARNSTABLE & WEST BARNSTABLE
Moderate
✪ **The Acworth Inn.** 4352 Rte. 6A (near the Yarmouth Port border), Cummaquid, MA 02637. ☎ **800/362-6363** or 508/362-3330. Fax 508/375-0304. www.acworthinn.com. 5 units. A/C. Summer $115–$150 double; $185 suite. Rates include full breakfast. AE, DC, DISC, MC, V. No children under 12.

Cheryl and Jack Ferrell know that it's the small touches that make a stay memorable, and anyone lucky enough to land in this sunnily rehabbed house is sure to remember every last one, from the cranberry spritzer offered on arrival to the handmade chocolates that take the place of pillow mints. Cheryl, who does baking demonstrations locally, even grinds the whole grains that go into her home-baked breakfasts, in the form of cranberry-orange rolls or whole-wheat pancakes. Anyone looking to avoid the excess of Victorian furnishings in many B&Bs will delight in the simple, fresh, immaculate decor here, mainly in shades of white and beige. Two rooms in the carriage house have been combined into a romantic luxury suite with whirlpool bath, TV/VCR, working fireplace, air-conditioning, and minifridge. The inn is close to Barnstable Village and popular Cape Cod Bay beaches, so the complimentary bikes may be all you need in the way of wheels.

✪ **Ashley Manor Inn.** 3660 Rte. 6A (just E of Hyannis Rd.), Barnstable, MA 02630. ☎ **888/535-2246** or 508/362-8044. Fax 508/362-9927. www.ashleymanor.net. E-mail: ashleymn@capecod.net. 6 units. A/C. Summer $135–145 double; $185–$195 suite. Rates include full breakfast. DISC, MC, V.

A lovely country inn along the Old King's Highway, this house is a much-modified 1699 colonial mansion that still retains many of its original features, including a hearth with beehive oven (the perfect place to sip Port on a blustery evening), built-in corner cupboards in the wainscoted dining room, and wide-board floors, many of them brightened with Nantucket-style splatter paint. The rooms, all but one of which boast a working fireplace, are spacious and inviting: a true retreat. All rooms have hairdryers. A deluxe room in its own wing has a separate entrance, whirlpool bath, glass-enclosed shower, canopy bed, and fireplace. The 2-acre property itself is shielded from the road by an enormous privet hedge, and fragrant boxwood camouflages a Har-Tru tennis court. (You'll find loaner bikes beside it, ready to roll.) Romantics can sequester themselves in the flower-fringed gazebo. Breakfast on the brick patio is worth waking up for: You wouldn't want to miss the homemade granola, much less the main event—quiche, perhaps, or crêpes.

✪ **Beechwood Inn.** 2839 Rte. 6A (about 1½ miles E of Rte. 132), Barnstable, MA 02630. ☎ **800/609-6618** or 508/362-6618. Fax 508/362-0298. www.beechwoodinn.com. E-mail: info@beechwoodinn.com. 6 units. A/C. Summer $140–$180 double. Rates include full breakfast. AE, DISC, MC, V.

Look for a butterscotch-colored 1853 Queen Anne Victorian all but enshrouded in weeping beech trees. Admirers of late–19th-century decor are in for a treat: The interior remains dark and rich, with a red-velvet parlor and tin ceilings in the dining room where innkeeper Debbie Traugot serves a three-course breakfast featuring home-baked delights such as applesauce pancakes and raspberry bread. Two of the upstairs bedrooms embody distinctive period styles: The Cottage Room contains furniture painted in an 1860s mode, and the Eastlake Room is modeled on the aesthetic precepts of William Morris that flourished in the 1880s. Each affords a distant view of the sparkling bay. All rooms have Sealy Posturepedic Plush mattresses. The Traugots are always making improvements; most recently they've added two more fireplaces. Rooms range from quite spacious (Lilac) to romantically snug (Garret).

✪ **Lamb and Lion Inn.** 2504 Main St. (Rte. 6A), Barnstable, MA 02630. ☎ **800/909-6923** or 508/362-6823. Fax 508/362-0227. www.lambandlion.com. E-mail: info@lambandlion.com. 10 units. A/C TEL TV. Summer $125–145 double; $140–$250 suite. Rates include continental breakfast. MC, V. Well-behaved pets allowed.

This is an unusual property: part B&B, part motel. From the roadside, it's one of those charming old Cape Cod cottages (ca. 1740) along the Old King's Highway (where charming "capes" are ubiquitous), set up on a knoll with a sloping lawn full of colorful flowers. Inside, it's a motellike space with units encircling a pool and hot tub. The rooms are all individually decorated, and there are several are suites with kitchenettes. All rooms in the main inn building are air-conditioned. The multilevel barn suite, with three loft-type bedrooms, is a funky space, filled with rustic nooks and crannies.

⊕ Family-Friendly Hotels & Restaurants

Baxter's Boat House in Hyannis *(see p. 112)*   Set not just on but over the harbor, this self-service eatery is the perfect spot to stage a messy seafood feast alfresco.

The Beach House Inn in West Dennis   Equipped with its own playground, guest kitchen, and cookout deck, this B&B right on the beach is the answer to every parent's prayers.

✪ **Jack's Outback** in Yarmouth Port *(see p. 120)*   Kids get a kick out of all the funny "stern" signs and the silly communal menu at this rambunctious neighborhood diner.

Lighthouse Inn in West Dennis *(see p. 126)*   It's the 1950s again at this classic family resort right on the beach. If the sun is shining, the kids will want to romp in the surf all day; otherwise there are children's programs. Families often know each other here, because they've been coming back for generations.

WHERE TO DINE
IN HYANNIS
Expensive

Alberto's Ristorante. 360 Main St., Hyannis. ☎ **508/778-1770.** Reservations recommended. Main courses $11–$27. AE, CB, DC, DISC, MC, V. Mon–Sat 3–10pm; Sun noon–10pm. ITALIAN.

Alberto's explores the full range of Italian cuisine, with a classicist's attention to components and composition. Owner/chef Felisberto Barreiro's most popular dishes are his treatments of lobster, rack of lamb, and beef tenderloin. Hand-cut pasta is also a specialty, including the ultra-rich seafood ravioli cloaked in saffron-cream sauce. Though the atmosphere is elegant, with sconces shedding a warm glow over well-spaced, linen-draped tables, it is not one of hushed reverence: People clearly come here to have a good time, and the friendly service and fabulous food ensure that they do. Locals who appreciate a bargain know to come between 3 and 6pm, when a full dinner, with soup, salad, and dessert, costs as little as $10 to $15. There's live jazz or piano music daily year-round.

The Black Cat. 165 Ocean St. (opposite the Ocean Street Dock), Hyannis. ☎ **508/778-1233.** Main courses $15–$29. AE, DC, DISC, MC, V. Apr–Oct daily 11:30am–10pm; call for off-season hours. NEW AMERICAN.

Conveniently located less than a block from the Hy-Line ferries, this is a fine place to catch a quick bite or full meal while you wait for your boat to come in. The menu is pretty basic—steak, pasta, and, of course, fish—but attention is paid to the details; the onion rings, for instance, are made fresh. The dining room, with its bar of gleaming mahogany and brass, will appeal to chilled travelers on a blustery day; in fine weather, you might prefer the porch. There's live jazz on the weekends in season.

The Paddock. West End rotary (at the intersection of W. Main St. and Main St.), Hyannis. ☎ **508/775-7677.** Reservations recommended. Main courses $15–$25. AE, DC, DISC, MC, V. Apr to mid-Nov Mon–Sat 11:30am–2:30pm and 5–10pm; Sun noon–10pm. Closed mid-Nov to Mar. CONTINENTAL.

In the almost 30 years that the Zartarian family has run this large, traditional restaurant, they have maintained a solid reputation in the community with consistently good food and service. The decor might be a little dated, but grandma will love the Victorian motifs; better yet, you can dine on the plant-and-wicker-filled summer porch. Chef John Anderson has been with The Paddock since it opened in 1970, and traces of the original saucy continental menu remain (you can still order extra béarnaise sauce on the side). The menu combines traditional with creative touches. For appetizers, there's clams casino, but also polenta custard with mild mushroom ragout. For main courses there's prime rib, but also sesame-encrusted yellowfin tuna served rare with Asian greens. The 300-bottle wine list has received awards from *Wine Spectator* for 16 years. There is free valet parking, and a pianist entertains nightly in the pub area. Because the Cape Cod Melody Tent is right next door, you'll need to go after 9pm to avoid the crowds if there is an act playing.

✪ Penguin SeaGrill. 331 Main St. (in the center of town), Hyannis. ☎ **508/775-2023.** Reservations recommended. Main courses $15–$24. AE, CB, DC, DISC, MC, V. June–Sept Sun–Thurs 5–10pm; Fri–Sat 5–11pm; call for off-season hours. Closed Jan. INTERNATIONAL.

For years, this has been considered one of the top restaurants on the Cape. Chef/owner Bob Gold is one of those restless types who, having mastered one style of cuisine (Italian), can't wait to take on another. Hence the versatile menu, which bounces from Asian influences, like "Thai Jumpin' Squid," to mussels Portuguese-style. The specialty here is definitely seafood; pay attention to the specials and you can't go wrong. Large lobsters are served nightly; meats and fish are wood-grilled. The wine list is impressive with many fine vintages in all price ranges. The setting is contemporary, with brick walls, mirrored accents, and mammoth carved fish. There's even entertainment Friday nights in season.

✪ **Ristorante Barolo.** 1 Financial Place (297 North St., just off the West End rotary), Hyannis. ☎ **508/778-2878.** Reservations recommended. Main courses $8–$26. AE, DC, MC, V. June–Sept Sun–Thurs 4:30–10pm; Fri–Sat 4:30–11pm; call for off-season hours. NORTHERN ITALIAN.

This is the best Italian restaurant in town. Part of a smart-looking brick office complex, this thoroughly up-to-date establishment does everything right, from offering extra-virgin olive oil for dunking its crusty bread to getting those pastas perfectly al dente. Appetizers perfect for sharing are *Polpette Gartinate alla Romana* (homemade meatballs in a tomato-and-basil sauce) and *Gamberi al Martini* (shrimp sautéed with fresh scallions and martini-wine sauce). Entrees include a number of tempting veal choices, like *Vitello alla Sorrentina* (Provimi-brand veal, mozzarella, and basil with plum-tomato sauce), as well as such favorites as *Linguine al Frutti di Mare*, with littlenecks, mussels, shrimp, and calamari. The desserts are brought in daily from Boston's famed North End.

✪ **Roadhouse Cafe.** 488 South St. (off Main St., near the West End rotary), Hyannis. ☎ **508/775-2386.** Reservations recommended. Main courses $12–$25. AE, CB, DC, DISC, MC, V. Daily 4–11pm. AMERICAN/NORTHERN ITALIAN.

The humble name belies the culinary caliber of this intimate but ambitious restaurant. This is not the hybrid "Italian-American" fare that so poorly represents both. Instead, the extensive menu is pretty much split between American standards such as steak (not to mention oysters Rockefeller or casino) and real Italian cooking, unstinting on the garlic. There's also a less expensive lighter-fare menu, including what some have called "the best burger in the world," served in the snazzy bistro in back. Among the appetizers are such delicacies as beef carpaccio with fresh-shaved Parmesan, and vine-ripened tomatoes and buffalo mozzarella drizzled with balsamic vinaigrette. The latter also makes a tasty marinade for native swordfish headed for the grill. The signature dessert, a distinctly non-Italian cheesecake infused with Baileys Irish Cream, is itself an excuse to come check out the live jazz in the bistro (see "Hyannis & Environs After Dark," below).

Roo Bar. 586 Main St., Hyannis. ☎ **508/778-6515.** Main courses $9–$25. AE, DC, MC, V. Daily 5–10pm. BISTRO.

This moody, stylish bistro is the new kid on the block and one of the few hip bars in Hyannis. You may want to sit at the bar and have a few appetizers like the chicken pot sticker (pan-seared wonton wrappers filled with an Asian chicken and vegetable stuffing with an orange marmalade dipping sauce) or a simple plate of oysters on the half shell. The most popular entree may be the seafood Provençale (jumbo shrimp and sea scallops sautéed with fresh tomatoes and basil in a white-wine garlic sauce and served over fresh angel-hair pasta), but there are a number of other lobster, fish, and steak dishes. There's also a selection of delicious gourmet pizzas (see "Hyannis & Environs After Dark," below).

Moderate

Harry's. 700 Main St. (near the West End rotary), Hyannis. ☎ **508/778-4188.** Main courses $10–$19. MC, V. Daily 11:30am–1am. INTERNATIONAL.

Seemingly transported from the French Quarter, this small restaurant/bar—park benches serve as booths—has added some Italian and French options to its menu, but it's the authentic Cajun cooking that keeps customers coming back: ribs, jambalaya, hoppin' John, red beans, and rice. On the weekends, get set for a heaping serving of R&B (see "Hyannis & Environs After Dark," below).

Sweetwaters Grille. 644 Main St. (about ¼ mile E of the West End rotary), Hyannis. ☎ **508/775-3323.** Main courses $9–$19. AE, MC, V. Mid-June to early Sept Mon–Thurs 4–10pm; Fri–Sat 11:30am–11pm; Sun noon–10pm. Early Sept to mid-June Mon–Thurs 11:30am–10pm; Fri–Sat 11:30am–11pm; Sun noon–10pm. SOUTHWESTERN.

The Cape is no more immune to Tex-Mex fever than any other halfway-hip community—or to fusion influences, which explains the seafood spring roll (wrapped in a tortilla with green-chili sauce) and the Thai grilled beef with lemongrass salsa. Chili-heads can test themselves on the chicken Diablo, a brandy flambé with a red-chili garlic sauce chaser—masochists begging for more can slather on a side of "rattlesnake venom." There are plenty of less-incendiary choices, and the setting itself is soothing and understated, done in shades of sage green.

Tugboats. 21 Arlington St. (at the Hyannis Marina, off Willow St.), Hyannis. ☎ **508/775-6433.** Main courses $11–$15. AE, DC, MC, V. Late May–late Oct daily 11:30am–10:30pm; mid-Apr to late May Tues–Sun 11:30am–10:30pm. Closed Nov to mid-Apr. AMERICAN.

Yet another harborside perch for munching and ogling, this one's especially appealing. The two spacious outdoor decks are angled just right to catch the sunset, with cocktail/frappés to match, or perhaps a bottle of Moët et Chandon. Forget fancy dining and chow down on blackened-swordfish bites (topping a Caesar salad, perhaps) or lobster fritters or the double-duty Steak Neptune, topped with scallops and shrimp. Among the "decadent desserts" (must we constantly be reminded?) is a Key lime pie purportedly lifted straight from Papa's of Key West.

Inexpensive

Baxter's Boat House. 177 Pleasant St. (near the Steamship Authority ferry), Hyannis. ☎ **508/775-7040.** Main courses $8–$14. AE, MC, V. Late May–early Sept Mon–Sat 11:30am–10pm; Sun 11:30am–9pm; hours may vary at the beginning and end of the season. Closed mid-Oct to Mar. SEAFOOD.

A shingled shack on a jetty jutting out into the harbor, Baxter's has catered to the boating crowd since the mid-1950s with Cape classics such as fried clams and fish virtually any way you like it, from baked to blackened, served on paper plates at picnic tables. This is a good place to bring a brood of kids. If you sit out on the deck, be wary of swooping seagulls looking to spirit away your lunch.

Common Ground Cafe. 420 Main St., Hyannis. ☎ **508/778-8390.** Most items under $6. AE, DC, DISC, MC, V. Mon–Thurs 10am–10pm; Fri 10am–3pm. AMERICAN.

Talk about an out-of-body experience: Step off tacky Main Street Hyannis into this New Age-y sandwich shop run by a commune. The barn-board walls and wide-board floors surround alcoves with private booths containing amorphous tree-stump tables. You can see straight up to the second floor juice and smoothie bar, where they also sell some health and beauty products. But enough about atmosphere; this place makes the best iced tea on Cape Cod (the house blend—a mixture of mint teas and lemon). Everything is made from scratch here. The sandwiches and salads are, as you'd expect, wholesome and delicious. They also have some South of the Border choices: The burrito with turkey is a winner. If I understand correctly from their literature (available at the door), the "Common Ground" is love. Count me in.

Mayflower Cape Cod Diner. 50 Sea St. (at the corner of South St.). ☎ **508/771-3554.** All items under $9. AE, MC, V. Late May–Sept Mon–Sat 7am–8pm, Sun 7am–1pm; call for off-season hours. DINER.

In the tradition of great diners, this one has a tin ceiling, comfy booths, and a shiny counter. It also serves breakfast all day and has sassy waitresses who pour really good coffee. Selections from the children's menu are under $4. Wash down a tuna melt with a root beer float or splurge on the roast turkey dinner. It's a block from Main Street and about a ½ mile from the Hy-Line ferry terminal with boats to Nantucket.

Spiritus. 500 Main St. (in the center of town), Hyannis. ☎ **508/775-2955.** Most items under $10. MC, V. June–Aug daily 11:30am–2am; call for off-season hours. ITALIAN/ECLECTIC.

A branch of the Provincetown pizza palace, this one sports a ceiling mural of demented cherubs and tends to attract local young folks and artistes, who may take the floor on Tuesday nights off-season to recite poetry. Most everything's homemade, from the soup to the carrot juice, even the biscotti. The whole scene is very low-key.

Starbuck's. 668 Rte. 132 (near the airport), Hyannis. ☎ **508/778-6767.** Main courses $7–$14. AE, CB, DC, DISC, MC, V. Daily 11:30am–midnight. AMERICAN.

This is not the famous Seattle coffee chain; it's a fun-loving family restaurant with a hopping bar scene. This hangarlike space actually contains an airplane, a decommissioned Fokker D-7, suspended from the ceiling, along with a lot of other odd conversation pieces conducive to the singles-mingling going on below. The bar tends to attract a slightly older (post-college) crowd, and it's a fun place for families as well. Kids can order scaled-down desserts as well as entrees—provided you can talk them out of the Oreo-cookie pie. Or you can slap together a multicultural meal spanning baked brie and Philly cheesesteak, jambalaya, and Thai scallops. Go traditional with their chunky clam chowder served in a bread bowl.

✪ Ying's. 59 Center St. (Center Plaza, 1 block N of Main St.), Hyannis ☎ **508/790-2432.** All items under $15. AE, MC, V. Daily 11:30am–10:30pm. THAI/JAPANESE/KOREAN.

Not only is this the best Asian food served in Hyannis, but the atmosphere here provides a much-needed dose of tranquility in hectic Hyannis. There's a water garden at the entrance and an eight-seat sushi bar, in addition to tables. While specializing in three distinct Asian cuisines may seem risky, Ying's handles the challenge with aplomb. The sushi menu is extensive, but there are also Thai and Korean specialties, including many vegetarian dishes.

Coffee & Desserts

Hyannis does have an authentic French cafe. **La Petite France Cafe,** 349 Main St., in the center of town (☎ **508/771-4445**), owned by Lucien Degioanni of San Remy, serves scrumptious croissants, breads, and pastries, all baked on-site. For lunch, there are homemade soups and quiches, as well as popular sandwiches and salads. Closed January to March.

Vermont's favorite sons, **✪ Ben & Jerry,** have one of their playful ice-cream parlors at 352 Main St., Hyannis (☎ **508/790-0910**).

A modest luncheonette may make an unlikely shrine, but since 1934, several generations of summer goers—including enthusiastic Kennedys—have fed their ice-cream cravings at **✪ Four Seas,** 360 S. Main St., at Main Street, in the center of Centerville (☎ **508/775-1394**). Founder Richard Warren was into exotic flavors long before they became the norm. His specialties include rum-butter toffee, cantaloupe, and—at the height of the season—Cape Cod beach plum. Closed early September to late May.

Take-Out & Picnic Fare

Another branch of the popular **Box Lunch** (☎ **508/790-5855**), serving pita "rollwiches," is right on Main Street (no. 357) in Hyannis. These are the best—and fastest—sandwiches in town.

In Barnstable Village, Osterville & Cotuit

Very Expensive

✪ The Regatta of Cotuit at the Crocker House. 4631 Rte. 28 (near the intersection of Rte. 130), Cotuit. ☎ **508/428-5715.** Reservations recommended. Main courses $22–$35. AE, MC, V. Apr–Dec daily 5–10pm; Jan–Mar Tues–Sun 5–10pm. NEW AMERICAN.

One of the best restaurants on Cape Cod, this year-round cousin of The Regatta of Falmouth-by-the-Sea (see "Where to Dine," under "Falmouth" in chapter 4) serves fine cuisine in a suite of charmingly decorated Federal-era rooms: This 1790 Cape was once a stagecoach inn. Nightly specials might include such hearty offerings as roasted buffalo tenderloin with blackberry Madeira sauce served with braised fresh greens and a stilton sage bread pudding; or sautéed fillet of halibut with a citrus beurre blanc, lobster mashed potatoes and a marinated vegetable salad. The cuisine is exquisitely prepared and presented, fortified by herbs and vegetables plucked fresh from the kitchen garden, and the mood is invariably festive. You're likely to experience the best service on Cape Cod at this enchanting locale.

For budget-minded gourmands, The Regatta also serves an affordable fixed-price ($22 to $26) three-course "early dinner" from 5 to 6pm.

Moderate

Barnstable Tavern & Grille. 3176 Main St., Barnstable. ☎ **508/362-2355.** Main courses $12–$22. AE, MC, V. May–Oct Sun–Thurs 11:30am–10pm; Fri–Sat 11:30am–11pm; call for off-season hours. REGIONAL.

From the outside, this restaurant—a former stagecoach stop smack dab in the middle of Barnstable Village—feels like it's been here forever, but the interior has been cheerfully revamped. The tavern area is now separate from the main dining room, so you're assured a smoke-free experience. In season, you'll want one of the tables in the courtyard with views of the majestic courthouse across the street. The restaurant offers 38 wines by the glass and serves food until midnight. Specialties here include Black Angus sirloin and fresh grilled swordfish. In the off-season, there's a large Sunday brunch buffet.

Dolphin Restaurant. 3250 Rte. 6A (in the center of town), Barnstable. ☎ **508/362-6610.** Main courses $14–$21. AE, DC, MC, V. May–Oct Mon–Sat 11:30am–3pm; daily 5–9:30pm; call for off-season hours. NEW AMERICAN.

It looks like just another run-of-the-mill roadside eatery, so it's easy to miss from the road. Never mind the corny decor (pine paneling and clunky captain's chairs) or the little plate of crackers and cheese dip that greets you at the table, both carryovers from the restaurant's 1953 debut. The finesse is to be found in the menu, where amid the more typical fried fish you'll find such delicacies as Chilean sea bass with roasted corn salsa and lime vinaigrette, roast duck with mango glaze and toasted coconut, or arctic char with caramelized onions and citrus butter. It's a painless segue from there to the signature dessert: amaretto bread pudding.

Mattakeese Wharf. 271 Mill Way (about ½ mile N of Rte. 6A), Barnstable. ☎ **508/362-4511.** Reservations recommended. Main courses $12–$25. AE, MC, V. June–Oct daily 11:30am–10pm; call for off-season hours. Closed Nov–Apr. SEAFOOD.

This water-view fish house, with broad decks jutting out into the harbor, gets packed in season; don't even bother on summer weekends. The outdoor seating fills up first, and no wonder, with Sandy Neck sunsets to marvel over and fish so fresh it could have flopped on deck. There's a Mediterranean subtext to the extensive menu. The bouillabaisse is worthy of the name, and the varied combinations of pasta, seafood, and sauce—from Alfredo to *fra diavolo*—invite return visits. There's live piano music most nights in season.

Take-Out & Take-Home Food

Area residents like to think of ✪ **Mill Way,** Mill Way Road, on Barnstable Harbor, about a ⅓ mile north of Route 6A (☎ **508/362-2760**), a high-falutin' fish shack, as their own little secret. Certainly there are no outward signs to suggest that chef/co-owner Ralph Binder is a product of the prestigious Culinary Institute of America. You can order the usual Cape specialties, from chowder to fried clams to lobster, from the take-out window, but be sure to step inside to see what else is available—perhaps a pungent calamari salad, or seafood sausage, a delicately seasoned mélange of lobster, shrimp, and scallops. Closed mid-October through April.

HYANNIS & ENVIRONS AFTER DARK
LOW-KEY EVENINGS

Baxter's Boat House. 177 Pleasant St. (see "Where to Dine," above), Hyannis. ☎ **508/775-7040.** No cover.

This congenial little lounge, with map-topped tables and low-key blues piano, draws an attractive crowd, including the occasional vacationing celebrity.

✪ **Roadhouse Cafe.** 488 South St. (see "Where to Dine," above), Hyannis. ☎ **508/775-2386.** No cover.

If raucous rock is the last thing you seek in after-dinner entertainment, duck into this dark-paneled bar, decorated like an English gentlemen's club in burgundy leather. The bar stocks 48 boutique beers, in addition to all the usual hard, soft, and sweet liquors, and you won't go hoarse trying to converse over the soft jazz. The new bistro area next to the bar has live jazz piano nightly. Insiders know to show up Monday nights to hear local jazz great Dave McKenna.

Roo Bar. 586 Main St., Hyannis. ☎ **508/778-6515.** No cover.

This bistro feels very Manhattan, with ultra-cool servers, a long sleek bar area, and lots of attitude. Food is good, too (see "Where to Dine," above). Trendy cigar smoking commences after 10pm.

Windjammer Lounge. Airport Shopping Plaza, Hyannis. ☎ **508/771-2020.** No cover.

How did this classic 1950s gin joint end up in a strip mall next to TJ Maxx? Best not to think about it too hard; just enjoy the live acoustic performers, Thursday through Sunday in season.

LIVE & LOUD

Duval Street Station. 477 Yarmouth Rd. (about 1 mile NE of Main St.), Hyannis. ☎ **508/771-7511.** Nominal cover charge Fri–Sat in season.

Hyannis's only gay bar occupies an old train station. The lower level is a comfortable lounge, and upstairs there's a dance bar complete with light show and DJ mixes that spin from Latin rhythms to New Wave to "gay disco classics" of the '70s and '80s.

Harry's. 700 Main St. (see "Where to Dine," above), Hyannis. ☎ **508/778-4188.** Cover Thurs–Sat $3–$4.

There's hardly room to eat here, let alone rock out, but the cramped dance floor makes for instant camaraderie. The classic blues music heard here, like Rick Russell and the Cadillac Horns, really demands to be absorbed in such an intimate space. Live performance reigns Thursday to Saturday in season and weekends year-round.

Starbuck's. 645 Rte. 132 (see "Where to Dine," above), Hyannis. ☎ **508/778-6767.** No cover.

Acoustic acts and soft-rock bands, like John Poussette Dart, attract a 30-plus crowd. But the drinks range from silly (for example, Grape Crush) to serious (27-oz. margaritas), and both the setting and staff contrive to ensure a good time.

Steamers Grill & Bar. 235 Ocean St., Hyannis. ☎ **508/778-0818.** No cover.

Everyone's glowing with the day's exertions as they cram onto the deck to enjoy liberal libations, a lingering sunset, and, on weekends, live bands. Upstairs, it's a young, sporty crowd for the most part; and by 9pm on Friday and Saturday in season, it's packed. Downstairs, the Putter's Pub with its fuddy-duddy duffers' motif is more sedate.

PERFORMANCES, READINGS & LECTURES

The Barnstable Comedy Club. 3171 Rte. 6A (in the center of town), Barnstable. ☎ **508/362-6333.** Tickets $10–$12; students and seniors $8–$10. Call for schedule.

A local favorite since 1922, the oldest amateur theater group in the country (Kurt Vonnegut is an admiring ex-member) offers a mix of old chestnuts and original farces off-season.

✪ **The Cape Cod Melody Tent.** West End rotary, Hyannis. ☎ **508/775-9100.** Curtain 8pm nightly July–early Sept. Tickets $18–$45. Most performances 8pm. Call for schedule.

Built as a summer theater in 1950, this billowy blue big-top proved even better suited to variety shows. A non-profit venture since 1990 (proceeds fund other cultural initiatives Cape-wide), the Melody Tent has hosted the major performers of the past half century, from jazz greats to comedians, crooners to rockers. Every seat is a winner in this grand oval, only 20 banked aisles deep. There's also a children's theater program Wednesday mornings at 11am.

2 Yarmouth

19 miles (31km) E of Sandwich; 38 miles (61km) S of Provincetown

This cross section represents the Cape at its best—and worst. Yarmouth Port, on Cape Cod Bay, is an enchanting town, clustered with interesting shops and architectural pearls, whereas the soundside "villages" of West to South Yarmouth are an object lesson in unbridled development run amuck. This section of Route 28 is a nightmarish gauntlet of tacky accommodations and "attractions." Yet even here, you'll find a few spots worthy of the name.

Legend has it that Leif Eriksson found the region very attractive indeed, and set up what was meant to be a permanent camp by the Bass River around A.D. 1000. No trace has yet been found—other than the puzzling "Bournedale stone," with its vaguely runic inscriptions, now housed at the Aptucxet Trading Post Museum in Bourne. Why Eriksson left—and whether, in fact, he came to Cape Cod at all, and not some similar spot—are mysteries still unanswered. We do know that Yarmouth, most likely named for an English port, was the second Cape town to incorporate, following closely on the heels of Sandwich; and that at the height of the shipping boom, Yarmouth Port boasted a "Captain's Row" of 50 fine houses, most of which remain showpieces to this day.

So, you've got the north shore for culture and refinement, and the south shore for kitsch. Take your pick, or ricochet, enjoying the best of both worlds.

ESSENTIALS

GETTING THERE   After crossing either the Bourne or Sagamore bridge, head east on Route 6 or 6A. Route 6A (north of Rte. 6's exit 7) passes through the village of

Yarmouth Port. The villages of West Yarmouth, Bass River, and South Yarmouth are located along Route 28, east of Hyannis; to reach them from Route 6, take exit 7 south (Yarmouth Rd.), or exit 8 south (Station St.), or fly into Hyannis (see "Getting There" in chapter 2).

If you need to get around the area without a car, the Yarmouth Easy Shuttle circles Route 28 from Hyannis's bus terminal; for details, contact the Yarmouth Area Chamber of Commerce (see below).

VISITOR INFORMATION   Contact the **Yarmouth Area Chamber of Commerce,** 657 Rte. 28, West Yarmouth, MA 02673 (☎ **800/732-1008** or 508/778-1008; fax 508/778-5114; www.yarmouthcapecod.com; e-mail: yarmouth@capecod.net); or the **Cape Cod Chamber of Commerce,** (see "Visitor Information" in the "Barnstable, Hyannis, Neighboring Villages & Environs" section, above). The Yarmouth Chamber is open Monday to Saturday 9am to 5pm and Sunday 10am to 3pm.

BEACHES & RECREATIONAL PURSUITS

BEACHES   Yarmouth boasts 11 saltwater and 2 pond beaches open to the public. The body-per-square-yard ratio can be pretty intense along the sound, but so's the social scene, so no one seems to mind. The beachside parking lots charge $10 a day and sell weeklong stickers ($40).

- **Bass River Beach,** off South Shore Drive in Bass River (South Yarmouth): Located at the mouth of the largest tidal river on the eastern seaboard, this sound beach offers bathroom facilities and a snack bar, plus a wheelchair-accessible fishing pier. The beaches along the south shore (Nantucket Sound) tend to be clean and sandy with comfortable water temps (kids will want to stay in all day), but they can also be quite crowded during peak times. You'll need a beach sticker to park here.
- **Grays Beach,** off Center Street in Yarmouth Port: This isn't much of a beach, but tame waters make this tiny spit of dark sand good for young children; adjoins the Callery-Darling Conservation Area (see "Nature & Wildlife Areas," below). The Bass Hole boardwalk offers one of the most scenic walks in the Mid Cape. Parking is free here, and there's a picnic area with grills.
- **Parker's River Beach,** off South Shore Drive in Bass River: The usual amenities like rest rooms and a snack bar, plus a 20-foot gazebo for the sun-shy.
- **Seagull Beach,** off South Sea Avenue in West Yarmouth: Rolling dunes, a boardwalk, and all the necessary facilities, like rest rooms and a snack bar, attract a young crowd. Bring bug spray, though: Greenhead flies get the munchies in July.

BICYCLING   The ✪ **Cape Cod Rail Trail** (☎ 508/896-3491) is just a few miles away on Route 134 (near the entrance to Rte. 6) in South Dennis. Rent a bike at the trailhead, and if you are feeling Olympian, bike all the way to Wellfleet (25 miles).

BOATING   Paddle Cape Cod (☎ **888/226-6393** or 508/564-4051; www. paddlecapecod.com; e-mail: cccanoe@capecod.net) runs naturalist-guided trips throughout the Cape. Trips (3 to 3½ hours)—daily, weather permitting, April through October—cost $30 for a solo kayak or $50 for a tandem kayak or canoe. Sunset trips are particularly popular. All equipment is supplied, and trips include juice and snacks. Call for schedule.

If you want to explore on your own by canoe, you can rent one at **Cape Cod Waterways,** 16 Rte. 28, Dennisport (☎ **508/398-0080**), and paddle along the Bass River, which flows between South Yarmouth and West Dennis on the south side of the Cape. A full-day canoe or kayak rental costs $30 to $40.

FISHING   Of the five fishing ponds in the Yarmouth area, **Long Pond** near South Yarmouth is known for its largemouth bass and pickerel; for details and a license (shellfishing is another option), visit **Town Hall** at 1146 Rte. 28 in South Yarmouth (☎ **508/398-2231**) or **Riverview Bait and Tackle** at 1273 Rte. 28 in South Yarmouth (☎ **508/394-1036**). Full-season licenses for Massachusetts residents cost $28.50; for out-of-staters, $38.50. You can cast for striped bass and bluefish off the pier at Bass River Beach (see "Beaches," above).

FITNESS   The **Mid-Cape Racquet Club** (see "Tennis," below) doubles as a fitness center.

GOLF   The township maintains two 18-hole courses: the seasonal **Bayberry Hills,** off West Yarmouth Road in West Yarmouth (☎ **508/394-5597**), and the **Bass River Golf Course,** off High Bank Road in South Yarmouth (☎ **508/398-9079**), founded in 1900 and open year-round. Two more 18-holers are open to the public: the par-54 **Blue Rock Golf Course** off High Bank Road in South Yarmouth (☎ **508/398-9295**), open year-round, and the seasonal **Kings Way Golf Club,** off Route 6A in Yarmouth Port (☎ **508/362-8870**).

NATURE & WILDLIFE AREAS   For a pleasant stroll, follow the 2 miles of trails maintained by the Historical Society of Old Yarmouth on 53 acres behind the Captain Bangs Hallet House (see "Museums," below). Park behind the post office, and check in at the gatehouse, whose herb garden displays a "Wheel of Thyme." The in-season trail fee (50¢ adults, 25¢ children) includes a keyed trail guide: Look for— but do not pick—the endangered pink lady's slipper, a local orchid. Your path will cross the transplanted 1873 **Kelley Chapel,** said to have been built by a Quaker grandfather to comfort his daughter after the death of her child.

In Yarmouth Port, follow Centre Street about a mile north and bear northeast on Homers Dock Road; from here a 2½-mile trail through the **Callery-Darling Conservation Area** leads to Grays Beach, where you can continue across the Bass Hole Boardwalk for a lovely view of the marsh.

TENNIS   There are four public courts at Flax Pond, off North Main Street in South Yarmouth; four more at Sandy Pond, on Buck Island Road off Higgins Crowell Road; plus 10 at Dennis-Yarmouth High School at Station Avenue in South Yarmouth. For details, contact the **Yarmouth Recreation Department** (☎ **508/398-2231**, ext. 284). The **Mid-Cape Racquet Club,** 193 Whites Path, South Yarmouth (☎ **508/394-3511**), has nine indoor courts ($28 per hour), plus racquetball and squash courts (one each) and health-club facilities ($10 per day).

MUSEUMS

Captain Bangs Hallet House. 11 Strawberry Lane (off Rte. 6A, about ½ mile E of the town center; park behind the post office at 231 Rte. 6A), Yarmouth Port. ☎ **508/362-3021.** Admission $3 adults, 50¢ children 12 and under. June, Sept, and Oct Sun 1–3:30pm (tours at 1, 2, and 3pm); July–Aug Thurs and Sun 1–3:30pm (tours at 1, 2, and 3pm). Groups by appointment. Closed Nov–May.

Typical of the sumptuous tastes of the time, this 1840 Greek Revival house is named for the China Trade seafarer who lived here from 1863 to 1893. The Historical Society of Old Yarmouth, which oversees the property, has filled its beautifully proportioned rooms with the finest furnishings of the day, from Hitchcock chairs to a Hepplewhite sofa. The rustic kitchen in back belongs to the 1740 core around which this showy edifice was erected. Note the nearly 200-year-old weeping beech tree and the herb garden beyond, which lead to a scenic 2-mile walking trail (see "Nature & Wildlife Areas," above).

✪ **Winslow Crocker House.** 250 Rte. 6A (about ¹/₂ mile E of the town center), Yarmouth Port. ☎ **508/362-4385.** Admission $4 adults, $3.50 senior citizens, $2 children 6–12, free to Cape Cod residents. Tours June to mid-Oct hourly Sat–Sun 11am–5pm (last tour at 4pm). Closed mid-Oct to May.

The only property on the Cape currently preserved by the prestigious Society for the Preservation of New England Antiquities, this house, built around 1780, deserves every honor. Not only is it a lovely example of the shingled Georgian style, it's packed with outstanding antiques—Jacobean to Chippendale—collected in the 1930s by Mary Thacher, a descendent of the town's first land grantee. Anthony Thacher and his family had a rougher crossing than most: Their ship foundered off Cape Ann in 1635 (near an island that now bears their name), and though their four children drowned, Thacher and his wife were able to make it to shore, clinging to the family cradle. You'll come across a 1690 replica in the parlor. Thacher's son, John, a colonel, built the house next door in around 1680, and—with the help of two successive wives—raised a total of 21 children. All the museum-worthy objects in the Winslow Crocker House would seem to have similar stories to tell. For antique lovers, as well as anyone interested in local lore, this is a valuable cache and a very worthwhile stop.

BASEBALL & SOCCER

The Dennis-Yarmouth Red Sox, part of the ✪ **Cape Cod Baseball League,** play at Dennis-Yarmouth Regional High School's Red Wilson Field off Station Avenue in South Yarmouth. For a schedule, contact the Yarmouth Chamber of Commerce, (☎ **508/778-1008**), the **Yarmouth Recreation Department** (☎ **508/398-2231,** ext. 284), or the **League** (☎ **508/432-6909**).

The **Cape Cod Crusaders** soccer team takes on a dozen other Atlantic-coast teams mid-May to early August, also at the Dennis-Yarmouth Regional High School. For details, contact the **Yarmouth Chamber of Commerce** (☎ **508/778-1008**).

KID STUFF

Children tend to crave the "junk" we adults condemn, so they're likely to be enthralled by the rainy-day enticements of Route 28. Among the more enduringly appealing miniature-golf courses clamoring for attention is **Pirate's Cove,** at 728 Main St./Rte. 28, South Yarmouth (☎ **508/394-6200;** open daily 9am to 11pm in season; closed November to mid-April), where the trap decor is strong on macabre humor. For something a little more wholesome, treat the kids to an ice-cream soda at **Hallet's,** an 1889 drugstore on Route 6A in Yarmouth Port (see "A Soda Fountain" under "Where to Dine," below).

ZooQuarium. 674 Rte. 28 (midway between West Yarmouth and Bass River), West Yarmouth. ☎ **508/775-8883.** Admission $8 adults, $5 children 2–9. July–early Sept daily 9:30am–6pm; mid-Feb to June, Sept–Nov 9:30am–5pm. Closed Dec to mid-Feb.

This slightly scruffy wildlife museum has made great strides in recent years toward blending entertainment with education. It's a little easier to enjoy the sea lion show once you've been assured that the stars do, in fact, like performing. They have been trained with positive reinforcement only and arrived with injuries that precluded their survival in the wild. The aquarium is arranged in realistic habitats, and the "zoo" consists primarily of indigenous fauna, both domesticated and wild (the pacing bobcat is liable to give you pause). Children will be entranced by the Zoorific theater (a live-animal education program) and the children's discovery center with hands-on activities. The new exhibit, *A Walk Through the Cape Cod Woods,* features some of the little creatures that inhabit the woodland floor. In addition, a very creditable effort is made to convey the need for ecological preservation.

SHOPPING

Driving Route 6A, the Old Kings Highway, in Yarmouth Port, you'll pass a number of antique stores and fine shops for the home. Unless you have children in tow, you may want to bypass Route 28 entirely and stay on the pretty north side of Yarmouth.

ANTIQUES/COLLECTIBLES   Check out **Town Crier Antiques,** 153 Rte. 6A (in the center of town), Yarmouth Port (☎ **508/362-3138**), for fun stuff including well-priced (if not museum-quality) quilts, glassware, and attendant paraphernalia. Closed mid-October to mid-May.

ARTS & CRAFTS   Ron Kusins's designs range from the traditional (for example, a burnished porringer) to the contemporary (for example, sleek and shiny asymmetrical candlesticks). There's a style to suit every look, and you can watch this nearly extinct art in action at **Pewter Crafters of Cape Cod,** 933 Rte. 6A (near the Dennis border), Yarmouthport (☎ **508/362-3407**).

BOOKS   The most colorful bookshop on the Cape (if not the whole East Coast) is ❂ **Parnassus Books,** 220 Rte. 6A (about a ¼ mile east of the town center), Yarmouth Port (☎ **508/362-6420**). This jam-packed repository—housed in an 1858 Swedenborgian church—is the creation of Ben Muse, who has been collecting and selling vintage tomes since the 1960s. Relevant new stock, including the Cape-related reissues published by Parnassus Imprints, is offered alongside the older treasures, and don't expect much hand-holding on the part of the gruff proprietor. You'll earn his respect by knowing what you're looking for or, better yet, being willing to browse until it finds you. The outdoor racks, maintained on an honor system, are open 24 hours a day, for those who suffer from *anbibliophobia*—fear of lacking for reading material.

GIFTS/HOME DECOR   To emulate that Cape look—breezy chic—study the key ingredients artfully assembled at **Design Works,** 159 Rte. 6A (in the center of town), Yarmouth Port (☎ **508/362-9698**): stripped-pine antiques, crisp linens, and colorful majolica. There are also books and cards.

The design approach at **Peach Tree Designs,** 173 Rte. 6A (in the center of town), Yarmouth Port (☎ **508/362-8317**), is much more adventurous and eclectic. A bold hand is evident in the juxtaposition of disparate elements, from hunting prints to beribboned hats, model ships to handwoven throws. The gift pickings are superlative as well—especially if you're shopping for yourself.

WHERE TO STAY

There are so many hotels and motels lining Route 28 and along the shore in West and South Yarmouth that it may be hard to make sense of the choices. The following are some that offer clean rooms and cater to families looking for a reasonably priced beach vacation. All are within a few miles of the beach or right on the beach. For those staying on Route 28, the town runs frequent beach shuttles in season.

The Tidewater Motor Lodge, 135 Main St./Rte. 28, West Yarmouth (☎ **800/338-6322** or 508/775-6322; www.tidewaterml.com; e-mail: tidewater@tidewaterml.com), is a short walk (a ½ mile) from a small beach on Lewis Bay and a not-so-short walk (about a mile) from Hyannis's Main Street and the ferries to Nantucket. Summer rates are $90 to $160 double. One of the more attractive motels along this strip, it's a white clapboard double-decker motel with green shutters and doors. The Tidewater also has an indoor pool, an outdoor pool, and a breakfast restaurant.

All Seasons Motor Inn, 1199 Main St./Rte. 28, South Yarmouth (☎ **800/527-0359** or 508/394-7600; www.allseasons.com), is popular with families. Summer rates are $99 to $125 double. It has indoor and outdoor pools, a breakfast restaurant, and exercise and game rooms.

Ocean Mist, 97 S. Shore Dr., South Yarmouth (☎ **800/248-6478** or 508/398-2633; www.capecodtravel.com/oceanmist), is a large motel right on the beach. There's also an indoor pool, just in case it rains. Summer rates are $169 to $189 double, $219 to $239 suites.

VERY EXPENSIVE

Red Jacket. 1 S. Shore Dr. (P.O. Box 88), South Yarmouth, MA 02664. ☎ **800/672-0500** or 508/398-6941. Fax 508/398-1214. www.redjacketinns.com/redjacket. 150 units, 13 cottages. A/C TV TEL. Summer $185–$280 double; $350–$570 cottages. MC, V. Closed Nov to mid-Apr.

Of the huge resort motels lining Nantucket Sound in South Yarmouth, Red Jacket has the best location. It is the last hotel at the end of the road and borders Parker's River on the west, so sunsets are particularly fine. Families who want all the fixings will find them here, though the atmosphere can be a bit impersonal. All rooms have a balcony or private porch; you'll want one overlooking the private beach on Nantucket Sound or looking out towards Parker's River. Also, all rooms have fridges, and some have Jacuzzis. Off-season, rooms can be as cheap as $85 a night.

Dining/Diversions: The dining room, serving breakfast, lunch, and dinner in season, may come in handy in the morning, though you'll probably want to try something more inspiring for dinner. There's a lounge/bar area open for cocktails nightly.

Amenities: Full concierge service; daily summertime children's program of supervised sports and activities, which may take advantage of the playground, minigolf, shuffleboard, horseshoes, and badminton; tennis, basketball and volleyball courts (one of each), as well as a putting green; indoor and outdoor heated pools, plus whirlpool, sauna, and exercise rooms; parasailing, kayaking, paddleboat and sailboat rentals, and catamaran cruises.

EXPENSIVE

✪ **Captain Farris House.** 308 Old Main St. (just W of the Bass River Bridge), Bass River, MA 02664-4530. ☎ **800/350-9477** or 508/760-2818. Fax 508/398-1262. www.captainfarris.com. E-mail: info@captainferris.com. 10 units. A/C TV TEL. Summer $110–$160 double; $175–$225 suite. Rates include full breakfast. AE, DISC, MC, V.

"Sumptuous" is the only way to describe this 1845 inn, improbably set amid a peaceful garden, a block off bustling Route 28. A skilled interior decorator has combined fine antiques and striking contemporary touches to lift this inn's interiors way above the average homey B&B decor. Some suites are apartment-size, containing sitting rooms equipped with a fireplace, and whirlpool-tub bathrooms bigger than the average bedroom. Next door, the 1825 Elisha Jenkins House contains an additional large suite with its own sundeck. Welcoming touches in rooms include chocolates, fresh flowers, and plush robes. All rooms are equipped with irons, hair dryers, dataports, and VCRs. Breakfast consists of three courses served in the formal dining room or the sunny courtyard. The central location puts the entire Cape, from Woods Hole to Provincetown, within a 45-minute drive, assuming you can tear yourself from this pampering environment.

The Inn at Cape Cod. 4 Summer St. (P.O. Box 96), Yarmouth Port, MA 02675. ☎ **800/850-7301** or 508/375-0590. Fax 508/362-9520. www.capecodtravel.com/innatcapecod. 8 units. A/C TV TEL. Summer $125–$185 double. Rates include full breakfast. AE, CB, DC, DISC, MC, V. No children under 10.

New innkeepers Mary and Doug Heywood have taken the reins at this captain's manse/stylish inn. You can't miss the building; it's the one that looks like a tall, thin Southern plantation manor with four towering Ionic columns. Upon entering, the

You Paid What?

47,000 hotels, 700 airlines, 50 rental car companies. And a few million ways to save money.

Travelocity.com
A Sabre Company

Go Virtually Anywhere.

AOL Keyword: Travel

Will you have enough stories to tell your grandchildren

Yahoo! Travel

DO YOU YAHOO!?

elegant foyer, with its grandly curving staircase, leads you into a comfortable common seating-and-breakfast area. Ceilings in the guest rooms are probably the highest you'll find in the area, and the rooms are furnished with well-chosen antiques and period reproductions. Some rooms have canopy beds, and one has a working fireplace. The inn is centrally located in Yarmouthport village with several shops and restaurants within walking distance. It also abuts the 500 acres of town-owned conservation trails behind the historic Captain Bangs Hallet House (see "Museums" above).

✪ **Wedgewood Inn.** 83 Main St./Rte. 6A (in the center of town), Yarmouth Port, MA 02675. ☎ **508/362-5157** or 508/362-9178. Fax 508/362-5851. www.wedgewood-inn. com. E-mail: info@wedgewood-inn.com. 9 units. A/C. Summer $140–$205 double. Rates include full breakfast. AE, MC, V.

This elegant 1812 Federal house sits atop its undulating lawn with unabashed pride. The first house in town to be designed by an architect, it still reigns supreme as the loveliest—one that happens to welcome strangers, though you won't feel like one for long. Innkeeper Gerrie Graham provides a warm welcome, complete with tea delivered to your room. In the main house, the four formal and spacious front rooms all have cherry-wood pencil-post beds, Oriental rugs, antique quilts, and wood-burning fireplaces, and the two downstairs rooms have private screened porches. All have ample bathrooms and thoughtful amenities like hair dryers. The two romantic hideaways under the eaves are decorated in a cheerful country-casual style. The picturesque barn in back has been completely revamped to include three very private, spacious suites, with canopy beds, fireplaces, decks, and sparkling contemporary bathrooms. These new barn suites also include telephones and televisions cleverly tucked into painted cabinets.

INEXPENSIVE

One Centre Street Inn. 1 Centre St. (at Rte. 6A, 1 mile from the village center), Yarmouth Port, MA 02675. ☎ **888/407-1653** or 508/362-8910. Fax 508/362-0195. www.bbonline. com/ma/onecentre/. 6 units, 2 with shared bathroom. Summer $105–$145 double. Rates include full breakfast. DISC, MC, V. No children under 8.

Guests staying in this handsome 1824 colonial on the historic Old King's Highway seem so content. And why not? In the morning, their gracious hostess Karen Iannello serves them a gourmet breakfast (orange French toast with strawberry Grand Marnier sauce or cranberry and toasted pecan pancakes, perhaps); her lovable Dalmatian, Chelsea, nuzzles them as they plan their day, and in the evenings, they can relax in their spacious, charming rooms. And the price is right. Rooms are cheerful with handmade quilts on antique beds of brass, wicker, iron, or mahogany. All rooms have plush terry robes; some are decorated with Waverly or Laura Ashley fabrics. One room features the inn's only working fireplace; another, the only television. The inn also serves as a gallery for the paintings of local artists.

WHERE TO DINE
EXPENSIVE

✪ **abbicci.** 43 Main St./Rte. 6A (near the Cummaquid border), Yarmouth Port. ☎ **508/ 362-3501.** Reservations recommended. Main courses $16–$28. AE, CB, DC, DISC, MC, V. Daily 5–10pm. NORTHERN ITALIAN.

Many consider this sophisticated venue *the* place to eat on Cape Cod these days, comparable to the stylish establishments found on the Islands or even in the big city. While the exterior is a modest mustard-colored 18th-century Cape, the interior features mosaic floors and mural-covered walls in several cozy dining rooms. The knowledgeable and efficient wait staff delivers delicious, artfully prepared, innovative dishes. In fact, the whole setup seems almost out of place in folksy Yarmouth Port. On the menu, you'll find seafood dishes, as well as veal, lamb, and, of course, pasta, all in a delicate Northern Italian style. A taste of the veal *nocciole* (with toasted hazelnuts and a splash of balsamic vinegar), and you'll be transported straight to Tuscany. This small restaurant can get overburdened on summer weekends, so expect a wait even with a reservation.

MODERATE

✪ **Inaho.** 157 Main St./Rte. 6A (in the village center), Yarmouth Port. ☎ **508/362-5522.** No reservations. Main courses $12–$20; sushi pieces and rolls $4–$9. MC, V. Tues–Sun 5–10pm; call for off-season hours. JAPANESE.

What better application of the Cape's oceanic bounty than fresh-off-the-boat sushi? You can sit in awe at the sushi bar and watch chef/owner Yuji Watanabe perform his legerdemain, or enjoy the privacy afforded by a gleaming wooden booth. From the front, Inaho is a typical Cape Cod cottage, but park in the back so you can enter through the Japanese garden. Inside, it's a veritable *shibui* sanctuary, with minimalist decor (the traditional shoji screens and crisp navy-and-white banners) softened by tranquil music and service. On chilly days, opt for the tempura or a steaming bowl of shabu-shabu.

Lobster Boat. 681 Rte. 28 (midway between West Yarmouth and Bass River), West Yarmouth. ☎ **508/775-0486.** Main courses $12–$22. AE, DISC, MC, V. May–Oct daily 4–10pm; call for off-season hours. Closed Nov–Mar. SEAFOOD.

Just about every town seems to have one of these barnlike restaurants plastered with flotsam and serving the usual array of seafood in the usual manner, from deep-fried to boiled or broiled. True to its soundside setting, this tourist magnet advertises itself rather flamboyantly with a facade that features the hull of a ship grafted onto a shingled shack.

INEXPENSIVE

✪ **Jack's Out Back.** 161 Main St./Rte. 6A (behind Main St. buildings, in the center of town), Yarmouth Port. ☎ **508/362-6690.** Most items under $7. No credit cards. Daily 6:30am–2pm. AMERICAN.

This is a neighborhood cafe as Dr. Seuss might have imagined it: hyperactive (okay, semi-crazed) and full of fun. Chef/owner Jack Braginton-Smith makes a point of dishing out good-natured insults along with the home-style grub, which you bus yourself from the open kitchen, thereby saving big bucks as well as time. This is a perfect place for impatient children, who'll find lots of familiar, approachable dishes on the hand-scrawled posters that serve as a communal menu.

Pizzas by Evan. 559 Rte. 6A (1 mile from the village center), Yarmouth Port. ☎ **508/362-7977.** Most items under $10. MC, V. Daily 10am–9pm. PIZZA.

This joint gets my vote as the best pizza on the Cape. The crust is crisp on the outside, doughy on the inside; the toppings are fresh and bountiful. There are also grinders, pasta, and salads. There are plenty of tables in this clean, if uninspiring, restaurant, but you may want to take your pie down the road to Grays Beach and watch the sun set over the marsh.

A SODA FOUNTAIN

Unsuspecting passersby invariably do a double take when they happen upon **Hallet's,** 139 Rte. 6A, Yarmouth Port (☎ **508/362-3362**), an 1889 drugstore where the sunfaded window displays seem to have been left untouched for decades. Not much has changed over the past 100-plus years: The biggest difference is that it is Charles Clark, the great grandson of town pharmacist (and postmaster and justice-of-the-peace) Thacher Taylor Hallet, who is now the one dishing out frappés and floats from the original marble soda fountain. Rumor has it that some years ago a couple of honchos from Walt Disney offered to buy the entire interior for their "Main Street USA" at Disneyland; fortunately, the generous offer was declined. Visit the display area upstairs for a look at old apothecary knickknacks and historic photos. Closed December to March.

EVENING FUN IN YARMOUTH

Yarmouth Summer Band Concerts (☎ 508/778-1008) are held Monday evenings in July and August from 7 to 9pm at the Mattacheese Middle School on Higgins Crowell Road in West Yarmouth. Bands in the past have featured traditional brass, jazz, and blues. Get there early and bring a picnic.

3 Dennis

20 miles (32km) E of Sandwich; 36 miles (58km) S of Provincetown

If Dennis looks like a jigsaw puzzle piece snapped around Yarmouth, that's because it didn't break away until 1793, when the community adopted the name of Rev. Josiah Dennis, who'd ministered to Yarmouth's "East Parish" for close to 4 decades. His 1736 home has been restored and now serves as a local-history museum.

In Dennis, as in Yarmouth, virtually all the good stuff—pretty drives, inviting shops, and restaurants with real personality—are in the north, along Route 6A. Route 28 is chockablock with more typical tourist attractions, RV parks, and family-oriented motels—some with fairly sophisticated facilities, but nonetheless undistinguished enough not to warrant even a drive by (the few exceptions are noted below). In budgeting your time, be sure to allocate the lion's share to Dennis Village and not its southern offshoots. It's as stimulating and unspoiled today as it was when it welcomed the Cape Playhouse, the country's oldest surviving straw-hat theater, during the anything-goes 1920s.

ESSENTIALS

GETTING THERE   After crossing either the Bourne or Sagamore bridge, head east on Route 6 or 6A. Route 6A passes through the villages of Dennis and East Dennis (which can also be reached via northbound Rte. 134 from Rte. 6's exit 9). Route 134 south leads to the village of South Dennis; if you follow Route 134 all the way to Route 28, the village of West Dennis will be a couple of miles to your west, and Dennisport a couple of miles east. Or fly into Hyannis (see "Getting There" in chapter 2).

The **Coach of Dennis Trolley** (☎ 800/352-7155) operates daily from late June to early September. Passengers may board at official stops (Patriot Square, Windmill Plaza, Dennisport beaches, and the intersection of Rtes. 28 and 134) or flag down the driver from anywhere on the route. Fares are 25¢ to 50¢. This shuttle connects with the Harwich Beach Shuttle and the Yarmouth Easy Shuttle.

VISITOR INFORMATION   Contact the **Dennis Chamber of Commerce,** 242 Swan River Rd., West Dennis, MA 02670 (☎ 800/243-9920 or 508/398-3568; www.dennischamber.com), or the **Cape Cod Chamber of Commerce** (see "Visitor Information" in the "Barnstable, Hyannis, Neighboring Villages & Environs" section, above). The Dennis Chamber is open May to October daily 10am to 4pm; November to April Monday to Friday 10am to 2pm.

BEACHES & RECREATIONAL PURSUITS

BEACHES   Dennis harbors more than a dozen saltwater and two freshwater beaches open to nonresidents. The bay beaches are charming and a big hit with families, who prize the easygoing surf, so soft it won't bring toddlers to their knees. The beaches on the sound tend to attract wall-to-wall families, but the parking lots are usually not too crowded, since so many beachgoers stay within walking distance. The lots charge $10 per day; for a weeklong permit ($34), visit **Town Hall** on Main Street in South Dennis (☎ **508/760-6159**).

- **Chapin Beach,** off Route 6A in Dennis: A nice, long bay beach pocked with occasional boulders and surrounded by dunes. No lifeguard, but there are rest rooms.
- **Corporation Beach,** off Route 6A in Dennis: Before it filled in with sand, this bay beach—with wheelchair-accessible boardwalk, lifeguards, snack bar, rest rooms, and a children's play area—was once a packet landing owned by a shipbuilding corporation comprised of area residents. It was donated to the town by Mary Thacher, owner of Yarmouth Port's Winslow Crocker House (see "Museums" in section 2 of this chapter).
- **Mayflower Beach,** off Route 6A in Dennis: This 1,200-foot bay beach has the necessary amenities, plus an accessible boardwalk. The tidal pools attract lots of children.
- **Scargo Lake** in Dennis: This large kettle-hole pond (formed by a melting fragment of a glacier) has two pleasant beaches: Scargo Beach, accessible right off Route 6A; and Princess Beach, off Scargo Hill Road, where there are rest rooms and a picnic area.
- **West Dennis Beach,** off Route 28 in West Dennis: This long (1½-mile) but narrow beach along the sound has lifeguards, a playground, a snack bar, rest rooms, and a special kite-flying area. The eastern end is reserved for residents; the western end tends, in any case, to be less packed.

BICYCLING   The 25-mile ✪ **Cape Cod Rail Trail** (☎ **508/896-3491**) starts— or, depending on your perspective, ends—here, on Route 134, a ½ mile south of Route 6's exit 9. Once a Penn Central track, this 8-foot-wide paved bikeway extends all the way to Wellfleet (with a few on-road lapses), passing through woods, marshes, and dunes. Sustenance is never too far off-trail, and plenty of bike shops dot the course. At the trailhead is **Bob's Bike Shop,** 430 Rte. 134, South Dennis (☎ **508/ 760-4723**), which rents bikes and inline skates and does repairs. Rates are $10 for a couple hours and up to $22 for the full day. Another paved bike path runs along Old Bass Road, 3½ miles north to Route 6A.

BOATING   **Paddle Cape Cod** (☎ **888/226-6393** or 508/564-4051; www. paddlecapecod.com; e-mail: cccanoe@capecod.net) runs naturalist-guided trips throughout the Cape. Trips (3 to 3½ hours)—daily, weather permitting, April through October—cost $30 for a solo kayak or $50 for a tandem kayak or canoe. Sunset trips are particularly popular. All equipment is supplied, and trips include juice and snacks. Call for schedule.

Located on the small and placid Swan River, **Cape Cod Waterways,** 16 Rte. 28, Dennisport (☎ **508/398-0080**), rents canoes, kayaks, and paddleboats for exploring 200-acre Swan Pond (less than a mile north) or Nantucket Sound (2 miles south). A full-day canoe or kayak rental costs $30–$40.

The 63-foot schooner *Freya,* Municipal Marina, Sesuit Harbor in East Dennis, (☎ **508/385-4399**), offers 2-hour sails around Cape Cod Bay, morning through sunset (higher rates prevail as the day progresses). Tickets are $12–$18 adults, $6–$10 children 2–12. Parking at the marina costs $6. Call for schedule.

Water Safaris, located at Bass River Bridge (at Rte. 28) in West Dennis, (☎ **508/362-5555**), explores the Bass and Weir rivers the way Leif Eriksson might have—by boat. This one, a poky but stable custom minibarge, the M/V *Starfish,* is motorized, so the whole circuit takes only 1½ hours. If some of the tales strike you as rather tall, there's still plenty of wildlife and prime real estate to ogle. Trips are offered mid-May through mid-October and tickets are $12–18 for adults and $6–$12 for children ages 2–12. Call for schedule.

FISHING   Fishing is allowed in **Fresh Pond** and **Scargo Lake,** where the catch includes trout and smallmouth bass; for a license (shellfishing is also permitted), visit **Town Hall** on Main Street in South Dennis (☎ **508/394-8300**) or **Riverview Bait and Tackle** at 1273 Rte. 28 in South Yarmouth (☎ **508/394-1036**). Plenty of people drop a line off the **Bass River Bridge** along Route 28 in West Dennis. Several charter boats operate out of the Northside Marina in East Dennis's Sesuit Harbor, including the *Albatross* (☎ **508/385-3244**).

FITNESS/JOGGING   **David's Gym** at 50 Rte. 134 in South Dennis (☎ **508/394-7199**) offers aerobics, weight training, and cardio equipment, plus Cybex equipment, nautilus, and boxing. A day pass costs $12.

For joggers, and fitness freaks in general, the 1½-mile Lifecourse trail, located at Old Bass River and Access roads in South Dennis, features 20 exercise stations along its tree-shaded path.

GOLF   The public is welcome to use two 18-hole championship courses: the hilly, par-71 **Dennis Highlands** on Old Bass River Road in Dennis (☎ **508/385-8347**), and the even more challenging par-72 **Dennis Pines** on Golf Course Road in East Dennis (☎ **508/385-8347**). Both are open year-round.

ICE-SKATING   During the drama that permeated the 1994 Olympics, regular Nancy Kerrigan rendered the **Tony Kent Arena** at 8 S. Gages Way in South Dennis (☎ **508/760-2415**) world-famous. This non-profit, donation-supported facility is open for public skating year-round; call for a current schedule.

NATURE & WILDLIFE AREAS   Behind the Town Hall parking lot on Main Street in South Dennis, a ½-mile walk along the **Indian Lands Conservation Trail** leads to the Bass River, where blue herons and kingfishers often take shelter. Dirt roads off South Street in East Dennis, beyond the Quivet Cemetery, lead to **Crow's Pasture,** a patchwork of marshes and dunes bordering the bay; this circular trail is about a 2½-mile round-trip.

TENNIS   Public courts are located at the Dennis-Yarmouth Regional High School in South Yarmouth and Wixon Middle School, Route 134 in South Dennis; for details, contact the **Dennis Recreation Department** (☎ **508/394-8300**). Or you may be able to book time at the **Mashantum Tennis Club** off Nobscussett Road in Dennis Village (☎ **508/385-7043**), which has clay courts, or **Sesuit Tennis Centre** at 1389 Rte. 6A in East Dennis (☎ **508/385-2200**). At Sesuit, singles are $12 per person; doubles are $10 per person.

MUSEUMS

Cape Museum of Fine Arts. 60 Hope Lane (off Rte. 6A in the center of town). ☎ **508/385-4477.** www.cmfa.org. Admission $5 adults, free for children under 16. May–Oct Mon–Sat 10am–5pm; Sun 1–5pm; Oct–May Tues–Sat 10am–5pm, Sun 1–5pm. Open year-round.

Part of the prettily landscaped Cape Playhouse complex, this museum has done a great job of acquiring hundreds of works by representative area artists dating back to the turn of the century. The main gallery has been recently renovated and expanded, and two galleries have been added to better display the collection and the revolving schedule of exhibits. Call ahead for a schedule of special shows, lectures, concerts, and classes.

Jericho House and Barn Museum. Trotting Park Rd. (at Old Main St., off Rte. 28 about ½ mile E of the Bass River Bridge), West Dennis. ☎ **508/394-6114.** Donations accepted. July–Aug Wed 2–4pm and Fri 10am–noon; also open by special request. Closed Sept–June.

For a century and a half, this classic 1801 Cape house remained in the family of its builder, Capt. Theophilus Baker, and was the model for Richard Henry Dana's *Two Years Before the Mast.* Its mostly Federal furnishings embody the understated elegance of the era. Among the displays are mannequins outfitted in antique clothing. Out back is an 1810 barn housing assorted displays, from a miniature saltworks (the clearest possible depiction of one of the Cape's earliest and most lucrative industries) to an ingenious "driftwood zoo" improvised several decades ago by a playful summer resident. In August, the museum sponsors demonstrations of skills of the 1800s.

Josiah Dennis Manse and Old West Schoolhouse. 77 Nobscusset Rd. (N of Rte. 6A, about ½ mile W of the town center). ☎ **508/385-2232.** Donations accepted. Late June–Sept Tues 10am–noon and Thurs 2–4pm. Closed Oct–late June.

This compact 1736 saltbox housed Rev. Josiah Dennis, the town's first minister. Though not necessarily original, the furnishings are fascinating, as is a diorama of the Shiverick Shipyard, the source, in the mid-1800s, of the world's swiftest ships. Costumed guides lead guests through a maritime room and a children's room. There is also a Native American exhibit. Don't miss the 1770 schoolhouse, where a comprehensive (if strict) approach to learning is beautifully preserved.

Scargo Tower. Scargo Hill Rd. (off Old Bass River Rd., S of Rte. 6A in the center of town). No phone. Free admission. Daily 6am–10pm.

All that remains of the grand Nobscusset Hotel, this 28-foot stone observatory looks out from its 160-foot perch over the entire Outer Cape, including the tightly furled tip that is Provincetown. In the foreground is Scargo Lake—the legacy, native legend has it, of either the giant god Maushop or perhaps a princess who bid her handmaidens to scoop it out with clamshells.

BASEBALL

The Dennis-Yarmouth Red Sox, part of the Cape Cod Baseball League, play at Dennis-Yarmouth High School's Red Wilson Field off Station Avenue in South Yarmouth. For a schedule, contact the **Yarmouth Area Chamber of Commerce,** 657 Rte. 28, West Yarmouth, MA 02673 (☎ **508/778-1008**), the **Yarmouth Recreation Department** (☎ **508/398-2231,** ext. 284), or the **League** (☎ **508/432-6909**).

KID STUFF

Dennisport boasts the best rainy-day—or any-day—destination for little kids on the entire Cape, the non-profit **Cape Cod Discovery Museum & Toy Shop,** at 444 Rte. 28 (☎ **508/398-1600**). Hours are 9:30am to 5:30pm daily in season; 9:30am to 4:30pm (except Thanksgiving, Christmas, and Easter) off-season. For a nominal admission fee ($2.50 adults, $4.50 children 1 to 15, $2 senior citizens), the entire family will enjoy this vast educational play space equipped with a frozen-shadow wall, a transparent piano, a pretend diner, a dress-up puppet theater, a veterinary shop, and all sorts of other fun stuff. Special workshops, including reptile shows, are offered daily.

On Friday mornings in season, at 9:30 and 11:30am, the **Cape Playhouse** at 820 Rte. 6A in Dennis (☎ 508/385-3911) hosts various visiting companies that mount children's theater geared toward kids 4 and up; at only $6, tickets go fast.

SHOPPING

You can pretty much ignore Route 28. There's a growing cluster of antique shops in Dennisport, but the stock is flea-market level and requires more patience than most mere browsers—as opposed to avid collectors—may be able to muster. Save your time and money for the better shops along Route 6A, where you'll also find fine contemporary crafts.

ANTIQUES/COLLECTIBLES   More than 136 dealers stock the co-op **Antiques Center of Cape Cod,** 243 Rte. 6A (about 1 mile south of Dennis Village center), Dennis (☎ 508/385-6400); it's the largest such enterprise on the Cape. You'll find all the usual "smalls" on the first floor; the big stuff—from blanket chests to copper bathtubs—beckons above.

Eldred's, 1483 Rte. 6A (about a ¼ mile west of Dennis Village center), East Dennis (☎ 508/385-3116), where the gavel has been wielded for more than 40 years, is the Cape's most prestigious auction house. Specialties include Oriental art, American and European paintings, marine art, and Americana. Call for a schedule.

The premier place for antique wicker furniture on the Cape is **Leslie Curtis Antiques** at two locations in Dennis Village, 776 Main St./Rte. 6A and 838 Main St./Rte. 6A (☎ 508/385-2921). Her wicker selection includes Victorian pieces and Bar Harbor wicker of the 1920s. She also specializes in French Quimper pottery and American 19th-century furniture.

ARTS & CRAFTS   The creations of **Ross Coppelman,** 1439 Rte. 6A (about a ¼ mile west of the town center), East Dennis (☎ 508/385-7900)—mostly fashioned of lustrous 22-karat gold—have an iconic drama to them: They seem to draw on the aesthetics of some grand, lost civilization.

♻ **Scargo Stoneware Pottery and Art Gallery,** 30 Dr. Lord's Rd. S. (off Route 6A, about 1 mile east of the town center), Dennis (☎ 508/385-3894), is a magical place. Harry Holl set up his glass-ceilinged studio here in 1952; today his work, and the output of his four grown daughters, fills a sylvan glade overlooking Scargo Lake. Much of it—such as the signature birdhouses shaped like fanciful castles—is meant to reside outside. The other wares deserve a place of honor on the dining-room table or perhaps over a mantle. Hand-painted tiles by Sarah Holl are particularly enchanting.

BOOKS   Bookstore junkies (you know who you are) will love **Armchair Bookshop,** 619 Rte. 6A, Dennis Village (☎ 508/385-0900), one of those quaint little bookshops that does everything right. This one seems to specialize (unofficially) in books about dogs, in tribute to the friendly golden retrievers in residence. But you'll find everything here, from best-sellers to books of local interest to children's books and more. There is also a large selection of cards and gift items. It's all very well-organized and a delight for browsers.

Booksmith at Patriot Square on Route 134 in South Dennis (☎ 508/398-8380) has a large selection and discounts on best-sellers.

HOME DECOR   If you've ever longed to commission a colonial-looking wool–braided rug, custom-made to match a specific color scheme or to fit an odd-size floor, here's your chance. Small samples go for as little as $25 at the **Cape Cod Braided Rug Co.,** 259 Great Western Rd. (near the Harwich border), South Dennis (☎ 508/398-0089).

WHERE TO STAY
VERY EXPENSIVE

✪ **Lighthouse Inn.** 1 Lighthouse Inn Rd. (off Lower County Rd., ½ mile S of Rte. 28), West Dennis, MA 02670. ☎ **508/398-2244.** Fax 508/398-5658. www.lighthouseinn.com. E-mail: inquire@lighthouseinn.com. 44 units, 24 cottages. TV TEL. Summer $206–$250 double; $405–$488 2-bedroom cottage. MC, V. Rates include full breakfast and all gratuities. Closed mid-Oct to mid-May.

Set smack dab on placid West Dennis Beach on Nantucket Sound, this popular resort has been welcoming families for over 60 years. In 1938, Everett Stone acquired a decommissioned 1885 lighthouse and built a charming inn and a 9-acre cottage colony around it. Today his grandsons run the show, pretty much as he envisioned it; the light has even been resuscitated. As they have for at least two generations, families still gather at group tables in the summer-camp-scale dining room to plot their day over breakfast and recap over dinner. Many coordinate their vacations so that they can catch up with the same group of friends year after year. With a private beach, heated outdoor pool, tennis courts, and motley amusements such as miniature golf and shuffleboard right on the premises, there's plenty to do. The rooms aren't what you'd call fancy, but some have great Nantucket Sound views. Also, they're stocked with conveniences like a hair dryer, VCR, in-room safe, and minifridge. There are four fully handicapped-accessible rooms.

Dining/Diversions: Serving three meals, the sail-loftlike dining room—with state flags rippling from the rafters—is open to the general public. The prices are quite reasonable (entrees rarely exceed $17), and the menu isn't half as stuffy as you might expect: In fact, it's enlivened by reverberations of the New American revolution. Lunch is served under umbrellas on the deck overlooking Nantucket Sound, a delightful setting to enjoy a club sandwich. In season, the poolside snack bar serves light lunches. Down the road, at the entrance to the complex, The Sand Bar, a classic bar with cabaret-style entertainment, serves as on-site nightspot (see "The Dennises After Dark," below).

Amenities: Outdoor heated pool with ample sunning deck, chairs, umbrellas, and pool house/changing rooms; one outdoor tennis court. "InnKids," a supervised play program offered in July and August, is free of charge. There's also a game room, shuffleboard, volleyball, and minigolf.

MODERATE

Corsair & Cross Rip Resort Motels. 41 Chase Ave. (off Depot St., 1 mile SE of Rte. 28), Dennisport, MA 02639. ☎ **800/201-1072** or 508/398-2279. Fax 508/760-6681. www.corsaircrossrip.com. E-mail: info@corsaircrossrip.com. 47 units. A/C TV TEL. Summer $135–$155 double; $155–$245 efficiency. Special packages and family weekly rates available. AE, MC, V.

Of the many family-oriented motels lining this part of the sound, these two neighbors are among the nicest, with fresh contemporary decor, two beach-view pools, and their own chunk of sand. As a rainy-day backup, there's an indoor pool, a game room, and a toddler playroom equipped with toys. All rooms have minifridges and coffeemakers; some have kitchenettes.

The Four Chimneys Inn. 946 Rte. 6A (about ½ mile E of the town center), Dennis, MA 02638. ☎ **800/874-5502** or 508/385-6317. Fax 508/385-6285. www.fourchimneysinn.com. E-mail: chimneys4@aol.com. 8 units. Summer $90–$155 double; $155 suite. Rates include continental breakfast. AE, MC, V. Closed mid-Oct to mid-Apr.

Scargo Lake is directly across the street, and the village is a brief walk away from this imposing 1880 Victorian, former home to the town doctor. Opulent tastes are evident in the high ceilings and marble fireplace of the front parlor. Rooms vary in size, but innkeeper Kathy Clough has rendered them all quite appealing, with hand-painted stenciling and summery wicker furnishings. Three of the rooms have outside decks overlooking the lovely landscaped grounds. Six of the rooms are equipped with televisions, and two have air-conditioning.

✪ **Isaiah Hall B&B Inn.** 152 Whig St. (1 block NW of the Cape Playhouse), Dennis, MA 02638. ☎ **800/736-0160** or 508/385-9928. Fax 508/385-5879. www.isaiahhallinn.com. E-mail: info@isaiahhallinn.com. 10 units. A/C TV TEL. Summer $102–$141 double; $171 suite. Rates include continental breakfast. AE, DISC, MC, V. Closed mid-Oct to late Apr. No children under age 7.

So keyed-in is this Greek Revival farmhouse to the doings at the nearby Cape Playhouse that you might as well be backstage. Many stars have stayed here over the past half century, and, if you're lucky, you'll find a few sharing the space. Your animated hostess, Marie Brophy, has been entertaining the entertainers for over 15 years. The "great room" in the carriage-house annex is a virtual green room: It seems to foment late-night discussions, to be continued over home-baked breakfasts at the long plank table that dominates the 1857 country kitchen. Room styles range from 1940s knotty pine to spacious and spiffy. They are quaint, countrified, spotlessly clean, and several have balconies. All rooms, including the spacious suite, have VCRs. The inn's location on a quiet side street in a residential neighborhood bodes well for a good night of sleep, but it's also just a short walk to restaurants, entertainment options, and Corporation Beach on Cape Cod Bay.

WHERE TO DINE
MODERATE

✪ **Gina's by the Sea.** 134 Taunton Ave. (about 1½ miles NW of Rte. 6A (off New Boston and Beach sts). ☎ **508/385-3213.** Reservations not accepted. Main courses $10–$23. AE, MC, V. June–Sept daily 5–10pm; Apr–May and Oct–Nov Thurs–Sun 5–10pm. Closed Dec–Mar. ITALIAN.

A landmark amid Dennis's "Little Italy" beach community since 1938, this intimate little restaurant has a few tricks up its sleeve, such as homemade ravioli stuffed with smoked mozzarella. Most of the fare here is the traditional Italian food of our youth, but nonetheless tasty: The ultra-garlicky shrimp scampi, for instance, needs no updating. Save room for Mrs. Riley's Chocolate Rum Cake made daily by owner Larry Riley's mother; it's scrumptious. This popular place fills up fast, so if you want to eat before 8:30pm, arrive before 5:30pm. Take a sunset or moonlight walk on the beach (just over the dune) to round out the evening.

✪ **The Red Pheasant Inn.** 905 Main St. (about ½ mile E of the town center). ☎ **508/385-2133.** Reservations recommended. Main courses $17–$27. DISC, MC, V. Apr–Dec daily 5–10pm; Jan–Mar Wed–Sun 5–10pm. CONTEMPORARY AMERICAN.

An enduring Cape favorite since 1977, this handsome space—an 18th-century barn turned chandlery—has managed not only to keep pace with trends, but to remain a front-runner. Favorites from Chef/owner Bill Atwood include roast rack of lamb, boneless roast duckling, and sole meuniere. In the fall, expect game specials like venison and ostrich. His signature cherrystone-and-scallop chowder gets its zip from fresh-plucked thyme. Two massive brick fireplaces tend to be the focal point in the off-season, drawing in the weary—and delighted—wanderer. In fine weather, you'll want to sit out in the garden room.

Scargo Cafe. 799 Main St./Rte. 6A (opposite the Cape Playhouse). ☎ **508/385-8200.** Main courses $11–$21. AE, DISC, MC, V. Mid-June to mid-Sept daily 11am–3pm, 4:30–11pm; mid-Sept to mid-June 11am–10pm. INTERNATIONAL.

A richly paneled captain's house given a modernist reworking, this lively bistro—named for Dennis's scenic lake—deftly spans old and new with a menu neatly split into "traditional" and "adventurous" categories. Traditionalists will find surf and turf, and the popular grilled lamb loins served with mint jelly (talk about traditional!); adventurous dishes include the likes of "wildcat chicken" (a sauté of sausage, mushrooms, and raisins, flambéed with apricot brandy). Lighter nibbles, such as burgers or "Scallop Harpoon"—a bacon–wrapped skewerful, served over rice—are available throughout the day, a boon for beachgoers who tend to return ravenous. Serving food until 11pm makes this the perfect (and only) place in the neighborhood to go after a show at the Cape Playhouse across the street.

Swan River Seafood. 5 Lower County Rd. (at Swan Pond River, about ⅔ mile SE of the town center), Dennisport. ☎ **508/394-4466.** Main courses $15–$20. AE, DISC, MC, V. Late May–Sept daily noon–9pm. Closed Oct–late May. SEAFOOD.

Every town has its own version of the "fish place with a fantastic view." Here the scenic vista is relatively low-key: a marsh punctuated by an old windmill. The fish—from the adjoining market—is snapping fresh and available deep-fried, as it is everywhere, but also smartly broiled or sautéed. Go for the assertive shark steak *au poivre* (with black pepper) and such specialties as scrod San Sebastian, fresh fillets poached in a garlic-infused broth.

INEXPENSIVE

✪ **Bob Briggs' Wee Packet Restaurant and Bakery.** 79 Depot St. (at Lower County Rd., about ⅓ mile S of the town center), Dennisport. ☎ **508/398-2181.** Main courses $6–$15. MC, V. Late June–early Sept daily 8am–8:30pm; May–late June daily 11:30am–8:30pm. Closed mid-Sept to Apr. SEAFOOD.

It's been Bob Briggs's place since 1949; otherwise, the name that might leap to mind would be "Mom's." This tiny joint serves all the requisite seafood staples, fried and broiled, plus steak and chicken dishes. Five generations have been known to commandeer a couple of Formica tables for a traditional summer feast topped off by a timeless dessert such as blueberry shortcake.

Captain Frosty's. 219 Rte. 6A (about 1 mile S of the town center). ☎ **508/385-8548.** All items under $15. No credit cards. June–Aug daily 11am–9pm; call for off-season hours. Closed late Sept–early Apr. SEAFOOD.

Here you won't find the typical, tasteless deep-fried seafood seemingly dipped in greasy cement. The breading is light (thanks to healthy canola oil), and the fish itself is the finest available—fresh off the local day boats, and hooked rather than netted (the maritime equivalent of clear-cutting a forest). You won't find a more luscious lobster roll anywhere, and the clam-cake fritters seem to fly out the door.

The Devon Tea Room. 294 Main St./Rte. 28, West Dennis. ☎ **508/394-6068.** All items under $10. AE, MC, V. June–Sept Mon–Sat 11am–4:30pm; Apr–May, Oct to mid-Dec Wed–Sat 11am–4pm. Closed mid-Dec to Mar. TEAROOM.

Grab a girlfriend and get out of the sun. Owner Jenny Hatch has created a cool little oasis in the heart of West Dennis village. Nine tables set with fine English bone china, linen, and floral tablecloths are tucked against the wall, while a small area with tea-related gifts occupies the other side of the room. Lunch specials include homemade soup, freshly baked quiches, or special sandwiches, but you may want to have the shepherd's pie (when in Rome, after all). Tea is served most properly with all the accoutrements. Music from the big-band era completes the old-fashioned mood.

✪ **The Dog House.** 179 Lower County Rd., Dennisport. ☎ **508/398-7774.** All items under $10. No credit cards. Late May to mid-Sept daily 11am–8pm; call for off-season hours. Closed Nov–Apr. HOT DOG STAND.

This just might be the ultimate hot dog stand, housed in a tiny peaked-roofed hut about a ½ mile from Nantucket Sound. Hot dogs, cheese dogs, and chili dogs with all the fixings are the specialty here, but there's also chili, hamburgers, and for non-carnivores there's the surf burger (salmon). French fries are thickly cut, and onion rings are hand-battered. Fresh lemonade is on hand to wash it down. There are 12 picnic tables in this pine glade.

Marathon Seafood. 231 Rte. 28, West Dennis. ☎ **508/394-3379.** Main courses $7–$15. MC, V. June–Sept daily 11:30am–11pm; call for off-season hours. Closed Dec–Feb. SEAFOOD.

Family-owned and -operated for over 15 years, this place holds its own among the Route 28 fast-food/clam-shack competition. You should order a heaping, steaming platter of fried fish, clams, scallops, shrimp, or a combo served with french fries, and onion rings. Wash it down with a chocolate milk shake. Hard on the heart, but easy on the wallet.

✪ **The Marshside.** 28 Bridge St. (at the junction of Rtes.134 and 6A), East Dennis. ☎ **508/385-4010.** Main courses $7–$15. AE, CB, DC, DISC, MC, V. Daily 7am–9pm. Open year-round. AMERICAN.

This is one of the Cape's best diners; it's a clean, well-run establishment overlooking a picturesque marsh and, in the distance, Sesuit Harbor. There's a relaxed atmosphere here that comes from having a year-round wait staff that knows what it's doing (a rarity on the Cape). The food is fresh, tasty, and cheap, be it a fried-fish platter, a cheeseburger with french fries, or a veggie melt. Save room for homemade desserts.

A FARM STAND

Tobey Farm. 352 Rte. 6A (about ½ mile W of the town center). ☎ **508/385-2930.**

The remarkable thing about this farm stand is that it has been in the same family since 1681. The fresh-picked corn should go straight into the pot; a dried flower arrangement might make a nice memento. In October, Tobey Farm comes alive with Halloween treats like Hobgoblin hayrides at night and not-so-scary hayrides during the day on weekends. Call for a schedule.

SWEETS

Ice Cream Smuggler. 716 Rte. 6A (about ¼ mile W of Dennis Village center). ☎ **508/385-5307.** Closed Oct–Mar.

A noteworthy stop on any Cape-wide ice-cream crusade, this cheerful parlor dispenses terrific custom flavors, as well as seductive sundae concoctions and "fudge-bottom pies."

✪ **Sundae School.** 387 Lower County Rd. (at Sea St., about ⅓ mile S of Rte. 28), Dennisport. ☎ **508/394-9122.** Summer daily 11am–11pm. Closed mid-Oct to mid-Apr.

For a time-travel treat, visit this spacious barn retrofitted with a turn-of-the-century marble soda fountain and other artifacts from the golden age of ice cream. Homemade flavors include Milky Way, Kahlua chip, and Grapenut. Local berries and real whipped cream make for especially tasty toppings.

Woolfie's Home Baking. 279 Lower County Rd. (about ½ mile SW of the town center), Dennisport. ☎ **508/394-3717.** Closed Oct–Apr.

The families clustered along the southern shore have a friend in Terri Moretti, who gets up before dawn to bake fabulous megamuffins as well as strudel, Danish, and other tasty eye-openers.

THE DENNISES AFTER DARK
PERFORMANCES

✪ **The Cape Playhouse.** 820 Rte. 6A (in the center of town). ☎ **877/385-3911** or 508/385-3911. Fax 508/385-8162. www.capeplayhouse.com. Tickets $15–$35. Performances mid-June to early Sept Mon–Sat at 8pm; Matinees Wed–Thurs at 2pm.

The oldest continuously active straw-hat theater in the country and still one of the best, this way-off-Broadway enterprise was the 1927 brainstorm of Raymond Moore, who'd spent a few summers as a playwright in Provincetown and quickly tired of the strictures of "little theater." Salvaging an 1838 meetinghouse, he plunked it amid a meadow, and got his New York buddy, designer Cleon Throckmorton, to turn it into a proper theater. Even with a roof that leaked, it was an immediate success, and a parade of stars—both established and budding—have trod the boards in the decades since, from Ginger Rogers to Jane Fonda (her dad spent his salad days there, too, playing opposite Bette Davis in her stage debut), Humphrey Bogart to Tab Hunter. Not all of today's headliners are quite as impressive (many hail from the netherworld of TV reruns), but the theater can be counted on for a varied season of polished work. On Friday mornings, performances of children's theater are at 9:30 and 11:30am. Admission is $6.

DANCING & LIVE MUSIC

Christine's Restaurant. 581 Rte. 28 (about ¼ mile E of the town center). ☎ **508/394-7333.** Cover varies.

The 300-seat showroom of this Lebanese/Italian restaurant draws some big acts nightly in season, and weekends off-season, including local jazz great pianist Dave McKenna and all sorts of oldies bands; also on the roster are comedy acts and novelty acts, like a hypnotist.

The Sand Bar. At the Lighthouse Inn (see "Where to Stay," above), West Dennis. ☎ **508/398-2244.** Cover varies. Free admission for guests of the Lighthouse Inn.

This homey cabana was built in 1949, the very year Dennis went "wet." Rock King, a combination boogie-woogie pianist and comedian, still rules the evening and wows the crowd.

A MOVIE THEATER

✪ **Cape Cinema.** 36 Hope Lane (off Rte. 6A, in the center of town). ☎ **508/385-2503** (recording) or 508/385-5644. www.capecinema.com. Early Apr to mid-Nov daily 4:30, 7, and 9pm.

In 1930, Raymond Moore—perceiving motion pictures as a complement rather than a threat to live theater—added a movie house, modeled on Centerville's Congregational Church, to the Cape Playhouse complex. The interior decoration is an art-deco surprise, with a Prometheus-themed ceiling mural and folding curtain designed by artist Rockwell Kent and Broadway set designer Jo Mielziner. Independent-film maven George Mansour, curator of the Harvard Film Archive, sees to the art-house programming. That, plus the setting and seating—black leather armchairs—may spoil you forever for what passes for cinemas today. From mid-November to early April, art-house films are shown in the small theater located in the complex.

The Lower Cape: Brewster, the Harwiches, Chatham & Orleans

The Cape's elbow requires an intentional detour, which has helped to preserve Harwich and Chatham from the commercial depredations evident elsewhere along the Nantucket Sound. The quaint village of Harwich Port was all set for an upscale overhaul when the recession struck; faltering funds have left it in an agreeable limbo. Here, the beach is a mere block off Main Street, so the eternal summertime verities of a barefoot stroll capped off by an ice-cream cone can still be easily observed. Chatham, a larger, more prosperous community, is being touted as "the Nantucket of the Cape." Its Main Street, a gamut of appealing shops and eateries, approaches an all-American, small-town ideal—complemented nicely by a scenic lighthouse and plentiful beaches nearby.

Occupying the easternmost portion of historic Route 6A, Brewster still enjoys much the same cachet that it boasted as a high roller in the maritime trade. But for a relatively recent incursion of condos and, of course, the cars, it looks much as it might have in the late 19th century, its general store still serving as a social center point. For some reason—perhaps because excellence breeds competition—Brewster has spawned several fine restaurants in recent years and has become something of a magnet for gourmands.

As the gateway to the Outer Cape, where all roads merge, Orleans is a bit too frantic to offer the respite most travelers seek. Its nearby cousin, East Orleans, is on the upswing as a destination, though, offering a couple of fun restaurants and—best of all—a goodly chunk of magnificent, unspoiled Cape Cod National Seashore.

1 Brewster

25 miles (40km) E of Sandwich; 31 miles (50km) S of Provincetown

One of the "youngest" of the Cape towns, Brewster—named for the Pilgrim leader William Brewster—dissociated itself from Harwich in 1803, the better to enjoy its newfound riches as a hotbed of the shipping industry. All along the winding curves of the Old King's Highway (now Rte. 6A), successful captains erected scores of proud houses—99 in all, according to the local lore. When Henry David Thoreau passed through in the mid-1850s, he remarked: "This town has more mates and masters of vessels than any other town in the country."

The Greek/Gothic Revival First Parish Church, built in 1834, embodies many of their stories. Among the more dramatic tales conjured by the gravestones in back is that of Captain David Nickerson, who is said to have rescued an infant during the French Revolution—possibly the son of Louis XVI and Marie Antoinette. Whatever his origins, "René Rousseau" followed in his adoptive father's footsteps, ultimately drowning at sea. His name was incised on the back of Nickerson's headstone, according to the custom of the day. Nickerson's name also appears on a pew in the white clapboard church.

Brewster still gives the impression of somehow setting itself apart. Mostly free of the commercial encroachments that have plagued the southern shore, this thriving community seems to go about its business as if nothing were amiss. It has even managed to absorb an intrusively huge development within its own borders, the 380-acre condo complex known as Ocean Edge, on what was once a huge private estate. The dust settled, the trees grew back, the buildings started to blend in, and it's life as usual, if a bit more closely packed. Brewster also welcomes the tens of thousands of transient campers and day-trippers who arrive each summer to enjoy the nearly 2,000 wooded acres of Nickerson State Park.

ESSENTIALS

GETTING THERE   After crossing either the Bourne or Sagamore bridge (see "Getting There" in chapter 2), head east on Route 6 or 6A. Route 6A passes through the villages of West Brewster, Brewster, and East Brewster. You can also reach Brewster by taking Route 6's exit 10 north, along Route 124. Or fly into Hyannis (see "Getting There," in chapter 2).

VISITOR INFORMATION   Contact the **Visitor Center** behind Brewster Town Hall, 2198 Main St./Rte. 6A, Brewster (☎ **508/896-3500;** fax 508/896-1086; www.capecodtravel.com/brewster; e-mail: infobrew@capecod.com); or the **Cape Cod Chamber of Commerce,** Routes 6 and 132, Hyannis, MA 02601 (☎ **888/332-2732** or 508/862-0700; fax 508/362-2156; www.capecodchamber.org; e-mail: info@ capecodchamber.org). The Brewster Visitor Center is open from mid-June to early September daily from 9am to 3pm and is closed from mid-October to late April. The Chamber of Commerce visitor center is open year-round Monday to Saturday from 9am to 5pm and Sundays and holidays from 10am to 4pm.

BEACHES & RECREATIONAL PURSUITS

BEACHES   Brewster's eight lovely bay beaches have minimal facilities. When the tide is out, the "beach" enlarges to as much as 2 miles, leaving behind tidal pools to splash in and explore, and vast stretches of rippled, reddish "garnet" sand. On a clear day, you can see the whole curve of the Cape, from Sandwich to Provincetown. That hulking wreck midway, incidentally, is the USS *James Longstreet,* pressed into service for target practice in 1943, and used for that purpose right up until 1970; it's now a popular dive site. You can purchase a beach parking sticker ($8 per day, $25 per week) at the **Visitor Center** behind Town Hall at 2198 Main St. (Route 6A; ☎ **508/ 896-4511**).

- **Breakwater Beach,** off Breakwater Road, Brewster: Only a brief walk from the center of town, this calm, shallow beach (the only one with rest rooms) is ideal for young children. This was once a packet landing, where packet boats would unload tourists and load up produce—a system that saved a lot of travel time until the railroads came along.
- **Flax Pond** in Nickerson State Park (see "Nature & Wildlife Areas," below): This large freshwater pond, surrounded by pines, has a bathhouse and offers water-sports rentals. The park contains two more ponds with beaches—Cliff and Little Cliff. Access and parking are free.

1. Cape Cod / Martha Vine

2. From the Cape Cod

3. Neva Change.

Clare

Republic National Bank

1185 Avenue of the Americas
New York, NY 10036

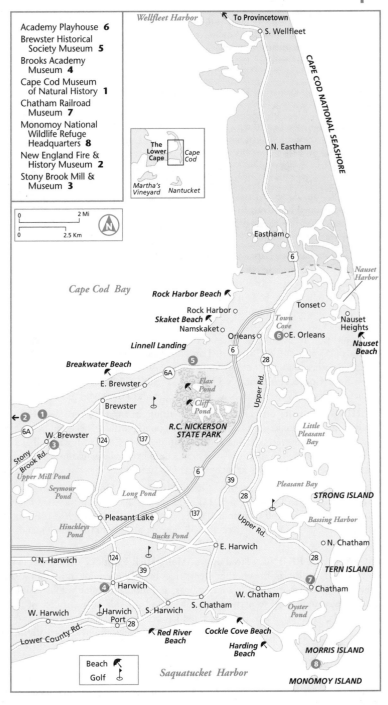

The Lower Cape

Academy Playhouse **6**
Brewster Historical Society Museum **5**
Brooks Academy Museum **4**
Cape Cod Museum of Natural History **1**
Chatham Railroad Museum **7**
Monomoy National Wildlife Refuge Headquarters **8**
New England Fire & History Museum **2**
Stony Brook Mill & Museum **3**

The Lower Cape
Cape Cod
Martha's Vineyard
Nantucket

0   2 Mi
0   2.5 Km

Wellfleet Harbor

To Provincetown
S. Wellfleet

CAPE COD NATIONAL SEASHORE

N. Eastham

Eastham
6

Nauset Harbor

Cape Cod Bay

Rock Harbor Beach
Rock Harbor
Skaket Beach
Namskaket
Linnell Landing

Tonset
Nauset Heights
Town Cove
Orleans
6 E. Orleans
Nauset Beach
6
28
Upper Rd.

Breakwater Beach
E. Brewster
5
Flax Pond
Cliff Pond

Brewster

2 **1**
6A
W. Brewster **3**
Stony Brook Rd.
Upper Mill Pond
Seymour Pond

124   137

R.C. NICKERSON STATE PARK

6

39

Little Pleasant Bay

Pleasant Bay   **STRONG ISLAND**

Long Pond

Hinckleys Pond
Pleasant Lake

28

137

28
Upper Rd.

Bassing Harbor

Bucks Pond
E. Harwich
N. Chatham

N. Harwich
124

39

28   **TERN ISLAND**

Harwich
4

7 Chatham

W. Chatham
W. Harwich
Harwich Port
28
S. Harwich
S. Chatham

Oyster Pond

Lower County Rd.
Red River Beach
Cockle Cove Beach
Harding Beach

MORRIS ISLAND

Beach
Golf

Saquatucket Harbor

8

MONOMOY ISLAND

133

- **Linnells Landing Beach,** on Linnell Road in East Brewster: This is a ½-mile, wheelchair-accessible bay beach.
- **Paines Creek Beach,** off Paines Creek Road, West Brewster: With 1½ miles to stretch out in, this bay beach has something to offer sun lovers and nature lovers alike. Your kids will love it if you arrive when the tide's coming in—the current will give an air mattress a nice little ride.

BICYCLING The ✪ **Cape Cod Rail Trail** intersects with the 8-mile **Nickerson State Park** trail system at the park entrance, where there's plenty of free parking; you could follow the Rail Trail back to Dennis (about 12 miles) or onward toward Wellfleet (13 miles). **Idle Times** (☎ 508/255-8281) provides rentals within the park, in season. Another good place to jump in is on Underpass Road about a ½ mile south of Route 6A. Here you'll find **Brewster Bicycle Rental,** 442 Underpass Rd. (☎ 508/896-8149), and Brewster Express, which makes sandwiches to go. Just up the hill is the well-equipped **Rail Trail Bike & Blade,** 302 Underpass Rd. (☎ **508/896-8200**). Both shops offer free parking. Bicycle rentals start at around $12 for 4 hours and go up to about $18 for 24 hours.

BOATING **Paddle Cape Cod** (☎ **888/226-6393** or 508/564-4051; www.paddlecapecod.com; e-mail: cccanoe@capecod.net) runs naturalist-guided trips throughout the Cape. Trips (3 to 3½ hours)—daily, weather permitting, April through October—cost $30 for a solo kayak or $50 for a tandem kayak or canoe. Sunset trips are particularly popular. All equipment is supplied, and trips include juice and snacks. Call for schedule.

If you want to explore on your own by canoe, you can rent one at **Jack's Boat Rentals** (☎ **508/896-8556**), located on Flax Pond within Nickerson State Park. To check out other canoeing locations in Brewster, you can rent a boat by the day or the week from **Goose Hummock** in Orleans (☎ **508/255-2620**) and paddle around Paines Creek and Quivett Creek, as well as Upper and Lower Mill ponds.

FISHING Brewster offers more ponds for fishing than any other town: 14 in all. Among the most popular are Cliff and Higgins ponds (within Nickerson State Park), which are regularly stocked. For a license, visit the Town Clerk at **Town Hall** at 2198 Rte. 6A (☎ **508/896-4506**). Brewster lacks a deep harbor, so would-be deep-sea fishers will have to head to Barnstable or, better yet, Orleans.

GOLF Part of a large resort, the 18-hole championship **Ocean Edge Golf Course** at 832 Villages Dr. (☎ **508/896-5911**) is the most challenging in Brewster, followed closely by **Captain's Golf Course** at 1000 Freemans Way (☎ **508/896-5100**). In season, a round at the Ocean Edge course will run you about $80 (including mandatory cart).

HORSEBACK RIDING Head over to **Moby Dick Farm** (☎ **508/896-3544**) at 179 Great Field Rd. in Brewster for scenic rides over 200 acres of conservation land, where you'll see kettle ponds, cranberry bogs, and inevitably some wildlife. All levels and all ages are invited to participate for $40, and the ride lasts a couple of hours. Owner Nick Rodday is a real character and has been riding these woods for a couple of decades. This is a great way to experience the Cape's terrain, particularly in the spring and fall.

NATURE & WILDLIFE AREAS Admission is free to the two trails maintained by the Cape Cod Museum of Natural History (see below). The **South Trail,** covering a ¾-mile round-trip south of Route 6A, crosses a natural cranberry bog beside Paines Creek to reach a hardwood forest of beeches and tupelos; toward the end of the loop, you'll come upon a "glacial erratic," a huge boulder dropped by a receding glacier.

Before heading out on the ¼-mile **North Trail,** stop in at the museum for a free guide describing the local flora, including wild roses, cattails, and sumacs. Also accessible from the museum parking lot is the **John Wing Trail,** a 1½-mile network traversing 140 acres of preservation land, including upland, salt marsh, and beach. (*Note:* This can be a soggy trip. Be sure to heed the posted warnings about high tides, especially in spring, or you might very well find yourself stranded.) Keep an eye out for marsh hawks and blue herons.

As it crosses Route 6A, Paines Creek Road becomes Run Hill Road. Follow it to the end to reach **Punkhorn Park Lands,** an undeveloped 800-acre tract popular with mountain bikers; it features several kettle ponds, a "quaking bog," and 45 miles of dirt paths composing three marked trails (you'll find trail guides at the trailheads).

Though short, the ¼-mile jaunt around the **Stony Brook Grist Mill** (see below) is especially scenic. In spring, you can watch the alewives (freshwater herring) vaulting upstream to spawn, and in the summer, the millpond is surrounded and scented by honeysuckle. Also relatively small, at only 25 acres, the **Spruce Hill Conservation Area** behind the Brewster Historical Society Museum (see below) includes a 600-foot stretch of beach, reached by a former carriage road reportedly favored by Prohibition bootleggers.

Just east of the museum is the 1,955-acre **Nickerson State Park** at Route 6 and Crosby Lane (☎ **508/896-3491**), the legacy of a vast, self-sustaining private estate that once generated its own electricity (with a horse-powered plant) and attracted notable guests, such as President Grover Cleveland, with its own golf course and game preserve. Today it's a back-to-nature preserve encompassing 418 campsites (reservations pour in a year in advance, but some are held open for new arrivals willing to wait a day or two), eight kettle ponds, and 8 miles of bicycle paths. The rest is trees—some

---

Biking the Cape Cod Rail Trail

The 25-mile ✪ **Cape Cod Rail Trail** is one of New England's longest and most popular bike paths. Once a bed of the Penn Central Railroad, the trail is relatively flat and straight. On weekends in summer months, you'll have to contend with dogs, inline skaters, young families, and bikers who whip by you on their way to becoming the next Greg LeMond. Yet, if you want to venture away from the coast and see some of the Cape's countryside without having to deal with motorized traffic, this is one of the few ways to do it.

The trail starts in South Wellfleet on Lecount Hollow Road or in South Dennis on Mass. 134, depending on which way you want to ride. Beginning in South Wellfleet, the path cruises by purple wildflowers, flowering dogwood, and small maples, where red-winged blackbirds and goldfinches nest. In Orleans, you have to ride on Rock Harbor and West roads until the City Council decides to complete the trail. At least you get a good view of the boats lining Rock Harbor. Clearly marked signs lead back to the Rail Trail, on which you'll soon enter Nickerson State Park bike trails, or continue straight through Brewster to a series of swimming holes—Seymour, Long, and Hinckleys ponds. A favorite picnic spot is the Pleasant Lake General Store in Harwich. Shortly afterwards, you cross over U.S. 6 on Mass. 124 before veering right through farmland, soon ending in South Dennis.

—by Stephen Jermanok

88,000 evergreens, planted by the Civilian Conservation Corps. This is land that has been through a lot but, thanks to careful management, is bouncing back.

TENNIS   Five public courts are located behind the police station; for details, contact the **Brewster Recreation Department** (☎ 508/896-9430). You may also be able to book one at the **Bambergh House Tennis Club** (☎ 508/896-5023), where singles play is only $4–$5 per person for an hour.

WATER SPORTS   Various small sailboats, kayaks, canoes, and even aqua bikes (a.k.a. sea cycles) are available seasonally at **Jack's Boat Rentals** (☎ 508/896-8556), located on Flax Pond within Nickerson State Park.

BREWSTER HISTORIC SIGHTS & MUSEUMS

Brewster Historical Society Museum. 3341 Rte. 6A (about 1 mile E of the town center). ☎ **508/896-9521.** Donation requested. July–Aug Tues–Fri 1–4pm; call for off-season hours. Closed early Sept–May.

This somewhat scattershot collection offers glimpses of Brewster's past. It includes a model of the town's first house (built in 1660), vestiges of an old post office and barber shop, and various relics of the China Trade—the import business that made the town's fortune.

Brewster Ladies' Library. 1822 Rte. 6A (about ⅛ mile SW of the town center). ☎ **508/896-3913.** www.gis.net/~brewllib. Free admission. Call for schedule; hours vary.

So inviting is the buttercup-yellow facade of this Victorian library, built in 1868, that curiosity will undoubtedly draw you inside. A major new addition has doubled the space and added meeting rooms, an auditorium, and a Brewster history room. The original pair of reading rooms remain, however, with facing fireplaces and comfy armchairs. The two young ladies who started up this enterprise in 1852 with a shelf full of books had the right idea. The library hosts special exhibits, lectures, and music programs.

✪ **Cape Cod Museum of Natural History.** 869 Rte. 6A (about 2 miles W of the town center). ☎ **800/479-3867** (eastern Mass. only), or 508/896-3867. www.ccmnh.org. Admission $5 adults, $4.50 seniors, $2 children 5–12. Mon–Sat 9:30am–4:30pm; Sun 11am–4:30pm. Closed major holidays. Open year-round.

Long before "ecology" had become a buzzword, noted naturalist writer John Hay helped to found a museum that celebrates—and helps to preserve—Cape Cod's unique landscape. Open since 1954, the museum was also prescient in presenting interactive exhibits. The display on whales, for instance, invites the viewer to press a button to hear eerie whale songs; the children's exhibits include an animal-puppet theater. All ages are invariably intrigued by the "live hive"—like an ant farm, only with busy bees. Four marine-room tanks (one 125-gallon tank and three 55-gallon tanks) contain freshwater and saltwater fish, turtles, frogs, crabs, lobster, starfish, and a variety of mollusks. The bulk of the museum, naturally, is outdoors, where 85 acres invite exploration (see "Nature & Wildlife Areas," above). Visitors are encouraged to log their bird and animal sightings upon their return. The museum features an on-site archaeology lab on Wing Island, thought to have sheltered one of Brewster's first settlers—the Quaker John Wing, driven from Sandwich in the mid–17th century by religious persecution—and before him, summering native tribes dating back 10 millennia or more. A true force in fostering environmental appreciation, the museum sponsors all sorts of activities, like lectures, concerts, marsh cruises, bike tours, and "eco-treks"—including a sleepover on uninhabited Monomoy Island off Chatham. Other activities include evening astronomy cruises, seal cruises, and Pleasant Bay excursions. Call for schedule.

Harris-Black House and Higgins Farm Windmill. 785 Rte. 6A (about 2 miles W of the town center). ☎ **508/896-9521.** Free admission. July–Aug Tues–Sun 1–4pm; May–June and Sept–Oct Sat–Sun 1–4pm. Closed Nov–Apr.

Most Cape towns can still boast a windmill or two, a few of them even still functioning, but this no-longer-working model is especially handsome. Built in 1795 in the "smock" style that can be traced back to colonial days, it boasts an unusual cap shaped like a boat's hull. A few steps away is a classic half-Cape house, built that same year, consisting of one square room, 16 feet to a side. Here, one of the poorer members of the community—a blacksmith who doubled as barber—lived simply, yet apparently happily, with his wife and 10 children.

New England Fire & History Museum. 1429 Rte. 6A (about 1 mile W of the town center). ☎ **508/896-5711.** Admission $5 adults, $4.50 seniors, $2.50 children 5–12, $1 children under 5. Late May to mid-Sept Mon–Fri 10am–4pm; Labor Day to mid-Oct Sat–Sun noon–4pm. Closed mid-Oct to late May.

The gaslit displays may come across as a little hokey (and murky), but little kids as well as grown-up fire-fighting aficionados will probably find the array of equipment pretty enthralling. More than 30 antique fire engines have found a home here, including an extraordinarily decorative 1837 French provincial rig from Philadelphia and a unique 1929 Mercedes Benz worth a cool million. Also on the grounds, and included with admission, is a smithy offering frequent demos and an old-fashioned Apothecary Shop.

Stony Brook Grist Mill and Museum. 830 Stony Brook Rd. (at the intersection of Satucket Rd.). ☎ **508/896-6745.** Free admission. July–Aug Fri 2–5pm; May–June Thurs–Sat 2–5pm. Closed Sept–Apr.

It may be hard to believe, but this rustic mill beside a stream was once one of the most active manufacturing communities in New England, cranking out cloth, boots, and ironwork for over a century, starting with the American Revolution. The one remaining structure was built in 1873, toward the end of West Brewster's commercial run, near the site of a 1663 water-powered mill, America's first. After decades of producing overalls and, later, ice cream (with ice dredged from the adjoining pond), the factory was bought by the town and fitted out as a corn mill, with period millstones. Volunteers now demonstrate and urge onlookers to get in on the action. The second story serves as a repository for all sorts of Brewster memorabilia, including some ancient arrowheads. Recent archaeological excavations in this vicinity, sponsored by the Cape Cod Museum of Natural History, have unearthed artifacts dating back some 10,000 years. As you stroll about the millpond (see "Nature & Wildlife Areas," above), be on the lookout—who knows what you'll stumble across?

BASEBALL
The Brewster Whitecaps of the **Cape Cod Baseball League** play at the Cape Cod Tech field off Route 6's exit 11. For a schedule, contact the **Brewster Chamber of Commerce** (☎ **508/255-7045**), the **Brewster Recreation Department** (☎ **508/896-9430**), or the **League** (☎ **508/432-6909**).

KID STUFF
For an educational experience that's also fun, take the kids to the ✪ **Cape Cod Museum of Natural History** and the **Stony Brook Grist Mill** (see above). Both have walking trails, and the museum has extensive exhibits geared toward children, including a number of interactive exhibits.

SHOPPING

ANTIQUES/COLLECTIBLES   Brewster's stretch of Route 6A offers the best antiquing on the entire Cape. Diehards would do well to stop at every intriguing-looking shop; you never know what you might find. There are several consistent standouts.

The artifacts gathered at **Kingsland Manor Antiques,** 440 Rte. 6A, about 1 mile east of the Dennis border (☎ **800/486-2305** or 508/385-9741), tend to be on the flamboyant side, accent pieces rather than serviceable, retiring classics—which makes browsing all the more fun.

There's always an interesting variety of items at **Monomoy Antiques,** 3425 Rte. 6A (☎ **508/896-6570**), including many fascinating finds from local estate sales. Specialties include rare books, English china, Native American artifacts, sterling silver, and decoys.

Imagine a town dump full of treasures all meticulously arranged, and you'll get an idea of what's in store at **Diane Vetromile's Antiques** at 3884 Rte. 6A in Brewster (no phone). If the sign that reads "Antiques" is out, it's open; if not, it's closed. This place is a tad kooky, but any junk aficionado will be thrilled by the pickings: hubcaps, wooden nails, iron rakes, wood shutters—the more peeled paint the better. Owner Diane Vetromile is herself a sculptor, who works with (surprise) found objects, and you'll find her work on view at Jacob Fanning Gallery and Farmhouse Antiques, both in Wellfleet.

ARTS & CRAFTS   Clayton Calderwood's **Clayworks,** 3820 Main St. (Rte. 6A), Brewster (☎ **508/255-4937**), is always worth a stop, if only to marvel at the famous mammoth urns. There's also a world of functional ware here like bowls, pots, and lamps, in porcelain, stoneware, and terra cotta.

At **The Spectrum,** 369 Rte. 6A, about 1 mile east of the Dennis border (☎ **800/ 221-2472** or 508/385-3322), you'll find the kind of crafts that gave crafts a good name: fun stuff, with a certain irony to it, but unmistakably chic. In 1966, two young RISD (Rhode Island School of Design) grads opened shop in a rural schoolhouse. Bob Libby and Addison Pratt now oversee six stores: three on the Cape and Islands (the other branches are in Hyannis and on Nantucket), and one each in Newport, Troy (Mich.), and Palm Beach. Their taste is top-of-the-line, as you'll see in a quick tour of this split-level, country-modern shop.

BOOKS   David L. Luebke is a neat freak—a desirable trait in an antiquarian book-seller. Visit his **Punkhorn Bookshop,** 672 Main St./Rte. 6A, about a ½ mile east of the Dennis border (☎ **508/896-2114**), and you'll notice that each volume logged in his carefully selected stock—strong on regional and natural history—is shelved according to the Dewey Decimal System and protectively coddled in a see-through wrapper to keep fingerprints and "foxing" (stains) to a minimum. If you're in the market for a vintage print, you'll find some beauties here. Closed Monday year-round; open by appointment only off-season.

GIFTS/HOME DECOR   Though quite a bit spiffier than a "real" general store, **The Brewster Store,** 1935 Main St./Rte. 6A, in the center of town (☎ **508/ 896-3744**), an 1866 survivor—fashioned from an 1852 Universalist church—is a fun place to shop for sundries and catch up on local gossip. The wares are mostly tourist-oriented these days but include some handy kitchen gear (cobalt glassware, for example) and beach paraphernalia. Give the kids a couple of dimes to feed the Nickelodeon piano machine, and relax on a sunny church pew out front as you pore over the local paper.

You don't have to be a foodie—though it helps—to go gaga over the exhaustive collection of culinary paraphernalia, from esoteric instruments to foodstuffs, at **The**

Cook Shop, 1091 Rte. 6A, about 1½ miles west of the town center (☎ **508/896-7698**). If you're stuck cooking up a practical yet unusual house gift, look no further.

SEAFOOD   Breakwater Fish and Lobster at 235 Underpass Rd. in Brewster (☎ **508/896-7080**) stocks the freshest fish in town and also sells smoked fish.

WHERE TO STAY
EXPENSIVE

✪ **Captain Freeman Inn.** 15 Breakwater Rd. (off Rte. 6A, in the town center), Brewster, MA 02631. ☎ **800/843-4664** or 508/896-7481. Fax 508/896-5618. www.captainfreemaninn. com. E-mail: visitus@capecod.net. 12 units. Summer $135–$250 double. Rates include full breakfast and afternoon tea. AE, MC, V. No children under age 10.

The creation of an exemplary country inn is part business and part art; Carol Edmondson—the ex-marketing director behind this beauty—poured plenty of both into her mint-green 1866 Victorian. The "luxury rooms"—each complete with fireplace and a private porch with a two-person hot tub—incorporate every extra you could hope to encounter: a canopied, four-poster queen-size bed, a love seat facing the cable TV/VCR (she has a store's worth of tapes available for loan), telephone with answering machine, even a little fridge pre-stocked with cold soda. The plainer rooms are just as pretty—one nice feature of the porch-encircled house is that the second-story windows reach almost to the floor. All rooms have hair dryers. Delectable yet healthy breakfasts—Edmondson, a culinary maven, hosts weekend cooking courses off-season—are served in the elegant parlor or on a screened porch overlooking the outdoor pool and a lush lawn set up for badminton and croquet. Breakwater Landing is a bucolic 5-minute walk away or just moments away if you avail yourself of a loaner bike. Bliss.

MODERATE

Beechcroft Inn. 1360 Rte. 6A (about 1 mile W of the town center), Brewster, MA 02631. ☎ **877/233-2446** or 508/896-9534. Fax 508/896-8812. www.beechcroftinn.com. E-mail: beechcroftinn@aol.com. 8 units. Summer $110–$165. Rates include full breakfast. AE, CB, DC, DISC, MC, V. Open year-round.

Though it looks every inch the gracious summer home, this 1828 building, an inn since 1852, began as a meetinghouse. Subtract one steeple, relocate atop a little hillock crowned with magnificent beeches, and presto—a made-to-order country retreat. New innkeepers, Jan and Paul Campbell from England, have spruced up the place with English antiques and have turned two of rooms into suites. Conveniently, there's a restaurant/tea room on the premises: The Brewster Tea Pot serves breakfast, lunch, and afternoon tea.

The Bramble Inn. 2019 Rte. 6A (about ⅓ mile E of the town center), Brewster, MA 02631. ☎ **508/896-7644.** Fax 508/896-9332. www.innbook.com. 8 units. A/C TV. Summer $115–$155 double. Rates include full breakfast. AE, DISC, MC, V. Closed Nov to mid-May.

Cliff and Ruth Manchester oversee two rambling mid–19th-century homes, decorated in a breezy, country-casual manner. The main inn building, built in 1861, houses one of the Cape's best restaurants (see "Where to Dine," below) on the first floor. The 1849 Greek Revival house next door has additional rooms, all very cozy, simple, and quaint, with antique touches like crocheted bedspreads. All rooms have hair dryers. Cliff makes creative breakfasts, such as mixed fruit Swedish pancakes, which are served outside in the courtyard garden.

Candleberry Inn. 1882 Main St./Rte. 6A, Brewster, MA 02631. ☎ **800/573-4769** or 508/896-3300. Fax 508/896-4016. www.candleberryinn.com. E-mail: candle@cape.com. 9 units. A/C. Summer $95–$225 double. Rates include full breakfast. AE, DISC, MC, V.

Innkeepers Gini and David Donnelly graciously welcome guests to their restored 18th-century Federal-style home. These spacious accommodations feature wide-board floors, wainscoting, and windows with original glass. The decor is country but not cutesy. Some rooms have working fireplaces and canopy beds. Extras include hair dryers and terry-cloth robes in every room. Three rooms in the carriage house are decorated in a more contemporary style; two share an outside deck, one is a deluxe suite, and all have TVs. In season, the three-course full breakfast is frequently served on the sunny porch overlooking the 2 acres of landscaped grounds—which have colorful flower beds throughout. Guests love the view of Main Street from the "glider" rocking benches on the lawn. The Donnellys also rent two offsite cottages: one on the beach in Brewster, the other in Chatham with marsh views.

High Brewster Inn. 964 Satucket Rd. (off Rte. 6A, about 2 miles SW of the town center), Brewster, MA 02631. ☎ **800/203-2634** or 508/896-3636. Fax 508/896-3734. 2 units, 4 cottages. Summer $95–$115 double; $165–$220 cottage. Rates include continental breakfast. AE, MC, V. Closed Jan–Mar. Dogs allowed in cottages.

There are just a few bedrooms topping the exquisite restaurant that occupies most of this 1738 farmhouse. An ancient stairway with mismatched high steps leads the way up, where rooms are appropriately furnished in the classic "Ye Olde" style. The boldly decorated cottages, on the other hand, are like having your own 3½-acre place in the country, prettily situated on a hill overlooking a millpond. Your hosts Catherine and Tim Mundy are most hospitable.

Isaiah Clark House. 1187 Main St./Rte. 6A, Brewster, MA 02631. ☎ **800/822-4001** or 508/896-2223. Fax 508/896-2138. www.isaiahclark.com E-mail: info@isaiahclark.com. 7 units. A/C TV. Summer $110–$150 double. Rates include full breakfast and afternoon tea. AE, DISC, MC, V.

Many mementos of bygone days are found throughout this expanded 1780 Cape cottage. Antique hardware and wide-board floors are original to the house, and innkeeper Richard Griffin can show you the 1836 newspaper the original owners used to line the wall of a closet. Many beds are canopied, but the most spectacular is the suspended canopy bed in the front room with its plaid curtains. Some rooms have telephones. For breakfast, keep your fingers crossed for the Belgian waffles with fresh-fruit (the strawberries, blueberries, and raspberries are all picked locally) and whipped-cream toppings.

Michael's Cottages. 618 Main St./Rte. 6A, Brewster, MA 02631. ☎ **800/399-2967** or 508/896-4025. Fax 508/896-3158. www.sunsol.com/michaels/. E-mail: mdivito@capecod.net. 7 units. A/C TV TEL. Summer $115 double. Weekly rates $625–$700 double; $1,025 2-bedroom. AE, DISC, MC, V. Closed mid-Nov to late Apr.

These kid-friendly cottages on an immaculately groomed compound are small yet centrally located. Across the street is Brewster's Drummer Boy park, which has a playground, historic windmill, and antique house. Brewster's summer band concerts are held there as well. The closest beach is Paine's Creek, about 1 mile away. There are three one-bedroom cottages, one small two-bedroom cottage, one efficiency, and two B&B rooms. The cottages have screened porches, fireplaces, and microwaves. The two-bedroom cottage also has a dishwasher and washer/dryer. In July and August, rentals are available by the week only.

✪ **Ruddy Turnstone Bed & Breakfast.** 463 Main St./Rte. 6A, Brewster, MA 02631. ☎ **800/654-1995** or 508/385-9871. Fax 508/385-5696. www.sunsol.com/ruddyturnstone/. 5 units. Summer $120–$175 double. Rates include full breakfast. DISC, MC, V. Closed Dec–Feb.

Bird lovers will be particularly entranced by this cozy B&B; the salt marsh makes for frequent sightings. In fact, the upstairs suite and the common room of this lovely early 1880s home offer distant Cape Cod Bay and sweeping marsh views, for about the same price as other inns along this stretch without panoramic views. The house is beautifully situated up on a knoll and is furnished with antiques, Oriental rugs, and some canopy beds. The 1860s barn, moved here from Nantucket, houses two additional rooms. Your country breakfast served out on the screened porch or in the old keeping room might feature home-baked apple French toast. Innkeepers "Swanee" and Sally Swanson are the kind you look forward to seeing year after year.

INEXPENSIVE

✪ **Old Sea Pines Inn.** 2553 Main St. (about 1 mile E of the town center), Brewster, MA 02631. ☎ **508/896-6114.** Fax 508/896-7387. www.oldseapinesinn.com. E-mail: seapines@ c4.net. 24 units, 5 with shared bathroom. Summer $65–$135 double; $125–$155 suite. Rates include full breakfast and afternoon tea. AE, CB, DC, DISC, MC, V. Closed Jan–Mar.

This reasonably priced, large historic inn is a great spot for families, and hosts Michele and Steve Rowan have done their best to re-create the gracious ambience of days gone by. In the main house, the parlor and expansive porch lined with rockers, and a handful of rather minuscule boarding-school-scale rooms on the second floor, recall the inn's days as the Sea Pines School of Charm and Personality for Young Women. (These bargain rooms with shared bathrooms are the only ones in the house without air-conditioning, but at $65 per night in season, who cares?) This is one of the few places on the Cape where solo travelers can find a single room and pay no surcharge. There are two other buildings, one of which is fully wheelchair-accessible (another rarity among historic inns). Whereas the main house has an air of exuberance muted by gentility, the annex rooms are outright playful, with colorful accoutrements, including pink TVs. Steve does double duty as the breakfast chef and prepares good old-fashioned food. Sunday evenings from mid-June through mid-September, Old Sea Pines is the site of a dinner/theater performance by the Cape Cod Repertory Theatre (see "Brewster After Dark," below).

WHERE TO DINE
VERY EXPENSIVE

✪ **The Bramble Inn Restaurant.** 2019 Main St. (about ⅓ mile E of Rte. 124). ☎ **508/ 896-7644.** Reservations suggested. Fixed-price dinner $48–$58. AE, DISC, MC, V. June to mid-Oct Tues–Sun 6–9pm; call for off-season hours. Closed Nov to mid-May. INTERNATIONAL.

Often named among the best restaurants on Cape Cod, there's an impromptu feel to this intimate restaurant, an enfilade of five small rooms each imbued with its own personality, from sporting (the Tack Room) to best-Sunday-behavior (the Elegant Parlor). One-of-a-kind antique table settings add to the charm. Such niceties fade to mere backdrop, though, beside Ruth Manchester's extraordinary cuisine. A four-course (8- to 10-option) menu that evolves every few weeks gives her free rein to follow fresh enthusiasms, as well as seasonal delicacies—and it's a thrill to be able to follow along. Any specifics are quickly history, but she has a solid grounding in Mediterranean cuisines and a gift for improvising exotic influences. Her assorted seafood curry (with lobster, cod, scallops, and shrimp in a light curry sauce with grilled banana, toasted almonds, coconut, and chutney) and her rack of lamb (with deep-fried beet-and-fontina polenta, pan-seared zucchini, and mustard port cream) were written up in *The New York Times.*

Chillingsworth. 2449 Main St. (about 1 mile E of the town center). ☎ **800/430-3640** or 508/896-3640. Reservations suggested. Jacket advised for men in fine dining section. Fixed-price meals $50–$68. Bistro $13–$24. AE, CB, DC, MC, V. Mid-June to mid-Oct Tues–Sun 11:30am–2:30pm and 6–9:30pm; call for off-season hours. Closed late Nov to mid-May. FRENCH.

This longtime contender for the title of best restaurant on the Cape now has two dining options: fancy with jackets suggested for men, and more casual with no reservations. The fancy dining room boasts antique appointments reaching back several centuries and a six-course Francophiliac table d'hôte menu that will challenge the most shameless gourmands. Focus on the taste sensations, which are indeed sensational. Specialties include steamed lobster over spinach and fennel with sea beans and lobster-basil butter sauce; and seared and roasted boneless rib eye of veal with fresh morels, mushroom torte, and asparagus. Finish it off with warm chocolate cake with pistachio ice cream and chocolate drizzle. Or try the moderately priced, à la carte Bistro, which operates from a separate kitchen and serves meals in the adjoining greenhouse or on the shady lawn.

✪ **High Brewster.** 964 Satucket Rd. (off Rte. 6A, about 2 miles SW of the town center). ☎ **508/896-3636.** Reservations required. Fixed-price dinner $45–$65. AE, MC, V. Late May to mid-Sept daily 5:30–9pm; call for off-season hours. Closed Dec–Mar. CLASSIC AMERICAN.

By candlelight, the close yet cozy keeping rooms and paneled parlors of this 1738 colonial are irresistibly romantic. It's difficult to decide between the Rooster Room, with its whimsical wallpaper, or the Front Room, with its clever hand-painted murals. Robert Hickey's sensual, sophisticated cuisine only serves to intensify the mood. Dishes tend to be bold—mushroom-filled ravioli, for instance, with fresh tomato salsa, or pan-seared salmon with sun-dried tomato vinaigrette—yet he's good at adapting local ingredients and traditional preparations to treats our ancestors could have imagined only in their dreams. What they would have given, heaven only knows, to be able to celebrate the harvest with apple crisp topped with homemade apple-rum ice cream.

MODERATE

The Brewster Fish House. 2208 Main St. (about ½ mile E of the town center). ☎ **508/896-7867.** Reservations not accepted. Main courses $14–$25. MC, V. May–Aug Mon–Sat 11:30am–3pm and 5–10pm; Sun noon–3pm and 5–9:30pm; call for off-season hours. Closed Jan–Mar. NEW AMERICAN.

Spare and handsome as a Shaker refectory, this small restaurant bills itself as "nonconforming" and delivers on the promise. The approach to seafood borders on genius: Consider, just for instance, squid delectably tenderized in a marinade of soy and ginger, or silky-tender, walnut-crusted ocean catfish accompanied by kale sautéed in Marsala. These are but two examples of the daily specials devised to take advantage of the latest haul. Besides seafood, there are always beef dishes, as well as vegetarian dishes, on the menu. No wonder the place is packed. Better get there early if you want to get in.

INEXPENSIVE

Brewster Inn & Chowder House. 1993 Rte. 6A (in the center of town). ☎ **508/896-7771.** Main courses $12–$16. AE, DISC, MC, V. Late May to mid-Oct daily 11am–3pm; Sun–Thurs 5–9:30pm, Fri–Sat 5–10pm; call for off-season hours. Open year-round. ECLECTIC.

To really get the gist of the expression "chow down," just observe the early-evening crowd happily doing so at this plainish century-old restaurant known mostly by word of mouth. The draw is hearty, predictable staples—the homemade chowder, various

---

ⓘ Family-Friendly Hotels & Restaurants

The Barley Neck Inn Lodge in East Orleans *(see p. 170)* Tastefully rehabbed, this motel offers basic, low-priced rooms, a small pool, and a pair of superb, unstodgy restaurants.

Binnacle Tavern in Orleans *(see p. 171)* Design-your-own pizzas are the draw at this often raucous eatery, decorated with nautical salvage.

Chatham Bars Inn in Chatham *(see p. 156)* This luxury beachside resort offers well-heeled tots the best of everything, including organized play programs morning, noon, and night.

Kadee's Gray Elephant in East Orleans *(see p. 168)* This cute little compound comprises a colorful, all-kitchenette inn; a lively open-air clam bar; and even a minigolf course.

Old Sea Pines Inn in Brewster *(see p. 141)* Children will appreciate the traditional food and friendly, informal atmosphere of this former finishing school.

---

fried, broiled, or baked fish—at prices geared to ordinary people rather than splurging tourists. Check the blackboard for some interesting variations—maybe mussels steamed in cream and curry. If you like to indulge in a martini before your meal, this place makes the best ones in town. There's also a good old bar, The Woodshed (see "Brewster After Dark," below), out back.

Cobie's. 3260 Rte. 6A (about 2 miles E of Brewster center). ☎ **508/896-7021.** Most items under $10. No credit cards. Late May to mid-Sept daily 11am–9pm. Closed mid-Sept to late May. AMERICAN.

Accessible to cars whizzing along Route 6A and within collapsing distance for cyclists exploring the Rail Trail, this picture-perfect clam shack has been dishing out exemplary fried clams, lobster rolls, foot-long hot dogs, black-and-white frappés, and all the other beloved staples of summer since 1948.

SWEETS

How unusual to find a bakeshop tucked away in a sweet little country gifts shop. **Hopkins House Bakery,** 2727 Main St. (☎ **508/896-3450**), is an especially good one, with hermit cookies (molasses, raisins, and nuts) a standout. Heather Baxter also bakes breads and terrific muffins, including what she calls "the best corn muffin ever." Homemade fruit pies are also a specialty. Closed October to May.

BREWSTER AFTER DARK

Performances at the **Cape Cod Repertory Theatre Company,** 3379 Rte. 6A, East Brewster, about 2½ miles east of Brewster center (☎ **508/896-1888**), are given Tuesday to Saturday at 8pm from early July to early September. In summer, this shoestring troupe tackles the Bard, as well as serious contemporary fare, at a 200-seat outdoor theater on the old Crosby estate (now state-owned and undergoing restoration). Tickets for outdoor performances are $6. In season, they also put on a Broadway-musical dinner revue Sunday nights at the **Old Sea Pines Inn** ($37.50 fixed-price; see "Where to Stay," above). Off-season they perform here and there; if you're lucky, you might find Chatham resident Julie Harris fronting a benefit. Call for off-season hours. Tickets cost $15 for adults and $8 for those under 22.

Hot local bands take the tiny stage seasonally at **The Woodshed,** at the Brewster Inn & Chowder House, 1993 Rte. 6A (☎ **508/896-7771**), a far cry from the glitzy discos on the southern shore. If your tastes run more to Raitt and Buffett than techno, you'll feel right at home in this dark, friendly dive. Cover charge $3 to $5.

2 The Harwiches

24 miles (39km) E of Sandwich; 32 miles (52km) S of Provincetown

Harwich Port is the quintessential sleepy seaside village, not too mucked up—as yet—by the creeping commercialization of Route 28. The town's main claim to fame is as the birthplace, in 1846, of commercial cranberry cultivation: The "bitter berry," as the Narragansetts called it, is now Massachusetts's leading agricultural product. The curious can find elucidating displays on this and other local distinctions at the Brooks Academy Museum in the inland town of Harwich. The incurious, or merely vacation-minded, can loll on the beach.

ESSENTIALS

GETTING THERE   After crossing either the Bourne or Sagamore bridge (see "Getting There," in chapter 2), head east on Route 6 and take exit 10 south along Route 124. Harwich is located at the intersection of Route 39, where the two routes converge. Head southwest to Harwich Port and West Harwich, both located on Route 28. East Harwich (more easily reached from Rte. 6's exit 11) is inland, a few miles northeast. Or fly into Hyannis (see "Getting There," in chapter 2).

VISITOR INFORMATION   Contact the **Harwich Chamber of Commerce,** Route 28, Harwich Port, MA 02646 (☎ 800/441-3199 or 508/432-1600; fax 508/430-2105; www.harwichcc.com; e-mail: harwichc@capecod.net), open late May to late September daily from 9am to 5pm; call for off-season hours. You can also contact the **Cape Cod Chamber of Commerce** (see "Visitor Information" in the "Brewster" section, above).

BEACHES & RECREATIONAL PURSUITS

BEACHES   The Harwich coast is basically one continuous beach punctuated by the occasional harbor. Harwich Port is so close to the sound that it's a snap to walk the block or two to the water—provided you find a parking place in town (try the lot near the Chamber of Commerce booth in the center of town). Parking right at the beach is pretty much limited to residents and renters, who can obtain a weekly sticker for $25 at the **Community Center,** 100 Oak St., Harwich (☎ **508/432-7638**).

- **Bank Street Beach,** at the end of Bank Street in Harwich Port: This is one of the few sound beaches in Harwich Port that has parking, but you will need a sticker. The sound beaches are generally warm and calm, very good beaches for swimming. This is a pretty (and popular) stretch where you'll see lots of families as well as the self-conscious college crowd.
- **Red River Beach,** off Uncle Venies Road south of Route 28 in South Harwich: This is the only sound beach in town offering parking for day-trippers (they still have to turn up early); the fee is $5 on weekdays or $10 weekends and holidays. Marked off with stone jetties, this narrow, 2,700-foot beach has full facilities.
- **Sand Pond,** off Great Western Road near Depot Street: This beach honors the weekly beach sticker, as do the two parking lots at Long Pond (between Rtes. 137 and 124).

- **Hinckleys Pond and Seymours Pond,** west of Route 124 and right off the Rail Trail, and **Bucks Pond,** off Depot Road at Route 39 northeast of Harwich. While Hinckleys and Bucks have limited parking, there is no parking sticker required. At Seymours, however, you will need a sticker.

BICYCLING   Transecting Harwich for about 5 miles, the Cape Cod Rail Trail skirts some pretty ponds in the western part before veering north and zigzagging toward Brewster along Route 124. For rentals and information, contact **Harwich Port Bike Co.,** 431 Rte. 28 (☎ 508/430-0200); they can also provide inline skates. A 24-hour bike rental costs $16.

BOATING   Paddle Cape Cod (☎ 888/226-6393 or 508/564-4051; www. paddlecapecod.com; e-mail: cccanoe@capecod.net) runs naturalist-guided trips throughout the Cape. Call for schedule and more information or see "Beaches & Recreational Pursuits" in the "Brewster" section, above.

   If you want to explore on your own by canoe, you can rent one by the day or the week at **Goose Hummock** in Orleans (☎ 508/255-2620) and paddle down the Herring River in West Harwich. Meandering from a reservoir south to the sound, the river is a natural herring run framed by a cattail marsh.

   Cape Sail, out of Saquatucket Harbor (☎ 508/896-2730), offers sailing lessons as well as private charters.

FISHING   There are six ponds available for fishing in the Harwich area, as well as extensive shellfishing in season; for details and a license, visit **Town Hall** at 732 Main St. in Harwich (☎ 508/430-7516). For supplies and instruction, visit **Fishing the Cape,** at the Harwich Commons, Routes 137 and 39 (☎ 508/432-1200); it's the official Cape headquarters for the **Orvis Saltwater Fly-Fishing School** (☎ 800/235-9763). Trips for two anglers cost $275 for a half day and $375 for a full day. Several deep-sea fishing boats operate out of Saquatucket Harbor (off Route 28, about a ½ mile east of Harwich Port), including the 33-footers *Fish Tale* (☎ 508/432-3783) and *Arlie Ex* (☎ 508/430-2454). The 65-foot *Yankee* (☎ 508/432-2520) is a party boat out of Saquatucket Harbor offering two 4-hour trips per day Monday through Saturday and one trip on Sundays. Trips cost $23 adults and $21 seniors and children. The deep-sea party boat *Golden Eagle* (☎ 508/432-5611), offering two fishing trips a day and evening bluefish trips Tuesday and Thursday, heads out from Wychmere Harbor. Rates for the *Golden Eagle* day trips are $21 for adults and $16 for children; the evening trips are $22 for adults and $16 for children.

GOLF   Both the championship 18-hole **Cranberry Valley Golf Course** at 183 Oak St. in Harwich (☎ 508/430-5234), which wends its way among cranberry bogs, and the 9-hole **Harwich Port Golf Club** on Forest and South streets in Harwich Port (☎ 508/432-0250), are open to the public. Harwich Port Golf Club charges $15 for 9 holes.

NATURE & WILDLIFE AREAS   The largest preserve in Harwich is the 245-acre **Bells Neck Conservation Area** north of Route 28 near the Dennis border. It encompasses the Herring River, ideal for birding and canoeing (see "Boating," above).

TENNIS   Public courts are available on a first-come, first-served basis at the Cape Cod Technical High School on Route 124 and Brooks Park on Oak Street, about a ¼ mile east of Harwich center off Route 29; for details, contact the **Harwich Recreation Department** (☎ 508/430-7553). Open late May through September, the **Wychmere Harbor Tennis Club** at 792 Main St. in Harwich Port (☎ 508/430-7012) comprises nine Har-Tru courts and two hard courts; lessons can be scheduled. Court time is a whopping $25 an hour.

HISTORICAL HARWICH

Brooks Academy Museum. 80 Parallel St. (at the intersection of Sisson Rd. and Main St., about 1 mile N of Harwich Port center). ☎ **508/432-8089.** Donations accepted. Early June to mid-Oct Tues–Fri 1–4pm. Closed mid-Oct to early June.

Gathered in an 1844 Greek Revival academy that offered the country's first courses in navigation, the collections of the Harwich Historical Society are good for a rainy afternoon's worth of wonderment. On permanent display is an extensive exhibition chronicling the early days of the cranberry industry, when harvesting was a back-breaking chore performed on hands and knees with a wooden scoop, mostly by migrant workers. (It simplified matters enormously once someone figured out that the bogs could be flooded and threshed so that the berries bob to the surface.) Other holdings include Native American tools, paintings by local artist C.D. Cahoon, nautical items of historical interest, and extensive textiles, imaginatively presented. The complex also includes a Revolutionary powder house and—kids might get a kick of out this—a nicely restored 1872 outhouse.

BASEBALL

The Harwich Mariners, part of the **Cape Cod Baseball League,** play at Whithouse Field behind the high school in Harwich. For a schedule, contact the **Harwich Chamber of Commerce** (☎ 508/432-1600), the **Harwich Recreation & Youth Department** (☎ 508/430-7553), or the **League** (☎ 508/432-6909).

KID STUFF

West Harwich gets some spillover from Dennis's overdevelopment, including such junior-tourist attractions as **Harbor Glen Miniature Golf** at 168 Rte. 28 (☎ 508/432-8240), the **Trampoline Center** at 296 Rte. 28 (☎ 508/432-8717), and **Bud's Go-Karts** at the intersection of Routes 28 and 39 (☎ 508/432-4964), which welcomes hot-rodders as young as 8, provided they meet the height requirement (54 inches). All three are open until 11pm in summer. For free self-entertainment, visit **Castle in the Clouds,** a community-built playground behind the Harwich Elementary School on South Street in Harwich. Young culture mavens might want to take in a performance at the **Harwich Junior Theatre** at 105 Division St. in West Harwich (☎ 508/432-2002), which has been satisfying summer customers since 1952; if you plan to stick around for a while, your youngsters could even take classes and possibly work their way onstage. Tickets cost $10 to $14.

SHOPPING

Route 28 harbors lots of minimalls and shops, big on gifts (on the trite side) and unsensational art. With a few exceptions, save your power shopping for Chatham.

ANTIQUES/COLLECTIBLES ✪ **The Barn at Windsong,** 245 Bank St., a ½ mile north of Harwich Port center, midway between Routes 28 and 39 (☎ 508/432-8281), is the kind of archetypal shop antiquers crave: a lovely old barn in the country, packed with premium goods. Offerings include furniture, glass, china, and rugs. Closed November through April.

The Mews at Harwich Port, 517 Rte. 28, in the center of town (☎ 508/432-6397), is a shop run by five specialist dealers. It attracts collectors with certain categories to fill out—such as handwoven baskets. Closed November through April.

ARTS & CRAFTS **Cape Cod Cooperage,** 1150 Queen Anne Rd., at the intersection of Route 137 (☎ 800/521-1809 or 508/432-0788), is the oldest surviving barrel factory in the state (in fact, the only one), and is packed to the rafters with useful wooden goods, mostly made on-site. You might come away with a naif-painted chest or just a set of Shaker pegs, but you're unlikely to depart empty-handed.

BOOKS   At **Wychmere Book & Coffee** at 587 Main St. (at the corner of Rte. 28 and Bank St.) in Harwichport (☎ **508/432-7868**), you'll find a large selection and a friendly staff.

WHERE TO STAY

In addition to the more expensive choices listed below, there are several affiliated above-average motels in Harwich. **The Tern Inn,** 91 Chase St., West Harwich (☎ **800/432-3718** or 508/432-3714; www.coastalinnkeepers.com), is in a quiet residential neighborhood. Summer rates are $89 to $130 double, and $500 to $925 per week for a cottage. The Tern has a small, unheated pool. Rooms do not have telephones, but all have televisions and minifridges. Most have air-conditioning. Just 75 yards from a wide Nantucket Sound beach, **The Commodore Inn,** 30 Earle Rd., West Harwich (☎ **800/368-1180** or 508/432-1180; www.commodoreinn.com), has lovely rooms resembling upscale condos with cathedral ceilings and handsome, functional furniture. Rates are $165 to $215 double and include a full buffet breakfast in season. All rooms have microwave ovens and minifridges, as well as air-conditioning, televisions, and telephones. Some have Jacuzzis and fireplaces. Closed December to March. **Sandpiper Beach Inn,** 16 Bank St., Harwich Port (☎ **800/433-2234** or 508/432-0485; www.coastalinnkeepers.com), is plunked right on a lovely Nantucket Sound beach. All rooms have air-conditioning, telephones, television, and fridges. Summer rates are $125 to $320 double, $295 to $310 for suites. Closed November to mid-April.

VERY EXPENSIVE

✪ **The Winstead Inn and Beach Resort.** 328 Bank St.; (S of Rte. 28 in the center of town), Harwich Port, MA 02646. ☎ **800/870-4405** or 508/432-4444. Fax 508/432-9152. www.winsteadinn.com. 32 units. A/C TV TEL. Summer $195–$325 double. Rates include continental breakfast. MC, V. Open year-round.

This property is composed of two buildings: the former Beach House Inn set on a private Nantucket Sound beach and the newly converted Winstead Inn nearby. The beach house is an antiques-filled 1920s inn with ship-like, narrow hallways leading to immaculate, spacious rooms. The original rooms still boast their varnished pine paneling, as well as updated whirlpool baths; and the four glorious front rooms each feature a fireplace or deck as well, plus sweeping views of Nantucket Sound. In fact, all but two of the rooms here have a view of the beach. The nearby Winstead, a handsome colonial-style building with a pool, has undergone a deluxe remodeling. In addition to air-conditioning, all rooms have ceiling fans (to circulate those ocean breezes), and amenities like hair dryers and minifridges. The inn is within walking distance of town, so you don't have to compete with summer traffic.

EXPENSIVE

✪ **The Augustus Snow House.** 528 Main St. (in the center of town), Harwich Port, MA 02646. ☎ **800/320-0528** or 508/430-0528. Fax 508/432-6638. www.augustussnow.com. E-mail: info@augustussnow.com. 6 units. A/C TV TEL. Summer $170–$225 double. Rates include full breakfast. AE, DISC, MC, V. Open year-round.

A local landmark for almost a century, you can't miss this Queen Anne Victorian with gabled dormers and wraparound veranda centrally located on Main Street. The house was precisely situated so that Captain Snow could look out the front door and see the ocean a block away at the end of Pilgrim Lane. Rooms are spacious, immaculate, and very comfortable, with interesting antique appointments throughout. All have fireplaces and minifridges. Several of the bathrooms are particularly unique, some with claw-foot tubs, old sink tables, and restored antique toilets. A new large room in the carriage house has a private entrance, fireplace, Jacuzzi tub, and shower. The full breakfast features such delicacies as peach kuchen, baked pears with raspberry and cream sauce, and cinnamon apple quiche. (Innkeeper Joyce Roth suggests you don't swim after breakfast.)

Dunscroft by the Sea. 24 Pilgrim Rd. (S of Rte. 28 near the beach), Harwich Port, MA 02646. ☎ **800/432-4345** or 508/432-0810. Fax 508/432-5134. www.dunscroftbythesea. com. E-mail: dunscroft@capecod.net. 8 units, 1 cottage. A/C TEL. Summer $165–$255 double; $295 cottage. Rates include full breakfast. AE, MC, V. No children under 12.

Most people, upon finding such a prime property (a block from town, 500 feet from the beach), would be tempted to keep it all to themselves. But this gracious shingled colonial-revival home had been taking in guests since 1950, so Alyce and Wally Cunningham decided to make the leap to innkeeping. They've enhanced the house and honeymoon cottage (formerly the chauffeur's quarters) with extensive renovations in a Valentine-ish vein. Several of the rooms have Jacuzzis and TVs/VCRs, including the cottage, which also has a kitchenette and a working fireplace. Alyce hails from Virginia originally, and her Southern hospitality is particularly evident in the bountiful breakfast, which may feature Virginia fried apples or Caribbean French toast.

WHERE TO DINE
MODERATE

♻ **The Cape SeaGrille.** 31 Sea St. (S of Rte. 28 in the center of town), Harwich Port. ☎ **508/432-4745.** Reservations recommended. Main courses $15–$23. AE, MC, V. June–Aug daily 5–10pm; call for off-season hours. Closed Dec–Mar. NEW AMERICAN.

Two ambitious chef/owners are the power behind the stove of this upscale enterprise occupying the pared-down, peach-toned shell of an ordinary beach house. The menu is under constant revision, the better to springboard off market finds, but among the keepers are a salmon carpaccio appetizer with grilled exotic mushrooms, lemon capers and Dijon sauce, and a grilled medley entree starring lobster, shrimp, and bacon-wrapped swordfish. City sophisticates who insist on creativity and innovation will find this the most consistently rewarding source in town.

L'Alouette. 787 Rte. 28 (about ½ mile E of the town center), Harwich Port. ☎ **508/ 430-0405.** Reservations recommended. Main courses $15–$23. AE, DC, DISC, MC, V. May–Oct Tues–Sun 5–9pm. Nov–late Feb and mid-Mar to Apr Wed–Sun 5–9pm. Closed late Feb to mid-Mar. CLASSIC FRENCH.

There's no way to fake the seductive aromas of an authentic French restaurant. The secrets are all in the stock, and chef Jean Louis Bastres, formerly of Biarritz, makes his from scratch. He's a strict classicist (none of this nouvelle nonsense): Specialties at this auberge-style restaurant include such time-honored tests of prowess as bouillabaisse and chateaubriand.

INEXPENSIVE

Seafood Sam's. 302 Rte. 28 (about ½ mile E of the town center), Harwich Port. ☎ **508/ 432-1422.** Most items under $12. DISC, MC, V. Mid-Feb to late Nov daily 11am–10pm. Closed late Nov to mid-Feb. SEAFOOD.

Strategically located within a big bounce of the Trampoline Center, this McDonald's-style clam shack—part of a Cape-wide chain—dishes out deep-fried seafood, fast.

PICNIC FARE

The Cafe at Thompson's Farm Market. 710 Main St./Rte. 28 (about ½ mile E of the town center), Harwich Port. ☎ **508/432-5415.**

Don't be dissuaded by the size: Yes, it's a full-size grocery store, but seek out the deli/bakery to throw together a beach lunch, or shop for some trendy comestibles.

SWEETS

✪ **Sundae School.** 606 Main St. (in the center of town), Harwich Port. ☎ **508/430-2444.** Closed mid-Oct to mid-May. ICE CREAM.

Another branch of the local chain (also in Dennisport and East Orleans), this is home-made ice cream and a sure crowd pleaser with the kids. Real whipped cream and real cherries will keep the parents happy, too.

THE HARWICHES AFTER DARK

Bishop's Terrace. 108 Rte. 28, West Harwich. ☎ **508/432-0253.** Cover varies.

There's usually a pops-oriented pianist playing in the barn-turned-bar, and on week-ends, you might encounter a jazz ensemble.

The Irish Pub. 126 Main St. (Rte. 28), West Harwich. ☎ **508/432-8808.** Cover varies.

For years, this has been the premier Irish bar on the Cape. It feels authentic because it is. A variety of live entertainment (it could be Irish music, karaoke, or anything in between) Thursday to Saturday in season is usually rollicking good fun.

3 Chatham

32 miles (52km) E of Sandwich; 24 miles (39km) S of Provincetown

Sticking out like a sore elbow (and out of the way of much of the Cape's tourist flow), Chatham was one of the first spots to attract early explorers. Samuel de Champlain stopped by in 1606 but got into a tussle with the prior occupants over some copper cooking pots; he ended up leaving in a hurry. The first colonist to stick around was William Nickerson of Yarmouth, who befriended a local *sachem* (tribal leader) and built a house beside his wigwam in 1656. One prospered; the other—for obvious reasons—didn't. To this day, listings for Nickersons still occupy a half page in the Cape Cod phone book.

Chatham, along with Provincetown, is the only area on the Cape to support a com-mercial fishing fleet—against increasing odds. Overfishing has resulted in closely monitored limits to give the stock time to bounce back. Boats must now go out as far as 100 miles to catch their fill. Despite the difficulties, it's a way of life few locals would willingly relinquish. As in Provincetown, there's surprisingly little animosity between the hard-working residents and the summerers at play, perhaps because it's clear that discerning tourist dollars are helping to preserve this lovely town for all.

ESSENTIALS

GETTING THERE   After crossing either the Bourne or Sagamore bridge (see "Get-ting There" in chapter 2), head east on Route 6 and take exit 11 south (Rte. 137) to Route 28. From this intersection, the village of South Chatham is about a ½ mile west, and West Chatham is about 1½ miles east. Chatham itself is about 2 miles far-ther east on Route 28.

To fly to Chatham, take a commercial flight into Hyannis (see "Getting There," in chapter 2), or contact **Chatham Air Charter** at the Chatham Municipal Airport (☎ **508/945-1976**); they can take up to five people in their twin-engine planes.

Air Service Inc. (☎ **800/872-1704**) can transport up to three people in their single-engine planes.

VISITOR INFORMATION   Visit the **Cape Cod Chamber of Commerce** (see "Visitor Information" in the "Brewster" section, above) or the **Chatham Chamber of Commerce,** 533 Main St., Chatham, MA 02633 (☎ **800/715-5567** or 508/945-5199; www.chathamcapecod.org), or the new **Chatham Chamber booth** (no phone) at the intersection of Routes 137 and 28. Hours for both are July and August Monday to Saturday from 10am to 6pm, Sunday from noon to 6pm; closed late October to April. Call for off-season hours.

A STROLL AROUND CHATHAM

Parking on Main Street can be a challenge at the height of summer, so pretend you're a turn-of-the-century traveler and start out at the **Chatham Railroad Museum** on 153 Depot St. (closed mid-September to mid-June), 1 block north of Main Street at the western end of town. You can't miss it: It's a gaudy 1887 Victorian station in the "Railroad Gothic" style, painted yellow with fanciful russet ornamentation. The building itself is full of railroading memorabilia, and the big exhibits—antique passenger cars—are out back.

If you've got children along, they'll surely want to stretch their legs (and imaginations) at the **Play-a-Round Park,** opposite the Railroad Museum. Dreamed up by prominent playground designer Robert Leathers, it's a marvelous maze of tubes and rope ladders, slides, and swings. The only way you'll get going again is to promise to come back.

Head west to the end of Depot Street and right on Old Harbor Road, which, followed past Main Street, becomes State Harbor Road. About a mile farther along, past Oyster Pond, you'll encounter the **Old Atwood House and Museums** at 347 Stage Harbor Rd. (☎ **508/945-2493;** closed October to mid-June). The 1752 house itself shelters the odds and ends collected by the Chatham Historical Society over the past 7 decades; piece by piece, they tell the story of the town. The Society even managed to save an entire 1947 "fishing camp," a run-down cottage that looks as if the occupant just stepped out to check a line.

Heading back toward Main Street, bear right on Cross Street and look for Chase Park and Bowling Green, presided over by the Old Grist Mill, built in the late 18th century. You might actually try some lawn bowling along the lovingly tended greens before returning to Main Street, where the shops are too prolific and special to pass up. Then head eastward toward the shore, but be sure to duck into the **Mayo House** at 540 Main St. (☎ **508/945-4084**), a sweet little three-quarter Cape built in 1818. Entrance is free, and—if you've studiously avoided lengthy historical house tours so far—it can give you, in just a couple of minutes, a good sense of what life might have been like here in centuries past.

Main Street veers right when it reaches the shore. Continue along for about a ¼ mile to view the **Chatham Light,** an 1876 beacon not open to the public, but still in operation: Its light shines 15 miles out to sea. This is a good vantage point from which to marvel over the "break" that burst through Chatham's barrier beach in 1987. In the years since, the newly created island, South Beach, has already glommed onto the coastline, becoming a peninsula. This is one landscape that rarely stays put for long.

Retrace your steps northward along the shore. In about ¾ mile, you'll pass the grand ✪ **Chatham Bars Inn** at Shore Road and Seaview Street (☎ **800/527-4884** or 508/945-0096), which started out life as a private hunting lodge in 1914. Passersbys are

Chatham Area

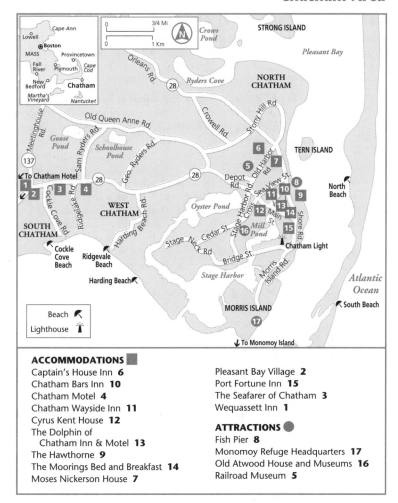

welcome to look around the lobby, restored to reflect its original Victorian splendor. Linger on the porch over coffee or a drink, if you like, before pressing on to the **Chatham Fish Pier,** about an ⅛ mile farther along Shore Road (☎ **508/945-5177**). If you've timed your visit right (from noon on), the trawlers should just now be bringing in the catch of the day: You can observe the haul from an observation deck. Also have a look at *The Provider,* an intriguing outdoor sculpture by Woods Hole artist Sig Pursin.

☕ **Winding Down** When you've had enough, or the insects seem to be insisting that you head on home, go back to Main Street down Seaview Street, past the Chatham Seaside Links golf course. One long block later (about a ½ mile), you're back in the center of town. You can relax and unwind at the **Chatham Wayside Inn** at 512 Main St. (☎ **508/945-5550**). Secure a table on the greenery-curtained patio and watch the world go by, as you fortify yourself with regionally inspired snacks and sweets on the large screened porch.

BEACHES & RECREATIONAL PURSUITS

BEACHES Chatham has an unusual array of beach styles, from the peaceful shores of the Nantucket Sound to the treacherous, shifting shoals along the Atlantic. For information on beach stickers ($8 per day, $35 per week), call the **Permit Department** on George Ryder Road in West Chatham (☎ **508/945-5180**).

- **Cockle Cove Beach, Ridgevale Beach,** and **Hardings Beach:** Lined up along the sound, each at the end of its namesake road south of Route 28, these family-pleasing beaches offer gentle surf suitable for all ages, as well as full facilities.
- **Forest Beach:** No longer an officially recognized town beach (there's no life-guard), this sound landing near the Harwich border is still popular, especially among surfboarders.
- **Oyster Pond Beach,** off Route 28: Only a block from Chatham's Main Street, this sheltered saltwater pond (with rest rooms) swarms with children.
- **Chatham Light Beach:** Located directly below the lighthouse parking lot (where stopovers are limited to 30 minutes), this narrow stretch of sand is easy to get to: Just walk down the stairs. Currents here can be tricky and swift, though, so swimming is discouraged.
- **South Beach:** A former island jutting out slightly to the south of the Chatham Light, this glorified sandbar can be equally dangerous, so heed posted warnings and content yourself with strolling or, at most, wading.
- **North Beach:** Extending all the way south from Orleans, this 5-mile barrier beach is accessible from Chatham only by boat; if you don't have your own, you can take the **Beachcomber,** a water taxi, which leaves from the fish pier. Call ☎ **508/945-5265** to schedule your trip. The round-trip cost is $12 for adults, $8 for children 3 to 15, and free for children under 3. Inquire about other possible drop-off points if you'd like to beach around. They also offer sunset cruises and seal watches. See "Boating" below.

BICYCLING Though Chatham has no separate recreational paths per se, a demarcated bike/blading lane makes a scenic, 8-mile circuit of town, heading south onto "The Neck," east to the Chatham Light, up Shore Road all the way to North Chatham, and back to the center of town. A descriptive brochure prepared by the **Chatham Chamber of Commerce** (☎ **800/715-5567** or 508/945-5199) shows the suggested route, and there are lots of lightly trafficked detours worth taking. Rentals are available at **Bikes & Blades,** 195 Crowell Rd., Chatham (☎ **508/945-7600**); rates are $15 per day; $20 per day for inline skates (including pads).

BIRD WATCHING In summer both the **Cape Cod Museum of Natural History** (☎ **508/896-3867**) and the Wellfleet Bay Wildlife chapter of the **Audubon Society** (☎ **508/349-2615**) offer bird-watching trips to the **Monomoy National Wildlife Refuge** on North Monomoy Island. On the Audubon Society tours of North Monomoy (3 hours) or South Monomoy (4 and 7 hours), after a 10-minute boat ride from Chatham, you'll embark on a guided tour, where you'll encounter a variety of species—from herring gulls and sandpipers to black-bellied plovers and willets. Tours cost around $30 to $60 and are recommended not just for avid bird watchers, but for anyone who enjoys the outdoors.

BOATING Paddle Cape Cod(☎ **888/226-6393** or 508/564-4051; www. paddlecapecod.com; e-mail: cccanoe@capecod.net) runs naturalist-guided trips throughout the Cape. Call for schedule and more information, or see "Beaches & Recreational Pursuits" in the "Brewster" section, above.

If you want to explore on your own by kayak, you can rent one (see below) and paddle down the Oyster River, past Hardings Beach, and over to Morris Island. You can also explore Pleasant Bay and reach the inside shore of the Outer Beach.

NautiJane's Boat Rental at 337 Rte. 28 in Harwich Port (☎ **508/432-7079**) also offers lessons and rentals on Ridgevale Beach in Chatham and at the Wequasett Inn: Available craft include kayaks, Sunfish, surfbikes, and sailboats up to 22 feet. Kayaks rent for $25 per hour or $39 for 2 hours, Sailboats rent for $65 to $95 for a couple hours or $115 to $175 for half a day.

Seaworthy vessels, from surf- and sailboards to paddle craft and Sunfish, can be rented from **Monomoy Sail and Cycle** at 275 Rte. 28 in North Chatham (☎ **508/945-0811**). Pleasant Bay, the Cape's largest bay, is the best place to play for those with sufficient experience; if the winds don't seem to be going your way, try Forest Beach on the South Chatham shore. Kayaks and sailboards rent for $45 for 24 hours; two-person kayaks rent for $55 for 24 hours.

The **Beachcomber** (☎ **508/945-5265**) is a new enterprise providing boat trips and water-taxi service in Chatham, as well as naturalist-guided trips. Chatham native Paul Avellar's business consists of three boats leaving out of Ryders Cove (for tours of Pleasant Bay and sunset cruises), Chatham Fish Pier (water-taxi service to North Beach; see "Beaches," above), and Stage Harbor (seal-watching cruises). Seal watches and Pleasant Bay trips cost $18 for adults, $12 for children 3 to 15, and are free for children under 3.

FISHING   Chatham has five ponds and lakes that permit fishing; Goose Pond off Fisherman's Landing is among the top spots. For saltwater fishing sans boat, try the fishing bridge on Bridge Street at the southern end of Mill Pond. First, though, get a license at **Town Hall** at 549 Main St. in Chatham (☎ **508/945-5101**). If you hear the deep sea calling, sign on with the ***Booby Hatch*** (☎ **508/430-2312**), a 33-foot sportfishing boat, or the 31-foot ***Banshee*** (☎ **508/945-0403**), both berthed in Stage Harbor. Sportfishing rates average around $550 to $600 for 8 hours. Shellfishing licenses are available at the **Permit Dept.** on George Ryder Road in West Chatham (☎ **508/945-5180**).

FITNESS   The **Chatham Health & Swim Club** at 251 Crowell Rd. in Chatham (☎ **508/945-3555**) offers bicycles and treadmills, weights and aerobics, steam rooms and a whirlpool, a five-lane indoor lap pool, and more. Day rates are $15.

GOLF   Once part of the Chatham Bars Inn property and now owned by the town, the scenic 9-hole, par-34 **Chatham Seaside Links** at 209 Seaview St. in Chatham (☎ **508/945-4774**) isn't very challenging, but fun for neophytes; inquire about instruction. A 9-hole round costs $15.

NATURE & WILDLIFE AREAS   Heading southeast from the Hardings Beach parking lot, the 2-mile, round-trip **Seaside Trail** offers beautiful parallel panoramas of Nantucket Sound and Oyster Pond River; keep an eye out for nesting pairs of horned lark. Access to 40-acre Morris Island, southwest of the Chatham Light, is easy: You can walk or drive across and start right in on a marked ¾-mile trail. Heed the high tides, as advised, though—they can come in surprisingly quickly, leaving you stranded.

The **Beachcomber** (☎ **508/945-5265**) runs seal-watching cruises out of Stage Harbor. Parking is behind the former Main Street School just on the left before the rotary. The cruises cost $18 for adults, $12 for children 3 to 15, and are free for children under 3.

Chatham's natural bonanza lies southward: The uninhabited ✪ **Monomoy Islands,** 2,750 acres of brush-covered sand favored by some 285 species of migrating birds, is the perfect pit stop along the Atlantic Flyway. Harbor and gray seals are catching on, too: Hundreds now carpet the coastline from late November through May. If you go out during that time, you won't have any trouble seeing them—they're practically unavoidable. Both the **Wellfleet Bay Wildlife Sanctuary,** operated by the Audubon Society (☎ **508/349-2615**), and Brewster's **Cape Cod Museum of Natural History** (☎ **508/896-3867**) offer guided trips. The Audubon 3-, 4-, or 7-hour trips take place April through November, and they cost $30 to $60 per person. The boat to Monomoy leaves from Chatham, and the trip includes a naturalist-guided nature hike. About a dozen times each summer, the museum organizes sleepovers in the island's only surviving structure—a clapboard "keeper's house" flanked by an 1849 lighthouse. The cost is $130 per person (dinner and breakfast provided), and the trip lasts from 10am until returning the next day at 1pm. Reservations should be made at least a month prior, as there is only space for six people in the three rooms. It's just you and the birds and seals and lots of deer, plus various other species that are harder to spot.

TENNIS   Free public courts are located near the Railroad Museum on Depot Street and at Chatham High School on Crowell Road; for details contact the **Chatham Recreation Department** (☎ **508/945-5100**). In addition, you may be able to rent one of the three courts at the **Chatham Bars Inn** on Shore Road (☎ **508/945-6759**) or the **Chatham Beach and Tennis Club** at 12 Main St. (☎ **508/945-0464**). Courts at Chatham Bars Inn cost a whopping $30 an hour.

CHATHAM HISTORICAL SIGHTS

Chatham Railroad Museum. 153 Depot Rd. (off Main St., 1 block N of the rotary). No phone. Donations accepted. Mid-June to mid-Sept Tues–Sat 10am–4pm. Closed mid-Sept to mid-June.

Even if you're not a railroad fanatic, it's worth visiting this beautiful 1887 depot to imagine the sights that would greet a Victorian visitor. To begin, the building itself is a "Railroad Gothic" work of wooden art, topped by a tapering turret. Inside you'll find volunteers dispensing lore and explaining the many displays. The museum's major holding is lined up in back: a "walk-through" 1918 New York caboose.

Mayo House. 540 Main St. (in the center of town). ☎ **508/945-4084.** Free admission. Mid-June to Sept Tues–Thurs 11am–4pm. Closed Oct to mid-June.

For a speedy version of the historical-house tour (these can get awfully drawn out), duck into this cheerful little yellow cottage, a three-quarter Cape that has stood its ground on Main Street since 1818. Ask all the questions you like—or just zip through, admiring the needlepoint handiwork of local lasses long gone, or the economy of movement required to subsist in one of the tiny dormered bedrooms.

The Old Atwood House Museum. 347 Stage Harbor Rd. (about ⅔ mile S of Main St.). ☎ **508/945-2493.** Admission $3 adults, $1 students under 12. Mid-June to Oct Tues–Fri 1–4pm. Closed Oct to mid-June.

For further glimpses of Chatham's past, visit this gambrel-roofed 1752 homestead, divided (rather awkwardly) into assorted wings celebrating different phases and products of the local culture. The house harbors all sorts of odd collections, from seashells to the complete works of early–20th-century author Joseph C. Lincoln, a renowned Cape writer whose hokey books are avidly collected by locals. One room definitely worth a visit is the New Gallery, featuring admirably direct portraits of crusty sea-goers by local artist Frederick Stallknecht. His work, unfortunately, was always overshadowed by the oeuvre of his mother, Alice Stallknecht Wight, who executed pretend-primitive murals of villagers enacting religious scenes (a contemporary

Christ-as-fisherman, for instance, celebrating the Last Supper). Her work occupies an adjoining barn; see if you think she deserves it. By far, the most enchanting exhibit on hand is an entire 1947 fishing "camp"—a one-room old boy's club salvaged, complete with shabby furnishings, from the onslaught of the winter storms that brought about the "break" of 1987.

BASEBALL

The Chatham Athletics (or "A's"), part of the **Cape Cod Baseball League,** play at Veterans Field off Depot Street. For a schedule, contact the **Chatham Chamber of Commerce** (☎ 800/715-5567 or 508/945-5199), the **Chatham Recreation Center** (☎ **508/945-5175**), or the **League** (☎ **508/432-6909**).

KID STUFF

The **Play-a-Round Park** on Depot Street (see "A Stroll Around Chatham," above) will suffice to keep kids entertained for hours on end. Treat them to lunch at the quirkily casual Breakaway Cafe at the Chatham airport (perhaps followed by a sightseeing flight?). The weekly ✪ **band concerts** (☎ 508/945-5199) at Kate Gould Park, held Friday nights in summer, are perfectly gauged for underage enjoyment: There's usually a bunny-hop at some point in the evening. Junior connoisseurs get a chance, once a year in late July, to enjoy some really fine music, when the Monomoy Chamber Ensemble puts on a free morning children's performance at the **Monomoy Theatre** (☎ **508/945-1589**), and musicals there are always fun.

SHOPPING

Chatham's tree-shaded Main Street, lined with specialty stores, offers a terrific opportunity to shop and stroll. The goods tend to be on the conservative side, but every so often, you'll happen upon a hedonistic delight.

ANTIQUES/COLLECTIBLES   ✪ **The Spyglass,** 618 Main St., is located in the center of town (☎ 508/945-9686). Ancient nautical instruments are the raison d'être of this intriguing shop: antique telescopes, sextants, barometers, captain's desks, maps, and charts.

ARTS & CRAFTS   The **Artful Hand Gallery,** 459 Main St., in the center of town (☎ **508/945-4933**), Boston's premier purveyor of superlative contemporary crafts, is always worth a visit for colorful and intriguing fine crafts and gifts.

Headed for such prestigious outlets as Neiman Marcus, the handblown glassworks of James Holmes originate at **Chatham Glass,** 758 Main St., just west of the Chatham rotary (☎ 508/945-5547), where you can literally look over their shoulders as the pieces take shape. Luscious colors are their hallmark; the intense hues, combined with a purity of form at once traditional and cutting-edge contemporary, add up to objects that demand to be coveted.

At **Chatham Pottery,** 2058 Rte. 28, east of intersection with Route 137 (☎ **508/ 430-2191**), striking graphics characterize the collaborative work of Gill Wilson (potter) and Margaret Wilson-Grey (glazer). Their work consists primarily of blue block-print-style designs set against off-white stoneware. The most popular design may be the etched pair of swimming fish, based on sketches over 100 years old. It's a look that's somewhat addictive. Luckily, it's available in everything from platters and bowls to lamps and tiles.

One of Chatham's oldest and most respected galleries is **Falconer's,** 492 Main St., Chatham (☎ **508/945-2867**), which started by showing just the work of Marguerite Falconer: oil paintings of Cape Cod scenes. Since 1991, her daughter Susan has managed the gallery and expanded the work on display to include some of the more interesting fine crafts available in town. This is a good place to look for that one-of-a-kind gift.

BOOKS   **Yellow Umbrella Bookstore,** 501 Main St., in the center of town (☎ 508/945-0144), offers both new and used books (from rare volumes to paper-backs perfect for a disposable beach read). This full-service, all-ages bookstore invites protracted browsing.

Cabbages and Kings Bookstore, 628 Main St., in the center of town (☎ 508/945-1603), carries books, toys, and cards. They have frequent in-store author signings as well as special events held at the Chatham Bars Inn.

FASHION   Catering to fashionable parents and their kids, ages newborn well into the teens, **The Children's Shop,** 515 Main St., in the center of town (☎ 508/945-0234), is the best children's clothing store in a 100-mile radius. While according a nod to doting grannies with such classics as hand-smocked party dresses, Ginny Nickerson also stays up-to-speed on what kids themselves prefer.

The flagship store of **Puritan Clothing Company** is at 573 Main St., Chatham (☎ 508/945-0326). This venerable institution, with stores all over the Cape, has updated its clothing considerably in the last 10 years. You'll find a wide range of quality men's and women's wear, including Polo, Nautica, Eileen Fisher, and Teva, at good prices.

Another Cape Cod institution, the elite **Mark, Fore & Strike** at 482 Main St., Chatham (☎ 508/945-0568), offers upscale and classic men's and women's sports-wear. There's also a branch in Osterville.

GIFTS/HOME DECOR   For quintessentially Cape-y gifts, stop in the **Regatta Shop,** 483 Main St., Chatham (☎ 800/432-1365 or 503/945-4999). It's a colorful shop with popular regional gift items like Claire Murray rugs, boat models, wedge-wood, china, and the intriguing weather glass that supposedly predicts the weather.

WHERE TO STAY

Chatham's lodging choices tend to be more expensive than those of neighboring towns, because it's considered a chichi place to vacation. But for those allergic to fussy, fancy B&Bs and inns, Chatham has several good motel options.

Practically across the street from the Chatham Bars Inn, **The Hawthorne,** 196 Shore Rd. (☎ 508/945-0372; www.thehawthorne.com) is a very basic, no-frills motel with one of the best locations in town: right on the water, with striking views of Chatham Harbor, Pleasant Bay, and the Atlantic Ocean. Rates are $150 to $170 double.

The Seafarer of Chatham, 2079 Rte. 28 (about a ½ mile east of Rte. 137), West Chatham (☎ 800/786-2772 or 508/432-1739; www.seafarerofchatham.com), is a lovely, personable, well-run motel on Route 28. Though it does not have a pool, it's only about a ½ mile from Ridgevale Beach. Rates are $120 to $145 double.

The least expensive option is **The Chatham Motel,** 1487 Main St./Rte. 28, Chatham (☎ 800/770-5545 or 508/945-2630; www.chathammotel.com), 1½ miles from Hardings Beach. Look for the shingled motel with yellow shutters. There's an outdoor pool, shuffleboard, and plenty of BBQ grills. Summer rates are $115 double, $165 for suites.

VERY EXPENSIVE

✪ **Chatham Bars Inn.** Shore Rd. (off Seaview St., about ½ mile NW of the town center), Chatham, MA 02633. ☎ **800/527-4884** or 508/945-0096. Fax 508/945-5491. www.chathambarsinn.com. E-mail: welcome@chathambarsinn.com. 205 units. A/C TV TEL. Summer $210–$420 double; $425–$540 1-bedroom suite; $580–$1,300 2-bedroom suite. AE, CB, DC, MC, V.

Set majestically above the beach in Chatham and commanding views out to a barrier beach and the Atlantic Ocean beyond, the grand old Chatham Bars Inn is the premier hotel on Cape Cod. A private hunting lodge built for a Boston family in 1914, this curved and colonnaded brick building—surrounded by 26 shingled cottages on 20 acres—has regained its glory days with recent renovations. The latest undertaking is a Victorian makeover, meant to lend the lovely behemoth a more imposing air. The large and cushy lobby clearly invites lingering, as the professional staff bustles around fluffing pillows and tending to guests' every whim. The best spot to take in the grandeur—as well as the sweeping ocean views—is the breezy veranda, from whence you can order a drink (make mine an old-fashioned) and recline in an Adirondack chair. Most rooms have had tasteful makeovers within the last few years; all have VCRs (borrow classics and some new selections gratis), iron/ironing boards, hair dryers and minifridges; many have private balconies with views of the beach or the prettily land-scaped grounds. Cottage rooms are cheery with painted furniture and Waverly fabrics.

Dining/Diversions: Options include the formal Main Dining Room (see "Where to Dine," below); the new fireplaced Tavern, with choices like burgers, ribs, and grilled fish; and the seasonal Beach House Grill located right on the beach, which, in addition to offering a breakfast buffet and lunch (7 to 10am and 11:30am to 3pm, respectively), puts on a fixed-price theme feast with live bands 3 evenings a week.

Amenities: There is an outdoor heated pool beside the ¼-mile private beach, where you can also catch a complimentary launch to Nauset Beach; three all-weather tennis courts and a putting green (Seaside Links, a 9-hole course open to the public, adjoins the resort; guests play for a fee); plus shuffleboard, croquet, and volleyball. There is also a basic fitness room. "Beach Buddies," a complimentary children's program for ages 3½ and up, is available morning through night in summer; baby-sitters are on call for younger guests. Room service is available from 7am to 10pm in season, 7am to 9pm off-season, and the concierge can offer advice on local excursions.

✪ **Pleasant Bay Village.** 1191 Orleans Rd./Rte. 28 (about 3 miles N of Chatham center), Chathamport, MA 02633. ☎ **800/547-1011** or 508/945-1133. Fax 508/945-9701. www. pleasantbayvillage.com. E-mail: pbv@cape.com. 58 units. A/C TV TEL. Summer $165–$255 double; $355–$455 1- or 2-bedroom suite (for 4 occupants). AE, MC, V. Closed Nov–Apr.

Set across the street from Pleasant Bay, a few minutes' walk from Pleasant Bay beach, this is one fancy motel (with prices set accordingly). Owner Howard Gamsey is a prodigious gardener: Over the past ¼ century, he has transformed this property into a playful Zen paradise, where waterfalls (five) cascade through colorful rock gardens into a stone-edged pool dotted with lily pads and flashing koi. Actually, he has poured that kind of attention into the entire 6-acre complex. The rooms and cottages, done up in restful pastels, are unusually pleasant. Many bathrooms feature marble counter-tops and stone floors. Howard is an art collector, and all rooms display wonderful pieces he has picked up at Wellfleet's finest galleries. All rooms have hair dryers and refrigerators; suites have kitchenettes. The breakfast room features antique kilims, crewel curtains, and antique tables. In summer, you can order lunch from the grill without having to leave your place at the heated pool. In July and August, dinner is also served here.

✪ **Wequassett Inn Resort and Golf Club.** 2173 Rte. 28 (about 5 miles NW of the town center, on Pleasant Bay), Chatham, MA 02633. ☎ **800/225-7125** or 508/432-5400. Fax 508/432-5032. www.wequassett.com. 104 units. A/C MINIBAR TV TEL. Summer $315–$800 double. AE, CB, DC, DISC, MC, V. Closed late Nov to mid-Apr.

A virtual village occupying its own little "crescent on the water" (the Algonquin name for Round Cove on Pleasant Bay), this low-key, 22-acre complex now has an 18-hole golf course adjacent called Cape Cod National Golf Club. Inn guests enjoy exclusive non-member privileges to the new course. Tucked amid the woods along the shore, 15 modest dwellings, built in the 1940s, harbor roomy quarters done up in an opulent country-style: They cost a bit more than the 56 more modern "villa" rooms but, with their picturesque settings, are definitely worth the surcharge. This is one of those places where—well-housed, well-fed, and pleasantly occupied indeed—you're assured of a temporary respite from the "real" world. And that has its price.

Dining/Diversions: The 18th-century Eben Ryder House is home to an elegant and very expensive restaurant with lovely Pleasant Bay views. Three meals a day are served here and are open to the public. Jackets are preferred for gentlemen in the evenings.

Amenities: Guests have access (for a fee) to four all-weather Plexipave tennis courts, plus a pro shop. Bikes and water crafts—sailboards, Sunfish, Daysailers, and Hobie Cats—may be rented on-site. Croquet and volleyball equipment may be borrowed gratis. A fitness room (with weights and aerobics videotapes) adjoins the heated pear-shaped pool set at the neck of Clam Point, a calm beach. Nauset Beach is a 15-minute ride via the inn's Power Skiff (cost $10); bay tours and fishing charters can also be arranged.

Instruction is available in tennis (there are two pros on-site), sailing (coordinated by Cape Cod Water Sports), and saltwater fly-fishing (a branch of the Orvis School); inquire about clinic packages. Complimentary van service is offered to two public golf courses, Cranberry Valley in Harwich and Captain's Course in Brewster, and to the private and exclusive new Cape Cod National Golf Club, a challenging course with water views (cost: $100 per round plus $20 for a cart). Van service is also available to Chatham and Orleans villages for shopping; box lunches are available on request. A concierge is on hand to recommend activities; a recreation manager to facilitate them.

EXPENSIVE

✪ **Captain's House Inn.** 369–377 Old Harbor Rd. (about ½ mile N of the rotary), Chatham, MA 02633. ☎ **800/315-0728** or 508/945-0127. Fax 508/945-0866. www. captainshouseinn.com. E-mail: info@captainshouse.com. 19 units. A/C TEL. Summer $125 single; $165–$375 double. Rates include full breakfast and afternoon tea. AE, DISC, MC, V.

This 1839 Greek Revival house set—along with a cottage and carriage house—on 2 meticulously maintained acres is a shining example of its era and style. The rooms, named for clipper ships, are richly furnished, with a preponderance of canopied four-posters, beamed ceilings, and, in some cases, brick hearths. All have hair dryers, robes, and slippers. Most have TV/VCRs, and some are equipped with Jacuzzis. Bikes are available for guests intent on exploring. Morning repast is served at non-communal tables (a thoughtful touch for those of us slow to rev up, sociability-wise), and the window-walled breakfast room is also the site of a traditional tea—presided over by innkeeper Jan McMasters, formerly of Bournemouth in Great Britain, who knows how to pour a proper cuppa.

Chatham Wayside Inn. 512 Main St. (in the center of town), Chatham, MA 02633. ☎ **800/391-5734** or 508/945-5550. Fax 508/945-3407. www.waysideinn.com. E-mail: info@waysideinn.com. 56 units. A/C TV TEL. Summer $165–$265 double; $285–$365 suite; off-season packages available. DISC, MC, V.

Centrally located on Chatham's Main Street, this former stagecoach stop, dating from 1860, has undergone a thoroughly modern renovation. Don't expect any musty antique trappings: it's lush carpeting, a warehouse's worth of Waverly fabrics, and polished reproduction furnishings, including four-posters. There's an outdoor heated pool in the back. The restaurant serves sophisticated New American fare, indoors and out, and the prize rooms boast patios or balconies overlooking the town bandstand. This is one of the few inns on the Cape with fully handicapped-accessible rooms and restaurant.

MODERATE

The Cyrus Kent House Inn. 63 Cross St. (1 block S of Main St. in the center of town), Chatham, MA 02633. ☎ **800/338-5368** or tel/fax 508/945-9104. www.capecodtravel.com/cyruskent. E-mail: cyrus@cape.com. 11 units. A/C TV TEL. Summer $155–$185 double; $205–$225 suite; $290 2-bedroom suite. Rates include continental breakfast. AE, MC, V. No children under 8.

Built in 1877, when sea captains lived like modern-day software moguls, this tall Victorian beauty was lavished with the latest in fancy fixings, including marble fireplaces (in both the butterscotch-yellow parlor and the wainscoted dining room) and a heavy helping of decorative plasterwork. Rooms, with very high ceilings, have canopy beds and are elegantly decorated with antiques. Fireplaces grace each of the slightly more modern carriage-house suites, rendered light and airy by a lofty Palladian window on the top floor and, below, French doors that give onto the garden. You'll find an open hearth in the lovely country kitchen. In the morning, an elaborate continental breakfast (perhaps hot fruit compote, oatmeal brûlée, or baked French toast) is served on individual tables set with Limoges china and sterling silver. New innkeepers Sandra and Steve Goldman have worked hard on recent renovations, improvements, and landscaping.

The Dolphin of Chatham. 352 Main St. (at the E end of Main St.), Chatham, MA 02633-2428. ☎ **800/688-5900** or 508/945-0070. Fax 508/945-5945. www.dolphininn.com. E-mail: romance@dolphininn.com. 34 units, 3 cottages. A/C TV TEL. Summer $149–$209 double; $209–$275 2-bedroom suite; cottages $1,700 weekly. Rates include continental breakfast. AE, DC, DISC, MC, V.

With an 1805 main inn building, motel units, and several cottages, The Dolphin offers a wide range of lodging options in the heart of Chatham. Even on exquisitely groomed Main Street, this property's extensive and colorful gardens stand out. The main inn has seven individually decorated rooms with romantic touches like beamed ceilings, canopied beds, and lacy curtains. The rest of the units are standard motel issue, except for the honeymoon suite, which is housed in a whimsical windmill. All rooms have minifridges and hair dryers, and several have Jacuzzis. In the center of the complex is a heated outdoor pool and hot tub with a pool bar that serves lunch and drinks. The inn also has a terrific bar area, serving light dinner fare, where guests can watch the world go by from a screened porch overlooking Main Street. Lighthouse Beach is a pleasant stroll away.

The Moorings Bed and Breakfast. 326 Main St. (at the E end of Main St.), Chatham, MA 02633. ☎ **800/320-0848** or 508/945-0848. Fax 508/945-1577. www.mooringscapecod.com. E-mail: moorings@capecom.net. 14 units, 1 cottage. A/C TV TEL. Summer $140–$198 double; $180–$225 suite; cottages $1,765 weekly. Rates include full breakfast. AE, DISC, MC, V.

This is a charming, well-run property on the east end of Chatham's Main Street. Whether you end up in the main house, a Victorian beauty built by Admiral Charles H. Rockwell, or the individualized units in the carriage houses in the back, you'll enjoy a full breakfast in the gazebo surrounded by flower gardens. Several rooms in the carriage houses are spacious, with kitchenettes and private decks or courtyards. Some rooms have VCRS and hair dryers. All are immaculate and quaintly decorated, joined by a central courtyard area and porches lined with rocking chairs. In addition, everything you need to enjoy Chatham's winding roads and beautiful beaches is provided: bikes, beach chairs, and umbrellas.

✪ **Moses Nickerson House.** 364 Old Harbor Rd. (about ½ mile N of Main St.), Chatham, MA 02633. ☎ **800/628-6972** or 508/945-5859. Fax 508/945-7087. www.capecodtravel. com/mosesnickersonhouse. E-mail: tmnhi@mediaone.net. 7 units. A/C TV TEL. Summer $139–$199 double. Rates include full breakfast and afternoon tea. AE, DISC, MC, V.

Your host George "I am not Moses" Watts and his wife Linda run this gem of a B&B with a sense of humor mixed with gracious hospitality. A grand captain's home in the classicist style, this 1839 manse is every inch devoted to stylish comfort. Whether you opt for a canopied bed with freshly scented linens or a ruggedly handsome, hunt-club-style room, rest assured you'll be pampered—with a home-baked breakfast in the garden-view solarium, and later a late-afternoon pick-me-up in the dazzling parlor, which is mostly white, with glints of vintage cranberry glass.

Port Fortune Inn. 201 Main St. (on the shore, near Chatham Light), Chatham, MA 02633. ☎ **800/750-0792** or 508/945-0792. Fax 508/945-0792. www.capecod.net/portfortune. E-mail: portfor@capecod.net. 14 units. A/C TEL. Summer $130–$190 double. Rates include continental breakfast. AE, MC, V. No children under 12.

This classic shingled cottage (formerly named Inn Among Friends), newly restored and redecorated, is just a short stroll from Lighthouse Beach. The cheerful name comes from explorer Samuel de Champlain, who named this area Port Fortune when he landed in Chatham in 1606. A couple of the spacious, traditionally decorated rooms have water views, and all have queen beds, some of them four-poster. All have hair dryers; some have televisions. Breakfast with an ocean view is served in the front building, which also has a few rooms upstairs that share the view.

WHERE TO DINE
EXPENSIVE
✪ **The Main Dining Room at the Chatham Bars Inn.** Shore Rd. (about ⅓ mile NW of the town center). ☎ **508/945-0096.** Reservations recommended. Main courses $21–$35. AE, DC, MC, V. June–Nov daily 7:30–11am and 6:30–9:30pm; call for off-season hours. NEW AMERICAN.

If it's grandeur you're after, the setting here supplies a surplus. The dining room is vast, the ballroom dimensions all but lost in the modern age, and the view is of the million-dollar variety—the Atlantic Ocean. Your fellow diners are decked out in their summer finery, and in the background, a live pianist tinkles the ivories. Dinners consist of hearty traditional fare like roasted duckling with orange mandarin ginger sauce and wild rice, roasted quail stuffed with foie gras and raisins with an Armagnac sauce and sautéed green grapes, and fillet of haddock with lobster stuffing and a Newburg sauce. This is not delicate food, but it is delicious; and the clam chowder may be the best on Cape Cod. Dessert choices are equally dense, like the hot-fudge sundae. Unusual on the Cape, a 17% service charge (gratuity) is added onto your check here.

MODERATE
Chatham Wayside Inn. 512 Main St. (in the center of town). ☎ **508/945-5550.** Main courses $13–$22. DISC, MC, V. May–Oct daily 8–11am, 11:30am–4pm, and 5–9pm; Nov–Apr Tues–Sun 8–11am, 11:30am–4pm, 5–9pm. NEW AMERICAN.

The Wayside's central location on Main Street makes it a good spot for a reasonably priced meal in Chatham. Diners have several seating choices depending on their mood (and the weather): the clubby tavern with gleaming wood tables surrounded by comfy Windsor chairs, the front room with cozy booths, or the large screened terrace, perfect during summer's dog days. More important, perhaps, is what's on the plate. Wayside specialties include crab cakes, or entrees like rack of lamb and pesto cod. For something a little different, try the chowder; it's prepared Portuguese-style with double-smoked bacon, fresh quahogs, and red bliss potatoes. Whether summer or winter, you'll want to end your meal with the apple-and-cranberry crisp; the secret is the oatmeal and brown-sugar crust. The Wayside is an even better choice at lunchtime, when the terrace is the perfect spot to watch Main Street's parade of shoppers.

Christian's. 443 Main St. (in the center of town). ☎ **508/945-3362.** No reservations. Main courses $9–$24. DISC, MC, V. May–Dec daily 5–10pm; call for off-season hours. Open year-round. NEW AMERICAN.

This popular boîte owned by the Chatham Wayside Inn is a good choice for a medium-priced dinner. The downstairs dining rooms enjoy an auberge-like French country decor, whereas Upstairs at Christian's (open year-round) is British clubby, with leather couches, mahogany paneling, a piano bar, and a smattering of classic movie posters. The same cinematic-motif menu applies to both venues: Famous movie titles are accorded to such specialties as salmon fillets sautéed with mushrooms, capers, white wine, and lemon—a.k.a. A Fish Called Wanda. Upstairs in the bar or on the outside deck, you can also order small pizzas, burgers, and fries.

The Impudent Oyster. 15 Chatham Bars Ave. (off Main St., in the center of town). ☎ **508/945-3545.** Reservations recommended. Main courses $13–$23. AE, MC, V. Mon–Sat 11:30am–3pm, Sun noon–3pm; daily 5–10pm. INTERNATIONAL.

All but hidden off the main drag, this perennially popular 1970s-era eatery—complete with decorative stained glass—continues to cook up fabulous fish in exotic guises, ranging from Mexican to Szechuan, but mostly continental. The flavorful specialties of the house are the *salmon piche* (baked with a dijon and herb bread-crumb crust), the *steak au poivre,* and *the chicken Français* (with rosemary-mustard butter sauce). Their interpretation of bouillabaisse is a hearty mixture of oysters, littlenecks, mussels, and four types of fish, marinated in white wine and topped with a lobster garnish. There is also a children's menu here.

Two Turtles at the Chatham Town House Inn. 11 Library Lane (just past the rotary on Main St.). ☎ **508/945-1234.** Reservations recommended. Main courses $15–$22. AE, CB, DC, DISC, MC, V. Mid-May to Oct Tues–Sun 5:30–9:30pm. Closed Nov to mid-May. AMERICAN/CONTINENTAL.

On a clear night, try to get one of the two tables out on the porch of this undiscovered gem, and you may enjoy one of the best meal deals in town. Because the inn sits above Main Street, the tables set up on the porch have a great view of the strolling scene. Meanwhile in the kitchen, Chef David Peterson, a Culinary Institute of America graduate, makes the best seafood paella in town. His concoction includes mussels, clams, shrimp, salmon, squid, chicken, and chorizo sausage. The menu is weighted with wonderful seafood dishes, but there are also fine meat and fowl choices, including a pan-seared breast of duck festively served with cranberry sauce and garlic mashed potatoes. The three intimate, candlelit dining rooms are somewhat generic, though the SS *United States* room displays the famous ship's set of dinnerware, coveted by none other than Malcolm Forbes.

Vining's Bistro. 595 Main St. (in the center of town). ☎ **508/945-5033.** Reservations not accepted. Main courses $15–$20. AE, DC, MC, V. June–early Sept daily 5:30–10pm; call for off-season hours. FUSION.

If you're looking for cutting-edge cuisine in a sophisticated setting, venture upstairs at Chatham's innocuous-looking minimall and into this ineffably cool cafe. The film-noirish wall murals suggest a certain bohemian abandon, but the food is up-to-the-minute and priced to suit young people. The menu offers compelling juxtapositions such as the warm lobster tacos with salsa fresca and crème fraîche, or the spit-roasted chicken suffused with achiote-lime marinade and sided with a salad of oranges and jicama. These creative choices are reason enough to return here.

INEXPENSIVE

Carmine's Pizza. 595 Main St. (in the center of town). ☎ **508/945-5300.** Most items under $15. No credit cards. May–Sept daily 11am–9pm; call for off-season hours. Closed Jan–Mar. ITALIAN.

A new-wave pizzeria that pays homage to the old ways with checkered tablecloths and soda-parlor chairs, this little eatery takes a bold approach to toppings—for example, pineapple, jalapeños, and hot cherry-pepper rings, in addition to the traditional garlic and crushed red pepper. Actually, that's the lineup of special ingredients for the "Pizza from Hell," sure to be a hit with hotheads. Cool down with creamy gelato.

TAKE-OUT & PICNIC FARE

✪ **Chatham Cookware.** 524 Main St. (in the center of town). ☎ **508/945-1550.**

Though it's no longer a mom-and-pop business (the acquisitive Wayside Inn has purchased it), this classic local deli still stocks most of the longtime favorites. Stop in and you're bound to walk out with some edible goods: a stunning soup du jour accompanied by some tasty hors-d'oeuvres-to-go, or perhaps some knockout pastries, as pretty as they are delectable. You might even end up lunching in the tiny dining room so thoughtfully provided.

Marion's Pie Shop. 2022 Rte. 28 (about ½ mile E of Rte. 137). ☎ **508/432-9439.**

Nearly a ½-century's worth of summer visitors have come to depend on this bakery for dinner and dessert pies, from sea clam to lemon meringue. Load up on the fruit breads and sweet rolls, and you can pretend you're having a four-course B&B breakfast—on the beach.

FRESH SEAFOOD

Nickerson Fish & Lobster. Chatham Fish Pier, Shore Rd. ☎ **508/945-0145.** Closed mid-Oct to late May.

The fish have to travel all of 50 yards from the boat, so you can imagine how fresh they are. And you don't need a kitchen to partake: They sell homemade quahog (giant clam) chowder and precooked frozen entrees to go.

SWEETS

Chatham Candy Manor. 484 Main St. (in the center of town). ☎ **800/221-6497** or 508/945-0825.

Normally, I cross the street to avoid this type of temptation, but Naomi Turner's hand-dipped chocolates (her mother opened the shop in the 1940s) are just too good to pass up. Surely there can't be anything too terribly harmful in an occasional "cranberry cordial" or chocolate-dipped strawberry, right? But once you start perusing the old-fashioned oak cases, it can be very hard to stop. Turtles, truffles, and the homemade fudge are tops. Children line up to watch them make candy canes here at Christmastime.

CHATHAM AFTER DARK

While most towns boast some comparable event, Chatham's free **band concerts**—40 players strong—are arguably the best on the Cape and attract crowds in the thousands. This is small-town America at its most nostalgic, as the band, made up mostly of local folks, plays those standards of yesteryear that never go out of style. Held in Kate Gould Park (off Chatham Bars Ave., in the center of town) from July to early September, it kicks off at 8pm every Friday. Better come early to claim your square of lawn (it's already checkerboarded with blankets by late afternoon), and be prepared to sing—or dance—along. Call ☎ **508/945-5199** for information.

PERFORMANCE ARTS

Monomoy Theatre. 776 Rte. 28 (about ¼ mile W of the rotary). ☎ **508/945-1589.** Tickets $14–$25. Performances mid-June to Aug Tues–Wed at 8pm; Fri–Sat at 8:30pm; Thurs 2 and 8pm. Closed Sept to mid-June.

Every summer since 1958, the Ohio University Players have commuted to this jewel box of a 1930s theater to put on a challenging play a week, from musicals to Shakespeare. In late July, they take a well-earned week off to cede the stage to the highly accomplished Monomoy Chamber Ensemble.

BARS & LIVE MUSIC

✪ **The Chatham Squire.** 487 Main St. (in the center of town). ☎ **508/945-0945.** No cover.

A great leveler, this local institution attracts patrons from all the social strata in town. CEOs, seafarers, and collegiates alike convene to kibitz over the roar of a jukebox or band (Fridays and Saturdays off-season) and the din of their own hubbub.

Upstairs at Christian's. 443 Main St. (in the center of town). ☎ **508/945-3362.** No cover.

Beloved of moneyed locals, this sporting piano bar has the air of a vintage frat house— it summons up young scions gracefully slumming it among scuffed leather couches and purloined movie posters. The live music is offered nightly in season and weekends year-round. Cinematically themed nibbles are always available to offset the generous movie-motif drinks. Piano music begins at 7pm.

4 Orleans

31 miles (50km) E of Sandwich; 25 miles (40km) S of Provincetown

Orleans is where the "Narrow Land" (the early Algonquin name for the Cape) starts to get very narrow indeed: From here on up—or "down," in paradoxical local parlance—it's never more than a few miles wide from coast to coast, and in some spots as little as one. All three main roads (Rtes. 6, 6A, and 28) converge here, too, so on summer weekends, it acts as a rather frustrating funnel.

But this is also where the oceanside beaches open up into a glorious expanse some 40 miles long, framed by dramatic dunes and blessed—from a swimmer's or boarder's perspective—with serious surf. The thousands of ship crews who crashed on these shoals over the past 4 centuries could hardly be expected to assume so sanguine a view. Shipwrecks may sound like the stuff of romance, but in these frigid waters, hitting a sandbar usually spelled a death sentence for all involved. So enamored were local inhabitants of the opportunity to salvage that some improved their odds by becoming "mooncussers"—praying for cloudy skies and luring ships toward shore by tying a lantern to the tail of a donkey, so as to simulate the listing of a ship at sea.

Such dark deeds seem very far removed from the Orleans of today, a sedate town that shadows Hyannis as a year-round center of commerce. Lacking the cohesiveness of smaller towns, and somewhat chopped up by the roadways coursing through, it's not the most ideal town to hang out in, despite some appealing restaurants and shops. The village of East Orleans, however, is fast emerging as a sweet little off-beach town with allure for both families and singles. About 2 miles east is seemingly endless (nearly 10 miles long) Nauset Beach, the southernmost stretch of the Cape Cod National Seashore preserve, and a magnet for the young and the buff.

ESSENTIALS

GETTING THERE   After crossing either the Bourne or Sagamore bridge (see "Getting There" in chapter 2), head east on Route 6 or 6A; both converge with Route 28 in Orleans. Or fly into Hyannis (see "Getting There" in chapter 2).

VISITOR INFORMATION   Contact the **Orleans Chamber of Commerce,** 44 Main St. (P.O. Box 153), Orleans, MA 02653 (☎ **800/865-1386** or 508/255-1386; www.capecod-orleans.com; E-mail: visit@capecod-orleans.com), open year-round Monday to Friday from 9am to 2pm; or the **Cape Cod Chamber of Commerce** (see "Visitor Information" in the "Brewster" section, above). There's an **information booth** at the corner of Route 6A and Eldredge Parkway (☎ **508/240-2484**). Its hours are early June to mid-October Monday to Saturday from 9am to 6pm and Sunday from 10am to 3pm. Closed late November to mid-May.

BEACHES & RECREATIONAL PURSUITS

BEACHES   From here on up, on the eastern side you're dealing with the wild and whimsical Atlantic, which can be kittenish one day and tigerish the next. While storms may whip up surf you can actually take a board to, less confident swimmers should definitely wait a few days until the turmoil and riptides subside. In any case, current conditions are clearly posted at the entrance. Weeklong parking permits ($25 for renters, $40 for transients) may be obtained from **Town Hall** on School Road (☎ **508/240-3775**). Day-trippers who arrive early enough—better make that before 9am—can pay at the gate (☎ **508/240-3780**).

- ✪ **Nauset Beach,** in East Orleans (☎ **508/240-3780**): Stretching southward all the way past Chatham, this 10-mile-long barrier beach, which is part of the Cape Cod National Seashore but is managed by the town, has long been one of the Cape's gonzo beach scenes—good surf, big crowds, lots of young people. Full facilities, including a terrific snack bar complete with fried fish offerings, can be found within the 1,000-car parking lot; the in-season fee is $8 per car, which is also good for same-day parking at Skaket Beach (see below). Substantial waves make for good surfing in the special section reserved for that purpose, and boogie boards are ubiquitous. In July and August, there are concerts from 7 to 9pm in the gazebo.

- **Skaket Beach,** off Skaket Beach Road to the west of town (☎ **508/255-0572**): This peaceful bay beach is a better choice for families with young children. When the tide recedes (as much as a mile), little kids will enjoy splashing about in the tide pools left behind. Parking costs $8, and you'd better turn up early.

- **Pilgrim Lake,** off Monument Road about 1 mile south of Main Street: This small freshwater beach is covered by a lifeguard in season, You must have a beach parking sticker.

- **Crystal Lake,** off Monument Road about a ¾ mile south of Main Street: Parking—if you can find a space—is free, but there are no facilities.

BICYCLING   Orleans presents the one slight gap in the 25-mile off-road ✪ **Cape Cod Rail Trail** (☎ **508/896-3491**): Just east of the Brewster border, the trail merges with town roads for about 1½ miles. The best way to avoid vehicular aggravation and breathing fumes is to zigzag west to scenic Rock Harbor. Bike rentals are available at **Orleans Cycle** at 26 Main St. in the center of town (☎ **508/255-9115**), and there are several good places (see "Take-Out & Picnic Fare," below) to grab some comestibles.

BOATING Paddle Cape Cod(☎ **888/226-6393** or 508/564-4051; www. paddlecapecod.com; e-mail: cccanoe@capecod.net) runs naturalist-guided trips throughout the Cape. Call for schedule and more information or see "Beaches & Recreational Pursuits" in the "Brewster" section, above.

If you want to explore on your own by canoe, you can rent one (see below) and paddle around Town Cove, Little Pleasant Bay (to Sampson Island, to Hog Island, and to Pochet Island), and the body of water called simply The River. Experienced paddlers can paddle through Pleasant Bay to the inside shore of the Outer Beach.

Arey's Pond Boat Yard, off Route 28 in South Orleans (☎ **508/255-7900**), offers sailing lessons on Daysailers, Catboats, and Rhode 19s in season on Little Pleasant Bay. Individual lessons are $60 per hour; weekly group lessons are around $160 to $250. The **Goose Hummock Outdoor Center** at 15 Rte. 6A, south of the rotary (☎ **508/255-2620;** www.goose.com), rents out canoes, kayaks, and more, and the northern half of Pleasant Bay is the perfect place to use them; inquire about guided excursions. Canoe and kayak rentals are $40 per day or $150 per week. Half-day guided trips are about $80.

FISHING Fishing is allowed in Baker Pond, Pilgrim Lake, and Crystal Lake; the third is a likely spot to reel in trout and perch. For details and a license, visit **Town Hall** at Post Office Square in the center of town (☎ **508/240-3700,** ext. 305) or **Goose Hummock** (see above). Surf casting—no license needed—is permitted on Nauset Beach South, off Beach Road. **Rock Harbor,** a former packet landing on the bay (about 1¼ miles northwest of the town center) shelters New England's largest sportfishing fleet: some 18 boats at last count. One call (☎ **800/287-1771** in Mass., or 508/255-9757) will get you information on them all. Or go look them over. Rock Harbor charter prices range from $400 for 4 hours to $550 for 8 hours. There are also individual prices available ($100 per person for 4 hours; $110 per person for 8 hours).

You can rent fishing rods and other gear from **Goose Hummock** at 15 Rte. 6A, just south of the rotary (☎ **508/255-2620**).

FITNESS If you're here for a while and need a place to stay in shape on rainy days, check out **Willy's Gym, Fitness, and Wellness Center** at 21 Old Colony Way at Orleans Marketplace (☎ **508/255-6826**). The Cape's biggest (21,000 sq. ft.) exercise facility is air-conditioned and open year-round. Dozens of classes are offered weekly, from basic aerobics to t'ai chi and Indonesian martial arts. Willy's also provides child care.

ICE-SKATING Orleans boasts a massive municipal rink, the **Charles Moore Arena** on O'Connor Way, off Eldredge Park Way, about 1 mile southwest of town center (☎ **508/255-2971;** call for schedule and fees). In season, it's open to the public Tuesday, Wednesday, and Thursday 2 to 4pm, Sunday 6 to 8pm. From September through March, it's open to the public Monday and Wednesday from 11am to 1pm, Thursday from 3:30 to 5pm, and Sunday from 2 to 4pm. Friday night is "Rock-Nite" for party animals aged 9 through 14. The cost is $4 adults, $3 for children 12 and under, $2 skate rentals.

NATURE & WILDLIFE AREAS Inland there's not much, but on the Atlantic shore is a biggie: **Nauset Beach.** Once you get past the swarms of people near the parking lot, you'll have about 9 miles of beach mostly to yourself. You'll see lots of birds (take a field guide) and perhaps some harbor seals off-season.

TENNIS Hard-surface public courts are located at the Nauset Middle School in Eldredge Park on a first-come, first-served basis; for details, contact the **Orleans Recreation Department** (☎ **508/240-3785**).

WATER SPORTS   The ✪ **Pump House Surf Co.** at 9 Cranberry Hwy./Rte. 6A
(☎ **508/240-2226**) rents and sells wet suits, body boards, and surfboards, while providing up-to-date reports on where to find the best waves. **Nauset Sports** at Jeremiah
Square, Route 6A at the rotary (☎ **508/255-4742**) also rents surfboards, body
boards, skim boards, and wet suits.

HISTORICAL MUSEUMS

French Transatlantic Cable Station Museum. 41 Rte. 28 (corner of Cove Rd., N of Main
St.). ☎ **508/240-1735.** Free admission. July–Aug Mon–Sat 1–4pm; June and Sept Fri, Sat,
and Sun 1–4pm. Closed Oct–May.

This ordinary-looking house was, from 1890 to 1940, a nexus of intercontinental
communications. Connected to France via a huge cable laid across the ocean floor,
local operators bore the responsibility of relaying stock-market data, keeping tabs
on World War I troops, and receiving the joyous news of Lindbergh's 1927 crossing.
Service was discontinued with the German invasion of France in 1940, and resumed
briefly between 1952 and 1959, when newer, automated technologies rendered the
facility obsolete. The exhibits, prepared with the assistance of the Smithsonian, are a
bit technical for non-scientists, but there are docents on hand who will patiently fill
in the blanks.

Jonathan Young Windmill. Rte. 6A (just S of the rotary). ☎ **508/240-1329.** Free admission; donations accepted. Late June–Aug daily 11am–4pm; call for off-season hours.

The majestic old windmill in Cove Park (next to Town Cove) has been authentically
restored and is open for guided tours in season. Though it is no longer grinding corn
and barley, the mill's works are fully operable. Most mills on the Cape have been
moved many times from town to town, and the Orleans mill has certainly seen more
than its share of relocations. The mill was built in the early 1700s in South Orleans.
In 1839, it was moved to Orleans center and then to Hyannisport. In 1983, it was
moved back to Orleans and donated to the Orleans Historical Society. Some of the
guides at the mill are actual millers, who give visitors an entertaining spiel about the
millwrights (the men who built the mills and kept the gears in working order) and
millers (who ground the corn) who have worked on this mill over the centuries.

Orleans Historical Society at The Meeting House Museum. 3 River Rd. (at Main St.,
about 1 mile E of the town center). ☎ **508/240-1329.** www.capecodhistory.org. Donation
$2. July–Aug Thurs–Sat 10am–1pm; off-season by appointment.

Other towns may have fancier facilities to house their historical societies, but few have
quite so colorful a history as Orleans—the only town on the Cape with a non-
English, non-native name. Upon separating from Eastham in 1797, Orleans assumed
the name of an honored guest: future king Louis-Philippe de Bourbon, Duke of
Orleans, who safely sat out the Revolution abroad, earning his living as a French tutor.
Not that all remained quiet on these shores either: Orleans suffered British naval attacks
during the War of 1812, and German submarine fire in 1918. You'll find a great many
mementos in this 1833 Greek Revival church, along with assorted artifacts—from
arrowheads to hand-hewn farm tools—and a thinly veiled terrorist threat, dated 1814,
from a British captain offering to spare the town's saltworks in Rock Harbor for a pal-
try $1,000. The townspeople balked, a warship struck, and the home team triumphed
in the Battle of Orleans. Though the displays are far from jazzy, a great many have
interesting stories attached and could spark an urge to learn more. Head over to Rock
Harbor to see a gold-medal-award-winning Coast Guard rescue boat and shipwreck
items from the wreck of the *Pendleton* tanker in 1952 that the Historical Society has
installed as an additional exhibit.

BASEBALL

The Orleans Cardinals, the easternmost team in the **Cape Cod Baseball League,** plays at Eldredge Park (off Eldredge Park Way between Rtes. 6A and 28). For a schedule, call the **Orleans Chamber of Commerce** (☎ **800/865-1386** or 508/255-1386), the **Orleans Recreation Department** (☎ **508/240-3785**), or the **League** (☎ **508/ 432-6909**).

KID STUFF

The **Charles Moore Arena** (see "Ice-Skating," above) offers respite from a rainy day. Young skaters—and anxious parents—might be interested to know that the Nauset Regional Middle School in Eldredge Park has its own **skateboard park,** with four ramps and a "fun box"; helmets are required.

SHOPPING

Though shops are somewhat scattered, Orleans is full of great finds for browsers and grazers.

ANTIQUES/COLLECTIBLES   Got an old house in need of illumination, or a new one in want of some style? You'll find some 400 vintage light fixtures at **Continuum Antiques,** 7 S. Orleans Rd., Route 28, south of the junction of Route 6A (☎ **508/ 255-8513**), from Victorian on down, along with a smattering of old advertising signs and venerable duck decoys.

Deborah Rita, proprietor of **Countryside Antiques,** 6 Lewis Rd., south of Main Street in the center of East Orleans (☎ **508/240-0525**), roams the world in search of stylish furnishings, mostly old, though age—and price—are evidently no object.

ARTS & CRAFTS   As a publicist, Helen Addison has forged friendships with some of the most interesting artists now working on the Cape. Her gallery, **Addison Holmes Gallery,** 43 Rte. 28, north of Main Street (☎ **508/255-6200**), run with partner Herb Holmes, represents such diverse artists as Lois Griffel of Provincetown, whose luminous oils and watercolors typify "Cape Cod impressionism"; and Gary Gilmartin of Truro, a realist working in egg tempera and watercolor, who paints Cape-inspired subjects.

The **Artful Hand Gallery,** 47 Main St., between Routes 6A and 28 (☎ **508/ 255-2969**), is a branch of a top crafts gallery based in Boston's haute Copley Place; the selections tend to be fun, but smart, too. Jewelry and glass are among what you'll find.

Stop by **Kemp Pottery,** 9 Cranberry Hwy./Rte. 6A, about an ⅛ mile south of the rotary (☎ **508/255-5853**), and check out Steve Kemp's turned and slab-built creations—from soup tureens to fanciful sculptures; they're remarkably colorful and one of a kind.

✪ **Tree's Place,** Route 6A at the intersection of Route 28, Orleans (☎ **888/ 255-1330** or 508/255-1330), is considered the premier gallery for contemporary realist work in the region. There is also an extensive fine craft, gift, and tile shop here.

BOOKS   **Compass Rose Book Shop,** 43–45 Main St., in the center of town (☎ **508/255-1545**), is well laid-out and offers a strong collection in the areas of local lore, nature, and nautical know-how; inquire about the bargains upstairs. In the Skaket Corners shopping center on Route 6A is a branch of the large retailer **Booksmith/Musicsmith** (☎ **508/255-4590**).

FASHION   With her main headquarters in trendy Northampton, Massachusetts, designer/buyer Susan Hannah displays her casual yet elegant chic at **Hannah,** 47

Main St., in the center of town (☎ 508/255-8324). Look for her larger shop when in Wellfleet.

Karol Richardson, 47 Main St., in the center of town (☎ 508/255-3944), is a preview of Richardson's main showroom in Wellfleet; stop in to see the latest from this gifted ex-Londoner.

GIFTS   Birders will go batty over ✪ **Bird Watcher's General Store,** 36 Rte. 6A, south of the rotary (☎ 800/562-1512 or 508/255-6974). The brainchild of local aficionado Mike O'Connor, who'd like everyone to share his passion, it stocks virtually every bird-watching accessory under the sun, from basic binoculars to costly telescopes, modest birdhouses to birdbaths fit for a tiny Roman emperor. Recorded birdsong trills through the rafters, and, in addition to CDs and field guides to take home, the store offers hundreds of bird-motif gifts, from mobiles to mugs.

The tasteful selections—tapes, books, jewelry, clothing, and more—found in **Oceana,** 1 Main St. Sq., north of Main Street, in the center of town (☎ 508/240-1414), celebrate the myriad gifts of nature.

WHERE TO STAY
MODERATE

The Barley Neck Inn Lodge. 5 Beach Rd. (in the center of town), East Orleans, MA 02643. ☎ 800/281-7505 or 508/255-0212. Fax 508/255-3626. www.barleyneck.com. E-mail: reservations@barleyneck.com. 18 units. A/C TV TEL. Summer $95–$159 double. Rates include continental breakfast. Open year-round. AE, MC, V.

Having radically transformed the Barley Neck Inn restaurant (see "Where to Dine," below), owners Kathi and Joe Lewis treated the adjoining motel to an equally intensive makeover. Every room is a little different, but all boast fluffy designer comforters, minifridges, and stylish appointments. There's a small outdoor pool within the complex. Nauset Beach is a mile down the road, and the motel provides beach–parking stickers.

The Cove. 13 S. Orleans Rd. (Rte. 28, N of Main St.), Orleans, MA 02653. ☎ 800/343-2233 or 508/255-1203. Fax 508/255-7736. www.thecoveorleans.com. E-mail: thecove@c4.net. 47 units. A/C TV TEL. Summer $109–$189 double; $169–$189 suite or efficiency. Open year-round. AE, CB, DC, DISC, MC, V.

Sensibly turning its back on busy Route 28, this well-camouflaged motel complex focuses instead on placid Town Cove, where guests are offered a free minicruise in season. The interiors are adequate, if not dazzling, and a small heated pool and a restful gazebo overlook the waterfront. All rooms have hair dryers, VCRs, microwaves, coffeemakers, and minifridges. Some have kitchenettes, and balconies with cove views.

High Nauset. 227 Beach Rd., East Orleans, MA 02643. ☎ 508/255-1658. www.highnauset.com. E-mail: highnaus@highnauset.com. 4 units. TV. Summer $140–$150 double. Rates include continental breakfast. Open year-round. MC, V. No children under 12.

The newest entry in the Orleans B&B scene is just a stone's throw from Nauset Beach, and all of the rooms, which are on the second floor of the house, have large picture windows with ocean views. This is one of the very few B&Bs adjacent to the National Seashore, and it's a real treat to be so close to the famous "Great Beach." Rooms have ceiling fans to circulate the fresh ocean breezes. Continental breakfast served in the guest living room might feature homemade muffins and coffeecake.

✪ **Kadee's Gray Elephant.** 216 Main St., East Orleans, MA 02643. ☎ 508/255-7608. Fax 508/240-2976. E-mail: kadees@capecod.net. 6 units. A/C TV TEL. Summer $110–$140, double. Weekly rates available. Closed mid-Oct to Mar. MC, V.

Available short or long term, these exuberantly decorated studio apartments are extremely cheery and ideal for families. Nauset Beach is a few miles down the road; meanwhile, everything you'll need is right in town—or right on the grounds. There's a friendly restaurant/snack bar right next door (see "Where to Dine," below), and the little minigolf course out back is geared just right for kids.

Nauset Knoll Motor Lodge. 237 Beach Rd. (at Nauset Beach, about 2 miles E of the town center), East Orleans, MA 02643. ☎ **508/255-2364.** 12 units. TV. Summer $135 double. MC, V. Closed late Oct to mid-Apr.

If you're the type who's determined to keep the sea within sight at all times—past a very busy beach, in this case—this nothing-fancy motel with picture windows should suit you to a T. The simple, clean rooms are well maintained, and by staying here, you'll save on daily parking charges at Nauset Beach (one of the most popular on Cape Cod). The whole complex is owned by Uncle Sam and is under the supervision of the National Park Service.

✪ **The Orleans Inn.** Rte. 6A (P.O. Box 188) (just S of the Orleans rotary), Orleans, MA 02653. ☎ **508/255-2222.** Fax 508/255-6722. www.orleansinn.com. E-mail: info@orleansinn.com. 11 units. TV TEL. Summer $125–$250 double. Rates include continental breakfast. AE, MC, V.

You can't miss this mansard-roofed beauty, perched right on the edge of Town Cove. Absolutely, get one of the rooms facing the water. Built in 1875, the inn was recently restored to its former grandeur. The simple rooms, some with twin beds or sleeper sofas, are cheerful with modern amenities and extra touches like a box of chocolates on the bureau. Downstairs is a bar and restaurant with wonderful views of the cove.

INEXPENSIVE

✪ **Nauset House Inn.** 143 Beach Rd., (P.O. Box 774) (about 1 mile E of the town center), East Orleans, MA 02643. ☎ **508/255-2195.** Fax 508/240-6276. www.nausethouseinn.com. E-mail: info@nausethouseinn.com. 14 units, 6 with shared bathroom. Summer $60–$140 double. Rates include full breakfast. DISC, MC, V. Closed Nov–Mar. No children under 12.

Just ½ mile from Nauset Beach, this reasonably priced country inn is a cozy setting for those seeking a quiet retreat. Several of the rooms in greenery-draped outbuildings feature such romantic extras as a sunken bath or private deck. The most romantic hideaway here, though, is a 1907 conservatory appended to the 1810 farmhouse inn. It's the perfect place to lounge as the rain pounds down, prompting the camellias to waft their heady perfume. Breakfast would seem relatively workaday, were it not for the setting—a pared-down, rustic refectory—and innkeeper Diane Johnson's memorable muffins and pastries.

The Parsonage Inn. 202 Main St. (P.O. Box 1501), East Orleans, MA 02643. ☎ **888/ 422-8217** or 508/255-8217. Fax 508/255-8216. www.parsonageinn.com. E-mail: innkeeper@ parsonageinn.com. 8 units. A/C. Summer $110–$140 double. Rates include full breakfast. Closed Jan to mid-Feb. AE, MC, V.

Blessed with charming British innkeepers, this 1770 full Cape—whose name describes its original function—offers the kind of unique, personalized experience especially prized by "innies" (the country-inn counterpart to foodies). Elizabeth Browne is an accomplished pianist who might, if the evening mood is right, take flight in a Chopin mazurka or Mozart sonata, as her husband, Ian, treats guests to a glass of wine. Rooms are prettily decorated and are equipped with coffee- and teamakers, as well as hairdryers. Most have televisions, and several have minifridges. The most expensive room is quite a bargain with its separate entrance, pullout couch, and kitchenette, for little more than a standard room.

WHERE TO DINE
EXPENSIVE

✪ **The Barley Neck Inn.** 5 Beach Rd. (about ½ mile E of the town center). ☎ **800/ 281-7505** or 508/255-0212. Reservations recommended. Main courses $14–$24. AE, MC, V. June–early Sept daily 5–10pm; call for off-season hours. Open year-round. FRENCH.

Recently rescued from dereliction and tastefully restored—complete with fanlight door and mullioned windows—this 1857 captain's house immediately ascended into the first rank. The owners, enterprising ex–New Yorkers Joe and Kathi Lewis, have recruited a superb chef in Franck Champely, who arrived from Taillevent and Maxim's by way of New York's Four Seasons. His classical background shines in straightforward yet subtle dishes such as grilled Atlantic salmon fillet with a red-pepper coulis and basil vinaigrette, or sautéed shrimp in a sauce of sweet garlic and Chablis atop lemon angel-hair pasta and shiitake mushrooms. The cuisine may be worship worthy, the wine list a connoisseur's delight, but the ambience is populist and festive, verging on boisterous. It's a very good mix.

Captain Linnell House. 137 Skaket Beach Rd. (about 1 mile NW of Rte. 6A). ☎ **508/ 255-3400.** www.linnell.com. Reservations recommended. Main courses $17–$27. AE, MC, V. Late May–Oct daily 5–9pm; call for off-season hours. Open year-round. AMERICAN.

The plantationlike facade of this colonnaded 1854 mansion, modeled on a Marseilles villa, foreshadows the romantic ambience that awaits within. This is really an old-style New England restaurant with a traditional menu and dependable service, making this a reliable choice for fine dining, and, for some, the best restaurant in town. Chef/owner William Conway's lobster bisque, bolstered with bourbon, is the kind that lingers in memory. Ask to be seated in the garden room, where the pleasing view will enable you to accord the food the undivided focus it deserves. Better yet, be really smart and come early (before 6pm) to score free soup and dessert.

MODERATE

Academy Ocean Grille. 2 Academy Place (in the center of town). ☎ **508/240-1585.** Reservations recommended. Main courses $16–$25. AE, DISC, MC, V. Apr–Dec daily noon–2pm; 5:30–9:30pm. Closed Jan–Mar. NEW AMERICAN.

Just the basics here, but it's fresh food prepared simply, and sometimes that's just what you want. Seafood specialties include sole Mediterranean, pan-fried with lemon, capers, olives, roasted tomatoes, and fresh basil; and cod pesto baked with bread crumbs and a tomato basil beurre blanc sauce. There's also pasta, steak, and chicken. On sunny days, lunch is served outside on the trellised patio, which is quite lovely. The interior of the restaurant is on the bland side.

✪ **Joe's Beach Road Bar & Grille.** The Barley Neck Inn, 5 Beach Rd. (about ½ mile E of the town center). ☎ **508/255-0212.** Reservations not accepted. Main courses $9–$18. AE, MC, V. Daily 5–10pm. Open year-round. NEW AMERICAN.

Joe Lewis has decorated this spacious beamed tavern with World War II posters and snazzy Roaring Twenties menswear ads. Off-season a fire blazes in the huge fieldstone fireplace. Inviting navy-blue armchairs are in the quieter dining room, around the corner from the 28-foot mahogany bar. Once you've secured your own table—the tablecloths are denim, the napkins bandannas—you have the run of a terrifically varied menu, which includes the exquisite dishes served in the more formal restaurant next door (see above). Asian specials like sushi are offered nightly but also traditional favorites like mussels to start, and then a succulent lamb shank. If you just want to nosh, consider Joe's pizza (with goat cheese, roasted peppers, and spinach) or high-falutin' fish-and-chips—beer-battered, with watercress aioli.

⊙ **Kadee's Lobster & Clam Bar.** 212 Main St., East Orleans. ☎ **508/255-6184.** Reservations not accepted. Main courses $7–$24. MC, V. Late June–early Sept daily noon–9pm; late May–late June Mon–Thurs 5–9pm, Fri–Sun noon–9pm. Closed early Sept–late May. SEAFOOD.

Achieving an air of effortless authenticity, this atmospheric sea shanty has been rigged to improve on the climate. When the sun's out, the brightly colored umbrellas pop up on the patio; as soon as the chilly seaborne fog moves in, a curtained awning drops down. The menu is equally adaptable: There's nothing like the classic chowders and stews or a healthy seafood kabob to take the chill off; fine weather, on the other hand, calls for a lobster roll, or perhaps the obligatory (at least once a summer) Fisherman's Feed combo platter splurge. There is also a raw bar with oysters, clams, and shrimp. Early birds can eat cheap from Monday to Thursday from 4 to 5pm. Due to meticulous management, the staff is a particularly sunny gang here. Befitting the playful atmosphere (minigolf next door), there's a fine kiddie menu here.

The Lobster Claw Restaurant. Rte. 6A (just S of the rotary), Orleans. ☎ **508/255-1800.** Main courses $10–$19. AE, CB, DISC, MC, V. Daily 11:30am–9pm. Closed Nov–Mar. SEAFOOD.

This family-owned and -operated business has been serving up quality seafood for almost 30 years. There's plenty of room for everyone in this sprawling restaurant, where booths spill over with boisterous families, and the usual flotsam and jetsam hang artfully from the ceiling. Get the baked stuffed lobster here with all the fixings. There's a children's menu, as well as early-bird specials served daily from 4 to 5:30pm.

Mahoney's Atlantic Bar & Grill. 28 Main St. (in the center of town). ☎ **508/255-5505.** Reservations recommended. Main courses $12–$21. AE, MC, V. Daily 8am–10pm. NEW AMERICAN.

Seafood is the specialty here at this casual bar/restaurant on Main Street. Dishes like tuna sashimi, grilled sea bass, and pan-seared lobster explain why you came to Cape Cod. There are also poultry, meat, pasta and vegetarian dishes on the menu. Sixteen wines are available by the glass for those who like to sample. Grab a booth and stay awhile. Some nights in season, there's live jazz and blues.

Nauset Beach Club. 222 Main St. (about ½ mile E of the town center). ☎ **508/255-8547.** Reservations suggested. Main courses $14–$19. AE, DISC, MC, V. Late May to mid-Oct daily 5:30–9:30pm; mid-Oct to late May Tues–Sat 5:30–9:30pm. NORTHERN ITALIAN.

The first thing you may notice about this peachy roadside trattoria (once a duck-hunter's cottage) is the tantalizing aromas. Unfortunately, the next impression is apt to be a surfeit of attitude, when, for example, the maitre d' informs you, unbidden, that each person in your party must order an entree—no exceptions made for young diners or small appetites. If you're willing to play by the rules, the reward is apt to be worth it: lusciously sauced, perfectly al dente pastas and other Italian-accented regional fare.

INEXPENSIVE

Binnacle Tavern. 20 S. Orleans Rd./Rte. 28 (N of Main St.). ☎ **508/255-7901.** Reservations not accepted. Most items under $12. AE, MC, V. Mid-May to mid-Oct daily 5–11:30pm; mid-Oct to mid-May Wed–Sun 5–11:30pm. AMERICAN.

All sorts of strange nautical salvage adorn the barn-board walls of this popular pizzeria, where the pies—reputed to be the Cape's best—come with some very peculiar toppings (Thai pizza with chicken, ginger, cilantro, scallions, and peanut sauce, and topped with mozzarella cheese!) for those so inclined. More conservative combos are available, along with traditional Italian fare.

✪ **Cap't Cass Rock Harbor Seafood.** 117 Rock Harbor Rd. (on the harbor, about 1½ miles NW of the town center). No phone. Most main courses under $12. No credit cards. Late June to mid-Oct daily 11am–2pm and 5–9pm. Closed mid-Oct to late June. SEAFOOD.

Most tourists figure that a silvered shack sporting this many salvaged lobster buoys has an inside track on the freshest of seafood. The supposition makes sense, but the stuff here is about par for the area and the preparations are plain. Nevertheless, it's fun to eat in a joint left untouched for decades as time—and dining fads—marched on.

Land Ho! 38 Main St. (at Rte. 6A, in the center of town). ☎ **508/255-5165.** Reservations not accepted. Main courses $9–$15. AE, DISC, MC, V. Mon–Sat 11:30am–10pm; Sun noon–10pm. Open year-round. AMERICAN.

A longtime hit with the locals (who call it, affectionately, "the Ho"), this rough-and-tumble pub attracts its share of knowledgeable tourists as well, drawn by the reasonable prices and relaxed feeling. The food may be nothing to write home about, but it's satisfying and easy on the budget. Light fare is served until midnight. Just being there (provided you can find the door: it's around back) will make you feel like an insider.

The Yardarm. 48 Rte. 28. (just E of Main St.). ☎ **508/255-4840.** Most items under $15. AE, DC, MC, V. Daily 11:30am–3pm, 5:30–9pm. Open year-round. PUB GRUB.

This rough and rowdy joint serves the best chowder in town. It's a delectable seafood concoction that comes in three sizes: little predicament, big predicament, and huge dilemma. It's also available frozen in pint and half-pint sizes. Locals also flock to Prime Rib Night (Monday and Thursday), Mexican Night (Tuesday and Wednesday), and Steak Night (Friday and Saturday). But you'll go to watch the colorful characters bellying up to the bar for a burger and a brew.

TAKE-OUT & PICNIC FARE

Fancy's Farm. 199 Main St., East Orleans. ☎ **508/255-1949.**

Rarely are vegetables rendered so appealing. They're especially prime whether domestic or imported from halfway across the world. The charming barnlike setting helps, as do the extras—fresh breads, pastries, juices, sandwiches, and exotic salads and soups to go. This is a great place to stop on the way to Nauset Beach for picnic supplies.

New York Bagels. 125 Rte. 6A (S of Main St.). ☎ **508/255-0255.**

Longing for the real thing, a real mouth wrestler? These chewy rounds are authentic and tasty; add the customary accompaniments for a satisfying sandwich. Among the other "Noo Yawk" mainstays are knishes and potato pancakes—and, of course, chicken soup. While awaiting your order, you can study the decorative pastiche of nostalgic tchotchkes.

Orleans Whole Food. 46 Main St. (in the center of town). ☎ **508/255-6540.**

The largest health-food store on the Cape, this bright and cheerful porch-fronted grocery offers all sorts of freshly made snacks and sandwiches to take out—or to tear into during an impromptu picnic in the adjoining garden.

Nauset Fish & Lobster Pool. Just S of the rotary on Rte. 6A in Orleans. ☎ **508/255-1019.**

The area's premier spot for fresh seafood; the selection is extensive and bountiful.

SWEETS

The Hot Chocolate Sparrow. 85 Rte. 6A (Lowell Square). ☎ **508/240-2230.** Open year-round.

Success means a larger location for this coffeehouse-cum-bakery. Chocolate manufacturing takes place here and at a sister shop in North Eastham. Real fudge flavors the hot chocolate and all mocha derivatives thereof. Frozen hot chocolate and frozen mochas are summer specialties. It's a good place to stop in, casually check the posters announcing local happenings, then dive in for a remorseless pig-out. This place serves the best coffee and cappuccinos in town, too.

✪ **Sundae School.** 210 Main St., East Orleans. ☎ **508/255-5473.**

A smaller branch of the Dennisport institution (and now in Harwich Port, too), this little ice-cream shop offers some mighty sophisticated flavors, drawing on fruits in season and even the liqueur cabinet.

ORLEANS AFTER DARK

Joe's Beach Road Bar & Grille (☎ 508/255-0212; see "Where to Dine," above) is a big old barn of a bar that might as well be town hall: It's where you'll find all the locals exchanging juicy gossip and jokes. On Sunday evenings in season, the weekend warriors who survived in style can enjoy live "Jazz at Joe's." Other nights there's Jim Turner, a blind piano player, who entertains with show tunes and boogie-woogie. There's never a cover charge.

There's live music on weekends at the **Land Ho!** (☎ 508/255-5165; see "Where to Dine," above), the best pub in town on Monday and Tuesday nights in season, and Thursday and Saturdays off-season. There's usually no cover charge.

The Academy Playhouse, 120 Main St., about a ¾ mile southeast of the town center (☎ 508/255-1963), makes a fine platform for local talent in the form of musicals and drama, recitals and poetry readings. The 162-seat arena-style stage is housed in the town's old town hall (built in 1873). Tickets are $14 to $16. Shows take place July through August Monday to Saturday at 8:30pm; call for off-season hours. There's a children's theater series from late June to early September on Saturday mornings. Cost is $5.

7

The Outer Cape: Eastham, Wellfleet, Truro & Provincetown

The rest of the Cape may have its civilized enticements, but it's only on the Outer Cape that the landscape and even the air feel really beachy. You can smell the seashore just over the horizon—in fact, everywhere you go because you're never more than a mile or two away from sand and surf.

You won't find any high-rise hotels along the shoreline here. No tacky amusement arcades. Just miles of pristine beaches and dune grass rippling in the wind. You'll also see the occasional cottage inhabited by some lucky soul who managed to get his or her hands on it (inevitably through some grandfather clause) before the coastline became the federally protected Cape Cod National Seashore in the early 1960s.

Henry David Thoreau witnessed virtually the same peaceful panorama when he roamed here in the 1850s. With luck and determination on the part of current inhabitants and visitors, the landscape will remain untouched. The Outer Cape, after all, is a place to play—in the sand, and in the delightful, non-conformist towns that sprouted up here, far from the censures of civilization.

While they share the majestic National Seashore, Outer Cape towns are quite diverse. Eastham, as the official gateway to the National Seashore, certainly gets its share of visitors, yet there is also a sleepy quality to this town, which used to have the distinction of being the turnip capital of the country. Grab a stool at a locals' joint like Flemings Donut Shop on Route 6 for a taste of old Cape Cod before there was ever any talk of a National Seashore.

Wellfleet, called the art-gallery town, is in my view one of the nicest towns on Cape Cod. The very strollable Main Street is lined with intriguing shops in historic buildings. Commercial Street, which leads to the harbor, has the art galleries, filled with work by mainly local artists inspired by this region. Wellfleet was for years one of the premier fishing villages on Cape Cod, and it still has the bustling and picturesque harbor to prove it. There are also freshwater ponds and National Seashore beaches; some of Cape Cod's finest swimming holes and most spectacular beaches line the coast of Wellfleet.

Tiny Truro is the least developed of the Cape's towns; it has the smallest population and the highest percentage of acres reserved for the National Seashore. The center of town is one of those blink-and-you-missed-it affairs, though the fact that Truro has four libraries should tell you something about the property owners here.

Provincetown is a former Portuguese fishing village turned into an internationally famous art and gay colony with a flamboyant nightlife.

The main drag (so to speak) is Commercial Street, with the best shopping on Cape Cod. Families come for the strolling, museums, and whale watching; sophisticates for the restaurants, cafes, and entertainment; and gays come for the camaraderie. And the beaches? On a clear day, they say you can see Europe.

1 Eastham

35 miles (56km) E of Sandwich; 21 miles (34km) S of Provincetown

Despite its optimal location (the distance from bay to ocean is as little as 1 mile in spots), Eastham is one of the least pretentious locales on the Cape—and yet highly popular as the gateway to the magnificent Cape Cod National Seashore.

The downside—or upside, depending on how you look at it—is that there aren't many shops or attractions worth checking out. Even Eastham's colorful history, as the site of the Pilgrims' "First Encounter" with hostile natives, has faded with time. One prominent vestige remains as a reminder of the days when, according to Cape historian Arthur Wilson Tarbell, Eastham served as "the granary of eastern Massachusetts": the smock-style 1680s windmill in the center of town. Also, those who take the trouble to track them down will find the graves of three "First Comers" in the Old Cove Burying Ground, near a condo complex across from Arnold's clam shack.

Most visitors won't bother, though—this is a place to kick back and let the sun, surf, and sand dictate your day.

ESSENTIALS

GETTING THERE   After crossing either the Bourne or Sagamore bridge, head east on Route 6 or 6A to Orleans, and north on Route 6. Or fly into Hyannis or Provincetown (see "Getting There" in chapter 2).

VISITOR INFORMATION   An information booth run by the town of Eastham is located on Route 6 at Governor Prence Road (☎ **508/255-3444**) and is open Memorial Day to late September. Call or write the Eastham Chamber of Commerce for an informational brochure: P.O. Box 1329, Eastham, MA 02642 (☎ **508/240-7211;** www.capecod.net/eastham/chamber). You may also contact the Cape Cod Chamber of Commerce, Routes 6 and 132, Hyannis, MA 02601 (☎ **888/332-2732** or 508/ 862-0700; fax 508/362-2156; www.capecodchamber.org; e-mail: info@capecodchamber. org), open year-round Monday to Saturday from 9am to 5pm and Sunday and holidays from 10am to 4pm.

BEACHES & RECREATIONAL PURSUITS

BEACHES   From here on up, the Atlantic beaches are best reserved for strong swimmers: Waves are *big* (often taller than you), and the undertow can be treacherous. The flat, nearly placid bay beaches, on the other hand, are just right for families with young children. The sand slopes so gradually that you won't have to worry about them slipping in over their heads. When the tide recedes (twice daily), it leaves a mile-wide playground of rippled sand full of fascinating creatures, including horseshoe and hermit crabs.

✪ **Coast Guard** and **Nauset Light,** off Ocean View Drive: Connected to outlying parking lots by a free shuttle, these pristine National Seashore beaches have lifeguards and rest rooms. In 1998, Coast Guard Beach was ranked the 18th best beach in the United States by a beach expert. Though National Seashore beaches can be chilly (this is the Atlantic Ocean, after all), the water is clean and clear. Like at all National Seashore beaches, the vistas are lovely (just 30 miles of beach), and the old white Coast Guard building is scenically perched up on a bluff. Parking is $7 per day, $20 per season.

- **First Encounter, Thumpertown, Campground,** and **Sunken Meadow:** These town-operated bay beaches generally charge $5 a day; permits ($20 per week) can be obtained from the Highway Department on Old Orchard Road in North Eastham (☎ **508/255-5972**).
- **Great Pond** and **Wiley Park beaches:** These two town-run freshwater beaches are also open to the public, on the same terms as the bay beaches.

BICYCLING   With plenty of free parking available at the Cape Cod National Seashore's **Salt Pond Visitor Center** (☎ **508/255-3421**), Eastham makes a convenient access point for the ✪ **Cape Cod Rail Trail** (☎ **508/896-3491**). Northward, it's about 5 wildflower-lined miles to Wellfleet, where the trail currently ends (further expansion is planned); Dennis is about 20 miles southwest. A 1.6-mile spur trail, winding through locust and apple groves, links the visitor center with glorious Coast Guard Beach: It's for bikes only (no blades). Rentals are available at the **Little Capistrano Bike Shop** (☎ **508/255-6515**), on Salt Pond Road just west of Route 6. Bikes cost about $17 per day. The best trailside eatery—fried clams, lobster, and the like—is **Arnold's** (☎ **508/255-2575**), located on Route 6 about 1 mile north of the visitor center.

BOATING   The best way to experience Nauset Marsh is by kayak or canoe. Rentals are available in neighboring towns: The closest source would be the **Goose Hummock Outdoor Center** at 15 Rte. 6A in Orleans (☎ **508/255-2620**).

   Jack's Boat Rentals (☎ **508/349-9808**) is located on Route 6 next to the Cumberland Farms in Wellfleet. Canoes rents for $38 a day. Jack's also rents kayaks, Sunfish sailboats, and yakboards (small kayaks). If you rent for 2 days, the third day is free. They have a seasonal outlet from mid-June to early September on Wellfleet's Gull Pond (☎ **508/349-7553**). Kayak and canoe rentals at Gull Pond cost $20 for an hour and $12 for each additional hour. After 3 hours, the fourth hour is free. In addition to watercraft to go, Jack's is also the place for info about **Eric Gustavson's guided kayak tours** (☎ **508/349-1429**), which include tours of Eastham's Herring River and Nauset Marsh. They cost $30 for a 2½-hour trip. For information about other excellent naturalist-guided tours, inquire about trips sponsored by the **Cape Cod Museum of Natural History** (☎ **800/479-3867** or 508/896-3867) and the **Wellfleet Bay Wildlife Sanctuary** (☎ **508/349-2615**).

   Paddle Cape Cod (☎ **888/226-6393** or 508/564-4051; www.paddlecapecod.com; e-mail: cccanoe@capecod.net) runs naturalist-guided trips throughout the Cape. Trips (3 to 3½ hours)—daily, weather permitting, April through October—cost $30 for a solo kayak or $50 for a tandem kayak or canoe. Sunset trips are particularly popular. All equipment is supplied, and trips include juice and snacks. Call for schedule.

FISHING   Eastham has four ponds open to fishing; **Herring Pond** is stocked. Freshwater-fishing licenses (starting at $28.50 for residents of Massachusetts) can be purchased at **Goose Hummock,** Route 6A, Orleans (☎ **508/255-0455**), or from the town clerk at **Town Hall,** Route 6 (☎ **508/240-5900**). For a shellfishing license, visit the **Natural Resources Department** at 555 Old Orchard Rd. (☎ **508/255-5972**). Surf casting is permitted at **Nauset Beach North** (off Doane Rd.) and **Nauset Light Beach** (off Cable Rd.).

FITNESS   The **Norseman Athletic Club,** 4730 Rte. 6, North Eastham (☎ **508/255-6370**), offers racquet sports, plus Nautilus and free weights, various classes, an Olympic pool, saunas, steam rooms, and whirlpools. Non-members pay $12 a day.

NATURE TRAILS   There are five "self-guided nature trails" with descriptive markers—for walkers only—within this portion of the Cape Cod National Seashore

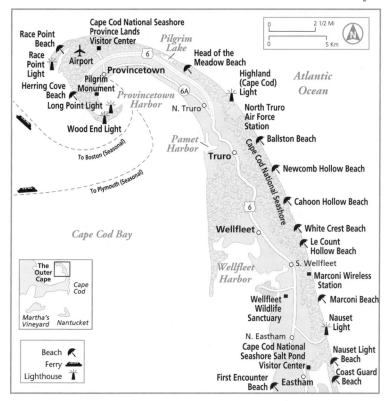

The map shows the Outer Cape region with the following labeled locations:

Race Point Beach, Race Point Light, Herring Cove Beach, Airport, Pilgrim Monument, Long Point Light, Wood End Light, Provincetown, Cape Cod National Seashore Province Lands Visitor Center, Pilgrim Lake, Head of the Meadow Beach, Highland (Cape Cod) Light, Atlantic Ocean, Provincetown Harbor, N. Truro, North Truro Air Force Station, Pamet Harbor, Truro, Ballston Beach, Newcomb Hollow Beach, Cahoon Hollow Beach, White Crest Beach, Le Count Hollow Beach, Wellfleet, S. Wellfleet, Marconi Wireless Station, Marconi Beach, Wellfleet Harbor, Cape Cod Bay, Wellfleet Wildlife Sanctuary, Nauset Light, N. Eastham, Cape Cod National Seashore Salt Pond Visitor Center, Nauset Light Beach, Coast Guard Beach, First Encounter Beach, Eastham, To Boston (Seasonal), To Plymouth (Seasonal)

Inset map: The Outer Cape, Cape Cod, Martha's Vineyard, Nantucket

Legend: Beach, Ferry, Lighthouse

(CCNS). The 1½-mile **Fort Hill Trail** off Fort Hill Road (off Rte. 6, about 1 mile south of the town center) takes off from a free parking lot just past the **Captain Edward Penniman House,** a fancy multicolored 1868 Second Empire manse maintained by rangers from the Cape Cod National Seashore. Seashore rangers lead occasional tours of the interior of the house in season. For times, call the visitor center at ☎ **508/255-3421.** But the exterior far outshines the interior, and more interesting sights await outside. Check out the huge whale-jawbone gate before walking across the street to the trail. Following the trail markers, you'll pass "Indian Rock" (bearing the marks of untold generations who used it to sharpen their tools) and enjoy scenic vantage points overlooking the channel-carved marsh—keep an eye out for egrets and great blue herons—and out to sea. The Fort Hill Trail hooks up with the ½-mile Red Cedar Swamp Trail, offering boardwalk views of an ecology otherwise inaccessible.

Three relatively short trails fan out from the Salt Pond Visitor Center. The most unusual is the ¼-mile **Buttonbush Trail,** specially adapted for the sight-impaired, with a guide rope and descriptive plaques in both oversize type and Braille. The **Doane Loop Trail,** a ½-mile woodland circuit about 1 mile east of the visitor center, is graded to allow access to wheelchairs and strollers. The 1-mile **Nauset Marsh Trail** skirts Salt Pond to cross the marsh (via boardwalk) and open fields before returning by way of a recovering forest. Look both ways for bike crossings!

TENNIS Five public courts are located at the Nauset Regional High School in North Eastham and can be used on a first-come, first-served basis; for details, contact

Road Tip

There have been many serious accidents on Route 6 in Eastham, and as a result, the speed limit here declines rather abruptly from 55 to 40. Eastham police are vigilant about enforcement.

the **Nauset High School** (☎ 508/255-1505). The **Norseman Athletic Club,** 4730 Rte. 6, North Eastham (☎ 508/255-6370), offers six indoor courts for a fee.

TWO MUSEUMS

The 1869 Schoolhouse Museum. Nauset Rd. (off Rte. 6, opposite the Salt Pond Visitor Center). ☎ 508/255-0788. Free admission. July–Aug Mon–Fri 1–4pm; Sat in Sept 1–4pm. Closed Sept–June.

Run by the volunteers of the Eastham Historical Society, this former one-room schoolhouse—with separate entrances for boys and girls—encapsulates the town's accomplishments. Exhibits range from early Native American tools to mementos of author Henry Beston's yearlong stay on Coast Guard Beach, which resulted in *The Outermost House,* as compelling a read today as it was back in 1928. And in case you were wondering—yes, that strange garden gate is in fact the washed-up jawbones of a rather large whale.

✪ **Salt Pond Visitor Center.** Salt Pond Rd. (E of Rte. 6). ☎ 508/255-3421. www.nps.gov/caco. Free admission. Late May to mid-Oct daily 9am–5pm; mid-Oct to late May daily 9am–4:30pm.

Plans are to close the visitor center for renovations when funding is available within the next 2 years. If this visitor center is closed, you can still enjoy the trails around the center. For more information about the Cape Cod National Seashore, journey up to Race Point in Provincetown, where another visitor center is tucked into the dunes.

If the Salt Pond Visitor Center is open, it's definitely worth a stop for exhibits and information about the seashore. After all, since you're undoubtedly going to spend a fair amount of time on the beach, you might as well find out how it came to be, what other creatures you'll be sharing it with, and how not to harm it or them.

Occupying more than half the land mass north of Orleans and covering the entire 30-mile oceanfront, the 44,000-acre Cape Cod National Seashore is a free gift from legislators who had the foresight to set it aside as a sanctuary in 1961. Take advantage of the excellent educational exhibits and continuous film loops offered here; particularly fascinating is a video about the 1990 discovery of an 11,000-year-old campsite amid the storm-ravaged dunes of Coast Guard Beach, which was about 5 miles inland when these early settlers spent their summers here. After absorbing some of the local history, be sure to take time to venture out—on your own or with a ranger guide—on some of the surrounding trails (see "Nature Trails," above).

KID STUFF

No one will look askance if you let your kids try the **Buttonbush Trail** (see "Nature Trails," above) in a blindfold: In fact, it's encouraged, not only as a good way to foster empathy for the blind but also to heighten "multisensory awareness." You'll find more predictable pastimes, such as miniature golf, along Route 6, and, of course, at the beaches.

SHOPPING

Eastham has fewer businesses than its southern neighbors, but poking around in unexpected places can pay off.

ANTIQUES   It would be easy to pass by **Collectors' World,** on Route 6 in Eastham, 1 mile north of the Salt Pond Visitor Center (☎ **508/255-3616**), without ever realizing the prime pickings inside. Interesting items line every square inch of the shop, from nautical antiques and weather vanes to lamps, toys, furniture, and, of course, collectibles.

ARTS & CRAFTS   **Sunken Meadows Basketworks and Pottery,** Sunken Meadow Road (off Aspinet Rd.), North Eastham (☎ **508/255-8962**), is a hidden gem tucked into the pines of North Eastham. Paulette Penney and her husband Hugh make stoneware-pinched pots, begging bowls, and wall pieces, as well as woven baskets and sculptures.

WHERE TO STAY
EXPENSIVE

✪ **The Whalewalk Inn.** 220 Bridge Rd. (about ¾ mile W of the Orleans rotary), Eastham, MA 02642. ☎ **800/440-1281** or 508/255-0617. Fax 508/240-0017. www.whalewalkinn.com. E-mail: whalewak@capecod.net. 16 units. A/C. Summer $160–$300 double; $235–$300 suite. Rates include full breakfast. AE, MC, V. Closed mid-Dec to mid-Feb.

Regularly hailed as one of the Cape's prettiest inns, this 1830s Greek Revival manse—sequestered in a quiet residential area just a few blocks off the Rail Trail—fully deserves its reputation. Innkeeper Carolyn Smith has dressed up every last space in a tasteful, mostly pastel, palette. Eclectic furnishings cohabit harmoniously in the common rooms, where complimentary evening hors d'oeuvres are served. The rooms are spacious, and all have amenities like hair dryers, irons, and minifridges. A new six-room carriage house sports deluxe rooms with antique four-poster beds, fireplaces, and some with private decks and whirlpool baths for two. Some of the suites have kitchenettes. Both Carolyn and Dick, who is responsible for the indulgent gourmet breakfasts, can knowledgeably steer you to the best the area has to offer and will lend you a bike if you like.

MODERATE

Over Look Inn. 3085 County Rd./Rte. 6 (opposite Salt Pond Visitor Center), Eastham, MA 02642. ☎ **508/255-1886.** Fax 508/240-0345. www.overlookinn.com. E-mail: stay@ overlookinn.com. 14 units. Summer $135–$175 double. A/C. Rates include full breakfast and afternoon tea. AE, CB, DC, DISC, MC, V. Pets allowed in cottage.Open year-round.

Scottish innkeepers Nan and Ian Aitchison took over this 1869 Queen Anne Victorian in 1983, and the house reflects their many enthusiasms: The library, for instance, is dedicated to Winston Churchill, and the Ernest Hemingway Billiard Room is lined with trophies that would have done Papa proud. Some rooms have brass beds and claw-foot tubs. All of the rooms have either ceiling fans or air-conditioning. The carriage house in back has several larger rooms, and there is a separate two-bedroom cottage that is rented seasonally. Pilgrims hiking along the Rail Trail will appreciate the hearty breakfasts, including an authentic "kedgeree," whose contents are best left unlisted until you've had a taste.

The Penny House. 4885 Rte. 6, Eastham, MA 02651. ☎ **800/554-1751** or 508/255-6632. Fax 508/255-4893. www.pennyhouseinn.com. E-mail: pennyhouse@aol.com. 12 units. A/C. Summer $165–$265 double. Rates include full breakfast. AE, DISC, MC, V.

Whizzing past on Route 6, you'd scarcely suspect there's a peaceful inn tucked away behind a massive hedge. This neat, comfortable B&B, graced with the warmth of Australian innkeeper Margaret Keith, is clustered around a 1690 saltbox, now the setting for rather rich homemade breakfasts. The rooms vary widely in terms of space and price, but all are nicely appointed with extras like hairdryers. Several have fireplaces.

Five deluxe rooms are equipped with bathrobes, phones, hair dryers, televisions, and minifridges. A communal TV in the cathedral-ceilinged "gathering room" encourages socializing.

INEXPENSIVE

Beach Plum Motor Lodge. 2555 Rte. 6 (about ¼ mile N of the town center), Eastham, MA 02642. ☎ **508/255-7668.** 5 units, 2 with shared bathroom. Summer $59–$65 double. Rates include continental breakfast. AE, MC, V. Closed mid-Oct to mid-May.

Look for the riot of flowers that Gloria Moll tenderly cultivates each year around her tiny front-yard pool, which is just big enough for a cool dip and some fragrant sunning. The rooms—in classic little cabins out back—are also smallish, but more than adequate for most people's needs and very generously priced, especially when you take into account the home-baked breakfast treats. After 20 years in business, Beach Plum's regulars may outnumber new guests, so make your reservations early.

Mid-Cape American Youth Hostel. 75 Goody Hallet Dr. (off Bridge Rd., about ½ mile W of the Orleans rotary), Eastham, MA 02642. ☎ **508/255-2785.** 50 beds. $14 for members, $17 for non-members. $45 private cabins. MC, V. Closed mid-Sept to mid-May.

Though nowhere near as picturesque as the Little America AYH-Hostel 14 miles north (see "Where to Stay" in section 3 of this chapter), this inland cluster of cabins makes a good stopover along the almost adjacent Rail Trail, and the bay is a quick glide away.

WHERE TO DINE
MODERATE

Eastham Lobster Pool. 4380 Rte. 6 (in the center of town). ☎ **508/255-9706.** Reservations not accepted. Main courses $11–$28. AE, DC, DISC, MC, V. Early July–early Sept daily 11:30am–10pm; Apr–early July and early Sept–Oct daily 11:30am–9:30pm. Closed Nov–Mar. AMERICAN.

For 3 decades, the scrape of metal chairs against the cement floor of this no-frills dining hall has been synonymous with seafood feasts. You can eye your potential entree—scrambling among a tankful of feisty lobsters—as you wait in line to gain admittance. (Smart diners know to show up in the early, early evening—as in, late afternoon.) Beyond the lobsters, there are all sorts of fish, all available grilled, broiled, baked, fried, stuffed, or poached. As far back as the early 1980s, the specials were exhibiting harbingers of New American panache, and they still pack some sophisticated surprises: Champagne-shallot butter, perhaps, to top a halibut steak. The bluefish, always affordable, is fabulous. Some rather nice wines are available by the glass.

INEXPENSIVE

Arnold's. 3580 Rte. 6 (about 1¼ miles N of the town center). ☎ **508/255-2575.** Main courses $7–$16. No credit cards. Mid-May to mid-Sept daily 11am–10pm. Closed mid-Sept to mid-May. AMERICAN.

Offering a take-out window on the Rail Trail and a picnic grove for those who hate to waste vacation hours sitting indoors, this popular eatery dishes out all the usual seashore standards, from rich and crunchy fried clams (cognoscenti know to order whole clams, not strips) to foot-long chili dogs.

TAKE-OUT & PICNIC FARE

Box Lunch. 4205 Rte. 6, North Eastham. ☎ **508/255-0799.**

And yet another source of the popular, Cape-invented pita "rollwiches."

ⓘ   Family-Friendly Hotels & Restaurants

Best Western Tides Beachfront in Provincetown *(see p. 209)*   Well removed from the road, this manicured beachfront motel offers everything a child could want: sun, sand, salt water, and a freshwater pool for variation.

Even'tide in South Wellfleet *(see p. 188)*   Shaded by towering pines, this roomy complex has its own huge heated indoor pool and a wooded path leading straight to the seashore.

Kalmar Village in North Truro *(see p. 195)*   A spiffy standout among the motels and cottage colonies lined up along the bay, this one—a family enterprise since the early 1940s—has its own personality; wholesome and fun.

The Lobster Pot in Provincetown *(see p. 216)*   Even the self-styled sophisticates in town willingly line up for the straightforward seafood and fabulous views.

SWEETS

Ben & Jerry's Scoop Shop. 50 Brackett Rd. (at Rte. 6), North Eastham. ☎ **508/255-2817.**

This premium ice-cream parlor is just about all most Eastham residents need in the way of evening entertainment.

The Chocolate Sparrow. 4205 Rte. 6, North Eastham. ☎ **508/240-0606.**

Let the seductive aroma of simmering chocolate lead you to this source of hand-dipped delights.

Hole-in-One Donut Shop. 4295 Rte. 6 (about ¼ mile S of the town center). ☎ **508/255-9446.**

Old-timers convene at the counter of this tiny shop (open 5am to noon daily) to ponder the state of the world. You can join in, or scurry home with your haul of hand-cut donuts and fresh-baked muffins and bagels.

EASTHAM AFTER DARK

The young crowd is now heading to the **Beach Break Grill and Lounge** at the Main Street Mercantile (Rte. 6) in North Eastham (☎ **508/240-3100**) for evening fun. There's an outdoor deck, raw bar, late-night menu, and frozen cocktails.

Most Saturday nights in season (the schedule is somewhat erratic), the **First Encounter Coffee House,** Chapel in the Pines, 220 Samoset Rd. (off Rte. 6, a ¼ mile west of town center), Eastham (☎ **508/255-5438**), a tiny 1899 church, hosts some very big names on the folk/rock circuit, such as Livingston Taylor and Patty Larkin. Tickets are $10; call for schedule. Closed May and September.

The **Salt Pond Visitor Center,** on Salt Pond Road in Eastham (east of Rte. 6; ☎ **508/255-3421**), puts on a varying schedule of entertainment (including concerts and guest presentations) in season. A nominal fee ($2 to $3) may apply. Call for schedule.

---

2 Wellfleet

42 miles (68km) NE of Sandwich; 14 miles (23km) S of Provincetown

Wedged between tame Eastham and wild Truro, Wellfleet—with the well-tended look of a classic New England village—is the golden mean, the perfect destination for artists, writers, off-duty psychiatrists, and other contemplative types who hope to find more in the landscape than mere quaintness or rusticity. Distinguished literati such as Edna St. Vincent Millay and Edmund Wilson put this rural village on the map in the 1920s, in the wake of Provincetown's bohemian heyday. In her brief and tumultuous tenure as Wilson's wife, Mary McCarthy pilloried the pretensions of the summer population in her novel, *A Charmed Life,* but had to concede that the region boasts a certain natural beauty: "steel-blue freshwater ponds and pine forests and mushrooms and white bluffs dropping to a strangely pebbled beach."

To this day, Wellfleet remains remarkably unspoiled. Once one departs from Route 6, commercialism is kept to a minimum, though the town boasts plenty of appealing shops—including a number of distinguished galleries—and a couple of excellent New American restaurants. It's hard to imagine any other community on the Cape supporting so sophisticated an undertaking as the Wellfleet Harbor Actors' Theatre, or hosting such a wholesome event as public square dancing on the adjacent Town Pier. And where else could you find, right next door to an outstanding nature preserve (the Wellfleet Bay Wildlife Sanctuary), a thriving drive-in movie theater?

ESSENTIALS

GETTING THERE   After crossing either the Bourne or Sagamore bridge, head east on Route 6 or 6A to Orleans, and north on Route 6. Or fly into Provincetown or Hyannis (see "Getting There" in chapter 2).

VISITOR INFORMATION   Contact the **Wellfleet Chamber of Commerce,** off Route 6, Wellfleet, MA 02663 (☎ **508/349-2510;** fax 508/349-3740; www.capecod. net/wellfleetcc; e-mail: wellfleet@capecod.net), or the **Cape Cod Chamber of Commerce** (see "Visitor Information" in the "Eastham" section, above).

BEACHES & RECREATIONAL PURSUITS

BEACHES   Though the distinctions are far from hard and fast, Wellfleet's fabulous ocean beaches tend to sort themselves demographically: LeCount Hollow is popular with families, Newcomb Hollow with high-schoolers, White Crest with the college crowd (including surfers and off-hour hang gliders), and Cahoon with 30-somethings. Alas, only the latter two beaches permit parking by non-residents ($10 per day). To enjoy the other two, as well as Burton Baker Beach on the harbor and Duck Harbor on the bay, plus three freshwater ponds, you'll have to walk or bike in, or see if you qualify for a sticker ($25 per week). Bring proof of residency to the seasonal Beach Sticker Booth on the Town Pier, or call the **Wellfleet Recreation Department** (☎ **508/349-9818**). Parking is free at all beaches and ponds after 4pm.

- **Marconi Beach,** off Marconi Beach Road in South Wellfleet: A National Seashore property, this cliff-lined beach (with rest rooms) charges an entry fee of $7 per day, or only $20 for the season. *Note:* The bluffs are so high that the beach lies in shadow by late afternoon.
- **White Crest and ۞ Cahoon Hollow Beaches,** off Ocean View Drive in Wellfleet: These two town-run ocean beaches—big with surfers—are open to all. Both have snack bars and rest rooms. Parking costs $10 per day.
- **Mayo Beach,** Kendrick Avenue (near the Town Pier): Right by the harbor, facing south, this warm, shallow bay beach (with rest rooms) is hardly secluded but will please young waders and splashers. And the price is right; parking is free. You could grab a bite (and a paperback) at The Bookstore Restaurant across the street, which serves three meals a day and sells used books around back.

BICYCLING   The end (to date) of the 25-mile (and growing) ۞ **Cape Cod Rail Trail** (☎ **508/896-3491**), Wellfleet is also among its more desirable destinations:

A country road off the bike path leads right to LeCount Hollow Beach. Located at the current terminus, the **Black Duck Sports Shop** at 1446 Rte. 6 in Wellfleet, at the corner of LeCount Hollow Road (☎ 508/349-9801), stocks everything from rental bikes to "belly boards" and inflatable boats; the deli at the adjoining **South Wellfleet General Store** (☎ 508/349-2335) can see to your snacking needs.

BOATING **Jack's Boat Rentals,** located on Gull Pond off Gull Pond Road, about a ½ mile south of the Truro border (☎ 508/349-9808), rents out canoes, kayaks, sailboards, and Sunfish, as well as sea cycles and surf bikes. Gull Pond connects to Higgins Pond by way of a placid, narrow channel lined with red maples and choked with yellow water lilies. Needless to say, it's a great place to paddle. Renting a kayak or canoe at Gull Pond for a couple of hours costs $32. If you'd like a canoe for a few days, you'll need to go to the Jack's Boat Rentals location on Route 6 in Wellfleet (next to the Cumberland Farms). There, a canoe rents for about $38 for 24 hours, but only $76 for 3 days. Rentals come with a roof rack if you need it. There are many wonderful places to canoe in Wellfleet. A trip from Wellfleet's Town Pier across the harbor to Great Island, for instance, will get you nowhere fast, beautifully.

In addition to watercraft to go, Jack's is also the place for information about **Eric Gustavson's guided kayak tours** (☎ 508/349-1429) of nearby kettle ponds and tidal rivers. The cost is $30 for a 2½-hour tour. Eric also offers windsurfing lessons and rentals ($40 an hour), surfing lessons ($40 an hour), mountain-bike tours ($10 per person, per hour), and for the most adventurous, kitesurfing ($75 an hour). For information about other excellent naturalist-guided tours, inquire about trips sponsored by the **Cape Cod Museum of Natural History** (☎ 800/479-3867 or 508/896-3867) and the **Wellfleet Bay Wildlife Sanctuary** (☎ 508/349-2615).

The **Chequessett Yacht & Country Club** on Chequessett Neck Road in Wellfleet (☎ 508/349-3704) offers group sailing lessons. Call for rates. For experienced sailors, **Wellfleet Marine Corp.,** on the Town Pier (☎ 508/349-2233), rents 14- to 20-foot sailboats in season. The cost is $30 to $50 for the first hour, $12 to $20 for each additional hour, or $90 to $150 for the day.

FISHING For a license to fish at Long Pond, Great Pond, or Gull Pond (all stocked with trout and full of native perch, pickerel, and sunfish), visit **Town Hall** at 300 Main St. (☎ 508/349-0301) or the **Town Pier** (☎ 508/349-9818). Costs vary, but in general, Massachusetts residents pay $13.50 for a 3-day pass or $28.50 for a season pass; non-residents pay $24.50 for a 3-day pass or $38.50 for a season pass. Surf casting, which doesn't require a license, is permitted at the town beaches. Shellfishing licenses—Wellfleet's oysters are world-famous—can be obtained from the **Shellfish Department** on the Town Pier off Kendrick Avenue (☎ 508/349-0300). Shellfish licenses are $40 per season for residents, $125 per season for non-residents. Also heading out from here, in season, is the 60-foot party fishing boat *Navigator* (☎ 508/349-6003), and three smaller boats: the *Erin-H* (☎ 508/349-9663), *Jac's Mate* (☎ 508/255-2978), and *Snooper* (☎ 508/349-6113).

GOLF Hugging a pretty cove, the **Chequessett Yacht & Country Club** on Chequessett Neck Road (☎ 508/349-3704) has one of the loveliest 9-hole courses on the Cape; non-members need to reserve at least 3 days ahead. Greens fees are $27 for 9 holes, $40 for 18 holes.

NATURE & WILDLIFE AREAS You'll find 6 miles of very scenic trails lined with lupines and bayberries—Goose Pond, Silver Spring, and Bay View—within the **Wellfleet Bay Wildlife Sanctuary** in South Wellfleet (see below). Right in town, the short, picturesque boardwalk known as **Uncle Tim's Bridge,** off East Commercial Street,

Cape Cod National Seashore

No trip to Cape Cod would be complete without a visit to the Cape Cod National Seashore on the Outer Cape and an afternoon barefoot stroll along the **"The Great Beach,"** where you see exactly why the Cape attracts artists and poets. On August 7, 1961, President John F. Kennedy signed a bill designating 27,000 acres in the 40 miles from Chatham to Provincetown as the Cape Cod National Seashore, a new national park. Unusual in a national park, the Seashore includes 500 private residences, the owners of which lease land from the park service. Convincing residents that a National Seashore would be a good thing for Cape Cod was an arduous task back then, and Provincetown still grapples with Seashore officials over town land issues.

The Seashore's claim to fame is its spectacular beaches—in reality, one long beach—with dunes 50 to 150 feet high. This is the Atlantic Ocean, so the surf is rough (and cold), but a number of the beaches have lifeguards. Seashore beaches include Coast Guard and Nauset Light Beaches in Eastham, Marconi Beach in Wellfleet, Head of the Meadow Beach in Truro, and Provincetown's Race Point and Herring Cove beaches. A $20 pass will get you into all of them for the season, or you can pay a daily rate of $7.

The Seashore also has a number of walking trails—all free, all picturesque, and all worth a trip. In Eastham, ✪ **Fort Hill** (off Route 6) has one of the best scenic views on Cape Cod and a popular boardwalk trail through a red maple swamp. The **Nauset Marsh Trail** is accessed from the Salt Pond Visitor Center on Route 6 in Eastham. **Great Island** on the bay side in Wellfleet is surely one of the finest places to have a picnic; you could spend the day hiking the trails. On **Pamet Trail** off North Pamet Road in Truro, hikers pass the decrepit old cranberry-bog building (restoration is in the works) on the way to a trail through the dunes. Don't try the old boardwalk trail over the bogs here; it has flooded and is no longer in use. The **Atlantic White Cedar Swamp Trail** is located at the Marconi Station site, **Small Swamp** and **Pilgrim Spring** trails are found at Pilgrim

crosses Duck Creek to access a tiny island crisscrossed by paths. The Cape Cod National Seashore maintains two spectacular self-guided trails. The 1¼-mile **Atlantic White Cedar Swamp Trail,** off the parking area for the Marconi Wireless Station (see below), shelters a rare stand of the lightweight species prized by Native Americans as wood for canoes; red maples are slowly crowding out the cedars, but meanwhile the tea-tinted, moss-choked swamp is a magical place, refreshingly cool even at the height of summer. A boardwalk will see you over the muck (these peat bogs are 7 feet deep in places), but the return trip does entail a calf-testing ½-mile trek through deep sand. Consider it a warm-up for magnificent **Great Island,** jutting 4 miles into the bay (off the western end of Chequessett Neck Rd.) to cup Wellfleet Harbor. Before attaching itself to the mainland in 1831, Great Island harbored a busy whaling post; a 1970 dig turned up the foundations of an early–18th-century tavern. These days the "island" is quite uninhabited and a true refuge for those strong enough to go the distance. Just be sure to cover up, wear sturdy shoes, bring water, and venture to **Jeremy Point**—the very tip—only if you're sure the tide is going out.

A spiffy eco-friendly visitor center serves as both introduction and gateway to the ✪ **Wellfleet Bay Wildlife Sanctuary,** (off Route 6, a couple hundred yards north of the Eastham border, in South Wellfleet (☎ **508/349-2615;** fax 508/349-2632;

Heights Beach, and **Beech Forest Trail** is located at Race Point in Provincetown. The best bike path on Cape Cod is the **Province Lands Trail,** 5 swooping and invigorating miles, at Race Point Beach. If that's not enough in the way of sports, surf casting is allowed from the ocean beaches—Race Point is a popular spot.

The Seashore also includes several historic buildings that tell their part of the region's history. At Race Point Beach in Provincetown, the **Old Harbor Lifesaving Station** serves as a museum of early lifesaving techniques. **Captain Edward Penniman's 1868 house** at Fort Hill in Eastham is a grandly ornate Second Empire home, and the 1730 **Atwood-Higgins House** in Wellfleet is a typical Cape-style home; both are open for tours. Five lighthouses dot the Seashore, including Highland Light in Truro and Nauset Light in Eastham, both recently moved back from precarious positions on the edge of dunes.

Most of the Seashore beaches have large parking lots, but you'll need to get there early (before 10am) on busy summer weekends. If the beach you want to go to is full, try the one next door—most of the beaches are 5 to 10 miles apart. Don't forget your beach umbrella; the sun exposure here can get intense.

Getting There: Take Route 6, the Mid-Cape Highway, to Eastham (about 50 miles). Pick up a map at the Salt Pond Visitor Center in Eastham. There is another visitor center at Race Point. Both centers have ranger activities, maps, gift shops, and rest rooms. Seashore beaches are all off Route 6 and are clearly marked. Additional beaches along this stretch are run by individual towns, and you must have a sticker or pay a fee.

Recommended Reading: Henry David Thoreau's *Cape Cod* is an entertaining account of Thoreau's journeys on the Cape in the late 19th-century—the writer/naturalist walked along the beach from Eastham to Provincetown. You can follow in his footsteps. Henry Beston's *The Outermost House* describes a year of living on the beach in Eastham in a simple one-room dune shack. The shack washed out to sea about 20 years ago, but "The Great Beach" remains.

www.wellfleetbay.org) a 1,000-acre refuge maintained by the Massachusetts Audubon Society. Passive solar heat and composting toilets are just a few of the waste-cutting elements incorporated into the seemingly simple $1.6-million building, which nestles into its wooded site like well-camouflaged wildlife. You'll see plenty of the latter—especially lyrical red-winged blackbirds and circling osprey—as you follow 5 miles of looping trails through pine forests, salt marsh, and moors. To hone your observation skills, avail yourself of the naturalist-guided tours offered during the day and sometimes at night (see "Wellfleet After Dark," below): You'll see and learn much more. Also inquire about special workshops for children (some, like the Japanese "fish-printing" session, are truly ingenious), and about canoeing, birding, and seal-watching excursions. Seal-watching trips are $30 to $35 for a 1½-hour tour by boat. Canoe trips for experienced paddlers (over age 12) are scheduled in season Tuesday, Wednesday, and Friday throughout the Lower Cape. The cost is $14 to $18. A 3-hour boat tour of Pleasant Bay that includes exploring an island is $25 to $35. A listing of all Wellfleet Bay Wildlife Sanctuary events with dates and times is posted in the main building.

Trail use is free for Massachusetts Audubon Society members; the trail fee for non-members is $3 for adults and $2 for seniors and children. Trails are open July through

August from 8am to 8pm, and September through June from 8am to dusk. The visitor center is open Memorial Day to Columbus Day daily from 8:30am to 5pm; during the off-season, it's closed Monday.

Note: It's worth joining the **Massachusetts Audubon Society** just for the chance—afforded only to members—to camp out here.

TENNIS Public courts are located at Mayo Beach on Kendrick Avenue near the harbor; for details and exact fees, contact the **Wellfleet Recreation Department** (☎ 508/349-0330). Also for a fee, book one of the five clay courts at the **Chequessett Yacht & Country Club** on Chequessett Neck Road (☎ 508/349-3704) or the eight at **Oliver's Clay Courts** at 2183 Rte. 6, about 1 mile south of town (☎ 508/349-3330). At Chequessett, 1 hour of singles play costs $18, doubles $25. Both settings are beautiful.

WATER SPORTS Surfing is restricted to White Crest Beach, and sailboarding to Burton Baker Beach at Indian Neck during certain tide conditions; ask for a copy of the regulations at the Beach Sticker Booth on the Town Pier.

WELLFLEET HISTORICAL SIGHTS

Marconi Wireless Station. Marconi Site Rd. (off Rte. 6, about ¾ mile S of the town center). ☎ 508/349-3785. www.nps.gov/caco. Free parking and admission. Open dawn–dusk.

It's from this bleak spot that Italian inventor Guglielmo Marconi broadcast, via a complex of 210-foot cable towers, the world's first wireless communiqué: "cordial greetings from President Theadore [*sic*] Roosevelt to King Edward VII in Poldhu, Wales." It was also here that news of the troubled *Titanic* first reached these shores. There's scarcely a trace left of this extraordinary feat of technology (the station was dismantled in 1920); still, the displays convey the leap of imagination that was required.

Wellfleet Historical Society Museum. 266 Main St. (in the center of town). ☎ 508/349-9157. Admission $1 adults, free for children under 12. Late June–early Sept Tues and Fri 10am–noon; Tues–Sat 1–4pm. Closed early Sept–late June.

Every last bit of spare Wellfleet memorabilia seems to have been crammed into this old storefront. The volunteer curators have taken pains to arrange the surfeit of artifacts so that visitors can follow up on a particular interest—the United Fruit Co., say, which got its start here in 1870 when one of Lorenzo Dow Baker's swift clipper ships delivered a cargo of exotic bananas, or Marconi's mysterious transoceanic experiments. Even restless children are likely to find something of interest, particularly among the antique toys in the attic. Inquire about the lecture schedule: The museum hosts some fascinating speakers and sponsors a chowder supper once a summer. Historical walking tours around town take 1¼ hours, cost $3, and leave at 10:30am.

KID STUFF

No conceivable nocturnal treat beats an outing to the **Wellfleet Drive-In Theater**—unless it's a double-feature prefaced by a game of on-site minigolf while you're waiting for the sky to darken. The restaurant on-site is the **Intermission Grill** (☎ 508/349-7007), which specializes in grilled seafood and beef, and is open from 11:30am to 10pm daily in season. There's also a children's menu. During the day, check out what's up at the Wellfleet Bay Wildlife Sanctuary (see "Beaches & Recreational Pursuits," above).

SHOPPING

Boasting over a dozen arts emporia, Wellfleet has begun hailing itself as "the art-gallery town." Though it may lag behind Provincetown in terms of quantity, the quality does achieve comparable heights. Crafts make a strong showing, too, as do contemporary women's clothing and eclectic home furnishings. Just one drawback: Unlike Provincetown, which has something to offer virtually year-round, Wellfleet pretty much closes up come Columbus Day, so buy while the getting's good.

ANTIQUES/COLLECTIBLES   Wheeler-dealers should head for the **Wellfleet Flea Market,** 51 Rte. 6, north of the Eastham-Wellfleet border (☎ **800/696-3532** or 508/349-2520). A few days a week in summer and during the shoulder seasons, the parking lot of the Wellfleet Drive-In Theater "daylights" as an outdoor bazaar featuring as many as 300 booths. Though a great many vendors stock discount surplus, there are usually enough collectibles dealers on hand to warrant a browse through. An added bonus: Kids can kick loose in the little playground or grab a quick bite at the snack bar. Lookers are charged $1 to $2 per carload. Open weekends and Monday holidays, from mid-April through June, September, and October, from 8am to 4pm; Wednesdays, Thursdays, weekends, and Monday holidays in July and August from 8am to 4pm.

   Farmhouse Antiques, Route 6 at Village Lane, South Wellfleet (☎ **508/349-1708**), is a large storehouse filled with an enormous variety of goods, including a wide array of furniture, stacks of books and ephemera, and the antique chandeliers that didn't fit in the Orleans shop, Continuum (Farmhouse is a dealer for Continuum's wares).

ARTS & CRAFTS   ✪ Cherrystone Gallery, 70 E. Commercial St., about ⅛ mile south of East Main Street (☎ **508/349-3026**), is slightly off the main arts drag and intentionally out of step, but this tiny gallery is probably more influential than all the others put together. It got a head start—opening in 1972, and showing such luminaries as Rauschenberg, Motherwell, and, more recently, Wellfleet resident Helen Miranda Wilson. Closed late September to mid-June.

   One of the more distinguished galleries in town, the smallish ✪ **Cove Gallery,** 15 Commercial St., by Duck Creek (☎ **508/349-2530**)—with a waterside sculpture garden—carries the paintings and prints of many well-known artists, including Barry Moser and Leonard Baskin. John Grillo's work astounds every summer during his annual show, which recently featured boldly painted tango-themed paintings, watercolors, and prints. Alan Nyiri, whose dazzling color photographs are collected in the coffee-table book *Cape Cod,* shows regularly, as does Carla Golembe, whose lively Caribbean-influenced tableaux have graced several children's books. Closed mid-October through April.

   Crafts make a stronger stand than art at **Left Bank Gallery,** 25 Commercial St., by Duck Creek (☎ **508/349-9451**). A 1933 American Legion Hall, it's an optimal display space. Whereas the paintings occupying the former auditorium sometimes verge on hackneyed, the "Potter's Room" overlooking the cove is packed with sturdy, handsome, useful vessels, along with compatible textiles. Also worth hunting out are the curious collages of Kim Victoria Kettler. The **Left Bank Small Works & Jewelry Gallery,** 3 W. Main St., in the center of town (☎ **508/349-7939**), features the spillover from the Left Bank Gallery, and in some ways, it is superior. There's also an irresistible sampling of new-wave jewelry designs, collected from over 100 noted artisans across the nation and arrayed in clever thematic displays.

FASHION   At ✪ **Hannah,** 234 Main St. (☎ **508/349-9884**), Susan Hannah, whose main store is in ultra-hip Northampton, Massachusetts, shows her own private label in this nicely rehabbed house, along with other designers' works. The emphasis is on flowing lines and relaxed fabrics—slinky rayons, soft cotton jersey, and nubby linen. Closed mid-September to late May.

   Slightly more citified is **Off Center,** 354 Main St. (☎ **508/349-3634**), where the clothes are neither traditional nor trendy, but right on, go-anywhere chic. Closed January through March.

Somewhat to the left of—and across the street from—its parent shop, Off Center, is **Eccentricity,** 361 Main St., in the center of town (☎ **508/349-7554**), which lives up to its name with dramatic antique kimonos and artifacts from Japan, India, and Africa. Closed January through March.

✪ **Karol Richardson,** 3 W. Main St. (☎ **508/349-6378**), is owned and operated by its namesake, an alumna of the London College of Fashion and a refugee from the New York rag trade. She has a feel for sensual fabrics and a knack for fashions that, in her own words, are "wonderfully comfortable but sophisticated at the same time and very flattering to the less-than-perfect body." The lovely clothes that are seasonally displayed in this barn showroom, and slavered over by several generations, bear out the claim. Closed mid-October through April.

GIFTS   ✪ Jules Besch Stationers, 15 Bank St. (☎ **508/349-1231**), specializes in stationery products, including papers, ribbon, gift cards, handmade journals and albums, desktop pen sets, guest books, and unusual gift items. This is an exquisite store in a mansard-roofed former bank building and certainly worth a browse.

WHERE TO STAY
MODERATE

Aunt Sukie's Bayside Bed & Breakfast. 525 Chequessett Neck Rd., Wellfleet, MA 02667. ☎ **800/420-9999** or 508/349-2804. www.auntsukies.com. E-mail: auntsukies@mediaone.net. 3 units, 1 cottage. TEL. Summer $150–$200. Cottage $1200–$1400 per week. Room rates include continental breakfast. MC, V. Closed mid-Jan to mid-Mar.

Sue and Dan Hamar's house is perched on a bluff in an exclusive residential neighborhood overlooking Cape Cod Bay. Behind the house, a boardwalk path leads to a private bay beach. They also own a two-bedroom cottage located about a mile away in the pines that is available by the week and offers, among other features, a galley kitchen, washer/dryer, and barbecue. The main house was built in 1830 but has been modernized and added on to over the years. The Nickerson Suite is in the old part of the house and has wide-board wood floors and a fireplace. The Chequessett and Billingsgate rooms are more contemporary as befits the addition completed in 1993. All rooms have sweeping bay views. There are beautiful gardens in front of the house, and in the back is a large deck where guests eat breakfast and can sunbathe during the day.

✪ **Surfside Cottages.** Ocean View Dr. (at LeCount Hollow Rd.) (P.O. Box 937), South Wellfleet, MA 02663. ☎/fax **508/349-3959.** www.capecod.net/surfside. E-mail: surfside@capecod.net. 18 cottages. TEL. Summer $750–$1,350 weekly; off-season $70–$125 per day. MC, V. Pets allowed off-season.

This is where you want to be: smack dab on a spectacular beach with 50-foot dunes, within biking distance of Wellfleet Center, and a short drive to Provincetown for dinner. These cottages, fun and modern in a 1960s way, have one, two, or three bedrooms. All cottages have kitchens including microwaves, as well as fireplaces, barbecues, and screened porches. Some have dishwashers, outdoor showers and (most important) roof decks. From mid-May to mid-October, the cottages rent weekly. It's best to bring your own sheets and towels; renting a set costs $10 per person. Reserve early.

INEXPENSIVE

Even'tide. 650 Rte. 6 (about 1 mile N of the Eastham border), South Wellfleet, MA 02663. ☎ **800/368-0007** in MA only, or 508/349-3410. Fax 508/349-7804. www.eventidemotel. com. E-mail: eventide@capecod.net. 31 units. A/C TV TEL. Summer $89–$120 double; $122–$149 efficiency. AE, CB, DC, DISC, MC, V.

Set back from the road in its own roomy compound, complete with playground, this motel feels more like a friendly village centered around a 60-foot, heated indoor pool—a godsend in inclement weather and a rarity in this part of the Cape. All rooms have minifridges and coffeemakers; and four "apartments" have kitchenettes. There are seven cottages on the property with one, two, and three bedrooms. There's also a self-service Laundromat on-site. The Rail Trail goes right by the motel, and a 1-mile footpath through the woods leads to Marconi Beach.

The Inn at Duck Creeke. 70 Main St. (P.O. Box 364), Wellfleet, MA 02667. ☎ **508/349-9333.** Fax 508/349-0234. www.capecod.net/duckinn. E-mail: duckinn@capecod.net. 27 units, 8 with shared bathroom. Summer $70–$100 double. Rates include continental breakfast. AE, MC, V. Closed Nov–Apr.

This historic complex consists of four buildings set on 5 woodsy acres overlooking a tidal creek and salt marsh. Three lodging buildings include the main building, an 1880s captain's house with wide-board floors and charming but basic rooms, many with shared bathrooms; the carriage house with a few light and airy cabin-style rooms; and the 1715 saltworks building with smaller cottage-type rooms with antique decor. In the main building, the shared bathrooms adjoin two rooms, so there's an intimacy here those in search of privacy might not desire. And if the adjoining room houses a family of four, it might be a rough night. All rooms have fans, and the third floor rooms in the main house have air-conditioning. The rooms in the carriage house and saltworks building are quieter and can be downright romantic. But there's definitely a no-frills quality to this lodging option—towels are thin, and so are walls. Even the continental breakfast is very basic: a buffet of tiny muffins on paper plates. A big plus is that there are two good restaurants (see "Where to Dine," below) on-site: Sweet Seasons, the more expensive, and the Duck Creeke Tavern, with a publike atmosphere and live entertainment in season.

WHERE TO DINE
EXPENSIVE

Aesop's Tables. 316 Main St. (in the center of town). ☎ **508/349-6450.** Reservations recommended. Main courses $15–$27. AE, CB, DISC, MC, V. July–Aug Wed–Sun noon–3pm; daily 5:30–9:30pm; call for off-season hours. Closed Nov–Apr. NEW AMERICAN.

This delightful restaurant—offbeat and avant-garde enough to stay interesting year after year—has it all: a handsome, historic setting; a relaxed and festive atmosphere; and utterly delectable food, reliably and artistically turned out by executive chef Patricia Worthington. Brian Dunne is at once owner and host; it's he who sets the mood and oversees the sourcing of the superb local provender, even growing some of the edible flowers and delicate greens that go into the "Monet's Garden" salad. The scallops and oysters come straight from the bay. *Coeur del la Mer* is fresh lobster meat, mussels, clams, shrimp, and fish in a citrus-saffron broth. While some entrees have begun to show evidence of world-beat influences, the desserts are sacrosanct. Many followers simply could not get through the summer without enjoying at least one encounter with "Clementine's Citrus Tart," a rich *pâté sablée* (sablé pastry) offset by a piquant mousse blending fruit and white chocolate.

Sweet Seasons Restaurant. At the Inn at Duck Creeke, 70 Main St. (about ⅛ mile W of Rte. 6). ☎ **508/349-6535.** Reservations recommended. Main courses $16–$23. AE, MC, V. Late June to mid-Sept daily 5:30–10pm. Closed mid-Sept to late June. NEW AMERICAN.

The competition has grown heated of late, but chef-owner Judith Pihl's Mediterranean-influenced fare is still appealing after 20-plus years, as is this mullion-windowed dining room's peaceful pond view. Some of the dishes can be a bit heavy by contemporary standards, but there's usually a healthy alternative: Wellfleet littlenecks and mussels in a golden, aromatic tomato-and-cumin broth, for instance, as opposed to Russian oysters with smoked salmon, vodka, and sour cream. Specialties of the house include creamy sage-and-asparagus ravioli, swordfish with artichoke tapenade, and Seasons shrimp with feta and ouzo. Lighter fare is served in the adjoining Duck Creeke Tavern.

MODERATE

Finely JP's. 554 Rte. 6 (about 1 mile N of the Eastham border). ☎ **508/349-7500.** Reservations not accepted. Main courses $12–$15. DISC, MC, V. June–Aug daily 5–10pm; call for off-season hours. Closed mid-Dec to mid-Jan. NEW AMERICAN.

The passing motorist who happens upon this roadside eatery will feel like a clever explorer indeed, even if locals have long been in on the secret. Were it not for the venue—a rather non-descript wood-paneled box right by the busy roadway—chef-owner John Pontius could charge a lot more for his polished cuisine. As it is, you can feast on baked *oysters Bienville* (doused with wine and cream and topped with a mushroom-onion duxelle and grated Parmesan) and an improvised "Wellfleet paella," having barely broken a 20-note. Pass it on.

✪ **Painter's Restaurant.** 50 Main St. (near Rte. 6). ☎ **508/349-3003.** Main courses $8–$23. AE, MC, V. Late May to mid-Oct daily 6–10pm; mid-Oct to late May Wed–Sat 6–10pm. NEW AMERICAN/ASIAN.

The offspring of local literati, Kate Painter trained at some pretty fancy establishments: San Francisco's world-famous Stars, Boston top-spot Biba, and Cape Cod's own Chillingsworth. Still, if she had her druthers—and now she does, having set up her own restaurant in a rambling 1750 tavern—she'd prefer, in the words of her motto and mission statement, "simple food in a funky place." The modesty is misplaced; although the setting is pretty low-key (a wood-beamed bistro dressed up with friends' artwork), her culinary skills are top-notch. On the appetizer list, the crackling Asian cellophane shrimp served with tomato coulis is a flavorful delight; nori-wrapped grilled salmon is also very fine. The entrees include such dishes as Painter's Tuna, seared with sesame and mustard seed, served with a lovely orange-ginger Asian dipping sauce and wasabi; clams Cataplana (like a sunnily spiced Portuguese bouillabaisse); and an always affordable linguine with Painter's Red Sauce. Painter's sense of humor shows up in the desserts: "Something Chocolate" and "Something Lemon" are just that, an intriguing cross between cake and soufflé. A limited tavern menu is served until 11pm.

INEXPENSIVE

The Lighthouse. 317 Main St. (in the center of town). ☎ **508/349-3681.** Main courses $9–$18. DISC, MC, V. May–Oct daily 7am–10pm; call for off-season hours. Closed Mar. AMERICAN.

Nothing special in and of itself, this bustling year-round institution is an off-season haven for locals and a beacon to passing tourists year-round. Except on Thursday's "Mexican Night," the menu is all-American normal, from the steak-and-eggs breakfast to the native seafood dinners. Appreciative patrons usually keep up a dull roar throughout the day, revving up to a deafening roar as the Bass and Guinness flow from the tap.

✪ **Moby Dick's Restaurant.** Rte. 6, Wellfleet. ☎ **508/349-9795.** Reservations not accepted. Main courses $8–$20. MC, V. June–Sept daily 11:30am–10pm; call for off-season hours. Closed mid-Oct to Apr. SEAFOOD.

This is your typical clam shack, with the requisite netting and buoys hanging from the ceiling. Order your meal at the register, sit at a picnic table, and a cheerful college student brings it to you. Fried fish, clams, scallops, and shrimp are all good here; try the Moby's Seafood Special—a heaping platter of all of the above, plus coleslaw and fries.

Then there's the clambake special with lobster, steamers, and corn on the cob. Portions are huge; bring the family and chow down.

TAKE-OUT & PICNIC FARE

Box Lunch. 20 Briar Lane (N of Main St. in the town center). ☎ **508/349-2178.**

With a porch usually hemmed in by bicycles, this is the original source of the Cape's signature "rollwiches": rolled pita sandwiches with unusual fillings.

✪ **Hatch's Fish & Produce Market.** 310 Main St. (behind Town Hall). ☎ **508/349-6734** for produce, **508/349-2810** for fish market. Closed Oct–May.

This former fishing shack is the unofficial heart of Wellfleet. You'll find the best of local bounty, from fresh-picked corn and fruit-juice Popsicles to steaming lobsters and home-smoked local mussels and pâté. Virtually no one passes through without picking up a little something, along with the latest talk of the town. Closed late September to late May.

Mac's Seafood Market and Restaurant. Wellfleet Town Pier. ☎ **508/349-0404.** Daily 11am–9pm. Closed Oct–May.

Located on the town pier, this take-out shack with picnic tables features fresh local seafood unloaded from the boats just steps away. Besides grilled fish dinners, there are homemade chowders, seafood salads, sushi, and a raw bar.

SWEETS

The Chocolate Sparrow. 326 Main St. (in the center of town). ☎ **508/349-1333.**

This closet-size outlet of a local chocolatier is hard to pass by once you've happened upon it. There's also a room full of penny candy. Closed mid-September to late May.

Just Dessert. 91 Commercial St. (behind the Bayside Lobster Hutt). ☎ **508/349-6333.**

In a coveside cottage with a breezy deck and a deli case full of sweet finales, you can enjoy treats from sophisticated cheesecakes to "mile-high apple pie." There's ice cream, too. Closed early September to late June.

A Nice Cream Stop. 326 Main St. (in the center of town). ☎ **508/349-2210.**

This is Wellfleet's premier premium ice-cream parlor, scooping Emack & Bolio's, a luscious Boston boutique brand. Closed mid-September to mid-June.

WELLFLEET AFTER DARK
CLUBS & WATERING HOLES

✪ **The Beachcomber.** 1220 Old Cahoon Hollow Rd. (off Ocean View Dr. at Cahoon Hollow Beach). ☎ **508/349-6055.** www.beachcomber.com. Cover varies. Late June–early Sept daily noon–1am; call for off-season hours. Closed mid-Sept to late May.

Arguably the best dance club on Cape Cod, the 'Comber—housed in an 1897 life-saving station—is definitely the most scenic, and not just in terms of the barely legal-age clientele. It's right on Cahoon Hollow Beach—so close, in fact, that late beachgoers on summer weekends can count on a free concert: reggae, perhaps, or the homegrown "Toots and the Maytalls." Other nights, you might run into blues, ska, or rock, and often some very big names playing mostly for the fun of it. For victims of late-night munchies, the Beachcomber serves food until midnight.

Duck Creeke Tavern. At the Inn at Duck Creeke, 70 Main St. (about ⅛ mile W of Rte. 6). ☎ **508/349-7369.** Closed mid-Oct to late May. No cover.

Local talent—jazz, pop, folk, blues, and various hybrids—accompany the light fare here. Check out the bar itself, fashioned from old doors.

Upstairs Bar at Aesop's Tables. 316 Main St. (in the center of town). ☎ **508/349-6450.** No cover. July–Aug daily 5:30pm–1am; call for off-season hours. Closed mid-Oct to mid-May.

Locally spawned blues and jazz usually inhabit this cozy attic, where revelers can recline in comfy armchairs and velvet settees. A cafe menu from the superb restaurant downstairs (see "Where to Dine," above) can be enjoyed, along with the signature desserts and some seductive "special finales," blending coffee or tea and select liqueurs.

FROM BELFRIES TO BATS & OTHER ENTERTAINMENT

The First Congregational Church of the United Church of Christ, 200 Main St., about an ⅛ mile west of Route 6 (☎ **508/349-6877**), hosts organ concerts Sundays at 8pm during July and August on its elaborate 1873 instrument. They're a good excuse to stop in and take a look around—the soaring 1850 Greek Revival church has the world's only bell tower ringing ship's time (an innovation introduced in 1952). Admission is free.

Wednesday nights in July and August, Wellfleet's workaday fishing pier (off Kendrick Avenue) resounds to the footfalls of avid amateur **square dancers** of every age. Call ☎ **508/349-0330** for more information.

How about a night hike or bat walk? Both are offered at the **Wellfleet Bay Wildlife Sanctuary** (☎ **508/349-2615;** see "Beaches & Recreational Pursuits," above). Rates vary; call for schedule and reservations. Just don't take in any vampire movies at the drive-in beforehand.

The **Wellfleet Drive-In Theater,** 51 Rte. 6, just north of the Eastham border (☎ **800/696-3532** or 508/349-2520), clearly deserves National Landmark status: Built in 1957, it's the only drive-in left on Cape Cod and one of a scant half dozen surviving in the state. The rituals are unbending and every bit as endearing as ever: the playtime preceding the cartoons, the countdown plugging the allures of the snack bar, and finally, two full first-run features. The drive-in is open daily from late May through mid-September; show time is at dusk. Call for off-season hours. Admission is $6 for adults and $3.50 for seniors and children 5 to 11.

The principals behind the ✪ **Wellfleet Harbor Actors' Theatre,** 1 Kendrick Ave., near the Town Pier (☎ **508/349-6835**), aim to provoke—and usually succeed, even amid this very sophisticated, seen-it-all summer colony. Co-artistic directors Jeff Zinn and playwright Gip Hoppe go to great lengths to secure original work, some local and some by playwrights of considerable renown, with the result that the repertory rarely suffers a dull moment. Gip Hoppe's *Jackie O!* made it to Broadway a few years ago. Tickets are $14. Performances are given daily at 8pm from late May through October; call for schedule.

3 Truro

46 miles (74km) E of Sandwich; 10 miles (16km) S of Provincetown

Truro is one of those blink-and-you'll-miss-it towns. With only 1,600 year-round residents (fewer than it boasted in 1840, when Pamet Harbor was a whaling and ship-building port), the town amounts to little more than a smattering of stores and public buildings, and lots of low-profile houses hidden away in the woods and dunes. As in Wellfleet, writers, artists, and vacationing therapists are drawn to the quiet and calm. Edward Hopper lived in contented isolation in a South Truro cottage for nearly 4 decades.

If you find yourself craving cultural stimulation or other kinds of excitement, Provincetown is only a 10-minute drive away (you'll know you're getting close when you spot the wall-to-wall tourist cabins lining the bay in North Truro). Here, the natives manage to entertain themselves pretty well with get-togethers at the Truro Center for the Arts or, more simply, among themselves. However much money may be circulating in this rusticated community (the answer is: a lot), inconspicuous consumption is the rule of the day. The culmination of the social season, tellingly enough, is the late-September "dump dance" held at Truro's recycling center.

ESSENTIALS

GETTING THERE   After crossing either the Bourne or Sagamore bridge, head east on Route 6 or 6A to Orleans and north on Route 6. Or fly into Provincetown (see "Getting There" in chapter 2).

VISITOR INFORMATION   Contact the **Truro Chamber of Commerce,** Route 6A (at Head of the Meadow Rd.), Truro, MA 02666 (☎ **508/487-1288;** trurococ@ capecod.net) or the **Cape Cod Chamber of Commerce** (see "Visitor Information" in the "Eastham" section, above).

BEACHES & RECREATIONAL PURSUITS

BEACHES   Parking at all of Truro's exquisite Atlantic beaches, except for one Cape Cod National Seashore access point, is reserved for residents and renters. To obtain a sticker ($20 for 1 week; $30 for 2 weeks), inquire at the **beach-sticker office** at 14 Truro Center Rd. behind the post office in Truro Center (☎ **508/349-3635**). Walkers and bikers are welcome to visit such natural wonders as Ballston Beach, where all you'll see is silky sand and grass-etched dunes. Parking is free at all beaches after 4pm.

- ✪ **Head of the Meadow,** off Head of the Meadow Road: Among the more remote National Seashore beaches, this spot (equipped with rest rooms) is known for its excellent surf. A parking lot connected by a short boardwalk to the beach makes this beach more easily accessible than other National Seashore beaches. It is also connected by a short bike path to Pilgrim Heights (see "Bicycling," below). Parking costs $7 per day, or $20 per season.
- **Corn Hill Beach,** off Corn Hill Road: Offering rest rooms, this bay beach—near the hill where the Pilgrims found the seed corn that ensured their survival—is open to non-residents for a parking fee of $5 per day.

BICYCLING   Although it has yet to be linked up to the Cape Cod Rail Trail, Truro does have a stunning 2-mile bike path of its own: the **Head of the Meadow Trail,** off the road of the same name (look for a right-hand turn about a ½ mile north of where Routes 6 and 6A intersect). Part of the old 1850 road toward Provincetown—Thoreau traveled this same route—it skirts the bluffs, passing Pilgrim Heights (where the Pilgrims found their first drinking water) and ending at High Head Road. Being fairly flat as well as short, this stretch should suit youngsters and beginners. Rentals can be arranged at **Bayside Bikes,** 102 Shore Rd. (Rte. 6A), North Truro (☎ **508/487-5735**).

BOATING   The inlets of Pamet Harbor are great for canoeing and kayaking; when planning an excursion, study the tides so you won't be working against them. The closest rentals are in Wellfleet at **Jack's Boat Rentals** (☎ **508/349-9808**) on Route 6, next to the Cumberland Farms. **Eric Gustavson** (☎ **508/349-1429**) leads naturalist kayak tours along the Pamet River and other locations on the Outer Cape. You can get the schedule from Jack's Boat Rentals.

FISHING   Great Pond, Horseleech Pond, and Pilgrim Lake—flanked by parabolic dunes carved by the wind—are all fishable; for a license, visit **Town Hall** on Town Hall Road (☎ **508/349-3860**). For shellfishing licenses, call ☎ **508/349-3635.** Surf casting is permitted at Highland Light Beach, off Highland Road.

GOLF   North Truro boasts the most scenic—and historic—9-hole course on the Cape. Created in 1892, the minimally groomed, Scottish-style **Highland Links** at 10 Lighthouse Rd., off South Highland Road (☎ 508/487-9201), shares a lofty bluff with the 1853 Highland Light, where Thoreau used to crash during his Outer Cape expeditions. Greens fees at the federally owned, town-run Highland Links are reasonable ($16 for 9 holes, $32 for 18 holes), considering the spectacular setting.

NATURE TRAILS   The Cape Cod National Seashore, composing 70 percent of Truro's land, offers three informative self-guided nature trails. The ½-mile **Pamet Trail** off North Pamet Road leads you past an old cranberry-bog building and bogs that have reverted to marshland. Park in the lot to the left of the Little America youth hostel (see "Where to Stay," below) and walk back to the fire road entrance about 500 feet back down North Pamet Road. The **Pilgrim Spring Trail** and **Small Swamp Trail** (each a ¾-mile loop) head out from the National Seashore parking lot just east of Pilgrim Lake. Pilgrim Spring is where the parched colonists sipped their first freshwater in months. Small Swamp is named for Thomas Small, a rather overly optimistic 19th-century farmer who tried to cultivate fruit trees in a soil more suited to salt hay. Both paths overlook Salt Meadow, a freshwater marsh favored by hawks and osprey.

TENNIS   Courts are available at the **Pamet Harbor Yacht and Tennis Club** on Depot Road (☎ 508/349-3772). Hourly fees are $16 singles and $20 doubles.

AN ARTS CENTER & A MUSEUM

✪ **Truro Center for the Arts at Castle Hill.** 10 Meetinghouse Rd. (at Castle Rd., about ¾ mile NW of the town center). ☎ **508/349-7511.** www.castlehill.org. Admission varies. Call for schedule. Closed Oct–May.

Send ahead for a brochure, and you could work some learning into your vacation. A great many celebrated writers and artists—from poet Alan Dugan to painter Edith Vonnegut—emerge from their summer hideaways to offer courses, lectures, and exhibits at this bustling little complex, an 1880s horse barn with windmill (now home to the administrative offices). The roster changes slightly from year to year, but you can rest assured that the stellar instructors will be at the top of their form in this stimulating environment. The center also offers lots of children's workshops for artists age 7 and up.

✪ **Truro Historical Museum and Highland Lighthouse.** 6 Lighthouse Rd. (off S. Highland Rd., 2 miles N of the town center on Rte. 6). ☎ **508/487-1121.** Admission to both museum and lighthouse $5 adults, free for children under 12. Admission to museum or lighthouse $3; free for children under 12. June–Sept daily 10am–5pm. Closed Oct–May.

Built as a hotel in 1907, the Highland House is a perfect repository for the odds and ends collected by the Truro Historical Society: ship's models, harpoons, primitive toys, a pirate's chest, and so on. Be sure to visit the second floor, set up as if still occupied by 19th-century tourists.

In 1996, Highland Lighthouse was moved back from its perilous perch above a rapidly eroding dune. Now the lighthouse is within 800 feet of the museum and is also operated by the Truro Historical Society. Seasonal lighthouse tours run May through October. There is a 51-inch height requirement, so, unfortunately, little ones can't climb up the tower. The lighthouse lookout deck stays open through October.

SHOPPING

ANTIQUES/COLLECTIBLES   Want to stay one step ahead of the antiques dealers, while enjoying pre-markup prices? Make regular visits to **Estate Furniture/North Truro Art Factory,** 346A Rte. 6, behind Seamen's Savings Bank (☎ 508/487-2705), where Jack Albacker stores entire households of vintage furnishings and also does framing. His goal is to keep the stuff moving, at modest prices. Collectors could be in luck.

Trifles and Treasures, 11 Truro Center Rd. (☎ **508/349-1708**), is a darling little shop right in the center of town. Antique buffs will enjoy browsing through the furniture, mainly American country pine. There's also authentic ironwork and other kitchen items.

ARTS & CRAFTS ✪ **The Susan Baker Memorial Museum,** 46 Shore Rd., Route 6A, a ¼ mile northwest of Route 6 (☎ **508/487-2557**), showcases Ms. Baker's creative output, from fanciful/functional papier-mâché *objets* and to brightly colored European landscapes. Despite the place's name, Baker has not passed on; it seems that she herself has exaggerated rumors of her death so as to rate her own museum without actually croaking. You might guess that she is definitely a character, as original as her work. Her main stock in trade—here, and at her Provincetown outlet— is humor displayed in various media, from artist's books to very atypical T-shirts (among the more popular of slogans in Provincetown: "Too Mean to Marry"). Call ahead October through May.

WHERE TO STAY

Days Cottages. Rte. 6A. (a couple miles south of the Provincetown border), North Truro, MA 02652. ☎ **508/487-1062.** Fax 508/487-5595. www.capecod.net/dayscott/. E-mail: dayscot@ capecod.net. 23 cottages. Summer $790 weekly. No credit cards. Closed mid-Oct to late Apr.

These are the famous tiny cottages you always see in local paintings and photos. All lined up along the bay beach in North Truro, these absolutely identical cottages— named after flowers—are all white clapboard with sea-foam green shutters. Although lacking frills, each has a living room, two small bedrooms, a kitchen, and a bathroom. The downside is that these are somewhat rough accommodations: The bedrooms are miniscule, and in some of the cottages, the fireplace has about 10 years worth of graffiti written on the brick chimney. There is also the noise of passing cars on this busy stretch of road to contend with. The upside is miles of bay beach for walking and swimming with views of Provincetown's quirky skyline in the distance. In season, beginning June 1, the cottages are rented only by the week, and they usually book up far in advance. Nevertheless, you may be able to squeeze in.

Kalmar Village. 674 Shore Rd. (Rte. 6A, about ¼ mile S of the Provincetown border), North Truro, MA 02652. ☎ **508/487-0585.** Fax 508/487-5827. www.kalmarvillage.com. 16 units, 40 cottages. TV. Summer $100 double; $140 suite; $1,000–$1,900 cottages weekly. DISC, MC, V. Closed mid-Oct to late May.

Spiffier than many of the motels and cottages along this spit of sand between Pilgrim Lake and Pilgrim Beach, this 1940s complex resembles a miniaturized Edgartown, with little white cottages shuttered in black. There are picnic tables, grills, and daily maid service. Some cottages have air-conditioning. The clientele—mostly families— can splash the day away in the 60-foot freshwater pool or on the 400-foot private beach.

Little America AYH-Hostel. 111 N. Pamet Rd. (1¼ miles E of Rte. 6), Truro, MA 02666. ☎ **508/349-3889.** 42 beds. $15 for members, $17 for non-members. JCB, MC, V. Closed mid-Sept to mid-June.

By far the most scenic of the youth hostels on the Cape, this Hopperesque house on a lonely bluff a short stroll from Ballston Beach was once a Coast Guard station; these days, it winters as an environmental-studies center. During the all-too-short summer, it's a magnet for hikers, cyclists, and surfers.

Outer Reach Motel. 535 Rte. 6 (midway between North Truro center and the Provincetown border), North Truro, MA 02652. ☎ **800/942-5388** or 508/487-9090. Fax 508/487-9007. 58 units. TV. Summer $99–$124 double. MC, V. Closed late Oct to mid-May.

The only tradeoff worth forfeiting a spot right on the beach is a fabulous view of the beach. This sprawling motel—the last development to sneak under the wire pre–National Seashore—offers glorious vistas of Provincetown. On-site, you'll find an outdoor pool and tennis court, as well as a basketball hoop and shuffleboard; the ocean is 1 mile east. The rooms are standard issue with large fans, and all rooms have minifridges. There's a mediocre restaurant, Adrian's, within the complex.

Truro Vineyards of Cape Cod. 11 Shore Rd. (Rte. 6A, off Rte. 6, ½ mile S of the town center), North Truro, MA 02652. ☎ /fax **508/487-6200.** 5 units. Summer $99 double; $129 suite. Rates include continental breakfast. MC, V. Closed mid-Sept to mid-May.

You don't have to be a wine lover to appreciate this beautiful 1836 B&B set amid 5 vine-covered acres. If you are, though, you'll be in your element. Each of the five bedrooms—including the Vintage Suite, with its double Jacuzzi—comes with a four-poster bed draped in particular grape tones, ranging from claret to burgundy. These are comfortable rooms with ultra-thick wall-to-wall carpeting in matching deep tones. Horticulturist/innkeepers Kathy Gregrow and Judy Wimer uncorked their first homegrown Chardonnay and Cabernet Franc in the fall of 1996, the Muscadet in 1997, and the Merlot is well on its way. Guests enjoy breakfast in the slate-floored sunroom or the outdoor brick patio. The living room, with its exposed beams, is decorated with interesting oenological artifacts. Late May through October, free wine tastings are held daily from noon to 5pm. For the non-connoisseur, the draw is likely to be the bucolic setting (this is one of the last working farms on the Outer Cape), only 6 miles from the center of Provincetown.

WHERE TO DINE

Babe's Bakery and Restaurant. Rte. 6A (about ¼ mile north of the North Truro center), North Truro. ☎ **508/487-9473.** Most items under $8. No credit cards. Daily Mid-June to Sept 7:30am–12:30pm. Closed Oct to mid-June. DINER.

Perched on a windswept hill in North Truro, this terrific diner serves very basic but consistently good meals. The pastries are homemade and baked on-site daily. Babe's is popular, so expect a half-hour wait in season (timing is everything; the earlier the better). Hearty lunch selections include a Reuben sandwich, bacon-and-cheese burger, or perhaps quiche Lorraine. There's also a selection of fresh salads and sandwiches.

✪ **Terra Luna.** 104 Shore Rd. (Rte. 6A), North Truro. ☎ **508/487-1019.** Reservations recommended. Main courses $14–$20. AE, MC, V. Late May to mid-Oct daily 8am–1pm and 5:30–10pm. Closed mid-Oct to late May. FUSION.

People come from miles around to sample the outstanding breakfasts at this modest restaurant. The muffins and scones emerge fresh from the oven, and "entrees" such as the breakfast burrito or strawberry mascarpone-cheese pancakes call for a hearty appetite. You can start in again in the evening, on well-priced Pacific Rim and/or neo-Italian fare, such as *penne prosciutto* sautéed with garlic, black pepper, and a splash of vodka. Main courses include local seafood and lobster dishes, like lobster risotto with asparagus and saffron. There's even a creative children's menu here.

SWEETS & TAKE-OUT

✪ **Jams.** 14 Truro Center Rd. (off Rte. 6, in the center of town). ☎ **508/349-1616.**

Seeing as this deli/bakery/grocery is basically the whole enchilada in terms of down-town Truro, and seasonal to boot, it's good that it's so delightful. It's full of tantalizing aromas: fresh, creative pizzas (from pesto to pupu); rotisseried fowl sizzling on the spit;

or cookies straight from the oven. The pastry and deli selections deserve their own four-star restaurant, but are all the more savory as part of a picnic. Closed early September to late May.

Paradice. 1 Depot Rd. (at Old County Rd., about ½ mile W of Rte. 6). ☎ **508/349-2499.**

Hot, thirsty travelers will think they've died and gone to Hawaii when they happen upon "shave ice," a Pacific treat available here in 38 flavors, from Kahlúa to apple pie à la mode. Closed early September through June.

4 Provincetown

56 miles (90km) NE of Sandwich; 42 miles (68km) NE of Hyannis

You made it all the way to the end of the Cape: one of the most interesting, rewarding spots on the eastern seaboard. Explorer Bartholomew Gosnold surely felt much the same thrill in 1602, when he and his crew happened upon a "great stoare of codfysshes" here (it wasn't quite the gold they were seeking, but valuable enough to warrant changing the peninsula's name). The Pilgrims, of course, were overjoyed when they slogged into the harbor 18 years later: Nevermind that they'd landed several hundred miles off course—it was a miracle they'd made it 'round the treacherous Outer Cape at all. And Charles Hawthorne, the painter who "discovered" this near-derelict fishing town in the late 1890s and introduced it to the Greenwich Village intelligentsia, was besotted by this "jumble of color in the intense sunlight accentuated by the brilliant blue of the harbor."

He'd probably be aghast at the commercial circus his enthusiasm has wrought—though proud, perhaps, to find the Provincetown Art Association & Museum, which he helped found in 1914, still going strong. Although it's bound to experience the occasional off year or dull stretch, the town is wholeheartedly dedicated to creative expression, both visual and verbal, and right now, it's on a roll. Some would ascribe the inspiration to the quality of the light (and it is particularly lovely, soft and diffuse) or the solitude afforded by long, lonely winters. But the general atmosphere of open-mindedness plays at least as pivotal a role, allowing a very varied assortment of individuals to pull together in pushing the cultural envelope.

That same warm embrace of different lifestyles accounts for Provincetown's ascendancy as a gay and lesbian resort. During peak season, Provincetown's streets are a celebration of the individual's freedom to be as "out" as imagination allows. This isolated outpost has always been a magnet for the adventurous minded. In fact, the tightly knit Portuguese community mostly descends from fishermen and whaling crews who set out from the Azores in centuries past. One might think that a culture so bound by tradition and religion would look askance at a way of life so antithetical to their own, but "family values" enjoy a very broad definition here. Those who've settled in Provincetown (affectionately referred to as "P-town") know they've found a very special place, and in that, they have something precious in common.

ESSENTIALS

GETTING THERE After crossing either the Bourne or Sagamore Bridge (see "Getting There" in chapter 2), head east on Route 6 or 6A to Orleans, then north on Route 6.

If you plan to spend your entire vacation in Provincetown, you don't need a car because everything is within walking or biking distance. And since parking is a hassle in this tiny town, consider leaving your car at home and taking a boat from Boston or Plymouth. Another advantage is that you'll get to skip the horrendous Sagamore Bridge traffic jams and arrive like the Pilgrims did.

Bay State Cruises (☎ 617/748-1428; www.baystatecruisecompany.com) makes round-trips from Boston, daily from late June to early September and weekends in the shoulder seasons.

The regular boat, called Provincetown II, leaves Boston's Commonwealth Pier at 9am and arrives in Provincetown at noon. At 3:30pm, the boat leaves Provincetown, arriving in Boston at 6:30pm. On the slow boat, round-trip fare is $30 for adults, $21 for children under 13, and $23 for seniors.

The new **high-speed Provincetown Express** boat makes two round-trips daily from mid-May to mid-October, and it takes just under 2 hours. It leaves Boston's Commonwealth Pier at 8am and 4pm, and it arrives in Provincetown at 9:50am and 5:50pm, respectively. On the return trip, it leaves Provincetown at 10:30am and 6:30pm, and it arrives back in Boston at 12:20pm and 8:20pm, respectively. All tickets on the high-speed boat cost $39 one-way, $75 round-trip. Reservations are recommended.

Captain John Boats (☎ 508/747-2400) connects Plymouth and Provincetown in summer. The 1½-hour boat ride leaves Plymouth at 10am; it leaves Provincetown at 4:30pm. The adult round-trip fare is $26, seniors $21, children 12 and under $16; bikes are $2 extra. You can also fly into Provincetown (see "Getting There" in chapter 2).

As far as getting around once you're settled, you can enjoy the vintage fleet of the **Mercedes Cab Company** (☎ 508/487-3333).

VISITOR INFORMATION   Contact the **Provincetown Chamber of Commerce,** 307 Commercial St., Provincetown, MA 02657 (☎ 508/487-3424; fax 508/487-8966; www.ptownchamber.com; e-mail: info@ptownchamber.com), open late May to mid-September daily from 10am to 4pm (call for off-season hours); the gay-oriented **Provincetown Business Guild,** 115 Bradford St., P.O. Box 421, Provincetown, MA 02657 (☎ 800/637-8696 or 508/487-2313; fax 508/487-1252; www.ptown.org; e-mail: pbguild@capecod.net), open Monday to Friday from 9am to noon and 12:30 to 2pm; or the **Cape Cod Chamber of Commerce** (see "Visitor Information" in the "Eastham" section, above).

GETTING AROUND

Parking is at a premium in Provincetown. Illegally parked cars are ticketed (even on Sundays), and repeat offenders will be towed. If your inn provides parking, you may want to keep your car there and get around on foot, bicycle, or shuttle. **Provincetown's Summer Shuttle** (☎ 508/432-3400) loops through town daily from 8am to midnight traveling all along Bradford Street and to Macmillan Wharf off Commercial Street and all the way to North Truro. The bus runs daily late June to mid-September at 20-minute intervals from 7:15am to 12:15am. The Beach loop travels to Herring Cove on the hour from 9am to 7pm. Riders may flag the bus down at any intersection on Bradford Street. Service continues through October in Provincetown only, without the Truro stops. All rides cost $1 adults, 50¢ for seniors and kids 6 to 17.

A STROLL AROUND PROVINCETOWN

Park wherever you can—at the edge of town or in the big public lot on MacMillan Wharf. From there, it's just 1 block inland to **Provincetown Town Hall** at 260 Commercial St. (☎ 508/487-7000). The "meet rack"—a row of facing benches out front—is a good place to get acclimated while planning your assault. The 1878 building itself is worth poking around in for its cache of historic artworks by Charles Hawthorne and others; gay and lesbian couples might even want to consider registering as "domestic partners."

Provincetown

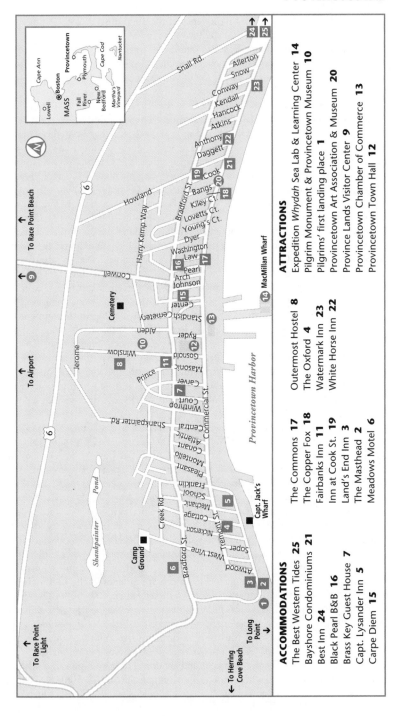

ATTRACTIONS

Expedition *Whydah* Sea Lab & Learning Center **14**
Pilgrim Monument & Provincetown Museum **10**
Pilgrims' first landing place **1**
Provincetown Art Association & Museum **20**
Province Lands Visitor Center **9**
Provincetown Chamber of Commerce **13**
Provincetown Town Hall **12**

ACCOMMODATIONS

The Best Western Tides **25**
Bayshore Condominiums **21**
Best Inn **24**
Black Pearl B&B **16**
Brass Key Guest House **7**
Capt. Lysander Inn **5**
Carpe Diem **15**

The Commons **17**
The Copper Fox **18**
Fairbanks Inn **11**
Inn at Cook St. **19**
Land's End Inn **3**
The Masthead **2**
Meadows Motel **6**

Outermost Hostel **8**
The Oxford **4**
Watermark Inn **23**
White Horse Inn **22**

One block west is the **Unitarian-Universalist Meetinghouse,** at 236 Commercial St. (☎ **508/487-9344**), an 1847 Greek Revival beauty with trompe l'oeil interiors by 19th-century architectural muralist Carl Wendte and pews adorned with whale-tooth scrimshaw emblems. These days, the congregation is dedicating most of its resources not to decorative finery but to caring for the needs of people with AIDS (P-town, tragically, has the second-highest per capita concentration of cases in the country). This also serves as a theater and concert hall in season.

Take your next right, on Masonic Place, to pass **The Atlantic House,** 6 Masonic Place (☎ **508/487-3821**). Built around a 1798 core, this has been the nation's foremost gay bar for several decades now. The owner once recounted how, in 1918, the town's only police officer here arrested Eugene O'Neill as a suspected German spy, having seen the fledgling playwright distractedly pacing the dunes.

Continuing on up a short flight of stone stairs, take a right on Bradford Street. On the northern side, you'll see several colonial-era houses (some transformed into B&Bs) and the bas-relief, a plaque by Cyrus Dalin commemorating the Pilgrims' landing on November 21, 1620. To quell a potential rebellion among the indentured servants (who could not be held to the laws of the Virginia colony), the founding fathers composed the Mayflower Compact, the text of which is reproduced here. In formulating the colonists' intent to "covenant & combine our selves togeather into a civill body politick," the document presaged the quest for self-government that would give rise to the Constitution.

Directly above the Town Green, off Winslow Street, is the **Pilgrim Monument & Provincetown Museum** on High Pole Hill Road (☎ **508/487-1310**). Modeled on Sienna's Torre del Mangia, P-town's not-so-little (252-foot) "Freudian joke"—the highest granite structure in the country—was erected between 1907 and 1910 by civic-minded locals ticked off that Plymouth was getting all the attention as the birthplace of the nation. It makes a fabulous vantage point from which to gaze down on the entire Cape, and the museum of local history at its foot deserves a close look (see "Provincetown Museums," below).

Returning to Bradford Street, follow it eastward a little over a ¼ mile and turn left on Pearl Street to visit the **Fine Arts Work Center** at 24 Pearl St. (☎ **508/487-9960**), formerly Day's Lumber Yard, where in 1911 the softhearted owner built studios to accommodate impecunious artists. At the munificent rate of $50 a season, many a painter—such as Hawthorne protégé Edwin Dickinson, who wrapped himself in canvas to survive the iciest nights—contrived to winter over. The 20 FAWC fellows who now spend the off-season here—plus the summer visitors who come to take advantage of weekend and weeklong workshops with outstanding instructors—have it much softer, and townspeople and tourists alike get the benefit of students' and mentors' shows, talks, and readings held at the adjoining **Hudson D. Walker Gallery.**

The works of Provincetown's most accomplished artists reside back on Commercial Street, another ¼ mile east, through a zone thick with galleries, at the ✪ **Provincetown Art Association & Museum,** 460 Commercial St. (☎ **508/487-1750**). Founded by Hawthorne and cohorts in 1914, this prescient organization was on hand to scoop up some of the seminal American works of the 20th century—some 1,700 items so far (see "Provincetown Museums," below). In the sculpture garden on the museum grounds, look for Chaim Gross's *Dance Rhythms.* Another spirited work by this longtime summerer, *Tourists,* can be found about a ½ mile west, signaling the former **Provincetown Heritage Museum** at 356 Commercial St. (☎ **508/487-7098**). Locals can't quite decide what to do with this handsome Italianate building, which was built in 1860 as a Methodist church. Most recently, it served as a modest local-history museum. The second floor shelters a huge half-scale schooner—and that's the problem. Some want to use the building for a library or an art center, and move the schooner, a replica of a local ship that won the prestigious Lipton Cup in 1907. Others want it to stay right where it is. The town is at an impasse.

From this point westward, you'll be entering the epicenter of Provincetown's tourist zone. Take in whatever shops appeal (see "Shopping," below) before seeking refuge on MacMillan Wharf, named for the town's illustrious native son, who made a name for himself exploring the North Pole in 1909. One of the few survivors among the 50-odd piers that once lined the shore, **MacMillan Wharf** is home to Provincetown's whale-watching fleet and other charter boats, as well as the new **Expedition Whydah Sea Lab & Learning Center** (☎ 508/487-8899), where relics from the 1717 shipwreck—discovered off Wellfleet in 1984—are undergoing painstaking reclamation. You can watch marine archaeologists at work while learning more about this pirate ship and its place in Cape Cod history.

☕ **WINDING DOWN   The Lobster Pot,** 321 Commercial St. (☎ 508/487-0842), is a longtime favorite of locals and visitors alike. They may also have the most extensive appetizer (read: midday munchies) selection in town. Stop here for a steaming cup of their award-winning clam chowder, a bucket of steamers, or even blackened tuna sashimi.

BEACHES & RECREATIONAL PURSUITS

BEACHES   With nine-tenths of its territory (basically, all but the "downtown" area) protected by the Cape Cod National Seashore (CCNS), Provincetown has miles of beaches. The 3-mile bay beach that lines the harbor, though certainly swimmable, is not all that inviting compared to the magnificent ocean beaches overseen by the National Seashore. The two official access areas (see below) tend to be crowded; however, you can always find a less densely populated stretch if you're willing to hike.

Note: Local beachgoer activists have been lobbying for "clothing-optional" beaches for years, but the rangers, fearful of voyeurs trampling the dune grass, are firmly opposed and routinely issue tickets, so stand forewarned (and fully clothed).

- **Herring Cove** and ✪ **Race Point:** Both National Seashore beaches are spectacular with long stretches of pristine sand, and they are very popular. Herring Cove, facing west, is known for its spectacular sunsets; observers often applaud. Race Point, on the ocean side, is rougher, and you might actually spot whales en route to Stellwagen Bank. Calmer Herring Cove is a haven for same-sex couples, who tend to sort themselves by gender. Parking costs $7 per day, $20 per season.
- **Long Point:** Trek out over the breakwater and beyond, or catch a water shuttle—$10 round-trip—from Flyer's Boat Rental (see "Boating," below) or slip 2 on Macmillan Wharf to visit this very last spit of land, capped by an 1827 lighthouse. Locals call it "the end of the Earth." Shuttles run hourly in July and August.

BICYCLING   North of town, nestled amid the Cape Cod National Seashore preserve, is one of the more spectacular bike paths in New England, the 7-mile ✪ **Province Lands Trail,** a heady swirl of steep dunes (watch out for sand drifts on the path) anchored by wind-stunted scrub pines. With its free parking, the **Province Lands Visitor Center** (☎ 508/487-1256) is a good place to start: You can survey the landscape from the observation tower to try to get your bearings before setting off amid the dizzying maze. With any luck, you'll find a spur path leading to one of the beaches—Race Point or Herring Cove—lining the shore. Bike rentals are offered seasonally, practically on-site, by **Nelson's Bike Shop** at 43 Race Point Rd. (☎ 508/487-8849). It's also an easy jaunt from town, where you'll find plenty of good bike shops—such as the centrally located **Ptown Bikes** at 42 Bradford St. (☎ 508/487-8735; reserve several days in advance)—as well as all the picnic fixings you could possibly desire. Bike rentals cost a few dollars an hour or $10 to $16 a day.

BOATING   In addition to operating a Long Point shuttle from its own dock (see "Beaches," above), **Flyer's Boat Rental** at 131 Commercial St. in the West End (☎ 508/487-0898)—established in 1945—offers all sorts of craft, from kayaks ($25 for half a day; $40 for a full day) and dinghies to sailboats of varying sizes; they also give sailing lessons ($75 for 2 hours) and organize fishing trips. They offer a special rate of $50 to rent a small boat with light tackle from 8am to noon.

Off the Coast Kayak Company at 3 Freeman St. in the center of town (☎ 508/487-2692) is a new company offering tours and rentals daily in season. A half-day tour costs $55 per person. Rentals cost $25 for half a day; $40 for a full day.

FISHING   Surf casting is permitted at **Herring Cove Beach** (off Rte. 6) and **Race Point Beach** (near the Race Point Coast Guard Station); also, many people drop a hand-line or light tackle right off the West End breakwater. For low-cost deep-sea fishing via party boat, board the **Cee Jay** (☎ 800/675-6723 or 508/487-4330); it costs $20 for adults and $15 for children. For serious sportfishing, sign on for the **Shady Lady II** (☎ 508/487-0182). Both depart from MacMillan Wharf.

FITNESS   For days when the weather's forcing your workouts indoors, the **Provincetown Gym** at 81 Shank Painter Rd. (☎ 508/487-2776) has the usual equipment and promises a "non-intimidating" atmosphere; the **Mussel Beach Health Club,** located at 35 Bradford St. (☎ 508/487-0001), attracts a rather buff clientele. Both gyms are $12 a day for non-members. For post-workout pampering, book a massage or herbal wrap at the **West End Salon & Spa,** 155 Commercial St. (☎ 508/487-1872).

NATURE TRAILS   Within the Province Lands (off Race Point Rd., a ½ mile north of Rte. 6), the CCNS maintains the 1-mile, self-guided **Beech Forest Trail,** a shaded path that circles a shallow freshwater pond blanketed with water lilies (also look for sunning turtles) before heading into the woods. You can see the shifting dunes (much of this terrain is soft sand) gradually encroaching on the forest.

Another wonderful walk is along the **West End breakwater** out to the end of Long Point, about 3 miles round-trip. The breakwater is located at the end of Commercial Street, next to the Provincetown Inn. It's about a 20-minute walk across the wide breakwater; then it's soft sand for the remainder of the hike. **Wood End Lighthouse** is directly across the spit of sand near the breakwater. It will take about another 40 minutes to reach **Long Point Light** at the very tip of Cape Cod. Hikers determined to reach the end of Long Point will want to bring a hat, water, and sunscreen for this intense trek along the beach. The outside of the arm tends to be the more scenic route for contemplative hikers; the inside coast can be crowded with picnicking families and surf casters. The Long Point Shuttle runs from MacMillan Wharf across to Long Point for about $10 round-trip. Service is continuous in season.

TENNIS   Three public courts are located at Motta Memorial Field at the top of Winslow Street (near the Provincetown Monument); for details, contact the **Provincetown Recreation Department** (☎ 508/487-7097). Open mid-May to mid-October, the **Provincetown Tennis Club** at 186 Bradford St. (☎ 508/487-9574) has seven courts—two asphalt, five clay—tucked away amid tall trees.

ORGANIZED TOURS

Art's Dune Tours. At the corner of Commercial and Standish sts. (in the center of town). ☎ **800/894-1951** or 508/487-1950. Tickets $12 adults, $8 children 4–11. Sunset tours $15 adults, $10 children. Call for schedule and reservations.

In 1946, Art Costa started driving sightseers out to ogle the decrepit "dune shacks" where such transient luminaries as Eugene O'Neill, Jack Kerouac, and Jackson Pollock found their respective muses; in one such hovel, Tennessee Williams cooked up the steamy *A Streetcar Named Desire*. The Park Service wanted to raze these eyesores, but luckily saner heads prevailed: They're now National Historic Landmarks. The tours conducted by Art's son and others, via Chevy Suburban, typically take about 1 to 1½ hours and are filled with wonderful stories of local literati and other characters. Don't forget your camera for the views of this totally unique landscape.

Bay Lady II. MacMillan Wharf (in the center of town). ☎ **508/487-9308.** www.sailcapecod.com. Tickets $10–15 adults, $5 children under 12. Mid-May to mid-Oct, 4 2-hr. sails daily; call for schedule and reservations. Closed mid-Oct to mid-May.

In sightseeing aboard this 73-foot reproduction gaff-rigged Grand Banks schooner, you'll actually be adding to the scenery for those onlookers onshore. The sunset trip is especially spectacular.

Provincetown Trolley. In front of Town Hall, 260 Commercial St. (in the center of town). ☎ **508/487-9483.** Tickets $8 adults, $7 seniors, $6 children 12 and under. Departures May–Oct daily every half hr. 10am–4pm and hourly 5–7pm. Closed Nov–Apr.

For a quick high-points tour, this 40-minute narrated circuit covers all the bases: West End, Province Lands, East End, and "home." Don't expect to learn a whole lot if you already have some sense of town history. On the other hand, with the ability to dismount and reboard at will, you can pretty much create your own tour, with stopovers for taking in the sights and/or shopping.

Willie Air Tours. Provincetown Municipal Airport, Race Point Rd. (2 miles NW of the town center). ☎ **508/487-9989.** Late May–late Oct, 15-min. flights $50 for 2 adults, $15 children 12 and under; call for schedule. Closed late Oct–late May.

Board a cheery yellow 1931 Stinson Detroiter for a quick look around: It's a great way to fathom the forces still shaping the land. It's hard to believe from the tiny exterior, but you can cram four slim friends (or parents and a couple of lucky kids) into this adorable biplane. Back-seat riders get to luxuriate on a red leather banquette, but the passenger next to the pilot gets the best view. If it weren't for the windshield, you could reach out and touch the propeller. The flight is smooth and gentle, an intoxicating way to experience the tip of the Cape.

PROVINCETOWN MUSEUMS

The Expedition Whydah Sea Lab & Learning Center. MacMillan Wharf (just past the whale-watching fleet). ☎ **508/487-8899.** www.whydah.com. Admission $5 adults, $3.50 children 6–12. June–Aug daily 10am–8pm; Sept–Dec and Apr–May daily 10am–5pm. Closed Jan–Mar.

Cape Cod native Barry Clifford made headlines in 1984 when he tracked down the wreck of the 17th-century pirate ship *Whydah* (pronounced "*Wid*-dah," like Yankee for "widow") 1,500 feet off the coast of Wellfleet, where it had lain undisturbed since 1717. Only 10 percent excavated to date, it has already yielded over 100,000 artifacts, including 10,000 gold and silver coins, plus its namesake bell, proving its authenticity. In this museum/lab, visitors can observe the reclamation work involving electrolytic reduction as it's done and discuss the ship, its discovery, and its significance

Whale Watching

In 1975, 4 years after the U.S. government—fearing the species' extinction—called an official halt to whaling, fisherman Al Avellar noticed that they seemed to be making a comeback in the Stellwagen Bank feeding area, 8 miles off Provincetown. Together with marine biologist Charles "Stormy" Mayo of the Center for Coastal Studies, he came up with the notion of a new kind of hunt, spearheaded by tourists bearing cameras. An immediate success, their ✪ *Dolphin* **Fleet,** on MacMillan Wharf (☎ **800/826-9300** or 508/349-1900), was widely copied up and down the coast. These are still the prime feeding grounds, however, which is why all the whale-watching fleets can confidently "guarantee" sightings—they offer a rain check should the cetaceans fail to surface.

Most cruises carry a naturalist (a very vague term) to provide running commentary: The difference of the *Dolphin* is that the CCS scientists are out there doing research crucial to the whales' survival, and part of the proceeds goes to further their worthwhile efforts. Serious whale aficionados will want to try one of the daylong trips to the Great South Channel, where humpbacks and finbacks are likely to be found by the dozen.

Some tips for first-timers: Dress very warmly, in layers (it's cold out on the water), and definitely take along a windbreaker, waterproof if possible. The weather's capricious, and if you stand in the bow of the boat, the best viewing point, you can count on getting drenched. Veteran whale watchers know to bring a spare set of dry clothes, as well as binoculars—although if the whales seem to be feeling friendly and frisky, as they often are, they'll play practically within reach. And last but not least, if you're prone to seasickness, you'd better bring along some motion-sickness pills: It can get pretty rough out there.

Tickets are $19 for adults, $17 for senior citizens, $16 for children 7 to 12, and free for children under 7. In season, there are nine 3½-hour trips daily. Call for a schedule and reservations (required). Closed November through March.

---

with the scientists and scholars on hand, while studying the many interpretive exhibits.

Old Harbor Life-Saving Museum. Race Point Beach (off Race Point Rd., about 2 miles NW of the town center). ☎ **508/487-1256.** Free admission; parking fee for Race Point is $7; bikes are $1. July–Aug daily 3–5pm; call for off-season hours. Closed Nov–Apr.

One of 13 lifesaving stations mandated by Congress in the late 19th century, this shingled shelter with a lookout tower was part of a network responsible for saving some 100,000 lives. Before the U.S. Life-Saving Service was founded in 1872 (it became part of the Coast Guard in 1915, once the Cape Cod Canal was in place), shipwreck victims lucky enough to be washed ashore were still doomed unless they could find a "charity shed"—a hut supplied with firewood—maintained by the Massachusetts Humane Society. The six valiant "Surfmen" manning each lifesaving station took a more active approach, patrolling the beach at all hours, sending up flares at the first sign of a ship in distress and rowing out into the surf to save all they could. When the breakers were too high to breach, they'd use a Lyle gun to shoot a line to be secured to the ship's mast, and over this, one by one, the crew would be pulled to shore astride a "breeches buoy"—like a lifesaving ring fitted out with canvas BVDs. All the old equipment is on view at this museum, and Thursday evening at 6pm, rangers re-enact a breeches-buoy rescue.

Pilgrim Monument & Provincetown Museum. High Pole Hill Rd. (off Winslow St., N of Bradford St.). ☎ **508/487-1310.** Admission $6 adults, $3 children 4–12. July–Aug daily 9am–7pm; off-season daily 9am–5pm. Last admission 45 min. before closing. Closed Dec–Mar.

You can't miss it: Anywhere you go in town, this granite tower looms, ever ready to restore your bearings. Climb up the 60 gradual ramps interspersed with 116 steps—a surprisingly easy lope—and you'll get a gargoyle's-eye view of the spiraling coast and, in the distance, Boston against a backdrop of New Hampshire's mountains. Definitely devote some time to the curious exhibits in the museum at the monument's foot, chronicling P-town's checkered past as both fishing port and arts nexus. Among the memorabilia, you'll find polar bears brought back from MacMillan's expeditions and early programs for the Provincetown Players.

Province Lands Visitor Center of the Cape Cod National Seashore. Race Point Rd. (about 1½ miles NW of the town center). ☎ **508/487-1256.** Free admission. Mid-Apr to late Nov daily 9am–5pm. Closed late Nov to mid-Apr.

Though much smaller than the Salt Pond Visitor Center, this satellite also does a good job of explicating this special environment, where plant life must fight a fierce battle to maintain its toehold amid shifting sands buffeted by salty winds. After perusing the exhibits, be sure to circle the observation deck for great views of the "parabolic" dunes. A variety of ranger-guided tours and programs is offered daily in July and August, and frequently during the shoulder seasons. Inquire about any special events scheduled, such as family campfires (reservations required). There are also canoe programs ($15 adults; $9 children) and surf-casting programs ($12), both with equipment provided.

☼ Provincetown Art Association & Museum. 460 Commercial St. (in the East End). ☎ **508/487-1750.** Suggested donation $3 adults, $1 seniors and children under 12. July–Aug daily noon–5pm and 8–10pm; call for off-season hours. Open year-round.

This extraordinary cache of 20th-century American art began with five paintings donated by local artists, including Charles Hawthorne, the charismatic teacher who first "discovered" this picturesque outpost. Founded in 1914, only a year after New York's revolutionary Armory Show, the museum was the site of innumerable "space wars," as classicists and modernists vied for square footage; an uneasy truce was finally struck in 1927, when each camp was accorded its own show. In today's less competitive atmosphere, it's not unusual to see an acknowledged Master sharing space with a less-skilled upstart. Juried members' shows usually accompany the in-depth retrospectives, so there are always new discoveries to be made. Nor is there a hard and firm wall between creators and onlookers. Fulfilling its charter to promote "social intercourse between artists and laymen," the museum sponsors a full schedule of concerts, lectures, readings, and classes, in such disciplines as dance, yoga, and life-drawing.

KID STUFF

Kids love going out on **whale-watching trips,** where sightings are guaranteed. To really tire them out, climb the **Provincetown Monument.** Toddlers will also enjoy the story hour held Wednesday and Saturday at 10:30am at the homey and historic (1873) **Provincetown Public Library** (☎ 508/487-7094).

SHOPPING

If you want to stay one step ahead of the fashion-victims' pack, you have come to the right place. Many mavens visit off-season just to stock up on markdowns that are still well ahead of the curve. Of the several dozen art galleries in town, only a handful (noted below) are reliably worthwhile. (For in-depth coverage of the local arts scene, look to *Provincetown Arts,* a glossy annual sold at the Provincetown Art Association & Museum shop.) In season, most of the galleries and even some of the shops open around 11am, then take a supper-time siesta from around 5 to 7pm, reopening and greeting visitors up to as late as 10 or 11pm. Shows usually open Friday evening, prompting a "stroll" tradition spanning the many receptions.

ANTIQUES/COLLECTIBLES

Remembrances of Things Past, 376 Commercial St. (☎ 508/487-9443) is a kitsch-fest with a jumble of 20th-century nostalgia ranging from Bakelite bangles to neon advertising art and vintage *True Confessions.*

At **Small Pleasures,** 359 Commercial St. (☎ 508/487-3712), proprietor Virginia McKenna, a.k.a. "Ginny Jewels," stocks fine estate jewelry, ranging from romantic Victorian settings to sleek silver for the 1920s-era male.

Tribal Offerings, 394 Commercial St. (☎ 508/487-4857) stocks the best selection of Native American jewelry on the Cape. Dianne Kennedy travels to the Southwest to buy directly from artists.

ART GALLERIES

Showing the work of distinguished figures from Provincetown's past and current luminaries, **Albert Merola Gallery,** 424 Commercial St. in the East End. (☎ 508/487-4424) gallery is simply one of the best galleries in town. Each summer, such respected figures as Michael Mazur (*Dante's Inferno*) and Helen Miranda Wilson deliver their latest musings. Closed mid-October to March.

Berta Walker is a force to be reckoned with, having nurtured many top artists through her association with the Fine Arts Work Center, before opening her own gallery in 1990. At ✪ **Berta Walker Gallery,** 208 Bradford St. in the East End (☎ 508/487-6411), the historic holdings span Charles Hawthorne, Milton Avery, and Robert Motherwell; and whoever has Berta's current attention, such as figurative sculptor Romolo Del Deo, warrants watching. Closed late October to late May.

Founded in 1994 by artist and publishing scion Nick Lawrence, ✪ **DNA (Definitive New Art) Gallery,** 288 Bradford St. above the Provincetown Tennis Club in the East End (☎ 508/487-7700), has risen to the top tier. It has attracted such talents as: photographer Joel Meyerowitz, Provincetown's favorite portraitist, known for such tomes as *Cape Light;* sculptor Conrad Malicoat, whose free-form brick chimneys and hearths can be seen and admired about town; painter Tabitha Vevers, who devises woman-centered shrines and "shields" out of goatskin vellum and gold leaf. Another contributor is local conceptualist/provocateur Jay Critchley. It's a very lively bunch, appropriately grouped under the rubric "definitive new art," and readings by cutting-edge authors add to the buzz. Closed mid-October to late May.

Julie Heller started collecting early P-town paintings as a child—and a tourist at that. She chose so incredibly well, her roster at **Julie Heller Gallery,** 2 Gosnold St. on the beach in the center of town (☎ 508/487-2169) reads like a who's who of local art. Hawthorne, Avery, Hofmann, Lazzell, Hensche—all the big names from Provincetown's past are here, as well as some contemporary artists. Closed weekdays January to April. Open winter weekends by chance or appointment.

The work of Anne Packard and her daughters Cynthia and Leslie are displayed in **The Packard Gallery,** 418 Commercial St. in the east end (☎ 508/487-4690), a majestic former church. Anne Packard's large canvases tend to depict emotive land and seascapes with the horizon as a focus. Cynthia's colorful figurative work has Fauvist elements, and Leslie's watercolors capture Provincetown landscapes. Closed mid-October to mid-June.

At **Rice/Polak Gallery,** 430 Commercial St. in the East End (☎ 508/487-1052), you'll find art with a decorative bent, which is not to say that it will match anyone's sofa, only that it has a certain stylish snap. Several gallery artists have fun with dimensions—such as painter Tom Seghi with his mammoth pears, and sculptor Larry Calkins with his assemblages of undersized, antique-look dresses. Peter Plamondon's oil paintings capture still lives with exquisite clarity. Closed December to April.

✪ **Schoolhouse Center for Art and Design,** 494 Commercial St. in the East End (☎ **508/487-4800**), is an impressive setup with two galleries, studios, arts programs, and an events series. The Driskel Gallery features photography and fine objects, while the Silas-Kenyon Gallery shows contemporary fine arts.

William-Scott Gallery, 439 Commercial St. in the East End (☎ **508/487-4040**), can be counted on to showcase the work of local emerging artists, as well as several who seem to have made it. In the latter category is John Dowd. Still quite young, he's shaping up as Hopper's heir apparent (patrons include the Schiffenhaus brothers, who inherited the Hoppers' Truro house). Other selections, such as John DiMestico's Cape landscapes on paper, Dan Rupe's bold portraits in oil, and Will Klemm's lush and mysterious pastel landscapes, augur well for an influential future. Closed November to late May.

BOOKS

Now Voyager, 357 Commercial St. in the East End (☎ **508/487-0848**), offers both new and collectible gay and lesbian books and also serves as an informal social center. There is also a large section of mystery and suspense books.

Provincetown Bookstore, 246 Commercial St. (☎ **508/487-0964**), has the most complete selection in town. You'll find all the best-sellers, as well as books about the region and local lore.

DISCOUNT SHOPPING

✪ **Marine Specialties,** 235 Commercial St. in the center of town (☎ **508/487-1730**), is packed to the rafters with useful stuff, from discounted Doc Martens to cut-rate Swiss Army knives and all sorts of odd nautical surplus whose uses will suggest themselves to you eventually. Be sure to look up: Hung from the ceiling are some real antiques, including several carillons' worth of ship's bells.

Provincetown Second Hand Store, 389 Commercial St. in the center of town (☎ **508/487-9163**), is a local institution selling drag for Guys and Dolls.

EROTICA

The dirtiest (and I don't mean dusty) store in Provincetown is **Shop Therapy,** 346 Commercial St. (☎ **508/487-9387**), a wildly muralled (or is it graffitied?) store filled with all manner of erotica. You'll want to wander in just for the sheer outrageousness of it all. Tall people beware; there's stuff hanging from the low ceiling that you might not want near your face.

FASHION

Giardelli/Antonelli Studio Showroom, 417 Commercial St. in the East End (☎ **508/487-3016**), is filled with Jerry Giardelli's unstructured clothing elements—shells, shifts, and palazzo pants—in vibrant colors and inviting textures. They demand to be mixed, matched, and perhaps offset by Diana Antonelli's statement jewelry.

Want to try on new identities? **Mad as a Hatter,** 360 Commercial St. (☎ **508/487-4063**), may be your best bet, with hats to suit every style and inclination, from folksy to downright diva-esque. Closed January to mid-February.

Moda Fina, 349 Commercial St. (☎ **508/487-6632**), specializes in women's clothing and accessories, including shoes and lingerie, and a variety of unique summer dresses.

Silk & Feathers, 377 Commercial St. in the East End (☎ **508/487-2057**), has seasonal styles, and the lingerie they sell is almost too pretty to cover up. Other indulgences include seaweed soaps and statement jewelry.

GIFTS/HOME DECOR

Christopher Pearson of **Pearson's Studio,** 214 Commercial St. in the East End (☎ **508/487-1101**), is the premier stained-glass maker in town; he's taught most of the others how it's done.

A breath of fresh contemporary design, **Utilities,** 393 Commercial St. in the center of town (☎ **508/487-6800**), is a kitchenware/tabletop shop that features sleek and colorful essentials.

A study in beiges and blacks, **Wa,** 184 Commercial St. in the West End (☎ **508/ 487-6355**), is a minimalist shop—its name means "harmony" in Japanese—specializing in decorative home accessories that embrace a Zen aesthetic. This might mean a trickling stone fountain or Chinese calligraphy stones.

Profits on the gifts and books you buy at **The Whale and Dolphin Information Center & Shop,** 307 Commercial St. in the center of town (☎ **508/487-6115;** www. provincetown.com/coastalstudies/), all help to support the cetacean research-and-rescue work carried out by the Center for Coastal Studies, a local non-profit organization. Identifying individual whales by their distinctive markings, Center staffers have managed to compile the world's largest whale population database to date and have participated in many a dramatic disentanglement. To appreciate the depth of their dedication, go whale watching with a Center scientist aboard a *Dolphin* Fleet cruise (see "Whale Watching," above). You might also inquire about Center-sponsored lectures, walks, and Elderhostel programs. Closed November to mid-April.

TOYS

The Curious Crocodile, 209 Commercial St. in the center of town (☎ **508/ 487-0125**), has games, toys, puzzles, yo-yos, and loads of fun stuff.

Norma Glamp's Rubber Stamps, 212 Commercial St. in the center of town (☎ **508/487-1870**) carries over 5,000 rubber stamps, as well as inks, papers, and stickers.

Take advantage of strong winds and wide-open beaches of the cape, and kite at **Outer Cape Kites,** 277A Commercial St. at Ryder St. Ext., near MacMillan Wharf (☎ **508/487-6133**). Closed November to March.

WHERE TO STAY

For those on a budget, you can't do much better than **The Meadows Motel,** 122 Bradford Ave. Ext. (in the far west end of town), Provincetown, MA 02657 (☎ **888/ 675-0880** or 508/487-0880; Meadowsmtl@aol.com). Rooms are clean with cable TV and minifridges. Rates in season are $70 to $80 a night. Closed November to mid-April.

VERY EXPENSIVE

✪ **Brass Key Guesthouse.** 67 Bradford St. (in the center of town), Provincetown, MA 02657. ☎ **800/842-9858** or 508/487-9005. Fax 508/487-9020. www.brasskey.com. E-mail: ptown@brasskey.com. 29 units, 4 cottages. A/C TV TEL. Summer $195–$395 double; $285–$395 cottage. Rates include continental breakfast and afternoon wine and cheese hour. AE, DISC, MC, V. Closed mid-Nov to early Apr. No children under 18.

After a multimillion-dollar expansion, Brass Key Guesthouse, now a compound consisting of four buildings, has been transformed into *the* place to stay in Provincetown. With Ritz-Carlton-style amenities and service in mind, Michael MacIntyre and Bob

Anderson have created a paean to luxury. These are the kind of innkeepers who think of everything: goose-down pillows, showers with wall jets, and gratis iced tea and lemonade delivered poolside in season. While all rooms share top-notch amenities like Bose radios, minifridges, hair dryers, safes, and VCRs, decorative styles are varied according to the building. The original 1828 Federal-style Captain's House and the Gatehouse are decorated in a playful country style—a loft is filled with teddy bears, for instance—while rooms in the Victorian-era building are classically elegant, with materials like mahogany, walnut, and marble. In the center is the extensively landscaped multileveled patio area with outdoor heated pool and large (17-foot) whirlpool. Most deluxe guest rooms have gas fireplaces and oversize whirlpool tubs. Fortunately, those bathrooms also include telephones, and some have televisions, so that you can be entertained while soaking. There are also two wheelchair-accessible rooms. In high season, the clientele here is primarily gay men, though all are made to feel welcome.

EXPENSIVE

Bayshore Condominiums. 493 Commercial St. (in the East End), Provincetown, MA 02657. ☎/fax **508/487-9133.** www.provincetown.com/bayshore. E-mail: bayshore@provincetown. com. 25 units. TV TEL. Summer $950–$1,695 weekly studio and 1-bedroom; $1,300–$2,000 weekly 2-bedroom. Shoulder season daily rates $95–$108 studio; $110–$185 1-bedroom; $125–$195 2-bedroom. AE, DISC, MC, V. Dogs allowed with advance notice. Open year-round.

This cherished beachfront complex continues to be a popular lodging choice. While retaining some of their improvised charm, such as a few select antiques and salvaged architectural details, the rooms have been lightened up, the better to reflect the waterside setting. All rooms have VCRs and kitchenettes, including microwave ovens. The prize rooms surround a flower-lined lawn, with pride of place going to a cathedral-ceiling loft right over the water; several more apartments, including a freestanding little house, can be found across the street. The bargain unit is in the "lower level" (read: basement) of this house; it's surprisingly quaint, but, as expected, dark. The decor is still not quite designer level, but the big plus is the opportunity to live among artworks on loan from the Walker Gallery, many of which could rightly hang on a museum wall. From late June to early September, rooms are available on a weekly basis only.

Best Western Tides Beachfront. 837 Commercial St. (near the Truro border), Province-town, MA 02657. ☎ **800/528-1234** or 508/487-1045. Fax 508/487-1621. www. bwprovincetown.com. 64 units. A/C TV TEL. Summer $139–$199 double; $249–$269 suite. AE, CB, DC, DISC, MC, V. Closed Nov to mid-May.

Families will be delighted with this beachfront motel, located on a 6-acre parcel well removed both from Provincetown's bustle and North Truro's ticky-tacky congestion. This surprise oasis, part of the Best Western chain, boasts every feature one might require, including a nice wide beach you can literally flop onto from the ground-level units. Most of the rooms overlook Provincetown's quirky skyline, as does the generously proportioned outdoor heated pool. Every inch of this complex has been groomed to the max, including the ultra-green grounds, the Wedgwood-blue breakfast room that seems to have been lifted whole from an elegant country inn, and the spotless rooms decorated in a soothing palette of ivory and pale pastels. All rooms have minifridges. Because the hotel is set back from busy Route 6A, the only sound you'll hear at night is the mournful refrain of a foghorn.

✪ **Captain Jack's Wharf.** 73A Commercial St., Provincetown, MA 02657. ☎ **508/ 487-1450.** www.ptown.com/ptown/captjacks. 14 units. Summer $750–$1,100 weekly. No credit cards. Closed Oct–May.

These apartments, located on one of P-town's last remaining wharves, are quintessential beach kitsch. Each space is individually and artistically decorated with exuberant splashes of color, funky artwork, and general panache. If you want the ultimate bohemian Provincetown lodging experience, you simply can't do any better than this. Be aware that your neighbors are fun loving, and since you are all sharing a rickety wharf, don't expect to get much sleep before 1am. From late June to early September, 1-week rentals are required. Off-season, the nightly rate (3-night minimum) is around $100.

◑ Land's End Inn. 22 Commercial St. (in the West End), Provincetown, MA 02657. ☎ **800/276-7088** or 508/487-0706 (also fax). www.landsendinn.com. 17 units, 1 with shared bathroom. Summer $125–$210 double; $145–$155 apartment; $285 suite. Rates include continental breakfast. MC, V. Open year-round.

Enjoying a prime 2-acre perch atop Gull Hill in the far West End, this magical, whimsical 1907 bungalow is stuffed to bursting with rare and often outlandish antiques. Some rooms would suit a 19th-century sheik, others your everyday hedonist. In the dark-paneled living room, it's always Christmas: The ornate decorations never come down. In other words, the place is quite unique, in a way that will delight some guests and overwhelm others. The loft suite, entered through a cabinet (very Narnia) must be one of the most unusual and spectacular lodging spaces on the Cape. From the spacious living room/kitchen, climb the ironwork spiral stairway to the bedroom, where an immense stained-glass window serves as your headboard. Through the encircling clerestory windows, the Atlantic Ocean beckons. There's also a wonderful octagonal room with windows wrapping halfway around, bay-view decks on two sides, and a blue glass turret. Some of the other rooms are tiny, but they're all positively dripping with kitschy Victorian and deco style. Though the inn is predominantly gay, cosmopolitan visitors will feel welcome, regardless of gender or orientation. The inn is part of a trust that donates its profits to the performing arts, in particular the Provincetown Repertory Theatre and the Provincetown Academy for the Performing Arts.

The Masthead. 31–41 Commercial St. (in the West End), Provincetown, MA 02657. ☎ **800/395-5095** or 508/487-0523. Fax 508/487-9251. www.capecodtravel.com/masthead. 21 units, 2 with shared bathroom; 4 cottages. A/C TV TEL. Summer $81–$197 double; $140–$166 efficiency; $229 2-bedroom apartment; $1,402–$1,905 cottages weekly. Off-season $63–$108 double; $76–$89 efficiency; $99–$126 2-bedroom apartment; $99–$168 cottage. AE, CB, DC, DISC, MC, V. Open year-round.

In its late-1950s heyday, glam types like Helena Rubenstein came to this funky resort on the beach at the far west end of Commercial Street to rough it. These days, it's one of the few places in town, other than the impersonal motels, that actively welcomes families, and the placid 450-foot private beach will delight young splashers. Many rooms are individually and creatively decorated, and all have minifridges and coffeemakers with complimentary tea and coffee. The cottages are fun, some with net stair railings, wicker furniture, and hand-painted antique furniture by Peter Hunt, as well as full (if tiny) kitchens, which include microwave ovens. In season, the cottage units rent weekly, but the rather generic motel units rent nightly. In some water-view rooms perched above the surf, with their 7-foot picture windows overlooking the bay and Long Point, you may feel like you are onboard a ship. Off-season rates here are a steal, considering the waterfront locale. The yachting crowd can take advantage of free deep-water moorings and launch service.

◑ Watermark Inn. 603 Commercial St. (in the East End), Provincetown, MA 02657. ☎ **508/487-0165.** Fax 508/487-2383. www.watermark-inn.com. E-mail: info@watermark-inn.com. 10 units. TV TEL. Summer $160–$320 suite. AE, MC, V. Open year-round.

If you'd like to experience P-town without being stuck in the thick of it (the carnival atmosphere can get tiring at times), this contemporary inn at the peaceful edge of town is the perfect choice. Resident innkeeper/architect Kevin Shea carved this beachfront manor into 10 dazzling suites: The prize ones, on the top floor, have peaked picture windows and sweeping views from their decks. All have kitchenettes that include dishwashers. Innkeeper/designer Judy Richland, Shea's wife, saw to the interior decoration—pastel handmade quilts brighten up clean, monochromatic rooms. From mid-May to mid-September, the suites rent only by the week. This inn is a favorite with families.

MODERATE

Best Inn. 698 Commercial St. (at Rte. 6A, in the East End), Provincetown, MA 02657. ☎ **800/422-4224** or 508/487-1711. Fax 508/487-3929. www.capeinn.com. E-mail: biptown@capecod.net. 78 units. A/C TV TEL. Summer $139–$179 double. Rates include continental breakfast. AE, CB, DC, DISC, MC, V. Closed Nov–Apr. Dogs allowed.

Formerly the Holiday Inn, this is a good choice for first-timers not quite sure what they're getting into. It's a no-surprises motel with a pool at the eastern edge of town, a bit far from the action but congenial enough. Guests get a nice view of town, along with cable TV and free movies in the restaurant/lounge. All rooms have minifridges, coffeemakers, irons, and hair dryers. Though this motel is a bit of a hike from the town's center, an in-season shuttle will whisk you down Commercial Street or to the beaches.

Carpe Diem. 12 Johnson St. (in the center of town), Provincetown, MA 02657. ☎ **800/487-0132** or 508/487-4242 (also fax). www.carpediemguesthouse.com. E-mail: carpediem@capecod.net. 13 units. A/C TV TEL. Summer $125–$165 double, $195 suites, $235 cottage. Rates include continental breakfast. AE, MC, V.

Rainer and Jurgen, two young, urbane Germans, run this stylish lodging option, an 1884 house with mansard roof, whose devil-may-care theme is "seize the day." The location, a quiet side street right in the center of town, would suit most Provincetown habitués to a T. The rooms here are exquisitely decorated with European antiques and brightly painted walls and wallpapers. Telephones in all rooms have voice-mail and dataports. All rooms have VCRs, down comforters, and bathrobes, and most have minifridges. There are two deluxe garden suites with private entrances, Jacuzzis, and fireplaces. The cottage has a two-person whirlpool and a wet bar. Continental breakfast features homemade German bread and muffins served at the family-size dining-room table. On clear days, sun worshippers prefer the patio where there's an eight-person hot tub.

The Commons. 386 Commercial St. (in the center of town), Provincetown, MA 02657. ☎ **800/487-0784** or 508/487-7800. Fax 508/487-6114. www.capecod.net/commons. E-mail: commons@capecod.net. 14 units. TV TEL. Summer $105–$160 double; $160 suite. Rates include continental breakfast. AE, MC, V. Closed Jan–Mar. Pets allowed.

Right in the thick of town, but removed from the hurly-burly by a street-side bistro (see "Where to Dine," below) and peaceful brick patio, this venerable old guest house has received a stylish renovation at the hands of co-owners Carl Draper and Chuck Rigg, a Washington, D.C., interior designer whose colorful landscapes decorate the rooms. The parlor is comfortable; the bedrooms, with their marble-look baths and (in most cases) bay views, are stylish and spacious. At the pinnacle is a beamed attic studio with its own deck overlooking MacMillan Wharf. All the delights of Provincetown are easily within reach, including—on-site—one of Provincetown's best up-and-coming restaurants.

Copper Fox. 448 Commercial St. (in the East End), Provincetown, MA 02657. ☎ and fax **508/487-8583.** www.provincetown.com/copperfox. E-mail: copperfox@provincetown.com. 5 units, 2 apartments. A/C TV TEL. Summer $140–$169 double; $185 apartments. Rates include continental breakfast and afternoon tea. MC, V. Open year-round.

Cheerful innkeeper John Gagliardi owns this majestic house with a large wraparound porch, set well back from the road. The expansive lawn, unusual in Provincetown where space is at a premium, is dotted with urns and a birdbath. Built in 1856, this 3-story, Federal-style captain's house is situated just a short walk from the galleries and restaurants of the East End. From the second floor deck, you have a perfect view of Provincetown harbor across the street. Several of the spacious rooms also have bay views. Two apartments have private entrances and kitchens. One has a private garden, and the other is large enough to accommodate six people comfortably (extra charge for more than two people). Bathrooms have been thoroughly modernized, but some have stylish claw-foot tubs and antique sinks.

✪ **The Fairbanks Inn.** 90 Bradford St. (near the center of town), Provincetown, MA 02657. ☎ **800/324-7265** or 508/487-0386. Fax 508/487-3540. www.fairbanksinn.com. E-mail: info@fairbanks.com. 14 units, 2 with shared bathroom. Summer $110–$225 double; $185 efficiency. Rates include continental breakfast. AE, MC, V. Open year-round.

This colonial mansion (built in 1776) looks its era without looking its age. Beautifully maintained, it boasts gleaming wooden floors softened by rich Orientals and romantic bedding—sleigh beds and four-posters. Most of the rooms have fireplaces. A patio, porch, and rooftop sundeck lend themselves to pleasant socializing. The attention to detail throughout the inn makes this one of the top places to stay in town.

The Inn at Cook Street. 7 Cook St. (at Bradford St., in the East End), Provincetown, MA 02657. ☎ **888/COOK-655** or 508/487-3894. www.innatcookstreet.com. E-mail: info@innatcookstreet.com. 6 units. A/C TV TEL. Summer $90–$115 double; $125–$175 suite. Rates include continental breakfast. MC, V.

This 1836 Greek Revival beauty, tucked away in a quiet neighborhood, positively exudes tasteful warmth, from its pale-yellow exterior trimmed with black shutters to its hidden garden complete with goldfish pool. All the handsomely appointed rooms are oriented to this oasis, with an assortment of private and shared decks. The suites have additional amenities like VCRs, hair dryers, minifridges, and coffeemakers. Innkeepers Paul Church and Dana Mitton arrived at their dream house by way of the elegant Cambridge House near Boston, and their enthusiasm is evident in every welcoming touch.

The Oxford. 8 Cottage St. (in the West End), Provincetown, MA 02657. ☎ **888/456-9103** or 508/487-9103. www.capecod.net/oxford/. E-mail: oxford@capecod.net. 6 units, 2 with shared bathroom. A/C TV TEL. Summer $100–$275 double. Rates include continental breakfast. AE, DISC, MC, V. Pets allowed in apartment.

British innkeepers Stephen Mascilo and Trevor Pinker have restored and refurbished this 1853 house in the far West End, adding yet another posh address to the town. This is truly affordable elegance. All rooms have upscale amenities like down comforters, bathrobes, hair dryers, telephones with voice-mail and dataport, minifridges, VCRs, and radio/CD players. One downstairs room is quite large, with 8-foot windows overlooking the landscaped grounds. Rooms with shared baths are smaller. The drawing room is especially cozy, with big down sofas and armchairs in front of a fireplace, above which a television is cleverly hidden. A new one-bedroom cottage will be ready in 2001. An extensive continental breakfast is served in the morning, when the inn fills with the scrumptious aroma of home-baked breads and coffeecake. You may want to take your coffee outside on the veranda overlooking the courtyard's fountain and pond.

INEXPENSIVE

✪ **The Black Pearl Bed & Breakfast.** 11 Pearl St. (off Commercial St., near the center of town), Provincetown, MA 02657. ☎ **508/487-6405.** Fax 508/487-7412. www.provincetown. com/blackpearl/index.html. E-mail: blkpearl@capecod.net. 5 units, 1 cottage. Summer

$95–$105 double; $190 suite; $165 cottage. Rates include continental breakfast. MC, V. Closed Jan–Mar.

Every room in this cheerily updated captain's house has a look all its own, from bold Southwestern to fanciful Micronesian murals covering the walls, and several boast skylights and private decks. The fully muralled Connemara Cottage takes the cake, with an antique bedstead, wood-burning fireplace, and double Jacuzzi, plus such niceties as air-conditioning, telephone, and a cable TV with VCR. The Lullwater suite consists of two rooms with TV/VCR, telephone, air-conditioning, minifridge, microwave, fireplace, and a separate entrance with French doors to a private deck with hot tub. All rooms have hair dryers and robes. One room is wheelchair-accessible.

Captain Lysander Inn. 96 Commercial St. (in the West End), Provincetown, MA 02657. ☎ **508/487-2253.** Fax 508/487-7579. 13 units, 6 with shared bathroom; 1 cottage. Summer $95 double with shared bathroom, $105 double with private bathroom; efficiency $125 daily, $1,400 weekly; apartment. $200 daily, $1,200 weekly; cottage $250 daily, $1,400 weekly. Rates include continental breakfast. MC, V. Open year-round.

This 1840 Greek Revival captain's house has definite curb appeal: Set back from the street in the quiet West End, it's fronted by a flower-lined path leading to a sunny patio. The conservatively furnished rooms are quite nice for the price, and some have lovely water views. Tall windows make these rooms light and airy; they're also spotlessly clean. Rooms with shared baths share with just one other room. The whole gang can fit in either the apartment or the cottage, both of which sleep six.

The Outermost Hostel. 28 Winslow St. (off Bradford St., ⅛ mile NW of the Provincetown Museum entrance), Provincetown, MA 02657. ☎ **508/487-4378.** E-mail: outermost@ mindspring.com. 40 beds. Summer $15 per bed. No credit cards. Reservations advised on weekends. Registration daily 8–9:30am and 6–9:30pm at cabin #4. Closed Nov to mid-May.

So what if these "European-style" dorms look more like an outtake from *The Grapes of Wrath*? Fifteen bucks a night! And, unlike the straitlaced American Youth Hostels, they're curfew free! For grungers (or misers) just looking for a place to crash, these bunks will fill the bill.

✪ **White Horse Inn.** 500 Commercial St. (in the East End), Provincetown, MA 02657. ☎ **508/487-1790.** 18 units, 10 with shared bathroom; 6 efficiencies. Summer $60 single with shared bathroom; $70–$80 double; $125–$140 efficiency. No credit cards.

Look for the house with the bright yellow door and oval window in the far East End of town. The rates are terrific, especially given the fact that this inn is the very embodiment of Provincetown's bohemian mystique. Frank Schaefer has been tinkering with this late–18th-century house since 1963; the rooms may be a bit austere, but each is enlivened by some of the 300 to 400 paintings he has collected over the decades. A number of his fellow artists helped him out in cobbling together the studio apartments out of salvage: There's an aura of beatnik improv about them still. Guests over the past 35 years have embodied a range of high and low art: Cult filmmaker John Waters stayed here often, as did poet laureate Robert Pinsky.

WHERE TO DINE
VERY EXPENSIVE

✪ **Chester.** 404 Commercial St. ☎ **508/487-8200.** Reservations recommended. Main courses $19–$32. AE, MC, V. July–early Sept daily 6–10pm; May–June and mid-Sept to Dec Thurs–Sun 6–10pm; call for off-season hours. Closed Jan–Apr. NEW AMERICAN.

Look for this grandly columned Greek Revival house for the newest entry to Provincetown's fine-dining scene. Chester specializes in local seafood, meats, and vegetables prepared simply yet with a flourish by Chef Michael McGrath. The restaurant is named after the owners' Airedale terrier, whose regal profile serves as their logo. The candlelit dining room, painted a summery yellow, is decorated with brightly colored paintings by local artists; you'll want to sit at the comfy banquettes lining the edges of the room. As is to be expected, service is exceptional, the food is beautifully presented, and the portions are hearty. Appetizers like spinach and scallop risotto take advantage of local provender, as does the entree Chatham cod with prosciutto and sage. Though I'm reluctant to order meat when I can see the ocean out the window, the braised leg of lamb with rosemary potato pancakes and French beans was a treat. The inn's extensive and well-priced wine list has been rewarded by *Wine Spectator.* For dessert, look no further than the warm Scharffen Berger chocolate cake. There's also home-made ice cream.

✪ **The Dancing Lobster Cafe Trattoria.** 373 Commercial St. (in the center of town). ☎ 508/487-0900. Reservations recommended. Main courses $17–$30. MC, V. July–Sept Tues–Sun 11:30am–5pm and 5:30–11pm; May–June and Oct 6–9pm. Closed Nov–Apr. MEDITERRANEAN.

Chef/owner Nils "Pepe" Berg virtually grew up at the restaurant Pepe's Wharf that was on this site for years, and he has now moved his lauded restaurant to this centrally located waterfront spot. This is a popular place, and you should expect to wait a half hour, even with a reservation. The food is still excellent, with seafood from local fishermen. The menu features Venetian specialties, among other special dishes. Start with the grilled-squid bruschetta, the saffrony Venetian fish soup, the crab ravioli, or perhaps the steamed mussels with a basil aioli. Main courses may include steak al "Pepe" with green and black peppercorns, brandy, demiglace, and cream; or Basque stew with littleneck clams, chicken, shrimp, linguica, squid, and mussels steamed with white beans.

✪ **Martin House.** 157 Commercial St. ☎ **508/487-1327.** Reservations recommended. Main courses $14–$30. AE, CB, DC, DISC, MC, V. May–Oct daily 6–11pm; Jan–May and Nov–Dec Thurs–Mon 6–10pm. Closed mid-Dec. FUSION.

Easily one of the most charming restaurants on the Cape, this snuggery of rustic rooms happens to contain one of the Cape's most forward-thinking kitchens. Co-owners Glen and Gary Martin conceived the inspired regional menu, and chef Alex Mazzocca creates it. The team favors regional delicacies, such as the Thai crab-and-shrimp soup with green curry and crispy rice noodles, or the local littlenecks that appear in a kafir-lime-tamarind broth with Asian noodles. Main courses might include local-lobster-stuffed squash blossoms with a warm porcini-saffron vinaigrette, or grilled rack of pork with mango salsa and cactus-pear demiglace on spicy masa. The peaceful, softly lit rooms make an optimal setting for exploring new tastes. In season, there's seating in the rose-choked garden terrace beside the small fountain.

EXPENSIVE

Cafe Edwige. 333 Commercial St. ☎ **508/487-2008.** Reservations recommended. Main courses $18–$21. MC, V. Late May–Aug daily 8am–1pm and 6–11pm; Sept to mid-Oct and Apr to mid-May daily 8am–1pm, Fri–Sun 6–10pm. Closed late Oct–Mar. NEW AMERICAN/FUSION.

The tourist throngs generally walk right on by this second-story eatery, little suspecting what they're passing up. To start: superlative, healthy breakfasts featuring everything from tofu stir-fry to broiled sole with stir-fried vegetables. The cathedral-ceilinged space, with hippie-era wooden booths and deco accents, is a great place to greet the day. At night, it's commensurately romantic, with subdued lighting and the cuisine of chef Stephen Frappolli, who has been praised in *The New York Times.* Start your meal with the Maine crabcake with Creole-mustard dressing and cucumber slaw.

Sake-and-plum-glazed Chilean sea bass served with wasabi mashed potatoes is another high point on the menu. Homemade desserts are exceptional here; you can't go wrong.

The Commons Bistro & Bar. 386 Commercial St. (see "Where to Stay," above). ☎ **508/487-7800.** Reservations recommended. Main courses $14–$23. AE, MC, V. Late June–early Sept daily 6–10:30pm; call for off-season hours. Closed Jan. ECLECTIC/FRENCH BISTRO.

It's a toss-up: The sidewalk cafe provides an optimal opportunity for studying P-town's inimitable street life, whereas the plum-colored dining room inside affords a refuge adorned with the owners' extraordinary collection of original Toulouse-Lautrec prints. Either way, you'll get to partake of Chach Breseno's tasty and creative fare. At lunchtime, her overstuffed lobster club sandwich on country bread is unbeatable, and the smoked-chicken and avocado salad is the ultimate summertime refresher. The Commons boasts the only wood-fired oven in town to date, which comes in handy in preparing the popular gourmet pizzas with combos like smoked salmon, crème fraîche, and golden caviar. Dinner appetizers include root-vegetable cake with smoked trout, and wood-oven roasted mussels with yellow Thai curry. As a main course, you must try the gingered and smoked salmon with scallion basmati rice and orange-soy vinaigrette. For dessert, choose the crème brûlée.

✪ **The Mews & Cafe Mews.** 429 Commercial St. ☎ **508/487-1500.** Reservations recommended. Main courses $18–$27. AE, CB, DC, DISC, MC, V. Late May to mid-Oct Mon–Fri 6–10pm, Sat and Sun 11am–2:30pm and 6–10pm; mid-Feb to late May and mid-Oct to late Dec Thurs–Mon 6–10pm and Sun 11am–2:30pm. Open year-round. INTERNATIONAL/AMERICAN FUSION.

Bank on fine food and suave service at this beachfront restaurant, an enduring favorite since 1961. Upstairs is the cafe with its century-old carved mahogany bar. The dining room downstairs sits right on the beach—and is practically of the beach, with its sand-toned walls warmed by toffee-colored Tiffany table lamps. The best soup in the region is the Mews' scrumptious summertime special, chilled cucumber miso bisque with curry shrimp timbale. Perennial pleasures include the Marsala-marinated portobello mushrooms and a mixed seafood carpaccio. Among the showier entrees is "captured scallops": prime Wellfleet specimens enclosed with a shrimp-and-crab mousse in a crisp wonton pouch and served atop a petite filet mignon with chipotle aioli. Desserts and coffees—you might take them upstairs in the cafe to the accompaniment of soft-jazz piano—are delectable. Awash in sea blues that blend with the view, Cafe Mews offers a lighter menu and serves as an elegantly informal community clubhouse almost year-round.

MODERATE

Bubala's by the Bay. 183 Commercial St. (in the West End). ☎ **508/487-0773.** Main courses $10–$21. AE, DISC, MC, V. Apr–Oct daily 8am–11pm. Closed Nov–Mar. ECLECTIC.

Once a nothing-special seaside restaurant, this trendy bistro—miraculously transformed with a gaudy yellow paint job and Picassoesque wall murals—promises "serious food at sensible prices." And that's what it delivers: from buttermilk waffles with real maple syrup to lobster tarragon salad and creative focaccia sandwiches to fajitas, Cajun calamari, and pad Thai. This is the only place on Cape Cod that serves ostrich. They're raised in Pennsylvania and served with a grilled pepper crust and a caramelized onion and balsamic glaze. In season, there's entertainment nightly from 10pm to 1am.

Cafe Heaven. 199 Commercial St. (in the center of town). ☎ **508/487-9639.** Reservations not accepted. Most items $11–$18. No credit cards. July–Aug daily 8am–3pm and 6:30–10pm; call for off-season hours. Closed Feb–May. AMERICAN.

Prized for its leisurely country breakfasts (served till mid-afternoon, for reluctant risers), this modern storefront—adorned with big, bold paintings by acclaimed Wellfleet artist John Grillo—also turns out substantive sandwiches, such as avocado and goat cheese on a French baguette. The salads are appealing as well—especially the "special shrimp," lightly doused with dilled sour cream and tossed with tomatoes and grapes. New chef Alan Cullinane has expanded the dinner choices to include local seafood, steaks, chops, and poultry, create-your-own-pasta options, and "heavenly" burgers with a choice of internationally inspired toppings. "No reservations" means long lines in July and August.

Gallerani's Cafe. 133 Commercial St. (in the West End). ☎ **508/487-4433.** Reservations accepted for parties of 5 or more only. Main courses $12–$23. DISC, MC, V. Late May to mid-Sept Mon–Thurs 6–10:30pm, Fri–Sun 6–11pm; mid-Sept to late May Thurs–Sun 6–9pm. Open year-round. INTERNATIONAL.

Tucked away as it is in the far western end of town, this congenial storefront cafe is likely to elude tourists, but locals keep it packed year-round. Here the fusion is not so much east-west as comfort-chic, as evidenced in dishes such as lobster cakes, sautéed and served with aioli; chicken with roasted red peppers, mozzarella, and pear chutney; or a dreamy banana-cream pie. Off-season the menu features old-time staples like pizza, lasagna, meat loaf, and chicken pot pie. This is one of the few places in town where you can have half-orders, the better to sample more of these diverse and luscious choices.

Little Fluke Cafe. 401½ Commercial St. (in the east end). ☎ **508/487-4773.** Reservations not accepted. Main courses $15–$24. No credit cards. July–Aug daily 8am–1pm and Wed–Sun 6–10pm; call for off-season hours. Closed Oct–Apr. NEW AMERICAN.

This tiny cafe with outdoor tables is a perfect people-watching spot during breakfast or lunch. For breakfast, try their famous blueberry cornmeal pancakes. Dinner is a bit pricey for this very casual atmosphere, but the small menu offers tasty choices for fish lovers, meat lovers, and even vegetarians. Good choices are the pan-seared fillet of salmon with a soy ginger reduction and wasabi cream, and the grilled marinated portobello mushrooms with sautéed baby spinach and seasonal vegetables.

The Lobster Pot. 321 Commercial St. (in the center of town). ☎ **508/487-0842.** Reservations not accepted. Main courses $14–$21. AE, CB, DC, DISC, MC, V. Mid-June to mid-Sept daily 11:30am–10:30pm; mid-Feb to mid-June and mid-Sept to Dec 11:30am–9:30pm. Closed Jan to mid-Feb. SEAFOOD.

Snobbish foodies might turn their noses up at a venue so flagrantly Olde Cape Coddish, but for Provincetown regulars, no season seems complete without at least one pilgrimage. You may feel like a long-suffering pilgrim waiting to get in: The line, which starts near the aromatic, albeit frantic, kitchen, often snakes into the street. While waiting, check out the hand-painted bar stools, which provide an architectural history of Provincetown. A lucky few will make it all the way to the outdoor deck; however, most tables, indoors and out, afford nice views of MacMillan Wharf. Spring for a jumbo lobster, by all means—boiled or broiled, sauced or simple. And definitely start off with the chowder, a perennial award winner.

✪ Lorraine's. 463 Commercial St. (in the East End). ☎ **508/487-6074.** Reservations suggested. Main courses $15–$22. MC, V. June–Sept daily 6–10pm; call for off-season hours. Closed Jan–Mar. MEXICAN/NEW AMERICAN.

Long-heralded by year-rounders as a spot for creative food and a festive atmosphere, Lorraine's has moved to a prestigious waterfront location—the site of Provincetown's oldest restaurant, The Flagship, where literati like Gertrude Stein and Anaïs Nin flocked after its early–1930s debut. Even those who shy away from Mexican restaurants should try Lorraine's; chef/owner Lorraine Najar brings a certain daring to bear on the cuisine she learned at her grandmother's knee. Abandon all caution and begin with *chile relleno de queso*, which is fresh chile peppers stuffed with the chef's choice nightly, rolled in corn meal and corn flour and lightly deep-fried. Maryland softshell crabs are lightly dusted in flour with chimayo chile power and pan-sautéed and served with a jalapeño aioli. For a main course, consider *viere verde*—sea scallops sautéed with tomatillos, flambéed in tequila, and cloaked in a green-chili sauce. On Fridays and Saturdays, tapas are served until 12am. This place is hopping; there's entertainment nightly in season.

The Moors. 5 Bradford St. Extension (at Province Lands Rd.). ☎ **800/843-0840** or 508/487-0840. Reservations recommended. Main courses $16–$20. AE, MC, V. May to mid-Oct daily 5:30–10pm; call for off-season hours. Closed Nov–Mar. PORTUGUESE.

A salty classic since 1939, this ramshackle restaurant, composed primarily of nautical salvage, serves traditional Azorean fare, such as *espadarte grelhado* (flash-broiled swordfish marinated in lemon juice, olive oil, parsley, and garlic) and *galinha à moda da Madeira* (chicken breast baked with a rich mushroom sauce). The standout is *porco em pau*, a Brazilian casserole of fork-tender pork tenderloin cubes in a spicy marinade. For meat lovers, the "Moors cut" of prime rib, served Friday through Sunday is extra thick.

Napi's. 7 Freeman St. (at Bradford St.). ☎ **800/571-6274** or 508/487-1145. Reservations recommended. Main courses $12–$24. AE, DC, DISC, MC, V. May–Oct daily 5–10pm; Nov–Apr daily 11:30am–4pm and 5–9pm. INTERNATIONAL.

Restaurateur Napi Van Dereck can be credited with bringing P-town's restaurant scene up to speed—back in the early 1970s. His namesake restaurant still reflects that *Zeitgeist*, with its rococo-hippie carpentry, select outtakes from his sideline in antiques, and some rather outstanding art, including a crazy quilt of a brick wall by local sculptor Conrad Malicoat. The cuisine is a lot less granola than it was when it started out, or maybe we've just caught up—hearty peasant fare never really goes out of style. And these peasants really get around, culling dumplings from China, falafel from Syria, and, from Greece, shrimp feta flambéed with ouzo and Metaxa. The lower-priced tavern menu available on weeknights ranges from $5 to $11.

INEXPENSIVE

Café Blasé. 328 Commercial St. (in the center of town). ☎ **508/487-9465.** Reservations not accepted. Main courses $9–$18. AE, MC, V. Mid-June to early Sept daily 9am–midnight; call for off-season hours. Closed late Sept–late May. ECLECTIC.

The turnover beneath these tasseled pink-and-navy umbrellas tends to be constant; everyone wants to see and be seen here. The full dinner menu, served 5 to 10pm, has been expanded to include pastas and dinner specials like hearty bourbon steak. You can also find some excellent salads, or subsist on sodas made from an assortment of esoteric European syrups (Richard Gere is said to have favored the *orzata*). The beers are pretty rarefied, too—everything from a microbrewed Vermont amber, courtesy of Catamount, to a pricey Belgian *framboise*.

Café Crudité. 336 Commercial St. (upstairs). ☎ **508/487-6237.** Most items under $10. No credit cards. June–early Sept daily noon–10pm; call for off-season hours. Closed Dec–Mar. VEGETARIAN.

With its tiny deck overlooking Provincetown's main drag, this health-conscious vegetarian/macrobiotic/vegan hideaway is a great place to sit out the hype and its empty-caloric enticements. In addition to the basic macrobiotic breakfast (a bowl of miso-and-rice soup), the many morning options include an unusual "Egg Saag"—two eggs poached and served atop seven-grain bread spread with Indian-spiced spinach. Cold sesame noodles are available throughout the day, as are double-bean burritos (featuring pinto and black beans). Coffees, including a wicked frozen cappuccino, represent the only departure from the straight and narrow.

✪ **Clem and Ursie's.** 85 Shankpainter Rd. (off Bradford St., a few blocks S of town). ☎ **508/487-2333.** Most main courses under $15. MC, V. Apr–Oct daily 11am–9pm. Closed Nov–Apr. SEAFOOD.

This is a great choice for a big family dinner on picnic tables. Make it a shoreman's dinner or a clambake. The menu is heavy on fried seafood, as well as BBQ chicken, ribs, and seafood. There are also more elaborate choices like bouillabaisse, *fra diavolo* (fish and shellfish in a spicy tomato sauce), and Japanese *udon* (fish, shellfish, and vegetables in a dashi broth over noodles). There's a children's menu, where for $5 your choice of six entrees comes with french fries, drink, dessert, and a surprise. Takeout is popular here, as is the separate ice-cream section.

Mojo's. 5 Ryder St. Ext. (on Fisherman's Wharf). ☎ **508/487-3140.** All items under $10. No credit cards. Call for hours; closed Oct–May. SEAFOOD.

This fried seafood shack is known for its lightly breaded fried fish. French fries are handcut daily. There are also veggie burgers, burritos, and chicken tenders. Eat at one of the six picnic tables on the patio or take it to the beach.

Spiritus. 190 Commercial St. (in the center of town). ☎ **508/487-2808.** All items under $15. No credit cards. Call for hours; closed Nov–Mar. PIZZA.

A local landmark, Spiritus is an extravagant pizza parlor known for post-last-call cruising: It's open until 2am. The pizza's good, as are the fruit drinks, specialty coffees, and four brands of premium ice cream, from Emack & Bolio's to Coconut Joe's. For a peaceful morning repast—and perhaps a relaxed round of bocce—check out the little garden in back.

ICE CREAM

Not only a good spot to satisfy any ice-cream cravings (how about a 20-scoop "Vermonster"?), **Ben & Jerry's,** 258 Commercial St., in the center of town (☎ **508/ 487-3360**), is also handy for refueling midstroll with a fresh-fruit drink.

TAKE-OUT & PICNIC FARE

The latest gourmet take-out shop is **Angel Foods,** 467 Commercial St., in the east end (☎ **508/487-6666**), which offers Italian specialties and other scrumptious prepared foods to go.

The rollwiches—pita bread packed with a wide range of fillings—at **Box Lunch,** 353 Commercial St., in the center of town (☎ **508/487-6026**), are ideal for a strolling lunch.

At **Flying Cups & Saucers,** The Aquarium Shops, 205 Commercial St., in the center of town (☎ **508/487-3780**), the offerings are limited but to the point: juice (vegetable and fruit), java, and pastries. Among the first category is a lovely concoction called the "Ruby Slipper Sipper," a smoothie made from pineapple, strawberries, and apple juice. Closed November to May.

Stop at **Fresh from the Oven,** 129 Bradford St., in the center of town (☎ **508/ 487-9331**), for more elaborate picnic supplies like smoked turkey–almond pasta salad, homemade hummus, and curried chicken salad pita. Closed November to May.

One thing you absolutely have to do while in town is peruse the cases of pasties (meat pies) and pastries at **Provincetown Portuguese Bakery,** 299 Commercial St., in the center of town (☎ **508/487-1803**). Point to a few and take your surprise package out on the pier for delectation. Though perhaps not the wisest course for the

Provincetown's Pooch Parade

Strolling down Provincetown's Commercial Street with a spirited dog on a leash has become de rigueur. As people stroll along this lively strip, the most common accessory appears to be a dog. No breed in particular: big and small, groomed and mangy. And why not? Provincetown is a perfect place to bring your best friend. There are a number of lodging establishments that allow dogs, and there are outdoor cafes all along Commercial Street that don't mind if your buddy lies under the table. There are several shops selling all manner of dog and cat accessories and a doggie bakery called **Paws and Whiskers** recently opened in the center of town (256 Commercial St.; ☎ **508/487-3441**).

Shops specializing in dog and cat accessories include **Tailwaggers** at 205–209 Commercial St. (☎ **508/487-6404**), **Big Bow Wow and Little Meow** at 372 Commercial St (☎ **508/487-2907**), and **Friends of Heart** at 234 Commercial St (☎ **508/487-1136**). You can also board your dog at **KC's Animal Resort,** 79 Shankpainter Rd. (☎ **508/487-7900**), where they allow you to pick up your dog for the day or just a few hours.

The Cape Cod National Seashore allows dogs with certain rules and regulations. Leashed dogs are allowed on all National Seashore beaches beyond posted seasonal shorebird nesting and lifeguard zones. Fire roads are accessible to pets year-round, though dogs are not allowed on bike trails or nature trails. From May 15 to October 15, dogs are not allowed at freshwater ponds within the National Seashore. Always pick up after your dog to keep this area pristine.

Lodging in Provincetown and North Truro where well-behaved dogs are welcome include a large motel just outside of town, **Best Inn,** 698 Commercial St. (☎ **800/422-4224** or 508/487-1711; www.capeinn.com.); **Outer Reach Resort,** Rte 6 in North Truro, a motel high on a bluff overlooking Provincetown; **Sutton Place East** on Rte. 6A, North Truro, (☎ **508/487-9420**); which are cottages right on the beach; The **Commons Guest House,** 386 Commercial, (☎ **800/487-0784** or 508/487-7800), which has one pet-friendly room on the first floor; The **Oxford** at 8 Cottage St. (☎ **888/456-9103** or 508/487-9103), a small, newly renovated inn in the west end of Provincetown; **Bayshore Condominiums** at 493 Commercial St. (☎ **508/487-9133**), which are very nice apartments in the east end of Provincetown. And there are more! Call the Provincetown Chamber of Commerce (☎ **508/487-3424**) for a complete list.

Cafes on Commercial Street where your dog will be seen to best advantage are **Bubalas** at 183 Commercial St. (☎ **508/487-0773**), **Little Fluke Cafe** at 401½ Commercial St. (☎ **508/487-4773**), and **Café Blasé** at 328 Commercial St. (☎ **508/487-9465**). Ask before sitting down to be sure they can accommodate your furry friend. Dogs are also welcome to lie under the picnic tables at Mojo, a fried fish shack on Fisherman's Wharf.

whale-watch-bound, it's the best way to sample the scrumptious international output of this beloved institution. Closed November through March.

PROVINCETOWN AFTER DARK

Note: There's so much going on in season on any given night that you might want to simplify your search by calling or stopping in at the **Provincetown Reservations System office** at 293 Commercial St., in the center of town (☎ **508/487-6400**).

THE CLUB SCENE

✪ **Antro.** 258 Commercial St. (beside Town Hall, 2nd floor). ☎ **508/487-8800.** Daily 7pm–1am. Cover varies. Closed Oct–May.

Long a contender for hottest nightclub in P-town, this is the current home of "Two Fags and a Drag" and the ever-popular all-star musical comedy drag revue "Big Boned Barbies," starring Kandi Kane. You'll see the two tall and svelte "barbies" outside the club welcoming all comers.

The Atlantic House. 6 Masonic Place (off Commercial St., 2 blocks W of Town Hall). ☎ **508/487-3821.** Cover for the Big Room $5–$10. Open year-round.

The "A-house"—the nation's premier gay bar—also welcomes straights of both sexes, except in the leather-oriented Macho Bar upstairs. Late in the evening, there's usually plenty going on in the Big Room dance bar. In the little bar downstairs—warm up at the fireplace—check out the Tennessee Williams memorabilia, including a portrait *au naturel;* there's more across the street in a new restaurant called Grand Central.

Boatslip Beach Club. 161 Commercial St. ☎ **508/487-1669.** Cover varies. Closed Nov–Apr. Cover $3–$10. Closed Nov–Apr.

If you're wondering where all the beachgoers went, come late afternoon; it's a safe guess that a goodly number are attending the gay-lesbian tea dance held daily in season from 3:30 to 6:30pm on the Boatslip hotel's pool deck. Later in the evening, after a post-tea T-dance at the Pied (see below), they'll probably be back for some disco or two-stepping.

Crown & Anchor. 247 Commercial St. (in the center of town). ☎ **508/487-1430.** www.thecrownandanchor.net. Cover $5–$15. Call or check Web site for schedule. Closed Nov–Apr.

The specialty bars at the large complex span leather ("The Vault"), disco, comedy, drag shows, and cabaret. Facilities include a pool bar and game room.

✪ **Pied.** 193A Commercial St. (in the center of town). ☎ **508/487-1527.** www. thepied.com. Cover varies. Closed Nov–Apr. Call for schedule.

In season, a "parade" of gay revelers descends in early evening from the Boatslip to "the Pied," for its After Tea T-Dance from 6:30 to 10pm. The late-night wave consists of a fair number of women, or fairly convincing simulacra thereof. For a glimpse of stars-in-the-making, check out "Putting on the Hits," a sampling of local talent held Tuesday nights at 10.

Vixen. Pilgrim House, 336 Commercial St. (in the center of town). ☎ **508/487-6424.** Cover varies. Call for schedule. Closed Nov–Apr.

This chic women's bar occupies the lower floors of a former hotel. On the roster are jazz, blues, and comedy acts. There are also pool tables.

THE BAR SCENE

✪ **Cafe Mews.** At The Mews (see "Where to Dine," above). ☎ **508/487-1500.**

This highly civilized venue, with its bay view and vintage mahogany bar, is one of the few nightspots in town to lend itself well to the art of conversation. The jazz piano enhances rather than intrudes. A light cafe menu, in addition to the dining room menu, is available.

Governor Bradford. 312 Commercial St. (in the center of town). ☎ **508/487-9618.** No cover. Call for schedule.

It's a good old bar, featuring pool tables, karaoke, and disco.

PERFORMANCE, ETC.

Meetinghouse Theatre and Concert Hall. At the Unitarian-Universalist Meetinghouse, 236 Commercial St. (in the center of town). ☎ **508/487-9344.** Ticket prices vary. Call for schedule.

In season, this glorious space (see "A Stroll Around Provincetown," above) is given over to a wide range of performances, from plays to opera to cabaret. Upstairs is an acoustically superb concert hall with a restored 1929 Steinway concert grand piano. Downstairs is an intimate theater. The season is usually capped off by a series of concerts by the Flirtations, a gay *a cappella* ensemble.

Post Office Cafe & Cabaret. 303 Commercial St. ☎ **508/487-3892.** Cover $10–$15. Call for schedule.

This cramped shoe-box space hardly leaves room for laughing in the aisles, but regulars like comedian Suzanne Westenhoffer, cabaret artist Valla Jean Merman, and drag show Guys and Dolls invariably exert that effect. Three shows, spanning drag and folk, are staggered throughout the evening.

LOW-KEY EVENINGS

Fine Arts Work Center. 24 Pearl St. (off Bradford St. in the center of town). ☎ **508/487-9960.** www.fawc.org. Most events free. Call for schedule.

Drawing on its roster of visiting artists and scholars, FAWC offers exceptional readings and talks (some serve as fund-raisers) year-round.

New Art Cinema. 214 Commercial St. (in the center of town). ☎ **508/487-9222.** Tickets $8. Closed mid-Sept to mid-May.

This small duplex theater shows the latest releases: usually a blockbuster pitted against an indie art film.

✪ **Provincetown Art Association & Museum.** 460 Commercial St. (in the East End). ☎ **508/487-1750.** Cover varies. Call for schedule.

Concerts, lectures, and readings attract an intellectually inclined after-hours crowd.

8 Nantucket

In his classic, *Moby Dick,* Herman Melville wrote, "Nantucket! Take out your map and look at it. See what a real corner of the world it occupies; how it stands there, away off shore. . . ." More than 100 years later, this tiny island, 30 miles off the coast of Cape Cod, still counts its isolation as a defining characteristic. At only 3½ by 14 miles in size, Nantucket is smaller and more insular than Martha's Vineyard. But charm-wise, Nantucket stands alone—20th-century luxury and amenities wrapped in an elegant 19th-century package.

The island has long appealed to wealthy visitors, but the recent economic boom has tipped the scales in their favor. Locals shake their heads over the changing demographics. "If they can't get a reservation at a restaurant, they buy the restaurant," one islander said. A well-known musician recently rented an entire 12-room inn for two people during his stay. Nevertheless, this is still a terrific spot for a family vacation or a romantic retreat. After all, window shopping at the island's exclusive boutiques and soaking up the sunshine on the pristine beaches are both free activities!

The Nantucket we see today is the result of a dramatic boom and bust that took place in the 1800s. Once the whaling capital of the world, the Nantucket of Melville's time was a bustling international port whose wealth and sophistication belied its size. But the discovery of crude oil put an end to Nantucket's livelihood, and the island underwent a severe depression until the tourism industry revived it at the turn of the century. Stringent regulations preserved the 19th-century character of Nantucket Town, and today 36 percent of the island (and counting!) is maintained as conservation land.

Nantucket Island has one town, also called Nantucket, which hugs the yacht-filled harbor. This sophisticated burg features bountiful stores, quaint inns, cobblestone streets, interesting historic sites, and pristine beaches. Strolling ensures you won't miss the scores of shops and galleries housed in wharf shacks on the harbor. The rest of the island is mainly residential, but for a couple of notable villages. Siasconset (nicknamed 'Sconset), on the east side of the island, is a tranquil community with picturesque, rose-covered cottages and a handful of businesses, including a pricey French restaurant. Sunset aficionados head to Madaket, on the west coast of the island, for the evening spectacular.

The lay of the land on Nantucket is rolling moors, heathlands, cranberry bogs, and miles of exquisite public beaches. The vistas are honeymoon-romantic: an operating windmill, three lighthouses, and a skyline dotted with church steeples. Although July and August are still the most popular times to visit the island, Nantucket's tourist season has lengthened considerably by virtue of several popular festivals: Daffodil Festival in April, Nantucket Harvest Weekend in October, and the monthlong Nantucket Noel, the granddaddy of all holiday celebrations in the region. Off-season, visitors enjoy a more tranquil and certainly less expensive vacation. While the "Grey Lady's" infamous fog is liable to swallow you whole, frequent visitors learn to relish this moody, atmospheric touch.

1 Essentials

GETTING THERE

BY FERRY   From Hyannis (South Street Dock), the **Steamship Authority** (☎ **508/477-8600;** www.islandferry.com; from Nantucket, ☎ **508/228-3274**) operates year-round ferry service (including cars, passengers, and bicycles) to Steamship Wharf in Nantucket. When planning to travel to the island with your car in summertime, you must reserve *months in advance* to secure a spot since only six boats make the trip daily in season (three boats daily off-season). Before you call have several alternatives for departure dates. Remember to arrive at least 1 hour before departure to avoid your space being released to standbys. If you arrive without a reservation and plan to wait in the standby line, there is no guarantee you will get to the island that day. There is a $10 processing fee for canceling reservations. No advance reservations are required for passengers traveling without cars.

Total trip time is 2 hours and 15 minutes. A round-trip fare for a car costs a whopping $316 from mid-May to mid-October; $194 from mid-October to mid-May. (Do you get the impression they don't want you to bring a car?) Car rates do not include drivers or passengers; you must get tickets for each person going to the island. For passengers, a one-way ticket is $12.50 ($25 round-trip) for adults, $6.25 one-way ($12.50 round-trip) for children 5 to 12, and $10 round-trip for bikes. Remember that Steamship Authority parking costs $8 to $10 per day; you do not need to make parking reservations.

The Steamship Authority's fast ferry to Nantucket, **The Flying Cloud** (☎ **508/ 495-3278**), is for passengers only and takes 1 hour and runs five to six times a day in season. It is cheaper than the Hy-Line ferry (see below), at $23 one-way ($42 round-trip) for adults, $17.25 one-way ($31.50 round-trip) for children 5 to 12. Parking costs $8 to $10. Passenger reservations are highly recommended.

From Hyannis, passenger ferries to Nantucket's Straight Wharf are operated by **Hy-Line Cruises,** Ocean Street Dock (☎ **888/778-1132** or 508/778-2600; for high-speed ferry reservations, call ☎ **800/492-8082** or 508/778-0404;

Travel Tip: Parking

You do not need a car on Nantucket, so plan to park your car in Hyannis before boarding the ferry to the island. For all **Hy-Line** ferry service, Ocean Street Dock (☎ **888/778-1132** or 508/778-2602) in July and August, it's a good idea not only to reserve tickets in advance, but also reserve a parking spot ahead of time. The all-day parking fee is $10 in season. Travellers on **Steamship Authority** (☎ **508/ 477-8600**) vessels do not need a parking reservation, but when the lots near the ferry terminal are full, satellite lots are used and passengers take shuttle buses to the terminal. Be sure to arrive at least 1 hour before sailing time to allow for parking.

www.hy-linecruises.com). Hy-Line offers year-round service with its high-speed passenger catamaran, The Grey Lady II, which makes five to six hourly trips per day. The cost of a one-way fare is $31.50 for adults ($56 round-trip), $25.50 for children 1 to 12 ($41 round-trip), and $5 extra for bicycles ($10 round-trip). This state-of-the-art vessel seats 70 and makes six round-trips daily to Nantucket in season—it's best to make a reservation in advance.

From early May through October, Hy-Line's standard, 1-hour-and-50-minute ferry service is also offered. Round-trip tickets are $26 for adults, $13 for children ages 4 to 12, and $10 extra for bikes. On busy holiday weekends, you may want to order tickets in advance; otherwise, be sure to buy your tickets at least half an hour before your boat leaves the dock.

Hy-Line's MV Great Point (less than a 2-hours trip) has a first-class section with a private lounge, bathrooms, bar, and snack bar; a continental breakfast or afternoon cheese and crackers is also served onboard. One-way fare is $21 for adults and children ($42 round-trip). No pets are allowed on the Great Point ferry.

Hy-Line's "Around the Sound" cruise is a 1-day round-trip excursion from Hyannis with stops in Nantucket and Martha's Vineyard that runs from early June to late September. The price is $36 for adults, $18 for children 4 to 12, and $15 extra for bikes.

Hy-Line runs three passenger-only ferries from Oak Bluffs, Martha's Vineyard to Nantucket from early June to late September (there is no car-ferry service between the islands). The trip time from Oak Bluffs is 2 hours and 15 minutes. The one-way fare is $12 for adults, $6 for children 5 to 12, and $5 extra for bikes.

From Harwich Port, you can avoid the summer crowds in Hyannis and board one of **Freedom Cruise Line's** (☎ 508/432-8999) passenger-only ferries to Nantucket. From mid-May to mid-October, boats leave from Saquatucket Harbor in Harwich Port; the trip takes 1 hour and 30 minutes. A round-trip ticket is $39 for adults, $34 for children 2 to 12, $5 for children under 2, and $10 extra for bikes. Parking is free for daytrippers; $12 per night. Advance reservations are highly recommended.

BY AIR You can also fly into **Nantucket Memorial Airport** (☎ 508/325-5300), which is about 3 miles south of Nantucket Road on Old South Road. The flight to Nantucket takes about 30 to 40 minutes from Boston, 15 minutes from Hyannis, and a little more than an hour from New York City airports.

Airlines providing service to Nantucket include: **Business Express/Delta Connection** (☎ 800/221-1212) from Boston (year-round) and New York (seasonally); **Cape Air/Nantucket Air** (☎ 800/352-0714) year-round from Hyannis ($74 round-trip), Boston (about $220 round-trip), Martha's Vineyard ($76 round-trip), and New Bedford ($71 round-trip); **Continental Express** (☎ 800/525-0280) from Newark, seasonally (about $325 round-trip); **Island Airlines** (☎ 508/228-7575) year-round from Hyannis ($74 round-trip); and **US Airways Express** (☎ 800/428-4322) year-round from Boston ($210 to $235 round-trip).

Island Airlines and Nantucket Airlines both offer year-round charter service to the island. Another recommended charter company is **Ocean Wings** (☎ 800/253-5039).

GETTING AROUND

Nantucket is easily navigated on bike, moped, or on foot, and also by shuttle bus or taxi. If you're staying outside of Nantucket Town, however, or if you simply prefer to explore by car, you might want to bring your own car or rent one when you arrive. Adventure-minded travelers may even want to rent a jeep or other four-wheel-drive

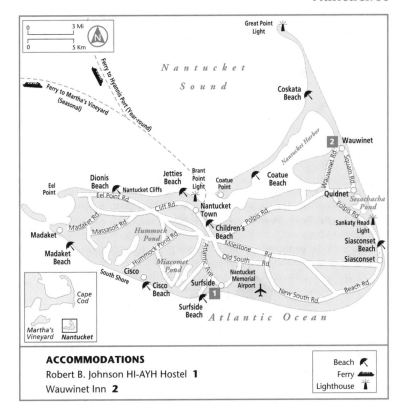

ACCOMMODATIONS

Robert B. Johnson HI-AYH Hostel **1**

Wauwinet Inn **2**

Beach 🏖
Ferry ⛴
Lighthouse 🗼

vehicle, which you can take out on the sand—a unique Island experience—on certain sections of the coast (permit required—see "By Car & Jeep," below). Keep in mind that if you do opt to travel by car, in-town traffic can reach gridlock in the peak season, and parking can be a nightmare.

BY BIKE & MOPED   When I head to Nantucket for a few days, biking is my preferred mode of transportation. The island itself is relatively flat, and paved bike paths abound—they'll get you from Nantucket Town to Siasconset, Surfside, and Madaket. There are also many unpaved back roads to explore, which make mountain bikes a wise choice when pedaling around Nantucket. *A word of warning for bikers:* One-way street signs apply to you, too! This law is enforced in Nantucket Town, and don't be surprised if a tanned but stern Island policeman requests that you get off your bike and walk. Helmets are required for children under 12. Mopeds are also prevalent, but watch out for sand on the roads. Be aware that local rules and regulations are strictly enforced. Mopeds are not allowed on sidewalks or bike paths. You'll need a driver's license to rent a moped, and state law requires that you wear a helmet. The following shops rent bikes and scooters; all are within walking distance of the ferries: **Cook's Cycle Shop, Inc.,** 6 S. Beach St. (☎ **508/228-0800**); **Holiday Cycle,** 4 Chester St. (☎ **508/228-3644**), rents just bikes; **Nantucket Bike Shops,** at Steamboat Wharf and Straight Wharf (☎ **508/228-1999**); and **Young's Bicycle Shop,** at Steamboat Wharf (☎ **508/228-1151**), which also does repairs. Bike rentals average around $18 to $25 for 24 hours.

Bumper to Bumper: Nantucket's Four-Wheel Jive

Natives of Nantucket have developed a complex social system to confer status; vehicles must be four-wheel drive and either very new—the bigger the better (Hummers have been spotted)—or ancient, beat-up army jeeps. And, as you will see, bumper stickers rule. A proper native's vehicle is slathered with at least five Over-Sand Vehicle Permits on the back window—lined up side by side to document longevity of association with the island. Other bumper stickers also indicate a Nantucketer in-the-know:

ACK   Usually seen in a square motif with a whale and a flag, this symbol is also prevalent on T-shirts, hats, and so on. What's ACK? The three-letter code for Nantucket Airport. Apparently the Navy has the letter N all wrapped up, so Nantucket reverted to the name of a previous local airport, Ackerly.

FOG HAPPENS   Nantucketers don't mind the fog; if you do, you'll be marked as an outsider.

TWENTY IS PLENTY IN 'SCONSET   Keep the speed limit down in this village, or you might hit a rose-covered cottage.

PIPING PLOVERS TASTE LIKE CHICKEN   Four-wheel drivers don't like it when the beaches are closed to accommodate nesting endangered piping plovers. Fist fights over this sticker are customary.

WHARF RAT CLUB   A bunch of old guys have been meeting in this shack on the wharf for about 1,000 years, it seems; during winter, they meet at the Pacific Club.

BAG THE MARKET   Nantucket voters cried an emphatic "No!" to developers wanting to build a new huge supermarket on the island.

BOX   Subtle and enigmatic, unlike the club that spawned the sticker. The Chicken Box, with live bands all summer, is the wildest club scene on the island.

UNIVERSITY OF NANTUCKET   *Hint:* This is a joke. The highest institute of learning on-island is The Chicken Box (see below).

BY SHUTTLE BUS   From June through September, inexpensive shuttle buses, with bike racks and accessibility for those with disabilities, make a loop through Nantucket Town and to a few outlying spots; for routes and stops, contact the **Nantucket Regional Transit Authority** (☎ **508/228-7025;** www.nantucket.net/trans/nrta) or pick up a map and schedule at the Visitors Service Center on Federal Street or the Chamber Office on Main Street (see "Visitor Information," below). The shuttle permits you to bring your clean, dry dog along, too. The cost is 50¢ to $1, and exact change is required. A 3-day pass can be purchased at the Visitors Center for $10.

Shuttle routes and fares are pretty simple. Downtown shuttle stops are located on the corner of Salem and Washington Streets (for South and Miacomet loops), Broad Street in front of the Foulger Museum (for Madaket loop and Beach Express), and Washington Street at the corner of Main Street (for 'Sconset loops).

- **South Loop** services Surfside Beach, Hooper Farm Road, and Pleasant Street area; every 15 minutes from 7am to 11:30pm; 50¢.
- **Miacomet Loop** services Fairgrounds Road, Bartlett Road, and Hummock Pond area; every 30 minutes from 7am to 11:30pm; 50¢.

- **Madaket Route** services Madaket (from Broad Street downtown) via Cliff Road and New Lane; every 30 minutes from 7:30am to 11:30pm; $1 each way.
- **'Sconset Route 1** services 'Sconset via Polpis Road; every 30 minutes from 8:20am to 11pm; $1 each way.
- **'Sconset Route 2** services 'Sconset via Old South Road/Nobadeer Farm Road and Milestone Road; every 30 minutes from 7:40am to 10:30pm; $1 each way. This route makes a stop about a ³⁄₁₀ mile from the airport. If you don't have a lot of bags, this is the cheapest way to go.
- **Beach Express** services Surfside and Jetties Beach. Downtown stop on Broad Street. $1 each way to Surfside; 50¢ each way to Jetties; every 30 minutes for Jetties Beach and every hour for Surfside Beach from 10:15am to 5:45pm.

BY CAR & JEEP   I'd recommend a car if you'll be here for more than a week or if you're staying outside Nantucket Town (or if you simply prefer to drive). However, there are no in-town parking lots; parking, although free, is limited to Nantucket's handful of narrow streets, which can be a problem in the busy summer months. Also, gas is much more expensive on Nantucket than it is on the mainland.

Four-wheel drives are your best bet, since many beaches and nature areas are off sandy paths; be sure to reserve at least a month in advance if you're coming in summer. If you plan on doing any four-wheeling in the sand, you need to get an **Over-Sand Permit** ($20) from the Nantucket Police Department (☎ **508/ 228-1212**). To drive in the Coskata-Coatue nature area, you need a separate permit from the **Trustees of Reservations,** at the gatehouse (☎ **508/228-0006**), which costs about $85 for a season pass plus a $20 gate fee.

The following on-island rental agencies offer cars, jeeps, and other four-wheel-drive vehicles: **Affordable Rentals of Nantucket,** 6 S. Beach Rd. (☎ **508/228-3501**); **Budget,** at the airport (☎ **800/527-0700** or 508/228-5666); **Don Allen Auto Service,** 24 Polpis Rd. (☎ **800/258-4970** or 508/228-0134), which specializes in Ford Explorers; **Hertz,** at the airport (☎ **800/654-3131** or 508/228-9421); **Nantucket Windmill Auto Rental,** at the airport (☎ **800/228-1227** or 508/ 228-1227); **Thrifty Car Rental,** at the airport (☎ **508/325-4616**); and **Young's 4 × 4 & Car Rental,** Steamboat Wharf (☎ **508/228-1151**). A standard car costs about $90 per day in season; a four-wheel-drive rental is about $180 per day (including an Over-Sand Permit).

BY TAXI   You'll find taxis (many are vans that can accommodate large groups or those traveling with bikes) waiting at the airport and at all ferry ports. During the busy summer months, I recommend reserving a taxi in advance to avoid a long wait upon arrival. Rates are flat fees, based on one person riding before 1am, with surcharges for additional passengers, bikes, and dogs. A taxi from the airport to Nantucket Town hotels will cost about $8. Reliable cab companies on the island include **A-1 Taxi** (☎ **508/228-3330**), **Aardvark Cab** (☎ **508/728-9999**), and **All Point Taxi** (☎ **508/228-5779**).

VISITOR INFORMATION

Contact the **Nantucket Island Chamber of Commerce** at 48 Main St., Nantucket, MA 02554 (☎ **508/228-1700;** www.nantucketchamber.org). When you arrive, you should also stop by the **Nantucket Visitors Service and Information Bureau** in Nantucket Town at 25 Federal St. (☎ **508/228-0925**), which is open daily June to September; Monday to Saturday October to May. There are also information booths at Steamboat Wharf and Straight Wharf. Always check the island's newspaper, the *Inquirer & Mirror,* for information on current events and activities around town.

Nantucket Accommodations, P.O. Box 217, Nantucket, MA 02554 (☎ **508/ 228-9559;** fax 508/325-7009; www.nantucketaccomodations.com; e-mail: nanacc@ nantucket.net) a 29-year-old private service, arranges advance reservations for inns, cottages, guest houses, bed-and-breakfasts, and hotels. You can call until the day of arrival, and they will arrange a booking based on your preferences. A member of the Chamber of Commerce, Nantucket Accommodations has access to 95 percent of the island's lodging facilities, in addition to houses and cottages available to rent by the night or week (as opposed to most realtors, who will only handle rentals for 2 weeks or more). The charge for the service is $15—a fee assessed only when a reservation is made. The customer pays Nantucket Accommodations by any major credit card or check, and N.A. then pays the inn or hotel. Last-minute travelers should keep in mind that the **Visitor's Service Center** (☎ **508/228-0925**), a daily referral service for available rooms rather than a booking service, always has the most updated list of accommodations availability and cancellations.

Automated teller machines (ATMs) can be difficult to locate on Nantucket. **Nantucket Bank** (☎ **508/228-0580**) has three locations: 2 Orange St., 104 Pleasant St., and the Airport lobby, all open 24 hours. **Pacific National Bank** has four locations: A&P Supermarket (next to the wharves), the Stop & Shop (open 24 hours seasonally), the Steamship Wharf Terminal, and Pacific National Bank lobby (open during bank hours only).

In case of a **medical emergency,** the **Nantucket Cottage Hospital,** 57 Prospect St. (☎ **508/228-1200**), is open 24 hours.

2 Beaches & Recreational Pursuits

BEACHES In distinct contrast to Martha's Vineyard, virtually all of Nantucket's 110-mile coastline is open to the public. Though the pressure to keep people out is sometimes intense (especially when four-wheel drivers insist on their right to go anywhere, anytime), islanders are proud that they've managed to keep the shoreline in the public domain.

Each of the following areas tends to attract a different crowd.

- **Children's Beach:** This small beach is a protected cove just west of busy Steamship Wharf. Appealing to families, it has a park, playground, rest rooms, lifeguards, snack bar (the beloved Downy Flake, famous for its homemade doughnuts), and even a bandstand for free weekend concerts.
- **Cisco Beach:** About 4 miles from town, in the southwestern quadrant of the island (from Main St., turn onto Milk St., which becomes Hummock Pond Rd.), Cisco enjoys vigorous waves—great for the surfers who flock here, not so great for the waterfront homeowners. Rest rooms and lifeguards are available.
- **Coatue:** This fishhook-shaped barrier beach, on the northeastern side of the island at Wauwinet, is Nantucket's outback, accessible only by four-wheel-drive vehicles, watercraft, or the very strong legged. Swimming is strongly discouraged because of fierce tides.
- **Dionis Beach:** About 3 miles out of town (take the Madaket bike path to Eel Point Rd.) is Dionis, which enjoys the gentle sound surf and steep, picturesque bluffs. It's a great spot for swimming, picnicking, and shelling, and you'll find fewer children than at Jetties or Children's beaches. Stick to the established paths to prevent further erosion. Lifeguards patrol here, and rest rooms are available.
- ✪ **Jetties Beach:** Located about a ½ mile west of Children's Beach on North Beach Street, Jetties is about a 20-minute walk, or even shorter bike ride, shuttle bus ride, or drive, from town (there's a large parking lot, but it fills up early on

summer weekends). It's another family favorite, for its mild waves, lifeguards, bathhouse, and rest rooms, and relatively affordable restaurant, The Jetties Cafe & Grille (☎ **508/325-6347**). Facilities include the town tennis courts, volley-ball nets, a skate park, and a playground; water-sports equipment, and chairs are also available to rent. Every August, Jetties hosts an intense sand-castle competi-tion, and the 4th of July fireworks are held here.

- **Madaket Beach:** Accessible by Madaket Road, the 6-mile bike path that runs parallel to it, and by shuttle bus, this westerly beach is narrow and subject to pounding surf and sometimes serious crosscurrents. Unless it's a fairly tame day, you might content yourself with wading. It's the best spot on the island for admiring the sunset. Facilities include rest rooms, lifeguards, and mobile food service.
- **Siasconset Beach:** The easterly coast of 'Sconset is as pretty as the town itself and rarely, if ever, crowded, perhaps because of the water's strong sideways tow. You can reach it by car, shuttle bus, or by a less scenic and somewhat hilly (at least for Nantucket) 7-mile bike path. There are usually lifeguards on duty, but the closest facilities (rest rooms, grocery store, and cafe) are back in the center of the village.
- **Surfside Beach:** Three miles south of town via a popular bike/skate path, broad Surfside—equipped with lifeguards, rest rooms, and a surprisingly accomplished little snack bar—is appropriately named and commensurately popular. It draws thousands of visitors a day in high season from college students to families, but the free-parking lot can only fit about 60 cars—you do the math, or better yet, ride your bike or take the shuttle bus.

BICYCLING   Several lovely, paved bike paths radiate out from the center of town to outlying beaches. The ✪ **main paths** run about 6.2 miles west to Madaket, 3.5 miles south to Surfside, and 8.2 miles east to Siasconset. To avoid backtracking from Siasconset, continue north through the charming village, and return on the new Polpis Road bike path. Strong riders could do a whole circuit of the island in a day, but most will be content to combine a single route with a few hours at a beach. You'll find pic-nic benches and water fountains at strategic points along all the paths.

On the way back to town, lighthouse enthusiasts will want to stop by Brant Point Light at the end of Easton Street. Located next to the Coast Guard station, this squat lighthouse is still used by boats maneuvering in and out of the harbor. It's a scenic spot to take a break and enjoy the view; you'll see ferries chugging by and immense yachts competing for prize berths along the wharves.

For a free map of the island's bike paths (it also lists Nantucket's bicycle rules), stop by **Young's Bicycle Shop,** at Steamboat Wharf (☎ **508/228-1151**). It's definitely the best place for bike rentals, from basic three-speeds to high-tech suspension models. In operation since 1931—check out the vintage vehicles they have on display—they also deliver door-to-door. See "Getting Around," above, for more bike-rental shops.

FISHING   For shellfishing, you'll need a permit from the **harbormaster's office** at 34 Washington St. (☎ **508/228-7261**). You'll see surf casters all over the island (no permit is required); for a guided trip, try Mike Mont of **Surf & Fly Fishing Trips** (☎ **508/228-0529**). Deep-sea charters heading out of Straight Wharf include Cap-tain Bob DeCosta's The Albacore (☎ **508/228-5074**), Captain Josh Eldridge's Monomoy (☎ **508/228-6867**), and Captain David Martin's Flicka (☎ **508/ 325-4000**).

FITNESS   **Nantucket Health Club** at 10 Youngs Way (☎ **508/228-4750**) offers all the usual equipment and classes. Non-members pay $20 a day.

GOLF   Two pretty 9-hole courses are open to the public: **Miacomet Golf Club,** 12 W. Miacomet Rd. (☎ 508/325-0333) and the **Siasconset Golf Club,** off Milestone Rd. (☎ 508/257-6596). You'll pay $29 for 9 holes to $55 for 18 holes. You need to be a member to play at the ultra-exclusive **Nantucket Golf Club** off Milestone Road. Annual memberships cost $250,000 to $500,000. This is where President Clinton played a round with Senator John Kerry and Microsoft CEO Bill Gates.

NATURE TRAILS   Through preservationist foresight, about one-third of Nantucket's 42 square miles are protected from development. Contact the **Nantucket Conservation Foundation** at 118 Cliff Rd. (☎ 508/228-2884) for a map of their holdings ($3), which include the 205-acre **Windswept Cranberry Bog** (off Polpis Rd.), where bogs are interspersed amid hardwood forests, and a portion of the 1,100-acre ✪ **Coskata-Coatue Wildlife Refuge,** comprising the barrier beaches beyond Wauwinet (see "Organized Tours," below). The **Maria Mitchell Association** (see "Museums & Historic Landmarks," below) also sponsors guided birding and wildflower walks in season.

TENNIS   The town courts are located next to Jetties Beach, a short walk west of town; call the **Nantucket Park and Recreation Commission** (☎ 508/325-5334) for information. Nine clay courts are available for rent nearby at the **Brant Point Racquet Club,** on North Beach Street (☎ 508/228-3700), for $30 an hour. Though it's not generally open to the public, the grand, turn-of-the-century **Siasconset Casino,** New St., Siasconset (☎ 508/257-6661), occasionally has courts available for rent from 1 to 3pm for $20 an hour.

WATER SPORTS   **Nantucket Community Sailing** manages the concession at **Jetties Beach** (☎ 508/228-5358), which offers lessons and rents out kayaks, sailboards, sailboats, and more. Rental rates for single kayaks are $15 per hour; Windsurfers $25 per hour; Sunfish $30 per hour. **Sea Nantucket,** on tiny Francis Street Beach off Washington Street (☎ 508/228-7499), also rents kayaks; it's a quick sprint across the harbor to beautiful Coatue. Single kayaks rent for $15 per hour or $30 for 4½ hours. **Nantucket Island Community Sailing** (☎ 508/228-6600) gives relatively low-cost private and group lessons from the Town Pier for adults (16 and up) and families; a seasonal adult membership covering open-sail privileges costs $150. One 3-hour lesson costs $100.

Gear for scuba-diving, fishing, and snorkeling are readily available at the souvenir shop **Sunken Ship** on South Water and Broad streets near Steamboat Wharf (☎ 508/228-9226). Fishing gear costs $15 per day; snorkeling gear costs $25 a day; scuba-diving gear and lessons costs $30–$40.

3 Museums & Historic Landmarks

Hadwen House. 96 Main St. (at Pleasant St., a few blocks SW of the town center). ☎ **508/228-1894.** Admission $4 adults, $3 children 5–14; also included in Nantucket Historical Association pass ($10 adults, $5 children). June–Sept daily 10am–5pm; call for off-season hours. Closed mid-Oct to late May.

During Nantucket's most prosperous years, whaling merchant Joseph Starbuck built the "Three Bricks" (nos. 93, 95, and 97 Main St.) for his three sons. His daughter married successful businessman William Hadwen, owner of the candle factory that is now the Whaling Museum, and Hadwen built this grand Greek Revival home across the street from his brothers-in-law in 1845. Although locals (mostly Quakers) were scandalized by the opulence, the local outrage spurred Hadwen on, and he decided to make the home even grander than he had first intended. The home soon became a showplace for entertaining the Hadwens' many wealthy friends. Soon after, Hadwen built the matching home next door for his niece, and it is assumed that he enjoyed using its grand ballroom for his parties, too. The Historical Association has done a magnificent job restoring the home and furnishing it with period furniture, fabrics, porcelains, wallpapers, and other decorative accessories thought to be original. The gardens are maintained in period style by the Nantucket Garden Club.

Jethro Coffin House. Sunset Hill Rd. (off W. Chester Rd., about ½ mile NW of the town center). ☎ **508/228-1894.** Admission $3 adults, $2 children 5–14; also included in Nantucket Historical Association pass ($10 adults, $5 children). Mid-June to early Sept daily 10am–5pm; call for off-season hours. Closed mid-Oct to late May.

Built around 1696, this saltbox is the oldest building left on the island. A National Historical Landmark, the brick design on its central chimney has earned it the nickname "The Horseshoe House." It was struck by lightning and severely damaged (in fact, nearly cut in two) in 1987, prompting a long-overdue restoration. Dimly lit by leaded glass diamond-pane windows, it's filled with period furniture such as lathed ladder-back chairs and a clever trundle bed on wooden wheels. Nantucket Historical Association docents will fill you in on all the related lore.

The Maria Mitchell Association. 4 Vestal St. (at Milk St., about ½ mile SW of the town center). ☎ **508/228-9198.** www.mmo.org. Museum pass (for birthplace, aquarium, science museum, and Vestal Street Observatory) $7 adults, $5 seniors and children age 6–14. Early June–late Aug Tues–Sat 10am–4pm; call for off-season hours.

This is a group of six buildings organized and maintained in honor of distinguished astronomer and Nantucket native Maria Mitchell (1818–89). The science center consists of astronomical observatories, with a lecture series, children's science seminars, and stellar observation opportunities (when the sky is clear) from the **Loines Observatory** at 59 Milk St. (☎ **508/228-8690**) and the **Vestal Street Observatory** at 3 Vestal St. (☎ **508/228-9273**). The Vestal Street Observatory is open June to September daily at 11am for a 1-hour tour. The Loines Observatory is open Monday, Wednesday, and Friday at 9pm. The cost is $10 adults, $6 children and seniors. Both observatories are open-round. Call for off-season hours.

The **Hinchman House Natural Science Museum** (☎ **508/228-0898**) at 7 Milk St. houses a visitor's center and offers evening lectures, bird watching, wildflower and nature walks, and discovery classes for children and adults. The **Mitchell House** (☎ **508/228-2896**) at 1 Vestal St., the astronomer's birthplace, features a children's history series and adult-artisan seminars, and has wildflower and herb gardens. The **Science Library** (☎ **508/228-9219**) is at 2 Vestal St. and the tiny, child-oriented aquarium (☎ **508/228-5387**) is at 28 Washington St.

Nantucket Life-Saving Museum. 158 Polpis Rd. ☎ **508/228-1855.** Admission $3 adults, $2 children. Mid-June to mid-Oct daily 9:30am–4pm.

Housed in a replica of the Nantucket Lifesaving Station (the original serves as the island's youth hostel), the museum has loads of interesting exhibits, including historic photos and newspaper clippings, as well as one of the last remaining Massachusetts Humane Society surf boats and its horse-drawn carriage.

✪ **Whaling Museum.** 13 Broad St. (in the center of town). ☎ **508/228-1894.** Admission $5 adults, $3 children 5–14; also included in the Nantucket Historical Association pass ($10 adults, $5 children). Late May to mid-Oct daily 10am–5pm; call for off-season hours. Closed early Dec to mid-Apr.

Housed in a former spermaceti-candle factory (candles used to be made from a waxy fluid that's extracted from sperm whales), this museum is a must-visit; if not for the awe-inspiring skeleton of a 43-foot finback whale (stranded in the 1960s), then for the exceptional collections of scrimshaw and nautical art (check out the action painting, *Ship Spermo of Nantucket in a Heavy Thunder-Squall on the Coast of California 1876,* executed by a captain who survived the storm). A wall-size map depicts the round-the-world meanderings of the *Alpha,* accompanied by related journal entries. The price of admission includes daily lectures on the brief and colorful history of the industry, like the beachside "whalebecue" feasts that natives and settlers once enjoyed. Pursued to its logical conclusion, this booming business unfortunately led to the near-extinction of some extraordinary species, but that story must await its own museum; this one is full of the glories of the hunt. Don't miss the gift shop on the way out.

4 Organized Tours

Christina. Slip 19, Straight Wharf. ☎ **508/325-4000.** Day sails $20 per person; sunset sails $30 per person. Reservations recommended. Closed Nov–Apr.

Built in 1926, the *Christina* is a classic solid mahogany cat boat. The boat makes seven 1½-hour trips daily in season, and the sunset trips tend to sell out a day or two in advance. Price-wise, a sail around the harbor on the *Christina* is probably the best entertainment bargain on Nantucket. Bring your own drinks and picnic supplies.

Coskata-Coatue Wildlife Refuge Natural History Tour. ☎ **508/228-6799.** $30 adult, $15 child 15 and under. Call for reservations. Mid-May to mid-Oct daily 9:30am and 2:30pm. Closed mid-Oct to mid-May.

The Trustees of the Reservations, a private statewide conservation organization that oversees the bulk of the Coskata-Coatue Wildlife Refuge, offers 3-hour naturalist-guided tours. The trip is over sand dunes via Ford Expedition out to the **Great Point Lighthouse,** a partly solar-powered replica of the 1818 original. Those interested can also tour the inside of the light. During the trip through this rare habitat, you might spot snowy egrets, ospreys, terns, and oystercatchers. Call to make a reservation and meet the group at the Wauwinet Inn parking lot.

Endeavor Sailing Excursions. Slip 15, Straight Wharf. ☎ **508/228-5585.** www.endeavorsailing.com. Rates are $22.50–$35 for a 1½-hr. sail (highest rates are July–Aug); reservations recommended. Closed Nov–Apr.

The Endeavor is a spirited 31-foot replica Friendship sloop, ideal for jaunts across the harbor into Nantucket Sound. Skipper James Genthner will gladly drop you off for a bit of sunbathing or beachcombing.

Gail's Tours. Departs from the Nantucket Information Bureau at 25 Federal St., and from pre-arranged pickup sites. ☎ **508/257-6557.** Reservations required. Rates $10 adults, free for children 3 and under. July–Aug departures at 10am, 1, and 3pm; call for off-season hours.

If you want to get some dirt on the island's colorful residents, Gail Nickerson Johnson—a seventh-generation native whose mother started a tour business back in the 1940s—has the inside track, and the charm, to keep a captive van-load rapt throughout a 1½-hour circuit of Island highlights, including lots of celebrity info.

Nantucket Harbor Cruises. Slip 11, Straight Wharf. ☎ **508/228-1444.** Rates $25 adults, $20 for children 4–12; call for reservations. MC, V. Closed May.

Adapting to the season, the *Anna W. II,* a lobster-boat-turned-pleasure-barge, offers lobstering demos in summer (passengers sometimes get to take home the proceeds) and seal-sighting cruises along the jetty from November through January ($15 adults, $10 children). In between, Capt. Bruce Cowan takes groups out just to view the lovely

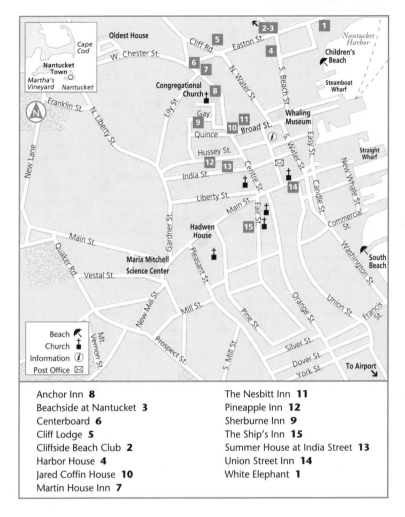

Anchor Inn **8**
Beachside at Nantucket **3**
Centerboard **6**
Cliff Lodge **5**
Cliffside Beach Club **2**
Harbor House **4**
Jared Coffin House **10**
Martin House Inn **7**

The Nesbitt Inn **11**
Pineapple Inn **12**
Sherburne Inn **9**
The Ship's Inn **15**
Summer House at India Street **13**
Union Street Inn **14**
White Elephant **1**

shoreline. In season, a 1-hour ice-cream cruise leaves at 3:30pm daily and costs $15 for adults and $10 for children.

Nantucket Historical Society Guided Walking Tours. Tour meets in front of Whaling Museum. ☎ 508/228-1894. $5 adults, $3 children or free with Historical Society visitor's pass. Late May–early Oct Mon–Sat 10:30am, 2:30pm. Call for off-season hours. Closed Dec–Mar.

Stroll along downtown's cobblestone streets on this Historical Society tour that spotlights the history and architecture of Nantucket. The tours are led by Nantucket Historical Society docents trained in Nantucket history.

5 Kid Stuff

The **Nantucket Park and Recreation Commission** (☎ 508/228-7213) organizes various free and low-cost activities for kids, like tennis clinics, Little League, a concert series, and tie-dye workshops (it's a bring-your-own-T-shirt proposition). The **Artists'**

A Peachy Idea

It was just over 11 years ago, on a cold December night on Nantucket, that two college buddies concocted a sweet peach drink in a blender. Nowadays, the hip and popular juices of Nantucket Nectars are available coast to coast, and the privately held company racked up sales of $70 million last year.

Juice Guys Tom First and Tom Scott, both in their 30s, are the photogenic chief operating officer and chief executive officer, respectively, of a thriving business they started on the island. They make frequent trips year-round to Nantucket and sponsor many local events. But these poster boys of entrepreneurship are quick to point out that success was neither easy nor immediate.

Their roots on Nantucket go back to childhood; both Toms vacationed on the island with their families. They first met at Brown University and continued to spend summers on the island working and playing. In the summer of 1989, while still in college, they started a harbor delivery service called Allserve, which catered to wealthy yacht owners.

With their Allserve business up and running, the two moved to Nantucket after college. Their juice epiphany occurred soon after. The two Toms were at a party and Tom First was fooling around with a blender, trying to duplicate a peach drink he had enjoyed in Spain. When their friends raved about the new drink, Tom and Tom christened it "Peach Nectar" and started selling it at Allserve. Soon local businesses were selling the hand-bottled drinks. Sales grew from 8,000 cases the first year to 20,000 the second year.

The Toms knew they were onto something, and invested their savings in the start-up, researched the juice business, and studied mass production. The business really turned around in 1993, when the Toms persuaded an investor they

---

Association of Nantucket (☎ 508/325-5251) sponsors a variety of classes for children in different media, and the **Nantucket Island School of Design and the Arts** (☎ 508/228-9248) offers all sorts of summer courses. The **Nantucket Atheneum** (☎ 508/228-1110) holds readings in its spiffy new children's wing, and the **Nantucket Historical Association** (☎ 508/228-1894) sponsors **Living History for Children,** 2-hour adventures for ages 6 to 10, which include grinding flour at the Old Mill, baking bread at the Oldest House, and trying your hand at knots and sailors' valentines. The cost is $25.

The **Actors' Theatre of Nantucket** at the Methodist Church, 2 Centre St. (☎ 508/228-6325), puts on theatrical performances for children by children from late July to mid-August, Tuesday to Saturday at 5pm; tickets are $10. **Nobadeer Minigolf,** at 12 Nobadeer Farm Rd., near the airport (☎ 508/228-8977), offers 18 fancily landscaped holes laced with lagoons; there's a great little Mexican restaurant, **Patio J,** on the premises. Little kids might like to get their hands on (and into) the touch tanks at the modest little **Maria Mitchell Aquarium** at 28 Washington St. (☎ 508/228-5387), which overlooks the harbor from whence the creatures came; the cost is only $1. It's open June through September Tuesday to Saturday from 10am to 4pm. For a real seafaring adventure, consider embarking on a treasure hunt aboard The Endeavor or signing on as crew with **Nantucket Whaleboat Adventures** (☎ 508/228-5585).

had met through their yacht delivery business—rent-a-car magnate Michael Egan, now pictured in the background of the bottles' label—to provide much-needed capital. That $50,000 allowed them to expand, and revenues soon broke the $1 million mark.

Today, Ocean Spray, a juice company owned by a cooperative of growers, owns an undisclosed portion of Nantucket Nectars, which expects sales of $80 million next year. But Tom and Tom are still running the show with their trademark humor and charisma.

A few Juice Guy tidbits:

Deciphering the label: That's Tom and Tom in their Allserve boat with their devoted dogs. Becky is part Lab, part Springer Spaniel, and part shortstop, according to owner Tom Scott. Pete, the black dog, is Tom First's Portuguese Water Dog.

Visitors to Nantucket hoping to live out the complete Juice Guy experience should make a beeline to their juice bar called, appropriately, **Juice Guys,** 4 Easy St. (☎ **508/228-4464**). Here, high-tech blenders mix potent combinations of fresh juice with vitamins, sorbet, yogurt, nuts, fruit, and holistic enhancers. The juice bar is open 8am to 8pm, spring through Christmas.

Those hoping to spot the Juice Guys might try some of their hangouts, such as the bar at **The Boarding House,** 12 Federal St. (☎ **508/228-9622**), and **Straight Wharf,** Straight Wharf (☎ **508/228-4499**), where they were employed one summer shucking scallops. The Juice Guys can also be found participating in local athletic competitions, like the annual Ironman triathlon in early summer. Juice Guy pilgrims can poke their heads into **Allserve,** Straight Wharf (☎ **508/228-8170**), the wharfside general store where it all started.

6 Shopping

Nantucket shopping is so phenomenal you'll be tempted to rent a U-Haul. It's as if all the best big-city buyers, from Bendel's to Brooks Brothers, got together and gathered up their favorite stuff. True, some tourist dreck has managed to drift in, but most of what you'll find for sale is as high in quality as it is in price—everything from $6 boxes of chocolate-covered dried cranberries to $900 cashmere sweaters.

ANTIQUES/COLLECTIBLES   Most tourists aren't looking to return home with a new living-room set, but **Lynda Willauer Antiques,** at 2 India St., between Federal and Centre streets (☎ **508/228-3631**), has such an exquisite selection of American, French and English furniture that it's worth stopping by just to gawk. All pieces are painstakingly tagged as to provenance and state of repair, and most are quite pricey. The shop also stocks paintings, Chinese export porcelain, Staffordshire china, samplers, ship wool works, Majolica, and brass and tortoise-shell boxes.

An island fixture since 1971, ✪ **Tonkin of Nantucket,** 33 Main St. (☎ **508/ 228-9697**), specializes in English and French antiques. Antique hounds will be in heaven browsing through the 9,000 square feet of showrooms, featuring such finery as silver, china, marine paintings, ship models, fireplace equipment, Quimper, and Majolica.

ART & CRAFTS   The Artists' Association of Nantucket has the widest selection of work by locals, and the gallery at 19 Washington St. (☎ **508/228-0294**) is impressive. Closed February and March.

Visit **The Golden Basket,** 44 Main St. (☎ **800/582-8205** or 508/228-4344), also known as **The Golden Nugget** at Straight Wharf (☎ **508/228-1019**). Widely copied, miniaturized jewelry versions of Nantucket's trademark lightship baskets were introduced here, and artisan Glenaan Elliot Robbins's rendition is still the finest. The baskets, complete with gold penny, represent a small portion of the inventory, all of which is exquisite.

The celebrated sculptor **David L. Hostetler** exhibits his work in one of the little galleries along Old South Wharf, 2 Old South Wharf (☎ **508/228-5152**). Private viewing appointments are also available in his large showroom. His work in various media appears as spiritual icons expressed in the female form.

Exquisite artful pieces can be found at **Nantucket Glassworks,** 28 Centre St. (☎ **508/228-7779**) where owners Robert and Jayne Dane show top-quality work. You'll be amazed at the colors and shapes of the glassware.

You'll definitely want to poke your head in **Sailor's Valentine** in the Macy Warehouse on lower Main Street (☎ **508/228-2011**), which houses an international collection of contemporary fine art, sculpture, folk art, and "outsider art." There are also new versions of the namesake craft, a boxed design of colorful shells, which 19th-century sailors used to bring back from the Caribbean for their sweethearts at home.

BOOKS   At **Mitchell's Book Corner,** 54 Main St. (☎ **508/228-1080**), Mimi Beman handpicks her stock, with an astute sampling of general-interest books and an entire room dedicated to regional and maritime titles.

Nantucket Bookworks, 25 Broad St. (☎ **508/228-4000**), is a charming bookstore, strong on customer service and with a central location.

FASHION   Martha's Vineyard may have spawned "Black Dog" fever, but this island boasts the inimitable "Nantucket reds"—cotton clothing that starts out tomato-red and washes out to salmon-pink. The fashion originated at **Murray's Toggery Shop,** 62 Main St. (☎ **800/368-2134** or 508/228-0437). Legend has it that the original duds were colored with an inferior dye that washed out almost immediately, but that customers so liked the thick cottons and instant aged look that the proprietor was forced to search high and low for more of the same fabric. Roland Hussey Macy, founder of Macy's, got his start here in the 1830s—his shop shows no signs of fading (no pun intended)—although today's management also manages to keep up with current trends. There's a bargain outlet on New Street.

Preppy patterns and bright colors are back! You'll find **Lilly Pulitzer's** latest, including sensational minidresses, at 5 S. Water St. (☎ **508/228-0569**).

GIFTS/HOME DECOR   A casual counterpart to its Madison Avenue boutique, ✪ **Erica Wilson Needle Works,** 25–27 Main St. (☎ **508/228-9881**), features the designs of its namesake, an Islander since 1958 and author of more than two dozen books on needlepoint. The shop offers hands-on guidance for hundreds of grateful adepts, as well as kits and handiwork of other noteworthy designers.

The also eponymous **Claire Murray,** 11 S. Water St. (☎ **508/228-1913**), is famous for its elaborate hand-hooked rugs. As a New York transplant running a Nantucket B&B in the late 1970s, Murray took up the traditional art of hooking rugs to see her through the slow season. She now runs a retail company grossing millions a year and is so busy creating new collections that she has hundreds of "hookers" (probably an old profession, but not the oldest) working for her around the world. Do-it-yourself kits ($100 to $500) are sold in the shop here for about two-thirds the price of the finished rugs and come with complimentary lessons.

Resembling an old-fashioned pharmacy, **The Fragrance Bar,** 5 Centre St. (☎ **800/ 223-8660** or 508/325-4740), is run by a colorful fellow who goes by the solo sobriquet of Harpo. A self-professed "nose," he has assembled some 400 essential oils with which he can duplicate designer scents or customize blends. Uncut by alcohol (unlike their commercial counterparts), these perfumes linger on the skin and do not cause associated problems such as allergies and headaches. Harpo won't discuss his clientele but admits to creating a custom scent for a certain recording megastar who also goes by a single name, starting with an "M."

Centrally located **Nantucket Looms,** 16 Main St. (☎ **508/228-1908**), is an elegant shop featuring beautifully textured woven items as well as fine furniture and gifts.

Although certain influences are evident (from Queen Anne to Shaker), the hand-fashioned furniture at **Stephen Swift,** 34 Main St. (☎ **508/228-0255**), is far too individualized to pass as reproduction. Such is its classicism, though, that Swift's work would blend into the most traditional of homes, or just as easily adapt to a modern setting. Among his signature pieces are wavy-backed Windsor chairs and benches (as sturdy as the original but more comfortable) and delicate, pared-down four-poster beds.

SEAFOOD   ✪ **Sayle's Seafood,** Washington Street Extension (☎ **508/228-4599**), sells fresh seafood from Nantucket waters and a new menu of take-out seafood platters. This is a great place to get a huge, steaming plate of fried clams to go.

TOYS   The Toy Boat, Straight Wharf (☎ **508/228-4552**), is keen on creative toys that are also educational. In addition to the top commercial lines, owner Loren Brock stocks lots of locally crafted, hand-carved playthings, such as "rainbow fleet" sailboats, part of the Harbor Series that includes docks, lighthouses, boats, and everything your child needs to create his or her own Nantucket Harbor. There are also stackable lighthouse puzzles replicating Nantucket's beams.

7 Where to Stay

Most visitors to Nantucket will wish to stay in the center of town. There's no need for a car here; in fact, parking can be a real problem in season. Everything is within walking distance, including beaches, restaurants, and the finest shopping in the region. Unless otherwise stated, hotels are open year-round.

VERY EXPENSIVE

✪ **Cliffside Beach Club.** 46 Jefferson Ave. (about 1 mile from town center), Nantucket, MA 02554. ☎ **508/228-0618.** Fax 508/325-4735. www.cliffsidebeach.com. 27 units, 1 cottage. A/C TV TEL. Summer $335–$535 double; $655–$1,310 suite; $655 apartment; $870 cottage. Rates include continental breakfast. AE. Closed mid-Oct to late May.

Right on the beach and within walking distance (about 1 mile) of town, this is the premier lodging on the island. It may not be as fancy as some, but there's a sublime beachy-ness to the whole setup, from the simply decorated rooms, the cheerful, youthful staff, the sea of antique wicker in the clubhouse, and of course, the blue, yellow and green umbrellas lined up on the beach. All rooms have such luxuries as French milled soaps, thick towels, and exceptional linens. Each room has a minifridge and a hair dryer. Turndown service is provided. Guests receive an umbrella, chairs, and beach towels. A very good continental breakfast is served in the large clubhouse room, its beamed ceilings draped with colorful quilts. Lucky guests on the 4th of July get a front-row seat for the fireworks staged at Jetties Beach nearby.

Dining: The Galley Restaurant is an elegant French bistro specializing in seafood and sunsets.

Amenities: Billed as Nantucket's finest exercise facility, the health club here boasts Cybex equipment and a trainer on staff. There's also an indoor hydrotherapy spa, steam saunas, and a climate-controlled massage room. These services are complimentary to guests.

Harbor House. S. Beach St. (in the center of town), Nantucket, MA 02554. ☎ **800/ 475-2637** or 508/228-1500. Fax 508/228-7639. 109 units. A/C TV TEL. Summer $310–$385, double, $370–$425 suites. AE, CB, DC, DISC, MC, V. Open year-round.

Close to the placid harbor cove at Children's Beach, the Harbor House, built in 1886, is a venerable hotel encircled by standard-issue, gray-shingled town houses. The larger, more luxurious rooms, which have country-pine furniture and private patios and decks, are located in six town houses, linked to one another and to an outdoor heated pool by nicely landscaped brick walkways. Rooms in the main house are prettily decorated with flowered fabrics and canopied or four-poster beds, but some can be a tight squeeze. All in all, this is a pleasant if generic place to stay, and for these prices, you might be able to do better.

Dining/Diversions: Food Fare serves traditional New England meals and is open for breakfast, dinner, and Sunday brunch. The elaborate buffet brunch is popular with islanders. You can also gather around the fire in this elegant wood-beamed hall and listen to live music most nights in season (see "Nantucket After Dark," below).

Amenities: Outdoor heated pool, concierge, baby-sitting for a fee, conference rooms, and business center.

✪ **The Wauwinet.** 120 Wauwinet Rd. (P.O. Box 2580) (about 8 miles E of Nantucket center), Nantucket, MA 02554. ☎ **800/426-8718** or 508/228-0145. Fax 508/228-6712. www. wauwinet.com. E-mail: email@wauwinet.com. 25 units, 5 cottages. A/C TV TEL. Summer $540–$890 double; $850–$1,500 cottage. Rates include full breakfast and afternoon wine and cheese. AE, DC, MC, V. Closed Nov–May.

This ultra-deluxe beachfront retreat is the most luxurious lodging choice on the island. With 25 rooms in the main building (which started out as a restaurant in 1850) and 10 more in five modest-looking shingled cottages, the complex can only hold about 80 decorously spoiled guests, outnumbered by 100 staffers. Each of the lovely rooms—all provided with a cozy nook from which to gaze out across the water—has a unique decorating scheme, with pine armoires, plenty of wicker, exquisite Audubon prints, handsome fabrics, and a lovely array of antique accessories. Extras include hair dryers, irons/ironing boards, Egyptian cotton bathrobes, and bottled water. Additional perks include a personalized set of engraved note cards. (Don't tell them I told you; it's supposed to be a surprise.) All rooms have CD players and VCRs, and if you order up a video from the extensive (400 videos) library, it is delivered on a tray by a steward with a couple of boxes of complimentary hot popcorn. That's service.

Dining: Guests can dine in the highly acclaimed Topper's restaurant on the premises (see "Where to Dine," below).

Amenities: The staff goes to great lengths to please, ferrying you into town, for instance, in a 1946 "Woody," or dispatching you on a 21-foot launch across the bay to your own private strip of beach in season. The inn is the last stop on an 8-mile road to nowhere (actually, a wildlife sanctuary), and it boasts two clay tennis courts with a pro shop and teaching pro, a croquet lawn, and plenty of boats and bikes to borrow.

White Elephant. Easton and Willard sts., (P.O. Box 1139) Nantucket, MA 02554. ☎ **800/ ISLANDS** or 508/228-2500. Fax 508/325-1195. www.whiteelephanthotel.com. 54 units, 12 cottages. A/C TV TEL. Summer $400–$750 double; $350–$1,160 cottage. Rates include full breakfast. AE, CB, DC, DISC, MC, V. Closed Nov–Apr.

This luxury property, right on the harbor, is the ultimate in-town lodging and has been newly renovated by the owners of The Wauwinet (see above). Rooms (distributed among one building and 12 cottages) are big and airy (the most spacious rooms on Nantucket), with country-chic decor and most with harbor views. In-room amenities include hair dryers and VCRs or DVD players. About half the rooms have working fireplaces. Guests can borrow from an extensive tape library of new and old movies. The hotel has pleasant commons rooms including a library, fitness center, and business lounge. The hotel's location welcomes "sail-in" guests. The same company owns Breakers, a 25-room hotel next door that offers a less bustling atmosphere.

Dining/Diversions: The Brant Point Grill (see "Where to Dine," below) is a lobster and steak house serving lunch and dinner daily. The view couldn't be better, and the quality of the service and food is excellent.

Amenities: Outdoor heated pool. This full-service hotel provides concierge, full room service, and newspapers. Laundry and dry-cleaning service are available for a fee.

EXPENSIVE

Beachside at Nantucket. 30 N. Beach St. (about ¾ mile W of the town center), Nantucket, MA 02554. ☎ **800/322-4433** or 508/228-2241. Fax 508/228-8901. www.beachside.com. E-mail: info@beachside.com. 90 units. A/C TV TEL. Summer $255–$270 double. Rates include continental breakfast. AE, DC, DISC, MC, V. Closed early Dec–late Apr.

No ordinary motel, the Beachside's 90 air-conditioned bedrooms and lobby have been lavished with Provençal prints and handsome rattan and wicker furniture; the patios and decks overlooking the central courtyard with its heated pool have been prettified with French doors and latticework. If you prefer the laissez-faire lifestyle of a motel to the sometimes constricting rituals of a B&B, you might find this the ideal base.

Centerboard. 8 Chester St. (in the center of town), Nantucket, MA 02554. ☎ **508/228-9696.** Fax 508/325-4798. www.nantucket.net/lodging/centerboard. E-mail: centerbo@nantucket.net. 7 units. A/C TV TEL. Summer $199–$235 double; $325–$395 suite. Rates include continental breakfast. MC, V. Open year-round.

Nantucket actually has very little in Victorian housing: The island was just too poor (and underpopulated) to build much in those days. The few to be found tend to get dolled up like this updated 1886 home, replete with parquet floors, Oriental rugs, lavish fabrics, a plush feather mattress, and lace-trimmed linens. The overall look is light, airy and less cluttered than the original Victorian look. Innkeeper Debbie Wasil has large-resort experience and is most hospitable. Of the inn's seven bedrooms, the first-floor suite is perhaps the most romantic, with a green-marble Jacuzzi and a private living room with fireplace. Other rooms and bathrooms are small, but all have bathrobes and minifridges.

Jared Coffin House. 29 Broad St. (at Centre St.), Nantucket, MA 02554. ☎ **800/248-2405** or 508/228-2400. Fax 508/228-8549. www.jaredcoffinhouse.net/. E-mail: jchouse@nantucket.net. 60 units. TV TEL. Summer $175–$325 double. AE, CB, DC, DISC, MC, V. Open year-round.

This grand brick manse was built in 1845 to the specs of the social-climbing Mrs. Coffin, who abandoned Nantucket for the big city after 2 years and left the house to boarders. Lovingly renovated to its original splendor by the Nantucket Historical Trust, it is the social center of town, as well as a mecca for visitors. Accommodations range from well-priced singles (rare in these parts) to spacious doubles. Rooms in the neighboring annex houses are equally grand. The concierge, Mrs. K., can't do enough to help, and refuses tips! The central location does have a drawback: The front rooms can be quite noisy. Twenty-minute waits for breakfast are not unusual because locals come, too. It's the best breakfast in town, though it is not included in the room rate. It's a good idea to call down ahead and put your name on the list.

✪ **The Pineapple Inn.** 10 Hussey St. (in the center of town), Nantucket, MA 02554. ☎ **508/228-9992.** Fax 508/325-6051. www.pineappleinn.com. E-mail: info@pineappleinn. com. 12 units. A/C TV, TEL. Summer $160–$295 double. Rates include continental breakfast. AE, MC, V. Closed early Dec to mid-Apr. No children under age 8.

This newly renovated historic inn has quickly become one of the premier places to stay on the island. The graceful Quaker entrance of this 1838 home bespeaks the hospitality to come from veteran innkeepers Bob and Caroline Taylor. Rooms are spacious and decorated in a Colonial style with fine reproductions and antiques, including handmade oriental rugs, marble bathrooms, and many four-poster canopy beds. There are five large king bedrooms with beds of tiger maple. The smaller, less expensive rooms are on the third floor. All rooms are equipped with such extras as hair dryers, goose-down comforters, voice-mail, dataports, and cable. The continental breakfast here is extra deluxe with fresh baked goods, espresso, cappuccino, and freshly squeezed orange juice among the offerings. The garden patio with climbing roses is a fine place to enjoy an afternoon cocktail and contemplate dinner plans.

Sherburne Inn. 10 Gay St. (in the center of town), Nantucket, MA 02554. ☎ **888/ 577-4425** or 508/228-4425. Fax 508/228-8114. www.sherburneinn.com. E-mail: sherinn@ nantucket.net. 8 units. A/C TV TEL. Summer $150–$275. Rates include continental breakfast. AE, DISC, MC, V. Open year-round. No children under 6.

You'd never guess from the gracious foyer of this 1835 house that it was once the headquarters of the Atlantic Silk Company, a short-lived 19th-century enterprise. Now it's an elegant and comfortable inn offering quiet comforts in the heart of Nantucket village. Innkeepers Dale Hamilton and Susan Gasparich, who bought the inn in 1994, are transplants from Pittsburgh who are active in a number of island organizations. Rooms vary in size, with smaller rooms a good value at lower rates. Ask for one on the sunny side of the house. Susan's recipes for baked goods like butterscotch coffee cake have been featured in *Gourmet* magazine.

Summer House at India Street. 31 India St. (in the center of town), Nantucket, MA 02554. ☎ **508/228-6609.** Fax 508/257-4590. www.thesummerhouse.com. 10 units. A/C TV TEL. Summer $225–$450. Rates include continental breakfast. AE, MC, V. Closed Jan–Apr.

The Summer House management now owns three properties: the very expensive cottages overlooking the beach in Siasconset, an inn on Fair Street, and this property on India Street. This India Street property is the most centrally located and is a handsome historic house, fully renovated with all new furnishings and top-notch amenities. All rooms have hair dryers and robes. Guests have access to complimentary jitney service to the Summer House beachfront property in 'Sconset and use of the pool there.

✪ **Union Street Inn.** 7 Union St. (in the center of town), Nantucket, MA 02554. ☎ **800/ 225-5116** or 508/228-9222. Fax 508/325-0848. www.union-street-inn.com. E-mail: unioninn@ nantucket.net. 12 units. A/C TV. Summer $150–$295 double; $325 suite. Rates include full breakfast. AE, MC, V. Closed Jan–Feb.

Sophisticated innkeepers Deborah & Ken Withrow have a terrific location for their historic 1770s property, just steps from Main Street yet in a quiet, residential section. Ken's experience in big hotels shows in the amenities and full concierge service offered here. The Withrows have completely restored the inn, highlighting its period charms and updating all amenities. Many rooms have canopied or four-poster beds; half have working fireplaces. All rooms are decorated with antique furniture and fixtures, and equipped with hair dryers. The comfortable beds are made up with Egyptian cotton linens. Unlike many Nantucket inns that are forbidden by zoning laws to serve a full breakfast, this inn's location allows a superb complete breakfast on the garden patio. If you are hanging around in the afternoon, there are usually home-baked cookies or other goodies to sample as well.

MODERATE

Anchor Inn. 66 Centre St. (P.O. Box 387, in the center of town), Nantucket, MA 02554. ☎ **508/228-0072.** www.anchor-inn.net. E-mail: anchorin@nantucket.net. 11 units. A/C (in season) TV TEL. Summer $165–$195. Rates include continental breakfast. AE, MC, V. Closed Jan–Feb.

Innkeepers Ann and Charles Balas have a historic gem in this sea captain's home located next to the Old North Church. Authentic details can be found throughout the house, in the antique hardware and paneling, wide-board floors, and period furnishings. All rooms are equipped with hair dryers and voice-mail. Guests enjoy continental breakfast with home-baked muffins at individual tables on the enclosed porch.

✪ **Cliff Lodge.** 9 Cliff Rd. (a few blocks from the center of town), Nantucket, MA 02554. ☎ **508/228-9480.** Fax 508/228-6308. www.nantucket.net/lodging/clifflodge. 11 units, 1 apartment. A/C TV TEL. Summer $115 single; $155–$195 double; $375 apartment. Rates include continental breakfast. MC, V. Open year-round. No children under 12.

Debby and John Bennett have freshened up this charming 1771 whaling captain's house with their own countrified style. It's located about a block from the center of town and has sunny, cheerful interiors featuring colorful quilts and splatter-painted floors. Rooms range from a first-floor beauty with king-size bed, paneled walls, and fireplace to the tiny third-floor rooms tucked into the eaves. All are spotlessly clean and blessed with quality beds and linens. The spacious apartment in the rear of the house is a sunny delight. The continental breakfast, serving home-baked breads and muffins on the garden patio, is congenial. Chat with Debby for a wealth of Island info and the latest goings-on, then climb up to the roof walk for a bird's-eye view of the town and harbor.

✪ **Martin House Inn.** 61 Centre St. (between Broad and Chester sts.; a couple blocks from town center), Nantucket, MA 02554. ☎ **508/228-0678.** Fax 508/325-4798. www.nantucket.net/lodging/martinn. E-mail: martinn@nantucket.net. 13 units, 4 with shared bathroom. Summer $75–$85 single; $125–$295 double. Rates include continental breakfast. MC, V. Open year-round.

This is one of the lower-priced B&Bs in town, but also one of the most stylish, with a formal parlor, dining rooms, and a spacious side porch, complete with hammock. Charming innkeeper Debbie Wasil, who also owns the nearby Centerboard (see above), keeps this historic 1803 mariner's home in ship shape. The garret single rooms with a shared bathroom are a bargain. Higher-priced rooms have four-posters and working fireplaces. The extensive continental breakfast, served at the long dining room table, includes Martin's famous granola, as well as home-baked breads, muffins, and fresh fruits.

The Ship's Inn. 13 Fair St., (a few blocks from town center) Nantucket, MA 02554. ☎ **508/228-0040.** Fax 508/228-6524. www.nantucket.net/lodging/shipsinn. E-mail: shipsinn@nantucket.net. 12 units, 2 with shared bathroom. TV TEL. A/C upon request. Summer $100 single with shared bathroom; $210 double. Rates include continental breakfast. AE, DISC, MC, V. Closed early Dec to mid-May.

This pretty, historic inn is on a quiet side street, just slightly removed—3 blocks—from Nantucket's center. Rooms are comfortable, spacious, and charming, and offer a good variety of bedding situations like single rooms and twin beds. All rooms have hair dryers and irons/ironing boards. The restaurant downstairs holds its own (see "Where to Dine," below).

INEXPENSIVE

The Nesbitt Inn. 21 Broad St., P.O. Box 1019, Nantucket, MA 02554. ☎ **508/228-0156** or 508/228-2446. 13 units (all with shared bathroom); 2 apartments. Summer $75 single; $85–$125 double; apartments $1,150 weekly. Rates include continental breakfast. MC, V. Closed mid-Dec to Feb.

This Victorian-style inn in the center of town has been run by the same family for 95 years. It's quite old-fashioned and a bargain for Nantucket. All rooms have sinks and share bathrooms, which are in the hall. There's a friendly, family atmosphere to the inn, and beloved innkeepers Dolly and Nobby Noblit are salt-of-the-earth Nantucketers, who will cheerfully fill you in on Island lore.

Robert B. Johnson HI-AYH Hostel. 31 Western Ave. (on Surfside Beach, about 3 miles S of Nantucket Town), Surfside, MA 02554. ☎ **508/228-0433.** Fax 508/228-5672. E-mail: nantuckethostel@juno.com. 49 beds. $15 for members, $18 for non-members. MC, V. Closed mid-Oct to mid-Apr.

This youth hostel enjoys an almost perfect location. Set right beside Surfside Beach, the former "Star of the Sea" is an authentic 1873 lifesaving station, Nantucket's first. Where seven Surfmen once stood ready to save shipwrecked sailors, 49 backpackers now enjoy gender-segregated bunk rooms; the women's quarters, upstairs, still contains a climb-up lookout post. The usual Hostel lockout (10am to 5pm) and curfew (11pm) rules prevail.

8 Where to Dine

Nantucket is filled with outrageously priced restaurants, in which star chefs create dazzling meals served in high style. Obviously, you don't need this kind of treatment every night, but you'll probably want to try at least one deluxe place here. Many of the best restaurants serve terrific lunches at half the price of their dinner menus. Thankfully, there are also a number of cafes scattered around town that serve reasonably priced lunches and dinners. Nantucket also has two old-fashioned drugstore soda fountains serving breakfast and lunch right next to each other on upper Main Street. If you dine in town, you may enjoy an evening stroll afterwards, since many stores stay open late. The supreme experience, though, may be to cruise on *The Wauwinet Lady,* a motor launch, over to Topper's, the fine restaurant at The Wauwinet. After dinner, you can stroll along the beach, reveling in your extravagance.

VERY EXPENSIVE

Chanticleer Inn. 9 New St., Siasconset. ☎ **508/257-6231** or 508/257-9756. Reservations recommended. Jacket required for men. Main courses $42–$45; fixed-price dinner $70. AE, DC, MC, V. Mid-May to mid-Oct Tues–Sun noon–2:30pm and 6:30–9:30pm. Closed mid-Oct to mid-May. FRENCH.

A contender for the priciest restaurant on the Cape and Islands, this rose-covered cottage-turned-French-auberge has fans who don't begrudge a penny, and who insist they'd have to cross an ocean to savor the likes of the classic cuisine that has been served here since the mid-1970s. Just to highlight a few glamorous options on the fixed-price menu: *gateau de grenouilles aux pommes de terre* (a frogs' legs "cake" in a potato crust); *tournedos de lotte marinée au gingembre, sauce au rhum, croquettes d'ail* (a gingered monkfish scaloppini with a lemon-rum sauce and sweet garlic fritters); and *pain perdu, glace au chocolat blanc, coulis d'abricots secs* (a very classy bread pudding with white-chocolate ice cream and apricot sauce). The restaurant's stellar wine cellar is stocked with 38,000 bottles.

Club Car. 1 Main St. ☎ **508/228-1101.** Reservations recommended. Main courses $32–$38. MC, V. July–Aug daily 11am–3pm and 6–10pm; call for off-season hours. Closed Jan–May. CONTINENTAL.

For decades one of the top restaurants on Nantucket, this posh venue is popular with locals, many of whom particularly enjoy beef-Wellington night on autumn Sundays. Executive chef Michael Shannon is chummy with Julia Child, and the menu has classic French influences. Interesting offerings include a first course of Japanese octopus in the style of Bangkok (with mixed hot peppers, tiparos fish sauce, mint, cilantro, lime, and tomato concassee) and an entree of roast rack of lamb Club Car (with fresh herbs, honey-mustard glaze, and minted Madeira sauce). Some nights, seven-course tasting menus are available for $65 per person. The lounge area is within an antique first-class car from the old Nantucket railroad; you'll want to have a drink while cuddled in the red leather banquettes before or after dinner. Lunch at the Club Car is a great deal for those on a budget; all that atmosphere and hearty food arrive without the soaring prices.

The Pearl. 12 Federal St. ☎ **508/228-9701.** Reservations recommended. Main courses $34–$40. AE, MC, V. Late June–early Sept daily 6:30–9:30pm; call for off-season hours. Closed mid-Oct to Apr. NEW AMERICAN.

It's Miami Beach on Nantucket at the newest and swankiest fine dining establishment on the island. The contemporary look here features bluish lighting and large fish tanks; it's definitely a different look for Nantucket. There are numerous stylish touches: appetizers and desserts served in martini glasses; local seafood prepared in innovative ways; an extensive champagne list. It's all very festive. Skip the *grande deluxe plateau de mer;* it's not a lot of shellfish for a lot of money. But do choose the wild mushroom galette with white truffle cream. As a main course, look no further than the pan-roasted striped bass with citrus tomato infusion and local lobster.

✪ **The Summer House.** 17 Ocean Ave., Siasconset. ☎ **508/257-9976.** Reservations recommended. Main courses $30–$42. AE, MC, V. July–Aug daily 6–10pm; mid-May to June and Sept to mid-Oct Wed–Sun 6–10pm. Closed mid-Oct to Apr. NEW AMERICAN.

The classic Nantucket atmosphere, 'Sconset-style, distinguishes this fine-dining experience from others on the island: wicker and wrought-iron, roses and honeysuckle. A pianist plays nightly—often Gershwin standards. The pounding Atlantic Ocean is just over the bluff. Service is wonderful, and the food is excellent, though expensive. Specialties of the house include fresh, locally caught seafood with Island vegetables delicately prepared and stylishly presented. Tempting appetizers include the grilled portobello mushrooms served with a pungent stilton-basil terrine, and the house-smoked salmon frisée with avocado salsa. The distinctive main courses are roast saddle of lamb with rosemary caponatina Port and feta mashed potatoes; the unusual and tasty lobster cutlets with coconut-jasmine risotto timbale and mint-tomato relish; and the grilled rib eye with wild mushrooms, foie gras, and Cabernet. Desserts are bountiful. Order the blueberry pie if it's in season.

✪ **Topper's at The Wauwinet.** 120 Wauwinet Rd. (off Squam Rd.), Wauwinet. ☎ **508/228-8768.** Reservations required for dinner and the launch ride over. Jacket requested. Main courses $34–$56. AE, DC, MC, V. May–Oct Mon–Sat noon–2pm and 6–9:30pm; Sun 10am–2pm and 6–9:30pm. Closed Nov–Apr. REGIONAL/NEW AMERICAN.

This 1850 restaurant—part of a secluded resort—is a tastefully subdued knockout, with wicker armchairs, splashes of chintz, and a two-tailed mermaid to oversee a chill-chasing fire. Try to sit at one of the cozy banquettes if you can. The menu features the finest regional cuisine: Lobster is a major event (it's often sautéed with champagne beurre blanc), and be on the lookout for unusual delicacies such as arctic char. Those are Gruyère-and-chive biscuits in the breadbasket, and you need to try one. Other recommendable house specialties include the lobster and crab cakes appetizer and the roasted Muscovy duck breast. Desserts are fanciful and fabulous: Consider the toasted brioche with poached pears and caramel sauce. The Wauwinet runs a complimentary launch service from mid-June to mid-September to the restaurant for lunch and dinner; it leaves from Straight Wharf at 11am and 5pm, takes 1 hour, and also makes the return trip.

EXPENSIVE

✪ **American Seasons.** 80 Centre St. (2 blocks from the center of town). ☎ **508/ 228-7111.** Reservations recommended. Main courses $24–$27. AE, MC, V. Apr–Nov daily 6–9pm. Closed Dec–Mar. REGIONAL AMERICAN.

This romantic little restaurant has a great theme: Choose your region (New England, Pacific Coast, Wild West, or Down South) and select creative offerings. You can mix or match your appetizers and entrees. For instance, begin with the Louisiana crawfish risotto with fire-roasted onion and fried parsnips in a sweet corn purée from Down South; then from the Pacific Coast, an aged beef sirloin with caramelized shallot and Yukon potato hash served with an Oregon blue-cheese salad with white-truffle oil and fried onions. Chef/Owner Michael L. Getter is having fun here, and you will, too.

Brant Point Grill. At the White Elephant Hotel (Easton and Willard sts.). ☎ **508/ 325-1320.** Jacket requested for gentlemen. Reservations recommended. Main courses $26–$39. AE, DC, DISC, MC, V. Mid-May to mid-Oct daily noon–2:30pm and 6–10pm. Closed mid-Oct to mid-May. NEW AMERICAN.

Recent renovations to the entire White Elephant complex on the harbor have converted this pretty dining room into a lobster, steak and chops house. If you can't sit on the terrace, try to snag a seat near one of the windows where you can watch the twilight fade over the harbor. The candlelight and white, airy dining room make for a perfectly romantic setting. Dinner at this establishment is an expensive proposition. For instance, the appetizer list includes Kobe Beef Tartare, "the caviar of beef," for $35. Prime New York strip steak is $35 to $39. There are also a range of fish dishes. You may want to consider having lunch here, a perfect idea for a rainy day, when prices are more reasonable.

Company of the Cauldron. 5 India St. (between Federal and Centre sts.) ☎ **508/ 228-4016.** Reservations required. Fixed-price $48–$50. MC, V. Tues–Sun, 2 seatings 7 and 9pm; call for off-season hours. Closed late Oct to mid-May. CONTINENTAL.

With its intimate candlelit dining room where, several nights a week in season, a classical harpist plays, this is one of the island's most romantic restaurants. Chef/owner All Kovalencik offers one intricate and distinct three- to four-course fixed-price meal each night, so would-be patrons must check the menu out front or telephone and then choose which evening's menu is most appealing. Dietary preferences, like vegetarianism, can be accommodated if you call ahead. The menu with classic American and continental influences changes nightly, and portions are generous. Don't miss the softshell crab appetizer when it is offered in season. The main course could be seafood, a special swordfish preparation for instance, or a meat dish, like rack of lamb or beef Wellington.

DeMarco. 9 India St. (between Federal and Centre sts.). ☎ **508/228-1836.** Reservations recommended. Main courses $18–$32. AE, MC, V. Mid-June to Sept daily 6–10pm; call for off-season hours. Closed mid-Oct to mid-May. NORTHERN ITALIAN.

This frame house carved into a cafe/bar and loft is the place to get the best Northern Italian food on the island. A forward-thinking menu and attentive service ensure a superior meal, which might include *antipasto di salmone* (house-smoked salmon rol-lantini, lemon-herb cream cheese, cucumber-and-endive salad with chive vinaigrette) and the delicate *capellini con scampi* (capellini with rock shrimp, tomato, black olives, capers, and hot pepper).

✪ **Òran Mór.** 2 S. Beach St. (in the center of town). ☎ **508/228-8655.** Reservations rec-ommended. Main courses $26–$32. AE, MC, V. July–Aug daily 6–10pm; Sept–June Mon–Sat 6–9pm, Sun noon–8pm. Open year-round. INTERNATIONAL.

Renowned Chef Peter Wallace runs this second-floor waterfront venue, which has quickly become the premier restaurant on the island. The unusual name is Gaelic and means "great song"; it's the name of Wallace's favorite single-malt scotch. Climb up the stairs of this historic building, and prepare yourself for a somewhat extravagant dining experience. The menu changes nightly, and there are always some surprising and unusual choices. Standouts are the appetizer lobster risotto and the entree roast loin of elk with oven-roasted tomato brushetta. There are always local seafood specials. Some say the grilled breast of duck with savory tapioca and local nectar jus is the best duck dish on the island. An excellent sommelier is on hand to assist wine lovers. On Sundays during the off-season, they sometimes serve a scrumptious brunch; call to check.

The Ship's Inn. 13 Fair St. (2 blocks SE of Main St.). ☎ **508/228-0040.** Fax 508/228-6524. Reservations recommended. Main courses $20–$32. AE, DISC, MC, V. July–Aug daily 5:30–9:30pm; call for off-season hours. Closed early Dec to mid-May. CALIFORNIA/FRENCH.

Within the peach walls of this romantic bistro, the chef finesses a flavorful hybrid of French and Californian cuisines. The island's homegrown produce is put to good use in the intensely flavored chilled soup of puréed vegetables. Local fish is a specialty, and recommendable main courses include the braised cod with pea purée, wild mush-rooms, and roasted shallots, and the steamed flounder and spring vegetables with sauce vierge.

Sushi by Yoshi. 2 E. Chestnut St. ☎ **508/228-1801.** Most dishes under $20; sushi $5–$15 per roll, most $6–$9. No credit cards. Apr to mid-Dec daily 11:30am–10pm. Closed mid-Dec to Mar. JAPANESE.

This tiny place is Nantucket's best source for great sushi. The incredibly fresh local fish is artfully presented by Chef Yoshihisa Mabuchi, who also dishes up such healthy, affordable staples as miso or udon (noodle) soup. It's tempting to order a raft of Rhoda rolls (with tuna, avocado, and caviar), especially when a portion of the proceeds goes toward AIDS support, but prices can add up. Be prepared for spotty service during the high season, however. In fact, this is an excellent place for take-out, but you'll want to allow an hour in season.

✪ **21 Federal.** 21 Federal St. (in the center of town). ☎ **508/228-2121.** Reservations rec-ommended. Main courses $24–$34. MC, V. June–Oct daily 6–10pm; call for off-season hours. Closed Jan–Mar. NEW AMERICAN.

Your agreeable host Chick Walsh has created an institution popular with locals, par-ticularly for the happening bar scene. With 4 years of *Wine Spectator* awards to its credit, 21 Federal features about 11 carefully selected wines available by the glass each night. Chef Russell Jaehnig seems to get better and more refined every year. Don't fill up on the cheddar-cheese bread sticks: There's a lot of good food to come. For melt-in-your-mouth pleasure, try the appetizer tuna tartare with wasabi crackers and cilantro aioli. Order a side of mashed potatoes if they don't come with your entree— not that you'll need more food; portions are generous. The fish entrees are most popular here, although you might opt for the fine breast of duck accompanied by

---

Readers Recommend

Something Natural, 50 Cliff Rd. (☎ **508/228-0504**), *is a local institution and a terrific value on pricey Nantucket. We love it so much we go back again and again. Something Natural turns out gigantic sandwiches, with fresh ingredients piled atop fabulous bread. Plan on sharing, so you'll have room for their addictive chocolate-chip cookies. It's a great place to stock up for a day at the beach, or you can eat your lunch right on the grounds, where there are picnic tables.*

And when only a bowl of chowder and a giant lobster will do, head for **The Lobster Trap,** 23 Washington St. (☎ **508/228-4200**), *where the big game is usually on the TV behind the bar. Main courses are $17 to $37. Closed mid-October to mid-May.*

—Lisa Renaud, New York, NY

---

pecan wild rice and shiitake mushrooms. I prefer the pan-crisped salmon with champagne cabbage and beet-butter sauce, which has been a staple on the menu for years. Desserts are tantalizing and sinful.

MODERATE

✪ **Black Eyed Susan's.** 10 India St. (in the center of town). ☎ **508/325-0308.** Reservations accepted for 6pm seating only. Main courses $17–$23. No credit cards. Apr–Oct daily 7am–1pm; Mon–Sat 6–10pm; call for off-season hours. Closed Nov–Mar. ETHNIC ECLECTIC.

This is supremely exciting food in a funky bistro atmosphere. It's small, popular with locals, and packed. Reservations are accepted for the 6pm seating only, and these go fast. Others must line up outside the restaurant (the line starts forming around 5:30pm), and the hostess will assign you a time to dine. If you don't mind sitting at the counter, you'll have a better choice. Inside, it may seem a bit too cozy, but that's all part of the charm. The menu is in constant flux, as chef Jeff Worster's mood and influences change biweekly. I always enjoy the spicy Thai fish cake when that is on the menu and also the tandoori chicken with green mango chutney. There's usually a southwestern touch like the Dos Equis beer-battered catfish quesadilla with mango slaw, hoppin' johns, and jalapeño. You'll mop up the sauce with the delectable organic sourdough bread. There's no liquor license, but you can BYOB. The corking fee is $1 per person.

Cioppino's. 20 Broad St. (between Federal and Centre sts.). ☎ **508/228-4622.** Main courses $19–$32. DC, DISC, MC, V. Mid-June to late Sept daily 5:30–10pm; call for off-season hours. Closed Nov to mid-Apr. NEW AMERICAN.

Sometimes it's the hosts that can make a restaurant stand out. Susie and Tracy Root want to be sure all their guests are enjoying themselves, and they are likely to stop by your table to see how you are doing. Ask Tracy Root for a wine recommendation because that's his specialty. He has more Steele single vineyards on his wine list than anyone in the country. The service is attentive and the food is hearty. On a clear night, you'll want to sit out on the patio and watch the strollers. The menu features simple, hearty dishes. Portions are generous; service is swift and friendly. Favorites on the menu include the Nantucket lobster bisque, scaloppini of pork picatta with lemon and capers, and Italian herb-crusted sea bass with a light citrus sauce. For the finale, try the peach and blueberry cobbler served warm with vanilla-bean ice cream.

Kendrick's. 5 Chestnut St. ☎ **508/228-9156.** Reservations recommended. Main courses $16–$29. AE, DISC, MC, V. June–Sept Mon–Sat 7:30–11:30am, Sun 9am–2pm; daily 6–10pm; call for off-season hours. Closed Jan–late Apr. NEW AMERICAN.

Owner Stephanie Silva has designed her restaurant to be a little less expensive (meaning entrees are under $30) than others; it concentrates on high quality, fresh ingredients, simple preparations, and ample portions. The menu is small but diverse; a mixed vegetarian-carnivore couple will be satisfied here. Every night there is a tofu vegetarian dish, a steak dish, and a few fish specials, in addition to other choices. Dishes tend to have strong international influences: Grilled rare tuna is served with bok choy and udon-noodle cake, and rack of lamb comes with eggplant turbans, feta, and couscous. Set in one of Nantucket's shingled historic inns in the center of town, Kendrick's has three small dining rooms, one lined with banquettes. Intriguing contemporary art, locally produced, is displayed. The bar menu, served till 11pm (with prices under $20), is popular with the late-night crowd.

Le Languedoc Cafe. 24 Broad St. ☎ **508/228-2552.** Reservations not accepted for cafe; reservations recommended for main dining room. Main courses $9–$19. AE, MC, V. June–Sept daily 6–10pm; Tues–Sun noon–2pm; call for off-season hours. Closed Jan–late May. NEW AMERICAN.

There's also an expensive dining room upstairs, but locals prefer the casual bistro atmosphere downstairs and out on the terrace. There's a clubby feel here as diners come and go, greeting each other and enjoying themselves. Soups are superb, as are the Angus-steak burgers. More elaborate dishes include the roasted tenderloin of pork stuffed with figs and pancetta, berlotti bean stew, and the napoleon of grilled tuna, tapenade, and roasted vegetables with pesto sauce.

INEXPENSIVE

Arno's. 41 Main St. ☎ **508/228-7001.** Reservations recommended. Main courses $16–$23. AE, CB, DC, DISC, MC, V. Apr–Dec daily 8am–9pm. Closed Jan–Mar. ECLECTIC.

A storefront facing the passing parade of Main Street, this institution packs surprising style between its bare-brick walls (Molly Dee's mostly monochrome paintings, like vintage photographs, are especially nice). The internationally influenced menu yields tasty, bountiful platters for breakfast, lunch, and dinner. Specialties include grilled sirloin steaks and fresh grilled fish. Generous servings of specialty pasta dishes like shrimp and scallop scampi Florentine are featured nightly.

The Brotherhood of Thieves. 23 Broad St. No phone. Main courses $9–$18. No credit cards. Mid-May to mid-Oct Sun–Thurs 11:30am–midnight, Fri–Sat 11:30am–12:30am; mid-Oct to mid-May Sun–Thurs11:30am–10:30pm, Fri–Sat 11:30am–11:30pm. PUB.

This classic whaling bar housed in the basement of an early–19th-century brick building in the center of town is a Nantucket institution. In July and August, tourists line up for a table in the dark tavern to chow on burgers and hand-cut curly fries. The specialty drink menu here is longer than the food menu and includes such playful concoctions as the "Dirty Girl Scout" and a wide selection of coffee and liquor drinks. In the fall and winter, locals enjoy the decently priced dinner offerings like chicken teriyaki and fried Cajun shrimp while sitting beside the cozy brick hearth.

✪ **Espresso Cafe.** 40 Main St. ☎ **508/228-6930.** Most items under $10. No credit cards. Late May–Oct daily 7:30am–10pm; Nov–late May daily 7:30am–4:30pm. INTERNATIONAL.

This reliable self-service cafe is in the heart of town. Pastries, sandwiches, soups, and international dishes are affordably priced, delicious, and made on-site. The cafe has some of the best coffee in town (the "Nantucket" and "Harvard" blends are perennial favorites). In good weather, enjoy a leisurely snack on the sunny patio out back.

Fog Island Cafe. 7 S. Water St. ☎ **508/228-1818.** Main courses $10–$20. MC, V. July–Aug Mon–Sat 7am–2pm and 5–10pm; Sun 7am–1pm and 5–10pm; call for off-season hours. Open year-round. NEW AMERICAN.

You'll be wowed by the creative breakfasts and lunches at this sassy cafe; they're reasonably priced, with super-fresh ingredients. Homemade soups and salads are healthy and yummy. The dinner menu features fresh seafood, pasta dishes, and a vegetarian alternative among the specialties. This local joint also has their cookbook for sale on-site.

TAKE-OUT & PICNIC FARE

Bartlett's Ocean View Farm. 33 Bartlett Farm Rd. ☎ **508/228-9403.** MC, V. Truck parked on Main St. in season.

You can get fresh-picked produce (in season, the tomatoes are incomparable) right in town from Bartlett's traveling market, or head out to this seventh-generation farm where, in June, you might get to pick your own strawberries. They also sell sandwiches, quiches, pastries, pies, and more.

Claudette's. Post Office Sq. (in the village center), Siasconset. ☎ **508/257-6622.** Closed Nov–May.

Home-baked goodies spruce up the breakfasts and lunches prepared here, which can be enjoyed on the small terrace or carted straight to the beach.

Nantucket Gourmet. 4 India St. ☎ **508/228-4353.** Daily 10am–5pm. Open year-round.

Besides an enticing array of kitchen items, Jonathan and Patty Stone have set up a deli full of scrumptious sandwiches, fixin's, and salads to take out.

Provisions. Harbor Sq., Straight Wharf. ☎ **508/228-3258.** Apr–late Nov daily 8am–6pm. Closed late Nov–Mar.

Before you bike out of town to the beach, stop by this gourmet sandwich shop for picnic staples including salads, soups, and muffins.

SWEETS

✪ **The Juice Bar.** 12 Broad St. ☎ **508/228-5799.** June–Aug daily 7am–11pm; Apr–May and Sept to mid-Dec 11am–9pm. Closed late Dec–Mar.

This humble hole-in-the-wall scoops up some of the best homemade ice cream and frozen yogurt around, complemented by superb homemade hot fudge. Waffle cones are homemade, too. The pastries are also excellent, and, yes, you can also get juice— from refreshing lime rickeys to healthful carrot cocktails.

9 Nantucket After Dark

The Nantucket Arts Alliance (☎ 800/228-8118 or 508/228-8118) operates Box Office Nantucket, offering tickets for all sorts of cultural events around town. They operate out of the Macy Warehouse on Straight Wharf in season, daily from 10am to 4pm.

Nantucket usually has an attractive crowd of barhoppers making the scene around town. The best part is, everything is within walking distance, so you don't have to worry about driving back to your inn. You'll find good singles scenes at **The Boarding House, 21 Federal,** or the **Club Car.** Live music comes in many guises on Nantucket, and there are a number of good itinerant performers who play at different venues. For instance, the talented P. J. Moody sings all your favorite James Taylor, Cat Stevens, and Van Morrison tunes; he can be found at the **Jared Coffin House's Tap Room, The Hearth at the Harbor House,** or **The White Elephant.** Meanwhile, it may be Reggae Night at **The Chicken Box,** when the median age of this rocking venue rises by a decade or two.

THEATER

Actors' Theatre of Nantucket. Methodist Church, 2 Centre St. ☎ **508/228-6325.** Tickets $15. Mid-May to mid-Sept Mon–Sat at 8:30pm; call for off-season hours. Children's production (tickets $10) mid-July to mid-Aug Tues–Sat at 5pm. Closed Nov–Apr.

Nantucket's Music Scene

If body boarding, bike riding, and windsurfing coupled with sun and salt air haven't taken their toll, several nightspots offer live music and dancing, while others cater to those content with toe tapping. The Grey Lady can kick up her heels after dark.

Conveniently located in town, **Rose & Crown,** 23 S. Water St. (☎ **508/ 228-2595;** closed January through March), has live music Thursday to Saturday ($3 to $5 cover) with bands whose repertoires range from reggae to R&B, Motown to rock. The rest of the week is divided among karaoke, DJs spinning dance tunes, and the Full Monty Night, where audience members are coaxed into dancing behind a shadow box. With the ambience of an off-campus beer hall, Rose & Crown attracts a decidedly postgraduate crowd that's anywhere from 25 to 50 in age.

A car or a taxi ride is necessary to visit the two other, large, live-band venues, The Muse and The Chicken Box. **The Muse,** 44 Atlantic Ave., about 1½ miles south of the town center (☎ **508/228-6873**), is where you'll find college-age kids and the island's summer employees wolfing pizza and subs, downing beer and exotic shots, and dancing to local and regional rock bands plus a scattering of name acts (George Clinton, Burning Spear, 10,000 Maniacs, and Maceo Parker are among recent headliners). The cover charge varies from $3 to the steep $50 required to lure George Clinton and his P-Funk All-Stars over from the mainland. Pool tables round out this 20-year-old club, which is open 365 days a year—there's a drastic upward shift in its demographics during the winter.

Pipe-smoking owner "Cap'n Seaweed" will tell you that ✪ **The Chicken Box,** 12 Dave St. (☎ **508/228-9717**), has been jumping since the mid-1970s, and if you want to work up a sweat on the dance floor, the Box is a good bet most any night. Beer, shots, mixed drinks, and pool tables draw a crowd slightly older than Muse's; the cover charge runs from $4 to $15, and ska bands, a staple of what might be called New England Beach Music, are a favorite, along with reggae, funk, and rock. NRBQ and The Dirty Dozen Brass band have both dropped anchor here.

At the end of the day (when else?), it comes down to which of these three clubs has booked the best band on a given night. Check the *Inquirer & Mirror*'s Music Beat column to find out.

There's live jazz Wednesday to Saturday at the **Tap Room,** downstairs at the Jared Coffin House, 29 Broad St. (☎ **508/228-2400**), and you'll find folk, blues, and low-key acoustic performers down the street at **The Brotherhood of Thieves,** 23 Broad St.; no phone; closed February. **The Hearth Pub & Patio** at Harbor House, South Beach Street (☎ **508/228-1500**), features cabaret-style entertainment in a handsome beamed hall. None of the above charges a cover.

Piano bars are numerous, including **The Club Car,** 1 Main St. (☎ **508/ 228-1101**), **The RopeWalk,** 1 Straight Wharf (☎ **508/228-8886**), **The Regatta,** at the White Elephant, Easton and Willart Streets (☎ **508/228-5500;** closed October through April), and **The Summer House,** 17 Ocean Ave., Siasconset (☎ **508/228-9976**). The latter, a fine restaurant on the east end of the island, fills whatever need there is on Nantucket for the Manhattan martini-and-cigar bar experience, complete with fabulous people. The RopeWalk is where the rich and famous yachting crowd meets for drinks, and it's a major social scene in July and August. In addition, it's one of the only outdoor raw bars on the island.

—Mark Scheerer, a Correspondent for CNN's *Showbiz Today.*

Drawing on some considerable local talent of all ages, this shoe-box theater assays thought-provoking plays as readily as summery farces.

MOVIES

Nantucket has two first-run movie theaters: **Dreamland Theatre,** 19 S. Water St. (☎ **508/228-5356**), and **Gaslight Theatre,** 1 N. Union St. (☎ **508/228-4435**). The **Siasconset Casino,** 10 New St., Siasconset (☎ **508/257-6661**), also shows films in season.

NANTUCKET LITERATI

✪ **Nantucket Atheneum.** Lower India St. ☎ **508/228-1110.** Free admission. Call for schedule.

Continuing a 160-year tradition, the Nantucket Atheneum offers readings and lectures for general edification year-round, with such local literati as David Halberstam, Frank Conroy, and Nathaniel Philbrick filling in for the likes of Henry David Thoreau and Herman Melville. The summer events are often followed by a charming garden reception.

Martha's Vineyard

Martha's Vineyard is a picturesque New England island with captain's houses and lighthouses, white picket fences and ice-cream shops, an authentic fishing village and a Native American community, miles of pristine beaches and rolling farmland. Unfortunately, it has been discovered, in a big way. If you can survive the hassles of getting to the island, and the crowds and traffic once you arrive, you may just have the perfect vacation. Better yet, visit the island off-season, in May or October, when the weather is often mild and the crowds have cleared out.

When the former First Family, the Clintons, chose to vacation on the island several years in a row, it only served to increase the worldwide fascination with this popular place. In fact, the island is loaded with celebrities, but you are unlikely to see them, as they prefer private house parties. But don't come to this island for the celebrities; it's considered impolite to gawk, and, like jaded New Yorkers, the locals barely seem to notice the stars in their midst.

Instead, visit the Vineyard to bicycle the shaded paths hugging the coastline. Admire the regal sea captain's houses in Edgartown, and stop by the Edgartown Scrimshaw Gallery for a memento of the sea. Stroll down Circuit Avenue in Oak Bluffs with a Mad Martha's ice-cream cone and then ride the Flying Horses Carousel, said to be the oldest working carousel in the country. Don't miss the cheerful "gingerbread" cottages behind Circuit Avenue, where the echoes of 19th-century revival meetings still ring out from the imposing Tabernacle. Marvel at the red-clay cliffs of Gay Head, now known as Aquinnah, a national historic landmark and home to the Wampanoag Tribe. Travel the country roads of West Tisbury and Chilmark, stopping at Allen Farm for sweaters made from the wool of their flock of over 200 sheep. Buy bread at the Scottish Bakehouse in North Tisbury and a lobster roll in the fishing village of Menemsha. There is no dearth of terrific vacation activities on the island.

Unlike much of New England, Martha's Vineyard has long been a melting pot in which locals, homeowners, and summer people coexist in an almost effortless comfort, united in their disapproval of traffic, their criticism of the Steamship Authority, and their protective attitude toward the island. The roots of Martha's Vineyard's diversity go back more than 100 years. In the late 19th century, Oak Bluffs, with its religious roots, was one of the first spots where African-Americans of means went on vacation. Today this community includes such notable

Going Native on Martha's Vineyard

Down-island: If you must buy a Black Dog T-shirt, wait until you get home to wear it. Don't loiter at the Charlotte Inn. Have cocktails on the porch of the Harborview Hotel. In Oak Bluffs, don't ask when Illumination Night is (it's a secret). Experience Edgartown on a snowy winter weekend or in spring when the lilacs are in bloom. Up-island: When in doubt, don't wear shoes. Sail a boat to a remote beach for a picnic. Don't view the rolling farmlands from a tour bus. By all means, bike. Canoe. Rent a cottage for a week or two. Don't be a day-tripper.

celebrities as film director Spike Lee and Washington power broker Vernon Jordan. In the tiny town of Aquinnah, the Wampanoags are the only Native American tribe in the region to have official status in Washington, D.C. And 12th-generation Vine-yarders farm the land in Chilmark and rub shoulders at Cronig's Market with posh Yankees from Edgartown.

There's always a lot of "hurry up and wait" involved in ferry travel, so allowing yourself just a weekend on the Vineyard may be less than you need. If you're traveling from New York, take an extra day off, allowing a minimum of 3 days for this trip. Four days will feel more comfortable. From Boston, a couple days is fine (the drive from Boston to Woods Hole takes 1½ hours with no traffic), but beware summer weekend bottlenecks (never aim for the last ferry). You really don't need to bring a car to get around this small island, but if you absolutely must be accompanied by four wheels, you'll need a car reservation for the ferry (see "Getting There," below, for details).

Try to savor the 45-minute ferry ride to and from this pastoral place. The Vineyard's pace is decidedly laid-back, and your biggest chore should be to try to blend in with the prevalent ultra-cool attitude. The six towns on Martha's Vineyard have distinct identities, but they can be divided into "down-island," referring to Vineyard Haven (officially called Tisbury), Edgartown, and Oak Bluffs; and "up-island," encompassing the towns of West Tisbury, Chilmark, and Gay Head.

1 Essentials

GETTING THERE

BY FERRY   Most visitors take the ferry service connecting the Vineyard and the mainland. If you're traveling via car or bus, you will most likely be catching the ferry from Woods Hole on Cape Cod; however, boats do run from Falmouth, Hyannis, New Bedford, New London, and Nantucket. On weekends in season, the Steamship Authority ferries make over 30 trips a day to Martha's Vineyard from Woods Hole (two other companies provide an additional 12 passenger ferries a day from Falmouth Harbor). Schedules are available from the **Martha's Vineyard Chamber of Commerce** (☎ 508/693-0085; fax 508/693-7589; www.mvy.com; e-mail: mvcc@vineyard.net) or the Steamship Authority (see below).

The state-run **Steamship Authority** (www.islandferry.com) runs the show in Woods Hole (☎ **508/477-8600** mid-April to mid-September daily 6am to 9pm, or 508/693-9130 daily 8am to 5pm; off-season office hours vary) and operates every day, year-round (weather permitting). It maintains the only ferries to Martha's Vineyard that accommodate cars, in addition to passengers, and they make about 25 crossings a day in season. These large ferries make the 45-minute trip to Vineyard Haven throughout the year; some boats go to Oak Bluffs from late May to late October (call for seasonal schedules). During the summer, you'll need a reservation to bring your car to the island, and you must reserve *months in advance* to secure a spot. If you are planning to bring your car over to the island, I suggest you get to the Woods Hole terminal at least 45 minutes before your scheduled departure.

Many people prefer to leave their cars on the mainland, take the ferry (often with their bikes), and then rent a car, Jeep, or bicycle on the island. You can park your car at the Woods Hole lots (always full in the summer) or at one of the many lots in Falmouth that absorb the overflow of cars during the summer months; parking is $10 per day. Plan to arrive at the parking lots in Falmouth at least 45 minutes before sailing time to allow for parking, taking the free shuttle bus to the ferry terminal, and buying your ferry ticket. Free shuttle buses (some equipped for bikes) run regularly from the outlying lots to the Woods Hole ferry terminal.

The cost of a round-trip passenger ticket on the ferry to Martha's Vineyard is $10 for adults and $5 for children 5 to 12 (kids under 5 ride free). If you're bringing your bike along, it's an extra $6 round-trip, year-round. You do not need a reservation on the ferry if you're traveling without a car, and there are no reservations needed for parking. The cost of a round-trip car passage from mid-May to mid-October is $104; in the off-season it drops to $62. Car rates do not include drivers or passengers; you must buy tickets for each person going to the island.

Once you are aboard the ferry, you have won the right to feel relieved and relaxed. Now your vacation can begin. Ferries are equipped with bathrooms and snack bars. Your fellow passengers will be a gaggle of kids, dogs, and happy-looking travelers.

From Falmouth, you can also board the ***Island Queen*** at Falmouth Harbor (☎ **508/548-4800**) for a 35-minute cruise to Oak Bluffs (passengers only). The boat runs from late May to mid-October; round-trip fare is $10 for adults, $5 for children under 13, and an extra $6 for bikes. There are seven crossings a day in season (eight on Friday and Sunday), and no reservations are needed. Parking will run you $10 or $12 a day.

Reservations-Only Policy for Car Passage to Martha's Vineyard

Vehicle reservations are required to bring your car to Martha's Vineyard on Friday, Saturday, Sunday, and Monday from mid-June to mid-September. During these times, standby is in effect only on Tuesday, Wednesday, and Thursday. Vehicle reservations are also required to bring your car to Martha's Vineyard on Memorial Day weekend. There will be no standby service available during these dates. Although technically, reservations can be made up to 1 hour in advance of ferry departure, ferries in season are almost always full, and you cannot depend on a cancellation during the summer months. Also be aware that your space may be forfeited if you have not checked into the ferry terminal 30 minutes prior to sailing time. Reservations may be changed to another date and time with at least 24 hours' notice; otherwise, you will have to pay for an additional ticket for your vehicle.

If you arrive without a reservation on a day that allows standby, come early and be prepared to wait in the standby line for hours. The Steamship Authority guarantees your passage if you're in line by 2pm on designated standby days only. For up-to-date **Steamship Authority** information, check out their Web site (**www.islandferry.com**).

The **Falmouth-Edgartown Ferry Service,** 278 Scranton Ave. (☎ **508/548-9400**), operates a 1-hour passenger ferry, called the *Pied Piper,* from Falmouth Harbor to Edgartown. The boat runs from late May to mid-October, and reservations are required. In season, there are five crossings a day (six on Friday). Round-trip fares are $22 for adults and $16 for children under 12. Bicycles are $6 round-trip. Parking is $10 per day.

From Hyannis, you can take the **Hy-Line,** Ocean Street Dock (☎ **508/ 778-2600;** www.hy-linecruises.com), to Oak Bluffs, May through October. They run three trips a day, and trip time is about 1 hour and 45 minutes; round-trip costs $26 for adults and $13.50 for children 5 to 12 ($10 extra for bikes). In July and August, it's a good idea to reserve a parking spot in Hyannis; the all-day fee is $10. From June through September, they also operate a 1-day cruise, called **Around the Sound,** with stops on the Vineyard and Nantucket ($37.50 adults; $18.75 children 5 to 12).

From Nantucket, Hy-Line runs three passenger-only ferries to Oak Bluffs on Martha's Vineyard from early June to late September (there is no car-ferry service between the islands). The trip time is 2 hours and 15 minutes. The one-way fare is $12.50 for adults, $6.25 for children 5 to 12, and $5 extra for bikes.

From New Bedford, Massachusetts, the *Schamonchi,* Billy Woods Wharf (☎ **508/997-1688;** www.mvferry.com), takes island-goers to Vineyard Haven from mid-May to mid-October. Trip time is about 1½ hours. A 1-day/round-trip ticket is $17 for adults, $9 for children under 12, and $5 extra for bikes. If you are staying overnight, the fare is $1 more, and parking is $8 per calendar day. No reservations are needed. This is a great way to avoid Cape traffic and to enjoy a scenic ocean cruise.

From New London, Connecticut, the *Tatobam* (☎ **888/SAILFOX;** www.foxnavigation.com) is a high-speed catamaran that makes the trip to Vineyard Haven in just over 2 hours (March to mid-October, but call ahead as schedule is subject to change). The boat is owned by Fox Navigation, a subsidiary of the Mashantucket Pequot Tribal Nation, which runs Foxwoods Casino in Ledyard, Connecticut. It leaves the Admiral Harold E. Shear State Pier in New London on Friday, Saturday, Sunday and Monday at 9am and arrives at West Dock in Vineyard Haven at 11:15am. It departs West Dock in Vineyard Haven at 4pm and arrives in New London at 6:15pm. A round-trip ticket is $89 first class and $59 clipper class. Parking at the state pier is free.

BY AIR   You can fly into **Martha's Vineyard Airport,** also known as Dukes County Airport (☎ **508/693-7022**), in West Tisbury, about 5 miles outside Edgartown.

Airlines serving the Vineyard include **Cape Air/Nantucket Airlines** (☎ **800/ 352-0714** or 508/771-6944), which connects the island year-round with Boston (trip time 33 min.; hourly shuttle service in summer for about $240 round-trip), Hyannis (trip time 20 minutes, cost $80), Nantucket (15 minutes, $76), and New Bedford (20 minutes, $83); **Continental Express/Colgan Air** (☎ **800/525-0280**), which has non-stop flights from Newark (seasonal) for about $240 round-trip (trip time 1 hour 15 minutes); and **US Airways Express** (☎ **800/428-4322**), which flies from Boston for about $100 round-trip and also has seasonal weekend service from La Guardia (trip time 1 hour 20 minutes), which costs approximately $300 round-trip.

The only company offering year-round charter service is **Direct Flight** (☎ **508/ 693-6688**). **Westchester Air** (☎ **800/759-2929**) also runs some charters from White Plains, New York.

BY BUS   **Bonanza Bus Lines** (☎ **800/556-3815**) connects the Woods Hole ferry port with Boston (from the new South Station), New York City, and Providence, Rhode Island. The trip from South Station in Boston takes about 1 hour and 35 minutes and

Martha's Vineyard

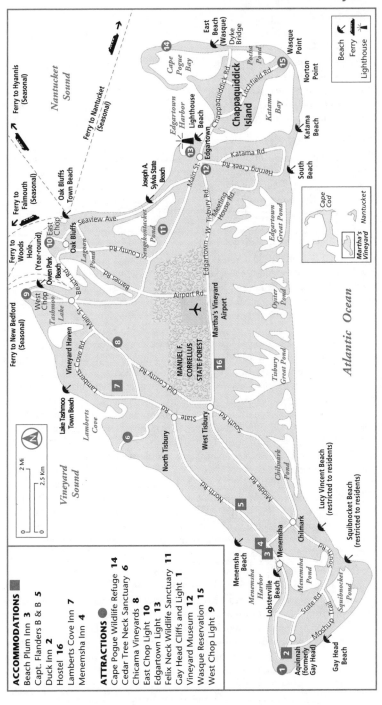

ACCOMMODATIONS ■

Beach Plum Inn **3**
Capt. Flanders B & B **5**
Duck Inn **2**
Hostel **16**
Lamberts Cove Inn **7**
Menemsha Inn **4**

ATTRACTIONS ●

Cape Pogue Wildlife Refuge **14**
Cedar Tree Neck Sanctuary **6**
Chicama Vineyards **8**
East Chop Light **10**
Edgartown Light **13**
Felix Neck Wildlife Sanctuary **11**
Gay Head Cliffs and Light **1**
Vineyard Museum **12**
Wasque Reservation **15**
West Chop Light **9**

Beach
Ferry
Lighthouse

Ferry to Hyannis (Seasonal)

Nantucket Sound

Ferry to Nantucket (Seasonal)

East Beach (Wasque)
Dyke Bridge
Wasque Point

Cape Pogue Bay

Litchfield Rd.
Pocha Pond
Norton Point

Chappaquiddick Rd.
Chappaquiddick Island
Katama Bay
Katama Beach

Edgartown Harbor
Lighthouse
Edgartown Harbor Beach
Katama Rd.
South Beach

Main St.
Edgartown
Herring Creek Rd.

Ferry to Falmouth (Seasonal)

Oak Bluffs Town Beach
Joseph A. Sylvia State Beach

Seaview Ave.

Cape Cod
Nantucket
Martha's Vineyard

Ferry to Woods Hole (Year-round)

East Chop
Oak Bluffs
Lagoon Pond
County Rd.
Barnes Rd.
Sengekontacket Pond
Meeting House Rd.

Edgartown – W. Tisbury Rd.
W. Tisbury Rd.

Edgartown Great Pond

Oyster Pond

Atlantic Ocean

Ferry to New Bedford (Seasonal)

West Chop
Owen Park Beach
Tashmoo Lake
Main St.
Beach Rd.
Vineyard Haven
Lamberts Cove Rd.

Airport Rd.
Martha's Vineyard Airport

MANUEL F. CORRELLUS STATE FOREST

Tisbury Great Pond

Lake Tashmoo Town Beach
Lambers Cove

North Tisbury
West Tisbury
State Rd.
Old County Rd.
South Rd.

Vineyard Sound

0   2 Mi
0   2.5 Km

North Rd.
Middle Rd.
Chilmark Pond

Lucy Vincent Beach (restricted to residents)
Squibnocket Beach (restricted to residents)

Menemsha
Chilmark
Menemsha Beach
Menemsha Harbor
Menemsha Pond
Lobsterville Beach

Aquinnah (formerly Gay Head)
Gay Head Beach
State Rd.
Moshup Trail
South Rd.
Squibnocket Pond

costs about $15 one-way, and from Boston's Logan Airport, it's $20 each way; from New York, it's about a 6-hour bus trip to Hyannis or Woods Hole, costing approximately $47 each way or $84 round-trip.

BY LIMO   Cape Cod Livery (☎ 800/235-5669 or 508/563-5669) will pick you up at Boston's Logan Airport and take you to meet your ferry in Woods Hole (or anywhere else in the Upper Cape area). The trip takes about 1 hour and 45 minutes depending on traffic, and costs about $115 each way for a carload or a vanload of people. You'll need to book the service a couple of days in advance.

GETTING AROUND

The down-island towns of Vineyard Haven, Oak Bluffs, and Edgartown are fairly compact, and if your inn is located in the heart of one of these small towns, you will be within walking distance of shopping, beaches, and attractions in town. Frequent shuttle buses can whisk you to the other down-island towns and beaches in 5 to 15 minutes. To explore the up-island towns, you will need to bike; it's possible to tour the entire island—60 some-odd miles—in 1 day. In season, you can also take the shuttle bus up-island. Otherwise, you will have to take a cab.

BY BICYCLE & MOPED   You shouldn't leave without exploring the Vineyard on two wheels, even if only for a couple of hours. There's a little of everything for cyclists, from paved paths to hilly country roads (see "Beaches & Recreational Pursuits," below, for details on where to ride), and you don't have to be an expert rider to enjoy yourself. Plus, biking is a relatively hassle-free way to get around the island.

Mopeds are also a way to navigate Vineyard roads, but remember that some roads tend to be narrow and rough—the number of accidents involving mopeds seems to rise every year, and many islanders are opposed to these vehicles. The renting of mopeds is banned in Edgartown. You'll need a driver's license to rent a moped.

Bike-, scooter-, and moped-rental shops are clustered throughout all three down-island towns. Bike rentals cost about $15 to $30 a day (the higher prices are for suspension mountain bikes), scooters and mopeds $30 to $80. In Vineyard Haven, try **Strictly Bikes,** Union Street (☎ 508/693-0782); **Martha's Bike Rentals,** Lagoon Pond Road (☎ 508/693-6593); or **Adventure/Thrifty Rentals,** Beach Road (☎ 508/693-1959), which rents mopeds only. In Oak Bluffs, there's **Anderson's,** Circuit Avenue Extension (☎ 508/693-9346), which rents bikes only; **DeBettencourt's Bike Shop,** 31 Circuit Ave. Extension (☎ 508/693-0011); **Ride-On Mopeds,** Circuit Avenue Extension (☎ 508/693-2076); **Sun 'n' Fun,** Lake Avenue (☎ 508/693-5457); and **Vineyard Bike & Moped,** Oak Bluffs Avenue (☎ 508/693-4498). In Edgartown, you'll find **R. W. Cutler Bike,** 1 Main St. (☎ 508/627-4052); **Edgartown Bicycles,** 190 Upper Main St. (☎ 508/627-9008); and **Wheel Happy,** 204 Upper Main St. and 8 S. Water St. (☎ 508/627-5928), which rents only bikes.

BY CAR   If you're coming to the Vineyard for a few days and you're going to stick to the down-island towns, I think it's best to leave your car at home, since traffic and parking on the island can be brutal in summer. Also, it's easy to take the shuttle buses (see below) from town to town, or simply bike your way around. If you're staying for a longer period of time or you want to do some exploring up-island, you should bring your car or rent one on the island—my favorite way to tour the Vineyard is by Jeep. Keep in mind that car-rental rates can soar during peak season, and gas is also much more expensive on the island. Off-road driving on the beaches is a major topic of debate on the Vineyard, and the most popular spots may be closed for nesting piping plovers at the height of the season. If you plan to do some off-road exploration, check with the Chamber of Commerce to see if the trails are open to vehicles before you rent. To drive off-road at Cape Pogue or Cape Wasque on Chappaquiddick, you'll need to purchase a permit from the **Trustees of Reservations** (☎ 508/627-7260); the cost is $70 to $110.

There are representatives of the national car-rental chains at the airport and in Vineyard Haven and Oak Bluffs. Local agencies also operate out of all three port towns, and many of them also rent Jeeps, mopeds, and bikes. The national chains include **Budget** (☎ 800/527-0700 or 508/693-1911), **Hertz** (☎ 800/654-3131), and **Thrifty** (☎ 800/874-4389).

In Vineyard Haven, you'll find **Adventure Rentals,** Beach Road (☎ 508/693-1959), where a Jeep will run you about $130 per day in season; **Atlantic/Consumer Car Rental,** 15 Beach Rd. (☎ 508/693-0480), which rents small cars for about $60 per day; and **Holmes Hole Car Rentals,** Water Street (☎ 508/693-8838), where a four-wheel-drive vehicle rents for about $120 per day in season. In Edgartown, try **AAA Island Rentals,** 141 Main St. (☎ 508/627-6800; also at Five Corners in Vineyard Haven, ☎ 508/696-5300). Another recommendable Island company that operates out of the airport is **All Island Rent-a-Car** (☎ 508/693-6868).

BY SHUTTLE BUS & TROLLEY   In season, shuttle buses certainly run often enough to make them a practical means of getting around. There are two different types of shuttle buses making the rounds, and they provide the cheapest, quickest and easiest way to get around the island during the busy summer season. Connecting Vineyard Haven (across from the ferry terminal), Oak Bluffs (near the Civil War statue in Ocean Park), and Edgartown (Church St., near the Old Whaling Church), the Island Transport yellow school buses cost about $1.50 to $4, depending on distance, and from late June to early September, they run from 6am to midnight every 15 minutes or half hour. Hours are reduced in spring and fall. From late June through August, buses go out to Gay Head (via the airport, West Tisbury, and Chilmark), leaving every couple of hours from down-island towns and looping about every hour through up-island towns. For information and a schedule, call **Island Transport** (☎ 508/693-0058).

The **Martha's Vineyard Transit Authority** (☎ 508/627-7448 or 508/627-9663) also operates several shuttle buses in season (white buses with a purple "come ride with us" logo). The Edgartown Downtown Shuttle and the South Beach buses circle throughout town or out to South Beach every 20 minutes in season. They also stop at the free parking lots just north of the town center—this is a great way to avoid circling the streets in search of a vacant spot on busy weekends. A one-way trip in town is just 50¢; a trip to South Beach (leaving from Edgartown's Church St. Visitor Center) is $1.50.

BY TAXI   Upon arrival, you'll find taxis at all ferry terminals and at the airport, and there are permanent taxi stands in Oak Bluffs (at the Flying Horses Carousel) and Edgartown (next to the Town Wharf). Most taxi outfits operate cars as well as vans for larger groups and travelers with bikes. Cab companies on the island include **Adam Cab** (☎ 800/281-4462 or 508/693-3332), **Accurate Cab** (☎ 888/557-9798 or 508/627-9798; which is the only all-night service), **All Island Taxi** (☎ 800/693-TAXI or 508/693-2929), **Martha's Vineyard Taxi** (☎ 508/693-9611 or 508/693-8660), and **Marlene's Taxi** (☎ 508/693-0037). Rates from town to town in summer are generally flat fees based on where you're headed and the number of passengers on board. A trip from Vineyard Haven to Edgartown would probably cost around $15 for two people. Late-night revelers should keep in mind that rates double after midnight until 7am.

THE CHAPPAQUIDDICK FERRY The **On-Time ferry** (☎ **508/627-9427**) runs the 5-minute trip from Memorial Wharf on Dock Street in Edgartown to Chappaquiddick Island from June to mid-October, every 5 minutes from 7am to midnight. Passengers, bikes, mopeds, dogs, and cars (three at a time) are all welcome. The one-way cost is $1 per person, $4 for one car/one driver, $2.50 for one bike/one person, and $3.50 for one moped or motorcycle/one person.

VISITOR INFORMATION

Contact the **Martha's Vineyard Chamber of Commerce** at Beach Road, Vineyard Haven, MA 02568 (☎ **508/693-0085;** fax 508/693-7589; e-mail: mvcc@vineyard. net) or visit their Web site at **www.mvy.com**. Their office is just 2 blocks up from the ferry terminal in Vineyard Haven and is open Monday to Friday 9am to 5pm year-round plus weekends in season. There are also information booths at the ferry terminal in Vineyard Haven, across from the Flying Horses Carousel in Oak Bluffs, and on Church Street in Edgartown. You'll want to poke your head into these offices to pick up free maps, tourist handbooks, and flyers on tours and events or to get answers to any questions you might have. Most inns also have tourist handbooks and maps available for guests.

Always check the two local newspapers, the *Vineyard Gazette* and the *Martha's Vineyard Times,* for information on current events.

In case of an **emergency,** call ☎ 911 and/or head for the **Martha's Vineyard Hospital,** Linton Lane, Oak Bluffs (☎ **508/693-0410**), which has a 24-hour emergency room.

2 A Stroll Around Edgartown

A good way to acclimate yourself to the pace and flavor of the Vineyard is to walk the streets of Edgartown. This walk starts at the Dr. Daniel Fisher House and meanders along for about a mile; depending on how long you linger at each stop, it should take about 2 to 3 hours.

If you're driving, park at the free lots at the edge of town (you'll see signs on the roads from Vineyard Haven and West Tisbury) and bike or take the shuttle bus (it only costs 50¢) to the Edgartown Visitor Center on Church Street. Around the corner are three local landmarks: the Dr. Daniel Fisher House, Vincent House Museum, and Old Whaling Church.

The **Dr. Daniel Fisher House,** 99 Main St. (☎ **508/627-8017**), is a prime example of Edgartown's trademark Greek Revival opulence. A key player in the 19th-century whaling trade, Dr. Fisher amassed a fortune sufficient to found the **Martha's Vineyard National Bank.** Built in 1840, his prosperous and proud mansion boasts such classical elements as colonnaded porticos, as well as a delicate roof walk. The only way to view the interior (now headquarters for the Martha's Vineyard Preservation Trust) is with a guided **Vineyard Historic Walking Tour** (☎ **508/627-8619;** see "Organized Tours," below). This tour originates next door at the **Vincent House Museum,** off Main Street between Planting Field Way and Church Street a transplanted 1672 full Cape considered to be the oldest surviving dwelling on the island. Plexiglas-covered cutaways permit a view of traditional building techniques, and three rooms have been refurbished to encapsulate the decorative styles of 3 centuries, from bare-bones colonial to elegant Federal. The tour also takes in the neighboring **Old Whaling Church,** 89 Main St., a magnificent 1843 Greek Revival edifice designed by local architect Frederick Baylies, Jr., and built as a whaleboat would have been, out of massive pine beams. With its 27-foot windows and 92-foot tower (a landmark easily

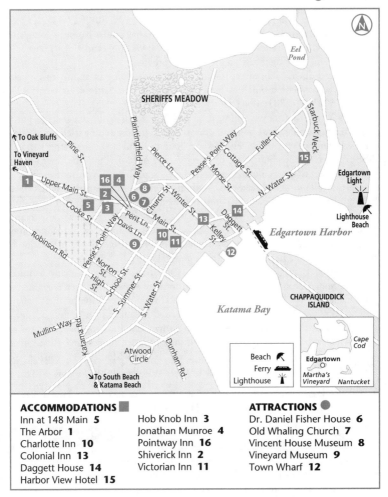

Eel Pond

SHERIFFS MEADOW

↑ To Oak Bluffs

To Vineyard Haven

Starbuck Neck

Edgartown Light

Lighthouse Beach

Edgartown Harbor

Pine St.

Plaintingfield Way

Pierce Ln.

Pease's Point Way

Fuller St.

Morse St.

Pease's Point Cottage St.

N. Water St.

1 Upper Main St.

16 **4**

2

5

3

Cooke St.

Church St.

Winter St.

8

6 **7**

Main St.

Pent Ln.

Davis Ln.

13

Daggett St.

Kelley St.

14

10 **11**

9

12

Robinson Rd.

Pease's Point Way

Norton St.

School St.

High St.

S. Summer St.

S. Water St.

Katama Rd.

Mullins Way

Atwood Circle

Dunham Rd.

Katama Bay

CHAPPAQUIDDICK ISLAND

↘ To South Beach & Katama Beach

Beach 🏖

Ferry ⛴

Lighthouse ⚓

Cape Cod

Edgartown

Martha's Vineyard

Nantucket

ACCOMMODATIONS ■
Inn at 148 Main **5**
The Arbor **1**
Charlotte Inn **10**
Colonial Inn **13**
Daggett House **14**
Harbor View Hotel **15**

Hob Knob Inn **3**
Jonathan Munroe **4**
Pointway Inn **16**
Shiverick Inn **2**
Victorian Inn **11**

ATTRACTIONS ●
Dr. Daniel Fisher House **6**
Old Whaling Church **7**
Vincent House Museum **8**
Vineyard Museum **9**
Town Wharf **12**

spotted from the sea), this is a building that knows its place in the community (central). Maintained by the Preservation Trust and still supporting a Methodist parish, the building is now primarily used as a performance site.

Continuing down Main Street and turning right onto School Street, you'll pass another Baylies monument, the 1839 **Baptist Church,** which, having lost its spire, was converted into a private home with a rather grand, column-fronted facade. Two blocks farther, on your left, is the **Vineyard Museum,** 59 School St. (☎ **508/627-4441**), a fascinating complex assembled by the Dukes County Historical Society. An absorbing display of island history, this cluster of buildings contains exhibits of early Native American crafts; an entire 1765 house; an extraordinary array of maritime art, from whalers' logs to WPA-era studies by Thomas Hart Benton; a carriage house to catch odds and ends; and the Gay Head Light Tower's decommissioned Fresnel lens.

Give yourself enough time to explore the museum's curiosities before heading south 1 block on Cooke Street. Catty-corner across South Summer Street, you'll spot the first of Baylies's impressive endeavors, the 1828 **Federated Church.** One block left are the offices of the *Vineyard Gazette,* 34 S. Summer St. (☎ **508/627-4311**). Operating out of a 1760 house, this exemplary small-town newspaper has been going strong since 1846; its 14,000 subscribers span the globe. If you are wandering by on a Thursday afternoon, you might catch a press run in progress.

Now head down Main Street toward the water, stopping in at any inviting shops along the way. Veer left on Dock Street to reach the **Old Sculpin Gallery,** 58 Dock St. (☎ **508/627-4881;** open late June to early September). The output of the Martha's Vineyard Art Association displayed here tends to be amateurish, but you might happen upon a find. The real draw is the stark old building itself, which started out as a granary (part of Dr. Fisher's vast holdings) and spent the better part of the 20th century as a boatbuilding shop. Keep an eye out for vintage beauties when you cross the street to survey the harbor from the deck at Town Wharf. It's from here that the tiny On-Time ferry makes its 5-minute crossing to **Chappaquiddick Island,** hauling three cars at a time and a great many more sightseers—not that there's much to see on the other side. Just so you don't waste time tracking it down, the infamous **Dyke Bridge,** scene of the Kennedy/Kopechne debacle, has been dismantled and, at long last, replaced. However, the island does offer great stretches of conservation land that will reward the hearty hiker or mountain biker.

Mere strollers might want to remain in town to admire the many formidable captain's homes lining **North Water Street,** some of which have been converted into inns. Each has a tale to tell. The 1750 **Daggett House** (no. 59), for instance, expanded upon a 1660 tavern, and the original beehive oven is flanked by a "secret" passageway. Nathaniel Hawthorne holed up at the **Edgartown Inn** (no. 56) for nearly a year in 1789 while writing *Twice Told Tales*—and, it is rumored, romancing a local maiden who inspired *The Scarlet Letter.* On your way back to Main Street, you'll pass the **Gardner-Colby Gallery** (no. 27), filled with beautiful island-inspired paintings.

🍵 **Winding Down**   After all that walking, you may need a refreshment. **Espresso Love,** at 2 S. Water St. (☎ **508/627-9211**), has legendary muffins and pastries.

3 Beaches & Recreational Pursuits

BEACHES   Most down-island beaches in Vineyard Haven, Oak Bluffs, and Edgartown are open to the public and just a walk or a short bike ride from town. In season, shuttle buses make stops at **State Beach** between Oak Buffs and Edgartown. Most of the Vineyard's magnificent up-island shoreline, alas, is privately owned or restricted to residents, and thus off-limits to transient visitors. Renters in up-island communities, however, can obtain a beach sticker (around $35 to $50 for a season sticker) for those private beaches by applying with a lease at the relevant **town hall:** West Tisbury, ☎ **508/696-0147;** Chilmark, ☎ **508/645-2113** or 508/645-2100; or Aquinnah, ☎ **508/645-2300.** Also, many up-island inns offer the perk of temporary passes to a hot spot such as Lucy Vincent Beach (see below). In addition to the public beaches listed below, you might also track down a few hidden coves by requesting a map of conservation properties from the **Martha's Vineyard Land Bank** (☎ **508/627-7141**). Below is a list of visitor-friendly beaches:

- **East Beach,** Wasque (pronounced *Way*-squee) Reservation, Chappaquiddick: Relatively few people go to the bother of biking or hiking (or four-wheel driving) this far, so this beach remains one of the Vineyard's best-kept secrets (and an ideal spot for bird watching). You should be able to find all the privacy you crave. If you're staying in Edgartown, the Chappy ferry is probably minutes by bike from your inn. Biking on Chappaquiddick is one of the great Vineyard experiences, but the roads can be quite sandy, and you may have to dismount during the 5-mile ride to Wasque. Because of its exposure on the east shore of the island, the surf here is rough. Pack a picnic, and make this an afternoon adventure. Sorry, no facilities.

- **South Beach** (Katama Beach), about 4 miles south of Edgartown on Katama Road: If you have time for only one trip to the beach and you can't get up-island, I'd go with this popular, 3-mile barrier strand that boasts heavy wave action (check with lifeguards for swimming conditions), sweeping dunes, and, most important, relatively ample parking space. It's also accessible by bike path or shuttle. Lifeguards patrol some sections of the beach, and there are sparsely scattered toilet facilities. The rough surf here is popular with surfers. *Tip:* Families tend to head to the left, college kids to the right.

- **Lucy Vincent Beach** (restricted to residents), off South Road, Chilmark: It's a shame that the island's most secluded and breathtaking beach is restricted to Chilmark town residents and guests only (don't forget that many up-island inns offer guest passes). Lined with red and brown clay cliffs, this wide stretch of sand and pounding surf is a virtual oasis. If you want to let it all hang out, head left down the beach.

- ✪ **Aquinnah Beach** (Moshup Beach), off Moshup Trail: Parking costs $15 a day (in season) at this peaceful ½-mile beach just east (Atlantic side) of the colorful cliffs. Go early, since the lot is small and a bit of a hike from the beach. I suggest that all but one person get off at the wooden boardwalk along the road with towels, toys, lunches, and so on, while the remaining one heads back up to park. In season, you can also take the shuttle buses from down-island to the parking lot at the Gay Head cliffs and walk to the beach. Although it is against the law, nudists tend to gravitate toward this beach. Remember that climbing the cliffs or stealing clay for a souvenir here is against the law for environmental reasons: The cliffs are suffering from rapid erosion. Rest rooms are near the parking lot.

- **Lobsterville Beach,** at the end of Lobsterville Road in Gay Head (restricted): This 2-mile beauty on Menemsha Pond boasts calm, shallow waters, which are ideal for children. It's also a prime spot for birding—just past the dunes are nesting areas for terns and gulls. Surf casters tend to gravitate here, too. The only drawback is that parking is for residents only. This is a great beach for bikers to hit on their way back from Gay Head and before taking the bike ferry over to Menemsha.

- **Menemsha Beach,** next to Dutchers Dock in Menemsha Harbor: Despite its rough surface, this small but well-trafficked strand, with lifeguards and rest rooms, is quite popular with families. In season, it's virtually wall-to-wall colorful umbrellas and beach toys. Nearby food vendors in Menemsha—selling everything from ice cream and hot dogs to steamers and shrimp cocktail—are also a plus here. *Tip:* This beach is the ideal place for a sunset. I suggest you get a lobster dinner to go at the famous **Home Port restaurant** right next to the beach in Menemsha (see "The Quintessential Lobster Dinner," below), grab a blanket and a bottle of wine, and picnic here for a spectacular evening. If you are staying at an up-island inn, Menemsha is a fun bike ride downhill. Energetic bikers can make it from down-island towns; plan to make it part of an entire day of scenic biking. Otherwise, you'll need a car to get here.

- **Lake Tashmoo Town Beach,** off Herring Creek Road, Vineyard Haven: The only spot on the island where lake meets the ocean, this tiny strip of sand is good for swimming and surf casting but is somewhat marred by limited parking and often brackish waters. Nonetheless, this is a popular spot, as beachgoers enjoy a choice between the Vineyard Sound beach with mild surf or the placid lake beach. Bikers will have no problem reaching this beach from Vineyard Haven; otherwise, you have to have access to a car to get to this beach.

- **Owen Park Beach,** off Main Street in Vineyard Haven: A tiny strip of harborside beach adjoining a town green with swings and a bandstand will suffice for young children, who, by the way, get lifeguard supervision. There are no rest rooms, but this is an in-town beach, which is probably a quick walk from your Vineyard Haven inn.
- **Oak Bluffs Town Beach,** Seaview Avenue: This sandy strip extends from both sides of the ferry wharf, which makes it a convenient place to linger while waiting for the next boat. This is an in-town beach, within walking distance for visitors staying in Oak Bluffs. The surf is consistently calm and the sand smooth, so it's also ideal for families with small children. Public rest rooms are available at the ferry dock, but there are no lifeguards.
- **Joseph A. Sylvia State Beach,** midway between Oak Bluffs and Edgartown: Stretching a mile and flanked by a paved bike path, this placid beach has views of Cape Cod and Nantucket Sound and is prized for its gentle and (relatively) warm waves, which make it perfect for swimming. The wooden drawbridge is a local landmark, and visitors and islanders alike have been jumping off it for years. Be aware that State Beach is one of the Vineyard's most popular; come midsummer, it's packed. The shuttle bus stops here, and roadside parking is also available—but it fills up fast, so stake your claim early. Located on the eastern shore of the island, this is a Nantucket Sound beach, so waters are shallow and rarely rough. There are no rest rooms, and only the Edgartown end of the beach, known as Bend-in-the-Road Beach, has lifeguards.
- **Lighthouse Beach,** off North Water Street, Edgartown: Even though tiny, unattended, lacking parking, and often seaweed-strewn, it's terribly scenic and a perfect place to watch the boats drifting in and out of the harbor. Fuller Beach nearby is popular with a college crowd. No lifeguards or rest rooms. Both these beaches are within walking distance of the center of Edgartown.
- **Wasque Beach,** Wasque Reservation, Chappaquiddick: Surprisingly easy to get to (via the On-Time ferry and a bike or car), this ½-mile-long beach has all the amenities—lifeguards, parking, rest rooms—without the crowds. Wasque Beach is a Trustees of Reservations property, and if you are not a member of this land-preservation organization, you must pay at the gatehouse (☎ **508/627-7260;** $3 per car and $3 per person) for access in season.

BICYCLING   What's unique about biking on Martha's Vineyard is that you'll find not only the smooth, well-maintained paths indigenous to the Cape, but also long stretches of virtually untrafficked roads that, while rough in spots, traverse breathtaking country landscapes with sweeping ocean views. Serious cyclists will want to do a 1-day ✪ **circle-the-island tour** through the up-island towns and out to Aquinnah, stopping in Menemsha before heading back down-island. You'll pass through all six Vineyard towns and some of unique off-the-beaten-track businesses.

For much of the trek, you'll be traveling country roads, so beware of sandy shoulders and blind curves. You'll avoid tour buses by taking routes outlined below, such as the Moshup Trail to Aquinnah or the triangle of paved bike paths between the down-island towns. These bike paths, roughly 8 miles to a side, link the down-island towns of Oak Bluffs, Edgartown, and Vineyard Haven (the sound portion along Beach

En-Route Shopping

When biking on the Edgartown–West Tisbury Road out to Gay Head, I always stop at **Campbell and Douglas Harness and Feed** at Rainbow Farm, South Road, Chilmark (☎ **508/645-7800**) (for the horsy at heart) and **Allen Farm Sheep and Wool Company,** South Road, Chilmark (☎ **508/645-9064**) (for the best hand-made wool sweaters). When biking back toward Vineyard Haven on State Road, I love to watch the glassblowing at **Martha's Vineyard Glass Works,** State Road, West Tisbury (☎ **508/693-6026**); and I can't live without the scones from **The Scottish Bake House,** State Road, Vineyard Haven (☎ **508/693-1873**). There are also a number of terrific galleries along the way, including **Granary Gallery at the Red Barn** (☎ **508/693-0455**) on Old County Road off Edgartown-West Tisbury Road in West Tisbury, **The Field Gallery** (☎ **508/693-5595**) on State Road across from Alley's General Store in West Tisbury, and **Etherington Fine Art** (☎ **508/ 693-9696**) on State Road in North Tisbury.

Road, flanked by water on both sides, is especially scenic). From Edgartown, you can also follow the bike path to South Beach (also known as Katama Beach). The bike paths are accessible off Edgartown–West Tisbury Road in Oak Bluffs, West Tisbury, and Edgartown.

The up-island roads leading to West Tisbury, Chilmark, Menemsha, and Aquinnah are a cyclist's paradise, with sprawling, unspoiled pastureland, old farmhouses, and brilliant sea views reminiscent of Ireland's countryside. But keep in mind that the terrain is often hilly, and the roads are narrow and a little rough around the edges. Try **South Road** from the town of West Tisbury to Chilmark Center (about 5 miles). En route, you'll pass stone walls rolling over moors, clumps of pine and wildflowers, verdant marshes and tidal pools, and, every once in awhile, an Old Vineyard farmhouse. About halfway, you'll notice the road becoming hillier as you approach a summit, **Abel's Hill,** home to the **Chilmark Cemetery,** where comedian John Belushi is buried. A mile farther, don't miss the view of **Allen Farm,** an operating sheep farm amongst picturesque pastureland. **Middle Road** is another lovely ride with a country feel and will also get you from West Tisbury to Chilmark (it's usually less trafficked, too).

My favorite up-island route is the 6-mile stretch from Chilmark Center out to Aquinnah via **State Road** and ✪ **Moshup Trail.** The ocean views along this route are spectacular. Don't miss the **Quitsa Pond Lookout,** about 2 miles down **State Road,** which provides a panoramic vista of Nashaquitsa and Menemsha ponds, beyond which you can see Menemsha, the Vineyard Sound, and the Elizabeth Islands—it's an amazing place to watch the sunset on a clear evening. A bit farther, just over the Aquinnah town line, is the Aquinnah spring, a roadside iron pipe where you can refill your water bottle with the freshest and coldest water on the island. At the fork after the spring, turn left on Moshup Trail—in fact, a regular road—and follow the coast, which offers gorgeous views of the water and the sweeping sand dunes. You'll soon wind up in Aquinnah, where you can explore the red-clay cliffs and pristine beaches. On the return trip, you can take the handy bike ferry ($7 round-trip) from Aquinnah to Menemsha. It runs daily in summer and weekends in May.

A word about Aquinnah: Almost every visitor to the Vineyard finds his or her way to the cliffs, and with all the tour buses lined up in the huge parking lot and the rows of tacky concession stands and gift shops, this can seem like a rather outrageous tourist trap. You're right; it's not the Grand Canyon. But the observation deck, with its view

En-Route Snacking

When tackling the Vineyard by bike, you'll have no trouble finding sustenance in the down-island towns. Up-island pit stops, however, are a bit scattered. The ones I prefer include **Alley's General Store** in the center of West Tisbury (☎ 508/693-0088), and right behind it, **Back Alley's** (☎ 508/693-7366), which has sandwiches and specializes in homemade muffins, cookies, and pies. Continuing up-island, you'll find the **Chilmark Store** (☎ 508/645-3739), which has great deli sandwiches and pizzas, and ✪ **The Bite,** on Basin Road in Menemsha (☎ 508/645-9239), a typical New England seafood shack.

---

of the colorful cliffs, the adorable brick lighthouse, and the Elizabeth Islands beyond, will make you glad you bothered. Instead of rushing away, stop for a cool drink and a clam roll at the snack bar with the deck overlooking the ocean.

The adventurous **mountain biker** will want to head to the trails in the **Manuel F. Correllus State Forest** (☎ 508/693-2540), a vast spread of scrub oak and pine smack-dab in the middle of the island that also boasts paved paths and hiking and horseback-riding trails. For those seeking an escape from the multitudes, the trails are so extensive that even during peak summer season it is possible to not see another soul for hours. On most of the conservation land on the Vineyard, however, mountain biking is prohibited for environmental reasons.

Bike-rental operations are ubiquitous near the ferry landings in Vineyard Haven and Oak Bluffs, and there are also a few outfits in Edgartown. For information on bike-rental shops, see "Getting Around," above.

A very good outfit out of Boston called **Bike Riders** (☎ 800/473-7040; www.bikeriderstours.com; e-mail: info@bikeriderstours.com) runs 6-day island-hopping tours of Martha's Vineyard and Nantucket. The cost is $1,395 per person plus $60 if you need to borrow one of their bikes. It's a perfect way to experience both islands.

The Chamber of Commerce has a great bike map available at its office on Beach Road in Vineyard Haven (see "Visitor Information," above).

BIRD WATCHING   **Felix Neck Wildlife Sanctuary,** Edgartown–Vineyard Haven Road, Edgartown (☎ 508/627-4850), is an easy 2-mile bike ride from Edgartown. A Massachusetts Audubon Property, it has a complete visitor center staffed by naturalists who lead bird-watching walks, among other activities. You'll see osprey nests on your right on the way to the center. Pick up a trail map at the center before heading out. Several of the trails pass Sengekontacket Pond, and the orange trail leads to Waterfowl Pond, which has an observation blind with bird-sighting information. While managed by the conservation group Sheriff's Meadow Foundation, the 300-acre **Cedar Tree Neck Sanctuary** (State Rd., follow to Indian Hill Rd. to Obed Daggett Rd. and follow signs), Tisbury (see "Nature Trails," below), was acquired with the assistance of Massachusetts Audubon. There are several trails, but you'll eventually arrive out on a picturesque bluff overlooking Vineyard Sound and the Elizabeth Islands. Check out the map posted at the parking lot for an overview of the property. The range of terrain here—ponds, fields, woods, and bog—provides diverse opportunities for sightings. ✪ **Wasque Reservation on Chappaquiddick,** Martha's Vineyard (see "Nature Trails," below), a sanctuary owned by the Trustees of Reservations and located on the easternmost reaches of the island, can be accessed by bike or four-wheel-drive vehicle (see "Getting Around," above). The hundreds of untouched acres here draw flocks of nesting shorebirds, including egrets, herons, terns, and plovers.

FISHING   For shellfishing, you'll need to get information and a permit from the appropriate town hall (for the telephone numbers, see "Beaches," above). Popular spots for surf casting include **Wasque Point** on Chappaquiddick (see "Nature Trails," below). The party boat Skipper (☎ **508/693-1238**) offers half-day trips out of Oak Bluffs harbor in season. The cost is $25 for adults and $15 for children 12 and under. Bring your own poles and bait. Deep-sea excursions can be arranged aboard **Big Eye Charters** (☎ **508/627-3649**) out of Edgartown, and **Summer's Lease** (☎ **508/693-2880**) out of Oak Bluffs. Up-island, there is **North Shore Charters** (☎ **508/645-2993**) and **Flashy Lady Charters** (☎ **508/645-2462**) out of Menemsha, locus of the island's commercial fishing fleet (you may recognize this weathered port from *Jaws*). Charter costs are about $400 for a half-day for five people and $750 for a full day.

IGFA world-record holder Capt. Leslie S. Smith operates **Backlash Charters** (☎ **508/627-5894**; e-mail: backlash@tiac.net), specializing in light tackle and fly-fishing, out of Edgartown. Cooper Gilkes III, proprietor of **Coop's Bait & Tackle** at 147 W. Tisbury Rd. in Edgartown (☎ **508/627-3909**), which offers rentals as well as supplies, is another acknowledged authority. He's available as an instructor or charter guide, and even amenable to sharing hard-won pointers on local hot spots.

FITNESS   Gym addicts can get their workout fix at the **Health Club at the Tisbury Inn** on Main Street in Vineyard Haven (☎ **508/693-7400**), which accepts visitors for a $10 fee.

GOLF   The 9-hole **Mink Meadows Golf Course** off Franklin Street in Vineyard Haven (☎ **508/693-0600**), which, despite occupying a top-dollar chunk of real estate, is open to the general public. There is also the semiprivate, championship-level 18-hole **Farm Neck Golf Club** off Farm Neck Road in Oak Bluffs (☎ **508/ 693-3057**). The Cafe at Farm Neck serves a wonderful lunch overlooking their manicured greens. In season, greens fees at Mink Meadows are $40 for 9 holes and $60 for 18 holes. In season greens fees at Farm Neck are $50 for 9 holes and $90 for 18 holes.

ICE-SKATING   The **Martha's Vineyard Ice Arena** on Edgartown–Vineyard Haven Road, Oak Bluffs (☎ **508/693-4438**), offers public skating from mid-July to mid-April; call for details.

INLINE SKATING   In-line skaters are everywhere on the island's paved paths. You'll find rentals at **Jamaikan Jam,** Post Office Square off Circuit Avenue (☎ **508/ 693-5003**), in Oak Bluffs. Another source is **Sports Haven,** 5 Beach St., Vineyard Haven (☎ **508/696-0456**). Rates are about $20 to $25 per day, including pads.

NATURE TRAILS   About a fifth of the Vineyard's land mass has been set aside for conservation, and it's all accessible to energetic bikers and hikers. The **West Chop Woods,** off Franklin Street in Vineyard Haven, comprise 85 acres with marked walking trails. Midway between Vineyard Haven and Edgartown, the **Felix Neck Wildlife Sanctuary** (see "Bird Watching," above) includes a 6-mile network of trails over varying terrain, from woodland to beach. Accessible by ferry from Edgartown, quiet Chappaquiddick is home to two sizable preserves: The **Cape Pogue Wildlife Refuge** and **Wasque Reservation** (gatehouse ☎ **508/627-7260**), covering much of the island's eastern barrier beach, have 709 acres that draw flocks of nesting or resting shorebirds. Also on the island, 3 miles east on Dyke Road, is another Trustees of Reservations property, the distinctly poetic and alluring ✪ **Mytoi,** a 14-acre Japanese garden that is an oasis of textures and flora and fauna.

The 633-acre **Long Point Wildlife Refuge** off Waldron's Bottom Road in West Tisbury (gatehouse ☎ **508/693-7392**) offers heath and dunes, freshwater ponds, a popular family-oriented beach, and interpretive nature walks for children. In season, the Trustees of Reservations charge a $7 parking fee, plus $3 per adult over age 16. The 4,000-acre **Manuel F. Correllus Vineyard State Forest** occupies a sizable, if not especially scenic, chunk mid-island; it's riddled with mountain-bike paths and riding trails. This sanctuary was created in 1908 to try to save the endangered heath hen, a species now extinct. In season, there are free interpretive and birding walks.

Up-island, along the sound, the **Menemsha Hills Reservation** off North Road in Chilmark (☎ 508/693-7662) encompasses 210 acres of rocks and bluffs, with steep paths, lovely views, and even a public beach. **The Cedar Tree Neck Sanctuary,** off Indian Hill Road southwest of Vineyard Haven (☎ 508/693-5207), offers some 300 forested acres that end in a stony beach (alas, swimming and sunbathing are prohibited). It's still a refreshing retreat.

Some remarkable botanical surprises can be found at the 20-acre **Polly Hill Arboretum,** 809 State Rd., West Tisbury (☎ 508/693-9426). Legendary horticulturist Polly Hill has developed this property over the past 40 years and allows the public to wander the grounds on Thursday to Tuesday from 7am until 7pm. This is a magical place, particularly mid-June to July when the Dogwood Allee is in bloom. Wanderers will pass old stone walls on the way to The Tunnel of Love, an arbor of pleached hornbeam. There are also witch hazels, camellias, magnolias, and rhododendrons. To get there from Vineyard Haven, go south on State Road, bearing left at the junction of North Road. The Arboretum entrance is .4 miles on the right. There is a requested donation of $5 for adults and $3 for children under 12.

TENNIS Public courts typically charge a small fee and can be reserved in person a day in advance. You'll find clay courts on **Church Street** in Vineyard Haven; non-clay in Oak Bluffs's **Niantic Park,** West Tisbury's **grammar school** on Old County Road; and the **Chilmark Community Center** on South Road. Three public courts—plus a basketball court, roller-hockey rink, softball field, and children's playground—are located at the **Edgartown Recreation Area** on Robinson Road. You can also book a court (1 day in advance only) at two semiprivate clubs in Oak Bluffs: the **Farm Neck Tennis Club** (☎ 508/693-9728) and **the Island Country Club** on Beach Road (☎ 508/693-6574). In season, expect to pay around $18 to $24 per hour for court time at these clubs.

WATER SPORTS **Wind's Up,** 199 Beach Rd., Vineyard Haven (☎ 508/693-4252), rents out canoes, kayaks, and various sailing craft, including windsurfers, and offers instruction on-site, on a placid pond; it also rents surfboards and boogie boards. Canoes and kayaks rent for $18 to $20 per hour. Rank beginners may enjoy towing privileges at **M. V. Parasail** at pier 44 off Beach Road in Vineyard Haven (☎ 508/693-2838), where you'll be airborne by parachute.

4 Museums & Historic Landmarks

Cottage Museum. 1 Trinity Park (within the Camp Meeting Grounds), Oak Bluffs. ☎ **508/ 693-7784.** Admission $1 (donation). Mid-June to Sept Mon–Sat 10am–4pm. Closed Oct to mid-June.

Oak Bluffs's famous "Camp Ground," a 34-acre circle with more than 300 multicolored, elaborately trimmed carpenter's Gothic cottages, looks very much the way it might have more than a hundred years ago. These adorable little houses, loosely modeled on the revivalists' canvas tents that inspired them, have been handed down through the generations. Unless you happen to know a lucky camper, your best chance of getting inside one is to visit this homey little museum, which embodies the late–19th-century *Zeitgeist* and displays representative artifacts: bulky black bathing costumes and a melodeon used for informal hymnal singalongs.

Oak Bluffs

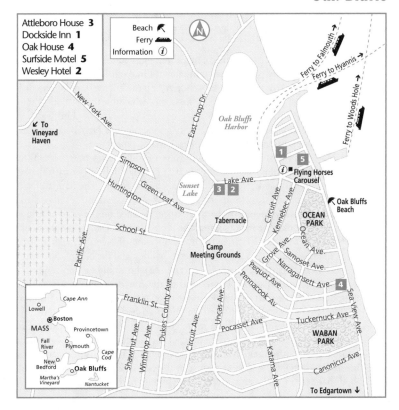

Attleboro House **3**
Dockside Inn **1**
Oak House **4**
Surfside Motel **5**
Wesley Hotel **2**

Beach
Ferry
Information *(i)*

New York Ave.
↙ To Vineyard Haven
East Chop Dr.
Oak Bluffs Harbor
Ferry to Falmouth
Ferry to Hyannis →
Ferry to Woods Hole →
Simpson
Huntington
Green Leaf Ave.
Sunset Lake
Lake Ave.
3 **2**
1 **5**
(i) ■ Flying Horses Carousel
Circuit Ave.
Kennebec Ave.
↖ Oak Bluffs Beach
OCEAN PARK
School St.
Tabernacle
Camp Meeting Grounds
Ocean Ave.
Grove Ave.
Samoset Ave.
Narragansett Ave.
Pequot Ave.
Pennacook Av.
4
Sea View Ave.
Franklin St.
Pacific Ave.
Dukes County Ave.
Shawmut Ave.
Winthrop Ave.
Uncas Ave.
Pocasset Ave.
Circuit Ave.
Katama Ave.
Tuckernuck Ave.
WABAN PARK
Canonicus Ave.
To Edgartown ↓

Cape Ann
Lowell ○
⊛ **Boston**
MASS
Provincetown ○
Fall River ○
Plymouth ○
Cape Cod
New Bedford ○
● **Oak Bluffs**
Martha's Vineyard
Nantucket

The compact architecture is at once practical and symbolic. The Gothic-arched French doors off the peak-roofed second-story bedroom, for instance, lead to a tiny balcony used for keeping tabs on community doings. The daily schedule was, in fact, rather hectic. In 1867, when this cottage was built, campers typically attended three lengthy prayer services daily. Today's denizens tend to blend in with the visiting tourists, though opportunities for worship remain: at the 1878 Trinity Methodist Church within the park, or just outside, on Samoset Avenue, at the non-sectarian 1870 Union Chapel, a magnificent octagonal structure with superb acoustics (posted signs give the lineup of guest preachers and musicians).

At the very center of the Camp Grounds is the striking Trinity Park Tabernacle. Built in 1879, the open-sided chapel is the largest wrought-iron structure in the country. Thousands can be accommodated on its long wooden benches, which are usually filled to capacity for the Sunday-morning services in summer, as well as for community sings (Wednesday in July and August) and occasional concerts (see "Martha's Vineyard After Dark," below). Give yourself plenty of time to wander this peaceful enclave, where spirituality is tempered with a taste for harmless frivolity.

✪ **Flying Horses Carousel.** 33 Circuit Ave. (at Lake Ave.), Oak Bluffs. ☎ **508/693-9481.** Tickets $1 per ride, or $8 for 10. Late May–early Sept daily 9:30am–10pm; call for off-season hours. Closed mid-Oct to mid-Apr.

You don't have to be a kid to enjoy the colorful mounts adorning what is considered to be the oldest working carousel in the country. Built in 1876 at Coney Island, this National Historic Landmark maintained by the Martha's Vineyard Preservation Trust

Fishing off Cuttyhunk Island

Like a misplaced Greek Island, tiny Cuttyhunk—just south of Cape Cod—sits at the tip of the mostly private and uninhabited Elizabeth Islands. On the eastern side of the island, homes are tightly clustered on the hill overlooking the sheltered harbor. Most of the remainder of the island, which measures about 2½ by ¾ miles, is conservation land and pristine beaches popular with bird watchers and solitude-seekers. Accessible from Martha's Vineyard and New Bedford, Cuttyhunk offers an unusual off-the-beaten-track island experience.

In the late 19th century, an exclusive group of millionaires from New York, Boston, and Philadelphia convened at the Bass Fishing Club, a 1-story, shingled bunkhouse on Cuttyhunk, for the ultimate anglers' vacation. The names of several U.S. presidents are scrawled in the guest book alongside those of railroad and oil magnates. For club members, days were spent perched on the edge of fishing stands jutting out over the rocky shores, while hired "chummers" baited the hooks and gaffed the prized catches. Evenings, over sumptuous five-course meals, relaxed industry titans would discuss the stock market, politics, and the best place to catch striped bass. Over cognac and cigars, they'd decide who would be president.

In 1906, William Madison Wood, head of the American Woolen Company and one of the richest men in America at the time, joined the club. Wood, a Horatio Alger poster boy, was born to an impoverished Portuguese family on Martha's Vineyard; by virtue of hard work, good sense, and a timely marriage to the boss's daughter, Wood rose to be head of the American Woolen Company. His passion for Cuttyhunk manifested itself in a keen acquisitive nature; by 1912, he had bought the club and most of the island. Though the Cuttyhunk Club disbanded in 1921 and the building is now a B&B, Cuttyhunk itself

predates the era of horses that "gallop." Lacking the necessary gears, these merely glide smoothly in place to the joyful strains of a calliope. The challenge lies in going for the brass ring that entitles the lucky winner to a free ride. Some regulars, adults included, have grown rather adept—you'll see them scoop up several in a single pass. In between rides, take a moment to admire the intricate hand-carving and real horsehair manes, and gaze into the horses' glass eyes for a surprise: tiny animal charms glinting within.

✪ **The Martha's Vineyard Historical Society/Vineyard Museum.** 59 School St. (corner of Cook St., 2 blocks SW of Main St.), Edgartown. ☎ **508/627-4441.** Fax 508/627-4436. Admission in season $6 adults, $4 children 6–15. Early June to mid-Oct Tues–Sat 10am–5pm. Off-season Wed–Fri 1–4pm; Sat 10am–4pm.

All of Martha's Vineyard's colorful history is captured here, in a compound of historic buildings. To acclimate yourself chronologically, start with the pre-colonial artifacts— from arrowheads to colorful Gay Head clay pottery—displayed in the 1845 **Captain Francis Pease House;** there's also an oral history exhibit, a gift shop, and a gallery to showcase local students' work.

The **Gale Huntington Reference Library** houses rare documentation of the island's history, from genealogical records to whale-ship logs. The recorded history of Martha's Vineyard (the name has been attributed, variously, to a Dutch seaman named Martin Wyngaard, and to the daughter and/or mother-in-law of early explorer Bartholomew Gosnold) begins in 1642 with the arrival of missionary Thomas Mayhew, Jr., whose father bought the whole chain of islands, from Nantucket through the Elizabeths, for £40, as a speculative venture. Mayhew, Jr. had loftier goals in mind, hasn't changed much in the ensuing 85 years. Wood's descendants are still prominent landowners on the island, and devoted anglers can still ply these waters for striped bass with some of the most skilled fishing guides on the East Coast. The fishing guides are **Capt. George Isabel** (☎ **508/991-7352,** or off-season 508/679-5675), **Capt. Duane Lynch** (☎ **508/522-4351**), **Capt. Jim Nunes** (☎ **508/993-7427**), and **Capt. Charlie Tilton** (☎ **508/992-8181**).

A word of warning: Cuttyhunk is a seasonal destination—mid-June to mid-September. Some years, the winter population dips to the single digits. The island has one road and few cars. Those who don't walk use golf carts. Dining and lodging options are quite limited.

How to get there: *By Ferry:* The **M/V** Alert II ferry (☎ **508/992-1432;** www.cuttyhunk.com; e-mail: alert2@cuttyhunk.com) departs New Bedford pier 3 once or twice daily in season. Reservations are highly recommended. Round-trip tickets are $17 for adults and $12 for children. Call for times. *By Seaplane:* **Bayside Air Service,** New Bedford (☎ **508/636-3762**), charges $90 to charter the plane, which holds three passengers. To sail on the Catamaran S/V *Arabella* from Menemsha on Martha's Vineyard to Cuttyhunk, call **Hugh Taylor** at ☎ **508/645-3511.**

Where to stay: The Cuttyhunk Fishing Club (☎ **508/992-5585**) has nightly rates (including continental breakfast) of $75 to $275; **Cuttyhunk Bed and Breakfast** (☎ **508/993-6490**) has two rooms at $70 to $100 per night.

Where to eat in season: Bart's Place at Four Corners is open for lunch and dinner and serves hamburgers, hot dogs, fish-and-chips, and even petit filet mignon. Cuttyhunk Shellfish Farms's **Floating Harbor Raw Bar** (☎ **508/ 971-1120**) offers lunch and dinner to go at the dock.

and it is a tribute to his methodology that long after he was lost at sea in 1657, the Wampanoags whom he had converted to Christianity continued to mourn him (a stone monument to his memory still survives by the roadside opposite the airport). In his relatively brief sojourn on-island, Mayhew helped to found what would become, in 1671, Edgartown (named for the British heir apparent). The library's holdings on this epoch are extensive, and some extraordinary memorabilia, including scrimshaw and portraiture, are on view in the adjoining **Francis Foster Maritime Gallery.** Outside, there's a reproduction "tryworks" to show the means by which whale blubber was reduced to precious oil.

To get a sense of daily life during the era when the waters of the East Coast were the equivalent of a modern highway, visit the **Thomas Cooke House,** a shipwright-built colonial, built in 1765, where the Customs collector lived and worked. A few of the house's 10 rooms are decorated as they might have been at the height of the maritime trade; others are devoted to special exhibits on other fascinating aspects of island history, such as the revivalist fever that enveloped Oak Bluffs. Further curiosities are stored in the nearby Carriage Shed. Among the vintage 19th-century vehicles are a painted peddler's cart, a whaleboat, a hearse, and a fire engine, and the odds and ends include some touching mementos of early tourism.

The Fresnel lens on display outside the museum was lifted from the Gay Head Lighthouse in 1952, after nearly a century of service. Though it no longer serves to warn ships of dangerous shoals (that light is automated now), it still lights up the night every evening in summer, just for show.

Menemsha: A New England Fishing Village

For an authentic slice of the Vineyard, leave the hordes down-island and take the winding roads up-island to picturesque Menemsha, one of the few remaining fishing villages in New England. Shuttle buses make the trip a few times daily, or you can take the bike ferry from Aquinnah—a spectacularly scenic but exhausting bike ride. It seems appropriate to approach Menemsha from its colorful harbor, alongside the commercial fishing fleet, the sportfishing vessels, and the pleasure boats. You can spend the afternoon strolling the wharves at leisure and watching the fishermen unloading their catches—lobsters, tuna, and swordfish. Or simply wander over to the town beach, a colorful mélange of umbrellas, plastic buckets, and splashing youngsters. The water here can be quite cold, but after all that biking, you'll appreciate it.

For charter fishing trips operating out of Menemsha, call **North Shore Charters** (☎ **508/645-2993**) and **Flashy Lady Charters** (☎ **508/645-2462**).

For a wonderful boat ride around Menemsha Harbor, take Hugh Taylor's catamaran *Arabella* (☎ **508/645-3511**). A sunset cruise before dinner at the Homeport (see below) will be a most perfect evening.

There are several charming clothing, craft, and antique shops in the village, as well as a fried-fish shack—✪ **The Bite** (☎ **508/645-9239**)—which some have dubbed the best restaurant on Martha's Vineyard. Or if you prefer, have a celebrity-monikered sandwich (I like the Art Buchwald) at the **Menemsha Deli** (☎ **508/645-9902**). Two family-owned fish markets within yards of each other enjoy a healthy competition. **Larsen's** (☎ **508/645-2680**) has picnic tables for on-site eating; **Poole's Fish Market** (☎ **508/645-2282**) is strictly take-out.

At dinnertime, you might prefer to eat at the casual **Homeport** (☎ **508/645-2679**), perhaps the most famous restaurant on the Vineyard; it has perfect sunset views. Places to stay in Menemsha with ocean views include the **Menemsha Inn and Cottages** (☎ **508/645-2521**), a serene compound; and the **Beach Plum Inn** (☎ **508/645-9454**), an antique farmhouse with a full-service restaurant.

5 Organized Tours

✪ **Arabella.** Menemsha Harbor (at North Rd.), Menemsha. ☎ **508/645-3511.** Evening sail $40 adults, $20 children under 12; day sail $60 adults, $30 children under 12. Departures mid-June to mid-Sept daily 10:30am and 6pm. Reservations required. Closed mid-Sept to mid-June.

Hugh Taylor (James's brother) alternates with a couple of other captains in taking the helm of his swift 50-foot catamaran for daily trips to Cuttyhunk, and sunset cruises around the Gay Head cliffs; you can book the whole boat, if you like, for a private charter. Zipping along at 15 knots, it's a great way to see lovely coves and vistas otherwise denied the ordinary tourist.

Good Fortune. Edgartown Harbor, Edgartown. ☎ **508/627-3445.** www.goodfortune. com. June–Oct $50 per person; call for details and reservations. Closed Nov–May.

Burly Captain Rick Hamilton sails his 1935 classic wooden schooner around Edgartown Harbor three times daily: from 10am to noon, noon to 4pm, and 4pm to sunset. It's a scenic, romantic harbor cruise.

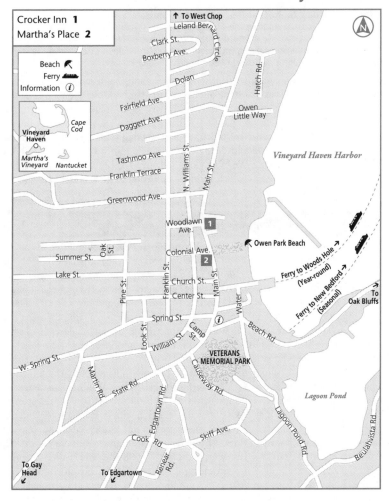

Crocker Inn **1**
Martha's Place **2**

Beach
Ferry
Information (i)

Cape
Cod

Vineyard
Haven

Martha's
Vineyard   Nantucket

↑ To West Chop
Leland Bernard Circle

Clark St.
Boxberry Ave.

Dolan

Fairfield Ave.

Daggett Ave.

Tashmoo Ave.

Franklin Terrace

Greenwood Ave.

Woodlawn
Ave. **1**

Colonial Ave. **2**

Summer St.

Lake St.

Franklin St.

Church St.

Center St.

Spring St.

W. Spring St.

Look St.

William St.

Pine St.

Oak St.

N. Williams St.

Main St.

Hatch Rd.

Owen
Little Way

Vineyard Haven Harbor

← Owen Park Beach

Ferry to Woods Hole →
(Year-round) →

Ferry to New Bedford →
(Seasonal)

To
Oak Bluffs

Water St.

Camp St.

Beach Rd.

VETERANS
MEMORIAL PARK

Martin Rd.

State Rd.

Edgartown Rd.

Causeway Rd.

Lagoon Pond

Lagoon Pond Rd.

Beulahvista Rd.

Cook Rd.

Renear Rd.

Skiff Ave.

To Gay
Head

To Edgartown

Soaring Adventures of America. Edgartown Airfield, Herring Creek Rd. (near South Beach), Edgartown. ☎ **508/627-3833.** Rates start at $59 per person; call for reservations. Open year-round.

Perhaps the best way to view the Vineyard is as an osprey might, circling silently on a cushion of thermal currents. If you've experienced this rush elsewhere (this company offers glider and balloon rides all over the country), you'll know just what's in store; if not, it may prove addictive.

Trustees of Reservations Natural History Tours. Cape Pogue, Chappaquiddick Island. ☎ **508/627-3599.** www.vineyard.net/org/trustees. In season, Mon–Fri 8am. $30 adults, $15 children. Call for reservations. Meet at Mytoi on Chappaquiddick. Closed mid-Oct to May.

The Trustees, a statewide land conservation group, offers several fascinating 2½-hour tours by safari vehicle or canoe around this idyllic nature preserve. The canoe tour on Poucha Pond and Cape Pogue Bay is designed for all levels. It also offers a tour of the Cape Pogue lighthouse at 10am and 1pm. The cost is $12 for adults and $6 for children.

Vineyard History Tours. From the Vincent House Museum, behind 99 Main St., Edgartown. ☎ **508/627-8619.** Also, from the Cottage Museum, 1 Trinity Park, Oak Bluffs and at the Steamship Authority kiosk in Vineyard Haven. $7–$10 adults, free for children 12 and under; inquire about combination passes including the Vineyard Museum (see above). June–Sept Mon–Sat 10:30am–3pm; call for off-season hours. Closed Nov–Apr.

Laced with local lore and often led by the entertaining local historian Liz Villard, hourlong tours provide access to the interiors of the 1672 Vincent House (the island's oldest surviving dwelling), the 1840 Dr. Daniel Fisher House (an elegant Greek Revival mansion), and the splendid Old Whaling Church, a town showpiece built in 1843. There are also a variety of other van and walking tours including 75-minute walking tours of Edgartown with intriguing titles like "Ghosts, Gossip, and Downright Scandal," "A-Whaling We Will Go," and, in Oak Bluffs, "Cottages, Campgrounds, and Flying Horses" (which includes admission to the Cottage Museum and a ride on the Flying Horses).

6 Kid Stuff

A must for tots to preteens is the unique **Flying Horses Carousel** in the center of Oak Bluffs (see above). Directly across the street is another great rainy-day diversion, the **Dreamland Fun Center** (☎ 508/693-5163), featuring dozens of video games, air hockey, skee-ball, and even a small bumper-car arena. For an atmospheric minigolf course, visit **Island Cove Mini Golf,** on State Road outside Vineyard Haven (☎ 508/693-2611), a family-friendly setup with a snack bar serving Mad Martha's ice cream, an Island favorite. On weekends, from 10am to 3pm, children might also enjoy visiting the **World of Reptiles** off Edgartown–Vineyard Haven Road on Bachelder Avenue, Edgartown (☎ 508/627-5634), where they'll meet various snakes, including a 21-foot python; turtles; and even an alligator. Admission is $3 for adults and $2 for children under 12. Nearby, the **Felix Neck Wildlife Sanctuary** (see "Beaches & Recreational Pursuits," above) (☎ 508/627-4850) on Edgartown–Vineyard Haven Road, is always a popular destination with its exhibit room and self-guided trails. On Sundays in season, there are natural history talks and activities geared to children. Pony-cart rides ($1.50) are offered summer afternoons at the **Nip 'n' Tuck Farm** on State Road in West Tisbury (☎ 508/693-1449). Many families plan their vacations around the **Agricultural Society Annual Livestock Show and Fair** (☎ 508/693-9549) in West Tisbury in mid-August. It's an old-fashioned country fair with animals, food, and entertainment. An island event that your kids will always remember is **Illumination Night** in Oak Bluffs, when all the cottages in the campground are lit up with Japanese lanterns. The exact day is a secret, but it's usually on a Wednesday evening at 7:30pm in mid-August.

7 Shopping

ANTIQUES/COLLECTIBLES For the most exquisite Asian furniture, lamps, porcelains, and jewelry, visit **All Things Oriental** at 123 Beach Rd. in Vineyard Haven (☎ 508/693-8375.) The treasures here are handpicked in China by owner Shirley Seaton.

You don't have to be a bona-fide collector to marvel over the museum-quality marine antiques at **C. W. Morgan Marine Antiques,** Beach Road, just east of the town center, Vineyard Haven (☎ 508/693-3622). Frank Rapoza's collection encompasses paintings and prints, intricate ship models, nautical instruments, sea chests, and scrimshaw.

ARTS & CRAFTS   Stop by **C. B. Stark Jewelers,** 53A Main St., Vineyard Haven
(☎ **508/693-2284**), and 27 N. Water St., Edgartown (☎ **508/627-1260**), where
proprietor Cheryl Stark started fashioning island-motif charms back in 1966.

No visit to Edgartown would be complete without a peek at the wares of scrimshan-
der Thomas J. DeMont, Jr. at ✪ **Edgartown Scrimshaw Gallery** at 43 Main St.
(☎ **508/627-9439**). In addition to DeMont's work, the shop carries the work of a
number of the country's top scrimshaw artists. All the scrimshaw in the gallery is
hand-carved using ancient mammoth ivory or antique fossil ivory.

In the center of Edgartown, stop in at ✪ **Gardner Colby Gallery** on 27 N. Water
St. (☎ **888/969-9500** or 508/627-6002), a soothing and sophisticated art showroom
filled with Vineyard-inspired paintings by such popular artists as Robert Cardinal,
whose landscapes often feature haunting purple skies; and Ovid Osborn Ward, who
paints graphically realistic portrayals of Vineyard motifs.

The **Chilmark Pottery,** off State Road (about 4 miles southwest of Vineyard
Haven), West Tisbury (☎ **508/693-6476**), features tableware fashioned to suit its
setting. Geoffrey Borr takes his palette from the sea and sky and produces highly serviceable stoneware with clean lines and a long life span. Summer pottery classes are
also available.

✪ **The Field Gallery,** State Road (in the center of town), West Tisbury (☎ **508/
693-5595**), set in a rural pasture, is where Marc Chagall meets Henry Moore and
where Tom Maley's playful figures have enchanted locals and passersbys for decades.
You'll also find paintings by Albert Alcalay and drawings and cartoons by Jules Feiffer.
The Sunday-evening openings are high points of the summer social season. Closed
mid-October to mid-May.

Don't miss the ✪ **Granary Gallery at the Red Barn,** Old County Road (off Edgartown–West Tisbury Road, about a ¼ mile north of the intersection), West Tisbury
(☎ **800/472-6279** or 508/693-0455), which displays astounding prints by the late
longtime summerer Alfred Eisenstaedt, dazzling color photos by local luminary Alison
Shaw, and a changing roster of fine artists—some just emerging, some long since discovered. A fine selection of country and provincial antiques is also sold here.

Another rather unique local artisans' venue is **Martha's Vineyard Glass Works,**
State Road, North Tisbury (☎ **508/693-6026**). World-renowned master glassblow-
ers sometimes lend a hand at this handsome rural studio/shop just for the fun of it.
The three resident artists—Andrew Magdanz, Susan Shapiro, and Mark Weiner—are
no slouches themselves, having shown nationwide to considerable acclaim. Their output is decidedly avant-garde and may not suit all tastes, but it's an eye-opening array
and all the more fascinating once you've witnessed a work in progress.

Nearby on State Road in North Tisbury, **Etherington Fine Art** (☎ **508/
693-9696**), housed in an old post office, features estimable work like Vineyard- and
Venice-inspired paintings by Rez Williams, nature collages by Lucy Mitchell, pastels
and oils by Wolf Kahn, and the colorful, iconographic sculptures by Sam Milstein that
grace the front yard. Gallery owner Mary Etherington's selection is a giant step up
from the usual seascapes and lighthouses offered by other Vineyard galleries. Big-name
museum people like Thomas Hoving and Agnes Gund all stop here when on the
island.

BOOKS   **Bickerton & Ripley Books,** Main Street (in the center of town), Edgartown (☎ **508/627-8463**), has a lively presentation of timely titles highlighting local
endeavors; inquire about readings and signings. Closed January to March.

Bunch of Grapes, 44 Main St. (in the center of town), Vineyard Haven (☎ **800/
693-0221** or 508/693-2291), offering the island's broadest selection (some 40,000
tomes), is a year-round institution and a browser's haven.

FASHION   ✪ The Great Put On, Dock Street (in the center of town), Edgartown (☎ 508/627-5495), dates back to 1969, but always keeps up with the latest styles, including lines by Vivienne Tam, Moschino, and BCBG.

Jamaikan Jam, Post Office Square (in the center of town), Oak Bluffs (☎ 508/693-5003), is one of the best ethnic shops along Circuit Avenue, carrying colorful and comfortable clothes and island tchotchkes. You can also buy or rent inline skates here.

Treading a comfortable middle ground between functional and fashionable, the varied women's and men's labels at **LeRoux,** 89 Main St. (in the center of town), Vineyard Haven (☎ 508/693-6463), include some nationally known names, such as Patagonia, Columbia Sportsware and Tommy Bahama. It also carries Woodland Waders, an island-made line of sturdy woolen outerwear—everyday clothes for both sexes that are neither staid nor trendy.

GIFTS/HOME DECOR   The owners of **✪ Bramhall & Dunn,** 23 Main St., Vineyard Haven (☎ 508/693-6437), have a great eye for the kind of chunky, eclectic extras that lend character to country homes. Expect to find the requisite rag rugs, rustic pottery, a smattering of English country antiques, bed linens, and a large selection of sweaters.

My favorite place for gifts in Oak Bluffs is **Craftworks,** 149 Circuit Ave. (☎508/693-7463), which is filled to the rafters with whimsical, colorful contemporary American crafts, some by local artisans.

Carly Simon's owns a shop called **✪ Midnight Farm,** 18 Water-Cromwell Lane, Vineyard Haven (☎ 508/693-1997), named after her popular children's book. This home store offers a world of high-end, carefully selected, and imaginative gift items starting with soaps and candles and including children's clothes and toys, rugs, furniture, books, clothes, and glassware.

✪ Paper Tiger, 29 Main St., Vineyard Haven (☎ 508/693-8970) is an old-fashioned stationery store with wonderful papers and envelopes, and the best selection of cards anywhere.

A handsome shop on upper Circuit Avenue (no. 73) is **Argonauta** (☎ 508/696-0097), which carries hand-painted vintage furniture, country pine, wicker, topiary, and artwork. **Third World Trading Co.,** 52 Circuit Ave., Oak Bluffs (☎ 508/693-5550), features well-priced clothing, accessories, and home accents gathered from around the globe.

SEAFOOD   Feel like whipping up your own lobster feast? For the freshest and biggest crustaceans on the island, head to **The Net Result,** 79 Beach Rd., Vineyard Haven (☎ 800/394-6071 or 508/693-6071). Run by the Larsen family, you'll find everything from shrimp, scallops, and swordfish to bluefish and tuna. Their spreadable seafood salad makes a perfect hors d'oeuvre, and if you're feeling sorry for your friends back home, they'll ship fresh lobsters, quahogs, and other aquatic delicacies anywhere in the United States overnight. If you're up-island, stop by **Poole's Fish Market** or **Larsen's Fish Market,** both right on the docks at Menemsha Harbor.

WINE   With a name like Martha's Vineyard, you probably expected to find wild grapes, which in fact have always grown on the island. But who knew whether fussy French vinifera would take? California transplants George and Catherine Mathiesen had high hopes when they started cultivating three backwoods acres in 1971, and their faith has been borne out in **✪ Chicama Vineyards,** Stoney Hill Road (off State Rd., about 3 miles southwest of Vineyard Haven), West Tisbury (☎ 508/693-0309), a highly successful winery yielding some 100,000 bottles a year. The dozen-plus varieties not only are very palatable drinking wines, but also lend themselves beautifully to such gourmet uses as jellies, jams, and flavored oils and vinegars, all prepared and sold on the premises. Visitors are always welcome for a tasting, and in high season, they're treated to an entertaining 20-minute tour of the production line.

8 Where to Stay

When deciding where to stay on Martha's Vineyard, you'll need to consider the type of vacation you prefer. The down-island towns of Vineyard Haven, Oak Bluffs, and Edgartown provide shops, restaurants, beaches, and harbors all within walking distance, and frequent shuttles to get you all over the island. But all three can be overly crowded on busy summer weekends. Vineyard Haven is the gateway for most of the ferry traffic; Oak Bluffs is a raucous town with most of the Vineyard's bars and nightclubs, and many visitors make a beeline to Edgartown's manicured Main Street. Up-island inns provide more peace and quiet, but you'll probably need a car to get around, including going to the beach. Nevertheless, there are some wonderful places to stay on the Vineyard, and all of the following choices have something special to offer.

EDGARTOWN
VERY EXPENSIVE

✪ **Charlotte Inn.** 27 S. Summer St. (in the center of town), Edgartown, MA 02539. ☎ **508/627-4751.** Fax 508/627-4652. 25 units. A/C. Summer $295–$525 double; $695–$850 suite. Rates include continental breakfast; full breakfast offered for extra charge. AE, MC, V. Open year-round. No children under 14.

Ask anyone to recommend the best inn on the island, and this is the name you're most likely to hear—not just because it's the most expensive, but because it's easily the most refined. Owners Gery and Paula Conover have been tirelessly fine-tuning this cluster of 18th- and 19th-century houses (five in all, counting the Carriage House, a Gery-built replica) since 1971. Linked by formal gardens, each house has a distinctive look and feel, though the predominant mode is English country, with fascinating antiques, hunting prints and quirky decorative accents. All rooms have hair dryers. All but one room have televisions, and some have VCRs. Bathrooms are luxurious, and some are enormous (bigger than most hotel rooms). In the elegant 1860 Main House, the common rooms double as the Edgartown Art Gallery and feature Ray Ellis's wonderful oil paintings. This is one of only two Relais & Châteaux properties on the Cape and Islands—a world-class distinction that designates excellence in hospitality.

Dining: However sterling the accommodations at the Charlotte Inn, the restaurant may actually gather more laurels: L'étoile is one of the island's finest. See "Where to Dine," below, for more information.

Amenities: Turndown service in the evenings; newspapers available at breakfast every morning.

Harbor View Hotel. 131 N. Water St. (about ½ mile NW of Main St.), Edgartown, MA 02539. ☎ **800/255-6005** or 508/627-7000. Fax 508/627-8417. www.harbor-view.com. 124 units. A/C TV TEL. Summer $285–$475 double; $485–$675 suite. AE, DC, MC, V. Open year-round.

Grander than grand, this shingle-style complex started out as two Gilded Age hotels, ultimately joined by a 300-foot veranda. Treated to a massive centennial makeover in 1991, it now boasts every modern amenity, while retaining its retro charm—and a lobby that's right out of an Adirondack lodge. Front rooms overlook little Lighthouse Beach; in back, there's a large pool surrounded by newer annexes, where some rooms and suites have kitchenettes. The hotel is located just far enough from "downtown" to avoid the traffic hassles, but close enough for a pleasant walk past impressive captain's houses.

Dining: The Carlos Fuentes cigar bar, is open daily for lunch and dinner; you can ask to be served by the pool, if you like. The recently renovated Coach House (see "Where to Dine," below) serves three meals a day in an elegant setting.

Amenities: A concierge is on hand to lend advice and assistance; room service, same day laundry, and baby-sitting are available. There is a heated outdoor pool with plenty of deck space and two tennis courts.

✪ **Hob Knob Inn.** 128 Main St. (on upper Main St., in the center of town), Edgartown, MA 02539. ☎ **800/696-2723** or 508/627-9510. Fax 508/627-4560. www.hobknob.com. E-mail: hobknob@vineyard.net. 20 units. A/C TV TEL. Summer $200–$525 double. Rates include full breakfast and afternoon tea. AE, MC, V. Open year-round.

Owner Maggie White has reinvented this 19th-century Gothic Revival inn as an exquisite destination now vying for top honors as one of the Vineyard's best places to stay. Her style is peppy/preppy, with crisp floral fabrics and striped patterns creating a clean and comfortable look. Sure it's meticulously decorated, but nothing is overdone or overstuffed. The inn has fitness equipment and massages are available on the premises (for an extra charge). All rooms are equipped with hair dryers and bathrobes. Maggie also rents bikes for the going rate (about $20 a day), and she and her attentive staff will pack a splendid picnic basket or plan a charter fishing trip on Maggie's 27-foot Boston Whaler. The full farm breakfast is a delight and is served at beautifully appointed individual tables in the sunny, brightly painted dining rooms. Bovine lovers will enjoy the agrarian theme, a decorative touch throughout the inn.

The Inn at 148 Main. 148 Main St. (on upper Main St.), Edgartown, MA 02539. ☎ **508/627-7248.** Fax 508/627-9505. E-mail: one48@vineyard.net. 8 units. A/C TV TEL. Summer $250–$400 double. Rates include continental breakfast. AE, DISC, MC, V. No children under 12. Open year-round.

This is a luxurious small inn, consisting of three buildings, two recently restored and one brand new. Though built in the 1840s, the main inn's interior is light and airy, and the spacious rooms are outfitted with every amenity, including VCRs, robes, and hair dryers. The luxurious carriage house suite with its gas fireplace and tiled Jacuzzi tub for two is exceptional. By the way, this is the only small lodging establishment on the Vineyard with an outdoor heated pool and hot tub.

The Point Way Inn. 104 Main St. (on upper Main St.), Edgartown, MA 02539. ☎ **888/711-6633** or 508/627-8633. Fax 508/627-3338. www.pointway.com. E-mail: pointwayinn@vineyard.net. 12 units. AC TV. Summer $225–$325 double; $375 suite. Rates include full breakfast. AE, DISC, MC, V. Closed Jan to mid-Feb.

This lovely inn has just undergone a multimillion-dollar freshening up, and it's just as pretty as it could be. While some of the rooms are on the small side, they are cheerfully decorated in a contemporary style with cozy bedding and amenities. All rooms have robes, and some have hair dryers and VCRs. In the sunlit breakfast room with individual tables, guests are served hearty morning meals that sometimes include crepes, stuffed French toast or quiche. In the afternoons, there are homemade cookies, and in the evenings, wine and cheese. In one unit, the garden room, which has a separate entrance, you are allowed to bring a well-behaved pooch for a $50 surcharge.

Shiverick Inn. 5 Pease's Point Way (just off upper Main St.), Edgartown, MA 02539. ☎ **800/723-4292** or 508/627-3797. Fax 508/627-8441. www.mvweb.com/shiv. E-mail: shiverickinn@vineyard.net. 10 units. A/C. Summer $260–$325 double; $360 suite. Rates include full breakfast and afternoon tea. AE, DISC, MC, V. No children under 12.

Of all the magnificent captain's houses in Edgartown, the Shiverick Inn, built in 1840 for the town physician, is perhaps the most glorious, with its mansard roof, elaborate portico, and belfry. As befits such a prominent home, the entrance is grand and has a curving staircase. The entire inn is furnished with American and English 18th- and 19th-century antiques, fine wallpapers, and oriental rugs. Rooms are uniformly lovely and spacious, with high ceilings; many have working fireplaces. The immense living room is formal yet comfortable, with welcoming couches and armchairs. There's a television in the upstairs library, and a private telephone booth in the hallway downstairs. The large conservatory/sunroom is set with china and stemware at individual tables for the full breakfast. Beach towels and chairs are provided in season.

EXPENSIVE

✪ **Colonial Inn of Martha's Vineyard.** 38 N. Water St., Edgartown, MA 02539. ☎ **800/627-4701** or 508/627-4711. Fax 508/627-5904. www.colonialinnmvy.com. 43 units. A/C TV TEL. Summer $170–$325 double; $350 suite or efficiency. Rates include continental breakfast. AE, MC, V. Closed Dec–Mar.

This 4-story 1911 inn in the center of Edgartown has been transformed into a fine modern hotel and recent extensive renovations have elevated it to what can accurately be described as "affordable luxury." Its lobby serves as a conduit to the Nevins Square shops beyond, and there are also two fine restaurants on the premises. The 43 rooms, decorated in soothing, contemporary tones (with pine furniture, crisp fabrics, hardwood floors, beadboard wainscoting, and four-poster beds), offer all one could want in the way of conveniences. Many rooms have hair dryers and telephones with data ports; some have private balconies and awesome harbor views. Guests whose rooms lack harborviews can wander onto one of the four common harborview decks to have a cocktail and enjoy the scenery. Suites have VCRs (complimentary videos) and kitchenettes. Be sure to visit the roof deck, ideally around sunset or, if you're up for it, sunrise over the water. There are two handicapped-accessible rooms.

The Daggett House. 59 N. Water St., Edgartown, MA 02539. ☎ **800/946-3400** or 508/627-4600. Fax 508/627-4011. www.mvweb.com/daggett. 31 units. A/C TV TEL. Summer $170–$265 double; $230–$575 suite. AE, DISC, MC, V. Open year-round.

What could be more Vineyard-y? Stay in the island's first tavern (the owner was fined for selling strong liquor), smack-dab on Edgartown Harbor and serving a hearty lunch and the best breakfast in town (for an extra charge). Actually, the property includes four buildings and one cottage, and the rooms vary greatly depending on the building. The main inn building has the most historical and charming accommodations (including a resident ghost; check out the photo on the way downstairs to the breakfast room). Request the secret staircase room, one of the many with a harbor view. The Warren House across the street is home to, among others, the dreaded "cozy fulls," which are tiny rooms (one is in a bay window). The newest acquisition is the Thomas House, an historic building on nearby Simpsons Lane whose rooms have been completely gutted and renovated. The cottage rooms are perhaps the nicest, located right on the harbor.

✪ **The Jonathan Munroe House.** 100 Main St., Edgartown, MA 02539. ☎ **508/627-5536.** Fax 508/627-5536. www.jonathanmunroe.com. 7 units, 1 cottage. A/C TEL. Summer $185–$250 double; $350 cottage. Rates include full breakfast. AE, MC, V. No children under 12. Open year-round.

With its graceful wraparound, colonnaded front porch, the Jonathan Munroe House stands out from the other inns and captain's homes on this stretch of upper Main Street. Inside, the formal parlor has been transformed into a comfortable gathering room with European flair. Guest rooms are immaculate, antique-filled, and dotted with clever details. Many rooms have fireplaces and baths with whirlpool jets. All have sitting areas, perfect for curling up with a bestseller (provided) or matching wits over a game of chess (also provided). At breakfast, don't miss the homemade waffles and pancakes, served on the sunny porch. Guests will immediately feel relaxed in the presence of genial host Chip Yerkes, an enthusiastic athlete, who will gladly assist guests with daily excursions that could include a trip around Sengekontacket Pond in one of his three canoes, fishing with one of his fly-fishing rods, a game of tennis, a bike ride, or a sail around Edgartown Harbor on his friend's sloop. Request the garden cottage, with its flowering window boxes, if you are in a honeymooning mood.

✪ **Victorian Inn.** 24 S. Water St. (in the center of town), Edgartown, MA 02539. ☎ **508/ 627-4784.** www.thevic.com. E-mail: victorianinn@vineyard.net. 14 units. A/C. Summer $165–$350 double. Rates include full breakfast and afternoon tea. MC, V. Dogs welcome Nov–Mar. Open year-round.

Do you ever long to stay at a quaint, reasonably priced inn that is bigger than a B&B but smaller than a Marriott? In the center of Edgartown, the Victorian Inn is a freshened-up version of those old-style hotels that used to exist in the center of every New England town. There are enough rooms here so you don't feel like you are trespassing in someone's home, yet there's a personal touch. With three floors of long, graceful corridors, the Victorian could serve as a stage set for a 1930s romance. Several rooms have canopy beds and a balcony with a harbor view. Each year innkeepers Stephen and Karen Caliri have improved and refined the inn, and they are always quick to dispense helpful advice with good humor.

MODERATE

The Arbor. 222 Upper Main St. (on the western edge of town, about ¾ mile from the harbor), Edgartown, MA 02539. ☎ **508/627-8137.** www.mvy.com/arborinn. 10 units, 2 with shared bathroom; 1 cottage. A/C. Summer $135–$185 double. Rates include continental breakfast. MC, V. Closed Nov–Apr.

This unassuming-looking house, hugging the bike path at the edge of town, packs surprising style: Innkeeper/antiquaire Peggy Hall tacked a lovely cathedral-ceilinged living room onto her 1880 farmhouse to add light and liveliness. And that's what you'll find as you compare notes with other travelers, or peruse a fine collection of coffee-table books from the comfort of an overstuffed chintz couch. The rooms range from tiny to spacious, but all are nicely appointed, largely with antiques. The rates are singularly gentle, especially considering the fresh-baked breakfast served on fine china.

✪ **Edgartown Inn.** 56 N. Water St., Edgartown, MA 02539. ☎ **508/627-4794.** Fax 508/627-9420. www.edgartowninn.com. 20 units, 4 with shared bathroom. A/C. Summer $100–$225 double. No credit cards. Closed Nov–Mar.

This centrally located historic inn offers perhaps the best value on the island. Nathaniel Hawthorne holed up here for nearly a year, and Daniel Webster also spent time here. It's a lovely 1798 Federal manse, a showplace even here on captain's row. Rooms are no-frills but pleasantly traditional; some have televisions. For an extra charge, breakfast is available in the dining room. Some rooms in the front of the house have harbor views. Modernists may prefer the two cathedral-ceilinged quarters in the annex out back, which offer lovely light and a sense of seclusion. Service is excellent here; be sure to say hello to Henry King, who has been on staff here for 50 years.

OAK BLUFFS

Those looking for a basic motel with a central location will want to stay at **Surfside Motel** across from the ferry dock on Oak Bluffs Ave. in Oak Bluffs (☎ **800/ 537-3007** or 508/693-2500). Summer rates are $150 to $160 double. Rooms are equipped with air-conditioning, televisions, minifridges, and telephones. Open year-round. Well-behaved pets allowed.

EXPENSIVE

✪ **The Oak House.** 75 Seaview Ave. (on the sound), Oak Bluffs, MA 02557. ☎ **800/ 245-5979** or 508/693-4187. Fax 508/696-7385. www.vineyard.net/inns. E-mail: inns@ vineyard.net. 10 units. A/C TV TEL. Summer $180–$220 double; $275–$280 suite. Rates include continental breakfast and afternoon tea. AE, DISC, MC, V. Closed late Oct–early May.

An 1872 Queen Anne bay-front beauty, this one-time home of former Massachusetts governor William Claflin has preserved all the luxury and leisure of the Victorian age. Innkeeper Betsi Convery-Luce trained at Johnson & Wales; her pastries (served at breakfast and tea) are sublime. The rooms toward the back are quieter, but those in front have Nantucket Sound views. The common rooms are furnished in an opulent Victorian mode, as are the 10 bedrooms (two are suites). This inn is very service-oriented, and requests for feather beds, down pillows, or non-allergenic pillows are accommodated. Anyone intent on decompressing is sure to benefit from this immersion into another era—the one that invented the leisure class.

MODERATE

The Dockside Inn. 9 Circuit Ave. Ext. (Box 1206), Oak Bluffs, MA 02557. ☎ **800/ 245-5979** or 508/693-2966. Fax 508/696-7293. 22 units. A/C TV TEL. Summer $150–$200 double; $250–$350 suite. Rates include continental breakfast. AE, DISC, MC, V. Closed late Oct–early Apr.

Set close to the harbor, the Dockside is perfectly located for exploring the town of Oak Bluffs and is geared for families. The welcoming exterior, with its colonnaded porch and balconies, duplicates the inns of yesteryear. Once inside, the whimsical Victorian touches will transport you immediately into the spirit of this rollicking town. Most of the standard-size rooms have either a garden or harbor view; they're decorated cheerfully in pinks and greens. All rooms have hair dryers. Suites have kitchenettes, and some have private decks. Location, charm, and flair mean this is a popular place, so book early.

Wesley Hotel. 70 Lake Ave. (on the harbor), Oak Bluffs, MA 02557. ☎ **800/638-9027** or 508/693-6611. Fax 508/693-5389. www.wesleyhotel.vineyard.net. E-mail: wesleyhotel@ aol.com. 95 units. TV. Summer $160–$220 double. AE, CB, DC, DISC, MC, V. Closed mid-Oct to early May.

Formerly one of the grand hotels of Martha's Vineyard, this imposing 1879 property, right on the harbor, has certainly seen sunnier times. There are still remnants from its years of grandeur—the rockers that line the spacious wraparound porch and the lobby with its old photographs, dark-stained oak trim, old-fashioned registration desk, and Victorian reproductions. The rooms, however, are quite spare and basic, with nary a picture on the wall. One suspects they've seen their share of rowdy guests. The Wesley Arms, behind the main building, contains 33 air-conditioned rooms with private baths. There are five handicapped-equipped rooms. *Note:* Reserve early to get harbor views, and you'll avoid the surcharge.

INEXPENSIVE

Attleboro House. 42 Lake Ave. (on the harbor), Oak Bluffs, MA 02557. ☎ **508/693-4346.** 11 units, all with shared bathroom. Summer $75–$95 double; $105–$175 suite. Rates include continental breakfast. MC, V. Closed Oct–May.

As old-fashioned as the afghans that proprietor Estelle Reagan crochets for every bed, this harborside guest house—serving Camp Meeting visitors since 1874—epitomizes the simple, timeless joys of summer. None of the 11 rooms is graced with a private bathroom, but the rates are so retro that you may not mind. What was good enough for 19th-century tourists more than suffices today.

VINEYARD HAVEN (TISBURY)
VERY EXPENSIVE

✪ **Martha's Place.** 114 Main St. (across from Owen Park, in the center of town), Vineyard Haven, MA 02568. ☎ **508/693-0253.** Fax 508/693-1890. www.marthasplace.com. E-mail: info@marthasplace.com. 6 units. A/C TV TEL. Summer $175–$425 double. Rates include continental breakfast. DISC, MC, V.

Martha's Place is exceptional for its elegance in the heart of this bustling port town. Owners Richard Alcott and Martin Hicks lovingly restored and refurbished this stately Greek Revival home and surrounded it with rosebushes. Swags and jabots line the windows; every knob has a tassel, every fabric a trim. If you enjoy admiring a neoclassical armoire or an antique bed draped in blue velvet, Martha's is the place. Rooms are spacious and feature antique beds with excellent mattresses, Egyptian cotton linens, and down comforters. The bathrooms here are quite luxurious: Ever seen one with a fireplace? Most rooms have harbor views. There's one limited-access room for guests with disabilities, too. Breakfast is served at the large dining room table set with china and silver, or you may have breakfast in bed, if you prefer. Rooms are equipped with hair dryers, robes, and dataports. Mountain bikes are available for exploring the island, and the innkeepers also run a luxury boat charter business that guests can book for a fee.

EXPENSIVE

Crocker House Inn. 12 Crocker Ave./P.O. Box 1658 (off Main St.), Vineyard Haven, MA 02568. ☎ **800/772-0206** or 508/693-1151. Fax 508/693-1123. www.crockerhouseinn. com. E-mail: crockerinn@aol.com. 8 units. A/C TV (on request) TEL. Summer $195–$285 double, $385 suite. Rates include continental breakfast. AE, MC, V. Open year-round. No children under 12.

Jynell and Jeff Kristal have recently renovated this 1920s home near the harbor into a comfortable and casually elegant place to stay. Rooms are particularly light and airy here; they've all been completely redone with new linens, beds, and furniture with a country flavor. Jynell has Mariott experience, and it shows in the room details and service-oriented hospitality. Jeff bakes the blueberry muffins in the morning, and guests rave about his chocolate chip cookies set out with ice tea and lemonade in the afternoon.

CHILMARK (INCLUDING MENEMSHA), WEST TISBURY & AQUINNAH
VERY EXPENSIVE

Beach Plum Inn. Beach Plum Lane (off North Rd., ½ mile NE of the harbor), Menemsha, MA 02552. ☎ **877/645-7398** or 508/645-9454. Fax 508/645-2801. www.beachpluminn.com. E-mail: info@beachpluminn.com. 5 units, 4 cottages. A/C TV TEL. Summer $200–$400 double or cottage. Rates include full breakfast in season; continental off-season. AE, DISC, MC, V. Closed Jan–Apr.

Completely renovated after a fire gutted the inn, this family-owned country inn is on 8 lush acres, with a lawn sloping graciously down to the water. There's a croquet course and Nova Grass tennis court on the grounds, plus bikes to take exploring (extra charge). The room decor is predominantly cottage-y, though some rooms lean towards elegance. All of the comfortable rooms are equipped with hair dryers, minifridges, irons, and ironing boards. Some, with canopied beds, are quite romantic. Linens are 300 count and above; towels are Egyptian cotton. Five of the rooms have a whirlpool bath. All but one room have decks, some with views of Menemsha Harbor.

Dining: The inn's restaurant is popular for its continental flair, and a full breakfast is served daily. Dinners are cooked to order. The menu changes nightly but may include *tournedos Rossini* prepared classically with foie gras and served atop a rich demiglace, or salmon *en papillote* with a saffron, mint, and orange butter.

Amenities: There is a concierge, laundry service for a charge, and twice-daily maid service. Arrangements can be made for baby-sitting, and in-room massage. On the grounds are tennis courts, a croquet court, and an exercise room. The inn has beach passes to the area's private beaches.

EXPENSIVE

Lambert's Cove Country Inn. Lambert's Cove Rd. (off State Rd., about 3 miles W of Vineyard Haven), West Tisbury, MA 02568. ☎ **508/693-2298.** Fax 508/693-7890. www. vineyard.net/biz/lambertscoveinn. 15 units. A/C. Summer $185–$250 double. Rates include full breakfast. AE, MC, V. Open year-round.

A dedicated horticulturist created this haven in the 1920s, expanding on a 1790 farmstead. You can see the old adzed beams in some of the upstairs bedrooms. Among his more prized additions is the Greenhouse Room, a bedroom with its own conservatory. You'll find an all-weather tennis court on the grounds, and the namesake beach 1 mile away. The inn's restaurant is known for skilled New American dinners (see "Where to Dine," below). Set far off the main road and surrounded by apple trees and lilacs, this secluded estate suggests an age when time was measured in generations. There's no better place to relax.

Dining: The inn's restaurant, serving dinner daily in season, is a romantic venue for traditional New England cuisine.

Menemsha Inn and Cottages. Off North Rd. (about ½ mile NE of the harbor), Menemsha, MA 02552. ☎ **508/645-2521.** Fax 508/645-9500. www.menemshainn.com. 15 units, 12 cottages. TV TEL. Summer $175–$215 double; $275 suite; cottages $1,800–$2,200 weekly. Rates include continental breakfast for rooms and suites. No credit cards. Closed Dec–Apr.

There's an almost Quaker-like plainness to this weathered waterside compound set in the pines near Menemsha Harbor, though many of the rooms are quite inviting. Mostly it's a place to revel in the outdoors (on 11 seaside acres) without distractions. The late *Life* photographer Alfred Eisenstaedt summered here for 4 decades, and the interior aesthetics would please any artist. There's no restaurant—just a restful breakfast room. Cottages have hair dryers, televisions, VCRs, outdoor showers, BBQ grills, and kitchenettes. The most luxurious suites are located in the Carriage House, which has a spacious common room with a fieldstone fireplace. All rooms have private decks; most have water views. Guests have access to complimentary passes and shuttle bus service the Lucy Vincent and Squibnocket private beaches.

MODERATE

The Captain R. Flanders House. North Rd. (about 1 mile NE of Menemsha), Chilmark, MA 02535. ☎ **508/645-3123.** 5 units, 2 with shared bathroom; 2 cottages. Summer $165 double; $250 cottage. Rates include continental breakfast. AE, DISC, MC, V. Closed mid-Nov to Apr.

Set amid 60 acres of rolling meadows crisscrossed by stone walls, this late–18th-century farmhouse, built by a whaling captain, has remained much the same for 2 centuries. The living room, with its broad-plank floors, is full of astonishing antiques, but there's none of that "for show" feel that's prevalent in more self-conscious B&Bs. This is a working farm, so there's no time for posing (even if it was featured in Martha Stewart's *Wedding Book*). Two new countrified cottages overlooking the pond have living rooms but not kitchenettes. After fortifying themselves with homemade muffins, island-made honey, and jam at breakfast, guests are free to fritter the day away. The owners will provide you with a coveted pass to nearby Lucy Vincent Beach, or perhaps you'd prefer a long country walk.

Duck Inn. 10 Duck Pond Way. (off State Rd. about ½ mile E of the lighthouse), Aquinnah, MA 02535. ☎ **508/645-9018.** Fax 508/645-2790. 5 units. Summer $105–$195 double. Rates include full breakfast. MC, V. Closed Nov–Apr.

Elise LeBovit knows that some guests will find her farmhouse B&B over the top, and that's fine with her. Others will find it just right, a place with real personality and glorious ocean views at every turn. Set on a meadow above the Gay Head cliffs, it's like a post-hippie pension, complete with hot tub. The five rooms, including one tucked into the 200-year-old stone foundation, are fancifully decorated (one is arrayed with antique kimonos) and runaway romantic. The pink stucco living room is agreeably cluttered and comfy, and LeBovit dishes out "gourmet organic" breakfasts, such as pear-couscous muffins and chocolate-raspberry crepes.

INEXPENSIVE

Manter Memorial AYH-Hostel. Edgartown–West Tisbury Rd. (about 1 mile E of the town center), West Tisbury, MA 02568. ☎ **508/693-2665.** Fax 508/693-2699. www.tiac.net/_users/hienec/. E-mail: marthasvineyardhostel@hostel.com. 78 beds. $15 for members, $18 for non-members. MC, V. Closed mid-Nov to Mar.

The first "purpose-built" youth hostel in the United States, this homey cedar shake saltbox set at the edge of a vast state forest is still a front-runner. It hums with wholesome energy, from the huge group kitchen with recycling bins and two communal fridges to the five sex-segregated dorms containing 78 beds. The hallways are plastered with notices of local attractions (some stores offer discounts to hostelers), and the check-in desk also serves as a tourist information booth. Outside, there's a volleyball court and a sheltered bike rack. By bike, the hostel is a little more than 7 miles from the Vineyard Haven ferry terminal; shuttle buses also make the rounds in summer. You'll have no trouble at all finding enjoyable ways to spend the 10am-to-5pm "lockout"; just don't forget the 11pm curfew.

9 Where to Dine

Restaurants tend to be rather expensive on the Vineyard, but the stiff competition has produced a bevy of places that offer excellent service, evocative settings, and creative cuisine. *A note on spirits:* Outside Oak Bluffs and Edgartown, all of Martha's Vineyard is "dry," including Vineyard Haven, so bring your own bottle; some restaurants charge a small fee for uncorking. **Great Harbour Gourmet & Spirits,** 40 Main St., Edgartown (☎ **508/627-4390**), has a very good wine selection.

EDGARTOWN
VERY EXPENSIVE

✪ **L'étoile.** Charlotte Inn, 27 S. Summer St. (off Main St.). ☎ **508/627-5187.** Reservations required. Jacket recommended for men. Fixed-price menus $68 and up. AE, MC, V. July–Aug daily 6:30–9:45pm; call for off-season hours. Closed Jan to mid-Feb. FRENCH.

Every signal (including the price) tells you that this is going to be one very special meal. Having passed through a pair of ormolu-laden sitting rooms, one comes upon a conservatory—a wonderfully summery room—sparkling with the light of antique brass sconces and fresh with the scent of potted citrus trees. Everything is perfection, from the table settings (gold-rimmed Villeroy & Boch) to a nouvelle-cuisine menu that varies seasonally but is always exquisite. Chef Michael Brisson, who came up through the kitchen of Boston's famed L'Espalier, is determined to dazzle, and he does, with an ever-evolving menu of delicacies flown in from the four corners of the earth. Sevruga usually makes an appearance—perhaps as a garnish for chilled leek soup. An étouffée of lobster with lobster, cognac and chervil sauce might come with littlenecks, bay scallops, and roasted corn fritters; or roasted pheasant breast in a cider, apple-brandy, and thyme sauce may be accompanied by apple, sun-dried cherry, and mascarpone-filled wild-rice crepes. When dinner with a decent wine runs over $100 a head, you expect revelation. You're likely to find it at L'étoile.

EXPENSIVE

Alchemy. 71 Main St. (in the center of town). ☎ **508/627-9999.** Reservations not accepted. Main courses $22–$33. AE, MC, V. Apr–Nov daily noon–11pm; call for off-season hours. Open year-round. FRENCH BISTRO.

Chef/owners Scott Caskey and Michael Presnol, who also own nearby Savoir Fare, have a spiffy new restaurant, and it's a little slice of Paris on Edgartown's Main Street. Such esoteric choices as oyster brie soup and Burgundy Vintners salad share the bill with escargot and chantarelle fricasse and lapin moutarde spatzle (yes, that's rabbit). As befits a true bistro, there's also a large selection of cocktails, liqueurs, and wines. In addition to lunch and dinner, a bar menu is served from 2:30 to 11pm. This choice isn't for everyone, but sophisticated diners will enjoy the continental flair here.

✪ **The Coach House.** At the Harbor View Hotel (see "Where to Stay" above), 131 N. Water St. ☎ **508/627-7000.** Reservations recommended. Main courses $22–$36. AE, MC, V. Mon–Sat 7–11am and noon–2pm, Sun 8am–1:30pm; daily 6–10pm; call for off-season hours. Open year-round. NEW AMERICAN.

A major makeover has opened up and transformed this restaurant from a stuffy blah room to a terrific place to have a drink, or to dine with an exquisite view of Edgartown Harbor and the lighthouse. The new long and elegant bar is particularly smashing. The menu is simple but stylish. To start, there's softshell crab with arugula and teardrop tomatoes. As a main course, try the carmelized sea scallops with a salad of Asian pear and apple. Service here is excellent; these are trained waiters, not your usual college surfer dudes. At the end of your meal, you may want to sit on the rockers on the Harborview Hotel's wraparound porch and just watch the lights twinkling in the harbor.

✪ **La Cucina Ristorante at the Tuscany Inn.** 22 N. Water St. (in the center of town). ☎ **508/627-8161.** Reservations recommended. Main courses $28–$42. MC, V. Late May–late Sept Wed–Mon 6–10pm. Closed Oct–May. NORTHERN ITALIAN.

Chef Marco Canora is the genius behind this exceptional Italian restaurant set in an elegant inn. Seating is outdoors under a verdant arbor with candles twinkling, or indoors in the tiled dining rooms. Specialties of the house are a bit more refined than at most local venues: marinated quail salad; roasted salmon with fennel, red onion, and mint salad, ginger-infused fig, and port compote; or rosemary- and lavender-marinated lamb chops with cannelini beans, oven-dried tomatoes, sage, and lamb jus. If you are unable to pop over to Tuscany this year, La Cucina will tide you over just fine.

✪ **Lattanzi's.** 19 Church St. (Old Post Office Sq., off Main St. in the center of town). ☎ **508/627-8854.** Reservations recommended. Main courses $22–$38. AE, CB, DC, DISC, MC, V. June–Sept daily 6–10pm; call for off-season hours. Open year-round. NORTHERN ITALIAN.

Some say Al Lattanzi cooks the best veal chops on Martha's Vineyard. Lattanzi's would be the ideal place to eat in the dead of winter, by the glow of the paneled living room's handsome fireplace. Service is exceptional, and the wine list has a wide range of well-priced bottles. Back to the veal chop. You have two choices: *Piccolo Fiorentina,* which is hickory-grilled veal porterhouse chop with black peppercorns and lemon, or *Lombatina di Vitello al Porcini,* which serves the chop with porcini-mushroom cream. If it's

The Quintessential Lobster Dinner

When the basics—a lobster and a sunset—are what you crave, head to **The Home Port** on North Road in Menemsha (☎ **508/645-2679**), a favorite of locals and visitors alike. At first glance, prices for the lobster dinners may seem a bit high, but note that they include an appetizer of your choice (go with the stuffed quahog), salad, amazing fresh-baked breads, a non-alcoholic beverage (remember, it's BYOB in these parts), and dessert. The decor is on the simple side, but who really cares? It's the riveting harbor views that have drawn fans to this family-friendly place for over 60 years. Locals not keen on summer crowds prefer to order their lobster dinners for pickup (less than half price) at the restaurant door, then head down to Menemsha Beach for a private sunset supper. Reservations are required. Fixed-price platters range from $25 to $45, and MasterCard and Visa are accepted. The Home Port is open mid-May to mid-October daily from 6 to 10pm. Closed mid-October to mid-April.

July, get the striped-bass special; from local waters, it's luscious. Lattanzi also owns the very good **brick-oven pizza joint** next door (☎ **508/627-9084**).

MODERATE

Among the Flowers Cafe. Mayhew Lane. ☎ **508/627-3233.** Main courses $14–$26. AE, DC, MC, V. July–Aug daily 8am–10pm; May–June and Sept–Oct daily 8am–4pm. Closed Nov–Apr. AMERICAN.

Everything's fresh and appealing at this outdoor cafe near the dock. Sit under the awning, and you'll just catch a glimpse of the harbor. The breakfasts are the best around, and all the crepes, waffles, and eggs are also available at lunch. The comfort-food dinners (chicken and black pepper sauté over pasta, butter-and-crumb-crusted baked haddock with a sautéed lobster-and-shallot-butter cream) are among the most affordable options in this pricey town. There's almost always a wait, not just because it's so picturesque, but because the food is homey, hearty, and kind on the wallet.

Chesca's. At the Colonial Inn, 38 N. Water St. ☎ **508/627-1234.** Main courses $13–$32. AE, MC, V. Reservations not accepted. Late June–early Sept daily 5:30–10pm; call for off-season hours. Closed Nov–Mar. ITALIAN.

Chesca's is a solid entry, with yummy food at reasonable prices, and you're sure to find favorites like paella (with roasted lobster and other choice seafood), risotto (with roasted vegetables), and ravioli (with portobello mushrooms and asparagus). Smaller appetites can fill up on homemade soup and salad.

INEXPENSIVE

Main Street Diner. Old Post Office Sq. (off Main St. in the center of town). ☎ **508/627-9337.** Most items under $10. MC, V. Daily 7am–9pm year-round. AMERICAN.

It's a little kitschy-cute, what with cartoon wallpaper decorated with vintage doodads, but tony Edgartown could use a place geared to folks not out to bust the budget. Kids and adults alike will enjoy this ersatz diner, where the food, as well as the trimmings, hearken back to the 1950s. A one-egg breakfast with home fries and a buttermilk biscuit will set you back only $2; the burgers and sandwiches (including a classic open-face hot turkey with gravy, potatoes, and cranberry sauce) less than $6. Grab a grilled cheese or BLT, and wash it down with a cherry Coke.

The Newes from America. At The Kelley House, 23 Kelley St. ☎ **508/627-4397.** Main courses $7–$10. AE, MC, V. Daily 11am–11pm. Open year-round. PUB GRUB.

The food is better than average at this subterranean tavern, built in 1742. The decor may be more Edwardian than colonial, but those who come to quaff don't seem to care. Locals love the French onion soup here. Beers are a specialty here. Try a rack of five esoteric brews, or let your choice of food—from a wood-smoked oyster "Island Poor Boy" sandwich with linguica relish to an 18-ounce porterhouse steak—dictate your draft; the menu comes handily annotated with recommendations. Don't miss their seasoned fries, accompanied by a savory Southwestern dipping sauce.

SWEETS

Espresso Love. 2 S. Water St., Edgartown. ☎ **508/627-9211.** Daily 6:30am–6pm. Closed Feb.

Enjoy the freshly baked pastries and muffins with strong coffee, and you're on your way for more shopping and sightseeing.

OAK BLUFFS
EXPENSIVE

✪ **Sweet Life Cafe.** 63 Circuit Ave. ☎ **508/696-0200.** Reservations recommended. Main courses $20–$32. AE, DISC, MC, V. Mid-May to mid-Sept daily 5:30–10pm; Apr to mid-May and mid-Sept to Dec Thurs–Mon 5:30–9:30pm. Closed Jan–Apr. FRENCH/AMERICAN.

Locals are crazy about this pearl of a restaurant, set in a restored Victorian house on upper Circuit Avenue and run by chef/owner Jackson Kenworth. In season, the most popular seating is outside in the gaily-lit garden. Fresh Island produce is featured, with seafood specials an enticing draw. The menu changes often, and everything is terrific. If the roasted lobster with potato-Parmesan risotto, roasted yellow beets, and smoked-salmon chive fondue is offered, order it.

✪ **Zephrus at the Tisbury Inn.** Main St. ☎ **508/693-3416.** Reservations recommended. Main courses $25–$35. AE, DC, DISC, MC, V. noon to 2:30, 5–10pm. Open year-round. INTERNATIONAL.

Chef Joe Da Silva who used to cook everyone's favorite dinners at the Stand By Café in Oak Bluffs has recently opened this hip restaurant at the Tisbury Inn in the center of Vineyard Haven. Seating is outside on Main Street or inside by the hearth in view of the open kitchen. Food is quite creative at this high-energy venue and portions are generous. For starters you might try the Thai-spiced grilled tiger shrimp with a cucumber salad or the smoked quail with glazed pearl onions and poached blood oranges. Main course winners are fish stew, a hearty broth with clams, shrimp, monkfish and potatoes. Though the menu is in constant flux, there is always a good vegetarian choice like the delicious vegetable ragout. Since it's in Vineyard Haven, you must BYOB, so you'll want to bring your favorite wine to compliment this winning cuisine.

MODERATE

Jimmy Seas Pan Pasta Restaurant. 32 Kennebec Ave. ☎ **508/696-8550.** Reservations not accepted. Main courses $16–$23. MC, V. May–Oct daily 5–10pm; call for off-season hours. Open year-round. MEDITERRANEAN.

If you're wondering why the luncheonette-level decor at this restaurant, where Frank Sinatra's crooning resounds at all times, doesn't quite match up with the menu prices, it's because chef Jimmy Cipolla gives his all to his one-pot pasta dishes, served right in the pan. Pasta comes in such intriguing guises as pumpkin tortellini in a creamy sage sauce, and everything's fair game for toppings, from chicken and shrimp with fresh pesto to swordfish in a balsamic vinaigrette. Portions are enormous.

Lola's Southern Seafood. At the Island Inn, Beach Rd. ☎ **508/693-5007.** Reservations accepted only for 5 or more. Main courses $20–$30. DC, MC, V. Sun 10am–2pm; daily 5–11pm. Open year-round. SOUTHERN.

This sultry New Orleans-style restaurant drips with atmosphere: crystal chandeliers, intricate wrought-iron, arched doorways, and starched linens in an ochre palette. Specialties include the chicken-and-seafood jambalaya and the rib-eye steak spiced either "from heaven or hell." There's live entertainment nightly in season, while Sunday brunch features live music. Off-season, there's live music Thursday through Saturday nights. A less-expensive pub menu is served in the bar with its mural of island personalities.

Zapotec. 14 Kennebec Ave. (in the center of town). ☎ **508/693-6800.** Reservations not accepted. Main courses $14–$18. AE, MC, V. June–Oct daily noon–2pm and 5–10pm; call for off-season hours. Closed Nov–Apr. MEXICAN/SOUTHWESTERN.

Look for the chili-pepper lights entwining the porch of this clapboard cottage: They're a beacon leading to tasty regional Mexican cuisine, from *mussels Oaxaca* (with chipotle peppers, cilantro, lime, and cream) to *crab cakes Tulum* (mixed with grilled peppers and cilantro, served with dual salsas), plus the standard chicken and beef burritos. There are also tasty fish tacos, topped with a creamy yogurt dressing. There's also a small children's menu. A good mole is hard to find this far north; here you can accompany it with Mexico's unbeatable beers (including several rarely spotted north of the border), refreshing sangria, or perhaps a hand-picked, well-priced wine.

INEXPENSIVE

Papa's Pizza. 53 Circuit Ave. ☎ **508/693-1400.** Most items under $8. MC, V. June–Aug Sun–Thurs 11am–9pm, Fri–Sat 11am–10pm; call for off-season hours. Open year-round. PIZZA.

The pizza at this vintage-look parlor is on the tame side; nevertheless, some call it the best on the Vineyard. For families with kids, it's ideal. Stop in if only to see the vintage photos of one-time "campers."

SWEETS

Hilliard's Kitch-in-Vue. 51 Circuit Ave. (in the center of town). ☎ **508/693-2191.**

Not even Candyland could match this pastel-painted cottage, where tantalizing renditions of white, milk, and dark chocolate are whipped up daily.

✪ **Mad Martha's.** 117 Circuit Ave. (in the center of town). ☎ **508/693-9151.** Branches at 8 Union St., Vineyard Haven (☎ **508/693-9674**), and 7 N. Water St., Edgartown (☎ **508/627-8761**). Closed ✪ Oct to Apr.

Vineyarders are mad for this locally made ice cream, which comes in two dozen enticing flavors. President Clinton opts for a restrained mango sorbet, which isn't to say you shouldn't go for a hot-fudge sundae.

Murdick's Fudge. 5 Circuit Ave. and 21 N. Water St., Edgartown. ☎ **888/553-8343** or 508/627-8047.

Since 1887, the Murdick family has been serving up homemade fudge, brittle, clusters, and bark. Bring the kids and watch the candy-makers in progress.

VINEYARD HAVEN (TISBURY)
EXPENSIVE

✪ **Black Dog Tavern.** Beach St. Extension (on the harbor), Vineyard Haven. ☎ **508/693-9223.** Reservations not accepted. Main courses $14–$27. AE, MC, V. June–early Sept Mon–Sat 7–11am, 11:30am–2:30pm, and 5–10pm; Sun 7am–1pm and 5–10pm; call for off-season hours. Open year-round. NEW AMERICAN.

How does a humble harbor shack come to be a national icon? Location helps. So do cool T-shirts. Soon after *Shenandoah* captain Robert Douglas decided, in 1971, that this hard-working port could use a good restaurant, influential vacationers, stuck waiting for the ferry, began to wander into this saltbox to tide themselves over with a bit of "blackout cake" or peanut-butter pie. The rest is history, as smart marketing moves extrapolated on word of mouth. The smartest of these moves was the invention of the signature "Martha's Vineyard whitefoot," a black Lab whose stalwart profile now adorns everything from baby's overalls to doggy bandannas, golf balls, and needlepoint kits. Originally the symbol signaled Vineyard ties to fellow insiders; now it merely bespeaks an acquaintance with mail-order catalogs.

Still, tourists love this rough-hewn tavern, and it's not just hype that keeps them happy. The food is still home-cooking good—heavy on the seafood, of course, (including grilled swordfish with banana, basil, and lime; and bluefish with mustard soufflé sauce)—and the blackout cake has lost none of its appeal. Though the lines grow ever longer (there can be a wait to get on the wait list!), nothing much has changed at this beloved spot. Eggs Galveston for breakfast at the Black Dog Tavern is still one of the ultimate Vineyard experiences—go early, when it first opens, and sit on the porch, where the views are perfect.

Le Grenier. 96 Main St. (in the center of town), Vineyard Haven. ☎ **508/693-4906.** Reservations suggested. Main courses $21–$30. AE, DC, DISC, MC, V. Daily 5:30–10pm. Open year-round. FRENCH.

If Paris is the heart of France, Lyons is its belly—and that's where chef-owner Jean Dupon grew up on his *Maman*'s hearty cuisine (she now helps out here, cooking lunch). Dupon has the continental moves down, as evidenced by such classics as steak au poivre, calf's brains Grenobloise with beurre noir and capers, and lobster Normande flambéed with calvados, apples, and cream. Despite the fact that Le Grenier means (and, in fact, is housed in) an attic, the restaurant is quite romantic, especially when aglow with hurricane lamps.

TAKE-OUT & PICNIC FARE

Black Dog Bakery. Water St. (near the harbor), Vineyard Haven. ☎ **508/693-4786.**

In need of a snack at 5am? That's when the doors to this fabled bakery open; from midmorning on, it's elbowroom only. This selection of freshly baked breads, muffins, and desserts can't be beat. Don't forget some homemade doggie biscuits for your pooch.

CHILMARK (INCLUDING MENEMSHA) AND WEST TISBURY
MODERATE

✪ **The Bite.** Basin Rd. (off North Rd., about ¼ mile NE of the harbor), Menemsha. ☎ **508/645-9239.** Main courses $18–$30. No credit cards. July–Aug daily 11am–9pm; call for off-season hours. Closed Oct–Apr. SEAFOOD.

It's usually places like "The Bite" that we crave when we think of New England. This is your quintessential "chowdah" and clam shack, flanked by picnic tables. Run by two sisters using their grandmother's recipes, this place makes superlative chowder, potato salad, fried fish, and so forth. The food comes in graduated containers, with a jumbo portion of shrimp topping out at around $26.

TAKE-OUT & PICNIC FARE

Alley's General Store. State Rd. (in the center of town), West Tisbury. ☎ **508/693-0088.**

That endangered rarity, a true New England general store, Alley's—in business since 1858—nearly foundered in the profit-mad 1980s. Luckily the Martha's Vineyard

Preservation Trust interceded to give it a new lease on life, along with a much-needed structural overhaul. The stock is still the same, though: basically, everything you could possibly need, from scrub brushes to fresh-made salsa (sold, along with other appealing picnic fixings, from **Back Alley's Bakery & Deli**). Best of all, the no-longer-sagging front porch still supports a popular bank of benches, along with a blizzard of bulletin-board notices. For a local's-eye view of noteworthy activities and events, this is the first place to check.

West Tisbury Farmer's Market. Old Agricultural Hall, West Tisbury. ☎ **508/693-3638.**

This seasonal outdoor market, open Wednesday from 2:30 to 5:30pm and Saturday from 9am to noon, is among the biggest and best in New England, and certainly the most rarefied, with local celebrities loading up on prize produce and snacking on pesto bread and other international goodies. The fun starts in June and runs for 18 Saturdays and 10 Wednesdays.

10 Martha's Vineyard After Dark

The Vineyard has an active summer social life. TV journalism and pop-culture firmament types such as Diane Sawyer, Mike Wallace, Walter Cronkite, Carly Simon, and Art Buchwald may be busy attending private dinner parties, but they are apt to join the rest of us later at a nightspot. While the number one club on the island is the Hot Tin Roof at the airport, there are plenty of other places within walking distance in the down-island towns. Hit Oak Bluffs for the rowdiest bar scene and best nighttime street life. In Edgartown, you may have to hop around before you find the evening's most happening spot; for instance, you could happen upon an impromptu performance by Vineyard Sound, a grooving all-male *a cappella* group. In addition, there are interesting cultural offerings almost every night in summer, so check local papers for details.

PUBS, BARS, DANCE CLUBS & LIVE MUSIC

Atlantic Connection. 124 Circuit Ave. (in the center of town), Oak Bluffs. ☎ **508/693-7129.** Cover $3–$10 June–early Sept 9pm–1am; call for off-season hours. Call for schedule.

Disco lives! As do karaoke and comedy, on occasion. Locals such as Spike Lee and Ted Danson seem to love the hodgepodge, and the unofficial house band, Entrain, has begun to attract a wide following (both on the island and on the mainland) with their funky, reggae-laced rock.

David Ryans. 11 N. Water St., Edgartown. ☎ **508/627-4100.** No cover. June–Sept daily 11:30am–1am; call for off-season hours.

People have been known to dance on the tables at this boisterous bar. You can hear the music blaring from Main Street. The bartender decides the canned tunes, from Sinatra to the Smashing Pumpkins.

✪ **Hot Tin Roof.** Airport Rd. (at Martha's Vineyard Airport), Edgartown. ☎ **508/693-1137.** www.mvhottinroof.com. E-mail: theroof@vineyard.net. Cover varies. Call for schedule. Closed Nov–May.

Carly's back, and the joint is jumping. Simon first opened this nightclub-in-a-hangar in the early 1970s and eventually lost interest (while it lost cachet). Now with multi-million-dollar backing from such high-rollers as hotelier Richard Friedman (who hosts the Clintons), it's on a roll again. Notoriously stage-shy, Carly will sometimes take the mike herself, but she's mostly content to attract an eclectic roster including such notables as Jimmy Cliff, Peter Wolf, Hall & Oates, the "Bacon Brothers" (including Kevin), and Kate Taylor, James's equally talented sister. Comedians command the stage on Tuesday. All in all, it's a family affair, where outsiders in sync with global-family values will feel right at home.

The Lampost/Rare Duck. 111 Circuit Ave. (in the center of town), Oak Bluffs. ☎ **508/696-9352.** Cover varies $1–$5. Call for schedule. Closed Nov–Mar.

Young and loud are the watchwords at this pair of clubs; the larger features live bands and a dance floor, the smaller (down in the basement), acoustic acts. This is where the young folk go, so entertainment includes such prospects as "'80s night" and "male hot-body contest."

Offshore Ale Company. 30 Kennebec Ave., Oak Bluffs. ☎ **508/693-2626.** June–Sept daily noon–midnight; call for off-season hours. Cover varies.

In 1602, the first barley in the New World was grown on Martha's Vineyard. A few years ago, the Vineyard's first and only brew pub opened, featuring eight locally made beers on tap ($2.75 to $5). It's an attractively rustic place, with high ceilings, oak booths lining the walls, and peanut shells strewn on the floor. There's a raw bar, and late-night munchies are served till 10pm, featuring pizza and hamburgers, among other offerings. Local acoustic performers entertain several nights a week in season.

The Ritz Cafe. 1 Circuit Ave. (in the center of town), Oak Bluffs. ☎ **508/693-9851.** Cover $2–$3. Call for schedule.

Locals and visitors alike flock to this down-and-dirty blues club that features live music every night in season and on weekends year-round.

LOW-KEY EVENINGS
Old Whaling Church. 89 Main St. (in the center of town), Edgartown. ☎ **508/627-4442.** Ticket prices vary. Call for schedule.

This magnificent 1843 Greek Revival church functions primarily as a 500-seat performing-arts center offering lectures and symposia, films, plays, and concerts. Such Vineyard luminaries as the actress Patricia Neal have taken their place at the pulpit, not to mention Livingston Taylor and Andre Previn, whose annual gigs always sell out.

THEATER AND DANCE
✪ **The Vineyard Playhouse.** 24 Church St. (in the center of town), Vineyard Haven. ☎ **508/696-6300** or 508/693-6450. Tickets $17.50–$27.50. June–Sept Tues–Sun at 8pm; call for off-season hours.

In an intimate (112-seat) black-box theater, carved out of an 1833 church-turned-Masonic lodge, Equity professionals put on a rich season of favorites and challenging new work, followed, on summer weekends, by musical or comedic cabaret in the gallery/lounge. Children's theater selections are performed on Saturdays at 10am. Townspeople often get involved in the outdoor Shakespeare production, a 3-week run starting in mid-July at the Tashmoo Overlook Amphitheatre about 1 mile west of town, where tickets for the 5pm performances Tuesday to Sunday run only $5 to $10.

The Yard. A Colony for the Performing Arts (off Middle Rd. near Beetlebung Corner), Chilmark. ☎ **508/645-9662.** www.tiac.net/users/theyard. Late May–early Sept. Performances at 8:30pm. Tickets $12 adults, $9 students.

For over 25 years, The Yard has been presenting modern dance performances on Martha's Vineyard. The choreographer residency program here is nationally recognized, and there are classes open to the public.

MOVIES

The **Entertainment Cinemas** at 65 Main St. (☎ **508/627-8008**) in Edgartown has two screens. Call ☎ **508/627-5900** or check local newspapers or schedules at the three vintage art-deco movie theaters: **Capawok,** Main Street, Vineyard Haven; **Island Theater,** at the bottom of Circuit Avenue, Oak Bluffs; and **The Strand,** Oak Bluffs Avenue Extension, Oak Bluffs.

ONLY ON THE VINEYARD

Gay Head Lighthouse. Off State Rd., Aquinnah. ☎ **508/645-2211.** Admission $2 adults, free for children under 12. Late June–late Sept Fri–Sun 7–9pm.

Though generally closed to the public, this 1856 lighthouse opens its doors on summer-weekend evenings to afford an awe-inspiring view of the sunset over the Devil's Bridge shoals. The light has been automated since 1952 (the original lens lights up the night sky in Edgartown), but the experience continues to be romantic. Tour time varies nightly. It begins an hour and a half before sunset and ends a half hour past sunset.

✪ **Trinity Park Tabernacle.** Trinity Park (within the Camp Meeting Grounds), Oak Bluffs. ☎ **508/693-0525.** July–Aug Wed at 8pm and occasional weekend evenings. Free admission. Call for schedule.

Designed by architect J. W. Hoyt of Springfield, Massachusetts, and built in 1879 for just over $7,000, this open-air church, now on the National Register of Historic Places, is the largest wrought-iron-and-wood structure in America. Its conical crown is ringed with a geometric pattern of amber, carmine, and midnight-blue stained glass. Old-fashioned community sings take place Wednesday at 8pm, and concerts are scheduled irregularly on weekends. James Taylor and Bonnie Raitt have regaled the faithful here, but usually the acts are more homespun.

Appendix A: Cape Cod in Depth

1 History 101

PRE-"DISCOVERY"   Compared to the rest of the continental United States, the Cape and Islands truly do represent a new land. The area is only some 12,000 to 15,000 years old and, from the archaeological evidence found to date, was only inhabited during the late Pleistocene (about 10,000 to 12,000 years ago), by nomadic hunter-gatherers. By the time the first European explorers arrived at the turn of the 17th century (a rumored ca. A.D. 1000 visit by Viking Leif Eriksson has yet to be substantiated), Algonquian tribes had set up permanent winter and summer camps and were farming, fishing, and hunting.

The interlopers proved deadly, not just because of their greed for land and resources (including human: long before the Pilgrims arrived, English scouts kidnapped several Indians to be displayed as curiosities in London), but because they bore diseases against which the natives had no immunity. From a population thought to number around 30,000 in the early 17th century, their numbers quickly plummeted to mere hundreds.

THE PILGRIMS' SPEEDY PROGRESS   The decimation of native tribes left the fields, quite literally, wide open to this band of 102 "saints and sinners" (religious dissidents and mercenary adventurers), who set anchor on the morning of November 11, 1620 off what would become Provincetown. The *Mayflower* had been bound for the Hudson River, at that point part of the Virginia Colonies, and with no established government—in fact, nothing at all—awaiting them on shore, the Pilgrims paused to make a covenant intended to prevent anarchy. Stating the case for self-rule, as well as for the full participation of every citizen, the "Mayflower Compact" has since been heralded as a forerunner of the U.S. Constitution.

Though the Pilgrims were fairly lucky in their choice of harbor—a scouting party led by Captain Miles Standish managed to steal some seed corn stored in what is now Truro and met with no hostility until reaching Eastham's "First Encounter Beach"—Provincetown's climate did not strike them as conducive to agriculture. They kept searching until they found "Plimoth," an ideal spot across the bay, with freshwater springs close at hand and a relatively safe vantage point overlooking the harbor. The Pilgrims dug in and, despite losing half their number that first harsh winter, stayed put.

Cape Cod in Depth

- **1614** Captain John Smith reconnoiters the New England coast and sends back glowing reports of fecund land and fabulous natural resources.

- **1620** In November, the Pilgrims touch down at what is now Provincetown. Finding the land and its inhabitants inhospitable, they cross the bay in December to settle an abandoned indigenous campsite in Plymouth.

- **1627** The Pilgrims set up America's first trading post at Aptucxet, in what is now Bourne.

- **1637** Puritan dissidents settle Sandwich, the first town to be incorporated on the Cape.

- **1660** Missionary Richard Bourne persuades the Plymouth court to accord the decimated Wampanoag tribe 10,500 acres in Mashpee "in perpetuity"—a land grant that a 1976 court refused to recognize.

- **1690** Nantucketers hire Ichabod Paddock of Truro to instruct them in the art of hunting "right" whales—so-called because they stick close to shore and float once killed.

- **1712** Nantucket's Captain Christopher Hussey happens to harpoon a sperm whale, whose oil proves far superior to that of near-shore whales. The tiny island soon takes the lead in worldwide whaling.

- **1770** Nantucket abolishes slavery 13 years before the rest of the state.

- **1779** The British attempt to land in Falmouth but are repelled by the local militia.

- **1816** Henry Hall of Dennis notices his wild cranberries flourish when

continues

However, just as the Puritans themselves had fled England in search of religious freedom, splinter groups soon tired of the Puritans' own intolerance and set off to forge their own destinies. The first such settlement on the Cape was Sandwich, settled in 1637. Colonization quickly spread along the bay, into Barnstable and Yarmouth, where the fringe of salt marsh proved an excellent source of hay.

Martha's Vineyard was also among the earliest settlements. In 1642, speculator Thomas Mayhew bought all the islands, including the Elizabeths, from an English noble for the grand sum of £40. His missionary son immediately set about converting the natives of Martha's Vineyard and succeeded in swaying some 1,600 within a few short years, before perishing at sea. In 1659, Mayhew, Sr. sold Nantucket to a group of settlers—some of them *non grata* on the mainland for having evidently sympathized with Quakers—for £30, plus "two Beaver Hatts."

Early peace treaties made in Plymouth and massive conversions sufficed to keep a wary peace with the Wampanoag tribe for over 50 years—until the 1675–76 uprising known as King Philip's War, a last-ditch effort by East Coast tribes to contain colonial expansion. Greatly outnumbered, the natives were crushed, and with them, in large part, their way of life.

ON THE WATERFRONT   Among the useful skills passed on by natives to newcomers was the practice of feasting off the occasional beached whale—or better yet, canoeing in pursuit of the "right" whales, which, once speared, stayed afloat and could be towed into shore. Using sailboats, the settlers set off in pursuit, and in 1712, a Nantucket ship blown out to sea managed to harpoon a sperm whale, which boasted not only blubber but spermaceti, a waxy substance that turned out to be ideal for candle making and lamp fuel. The hunt was on, and over the next 1½ centuries—until kerosene supplanted whale oil in 1859—Nantucket would remain in the forefront of the hugely lucrative whaling industry. Captains from the Cape and Islands tracked their quarry to the four corners of the earth, while initiating the China Trade in luxury goods like fine porcelain and dressing up their home towns with fine mansions.

Pro-independence forces along the coast were especially avid, either because they were a self-select band of dissidents to begin with or because they'd long been subject to excessive taxation. One of the revolution's most influential orators was lawyer James Otis of West Barnstable, who in 1761 quit his post as a customs agent to protest writs authorizing British soldiers to conduct searches at will: "A man's home is his castle," Otis declaimed to a receptive crowd at Old South Meeting House in Boston. His outspokenness earned him a near-fatal beating at a Tory pub in 1769, and a year later, the Boston Massacre definitively turned the tide of public opinion. By the time the Continental Congress declared independence on July 4, 1776, most Tory sympathizers along the coast were quietly planning to decamp. Though most of the action was far removed, the Cape did see a few skirmishes: Falmouth's volunteer militia, for instance, fended off an invading British fleet in 1779—several houses still bear the mark of cannon fire. And the ocean itself accomplished one of the most significant victories of 1778 in sinking the warship *Somerset* (the very boat Paul Revere had quietly paddled past en route to his famous ride of April 17, 1775) off North Truro. Townspeople rounded up the 480 soldiers who managed to make it to shore and hustled them back to Boston as prisoners of war.

The shipping trade remained dangerous right through the War of 1812, as British ships continued to conscript any American crews unlucky enough to cross their path. Some dangers—such as the risk of shipwreck—never abated, but the valiant captains of the Cape and Islands pressed on, broadening both commercial and intellectual horizons.

A SOMEWHAT GOLDEN AGE The early 18th century was a time of unprecedented prosperity. With shipping routes well-established for the distribution of goods, the Cape caught a touch of the Industrial Revolution fever then sweeping the mainland. The largest local enterprise was the Boston & Sandwich Glass Company (1828–88), which successfully applied glassblowing techniques on a factory scale, rendering glassware accessible to the masses for the first time in history.

Although the mostly immigrant labor force was often exploited, the newly emerging leisure class did feel an obligation to enlighten and instruct; hence, the proliferation of public libraries. Such was the mandate of the Nantucket Atheneum, whose brilliant young director, the amateur astronomer Maria

covered with a light dusting of sand; his tips, and a favorable environment, eventually elevate Massachusetts to the world's largest cranberry-producer.

- **1846** The Great Fire levels the port of Nantucket but the town quickly rebounds.
- **1849** Henry David Thoreau embarks on the first of several walking tours of Cape Cod, observing native customs with astringent wit.
- **1859** The introduction of kerosene sounds the death knell for the whaling industry.
- **1871** The U.S. Commission of Fish and Fisheries sets up a collection station in Woods Hole to support the study of oceanography.
- **1892** President Cleveland establishes the first "summer White House" at Gray Gables in Bourne.
- **1899** Artist Charles W. Hawthorne founds the Cape Cod School of Painting in Provincetown.
- **1914** The Cape Cod Canal is completed 17 days before the Panama Canal.
- **1916** Attracted by rumors of a radical new theater enterprise at the tip of the Cape, Eugene O'Neill shyly offers his first works to the Provincetown Players.
- **1918** A German sub fires on Orleans (while a Naval Air Station crew plays baseball).
- **1926** Raymond Moore founds the Cape Playhouse in Dennis, attracting such raw talent as Bette Davis, Humphrey Bogart, and others.
- **1935** Hans Hoffman revives the Cape Cod School of Art and turns Provincetown into a

continues

hotbed of abstract expressionism.

- **1950** Broadway star Gertrude Lawrence and her husband, Richard Aldrich, found the Cape Cod Melody Tent in Hyannis.
- **1961** Roughly 44,000 acres of the Outer Cape—a 30-mile swath of coast—is placed under National Park Service stewardship as the Cape Cod National Seashore.
- **1989** After much debate, Cape Codders vote for a Cape Cod Commission, a regulatory agency that seeks to control development on Cape Cod.
- **1994** Stellwagen Bank, an underwater reef that serves as a primary feeding ground for migrating whales, is declared a National Marine Monument.
- **1995** With the backing of the Mashpee Wampanoags, senators Edward Kennedy and John Kerry successfully mobilize the Mashpee National Wildlife Refuge along Waquoit Bay.
- **1996** Within a few months of each other, the Highland Lighthouse in North Truro and the Nauset Lighthouse in Eastham are moved back from their rapidly eroding cliffs.
- **1998** The Cape Cod Land Bank Bill, which preserves land in all 15 towns by using money from a real estate tax, is signed into law.
- **2000** Gov. Cellucci crafts a bill that would turn the 20,000-acre Massachusetts Military Reservation in Bourne into a wildlife preserve.

Mitchell, drew to her remote island such eminent contemporary figures as Frederick Douglass, John James Audubon, and Melville, Emerson, and Thoreau. Mitchell's accomplishments (she discovered a comet at the age of 29 and later became the country's first female college professor) are fairly indicative of the de facto feminism operative in a region where a good portion of the men spent most of their time at sea. As for Thoreau, he was clearly smitten with the Cape, returning repeatedly in the 1850s to report with acerbic relish on this "wild, rank place."

FROM BACKWATER TO SPA With the abrupt demise of whaling in the 1860s, recession-struck residents streamed northward to seek work in the factory towns surrounding Boston—or westward in search of gold. The population of the Cape and Islands declined steadily over the next 60 years, not recovering until the advent of the automobile.

Meanwhile, however, tourists had begun to take over. The first wave, in the 1830s, consisted of Methodist revivalists who camped in Eastham and Centerville before permanently pitching their tents—and later, gingerbread houses—in Martha's Vineyard's Oak Bluffs. Erected in the 1860s and 1870s, their colorful "Cottage City" survives as one of the earliest instances of successful urban planning. Another beneficiary of the region's long economic sleep is the beautiful port town of Nantucket. Preserved in near pristine condition, with minimal accommodation to modern amenities, it represents the largest concentration of pre-1850 structures in the United States. Except for the cars and crowds, you'd swear that scarcely any time had passed.

Nantucket began bouncing back as a tourist destination in the 1870s (it even supported an actors' colony in rose-covered 'Sconset). Falmouth became another popular destination with the coming of the railroad. At the turn of the century, Provincetown, hitherto a hard-scrabble fishing town, started attracting artists and writers from Greenwich Village. The radical theater movement that brought forth Eugene O'Neill also spawned more broadly appealing straw-hat ventures, including Dennis's still-thriving Cape Playhouse, where actors such as Bette Davis and Henry Fonda made their debuts.

The cast of characters may have changed over the years, but Provincetown—protectively encircled by the Cape Cod National Seashore preserve since 1961—

still takes itself seriously as an art colony. In particular, the off-season residency program at the Fine Arts Work Center, founded in 1968 by such local luminaries as painter Robert Motherwell and poet Stanley Kunitz, continues to elicit emerging talent; the "scholars," visual and literary, often settle in for good. Seductively diffuse light, scintillating company, great stretches of unspoiled nature close at hand—the very features that attracted the intelligentsia of the teens and '20s—are every bit as potent today as they were back then. By toeing the fine line between progress and preservation, those who love the region—residents and visitors alike—hope to perpetuate its charms for as long as the land lasts.

Appendix B: Planning Your Trip—An Online Directory

by Lynne Bairstow

Lynne Bairstow is the co-author of *Frommer's Mexico* and the editorial director of *e-com* magazine.

Day by day, the Internet becomes more integrated into our lives—including the way we plan and book our travel. By early 2000, one in every 10 trips was being booked online, a trend that's sure to accelerate.

The Internet not only provides a wealth of destination information, but also gives you the chance to compare experiences with fellow travelers, ask experts for pre-trip advice, seek out discounted fares once accessible only to travel-industry insiders, and stay in touch via e-mail while you're away. The instant communication and storehouse of information have revolutionized the way travel is researched, reserved, and realized.

The Frommer's Online Directory will help you take better advantage of the planning information available online, and it's best used in conjunction with this book. Section 1 lists general Internet resources that can make any trip easier, such as sites for obtaining the best possible prices on airline tickets. In section 2, you'll find some top online guides for Cape Cod, Nantucket, and Martha's Vineyard.

Please keep in mind that this is not a comprehensive list, but rather a discriminating selection to get you started. Recognition is given to sites based on their content value and ease of use, and are not paid for—unlike some Web-site rankings, which are based on payment. Finally, remember this is a press-time snapshot of leading Web sites—some undoubtedly will have evolved, changed or moved by the time you read this.

1 Top Travel-Planning Web Sites

While the Internet was once a conglomerate of sites for researching places to visit, several key companies have emerged that offer comprehensive travel planning and booking. In addition to Frommer's Online (see the box), we list the other top online travel agencies below, along with some more specialized services.

WHY BOOK ONLINE?

Online agencies have come a long way over the past few years, now providing tips for finding the best fare as well as giving you suggested dates or times to travel that yield the lowest price if your plans are at all flexible. Other sites even allow you to establish the price you're willing to pay, and then check the airlines' willingness to accept it. However, in some cases, these sites may not always yield the best price.

Editor's Note: What You'll Find at the Frommer's Site

We highly recommend **Arthur Frommer's Budget Travel Online** (**www.frommers.com**) as an excellent travel planning resource. Of course, we're a little biased, but you'll find indispensable travel tips, reviews, monthly vacation giveaways, and online booking. Among the most popular features of this site is the regular "Ask the Expert" bulletin boards, which feature one of the Frommer's authors answering your questions via online postings.

Subscribe to Arthur Frommer's Daily Newsletter (**www.frommers. com/newsletters**) to receive the latest travel bargains and insider travel secrets in your e-mailbox every day. You'll read daily headlines and articles from the dean of travel himself, highlighting last-minute deals on airfares, accommodations, cruises, and package vacations. You'll also find great travel advice by checking our "Tip of the Day" or "Hot Spot of the Month."

Search our Destinations archive (**www.frommers.com/destinations**) of more than 200 domestic and international destinations for great places to stay, tips for traveling there, and what to do while you're there. Once you've researched your trip, the online reservations system (**www. frommers.com/booktravelnow**) takes you to Frommer's favorite sites for booking your vacation at affordable prices.

Unlike a travel agent, for example, they may not have access to charter flights offered by wholesalers.

Online booking sites aren't the only places to reserve airline tickets—all major airlines have their own Web sites and often offer incentives—bonus frequent-flyer miles or Net-only discounts, for example—when you buy online or buy an e-ticket.

The new trend is toward conglomerated booking sites. By mid-2000, a consortium of U.S.- and European-based airlines are planning to launch an as-yet-unnamed Web site that will offer fares lower than those available through travel agents. United, Delta, Northwest, and Continental have initiated this effort, based on their success at selling airline seats at their own online sites.

The best of the travel-planning sites are now highly personalized—they store your seating preferences, meal preferences, tentative itineraries, and credit-card information, allowing you to quickly plan trips or check agendas.

In many cases, booking your trip online can be better than working with a travel agent. It gives you the widest variety of choices, control, and the 24-hour convenience of planning your trip when you choose. All you need is some time—and often a little patience—and you're likely to find the fun of online travel research will greatly enhance your trip.

WHO SHOULD BOOK ONLINE?

Online booking is best for travelers who want to know as much as possible about their travel options, for those who have flexibility in their travel dates and are looking for the best price, and for bargain hunters driven by a good value, who are open-minded about where they travel.

One of the biggest successes in online travel for both passengers and airlines is the offer of last-minute specials, such as American Airlines' weekend deals or

More people still look online than book online, partly due to fear of putting their credit-card numbers out on the Net. Secure encryption has removed this fear for most travelers. In some cases, however, it's simply easier to buy from a local travel agent who can deliver your tickets to your door (especially if your travel is last-minute or if you have special requests). You can find a flight online and then book it by calling a toll-free number or contacting your travel agent, though this is somewhat less efficient. To be sure you're in secure mode when you book online, look for a little icon of a key (in Netscape) or a padlock (in Internet Explorer) at the bottom of your Web browser.

other Internet-only fares that must be purchased online. Another advantage is that you can cash in on incentives for booking online, such as rebates or bonus frequent-flyer miles.

Business and other frequent travelers also have found numerous benefits in online booking, as the advances in mobile technology provide them with the ability to check flight status, change plans, or get specific directions from handheld computing devices, mobile phones, and pagers. Some sites will even e-mail or page passengers if their flight is delayed.

Online booking is increasingly able to accommodate complex itineraries, even for international travel. The pace of evolution on the Net is rapid, so you'll probably find additional features and advancements by the time you visit these sites. What the future holds for online travelers is ever-increasing personalization and customization.

TRAVEL-PLANNING & BOOKING SITES

Below are listings for sites for planning and booking travel. The following sites offer domestic and international flight, hotel, and rental-car bookings, plus news, destination information, and deals on cruises and vacation packages. Free (one-time) registration is required for booking.

Travelocity (incorporates Preview Travel). www.travelocity.com; www.previewtravel.com; www.frommers.travelocity.com
Travelocity is Frommer's online travel-planning and -booking partner. Travelocity uses the SABRE system to offer reservations and tickets for more than 400 airlines, plus reservations and purchase capabilities for more than 45,000 hotels and 50 car-rental companies. An exclusive feature of the SABRE system is its **Low Fare Search Engine,** which automatically searches for the three lowest-priced itineraries based on a traveler's criteria. Last-minute deals and consolidator fares are included in the search. If you book with Travelocity, you can select specific seats for your flights with online seat maps and also view diagrams of the most popular commercial aircraft. Its hotel finder provides street-level location maps and photos of selected hotels. With the **Fare Watcher** e-mail feature, you can select up to five routes and receive e-mail notices when the fare changes by $25 or more.

Travelocity's **Destination Guide** includes updated information on some 260 destinations worldwide—supplied by Frommer's.

Note to AOL Users: You can book flights, hotels, rental cars, and cruises on AOL at keyword: Travel. The booking software is provided by Travelocity/ Preview Travel and is similar to the Internet site. Use the AOL "Travelers Advantage" program to earn a 5% rebate on flights, hotel rooms, and car rentals.

Expedia. **expedia.com**

Expedia is Travelocity's major competitor. It offers several ways of obtaining the best possible fares: **Flight Price Matcher** service allows your preferred airline to match an available fare with a competitor; a comprehensive **Fare Compare** area shows the differences in fare categories and airlines; and **Fare Calendar** helps you plan your trip around the best possible fares. Its main limitation is that like many online databases, Expedia focuses on the major airlines and hotel chains, so don't expect to find too many budget airlines or one-of-a-kind B&Bs here.

TRIP.com. **www.trip.com**

TRIP.com began as a site geared toward business travelers, but its innovative features and highly personalized approach have broadened its appeal to leisure travelers as well. It is the leading travel site for those using mobile devices to access Internet travel information.

TRIP.com includes a trip-planning function that provides the average and lowest fare for the route requested, in addition to the current available fare. An on-site "newsstand" features breaking news on airfare sales and other travel specials. Among its most popular features are Flight TRACKER and intelliTRIP. **Flight TRACKER** allows users to track any commercial flight en route to its destination anywhere in the United States, while accessing real-time FAA-based flight monitoring data. **intelliTRIP** is a travel search tool that allows users to identify the best airline, hotel, and rental-car rates in less than 90 seconds.

In addition, the site offers e-mail notification of flight delays, plus city resource guides, currency converters, and a weekly e-mail newsletter of fare updates, travel tips, and traveler forums.

Yahoo! Travel. **www.travel.yahoo.com**

Yahoo! is currently the most popular of the Internet information portals, and its travel site is a comprehensive mix of online booking, daily travel news, and destination information. The **Best Fares** area offers what it promises, plus

Online Directory

Airline Web Sites

Below are the Web sites for the major airlines. These sites offer schedules and flight booking, and most have pages where you can sign up for e-mail alerts for weekend deals and other late-breaking bargains.

Air France. www.airfrance.com
Alitalia. www.alitalia.it
America West. www.americawest.com
American Airlines. www.aa.com
ATA. www.ata.com
British Airways. www.british-airways.com
Continental Airlines. www.continental.com
Delta. www.delta.com
Northwest Airlines. www.nwa.com
Southwest. www.southwest.com
Swissair. www.swissair.com
TWA. www.twa.com
United Airlines. www.ual.com
USAirways. www.usairways.com

provides feedback on refining your search if you have flexibility in travel dates or times. There is also an active section of Message Boards for discussions on travel in general and specific destinations.

SPECIALTY TRAVEL SITES

Although the sites listed above provide the most comprehensive services, some travelers have specialized needs that are best met by a site that caters specifically to them.

For adventure travelers, **iExplore** (www.iexplore.com) is a great source for finding information on and booking adventure and experiential travel. The site combines secure Internet booking functions with hands-on expertise and 24-hour live customer support by seasoned adventure travelers, catering to those interested in trips off the beaten path. The company is a supporting member of the Ecotourism Society and is committed to environmentally responsible travel worldwide.

Another excellent site for adventure travelers is **Away.com** (www.away.com), which features unique vacations for challenging the body, mind, and spirit. Trips may include cycling in the Loire Valley, going on an African Safari, or assisting in the excavation of a Mayan ruin. For those without the time for such an extended, exotic trip, offbeat weekend getaways are also available. Services include a customer service center staffed with experts to answer calls and e-mails, plus a network of over 1,000 pre-screened tour operators. Trips are listed according to cultural, adventure, and green-travel categories. Away.com also offers a Daily Escape e-mail newsletter.

GORP (Great Outdoor Recreation Pages; www.gorp.com) has been a standard for adventure travelers since its founding in 1995 by outdoor enthusiasts Diane and Bill Greer. Tapping their own experiences, they created this Web site that offers unique travel destinations and encourages active participation by fellow GORP visitors through the sophisticated menu of online forums, contests, and discussions.

For travelers who prefer more unique accommodations, **InnSite** (www.innsite.com) offers listings for inns and B&Bs in all 50 U.S. states and dozens of countries around the globe. Find an inn at your destination, have a look at images of the rooms, check prices and availability, and then send e-mail to the innkeeper if you have further questions. This is an extensive directory of bed-and-breakfast inns, but only includes a listing if the proprietor submitted one (*note:* it's free to get an inn listed). The descriptions are written by the innkeepers, and many listings link to the inn's own Web sites, where you can find more information and images.

Another good resource for mostly one-of-a-kind places in the U.S. and abroad is **Places to Stay** (www.placestostay.com), which focuses on resort accommodations.

"Have Kids, Still Travel!" is the motto of the **Family Travel Forum** (FTF; www.familytravelforum.com), a site dedicated to the promotion and support of travel with children. FTF is supported by memberships, which are available in flexible prices ranging from a $2.95 monthly fee to a heftier annual fee for more comprehensive services. Since no advertising is accepted, FTF provides its members with honest, unbiased information, informed advice, and practical tips designed to make traveling with children a healthier, safer, hassle-free experience, not to mention a better value.

TOP VACATION-PACKAGE SITES

Both **Expedia** and **Travelocity** (see above) offer excellent selections and searches for complete vacation packages. Travelers can search by destination and desired dates coupled with how much they are willing to spend. Travelocity has a valuable "Cruise Critic" function, to help would-be cruisers obtain first-hand accounts of the quality and details of a cruise from recent passengers.

Travel wholesalers, like **Apple Vacations** (**www.applevacations.com**) and **Funjet** (**www.funjet.com**), are also good starting points, but still require that the final booking be handled through a travel agent.

As travel agents tend to be more expert at sorting through the values in vacation packages, you might find **Vacation.com** (**www.vacation.com**) helpful in previewing packages and finding an appropriate agent to help you book the deal. This site represents a nationwide network of 9,800 local travel agencies that specialize in finding the best values in cruises, vacation packages, tours, and other leisure travel services.

LAST-MINUTE DEALS AND OTHER ONLINE BARGAINS

There's nothing airlines hate more than flying with lots of empty seats. The Net has enabled airlines to offer last-minute bargains to entice travelers to fill those seats. Most of these are announced on Tuesday or Wednesday and are valid for travel the following weekend, but some can be booked weeks or months in advance. You can sign up for weekly e-mail alerts at the airlines' sites (see the "Airline Web Sites" box, above) or check sites that compile lists of these bargains, such as **Smarter Living** or **WebFlyer** (see below). To make it easier, visit a site that will round up all the deals and send them in one convenient weekly e-mail. But last-minute deals aren't the only online bargains; other sites can help you find value even if you haven't waited until the eleventh hour. Increasingly popular are travel auction sites and services that let you name the price you're willing to pay for an air seat or vacation package.

Cheap Tickets. www.cheaptickets.com
Cheap Tickets has exclusive deals that aren't available through more mainstream channels. One caveat about the Cheap Tickets site is that it will offer fare quotes for a route, then later show this fare is not valid for your dates of travel—most other Web sites, such as Expedia, consider your dates of travel before showing what fares are available. Despite its problems, Cheap Tickets can be worth the effort because its fares can be lower than those offered by its competitors.

✪ 1travel.com. www.1travel.com
Here you'll find deals on domestic and international flights, cruises, hotels, and all-inclusive resorts such as Club Med. 1travel.com's **Saving Alert** compiles last-minute air deals so you don't have to scroll through multiple e-mail alerts. A feature called "Drive a little using low-fare airlines" helps map out strategies for using alternate airports to find lower fares. And **Farebeater** searches a database that includes published fares, consolidator bargains, and special deals exclusive to 1travel.com. *Note:* The travel agencies listed by 1travel.com have paid for placement.

Bid for Travel. www.bidfortravel.com
Bid for Travel is another of the travel auction sites, similar to Priceline (see below), which are growing in popularity. In addition to airfares, Internet users bid on vacation packages and hotels.

Go4less.com. www.go4less.com
Specializing in last-minute cruise and package deals, Go4less has some excellent offers. The Hot Deals section gives an alphabetical listing by destination of super-discounted packages.

LastMinuteTravel.com. **www.lastminutetravel.com**

Suppliers with excess inventory come to this online agency to distribute unsold airline seats, hotel rooms, cruises, and vacation packages. It's got great deals, but you have to put up with an excess of advertisements and slow-loading graphics.

Moment's Notice. **www.moments-notice.com**

As the name suggests, Moment's Notice specializes in last-minute vacation and cruise deals. You can browse for free, but if you want to purchase a trip, you have to join Moment's Notice, which costs $25. Go to World Wide Hot Deals for a complete list of special deals in international destinations.

✪ **Priceline.com.** **travel.priceline.com**

Even people who aren't familiar with many Web sites have heard about Priceline. com. Launched in 1998 with a $10-million ad campaign featuring William Shatner, Priceline lets you "name your price" for domestic and international airline tickets and hotel rooms. In other words, you select a route and dates, guarantee with a credit card, and make a bid for what you're willing to pay. If one of the airlines in Priceline's database has a fare lower than your bid, your credit card will automatically be charged for a ticket.

But you can't say when you want to fly—you have to accept any flight leaving between 6am and 10pm on the dates you selected, and you may have to make a stopover. No frequent-flyer miles are awarded, and tickets are non-refundable and can't be exchanged for another flight. So if your plans change, you're out of luck. Priceline can be good for travelers who have to take off on short notice (and who are thus unable to qualify for advance-purchase discounts). But be sure to shop around first, because if you overbid, you'll be required to purchase the ticket—and Priceline will pocket the difference between what it paid for the ticket and what you bid.

Priceline says that over 35 percent of all reasonable offers for domestic flights are being filled on the first try, with much higher fill rates on popular routes (New York to San Francisco, for example). It defines "reasonable" as not more than 30% below the lowest generally available advance-purchase fare for the same route.

Smarter Living. **www.smarterliving.com**

Best known for its e-mail dispatch of weekend deals on 20 airlines, Smarter Living also keeps you posted about last-minute bargains on everything from Windjammer Cruises to flights to Iceland.

SkyAuction.com. **www.skyauction.com**

An auction site with categories for airfare, travel deals, hotels, and much more.

Travelzoo.com. **www.travelzoo.com**

At this Internet portal, over 150 travel companies post special deals. It features a Top 20 list of the best deals on the site, selected by its editorial staff each

Know When the Sales Start

While most people learn about last-minute weekend deals from e-mail dispatches, it can pay to check the airline sites to find out precisely when they post their special fares. Because deals are limited, they can vanish within hours, sometimes minutes—often before you even read your e-mail. An example: Southwest's specials are posted at 12:01am Tuesdays (Central time). So if you're looking for a cheap flight, stay up late and check South-west's site to grab the best new deals.

Online Directory

One of the best sources of travel information is word-of-mouth, from someone who has just been there. Internet discussion groups are offering an unprecedented way for travelers around the globe to connect and share experiences. **Frommer's Online (www.frommers.com)** offers these message boards, as well as areas where you can pose questions to the guidebook writers themselves, in its section "Ask the Expert." **Yahoo! Travel, Expedia,** and **Travelocity** are other good sources of online travel discussion groups.

The granddaddy of specialized discussions on particular topics is **Usenet,** a collection of over 50,000 newsgroups. You'll find a comprehensive listing at **Deja News (www.dejanews.com/usenet)** or at **www.liszt.com**.

Wednesday night. This list is also available via an e-mail list, free to those who sign up.

WebFlyer. **www.webflyer.com**
WebFlyer is a comprehensive online resource for frequent flyers and also has an excellent listing of last-minute air deals. Click on "Deal Watch" for a round-up of weekend deals on flights, hotels, and rental cars from domestic and international suppliers.

ONLINE TRAVELER'S TOOLBOX
Veteran travelers usually carry some essential items to make their trips easier. Following is a selection of online tools to smooth your journey.

Visa ATM Locator. **www.visa.com/pd/atm/**

MasterCard ATM Locator. **www.mastercard.com/atm**
Find ATMs in hundreds of cities in the U.S. and around the world. Both include maps for some locations and both list airport ATM locations. *Tip:* You'll usually get a better exchange rate using ATMs than exchanging traveler's checks at banks, but check in advance to see what kind of fees your bank will assess for using an overseas ATM.

CDC Travel Information. **www.cdc.gov/travel/index.htm**
Health advisories and recommendations for inoculations from the U.S. Centers for Disease Control. The CDC site is good for an overview, but it's best to consult your personal physician to get the latest information on required vaccinations or other health precautions.

✪ Foreign Languages for Travelers. **www.travlang.com**
Learn basic terms in more than 70 languages and click on any underlined phrase to hear what it sounds like. (*Note:* Free audio software and speakers are required.) It also offers hotel and airline finders with excellent prices and a simple system to get the listings you're looking for.

Intellicast. **www.intellicast.com**
Weather forecasts for all 50 states and cities around the world. Note that temperatures are in Celsius for many international destinations, so don't think you'll need that winter coat for your next trip to Athens.

✪ Mapquest. **www.mapquest.com**
The best of the mapping sites that lets you choose a specific address or destination; in seconds, it will return back a map and detailed directions. It really is easier than calling, asking, and writing down directions. The site also links to special travel deals and helpful sites.

Net Café Guide. www.netcafeguide.com/mapindex.htm

Locate Internet cafes at hundreds of locations around the globe. Catch up on your e-mail, log onto the Web, and stay in touch with the home front, usually for just a few dollars per hour.

Tourism Offices Worldwide Directory. www.towd.com

An extensive listing of tourism offices, some with links to these offices' Web sites.

Travelers' Tales. www.travelerstales.com

Considered the best in compilations of travel literature, Travelers' Tales is an award-winning series of books grouped by destination (Mexico, Italy, France, China, and so on) or by theme (Love & Romance, The Ultimate Journey, Women in the Wild, and The Adventure of Food). It's a new kind of travel book that offers a description of a place or type of journey through the experiences of many travelers. It makes for a perfect traveling companion.

The Travelite FAQ. www.travelite.org

Tips on packing light, choosing luggage, and selecting appropriate travel wear—helpful if you always tend to pack too much, or are a compulsive list maker.

Universal Currency Converter. www.xe.net/currency

See what your dollar or pound is worth in more than a hundred other countries.

Check E-Mail at Internet Cafes While Traveling

Until a few years ago, most travelers who checked their e-mail while traveling carried a laptop—an expensive and often technologically problematic option. Thankfully, Web-based free e-mail programs have made it much easier to check your mail.

Just open an account at any one of the numerous "freemail" providers—the original leaders continue to be **Hotmail** (hotmail.com), **Excite** (www.excite.com), and **Yahoo! Mail** (mail.yahoo.com), though many are available. AOL users should check out **AOL Netmail**, and **USA.NET** (www.usa.net) comes highly recommended for functionality and security. You can find hints, tips, and a mile-long list of freemail providers at **www.emailaddresses.com**.

Then, all you'll need to check your mail is a Web connection, easily available at Net cafes and copy shops around the world. After logging on, just call up your freemail's Internet address, enter your username and password, and you'll have access to your mail. From these sites, you can download all of your e-mail—even from office accounts—or your local or national Internet Service Provider address. There will be a section generally called "check other mail" that allows you to add the names of other e-mail servers.

The downside is that most Web-based e-mail sites allow only a maximum of 3MB capacity per mail account, which can fill up quickly. Also, message sending and receiving is not immediate; some messages may be delayed by several hours, or even days.

Internet cafes have become ubiquitous, so for a few dollars an hour you'll be able to check your mail and send messages from virtually anywhere in the world. Interestingly, Internet cafes tend to be more common in very remote areas, where they may offer the best form of access for an entire community, especially if phone lines are difficult to obtain.

U.S. Customs Service Traveler Information.
www.customs.ustreas.gov/travel/index.htm

Wondering what you're allowed to bring in to the U.S.? Check at this thorough site, which includes maximum allowance and duty fees.

U.S. State Department Travel Warnings. travel.state.gov/
travel_warnings.html

Reports on places where health concerns or unrest might threaten U.S. travelers. Keep in mind that these warnings can be somewhat dated and conservative. You can also sign up to receive State Department briefings via e-mail.

Web Travel Secrets. www.web-travel-secrets.com

If this list leaves you yearning for more travel-oriented sites, Web Travel Secrets offers one of the best compilations around. One section offers advice and tips on how to find the lowest prices for airlines, hotels, and cruises. The other section provides a comprehensive listing of Web travel links for airfare deals, airlines, booking engines, cars, cruise lines, discount travel and best deals, general travel resources, hotels and hotel discounters, search engines, and travel magazines and newsletters.

2 Top Web Sites for Cape Cod, Nantucket & Martha's Vineyard

Note: Several of the sites listed in the Cape Cod section below include information on Nantucket and Martha's Vineyard.

CAPE COD

About.com: Cape Cod and the Islands. capecod.about.com

This collection of about 100 Web sites is categorized under about a dozen headings, including Arts and Entertainment, Dining, and Old Cape Cod. A section called "In the Spotlight" has short features on the island's myriad attractions (whale watching, wine tasting, and so on), and these stories include lots of links as well. Check the Lighthouses category and take an online tour of these historical structures.

Cape Cod Chamber of Commerce. www.capecodchamber.org

Click on Vacation Planning for an extensive if boosterish guide to the Cape's hotels, restaurants, shops, events, and top attractions. The lodging section lets you see images of the properties and, in some cases, reserve online. The dining listings are pretty thin, but in some cases, you can link to a restaurant's own site where you can preview menus. The events calendar can help you find out what's on during your visit.

Cape Cod History. www.capecodhistory.org

This umbrella site ranges from Tales of Cape Cod (a local preservation group) to a listing of recommended books (click on Cape Reading). At press time, seven towns were listed (scroll down and look in the left-side menu) and had pages detailing their history, with plans to add more soon.

Cape Cod Journal. www.capecodjournal.com

This local newspaper will get you up to speed on Cape news. Click on Entertainment Report for arts and nightlife advice. Also see the *Cape Cod Times* at **www.capecodonline.com/cctimes/**.

Cape Cod Life. www.capecodlife.com

This site features lots of inspiring photos, though the information can be a bit thin. The beach guide (under Recreation) has some nice images but very little concrete information. Other sections are more fleshed out, such as the boating guide. The calendar of events is well done, and the "Best of" section points to *Cape Cod Life*'s favorite restaurants, hotels, shops, marinas, and historic sites.

Cape Cod Magazine. www.capecodmagazine.com

Enjoy features from the current issue, or peruse the archive of past issues. Topics range from contentious local issues to tourists' pursuits to whimsical features such as "The Changing Face of the Pirate." This is a good site to visit to get a better idea of what's happening on Cape Cod.

Cape Cod Shops. www.capecodshops.com

If you can't wait to start shopping, this is the site for you. Or if you want to purchase something from the Cape after you get home, you can order through this site. Search for products by category (jewelry, furniture, and fragrances), or visit individual shops.

✪ CapeCodTravel.com. capecodtravel.com

This site has it all—from basics listings (attractions, lodgings, restaurants, and shops) to lively magazine features on everything from festivals to scallops. Produced by the *Best Read Guide to Cape Cod,* a free print publication, this guide has brief reviews of hotels and restaurants. But remember that the listings aren't comprehensive, and that properties may have paid to be listed. Essential sections worth checking include the events calendar, feature archive, and beach guide.

Cape Cod Visitors Center. www.allcapecod.com

This is a nice roundup of links to useful sites in categories including lodging, dining, and activities. Click on What to Do for sections on the arts, museums, outdoor activities, and Kids Korner.

Cape Week. www.capeweek.com

A weekly guide to what's happening on the Cape. Sections include best bets, dining, theater, galleries, films, and festivals.

Dolphin Fleet Whale Watching. www.whalewatch.com

From the home page, scroll down to learn about whale-watching opportunities and why Cape Cod is such a fine place for whale spotting. You can check schedules, prices, and a sighting update, and print a discount coupon from the Web site. Another whale-watch company, called **Portuguese Princess,** guarantees whale sightings. See their site at **www.princesswhalewatch.com**.

Kids on the Cape. www.kidsonthecape.com

If you're ever wondering what to do with the kids, this is the place to turn. You'll find dozens of recommended activities, as well as hotels and restaurants that help kids feel at home. Click on Town by Town for tips on what to do in each of the Cape's regions.

Massachusetts Office of Travel and Tourism. mass-vacation.com

This official statewide tourism site has a section on Cape Cod and the islands, though you won't find much that's not better covered in this guidebook. The site becomes worthwhile when seeking timely advice, such as fall foliage updates. A section called "Outdoor Adventures" leads to other sites that provide valuable information, while the lodging section can provide images of accommodations and offers online booking.

Melody Tent. www.melodytent.com

This venue has attracted artists from Liza Minelli to Eddie Murphy, bringing top-notch entertainment to the Cape. Learn who's on this year's bill and find out about tickets, schedules, and more.

OnCape. www.capecodonline.com/oncape
OnCape features guides to golf courses, beaches, and towns. A photo tour features many of the Cape's most stunning sights, while another link lets you send an online postcard via e-mail. Scroll down for Beyond Fifty, a guide for seniors, and a recreation guide called "Cape Outdoors."

Provincetown Guide. www.ptownguide.com
This tidy guide to the town at the tip of the Cape includes dining and lodging listings, as well as nightlife tips. Listings are limited, perhaps to companies that pay for placement.

NANTUCKET

Absolutely Nantucket. www.ackisland.com
This lively online magazine offers feature stories, photos, and essays about Nantucket. Though Absolutely Nantucket often focuses on the local communities, it can give travelers a better sense of the island.

Insider's Guide to Nantucket. www.insiders.com/capecod/ main-nantucket.htm
This is pretty much a watered-down version of a print guidebook, but you can find some nice images and get a better sense of what to do on Nantucket (scroll down for the events listings).

Nantucket Island Chamber of Commerce. www.nantucketchamber.org
This site boasts an engaging photo gallery and a short list of annual events. A special section for international visitors offers trip planning advice. The directory of members includes hotels, restaurants, shops, and outdoor outfitters.

Nantucket Island Information Center. www.allcapecod.com/nantucket
This guide doesn't have a whole lot of information on dining or lodging, but the General Information category includes ferry schedules and links to other Nantucket Web sites.

✪ Nantucket.net. www.nantucket.net/indexlong.html
You won't find much flash here, but the information is well-organized. Click on How to Get Here for links to air travel, bike rentals, and ferry information. A calendar of events can help you decide how to spend your time, a dining section features restaurants' pages, and you can see hotel images (and in some cases, reserve online).

✪ Yesterday's Island, Today's Nantucket. www.yesterdaysisland.com
An extensive guide to the island, including an events calendar, beach guide, kids' activities, as well as the basics. You'll also find magazine features with headlines such as "The Shy Man Who Talks with Paintbrushes." The restaurant guide has lengthy reviews of dozens of eateries, and the arts section includes theater reviews and gallery advice.

MARTHA'S VINEYARD

Best Read Guide to Martha's Vineyard. bestreadguide.com/ marthasvineyard
Though not nearly as extensive as the Best Read Guide to Cape Cod, this site features driving and walking tours, and some dining and lodging listings (which may be paid for by the restaurants and hotels, so read with a critical eye). The most valuable aspects of this site are its event listings and its feature stories (on topics ranging from Derby fishing to best sunset viewpoints).

Martha's Vineyard Chamber of Commerce. **www.mvy.com**

Though you won't get a complete listing of hotels and restaurants, you will find a nice selection. Most listings contain only basic information, but many places have links to their own Web pages where you can learn more. The boating and fishing section lists lots of charter companies.

Martha's Vineyard Historical Society. **www.vineyard.net/org/mvhs**

Consult this site for a short course in the island's compelling history. The images include a picture of an 1855 fire engine and vintage lighthouses.

Martha's Vineyard Online. **www.mvol.com**

This site features a Yahoo!-style directory. Though most of the categories aren't directly related to travel, many links can be useful, from fishing to shopping. You can even watch a short video tour of the island, (QuickTime software, which can be downloaded free, is required).

Martha's Vineyard Times. **www.mvtimes.com**

Everything you'd expect from a local newspaper: local issues, entertainment, weather, and sports/recreation. The menu in the left column has sections on fishing, dining, lodging, and shopping, but these listings are virtually useless—in most cases, all you'll find are business names and their phone numbers.

Online Directory

Index

See also Accommodations and Restaurant indexes below.

General Index

ACCOMMODATIONS INDEX

FROMMER'S® COMPLETE TRAVEL GUIDES

Alaska
Amsterdam
Arizona
Atlanta
Australia
Austria
Bahamas
Barcelona, Madrid &
  Seville
Beijing
Belgium, Holland &
  Luxembourg
Bermuda
Boston
British Columbia & the
  Canadian Rockies
Budapest & the Best of
  Hungary
California
Canada
Cancún, Cozumel &
  the Yucatán
Cape Cod, Nantucket &
  Martha's Vineyard
Caribbean
Caribbean Cruises & Ports
  of Call
Caribbean Ports of Call
Carolinas & Georgia
Chicago
China
Colorado
Costa Rica
Denmark
Denver, Boulder & Colorado
  Springs
England
Europe

European Cruises & Ports
  of Call
Florida
France
Germany
Greece
Greek Islands
Hawaii
Hong Kong
Honolulu, Waikiki & Oahu
Ireland
Israel
Italy
Jamaica
Japan
Las Vegas
London
Los Angeles
Maryland & Delaware
Maui
Mexico
Montana & Wyoming
Montréal & Québec City
Munich & the Bavarian
  Alps
Nashville & Memphis
Nepal
New England
New Mexico
New Orleans
New York City
New Zealand
Nova Scotia, New Brunswick
  & Prince Edward Island
Oregon
Paris
Philadelphia & the
  Amish Country

Portugal
Prague & the Best of the
  Czech Republic
Provence & the Riviera
Puerto Rico
Rome
San Antonio & Austin
San Diego
San Francisco
Santa Fe, Taos & Albuquerque
Scandinavia
Scotland
Seattle & Portland
Shanghai
Singapore & Malaysia
South Africa
Southeast Asia
South Florida
South Pacific
Spain
Sweden
Switzerland
Thailand
Tokyo
Toronto
Tuscany & Umbria
USA
Utah
Vancouver & Victoria
Vermont, New Hampshire
  & Maine
Vienna & the Danube Valley
Virgin Islands
Virginia
Walt Disney World &
  Orlando
Washington, D.C.
Washington State

FROMMER'S® DOLLAR-A-DAY GUIDES

Australia from $50 a Day
California from $60 a Day
Caribbean from $70 a Day
England from $70 a Day
Europe from $70 a Day

Florida from $70 a Day
Hawaii from $70 a Day
Ireland from $60 a Day
Italy from $70 a Day
London from $85 a Day

New York from $80 a Day
Paris from $80 a Day
San Francisco from $60 a Day
Washington, D.C.,
  from $70 a Day

FROMMER'S® PORTABLE GUIDES

Acapulco, Ixtapa &
  Zihuatanejo
Alaska Cruises & Ports of Call
Bahamas
Baja & Los Cabos
Berlin
California Wine Country
Charleston & Savannah
Chicago
Dublin

Hawaii: The Big Island
Las Vegas
London
Los Angeles
Maine Coast
Maui
Miami
New Orleans
New York City
Paris

Puerto Vallarta, Manzanillo
  & Guadalajara
San Diego
San Francisco
Sydney
Tampa & St. Petersburg
Venice
Washington, D.C.